SKATEBOARDING AND THE CITY

Iain Borden

SKATEBOARDING AND THE CITY

a complete history

BLOOMSBURY VISUAL ARTS

LONDON · NEW YORK · OXFORD · NEW DELHI · SYDNEY

BLOOMSBURY VISUAL ARTS
Bloomsbury Publishing Plc
50 Bedford Square, London, WC1B 3DP, UK
1385 Broadway, New York, NY 10018, USA
29 Earlsfort Terrace, Dublin 2, Ireland

BLOOMSBURY, BLOOMSBURY VISUAL ARTS and the Diana logo are trademarks of Bloomsbury
Publishing Plc

First published in Great Britain 2019
Reprinted 2020, 2021

Cover design: Richard Holland
Cover image: Erik J. Pettersson, Shanghai (2014). © Nikwen

A catalogue record for this book is available from the British Library.

Library of Congress Cataloging-in-Publication Data
Names: Borden, Iain, author.
Title: Skateboarding and the city : a complete history / Iain Borden.
Description: London ; New York : Bloomsbury Academic, 2019. | Includes bibliographical references
and index.
Identifiers: LCCN 2018015183 | ISBN 9781472583451 (flexiback : alk. paper) | ISBN 9781472583482
(epdf) | ISBN 9781472583475 (epub)
Subjects: LCSH: Skateboarding—History. | Skateboarding—Social aspects. | Skateboarding parks. |
Streets—Recreational use.
Classification: LCC GV859.8 .B66 2019 | DDC 796.22—dc23 LC record available at https://lccn.loc.
gov/2018015183

ISBN: PB: 978-1-4725-8345-1
         ePDF: 978-1-4725-8348-2
         eBook: 978-1-4725-8347-5

Typeset by Richard Holland
Printed and bound in India

for Sam

'Transform the world' –
all well and good. It is being
transformed. But into what?
Here, at your feet, is one
small but crucial element in
its mutation.'

Henri Lefebvre

LUAN OLIVEIRA

NYJAH HUSTON

Contents

Acknowledgements

This book has its earliest origins in the late 1980s, when I first wrote something academic about skateboarding. Since then, an enormous number of people have provided information, research materials, support and encouragement, and I fear that in seeking to thank all of those who have helped, I will inadvertently miss out far too many. But I will at least try to thank everyone, and here they are.

Dan Adams, Vernon Adams, Alena Agafonova, Dave Allen, Gerhard Andersson, Sabina Andron, Julie Angel, Andrew Armes, Rob Ashby, Gorm Ashurst, Jonny Aspen, Jon Aungier, Bill Bahne, Bob Bahne, Claire Baker, Iain Baker, Rob Ball, Larry Balma, Larry Barth, Becky Beal, Andy Beevers, David Belfrage, Michael Bennett, Johan Berglund, Francis Bernstein, Amanda Birch, Michael Blabac, Ole Bouman, Neil Bowen, Matt Bowles, Christine Boyer, Wilfred Brandt, Chris Bridger, Grant Brittain, Matt Broadley, Andrew Brooke, Angus Leadley Brown, Lucy Bullivant, Damien Burden, James Butcher, Warwick Cairns, Thom Callan-Riley, Claudio Caluori, Dobie Campbell, Ben Campkin, Matthew Carmona, Eray Cayli, Sarah Chaplin, Jonathan Charley, Swati Chattopadhyay, Dave Chesson, Ed Chester, Mike Christie, Marc Churchill, Dean Clarke, James Clarke, Phil Clarkson, Catherine Clayton, Nic Clear, Jono Coote, Matthew Cornford, Rachel Cottam, Paul Coupe, David Cross, Dan Cousins, Marcello Cruz, Allen Cunningham, Barry Curtis, Paul Davies, James Davis, Andy Day, Billy Deans, Jeremy Donaldson, Jacob Down, Kathryn Earle, Gustav Edén, Chris Eidem, Mackenzie Eisenhour, Søren Nordal Enevoldsen, Philip Evans, Kevin Fang, Tim Fitzgerald, John Flood, Mike Fordham, Adrian Forty, Sophie Friedel, David Frisby, Mikkel Frost, Brian Gaberman, Oskar Galewicz, Nathan Gallagher, Bradley Garrett, Jason Geralis, Richard Gilligan, Shaun Gladwell, Julien Glauser, Sean Goff, Matt Gold, David Goldsmith, Eric Gordon, Tim Greatrex, Ben Grieme, Sam Griffin, Erik Gross, Sam Haddad, Matt Harris, Serena Haywood, Jeppe Hein, Pete Hellicar, Hendrik Herzmann, Thomas S. Hines, Russ Holbert, Guy Hollaway, Emmi Holmer, Sander Hölsgens, Richie Hopson, Brad Horn, Ben Horton, Ed Houghton, Ocean Howell, James A. Hudson, Dan Hughes, Dan Hulme, Jon Humphries, Simon Inglis, Alex Irvine, Graham Ive, Mike John, Laurence Johns, Todd Johnson, Alasdair Jones, Peter Jones, Peter Joynt, Eddie Katz, Tiphaine Kazi-Tani, Jude Kelly, Jeff Kendall, Veith Kilberth, Greg King, Granville Kirkup, Kizz Kisby, Kristaps Kleinbergs, Lindsay Knight, Gunita Kulikovsky, Izumi Kuroishi, Garret LaCoss, Lesley Latimer, Graeme Larsen, Jack Layton, Katharina Ledersteger, Sandra Lenzhölzer, Austin Li, Nathan Livingston, Mark Logue, Kara-Jane Lombard, Mike Lorr, Jenny Lovell, Giancarlo Machado, Matt MacQueen, James Madge, Trevor Marchand, Michael Margraf, Doreen Massey, Demetrios Matheou, Mark Maunders, Mike McCart, Sandy McCreery, Matthew McDonald, Glen McDougall, Aaron McGowen, Mike McIntire, Jonathan Mehring, Jeremy Melvin, Pedro Mendes, William Menking, Paul Merrell, Daryl Mersom, Jeremy Millar, Paul Monaghan, Monkeyglove Matt, Alicia Moore, Belinda Moore, Brian Moore, Paula Morais, Alexander Morrison, Oli Mould, Charlie Mrusko, Bob Muckle, Sebastian Müller, Stefan Müller, Morag Myerscough, Simon Napper, Niall Neeson, Ben Nicholson, Ingrid Niehaus, Nikwen, Svein Nordrum, Kenny Omond, Tom Palmer, Tristan Palmer, Christian Parreno, James Parry, Paul Jelly Parsons, Grahame Paterson, Pearl Pelfrey, Dion Penman, Barbara Penner, Stacy Peralta, Jim Phillips, Steve Pile, David Pinder, Steve Pingleton, Alicia Pivaro, Pod, Alberto Polo, Ben Powell, George Powell, Nic Powley, Tony Presland, Paul Price, Richard Pyles, Claude Queyrel, Peg Rawes, Alan Read, Giovanni Reda, Alan Rendell, Beth Rendell, Jane Rendell, Ted Richards, Ed Riggins, Taina Rikala, Robert Rinehart, Leigh

Robinson, Charles Room, Jamie Ross, Norma Rosso, Lucas Rubeiro, Katerina Rüedi, Jeff Ryckebosch, Janne Saario, Nick Sable, Charlie Samuels, Leonie Sandercock, Zac Sanford, Ben Sansbury, Chiara Santini, Bart Saric, Chris Saunders, Helvijs Savickis, Joanna Saxon, Christian Sayer, Bill Schaffer, Philipp Schuster, Louise Scriven, Tim Sedo, Jenna Selby, Steve Sexton, Sangam Sharma, Justin Sharp, Rob Shaw, Sally Shaw, Bob Sheil, Kath Shonfield, Kieran Sills, Simparch, Jack Smith, Nick Smith, Richard Cándida Smith, David Snow, Craig Snyder, James Soane, Ed Soja, South London Shredders, Neil Spiller, Pete Staddon, Simon Staddon, Scott Starr, Brian Stater, Anne Strange Stelzner, Keith Stephens, Quentin Stevens, Bill Stinson, David Stokes, Andy Stone, David Stover, Elaine Stratford, Warren Stuart, Amy Sueyoshi, Paul Sunman, Paul Sweetman, Jon Swords, David Sypniewski, Philip Tabor, Risa Tadauchi, Graham Taft, Tricia Tarkington, Chris Taylor, Saul Taylor, Audrey Teichmann, Kevin Thatcher, Justin Thomas, Pete Thompson, Nigel Thrift, Michelle Tichtin, Jeremy Till, Jane Tobin, David Tong, Trawler, Helge Tscharn, Arthur Tubb, Andy Turner, Daniel Turner, Thomas Turner, Christian Unverzagt, Marc Vallée, Marc Vitelli, Dirk Vogel, Oliver Wainwright, Stefan Walz, Vicky Watson, Mauve Weinzier, Belinda Wheaton, Caroline Whitehead, Winstan Whitter, Kate aan de Wiel, Sarah Wigglesworth, Neftalie Williams, Shirley Wong, Helen Woolley, Jon Wood, Crys Worley, Freddy Worrell, Olly Zanetti, Raphaël Zarka and Daniel Zvereff.

Very special gratitude is due to all of the companies and photographers – and especially Glen E. Friedman, Jim Goodrich, Dave Van Laere, Tim Leighton-Boyce, the R.A.D. Archive and Wig Worland – who very generously allowed me to reproduce their work, and without whom this book would simply not have happened.

Richard Holland created the graphic design for the book, and has also been an active part in innumerable skateboard conversations, as have John Langton and Paul O'Connor. Many thanks also to Marije de Haas. At Bloomsbury, my profound gratitude to James Thompson and everyone else who supported the project. And a special acknowledgment is due to the Architecture Research Fund at the Bartlett School of Architecture, University College London, which has generously supported the book both financially and for research time.

Lastly, my ever-lasting thanks to my closest family – Claire Haywood, Sam Borden, Shelagh Borden, Tony Borden and Barbara Haywood – who have let skateboarding enter into their lives, and no doubt far more than they would ever have expected.

Figure 1.1
Go Skateboarding Day in
Manila (2015).
© Mark R. Cristino/Rex/
Shutterstock

1 Introduction

The scene is set, the playground open: unknown terrain, unknown features, unknown futures. Maybe.[1]
R.A.D.

Skateboarding today is a global phenomenon, with around fifty million riders and thousands of skateparks worldwide, and is recognized as an Olympic sport. From the full-on testosterone of *Thrasher* skateboard magazine to the fashionista lifestyling of *Vogue*, from the skater girls and boys of Kabul to the Native American reservations of South Dakota, from the skateparks of Brazil to the streets of Shenzhen, skateboarding is no longer just for street-based subcultural rebels, and is everywhere and for everyone (Figure 1.1).

As an active skateboarding advocate, writer and rider for over forty years, I have created *Skateboarding and the City* – and its accompanying YouTube channel – as a comprehensive study of this global phenomenon. We travel from the earliest skaters of surf-beach promenades in the 1950s and 1960s, encounter the suburban swimming pools and skatepark terrains of the 1970s, and come face-to-face with contemporary street-skateboarding, longboarding and hill-bombing. Along the way are developments in art, film, photography and DIY skatepark construction, alongside important matters of gender, community and professionalism, plus commerce, heritage and social enterprises. Throughout this journey, I show how skateboarding challenges many of our society's norms and conventions, positively contributes to contemporary culture and the economy and helps open out city spaces to everyone.

This may come as something of a surprise to those who still stereotype skateboarders as being teenage, male and white, and as punkish subcultural rebels. In fact, today a skater might well be Asian and hipster-cool, black and entrepreneurial, female and physically challenged, or older and gay – and every variation imaginable. Entering a skate shop, you are as likely to see branded shoes and T-shirts as actual skateboards. Alongside gritty urban streets, new skate terrains have emerged, from DIY constructions, flow-bowls and street plazas to longboard parks, multi-storey wonderlands and hybrid public spaces. And skateboarding is ever more associated with art and creativity, philanthropy and charity, and industry and commercialism, and even contributes to preservation, heritage, planning and urban politics. Inevitably, big companies are also involved, including the likes of Adidas, Levi's, New Balance, Nike and Vans. As a result of this, and from Brazil, the UK and the United States to Dubai, Nigeria and North Korea, skateboarding is being increasingly welcomed by a growing number of enlightened politicians, city managers and the general public, who all appreciate its help in addressing challenging social issues and in forming more diverse communities.

Other things have also changed, including, over the last two decades, the appearance of many new skateboarding books and sources of information. I identify these in the extensive references and bibliography, but of particular note are the accounts provided by Larry Balma *Tracker* (2015), Becky Beal *Skateboarding* (2013), Jürgen Blümlein and Dirk Vogel *Skateboarding Is Not a Fashion* (2018), James Boulter *Unemployable* (2015), Michael Brooke *The Concrete Wave* (1999), Cole Louison *The Impossible* (2011), Ben Marcus and Lucia Daniella Griggi *The Skateboard* (2011), Craig Snyder *A Secret History of the Ollie* (2015), and Raphaël Zarka *On a Day with No Waves* (2011).

Recent academic scholarship has also been significant, especially in erudite studies of local groups, professionalism and city policies, and which I also incorporate into this book. Nearly all these academic accounts, however, are single-topic investigations, and so are necessarily more focused than the range of artistic, cultural, design, spatial, theoretical and urban issues that I address here. As much as possible, I have made *Skateboarding and the City* broad in time span, detailed in history and comprehensive in its interpretations, as well as paying attention to events taking place beyond the United States.

Throughout this project, I additionally draw upon a wide array of magazines, films, DVDs, interviews, internet forums, blogs, YouTube, Facebook and social media. And while, in apparent contrast to all this popular culture, the appearance of various philosophers, theorists and other erudite thinkers in a book about skateboarding might seem rather unusual, it is, I think, worth persevering with their often-challenging formulations, for such ideas open our eyes to aspects of skateboarding that would otherwise remain hidden. In particular, I refer frequently to the work of French philosopher Henri Lefebvre on urban space and everyday life, as well as to his later writings on rhythmanalysis and architecture. Similarly, many other theorists are brought into play, from political philosopher Chantal Mouffe, psychologist Mihaly Csikszentmihalyi and architectural theorist Jill Stoner to cultural theorist Angela McRobbie, literary theorist Roland Barthes and urban geographer David Harvey.

Through these kinds of speculation, and of course also in close relation to skateboarding's ever-evolving terrains and culture, I move beyond the idea, particularly prevalent during the 1990s but still common today, of skateboarding somehow holding at its heart a single set of 'core' places, practices or values. Instead I show how skateboarding has been created from all manner of skaters, terrains and intentions. As Michele Donnelly notes, 'from skateboarding's earliest incarnations skateboarders have been involved for a variety of different reasons, in a variety of different ways and with a variety of different understandings or meanings,'[1] and I have endeavoured to reflect this diversity. Furthermore, skateboarding, like all cultural phenomena, is created not just by its practitioners but by innumerable commentators, media, magazines and films, and I therefore explore how these channels variously portray and influence the activity.

This book is then a 'complete history', although of course not in the sense of including every skate artwork, competition, local scene, rider, skatepark, skatespot or video ever involved, for that would be a fruitless task. But I do present an inclusive and encompassing arc of skateboarding's varied developments from the late 1950s through to the present day. *Skateboarding and the City* is 'complete' in that it at least touches on freestyle, downhill and slalom as well as street and skatepark riding, just as it moves across skateparks and skateboards, people and companies, ideas and attitudes, art and design, politics and money, photography and video, books and magazines, countries and regions; all these things are present, some more than others admittedly, but in a general composition that I think represents skateboarding's diverse activities and values. It is a balance. Others would tilt the scales another way, but this is my own reckoning of skateboarding's complex world over the last sixty years.

Thanks to the book's publishers and funders, to Richard Holland's design and to the many photographers who generously provided their work, I have been able to include substantial imagery. In addition to these photographs, the QR codes embedded in the pages connect to the accompanying *Skateboarding and the City* YouTube channel (www.bit.ly/ SkateboardingCity), thus letting readers become viewers, travelling though skateboarding history via one hundred short video clips, from the 1960s to the present day. These are not necessarily the very 'best' skateboarding videos – although many classic clips are indeed included – but rather give a wide-ranging overview of different kinds of skateboarding over the last six decades. Watch them alongside the book via tablet or smartphone, and skateboarding will spring even more dramatically to life.

Compared to *Skateboarding, Space and the City* – my earlier book on skateboarding, written back in the 1990s when skateboarding was a far narrower cultural phenomenon, media comprised mainly of a few printed magazines and VHS tapes, and academic research was being undertaken by just a handful of pioneers – this new volume is completely renewed, comprehensively expanded, more intensively researched and panoramic in outlook. To interrogate skateboarding's manifold constituents, *Skateboarding and the City* is divided into three main sections. Section One, 'Skateboard Scenes', covers skateboarding equipment, attitudes, industries and media. Within this section, Chapter 2, 'Skateboards', charts the developments in skateboards themselves, from the rudimentary surf-related devices of the 1950s and 1960s, through the urethane-wheeled advances of the 1970s, onward to equipment attuned to street-skateboarding and other riding specialisms. Chapter 3, 'Living by the Board', explores skate culture, including issues of class, gender, masculinity, ethnicity and territory.

The complementary Chapter 4, 'Affiliate Worlds', considers mainstream skateboarding qualities, including professionalism, corporate branding, regulations and entertainment-oriented events, while Chapter 5, 'Media Worlds', deals with the essential role of magazines, photography, movies, videos and social media.

Section Two, 'Skateboarding', explores the dynamic act of riding and the major terrains where skateboarders operate. Chapter 6, 'Found Space', engages with schoolyards, drainage ditches, swimming pools and water-management pipes, and introduces tactics of appropriation and colonization, mostly during the 1970s. Chapter 7, 'Skatopia', focuses on the same decade and its startlingly new concrete skateparks, before progressing to the wooden ramps of the 1980s. Chapter 8, 'Skatepark Renaissance', complements Chapter 7, providing an equivalent account of the second wave of skateparks that emerged after 2000, now enhanced by matters of innovative design, DIY construction, urbanism, neoliberalism and social integration. Chapter 9, 'Super-Architectural Space', explores how the rider's body, skateboard and architecture are reborn in the encounter between skateboarder and physical terrain, alongside the complex role of skateboarding images. Chapter 10, 'Skate and Destroy', moves to the emergence of urban street-skating in the 1980s and 1990s, leading to new ways of editing, mapping and recomposing the city, and Chapter 11, 'Movement Without Words', concludes this section by disclosing skateboarding's performative critique of society and urban space, alongside the censorship, conflicts and counter-reactions that often ensue.

Section Three, 'Skate and Create', focuses on two aspects of skateboarding that have most strongly emerged during the twenty-first century. Chapter 12, 'Artistry', investigates skateboarding's rich and varied relationship with graphic design, fine art, skateable sculptures and architecture, as well as creativity in general. Finally, Chapter 13, 'Do It for Others', shows how skateboarders increasingly engage with matters of public space, historic and architectural preservation, healthy and sustainable living and entrepreneurialism. This chapter closes with skate-based educational and social enterprise initiatives that today address challenging social issues like substance abuse, teenage suicide, and ethnic and religious intolerance, and so help build independence, confidence, trust and hope.

Last of all, Chapter 14, 'Skateboarding – A Magnificent Life?' reprises the ways in which skateboarding has, over the last sixty years, been both complex and contradictory, that is at once accepting and intolerant, aggressive and graceful, disorderly and clean-cut, free and paid-for, grassroots and organized, and individualistic and collective, as well as being local and global, physical and digital, street-based and skatepark-bound, technical and expressive, and urban and suburban. As I ultimately conclude, this diversity is not skateboarding's weakness but its very strength, and even suggests vital new approaches to city living. Indeed, as the whole book demonstrates, within skateboarding's distinctive outlook we find that the most valued of life attributes are not fame, wealth, winning or status but are – or should be – participation, expression, satisfaction and community. There is much here to celebrate and explore.

Section One
Skateboard Scenes

Chapter 2 Skateboards

A skateboard is a basic device, with just three main elements – one deck, two trucks and four wheels – and has had little of the complex technological advances seen in other board sports like windsurfing and snowboarding. The deck (riding surface) is usually made from wood, covered with high-friction grip tape similar to sandpaper. Bolted to the deck are two aluminium alloy trucks providing suspension and turning, usually by a 'double-action' mechanism where a metal hanger and split-axle pivot around two urethane bushings on a central kingpin. Turning and stability are tuned by tightening the bushing compression. Wheels, once metal or clay-composite, are now made from polyurethane, each typically measuring between 50 and 75 mm in diameter and containing two 608-format bearings. This standard specification was not immediately arrived at, however, but, as we shall see, took over twenty years to fully emerge, before moving into a series of further subtle evolutions and refinements.

Scooters and Surfing

Besides obvious forerunners to the skateboard such as the roller skate, other early idiosyncrasies included scooters like the Scooter Skate (1930s) and Skeeter Skate (1945), plus the sled-like Kne-Koster (1925) and Flexy-Racer (1932). Despite these various precursors, the skateboard almost certainly evolved from the kids' kick scooters, which had become popular during the first half of the twentieth century. From around 1910 onwards, these makeshift scooters were cobbled together from a 2 by 4 inch plank of wood, a fruit crate and a single roller skate, so providing independent urban mobility for cheeky kids. As recreated in *Ban This* (Stacy Peralta, 1989), holding on to the wooden handlebars and pushing with one foot, riders could rapidly navigate sidewalks and alleyways (Figures 2.1 and 2.2).[1]

The first skateboards then were essentially scooters shorn of the crate and handlebar components, as explained in Bruce Brown's early skateboarding short *America's Newest Sport* (1964). These primitive devices may

Figure 2.1
Scooters and roller-skate riders in the 'Anything on Wheels' derby in New York's Lower East Side (1952).
© Carl Nesensohn/ AP/Rex/Shutterstock.

Figure 2.2
Recreation of 1950s
scooter-riding in
Ban This (Powell-
Peralta, dir. Stacy
Peralta, 1989).
www.bit.ly/Scooters-
BanThis

have appeared in the 1930s and 1940s through the experimentations of La Jolla surfers like George 'Buster' Wilson and Peter Parkin, while African-American kids were skateboarding in Washington DC during the early 1950s.[2] Whoever did it first, the equipment was undoubtedly rudimentary. 'We were just using two by four and steel skates,' explained Denis Shufeldt.[3] Better still, the 2 by 4 inch wood strip could be replaced by a short wooden deck measuring around 20 inches long and 6 inches wide. Smaller, more manoeuvrable and easier to store than scooters, the skateboard still stopped whenever meeting a rough surface or small pebbles: 'the metal wheels hit those little rocks,' recalled Dick Metz, 'and you were history.'[4] The open-sided bearings also seized up easily: 'Sand and dirt had no problem getting in,' explained Bob Schmidt. 'You'd lock up and go flying at the worst possible time, usually when trying to avoid a parked car.'[5] Riding this rough-and-ready contraption was 'thirty seconds of gritty trundling' and enough to 'jar every bone in your body.'[6]

Around 1957, skaters like Jim Fitzpatrick in La Jolla were making skateboards for friends in batches of twenty, but the first truly commercial skateboards of the late 1950s and early 1960s were those like the AC Boyden/Humco with Sidewalk Swinger spring-loaded trucks and others by Skee-Skate, Chicago Roller Skate, Sport Flite, Carl Jensen and Roller Derby, some of which sold for as little as two dollars and came equipped with steel wheels measuring around 50 mm in diameter and 10 mm in width (Figure 2.3).[7] Better still were the wider 'composition' or 'clay' wheels adopted in the early 1960s from commercial roller skate rinks. Variously composed from clay, rubber, paper, ground walnut shells and polymer binders, these wheels offered a much smoother ride.

As early skaters were mostly concerned with simply riding downhill, 'hitting primitive hills at Roger Williams Park and Garden City', the greater turning capacity of these composition wheels also allowed for the heightened emulation of the burgeoning 1950s and 1960s surf culture.[8] Surfing, having originated in French Polynesia and Hawaii, was now being enthusiastically practised in hot spots across California, Florida, Hawaii and Australia, meaning that thousands of real and want-to-be surfers were ready for the similar experiences of skateboarding.[9] 'I was totally blown away by how similar grinding a turn on a skateboard was like doing a bottom turn in surfing,' recalled Dave Rochlen, while as Wentzle Ruml described skateboarding in Santa Monica, 'we just rode imaginary waves and blazed all over the city.'[10] *America's Newest Sport* directly compared surfing and skateboarding turns and other moves like walking-the-board and hanging ten (Figure 2.4).

Various entrepreneurs were quick to spot an opportunity. After making and selling a few basic skateboards, Val Surf shop in Los Angeles asked the Chicago Roller Skate company to supply double-action metal trucks (based on a 1935 patent) and composition wheels ready for assembly.[11] Other roller-skate derived trucks then available included the Super Surfer, Leesure Line, Roller Derby, Roller Sport, X-Caliber and Sure Grip, allowing surfers to make their own wood decks and then bolt on trucks and wheels. 'We'd chip the wood,' recalled one Californian surf-skater. 'They looked like custom surf designs in colored marker or airbrush, and we'd lacquer them on.'[12]

Alternatively, many preferred fully ready-to-ride boards, as offered by Larry Stevenson's Makaha Skateboards, founded in Venice Beach in 1963 and based in the offices of *Surf Guide* magazine. Makaha's overtly surfboard-shaped

BUILT FOR BALANCE AND SPEED!

OFFICIAL

ROLLER DERBY
SKATE BOARDS

Twist & Turn! Slide & Sled! Skim & Race!

There's a perfect size and style ROLLER DERBY
SKATE BOARD for everyone! Take your pick of 4
precision built models, each with perfectly balanced
wheels for smoother riding and easy gliding.

YOU'LL EXCELL WITH A ROLLER DERBY
SKATE BOARD!

THE ORIGINAL! THE FINEST!
Get your ROLLER DERBY SKATE BOARD today!

Figure 2.4
The Hobie skateboard team in
America's Newest Sport (dir. Bruce
Brown, 1964).
www.bit.ly/AmericasNewestSport

Commander, Red Commander and Malibu models cost around thirteen dollars and were promoted by famous surfers like Mike Hynson, Mike Doyle and Phil Edwards, generating some $4 million for Makaha in its first three years.[13] Surf companies like Gordon & Smith (G&S) also began making skateboards, deploying surfboard and archery technology to create Fibreflex decks laminated from maple and Bo-Tuff fibreglass epoxy resin.[14] But systematized skateboard production really took off when Ed Morgan persuaded the Vita-Pakt Juice Company to diversify into skateboard manufacture. Backed by hotel-heir investor Barron Hilton (father of skaters Dave and Steve Hilton), gaining design advice and backing from professional surfer Hobie Alter and poaching most of Makaha's team riders, in 1964 Vita-Pakt introduced the Hobie-branded 'Super Surfer' – 'Step on it . . . it's alive!' – heavily promoted in *America's Newest Sport* (Figure 2.4) and *The Quarterly SkateBoarder* magazine (Figure 2.5). The Vita-Pakt/Hobie collaboration went on to make over six million skateboards.[15]

Skateboarding now took off, with companies like Banzai, Bauer, Black Knight, Cooley, Nash, Sears, Sincor, Sokol Surf-Skate, Sport-Fun and Sterling among many others joining the action.[16] 'People don't realise how big skateboarding was in the 1960s', explains Curt Stephenson. 'It was an explosion from 1963 to 1965.'[17] By 1962 skateboarding had already reached places like Nevada and the US East Coast; the first skateboard competition was held in 1963 in Hermosa Beach, and in 1964 the first issue of *The Quarterly SkateBoarder* magazine appeared (quickly retitled *SkateBoarder*).[18] Corky Carroll demonstrated skateboarding on Johnny Carson's hugely popular 'The Tonight Show', as did the Makaha team for the Steve Allen show and a Kellogg's cereal commercial, and yet more national exposure came when Jan & Dean had a

top twenty-five Billboard chart hit with 'Sidewalk Surfin' (Figure 2.6). The Challengers and The Coastliners also released skate-related records.[19]

By the summer of 1965 skateboarding boasted fifteen million US-wide practitioners and $100 million in annual sales; Nash alone sold $1.3 million of equipment in two months, while the Chicago Skate Company was supplying trucks and wheels to ninety-two other brands.[20] ABC's *Wide World of Sports* televised the National Skateboard Championships at Anaheim's La Palma Stadium, where skaters from the United States, Mexico and Japan competed in downhill, slalom and freestyle for prizes of $500.[21] Skateboarding also took centre stage in the Academy Award–nominated *Skaterdater* (Noel Black, 1965), in which Torrance skaters carved downhill and jumped curbs, as shown to audiences nationwide alongside *Thunderball*.[22] The same year, *Life* magazine sported national girls' champion Patti McGee doing a handstand on its cover, *Popular Mechanics* ran a five-page feature on 'Skateboard Acrobatics', the *Wall Street Journal* amazedly reported on skateboarding's 'dizzying sales' and even famous cartoon dog Snoopy was seen expertly skateboarding.[23] Skate teams like Hobie, Jacks, Makaha, Palisades and Bayside sent team riders to exhibitions nationwide, and over fifty million skateboards had now been sold across the United States.[24]

Skateboarding was also starting internationally. As later documented in *Tic Tac 2 Heelflip* (Mike Hill, 2001), skateboarding was particularly popular in Australia. In 1964 and 1965, British Pathé news and British Movietone excitedly reported from Bondi on the new Australian pastime of 'roller boarding' and the exploits of the Midget Farrelly team. In *The Quarterly SkateBoarder* Roy Giles described the UK skateboarding scene in London and surfing centres like St. Ives in Cornwall and Langland

Figure 2.3
Roller Derby
skateboards.
*The Quarterly
SkateBoarder*
(Winter 1964).

Board shown—27" Hobie Fiberglass by Super Surfer

"Step on it...it's alive!"

New! Alive! The Hobie 27" Fiberglass Competition Model...The skateboard of champions.

Twenty-seven inches with room to walk the board, hang fives and tens, do the wheelie, just to name a few exciting skateboard tricks.

Terrific for traction! The embossed surface gives you firm footing and makes kick turns easy, slaloms smooth and safe.

Hobie 27" Fiberglass Competition Models have the famous and tough Super Surfer truck. With double-action cushions, Hobie skateboards are easily adjusted for greater maneuverability and more skillful performances. All that and a shock-absorber, too!

Now add four composition wheels, the kind that grip the skateboarding surface, and you're ready to roll.

Our Skateboard Team just placed #1 and #3 in the recent International Skateboard Championships held in Anaheim, California. These winners used Super Surfer and Hobie skateboards to win. That's why we can point with pride when we say—Super Surfer and Hobie are the Skateboards of Champions! Well, what are you waiting for?

SUPER SURFER

A Vita-Pakt PRODUCT
707 N. Barranca, Covina, Calif.

30" Hobie 22" Oak 30" Laminated 23" Laminated 25" Hobie 23" Pine

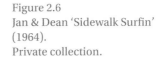

Figure 2.6
Jan & Dean 'Sidewalk Surfin''
(1964).
Private collection.

Figure 2.5
The Hobie Super
Surfer with 27 inch
fibreglass deck,
double-action trucks
and composition
wheels. *SkateBoarder*
(August 1965).
Courtesy Hobie.

Bay in South Wales.[25] Makaha promoted their equipment through Jim Fitzpatrick's tour around France, Spain, Italy, Lichtenstein, Switzerland, Germany, Netherlands, England, Scotland and Ireland.[26] In 1966, *Skaterdater* won Best Short Film at the Cannes Film Festival, Claude Jutra's *Rouli-roulant* (English version *The Devil's Toy*, 1969) was released by the National Film Board of Canada, and the UK's *Daily Mirror* proclaimed skateboarding as a new craze (Figure 2.7).[27] *Pilote* (1965), *Tintin* (1966) and *SkateBoarder* magazines all ran multi-page features on skateboarding in France.[28] Many 1960s celebrities like Tom Jones and Edward Heath in London, Clint Eastwood in Rome, Katharine Hepburn in Beverly Hills and John Lennon in the Bahamas were also depicted skateboarding, providing further promotional fuel.[29] In Japan, the All Japan Skateboard Association used surfing centres to introduce skateboarding during the 1960s,[30] while international manufacturers also sprang up, including Rollbrettl in Germany, GT, Surf Skate and Webcraft in Australia and Bauer, CCM, Dominion, Fox, Red Devil, Superskate and Surf 'n Ski in Canada.[31]

Despite this worldwide reach, skateboarding's first boom proved short-lived; after peaking by mid-1965, popularity fell away and by October

SkateBoarder magazine ceased publication with its fourth issue. With around thirty manufacturers creating over-supply in the US marketplace, retailers over-buying in advance of a retail boom that never materialized, and mounting criticism of skateboarding on health and safety grounds, the bubble burst; in November of 1965 companies like Makaha found orders worth hundreds of thousands of dollars being cancelled in a single day, and Larry Stevenson lost $250,000. As Hobie's Dick Metz explained, 'for two or three years you couldn't hardly give a skateboard away.'[32]

Nonetheless, skateboarding continued out of sight of the national media, with skaters like Jim Fitzpatrick, Torger Johnson, Steve Tanner and Dave Hilton becoming well-known. And while skateboarding still featured in other US states and overseas – *The Devil's Toy* even won a 1968 award at an Iranian film festival[33] – it prospered best as a US beach city phenomenon, including Californian venues like Santa Cruz and La Jolla, as well as Los Angeles areas like Ocean Park and Santa Monica. Skateboard teams even flourished on a small scale, including Makaha with skaters Ty Page, Bruce Logan and Brad Blank, while sales enjoyed a mini-resurgence around 1968.[34]

Figure 2.7
Skateboarding in
Montreal.
The Devil's Toy
(dir. Claude Jutra,
1966). www.bit.ly/
DevilsToy

Old School

Around 1972 and 1973, skateboarding entered
its second phase through new forms of
technology. Most significantly, the application
of polyurethane to skateboarding wheels was
famously pioneered by Frank Nasworthy.
Although Nasworthy was not wholly original
here – both Makaha and Vita-Pakt/Hobie had
rejected polyurethane wheels in the mid-1960s
on cost grounds – he was the first to persevere.[35]
During the summer of 1970, Nasworthy visited
Creative Urethanes in Purcellville, Virginia,
and discovered some plastic roller skate
wheels which he subsequently tried out in
Washington DC. 'There was so much concrete
and granite around,' remembered Nasworthy,
'so to skate all over it was a blast'. After moving
to California, Nasworthy formed the Cadillac
Wheels company and, working with Creative
Urethanes, went into production in 1973 with
the first urethane wheel purposely intended for
skateboarding.[36] As a slow roller skate wheel,
urethane wheels had previously been confined
to commercial rinks where longevity was key,
but softer skateboard-oriented compositions
hit a sweet spot of durability, speed and
traction. Long-term skateboard publisher and
manufacturer Fausto Vitello explains:

> Urethane has really good abrasion resistance,
> which means the wheel will last a while. Even
> more important, urethane gives a really good
> grip. It will slide if you push it hard, but it gives
> great traction. So that means you can control
> your board. And modern urethanes have a real
> high resiliency, or rebound, which means that
> although they're solid, they're very fast.[37]

Given this magical combination, skaters
unsurprisingly viewed moving from clay to
urethane wheels, in the words of UK surf-skater

Ben Liddell, as being like 'getting out of a beat-
up rusty Mini to a Porsche or Jaguar and having
a beautiful ride – instantly addictive'.[38]

During 1973 and 1974, Cadillac wheels were
initially sold through surf shops and magazines,
where Gregg Weaver, among other surf-
skaters, was seen exploiting the new urethane
compounds and 'contorting himself into
positions that were scarcely to be credited'.[39]
Others like Jack Smith were so impressed that
'after seeing an ad in *Surfer*, we jumped in a
car and drove 150 miles to a surf shop that
sold these new wonder rollers'.[40] By late 1974,
Nasworthy's mold-cast process wheels had
sold around 120,000 sets, clearly indicating that
skateboarding's new phase had truly taken off
(Figure 2.8). Other urethane offerings quickly
followed, including the injection-moulded
Metaflex developed by Oak Street Surf Shop
and manufactured in Canada.[41] Even more
popular was the 1975 Road Rider (designed
by Tony Roderick of Mearthane Products
Corporation, manufactured by Quality Products
in Rhode Island and distributed on the West
Coast by NHS), whose eye-catching translucent
red compound and sealed bearings allowed
for better riding and easier maintenance.[42]
Wheels like these – along with Tunnel Rocks
and SIMS Competition models – 'opened up
skateboarding for everyone' and allowed San
Diego riders like Jeff Tatum to 'bomb hills fast,
do slides, and take turns faster.'[43]

To match these new wheels, early 1970s
decks typically measured anywhere between
20 to 32 inches long and 6 ½ to 7 ½ inches
wide. Some were polypropylene, aluminium
or fibreglass (Bahne and G&S particularly
promoted fibreglass flex decks for slalom,
cruising and freestyle), while from 1976 decks

Figure 2.8
Bahne skateboard
with fibreglass deck,
Bahne trucks and
Cadillac urethane
wheels. *SkateBoarder*
(June 1976).
Courtesy Bahne
Skateboards.

Bahne: It's all the board you need.

Bahne is one of the oldest, most well-respected names in skate-boarding. It has been time-tested and proven under the most demanding conditions. We believe that the more you know about skateboarding, the better the board you'll choose. Bahne can give you all the board you need.

Bahne boards are wider to provide stability and maneuver-ability for high performance stunt riding. Made of unidirectional glass-struded fibreglass, the Bahne chassis combines strength with pliability. The non-skid deck is a must for safety. Six-weld unitized all-steel construction makes Bahne trucks the strongest and most durable on the market. New Cadillac wheels are available in four different models to offer varying combinations of speed control properties.

Bahne's high quality boards, trucks, and Cadillac wheels were custom designed to work together. However, every rider has unique needs, so the component parts are available separately to allow unlimited versatility to meet varying conditions and demands. Our broad price range ($30.00 to $60.00) puts Bahne quality within reach of any budget. All this allows you the freedom to design your own system to fit your individual specifications. Bahne: It's all the board you need.

BAHNE

Bahne Skateboards, Post Office Box 326A, Encinitas, California 92024, (714) 753-0255

were increasingly cut from solid beech, oak or teak. By now the angled rear 'kicktail' (patented by Larry Stevenson in 1969) had also become increasingly common.[44]

Other technical advances also aided skateboarding, including the rubberized riding surface of G&S Fibreflex decks and the introduction of deck grip tape by Bruce Walker (1973) and Ross Houston's Foot-Tred (1975); by the end of 1976 using grip tape – now commercialized by Jessup and 3M – was standard practice.[45] Underneath the deck, while early 1970s trucks from Sure Grip, X-Caliber, Bahne and Chicago were still derived from roller skates. engineer Rob Bennett's 1974 Bennett Hijacker design was purpose-designed for skateboarding, with a high aluminium hanger, recessed kingpin, wider axle and plastic baseplate, together offering increased manoeuvrability, stability and wheel clearance.[46] Even more significant was the launch a year later of Larry Balma, Dave Dominy and Gary Dodd's Tracker Fultrack, which effectively established the standard truck format, as later recognized by the Smithsonian.[47] The Tracker offered an even wider axle than the Bennett, along with a winged hanger made of A356-T6 aircraft-grade aluminium-magnesium alloy, a baseplate-welded kingpin tightened by a single nut, plus chrome-molybdenum axles and new four-hole mounting pattern, all of which dramatically improved strength, stability and convenience. Narrower Haftrack and Midtrack models soon followed.[48] By 1979, with odd exceptions like the Ermico Stroker multi-link (1976) and Rebound double-kingpin (1977), and reverse-angle variants like the Speed Spring (1975), Gullwing HPG IV and Phoenix (1977) and Variflex Connection (1979), nearly all trucks followed Tracker's arrangement.[49]

All these new innovations proved immensely successful commercially, and companies like ACS (American Cycle Systems) (Figure 3.11), Bennett, Black Knight, Cadillac, Free Former (Figure 4.2), G&S (Figure 2.9), Hobie, Logan, Makaha, Road Rider, Santa Cruz and SIMS were soon shifting substantial amounts of product; in 1975 around 150 US skate equipment manufacturers enjoyed $250 million of turnover. The same year, *SkateBoarder* magazine rapidly sold out the 75,000 copies of its re-launch issue (quickly rising to 300,000 copies), and Bahne peaked at a thousand complete skateboards a day (Figure 2.8).[50] In 1976, NHS sold over six million Road Riders,[51] GrenTec advertised its 20 inch GT and other plastic budget boards on

US television, and a year later toy giant Mattel rolled out its Magnum skateboard system with ribbed decks, quick-change wheels and torsion-turning trucks.[52]

Skateboarding's geographic spread was also now firmly established, refuting the impression often created by the specialist skateboard press that skateboarding was predominantly Californian. By 1975, Bahne was frantically fulfilling orders from Australia and worldwide,[53] while in 1977 *Skateboard Industry News* reported that 'extremely active' sales across South-Eastern, East Coast and Mid-West US states far exceeded those in California.[54] The same year, Morris Vulcan, the largest UK manufacturer, produced 15,000 boards every week.[55] G&S undertook the first skateboard tour of Japan in 1978, the same year its global sales hit $5.5 million (compared to $100,000 in 1974)[56] and Tracker's truck production hit 40,000 per month,[57] with *SkateBoarder*'s global sales nearing half a million.[58]

During the mid-1970s the modern global skateboard had arrived in the form of a wooden or fibreglass deck, aluminium alloy trucks with steel axles and urethane wheels. Various oddities like eight-wheeled, fuselage-covered, off-road, sail-driven or motorized skateboards have occasionally surfaced, and recent eccentricities include the complex automobile-inspired pendulum-suspension trucks and 110 mm wheels of the BMW StreetCarver (2000–2005), and even the sine wave grooved Shark wheels (2014). However, none of these innovations have affected the standard specification of a typical skateboard, which has instead remained remarkably constant in its fundamental design and construction.

That said, skateboards have certainly evolved in some subtle ways over the last forty years. Notably, in the later 1970s skateboards grew larger to provide extra stability on pool and skatepark walls. In 1977 a typical surfboard-shaped deck like the immensely popular G&S Warptail and Warp 2 (selling over 110,000 units during 1976 to 1978) was 7 ½ inches wide (Figure 2.9).[59] But by now a few skaters like Lonnie Toft were experimenting with 8 to 10 inch wide boards with blunt noses and square tails, and even 20 inch wide eight-wheeled versions.[60] In early 1978 the commercial 8 inch wide SIMS Superply and Lonnie Toft models appeared, while Wes Humpston and Jim Muir similarly experimented with wider boards.[61] Key here was laminated maple construction – allowing easy fabrication along with the greater rigidity, strength, lightness

Figure 2.9
Maple laminated G&S Warp 2 deck. *SkateBoarder* (November 1977). Courtesy G&S.

THE OUTER LIMITS

When it comes to high technology and proven performance one name stands out, Kryptonics. We pioneered the development of high rebound urethanes, precision hubs, composite decks and high technology wood boards. We were the first to explore the outer limits, now we control them.

COMPETITION SERIES WHEELS – The 64MM Double Conical and 60MM Freestyle are highly specialized, professional quality wheels. Both feature Dupont Zytel ST super tough glass reinforced nylon cores. The new black core is used only with the ultra-resilient 92A formulation developed after thorough testing during the Hester Series. The newly designed 64 is the lightest and fastest competitive bowl wheel we have ever produced.

RACING SERIES WHEELS – The 62MM Slalom and 70MM Downhill have no competition when it comes to street racing. Both designs have been refined and improved after years of testing and development. Both the Orange 88A Formulation and Red 78A Formulation feature the precision

molded black core and a smooth, fast ride. The soft red formula delivers the highest rebound of any wheel made, an incredible 80%.

HIGH PERFORMANCE DECKS – Kryptonics offers an extensive line of high quality skateboards including three Krypstik Models, two K-Beam 2 Models including a new Micke Alba Signature Model, two Freestyle Decks designed by Stuart Singer and two Foam/ Fiberglass Composite Decks.

THE PROVING GROUNDS – When we're done with a product in the lab it goes to the team for testing. While testing and developing the 1980 product line, the Kryptonics Skate Team happened to win the Prestigious Hester Series, the East Coast Amateur Championships at Cherry Hill, and the Florida Team Challenge. Results say a lot about the limits of both riders and equipment, those results speak for themselves.

When you're ready to explore the outer limits of your skill and equipment, stay on course. Follow the leader, Kryptonics.

Micke Alba winning at Boulder on his way to winning the 1979 Hester Series.

KRYPTONICS, INC.
5660 Central Avenue, Boulder, CO 80301
(303) 442-9173

© 1980 KRYPTONICS, INC.

and durability dictated by skatepark riding – a fabrication method that had been first pioneered by Tracker's Rockit decks in 1977 and licensed to G&S.[62] The same year, similar methods were being used by Wee Willi Winkels in Ontario, Canada and were brought back to the United States by Lonnie Toft, laminate deck construction subsequently being adopted by most manufacturers by late 1977.[63]

With *SkateBoarder* upgrading from bi-monthly to monthly publication in the June 1977 issue, and *Skateboard World* magazine launching the same month, things now progressed quickly. Californian pool- and skatepark-riding skaters were adopting 10 inch wide 'pig' decks by mid-1978, as first advertised by SIMS in the October 1978 *SkateBoarder*, and others quickly followed.[64] In the UK, Marc Sinclair and John Sablosky were riding 9 inch wide Benjyboard decks in 1978, Vancouver-based GNC/Skull Skates were producing a near 10 inch model, and by year's end Alva, Caster, Dogtown (Figure 12.1), Powell-Peralta (Figure 12.2) and Kryptonics (Figure 2.10) all offered fully 10 inch decks – the 'Old School' typology as it was later known.[65] Most of these decks comprised between five and nine maple layers, sometimes with additional fibreglass, and from around 1979 and 1980 many accommodated secure foot placement through a concave transverse profile, including the Santa Cruz Bevel, Z-Flex Z-Winger, Dogtown Jim Muir Triplane and Variflex Elguera/El Gato models. Other innovations included thinner decks with strengthening beams – such as the Alva LiteBeam, Kryptonics K-Beam, Dogtown Shogo Kubo Airbeam, Powell-Peralta Beamer and SIMS Dave Andrecht Beamer – many of which were created by Scott Peck and Boulder Boards in Colorado, as well as lightweight foam-cored and graphite decks such as the Kryptonics Foam Core (Figure 2.10) and SIMS Phase 3 Composite models.[66] Skaters also affixed hand-grabbing and board-saving devices like side rails and nose- and tail-protectors. Many decks enjoyed significant sales – the SIMS Andrecht Beamer model alone peaked at 10,000 per month.[67]

During 1978 and 1979, wider trucks appeared to match the bulkier decks, including the Tracker Extrack and Sixtrack, plus various extended widths from Lazer, Megatron and Independent. The Independent, with design input from Rick Blackhart, John Hutson, Tim Piumarta and Steve Olson, was a major challenge to Tracker, adding Bennett-style geometry to Tracker's standard feature-set.[68] Other refinements were also introduced, like the lightweight magnesium

models from ACS and Tracker (1978) (Figure 2.10), plus plastic Coper (Tracker) and Grindmaster (Independent) devices that clipped onto the truck hanger to decrease wear and friction.

Wheels also improved from better urethane, famously in late 1976 when Colorado-based Kryptonics introduced their Star*Trac and later variations offered in colour-coded red soft (street), intermediate blue (all terrain) and hard green (skatepark) formulations. Developed by Jim Ford, the Kryptonics wheels offered a unique combination of high rebound compounds, choice of hardness ('durometer'), speed, grip and smoothness, all aided by innovative advertising, and so proved massively popular. Bright colours also made these wheels instantly recognizable in magazine pictures. 'The product was pretty much NASA quality compared to all the other stuff,' recalled Brad Bowman. 'It had such a huge impact, it was like the magic carpet ride.'[69] Other companies also improved their products, with Powell-Peralta/ Bones, Road Rider, G&S, SIMS and Belair all introducing thicker edged skatepark-oriented wheels.[70] By late 1978, wheels like the SIMS Conical and Comp II, Alva Bevel, Kryptonics CX and UFO Saucer models sported front and/ or back bevelled profiles, intended to widen the track and prevent wheels from catching on the wall edge (Figure 2.10). More idiosyncratic wheels included the tyre-patterned Wizards, rubber and urethane Emotion (1977), cored wheels with aluminium (SIMS Gyro, 1979) or plastic (Kryptonics C-Series, 1978; Variflex X, 1981) hubs to reduce weight and increase stiffness, and even those near-spherical in shape (G&S Roller-balls, 1980).

After a boom period in the mid- to late-1970s, in which skateboarders enjoyed thousands of new skateparks worldwide and media exposure through national newspapers and mass-market US films like *Skateboard – the Movie* (George Gage, 1977) (Figure 4.1), as well as promotion through countless specialist publications worldwide, skateboarding underwent a serious decline in popularity. Nonetheless, skateboarding carried on, especially on the wooden ramps that mushroomed up to fill the gap left by skatepark closures. Skateboard designs changed accordingly. By the end of the 1980s, typical decks like those offered by SIMS and Santa Cruz featured a large upturned front end, a complex concave lateral profile and wide flared tail – features all aimed at riding half-pipes (Figures 2.11 and 12.3). Many others – including the Christian Hosoi Hammerhead (1985),

Zorlac Gargoyle (1986) and Vision Psycho Stick (1987) (Figure 12.5) – boasted eccentric shapes to provide different hand-holds. Most decks were made from seven-ply maple, but as with the late 1970s a few high-tech composite decks also surfaced, such as the wood and vulcanized cellulose laminated Boneite (Powell-Peralta, 1987), foam-cored Airtech (Santa Cruz, 1986) and foam-cored and fibreglass-skinned Fibrelite (G&S, 1986–1987). In the late 1980s a typical deck measured 31 inches long and 10 inches wide and weighed 1,500 g.[71]

For trucks, Tracker introduced its Ultralite nylon polyamide (1982) and Duralite carbon graphite (1988) baseplates, and by the end of the decade G&S, Tracker and Gullwing were similarly using plastic baseplates and hollow steel axles to reduce weight.[72] Many manufacturers also offered various enamel colourways, but, these minor variations excepted, truck design remained relatively constant. For their part, wheels like the Powell-Peralta T-Bones and Santa

Cruz Bullet (1988) were optimized for vertical riding on large half-pipes, now being harder at around 97a durometer, narrower in track and taller at around 66 mm diameter.[73] The first new street-oriented wheels also began to appear – such as G&S Bam Bams (1987), Vision Neutrons (1989) and Powell-Peralta Streetstyle (1987) – all slightly smaller at around 57 to 61 mm diameter and often sporting colour graphics. Other popular wheels included those by Toxic, Alva and the Australian-made Cockroach.

New School
In the second half of the 1980s into the early 1990s, skateboarding began its third boom, based largely on the emergence of street-based skating, and skateboard design consequently experienced its most significant evolution since the wide-boards of the late 1970s. By 1987, many US manufacturers were already selling over ninety per cent of their product for street-skateboarding, with designs responding accordingly.[74]

Figure 2.11
SIMS pro-model boards for Kevin Staab, Pierre André Senizergues, Buck Smith, Eric Nash, Henry Gutierrez and Jeff Phillips (L-R). *Thrasher* (July 1988). Courtesy SIMS.

Figure 2.12
One of the first new school
decks. World Industries
Mike Vallely pro model, with
'Barnyard' graphic design by
Marc McKee (1989).
Courtesy Stefan Müller.

Aiding this was a massive shake-up of the skateboard industry. By the end of the 1980s, the most established manufacturers included Alva, Dogtown, G&S, Independent, Kryptonics, Powell-Peralta, Santa Cruz, Schmitt, SIMS, Tracker, Vision and Walker, most of whom had been operating for well over a decade. But by 1992, many of these 'corporate behemoths' had become complacent. 'Just when they've settled into that rocking chair to watch the sun set and pat that mattress full of cash, all hell breaks loose', explained *Thrasher* magazine. 'Some big bears in the skateboard business may have disappeared by the time you read this.'[75]

Powell-Peralta did manage some overseas success, and in China they off-loaded dead stock via the Powell Golden Dragon Corporation in Qinhuangdao, creating a market dominance for many years.[76] But in the established US and European markets, a new pack of nimble manufacturers came to the fore, including Alien Workshop, Blind, Chocolate, Foundation, Girl, Hook-Ups, New Deal, Plan B, Real, Think, Toy Machine and World Industries. As Rodney Mullen explained of World Industries, 'Vision, Powell and Santa Cruz were humongous slick companies, but the kids liked our rawness.'[77] While several of the old guard have endured – notably Independent, Kryptonics, Powell, Santa Cruz and Tracker – since the early 1990s it is street-oriented companies that have dominated, including the likes of Antihero, Baker, Birdhouse, Black Label, Blueprint, Cliché, Consolidated, Creature, Darkstar, Dirty Ghetto Kids, Element, Enjoi, 5Boro, Flip, Heroin, Krooked, Magenta, Palace, Polar, Primitive, Raw, Shake Junt, Shorty's, Spitfire, Stereo, Supreme, Venture, Welcome, Zero and Zoo York.

Fuelled by these shifts in the manufacturing landscape and by the accompanying early 1990s domination of streetstyle, skateboards became narrower, lighter and 'new school' (and, from here onwards, the wider 1970s and 1980s skateboards were often termed 'old school'). The new streetstyle 'popsicle' deck format was longer and narrower (around 32 to 33 inches long and 7 ½ to 8 ½ inches wide), with parallel side rails, shorter wheelbase, shallow concave and near-identical, steep kicktails at both ends – these details accommodating various ollies, flips, nose-based moves and 'switch-stance' riding with either leg leading. In 1989, two of the first to display many of these characteristics were the Vision Double Vision and World Industries Mike Vallely pro model, which Rodney Mullen described as being a 'huge freestyle board' with double kicktails and a cartoon barnyard design on the underside (Figure 2.12).[78]

As Vallely's board suggests, another significant change concerned graphics. Older decks had often had some kind of painted underside design, with new models brought out annually or even longer; Powell-Peralta's Ollie Tank model for Alan Gelfand, for example, was effectively unaltered from 1980 to 1985.[79] However, by the mid-1990s the turnover rate for graphics was frantic, with new designs being generated every few months or even faster, and offering, as explored in Chapter 12, a massive range of different artistic styles, codes and attitudes. Essentially, most street deck manufacturers – by 2014 *Jenkem* estimated seventy in the United States alone[80] – now use the typical parallel-sided and rounded-end popsicle shape, as well as similar construction standards (nearly all top pro boards today use North American maple, with five length-wise and two cross-board layers), while deploying subtle variations in concave profile.[81] Some minor variants do exist, such as the Santa Cruz Everslick early 1990s series boasting a slippery thermoplastic underside layer, while over the last twenty-five years numerous manufacturers have played with different ply constructions and pressing techniques, such as Blind's Texalium decks with an aluminium and epoxy glass insert (2007).[82] More recently companies like Krooked, Welcome, Magenta and Creature have experimented with 'shaped' profiles, with Almost using carbon fibre and foam cores in their Uber Light series, and Flip, Creature, Toy Machine and others offering P2 decks with an aramid fibre insert to increase 'pop' and strength.

Similarly, specialist freestyle, slalom and downhill/longboard decks have also emerged from the likes of Decomposed, Pavel, Sk8Kings and Sector 9. Slalom decks can be particularly sophisticated, from the high-tech fibreglass-wrapped and foam-cored cambered Turner SummerSki of the 1970s, through the 2000s and the G&S Response and Duckrider decks designed by Attila Aszodi and Sean Mallard respectively, right up to modern rigid slalom decks such as those of Pavel and Sk8Kings, where 'money bump' and 'gas pedal' shape details, 'torsion box' construction, 'torsion tail' rear truck placement and camber or concave profiles are all finely tuned for racing.[83] Larger set-ups for longboarding and cruising have also become increasingly popular. Indeed, since the launch of Sector 9 and Gravity in 1993, longboards have sometimes even rivalled shortboard sales; in 2014, US sales of conventional completes (fully-assembled deck, trucks and wheel packages) for street- and skatepark-riding were only just ahead of longboard completes for downhill and cruising.[84]

But despite these occasional variants, most contemporary skateboard decks are street-riding models relying largely on vibrant graphics (often related to pro-skater signature models) to differentiate products and accelerate turnover. 'There are so many companies and so many pros,' explained Consolidated's art director Moish Brennan. 'So many angles have been tried. In the end, all you have to separate you from another company is your graphics.'[85]

Indeed, many 1990s brands also did not actually make their equipment, with wheels being poured by a few major producers for re-branding, and trucks predominantly being made at two US foundries.[86] Similarly, decks were typically brought in as unpainted blanks from large-scale producers like Taylor Dykema, Prime and PS Stix, while since 2000 decks have been sourced from producers like Bareback/Generator (USA and Mexico), Chapman (USA), Control (Canada), Crailtap (China), Dwindle/DSM (China), Master Core (USA), PS Stix (USA, China and Mexico) and Watson (USA).[87] Some of these are substantial operations – by 2006, Paul Schmitt's PS Stix factories were producing over 500,000 decks annually for the likes of Alien Workshop, Black Label, Element, Habitat and Stereo.[88] China has also become a large production location for many US manufacturers, some of whom began outsourcing manufacture there in the late 1990s. Significantly, once companies like Gift (Shanghai), She Hui/Society (Beijing), Fei Dian and Safari (Shenzhen) were geared up to make skateboards for US companies, they could also supply high-quality equipment directly into China.[89]

Truck design has also remained fundamentally unchanged for over two decades: 'Trucks have barely changed at all', recognizes Tim Piumarta of NHS/Independent. 'Two elastomers sandwiching a yoke that was connected to an axle and everything pivoted on one point.'[90] Truck developments have therefore largely been a matter of altering width, reducing weight and adding strength, and alongside enduringly popular Gullwing, Independent, Thunder and Tracker brands, additions in the 1990s included Destroyer, Destructo, Elevate, Fury, Grind King, Omega and Orion and since 2000 Bullet, Krux, Mini Logo, Royal and Theeve (Figure

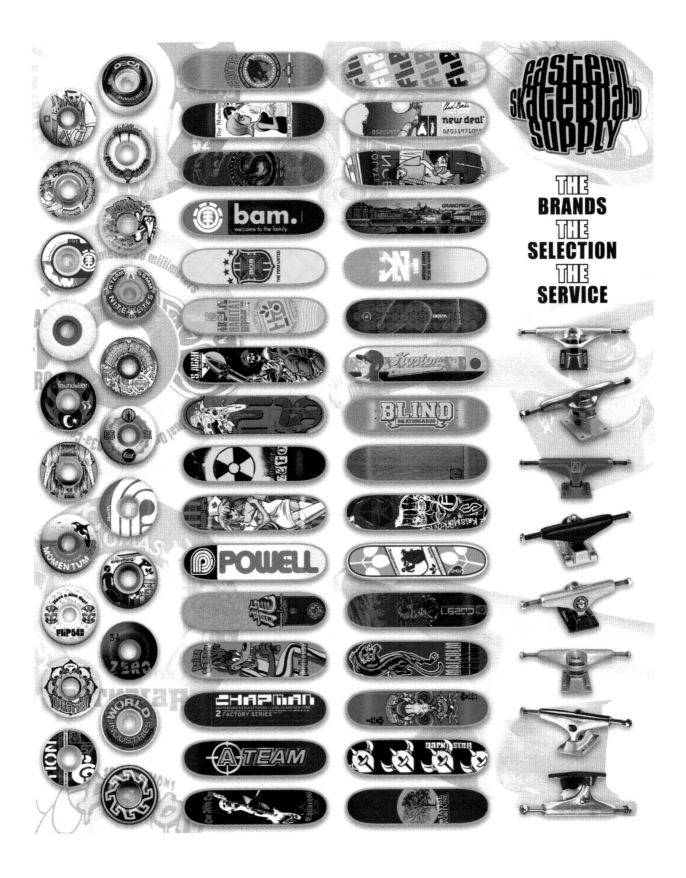

eastern skateboard supply

THE BRANDS
THE SELECTION
THE SERVICE

2.13). Some of these also introduced subtle refinements. Around 1992, Venture pioneered street-oriented trucks with low hangers to aid ollies, while the baseplate hole pattern shrank to accommodate boardslides and steeper kicktails. Rodney Mullen's patented Tensor design (1999) also included a polymer baseplate slider, interlocking bushings and splined kingpin (Figure 2.14).[91] More radically, some recent specialist longboard and slalom trucks, often with a high-angle reverse-kingpin design and sometimes with complex spring and/or torsion arrangements, have included those by Ace, Aera, Bear, Caliber, Fyre, Gullwing, Holey, Original, Other Planet, Paris, Randall, Sabre and Tracker. For example, Koastal's Revenge Alpha (2008) and The Edge (2015) torsion trucks, designed by surfer Brad Horn, are specifically aimed at cruising and flatland carving, emulating surf- and snowboard-style moves through tight-radius and fluid-turning characteristics.[92] Slalom truck arrangements can be particularly complex, with many skaters using a different, turn-oriented truck at the front, such as the Bennett Vector, Tracker RTX, GOG Foxy/Classic, Radikal Claw and Don't Trip Slalocybin, along with a more stable truck at the rear such as the Tracker RTS, GOG Mitchell, Radikal Dragon Tail, Splitfire and Airflows. Alternatively, models by CZ, 161 and Sk8Kings are used in either position, with angled wedges deployed to change turning characteristics.

Significant changes did occur in early streetstyle wheel sizes, averaging between 45 and 55 mm in diameter, but occasionally 40 mm or less, such as the Spitfire Fireballs 37 mm, Stereo Quarter Notes 37 mm, Toxic 39er (1992) and Powell-Peralta Mini Balls 39 mm diameter (1992) models. Small size here means a lower weight and centre of gravity, so aiding the ollie moves, faster acceleration and slides favoured by street-skaters. The wheels also became harder, such as the 101a durometer Toxic Meltdown (1992), and, unlike the multi-colour variations of the 1970s and 1980s, these 1990s wheels tended to be white with applied sidewall graphics. Some of the most popular 1990s models were offered by Birdhouse, Blind, Blueprint, Bones, Flip, Foundation, Formula One, Mad Circle, New Deal, Plan B, Powell, Ricta, Spitfire, Stereo and STM, which today have been supplemented by the likes of Autobahn, Chocolate, Enuff, Girl, Mini Logo, Pig, Portland, Speed Demon, Welcome, Wreck and Zero. In addition, companies like Abec, Alligator, Arbor, Cloud Ride, Divine, Gravity, Hawgs, Kryptonics, OJ, Orangatang, Santa Cruz, Satori, Sector

9, Seismic, These, Tunnel and Venom now produce larger and softer wheels for cruising, longboarding and downhill applications. One further development worth noting is the resurgence in the 2010s of the shortboard, suitable for both children and metropolitan dwellers looking for simple local transport. Lead by the Penny company – launched by Australian Ben Mackay in 2011 – these boards typically consist of a 1970s surf-inspired plastic deck (around 22 inches long, 6 inches wide and available in a huge range of colours and patterns) mounted on soft wheels.[93]

Despite these variations, the skateboard is a pretty basic piece of equipment, with technology mainly directed at increasing durability and speed while controlling traction and weight. Although some mainstream manufacturers have tried to sell skateboards with slogans like Powell-Peralta's 'avoid obsolete technologies', there have been very few truly path-breaking innovations.[94] Similarly, while some magazines, particularly the 1970s *SkateBoarder* and *Skateboard!*, undertook serious assessments of components and ran technical features on experimental deck construction and wheel characteristics, this has not been replicated in later magazines or media.[95] Technology- and performance-based reviewing may be of interest to specialist skateboarding practices such as slalom and longboarding and their associated publications and websites, but they are rarely featured in the more prevalent street- and skatepark-focused media. Skateboards are, then, usually sold on issues of style, brand, general reputation and reliability rather than performance measures, and for most skaters the issue is straightforward: 'A skateboard is a skateboard. They haven't changed. It's the same idea, right? You get on, you go.'[96]

As this last comment suggests, the skateboard as a device is relatively easy to understand, requiring little maintenance and no apparent skill to use other than balancing and movement. As such, when considering the full history of skateboarding, focusing on hardware alone – skateboards as decks, trucks and wheels – will provide only part of the picture, for the importance of the skateboard extends beyond manufacture and design into actual riding. It is with this complex inter-relation that Part Two of this book is largely concerned. Before doing so, however, the complex cultural, commercial and media scenes of skateboarding also merit investigation, and it is to these arenas that we now turn.

Figure 2.14 Advanced-design Tensor truck. *TransWorld Skateboarding* (October 2000). Courtesy Tensor Trucks.

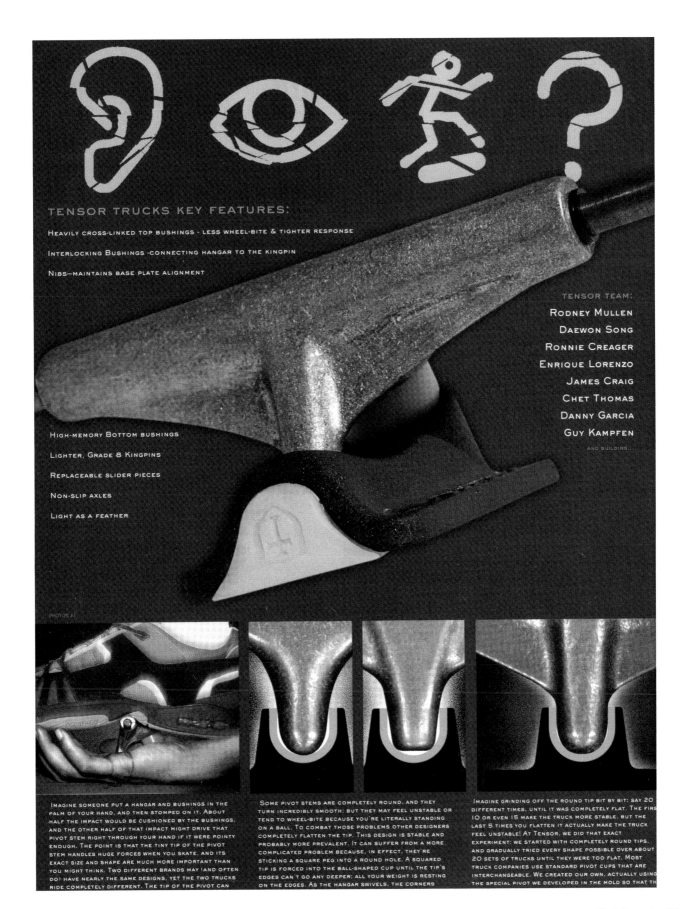

TENSOR TRUCKS KEY FEATURES:

HEAVILY CROSS-LINKED TOP BUSHINGS - LESS WHEEL-BITE & TIGHTER RESPONSE

INTERLOCKING BUSHINGS -CONNECTING HANGAR TO THE KINGPIN

NIBS—MAINTAINS BASE PLATE ALIGNMENT

HIGH-MEMORY BOTTOM BUSHINGS

LIGHTER, GRADE 8 KINGPINS

REPLACEABLE SLIDER PIECES

NON-SLIP AXLES

LIGHT AS A FEATHER

TENSOR TEAM:

RODNEY MULLEN

DAEWON SONG

RONNIE CREAGER

ENRIQUE LORENZO

JAMES CRAIG

CHET THOMAS

DANNY GARCIA

GUY KAMPFEN

AND BUILDING...

PHOTOS J.T.

IMAGINE SOMEONE PUT A HANGAR AND BUSHINGS IN THE PALM OF YOUR HAND, AND THEN STOMPED ON IT. ABOUT HALF THE IMPACT WOULD BE CUSHIONED BY THE BUSHINGS, AND THE OTHER HALF OF THAT IMPACT MIGHT DRIVE THAT PIVOT STEM RIGHT THROUGH YOUR HAND IF IT WERE POINTY ENOUGH. THE POINT IS THAT THE TINY TIP OF THE PIVOT STEM HANDLES HUGE FORCES WHEN YOU SKATE, AND ITS EXACT SIZE AND SHAPE ARE MUCH MORE IMPORTANT THAN YOU MIGHT THINK. TWO DIFFERENT BRANDS MAY (AND OFTEN DO) HAVE NEARLY THE SAME DESIGNS, YET THE TWO TRUCKS RIDE COMPLETELY DIFFERENT. THE TIP OF THE PIVOT CAN

SOME PIVOT STEMS ARE COMPLETELY ROUND, AND THEY TURN INCREDIBLY SMOOTH; BUT THEY MAY FEEL UNSTABLE OR TEND TO WHEEL-BITE BECAUSE YOU'RE LITERALLY STANDING ON A BALL. TO COMBAT THOSE PROBLEMS OTHER DESIGNERS COMPLETELY FLATTEN THE TIP. THIS DESIGN IS STABLE AND PROBABLY MORE PREVALENT. IT CAN SUFFER FROM A MORE COMPLICATED PROBLEM BECAUSE, IN EFFECT, THEY'RE STICKING A SQUARE PEG INTO A ROUND HOLE. A SQUARED TIP IS FORCED INTO THE BALL-SHAPED CUP UNTIL THE TIP'S EDGES CAN'T GO ANY DEEPER; ALL YOUR WEIGHT IS RESTING ON THE EDGES. AS THE HANGAR SWIVELS, THE CORNERS

IMAGINE GRINDING OFF THE ROUND TIP BIT BY BIT: SAY 20 DIFFERENT TIMES, UNTIL IT WAS COMPLETELY FLAT. THE FIRS 10 OR EVEN 15 MAKE THE TRUCK MORE STABLE, BUT THE LAST 5 TIMES YOU FLATTEN IT ACTUALLY MAKE THE TRUCK FEEL UNSTABLE! AT TENSOR, WE DID THAT EXACT EXPERIMENT: WE STARTED WITH COMPLETELY ROUND TIPS, AND GRADUALLY TRIED EVERY SHAPE POSSIBLE OVER ABOUT 20 SETS OF TRUCKS UNTIL THEY WERE TOO FLAT. MOST TRUCK COMPANIES USE STANDARD PIVOT CUPS THAT ARE INTERCHANGEABLE. WE CREATED OUR OWN, ACTUALLY USING THE SPECIAL PIVOT WE DEVELOPED IN THE MOLD SO THAT TH

Skateboard Scenes
Chapter 3 Living by the Board

Skateboarding is not a hobby and it's not a sport. Skateboarding is a way of learning how to redefine the world around you.[1]
Ian MacKaye

Living in complex worlds, many people today sense that their personal circumstances no longer guarantee their identity, but nevertheless, contend Paula Moya and Michael Hames-García, they still seek to build meaningful communities.[2] Furthermore, explains urban geographer Steve Pile, people are not passive individuals but are 'multiplied, dynamic, participating and determined', continually changing both the world around them and themselves.[3] Or in sociologist Pierre Bourdieu's terms, how groups like skateboarders develop their taste, style, cultural capital and social relations leads to a distinctive way of thinking and acting, in which they too are transformed.[4]

For skaters this means a form of *subculture* – Dick Hebdige's social worlds, which confront conventional codes and so help people to identify themselves.[5] When writing the earlier version of this book in the late 1990s, skateboarding subculture was largely cast as being oppositional to normative society. Skaters saw themselves as 'tired of the same old paralyzing stenchy activities' and instead as creating an alternative lifestyle of music, clothes, words, magazines and videos. This is still undoubtedly true, with many skaters today contending, along with Steve Rocco, that 'the opposite of skateboarding is golf'.[6]

Yet as I write this new book some twenty years later, skateboarding has moved inexorably from a seemingly singular subculture both into the mainstream – being now a pervasive yet less dominant presence in skaters' lives – and into myriad alternative identities. In this dispersed culture – which Julie Angel also notes[7] – skate-centric qualities like independence, cynicism, jocularity, creativity and resourcefulness combine in unpredictable ways. For example, Guan Mu, who runs the Chinese *Kicker Club* website, describes himself as 'father, skater, husband, Christian, developer.[8] And as the French-born, Malmö-based, transgender and non-binary-identifying Marie Dabbadie stated at the 2018 Pushing Boarders conference in London, 'cool dude masculinity no longer defines skateboarding'.

Just then as subculture scholars like Andy Bennett, Steve Redhead, David Muggleton and Rupert Weinzierl have gone beyond the work of Hebdige, identifying ways in which 'post-subculture' is more complex with regard to ethnicity, race, sexuality, gender and the cultural mainstream, so skateboarding has become more diverse in its practices and beliefs, as well as more global. It is to these complexities that we now turn.[9]

Freaks and Geeks

In its most distinctive social world, skateboarding, like many other kinds of subculture, has separated itself from cosy clubs, regulated schools and organized teams, being more irrational in organization, independently creative and exploitative of its 'sub-' status.[10] Skateboarders are also often disruptive, creating a distance from others, and so unsettle conventional society in an ambiguous yet challenging manner.

This was especially the case in the 1990s, when skaters typically equated with philosopher Henri Lefebvre's characterization of nineteenth-century romanticism, that is, an idealized present that involved coded dress, speech and body language, thus uniting individuals of different backgrounds and residing outside of society while simultaneously being within its heart.[11] As Rodney Mullen recalled, at this time 'skaters had their own look, own clothes, own way of looking at the world.'[12] These 1990s skaters also often saw themselves, in Jeff Grosso's words, as society's 'freaks and geeks', and ever since this period skateboard discourse has consistently characterized skaters as eccentrics, outcasts and rebels.[13]

Furthermore, skateboarding is typically practised by younger adults and teenagers; one 2009 estimate placed ninety-three per cent of US skaters below twenty-four years old.[14] With this comes the general attitude of youth, which in Lefebvre's words 'revolts against the Fathers', and which among skaters is frequently expressed as a dislike of routinized training and

Figure 3.1
Jason Jessee finds himself on death row for skateboarding. *Streets on Fire* (Santa Cruz, dir. Howard Dittrich, 1989). www.bit.ly/Jessee-StreetsOnFire

memberships.[15] Skateboarders are 'not kids whose dads gave them batting practice out in the front yard,' explained *Thrasher*. 'It's not a father-son deal.'[16] So instead of Little League institutions like school, family and teams, skaters opt for a sense of personal freedom. The opinions of someone like Shayne Stadnick are typical here, seeing that in skateboarding 'there is no coach to impress or teammates to let down, no rules or regulations' and 'no scheduled times.'[17]

An even more general critique of normative society is also discernible in skateboarding, what Beal has called a 'symbolic inversion' and a 'daily critique and alternative to mainstream relations.'[18] In 1983, Garry Scott Davis (GSD), for example, viewed things like 'baseball, hotdogs, apple pie, weed, beer, pills, needles, alcohol' as just the 'typical hobbies of all the typical people' in America. His conclusion was simple: 'Why be a clone?'[19] These views have been fairly constant within skateboarding; as Chris Joslin told the *Skateboard Mag* two decades later, 'you see those packed freeways? I don't really want to be another person on there.'[20]

Indeed, in its more extreme formulations, skate subculture involves everything, with practitioners like Christian Hosoi enjoying skateboarding 'because they want to totally live it', this kind of all-encompassing attitude also being evident in novels like Nick Hornby's *Slam* (2008), autobiographical texts like Jocko Weyland's *The Answer Is Never* (2002) and Justin Hocking's *Life and Limb* (2004), and in films like *Kids* (1995), *Ken Park* (2002), *Lords of Dogtown* (2005) and *Paranoid Park* (2007).[21] 'One way or another,' asserted Skatemaster Tate (Gerry Hurtado), 'skating relates to just about every part of my life.'[22] Or as *Thrasher* decreed, 'Live by the board, die by the board.'[23]

Everything in Between

Not everything is perfect in skateboarding's cultural garden, as many academic critiques have argued. Kusz has contended that extreme sports like skateboarding are a 'masculinising corrective' to the cultural feminization of 1990s US white males, whose practitioners regard themselves as superior to average citizens.[24] Studies of Michigan and Swedish skaters by Yochim and Hellmans concur, showing how some white male skaters can imagine themselves as victims and act non-inclusively.[25] And representations like Powell-Peralta's *Ban This* (1989) and Shorty's *Guilty* (2002) certainly cast skaters as misunderstood criminals, victimized because of their marginal and oppositional status; in Santa Cruz's *Streets on Fire* (1989), Jason Jessee is even placed on death row (Figure 3.1). According to Butz, skaters here understand the concept of marginalization, but erroneously present themselves as major victims, for, however much riders might face anti-skate legislation attitudes, they do not actually face the same level of pervasive repression or discrimination as do many other social groups.[26]

In addition, as academic studies have also shown, skateboarding culture can be equally reductive in other areas. Hence Leonard identifies how the *Tony Hawk* video games ignore poverty, violence and police brutality, and so aestheticize ghettos as 'exotic tourist destinations'. The privileged and largely white suburban consumers of this reductive landscape, the skater game-players, may then 'violate societal laws without consequences', enjoying an impunity not extended to youth of colour, and becoming reincarnations of white pioneers; 'Whereas the frontiersman defied the unnamed wilderness guarded by indigenous "savages"', argues Leonard, 'the extreme virtual skateboarder conquers this once dangerous space, demonstrating the ultimate "strength, coolness and confidence" of White masculinity.'[27] Brayton also shows how skateboard media regularly depict white-privileged travel alongside rebellious cool and supposedly 'black cultural' signifiers like hip-hop, gangsta criminality and virulent sexuality.[28] More overtly, Wheaton and Beal note how some skaters use racial stereotypes when claiming that African-Americans ollie higher and that Asian-Americans 'work harder', while Beal and Wilson have even postulated that black riders have to be better skaters before gaining recognition.[29] For street-skaters in particular, Atencio, Beal, McClain, Orpana, Wilson and Wright have all argued that the typically hyper-performing, overtly male and highly individualized body of this kind of rider aligns neatly with neoliberal patriarchal structures and their focus on risk, masculinist hierarchies and the denigration of women.[30] Consequently, Yochim calls all of this a 'corresponding culture' – analogous to Bourdieu's 'fields' – that critiques dominant masculinities (notably 'jock' athletes) without truly challenging the power of the dominant straight and white middle classes.[31]

However damning these academic interpretations might seem, they are complicated and refuted by skateboarding's social constitution and attitudes. Additionally, what was perhaps true years ago is not necessarily true today, just as skate *representations* do not always correlate with wider skate *practices*. Much skateboarding culture is far from the reactionary bastion which some have perceived.

In particular, skateboarding often transcends class, religion and ethnicity, and skaters have generally come from more varied backgrounds than occurs in traditional sports. Skaters like Jeremy Henderson welcome a scene where 'you see all different types of economic groups'. Andy Macdonald remembers Massachusetts as a place where rich and poor kids alike formed their local skate crew, while skateboarding similarly allowed Bob Burnquist to 'bridge social barriers' with Rio's favelas.[32] All this is aided by relatively low equipment costs – in the mid-2010s even a major brand set-up cost only between $100 and $150, and certainly skateboarding has avoided the kinds of technological advancements that have led windsurfing and snowboarding to outstrip many riders' budgets.[33] Less fashionable brands and second-hand equipment lower costs further, while street-skating and open-access skateparks reduce expenditure on transportation, fees or safety equipment. Today, notes Dinces, 'skaters hail from working- and upper-class backgrounds, and everything in between.'[34]

Religious categories can also be transcended, with skaters frequently crossing sectarian divides. As Drissel demonstrates in Belfast, skaters engage in 'collective identity work' and forge non-sectarian relationships.[35] Apart from the occasional punkish swastika, anti-Semitism is almost entirely absent, with Alan Gelfand (Figure 9.2), Torey Pudwill, Elliot Sloan and Yoshi Tanenbaum all being first-rank Jewish skaters.[36] Even modern rabbis like David Levinksy in Utah and ultra-orthodox Jews like Benad Eve-Chen in Jerusalem can be skaters.[37]

'Skateboarding community', considers Karl Watson, 'embraces all ways of life, whether you are black or white."[38] At first glance, however, a degree of caution is advisable here. In particular, there are commercial processes that some are keen to exploit. Pro skater Hosoi – himself of Japanese, Scottish-Irish, French, Chinese and Hawaiian extraction – frequently employed graffiti and gang symbols, which were quickly taken up by suburban skaters. One Team Hosoi advertisement, for example, depicted Hosoi and Monty Nolder caught in the glare of an arresting police torch, where gang-style board logos defy the camera, like offensive weapons.[39] Even earlier, 1970s Dogtown deck graphics had been derived from Los Angeles Hispanic gang culture (Figure 12.1), while later companies like Eightball, Grind King and Neighborhood also used gangster references.[40] For branding purposes, this strategy of interconnecting various combinations of skateboarding, ethnicity, street-level and gang culture has clearly worked. In 2004, Reebok sponsored skater Stevie Williams (Figure 13.1), who later formed the DGK (Dirty Ghetto Kids) sub-brand and by 2007 was regarded by the *New York Times* as a superstar successor to hip-hop's Jay-Z. Similarly, when rappers The Pack named their 2006 track 'Vans' after the skate shoe brand, many ethnic and low-income kids took up skateboarding.[41] Such tactics were important, given that during the 2000s the fast-expanding spending power of US ethnic groups was expected to reach $992 billion for Latinos and $965 billion for African-Americans.[42]

All of this could be seen as superficial consumerism in which ethnicity, in bell hooks's words, is used to 'liven up the dull dish that is mainstream white culture.'[43] Atencio, Beal and Yochim similarly argue that skateboarding is a predominantly white and male activity, using 'skurban' (skateboarding + urban) racialized images to sell goods and support neoliberalism. As they note, a 2009 Nike advertisement

Figure 3.2
Finnish Simo Makela
and Moroccan-
Belgian Youness
Amrani (2010).
@dvlphoto.

featuring Mexican-American skater Paul
Rodriguez and accompanied by Ice Cube's 'It
Was a Good Day' strips away any suggestions of
racial inequality and injustice. Instead, P-Rod
freely skates across an idealized playground
of multi-ethnic friends, traffic-free roads and
acquiescent police. Such representations
provide utopian glimpses of multi-ethnicity,
but simultaneously privilege individual status,
emphasize meritocracy, avoid critiquing real life
and ignore the need for social intervention in
complex urban conditions.[44]

Skateboarding's multi-ethnicity could then be
viewed as largely a matter of appearances and
branding, close to Brayton's 'crossover' culture
and 'limited to the consumption of essentialized
black culture such as rap and basketball apparel'.
Yet skate ethnic diversity does in fact frequently
extend into real friendships, and here comes
closer to Brayton's 'crossing over' with 'direct
engagement and communication between
people of color and Whites' (Figure 3.2).[45] 'In
skating, there is no segregation really', states Billy
Miller, because 'you don't become aware of their
skin color. It just doesn't matter.'[46] Similarly,
in *Sunlight* (Jordan Redila, 2012) African-
American Tayvion Posey notes how shared

skate experiences let 'different races, different
religions all get along'.

This pluralism is particularly true of recent
skateboarding, for, while 1970s skaters tended
to be white surfers called Jay, Bob or Brad –
according to John Tesoriero, many Australian
teams preferred their riders to be blond-haired
and blue-eyed[47] – from the 1980s onwards
skaters have been more ethnically varied, such
as 1980s pros Hispanic Steve Caballero (Figures
3.9 and 7.17), Japanese-American Lester Kasai
and African-American Steve Steadham, or 1990s
professionals like Armando Barajas, Omar
Hassan, Lavar McBride (Figure 4.7), Marcus
McBride, Kien Lieu and Willy Santos. By the
mid-1990s, street-skating particularly attracted
economically disadvantaged skaters of colour, as
with Keenan Milton and Chico Brenes appearing
in Chocolate's *Las Nueve Vidas de Paco* (1996),
while Asian-Americans formed twenty per cent
of National Skateboard Association members.[48]
Over the last twenty years, renowned skaters
have included, to name but a few, Chinese
ethnicity Jerry Hsu, African-Americans Ishod
Wair and Stevie Williams (Figure 13.1), Filipino-
American Willy Santos, Rastafarian-raised Nyjah
Huston (Figure 5.20), Hawaiian Jaime Reyes,

Figure 3.3
Lizzie Armanto in
*Tony Hawk's Pro
Skater 5* (2015).
Courtesy Activision
Press Center.

white Briton Geoff Rowley (Figure 10.13), Latina Patty Segovia-Krause, Latino Paul Rodriguez, Chinese-Vietnamese-American Kien Lieu, white Californians Ryan Sheckler and Julz Lynn, Russian-born and Dutch-raised Sewa Kroetkov, Danish Rune Glifberg (Figure 7.24), South Korean–born Daewon Song (Figure 7.20), Thai-American Eric Koston (Figure 11.5) and Brazilians Letícia Bufoni, Lincoln Ueda, Sandro Dias and Bob Burnquist. Such diversity is also now commonly replicated in mass-market representations; by 2015 the *Tony Hawk* video game included two black (Nyjah Huston and Ishod Wair), one Latino (David González) and two female skaters (Letícia Bufoni and Lizzie Armanto) among its ten headliners (Figure 3.3).

Outside professional circles, similar pattern are discernible. According to Sheldon Thompson, the Brooklyn Museum changed from a predominantly white skatespot to being for everybody;[49] elsewhere in New York, as shown by White and *Concrete Jungle* (Eli Morgan Gesner, 2009), between the 1980s and 2000s Bronx skateboarding went from a punk and 'whiteboy' activity to being undertaken by hip-hop-listening blacks, Dominicans and Puerto Ricans.[50] *Blackboard* (Marquis Bradshaw, 2016) records how black US youth were encouraged to skate by the likes of Lupe Fiasco and his track 'Kick, Push' (2006), and Forsyth notes how Aboriginal Canadians took up skateboarding.[51] In New Orleans, following hurricane Katrina (2005), a predominantly black scene emerged. As Edwards explains, encouraged partly by skateboarding rappers Lil Wayne and Pharrell Williams, and partly by the racialized marketing of skateboarding as mainstream culture,

skaters here resisted a culture of crime to form a community of trust.[52] Indeed, skate ethnic diversification is now a nationwide US trend. In 2007 the *New York Times* commented on how across the United States 'skateboarding has joined the fraternity of minority street games', and in 2014 some thirty-four per cent of skaters came from non-white backgrounds, roughly equivalent to the thirty-seven per cent of non-whites in the US population.[53] Today *Huffington Post* notes how 'black skaters are visible in skateparks, suburbs and inner city streets from New York to New Orleans.'[54]

Unsurprisingly, given this diversity, there are relatively few racial tensions within skateboarding, and indeed many skaters have fully embraced a varied class and ethnic life. East Coast skater Bryan Ridgeway recalled how his fellow African-Americans 'pretty much all had white, Asian, Hispanic buddies', and so when black Stevie Williams acknowledges white fellow Love Park local Josh Kalis as being the 'angel on my shoulder' who kept him on the straight and narrow, this is just one of a legion of similar stories.[55] And while the early surf-oriented history of skateboarding was infused with whiteness, notes Sueyoshi, in later years Asian-Americans have considered the skate community 'as one of racial tolerance where different people could come together and be judged purely for their skating ability.'[56]

Skateboarding at its heart shows a tendency towards openness and inclusivity, and, as discussed in Chapter 13, has been used for social empowerment worldwide. For now it is worth noting how, as Wheaton recounts, at the

Figure 3.4
Learning to skate at
the Zaatari refugee
camp, Jordan (2015).
© Daniel Zvereff.

Indigo Skate Camp and North Beach Park in
Durban, South Africa, and with aid from pro
Dallas Oberholzer, skateboarding has steered
kids away from drugs, alcohol and HIV and
towards healthier lifestyles and education.
Significantly, skateboarding here avoids the
whites-only connotations of colonial sports like
rugby and cricket, while its focus on individual
self-direction also renders it suitable for young,
black communities. Through hybridizing
vernacular cultures like Kwaito rap music with
US cultural forms like skateboarding, as one
skater explained, 'skating brings us all together'.
And, Wheaton concludes, skateboarding has
here produced a variety of complex cultural
flows and so has helped reconfigure lifestyle
sport cultures and identities.[57]

Home Turf and Foreign Lands

If skateboarding has any discernible tensions,
then these are often drawn up along lines of

geography. This was particularly true of the
late 1970s, when skaters often confronted
outsiders with hostility. 'It was a pretty heavy
scene,' described Tony Alva of his Santa Monica,
Ocean Park and Venice Beach locality. 'When
we're riding somewhere and someone put
our area down, we stood up for it.'[58] Here the
willingness for conflict enhanced both the sense
of belonging and intra-regional rivalries. 'There
is no energy down south,' declared Alva's fellow
Z-Boy skaters to their San Diego rivals. 'We
know that it is all located in Dogtown.'[59] Similar
rivalries existed between Australian groups like
the Sparx team, Radlanders and Badlanders.[60]

The early 1990s were another intense period
for this kind of locals-only home turf mentality
or what was now often called 'vibing'. At San
Francisco's Embarcadero, outsiders might get
shoulder-blocked or spat upon, and locals
like James Kelch ruled the roost, 'dismissing'

Figure 3.5
Riotous masculinity in *Beers, Bowls and Barneys* (Thrasher, dir. Preston Maigetter, 2004).
www.bit.ly/BeerBowlsBarneys

skaters he took exception to and 'defending his turf in countless brawls'.[61] As Vogel has pointed out, cliques also formed at other skatespots to spurn unwelcome visitors.[62] New York's Brooklyn Banks was particularly renowned for its 'survival-of-the-fittest' mentality, where new arrivals met with hazing, theft and intimidation, while Zoo York skaters would similarly steal outsiders' boards as 'primitive carjacking'.[63]

This was not, however, a ghettoization of different kinds of skateboarders, but merely a fragmentation of riders from different places. Today, a few occasionally complain of clique-like groupings, while some Chinese skaters, tired of their favourite local spots attracting unwanted attention from the authorities, have misdirected overseas visitors towards unfavourable locations.[64] But such spoiling tactics are rare, and instead, one normally finds easy allegiances between skaters. Forums and blogs are thus full with stories of newly met skaters in foreign lands who share food, drink, fuel and accommodation; Jonathan Mehring's *Skate the World* photographic collection shows skaters making friends in locations as diverse as Bangalore (India), Kharkiv (Ukraine), Kampala (Uganda), Almaty (Kazakhstan), Tehran (Iran), Ordos (China), Santarém (Brazil) and a Zaatari refugee camp (Jordan) (Figure 3.4). Given that social obscurity and loneliness are common urban conditions – as Fran Tonkiss comments after sociologist Georg Simmel, 'city life is characterized by anonymity, instrumentality and atomization'[65] – skaters here avoid such restrictions and make meaningful connections with others, and all without resorting to family, school and team institutions.

Travel is key here, and during the 2000s ever more skate videos have been based on road trips and distant journeys – not just across the United States, as typified by Shorty's *How to Go Pro* (2005), but increasingly in places like Australia, China, Cuba, Madagascar, Mongolia

(Figure 5.27), Oman, the Philippines and South America – typically emphasizing how skaters can find friends anywhere worldwide. As Kenny Anderson commented of the *Perros y Amigos* (2014) skate trip across Chile and Peru, 'I first started traveling internationally in 1998 and I haven't stopped since. To me, that's the best part about skateboarding. You'll always have something in common.' Despite its schmaltzy tone, *We Are Blood* (Ty Evans, 2015) displays similar sentiments, with pro skaters like Paul Rodriguez, Chris Colbourn and Sean Malto journeying across Brazil, China, Spain, United Arab Emirates and the United States, and generally evoking a spirit of skaters as one global community; 'some people see a skateboard as a symbol of hope,' narrates Rodriguez while visiting Brazil, 'that feeling of belonging or feeling included – it's like a family.' As Rodriguez somewhat portentously concludes, 'we come from many different cultures, but skateboarding brings us together.'

Beer and Barneys

Notwithstanding the welcome and increasing presence of female skaters discussed later in this chapter, masculinity, notes Yochim, is often the predominant identity within skateboarding.[66] And one place to locate this masculinity is *Thrasher* magazine, which, particularly after Jake Phelps's editorship commenced in 1993, has been especially connected with beer-drinking, hardcore-music, weed-smoking, party-seeking and all round rowdiness; 'I won't conform, I'm a piece of trash, fuck the established' sings Duane Peters in 'Love and Hate' with his punk band The Hunns.[67] This stance is typified by *Thrasher*'s video *Beers, Bowls and Barneys* (2004), directed by Preston Maigetter (aka P-Stone), with twenty-five minutes of on-the-edge riding, body-jarring slams, beer-drinking, hardcore music and raucous revelry (Figure 3.5).

How do we understand this masculinity? To begin with, as Judith Butler explains, gender

Figure 3.6
Diego Bucchieri bloodied and battered (2004).
© Jon Humphries.

and sexuality are fluid and 'performatively produced'.[68] Furthermore, note Connell and Brayton and others, there are multiple masculinities.[69] Nonetheless, at first sight skateboarding seems to be constituted as a determinedly singular heterosexual masculinity, marked by casual aggression, independence and rebellion. This is evident not only from *Thrasher* but in the *Big Brother* magazine of the 1990s and films like Larry Clark's *Kids* (1995), through to Ian Reid's *Sex, Hood, Skate and Videotape* (2006) and the *So What* (2016) video by London's With Section, which variously show irrepressible skateboarding energy mixed with a street milieu of weed, gangs, nudity, offhand violence and ad hoc DIY terrains. 'All I need is my girl, a chewy spliff, and a peanut butter and jelly sandwich to go along with my daily scorched earth domination', declares a 2014 Asphalt advertisement. 'No fucks given.'[70]

This riotous masculinity is also clearly evident in the product-tossing of many 1980s skate competitions, where pros threw stickers and T-shirts to a 'shark feeding-frenzy'.[71] For example, *Radical Moves* (1988) shows heaving mêlées at the 1986 Vancouver TransWorld Championships, while at a later Vancouver competition 'a riot broke out'.[72] In another variant, Mike Vallely's *Stand Strong* (2000) and *Greatest Hits* (2003) videos depict confrontations with officials and jocks, where countless brawls and slams emphasize skateboarding's outsider ethos and aggressive demeanour; 'within seconds', narrates one *Greatest Hits* sequence, 'Vallely comes in like a whirlwind, beats the crap out of every security guard in sight, then he's gone.'

Injuries sustained while skateboarding are another aspect of this male identity (Figure 3.6). 'The bruising of one's body', argues Beal, 'demonstrates a traditional masculine characteristic of risking bodily injury', while most skaters – male and female alike – accept that getting hurt is intrinsic to skateboarding; as Mark Gonzales says, 'you've gotta bleed to get paid'.[73] Although skateboarding is less dangerous than boxing, American football, snowboarding, ice hockey and mountain biking, and few skaters actively seek accidents, getting hurting is thus viewed as an essential part of skateboarding.[74] In 2001 *SkateBoarder* listed common injuries as sprained ankles, swollen elbows, cut palms, chipped teeth, sprained wrists, dislocated shoulders, hyper-extended knees, concussion and bruised genitalia.[75] And as *Thrasher* explained alongside a montage

of sixty gruesome wounds, 'without the pain, there'd never be any satisfaction'.[76]

Given the pervasiveness of pain, many videos unsurprisingly include numerous fails, bails and worse. *Thrasher*'s *911 Emergency* (1995) includes the hospitalization of Ricky Oyola, while its *Hall of Meat* (1999) details a gory series of collisions and falls; today, YouTube contains innumerable 'Best of' slam edits. Some individual failures even become notorious, as in 1997 when John Cardiel tried seventy-two times to boardslide a kinked handrail, hitting his head until his eyes bled.[77] Among innumerable other examples, *TransWorld*'s *The Reason* (1999) fully documents Paul Machnau's leg breakage – an episode that added considerably to his pro reputation[78] – and in *Lenz II* (Shinpei Ueno, 2013), Shun Hashimoto's perilous escapades include a high-level balcony drop down to a head-smashing encounter with the road below. During a 2015 Israel trip, Antihero's Raney Beres collided with a cobblestoned pillar, suffering a near-fatal brain haemorrhage.[79]

As this suggests, stunt-oriented skating can generate genuinely life-threatening risks. In 1997, just before Jeremy Wray famously ollied a high level gap between two water towers, photographer Daniel Sturt asked if there was a possibility of death. 'Actually, on this one, there is', Wray replied.[80] The same year, Jamie Thomas performed the infamous 'Leap of Faith' for Zero's *Thrill of It All*, where at Point Loma school he ollies into a 6 m void (Figure 5.18). Thomas later recalled, 'I remember dropping in the air and thinking, "Dude, this is way higher than I imagined. There's no way I'm going to be riding away from this."'[81] And before Geoff Rowley 180 ollied an ultra-high 5 m gap between some Long Beach port containers, he first instructed photographer Ryan Allan to pre-dial 911 in case of a serious fall.[82]

More recently, skaters like Aaron 'Jaws' Homoki and Brian Delatorre have gained notorious reputations for launching off buildings and undertaking rooftop moves.[83] One of Homoki's innumerable feats includes his 2015 successful jumping of the infamous twenty-five-stair set (around 4 ½ m drop and 7 m long) at Lyon's Centre de Congrès – a feat previously attempted by both Homoki (in 2014) and Ali Boulala (in Flip's *Sorry*, 2002) but resulting only in injury (Figure 3.7).[84] Similarly, *Tengu: God of Mischief* (Colin Read, 2013) starts with high-level rooftop New York manoeuvres, before Koki Loaiza ollies across the electrified train track of

Figure 3.7
Aaron 'Jaws' Homoki, twenty-five
stairs, Lyon (Thrasher, 2016).
www.bit.ly/LyonJaws

the 145th Street station, while the *Skate Near Death* 'skate-poem' (2016) shows Roma Alimov grinding a platform edge as a train rushes in and negotiating potentially fatal ledges, rails and bridges.

If skate videos often perform masculinity through dangerous stunts, another pervasive male representation involves the poses and attitudes struck in advertisements. To cite one classic example, in a 1988 photograph by Steve Gross for the Alva Posse team, twelve leather-clad 'Alva Boyz' stare defiantly at the camera, overtly displaying confrontational aggression and a 'gangster-don't-give-a-shit attitude'.[85] According to Alva, these were party-hard and skate-hard 'road warriors' and 'a total destruction machine'.[86]

At times, skateboarding's symbolism of gangs and semi-illegal activities has spilled over into drugs, violence and worse; renowned skaters convicted over the years including Jay Adams (drugs, assault), Ben Pappas (murder, cocaine smuggling), Tas Pappas (domestic violence, cocaine smuggling), Josh Swindell (second degree murder), Neil Heddings (manslaughter), Christian Hosoi (crystal meth smuggling), Mark 'Gator' Rogowski (rape, murder), Paul Hackett (matricide) and Duane Peters (domestic violence). Skater alcohol and/ or drug addiction has also occurred with some regularity, those affected including Dennis Agnew, Jake Anderson, Jason Dill, Christian Hosoi, Jeff Grosso, Matt Hensley, Andy Kessler, Bruce Logan, Lizard King, Guy Mariano, Dennis Martinez, Brandon Novak, Ben Pappas, Duane Peters, Lee Ralph, Andrew Reynolds, Wentzle Ruml, Per Viking, Danny Way and many others.[87]

Sometimes such criminality even becomes implicitly condoned. For example, Jay Adams's illegal activities are often dismissed as the kinds of minor errors typical of a 'bad boy skateboarder'. Hence while Adams indifferently

described his involvement in the fatal assault of a mixed-race gay couple – 'Beat up some homos. No big deal. We do that shit all the time' – his own untimely death in 2014 lead to eulogizing obituaries (according to Hosoi, Adams 'embodied our culture and lifestyle all in one') that typically dismissed such dark episodes as merely the acts of a 'colourful rebel'. Far rarer have been Keith Hamm's more balanced comments, recognizing that Adams was 'at his worst, a felon, junkie, and a racist and homophobic deadbeat dad', and simultaneously 'at his best, a legendary surfer and skateboarder, an honest and sober guy who goes to church on Sundays and sends his kid money each month'.[88]

Here lies a great contradiction within skateboarding, whose masculinity can be at once loud and contemplative, violent and considerate, intolerant and respectful. Indeed, *SkateBoarder* may have presented its favoured Dogtown skaters as unruly and rebellious, but its overall message was still of skateboarding as being clean-cut, progressive, professional and hierarchical; extreme behaviour went unreported and photographs showing underage skaters drinking beer were left unpublished.[89] Parents featured in *Skateboard Kings* (BBC, prod. Horace Ové, 1978) similarly praised skateboarding as a healthy outlet encouraging balance, agility and mobility, and it is to these kinds of skateboarding culture that we now turn.

Positive and Loving
That many skateboarders refute the 'jock' sports masculinity of physical domination, extreme competitiveness and overt sexism is, in part at least, evident from skaters' bodies. Of course, some skaters do have a pumped-up or otherwise formidable appearance; Vallely, for instance, was celebrated as a samurai-warrior 'burning with intensity', while Lizard King boasted 'hand tattoos, wild eyes and impressive alcohol tolerance'.[90] In this regard, skateboarding, for Beal, can be 'an alternative conduit for

Figure 3.8
Italo Romano, amputee and pro
skateboarder (2014).
www.bit.ly/RomanoItalo

promoting an ideology of male superiority and patriarchal relations.'[91]

Yet, notes Louison, most skaters are lithe or even scrawny.[92] Tony Hawk, Rodney Mullen, Nyjah Huston, Ben Raybourn, Lizzie Armanto and many others don't really look like sports athletes, their leanness offering power and agility that brawn would only hinder. And of course younger professionals – such as Ryan Sheckler (aged thirteen on turning pro in 2003), or Tom Schaar (aged twelve when winning gold at the Asia X Games) – have even more boyish physiques.

Some renowned skaters even contend with significant medical challenges, including Steve Caballero (scoliosis), Rodney Mullen (femoral anteversion) (Figures 9.5 and 10.3), Felipe Nunes and Italo Romano (amputated legs) (Figure 3.8), Steven 'Lefty' Breeding (no right arm), Auby Taylor (Asperger's), Andrew Reynolds (OCD), Tas Pappas (personality disorder) and Billy Rohan (manic-depression).[93] Similarly, deaf skaters have included Chris Weddle, Monty Nolder and Brandon White.[94] Skater-dancer-artist Bill 'Crutch' Shannon suffers from Legg-Calve-Perthes disease and uses crutches, and Aaron Fotheringham performs skate-derived wheelchair moves.[95] Among everyday skaters are John Coutis (spina bifida), Ian Parkinson and Clément Zannini (prosthetics), and Kanya Sesser and Rosie Davies (no legs).[96] Brett Devloo, Marcelo Lusardi, Dan Mancina and Nick Mullins are blind, and Erik Kondo balances his wheelchair on a skateboard.[97] Skateboarding also helps those with autism, disability, learning difficulties or even polymicrogyria brain deformation.[98]

If skaters rarely express masculinity through pumped muscularity or overt athleticism, other bodily expressions are nonetheless adopted. Most notable here are tattoos – popular designs include *Thrasher*'s Skate and Destroy, Independent's Iron Cross, Santa Cruz's

Screaming Hand and Spitfire's Fire Head – which *Skinned Alive* (Bart Saric, 2004) identifies as connecting skateboarding with punk music, individualism and anti-authoritarianism, but that also allow individuals to sidestep and avoid overtly stereotypical masculine personas. Hence someone like the small-framed Ben Raybourn sports nerdy Ray Ban spectacles and a few tattoos, while becoming globally renowned for his impulsive riding style. Similar to Raybourn in their individualistic yet non-aggressive character are the vast majority of everyday skaters, as well as professionals like Gregg Weaver, described by *SkateBoarder* as 'all the kid any parent could want', the artistic Mark Gonzales, widely acknowledged as the world's most influential skater, and the 'pathologically non-confrontational' Tony Hawk.[99] Andy Macdonald, a contemporary of Hawk's, adopted Ghandi's philosophy of non-violence; 'What really takes guts is to keep right on walking, confident in who you are.' Responding to a skater's father worried about illegality, profanities and violence, Macdonald argued that these things are actually more prevalent in other sports, and that skateboarding instead offers a drug-free path to self-fulfilment, financial success and civic-mindedness.[100]

In a similar vein, Davidson has argued vehemently that drugs and bad attitudes in skateboarding are largely promoted by a 'core' industry, whereas a 'silent majority' of everyday skaters actually possess different qualities, identified by Yochim as sensitivity, self-expression, transcendence, poetics and self-reflection.[101] This is also supported by Beal's interviews with a wide range of 1990s skaters, who included honour students, Christians, skinheads, feminists, teachers and drop-outs.[102] One scientific study similarly found no correlation between skateboarders and substance abuse, while Márquez and García show how Madrid skaters have diverse attitudes to skateboarding, music, drugs and fashion, and frequently reject beer and barneys lifestyles.[103] All this differs significantly from both the supposedly typical aggression of skaters (surliness, intoxication, brawling) and the mindlessness of jock athletes (aggression, intolerance, rigid codes). Just as Thorpe notes within snowboarding, skateboarding masculinities are increasingly plural and variable.[104]

This is not to say that all is perfect, and notably skateboarding, and here unfortunately in common with many other social practices, has frequently involved a strain of homophobia. Sometimes this is outright hostility, as with Adams's gay-bashing, while according to Bryce Kanights some skaters, even in the 2010s, are 'openly homophobic'.[105] More usually terms like 'gay' have frequently been used disparagingly, as with a 1992 Plan B advertisement depicting Mullen as 'just another gay freestyler', or the 2000s Australian skaters studied by Nolan who commonly identified non-skaters as 'poof' and 'faggot'.[106] As this suggests, skateboarding generally promotes heterosexuality as the dominant norm and ridicules those outside this stereotype. For example, freestyle has sometimes been described as skateboarding's feminine or homosexual 'other', its emphasis on grace and technique contrasting with the overt risk-taking of much transition and street-skating; for example, Hawk's 2000 autobiography described freestyle as skateboarding's 'dirty secret' in a confessional section called 'Coming Out of the Closet'.[107] Similarly, Hawk's Birdhouse were happy for amateur team rider Tim Von Werne to be gay, but dissuaded Werne from disclosing this sexuality in an interview (although Hawk himself backed Werne, and later supported gay marriage).[108] As Patrick Welch has discovered, at least seven current top skaters are probably gay, but apart from Brian Anderson, who came out in 2016, none, no doubt wary of their youth-oriented markets, have made this public; 'the reason why X pro doesn't come out as gay', argues Kanights, 'is that he won't sell any boards'.[109]

Rather than overt prejudices, these instances are part of a general unthinkingness and commercial fear that pervades skateboarding; as Willing and Shearer explain, skate media commonly ignore how skaters today are increasingly varied, including those who are older, female, lesbian, gay, bisexual or transgender.[110] Rare exceptions are *Monster*'s extended discussion of homosexuality, *Jenkem*'s coverage of openly gay photographer Sam McGuire and of transsexual skater Hillary

Thompson, and the interview in *Underexposed* (2013) with David Everly (previously pro skater Apryl Woodcock), *Skateism* magazine, and Unity's Queer Skate Days.[111]

Another form of masculinity is to see skateboarding as hardcore in its refusal of bodily abuse, where – and in contrast to the 'pathetic emptiness' of punk lifestyles, such as Josh Sandoval's aimless oscillation between pool-riding, beer-guzzling, bong-toking, party-puking and cigarette-scrounging – a more positive direction can be pursued.[112] This was especially evident among 1990s 'straight edge' adherents – including skaters like Bill Danforth, 'zines like *Skate Edge* and bands like Minor Threat – who abstained from risky sex, substances or meat-eating to focus on the purity of mind and body. According to some critics, straight edge was a white middle-class defence against drug-taking and sexuality, without embracing Moral Majority 'just say no' values.[113] But whatever its wider context, in skateboarding straight edge became particularly explicit through aggressively acting bodies, appropriative tactics and general subcultural attitudes. Indeed, some of this is latent in skateboarding generally, as when Lance Mountain declares that 'people that smoke and drink are fake'.[114] Tait Colberg has viewed skaters who drink beer in videos as being 'boring', and criticizes them for providing free advertising for alcohol companies, while pro skater and punk rocker Steve Caballero has called for 'more positive, loving and selfless attitudes' within skateboarding, alongside refraining from cigarettes, alcohol and drugs (Figure 3.9).[115] In this way, skateboarding provides an escape from drugs as both dangerous physiological abuse and entrapping social milieu; for Bob Burnquist (Figure 7.21), for example, skateboarding (and veganism) provided a way to break away from his teenage São Paulo indulgences of cocaine and glue-sniffing.[116]

Notably, Burnquist also drew upon beliefs in Christian Spiritism and reincarnation, while others who have similarly embraced Christianity include Ray Barbee, Tim Byrne, Steve Caballero, Eddie Elguera, Christian Hosoi, Josh Kasper, Lance Mountain, Rodney Mullen, Tas Pappas, Paul Rodriquez, Wentzle Ruml and Jamie Thomas.[117] For Hosoi, conversion came when facing a lengthy prison sentence, and after release he became an Outreach Pastor, using his skater reputation as 'a platform to preach the gospel'.[118] For others, God even actively participates in their skateboarding. 'I pray before dropping in', explains Sierra Fellers. '"God,

what do you want me to do?" I know it's going to be big, because you don't do little things.' Christianity has also impacted on everyday skaters, from G&S's promotion as a 'Christ-centred company' to Stephen Baldwin's 'Livin It' series of films, books and tours.[119] This part of skateboarding is rarely mentioned – particularly within the *Thrasher*-centred beer and barneys trope – but is nonetheless a pervasive and long-lasting element within skate culture.

Middle Age Shred

If skaters tend to avoid the regulated sports and behaviours often required of teenagers, then it is worth emphasizing that by no means are all skateboarders aged between thirteen and nineteen. Firstly, many younger skaters are having great success. Skateparks today frequently have kids aged below nine, some of whom have attained remarkably high standards; at age eight Sky Brown (Figure 3.15) competed in the Vans US Open Pro Series and Kristion Jordan made a boardslide down the notorious sixteen-step handrail at Hollywood High in Los Angeles. At nine C.J. Collins was sponsored and Sabre Norris completed a 540° aerial, at eleven Keegan Palmer won a Red Bull competition and Nyjah Huston had an X Games invite, and at

twelve Tom Schaar completed the world's first ever 1080° aerial and Alana Smith won a silver X Games medal.[120]

Another significant change has occurred at the opposite end of the spectrum. In the 1960s and 1970s, skaters in their thirties were a rarity. Yet by 1992 over ninety per cent of the riders at Davis skatepark were aged between eighteen and twenty-five, and when London's House of Vans skatepark (Figure 8.18) opened two decades later, over thirty-three per cent of skaters were over thirty.[121] In 2014, nineteen per cent of all visitors to the Skate Park of Tampa were over forty, compared to just over one per cent a decade earlier.[122] For the United States as a whole, in 2014 some twenty-eight per cent of US skaters were over twenty-five, and forty-five per cent over eighteen.[123]

As this suggests, many more skaters today are in their twenties and beyond, as reflected in internet forums such as Middle Age Shred (UK) and Old Kook Skating (US), plus numerous Facebook groups like Very Old Skateboarders and Skaters Over 50. Magazines like *Coping Block* and *Juice* also cater for this sector, while the *Tired Videos* (2014 and 2015) assembled

Figure 3.9
Steve Caballero (2015).
Courtesy bythelevel.com and Kieran Sills.

amateur footage from older skaters as a tribute to the belief that 'Some of us had it, then lost it. Most of us never had it, but still love it.'[124]

Sometimes, of course, even renowned older practitioners are discouraged by the 'scornful stares of the expert young' or by normalizing peer pressures.[125] 'The basic attitude I get,' lamented Stacy Peralta 'is "You're a professional skateboarder? How old are you?"'[126] Other difficulties include the diminished capacity to withstand body strains and minor breakages, and scheduling time to accommodate other commitments. Despite this, older skaters are increasingly common, and particularly in the skatepark, slalom, freestyle and longboarding genres. 'Age has got nothing to with it', reflects Australian bowl-rider Peter Rowe (born 1953). 'I just enjoy doing it.'[127]

Today, respected street-skaters over forty include Mike Carroll, Louie Barletta, Ronnie Creager, Daewon Song (Figure 7.20), Guy Mariano, Jason Dill, Eric Koston (Figure 11.5), Jamie Thomas (Figure 5.18) and Geoff Rowley (Figure 10.13), while masters-category transition-riders include the likes of Steve Caballero (Figure 3.9), Eddie Elguera (Figure 9.13), Sean Goff, Jeff Grosso, Nicky Guerrero, Tony Hawk (Figure 9.4), Peter Hewitt, Christian Hosoi, Lester Kasai, Chris Miller, Pat Ngoho, Brian Patch, Sluggo, Kevin Staab and Sergie Ventura. Particularly impressively, in 2015 at age fifty-one, Lance Mountain released a much-lauded video part in Nike SB's *Chronicles Vol. 3* showcasing a powerful range of street, pool and skatepark moves, and a year later won the Vans Pool Party Legends category to equal acclaim. Older beginners like Neal Unger (born Anaheim, 1954) are also well known for their open attitude. 'My goals for my skateboarding', explains Unger, 'are to research the quietness of my mind and how joyful that is. How old can I get and yet still act young?' Unger's additionally talks about applying lessons from skateboarding into friendships, family and creativity.[128]

As this suggests, older skaters are often thoughtful about their interactions with other riders. In particular, as demonstrated by Laurent and O'Connor, older riders frequently look out for younger kids, including how skate traditions are transferred to these new generations.[129] 'The older skateboarders truly understand this is something to pass down to the little guys', explains Heidi Lemmon, manager of a Venice Beach skatepark. 'A seven-year-old girl got on the ramp, and everyone stepped back. These skateboarders really look out for the little ones.'[130]

All Girl Skate Jam

Undoubtedly a few male skaters like Christian Hosoi, Craig Johnson and Nyjah Huston have in the past castigated women in skateboarding; 'I personally believe that skateboarding is not for girls at all,' commented Huston in 2013. 'Not one bit.'[131] Some males also attacked Toy Machine for placing Elissa Steamer on its team and in its video *Welcome to Hell*.[132] Kelly, Pomerantz and Currie even show how some Canadian females were harassed or dismissed by males as 'posers, flirts, and interlopers',[133] while feminist groups like Philadelphia's Shred the Patriarchy have similarly viewed skateparks as misogynistic, just as New York's Brujas skaters all experienced male intimidation.[134]

More usually, however, male skaters have displayed casual opposition, indifference or even welcoming attitudes towards females. For example, none of the 1990s male skaters interviewed by Beal overtly excluded female skaters, while a 2000s female Canadian reported how male skaters just ignored 'the girl in the corner teaching herself kickturns'.[135] Conversely, Laura, a south-eastern US skater, was fully integrated by males into conversations and repartee, and today enlightened males like Pontus Alv commonly argue that skateboarding should have 'less men, and more girls'.[136]

Whatever these varied attitudes, skateboarding has remained, apparently at least, a predominantly male activity. All-male line-ups dominate skateboarding, evidenced from a 1988 Powell-Peralta image showing 'just some skaters' to almost every team rider advertisement today, while more recent videos like *Hot Chocolate* (Spike Jonze, Ty Evans and Cory Weincheque, 2004) emphasize the all-male camaraderie of knuckle-bumps, room-sharing and sweaty mini-van travelling.[137] All this reinforces the notion that skateboarders are male, and that the absence of females is unproblematic.

Skateboarding is not alone is this regard, and Thorpe has shown how for action sports generally the media marginalizes and trivializes sportswomen through exclusion, gender marking and sexualization.[138] Just as challenging is how women are represented in advertisements. While 1970s and 1980s advertisements occasionally pictured scantily-clad females holding skateboards, in the 1990s this tactic became more commonplace. Most explicitly, *Big Brother* magazine – bought by pornographer Larry Flynt in 1997 – encouraged sexist, racist and offensive material, such as readers describing themselves as 'pussy getting machines', a Fuct clothing advertisement with women spanking each other with skateboards, and a Hooters advertisement with nipple graphics and the slogan 'urethane for men'.[139]

During the mid-1990s this misogynistic tone increased. Most extreme was company Bitch, whose 1993 logo depicted a man pointing a gun at a woman's head. Misogyny and sexism still pervade skateboarding, from a 2012 feature on 'The Ten Sexiest Female Skateboarders' to *Thrasher*'s *King of the Road* videos (2003–) where women seemingly exist solely to pole dance, stand around semi-naked and kiss male riders.[140] Companies like Sk8Mafia and Dirty Ghetto Kids have similarly produced numerous graphics of semi-naked girls, while Leonard shows how the *Tony Hawk Underground* game (2003) is defined by 'excessive female sexuality geared toward male pleasure'.[141] As Donnelly reveals, even Canadian television programme 'Hardcore Candy' (2002), which supposedly promoted women skaters, used male experts to measure women against male standards and so reaffirmed skateboarding's masculine associations.[142] Similarly, Beal and Dupont both found females being dismissed as inauthentic 'skate Betties' or 'ramp tramps' – girls without skateboards, or who supposedly skate only to meet boyfriends.[143] According to MacKay, Beal and Wilson, such depictions 'normalize, discipline and classify' women and render them 'sexualized, trivialized and marginalized'.[144]

Despite these adversarial conditions, there have been many females throughout skateboarding's history. In the early 1960s, surfer Linda Benson had a signature skateboard, while in 1965 Donna Cash, Wendy Bearer, Colleen Boyd and Laura (Laurie) Turner gained television coverage as competitors in the American National Skateboard Championship.[145] The same year, Hobie's Patti McGee appeared on *Life*'s cover and the 'What's My Line?' and 'Johnny Carson' television shows; her *SkateBoarder* interview opened by stating that 'skateboarding is 100 percent just as much for girls as it is for boys'.[146] In agreement, *The Devil's Toy* (Claude Jutra, 1966) included several shots of female skaters (Figure 2.7).

A decade later, females constituted some twenty-five per cent of Southern Californian skaters, while Cindy Berryman noted that ten per cent of Carlsbad riders were female.[147] Weir's *Advanced Skateboarding* (1979) included photographs of Yvonne Cucci and Kathy Bomeisler, while UK magazines provided similar coverage, notably *Skateboard Scene*'s 'Kate the Skate' column.[148] Many 1970s documentaries depicted female skaters, including *The Ultimate Flex Machine* (1975) (Figure 6.4), *Spinn'in Wheels* (1975), *The Magic Rolling Board* (1976), *Freewheelin'* (1976), *Blaze On* (1978) (Figure 5.9) and *Hot Wheels* (1978).

During this period women frequently joined established teams, as with Ellen Berryman (Bahne, Logan), Deanna Calkins (Hobie) (Figure 3.11), Debbie Eldredge (Unity), Pattie Hoffman (Pepsi, Variflex), Robin Logan (Logan) (Figure 3.11), Peggy Oki (Z-Boys) (Figure 5.12), Ellen O'Neal (G&S, Free Former, Pepsi) (Figures 3.11 and 4.1), Laura Thornhill (Logan), Desiree Von Essen (Free Former), Gale Webb (Powerflex), Laura Dickson, Laura Monahan and Edie Robertson.[149] Other notables included Teri Lawrence with a substantial pool-riding section in *Blaze On* (Al Benner, 1978) (Figure 5.9), plus Terry Brown, Brenda Devine, Sue Hazel, Jeannie Narducci, Judi Oyama and Peggy Turner.[150] Leslie Jo Ritzma, Mickey Horn and Tina Trefethen competed in the Signal Hill downhill competition, which by 1978 had women-only divisions.[151] Some, such as O'Neal and Berryman, helped develop freestyle skateboarding; *SkateBoarder* celebrated O'Neal's grace, poise, fast footwork and 'super style'.[152]

Other females showed prowess in pool, pipe and skatepark riding. Oki, Logan and Thornhill, along with Robin Alaway, Kim Cespedes (Hobie and Tracker), Jana Payne (G&S), Cindy Whitehead (SIMS and Tracker), Leilani Kiyabu, Leigh Parkin, Sheenagh Burdell and Vicki Vickers (Figure 5.6) all became renowned for transition skating; both Kiyabu and Vickers had *SkateBoarder* 'Who's Hot' features, and Vickers later gained a full interview; as early as 1976 Berryman's 'Let's Hear It for the Ladies' article in *SkateBoarder* depicted Thornhill, Cespedes and Logan riding skateparks, and Dodie Hackemack and Francine Hill carving pools. Logan, who had beaten males riding half-pipes and jumping barrels on the CBS 'Challenge of the Sexes' show, 'ventured onto heights of the bowl that less competent riders should not attempt'.[153] Cespedes gained extensive coverage in *Skateboard World*, while Thornhill was awarded a full *SkateBoarder* interview and was shown skating Montebello, Carlsbad and other skateparks.[154] ACS even devoted a two-page advertisement to female skaters riding freestyle, skateparks and banks (Figure 3.11).[155]

Into the 1980s, and despite some punk-inspired male hostility, many females persevered, including Cara-Beth Burnside, Michelle Kolar, Cyndy Pendergast, Debbie McAdoo, Jenny Byrd, Stephanie Person, Anita Tessensohn, Leaf Trienen, Lori Rigsbee, Wendy Zacks and many others in the United States, as well as Michelle Picktin and Sue Hazel in the UK.[156] A Powell-Peralta 1988 advertisement featuring Tessensohn and Trienen proclaimed that 'Some Girls Play With Dolls. Real Women Skate', while other highlights included McAdoo's Atlanta Ramp Ranch, Bonnie Blouin's 'Sugar and Spice' *Thrasher* article on female skaters, Tessensohn riding in Powell-Peralta's *Public Domain* (1988) and Burnside's *Thrasher* cover (August 1989) and appearance in *Hokus Pokus* (1989).[157] Hazel's considerable all-terrain endeavours are documented in Jenna Selby's later *As If, and What* (2008) and *Days Like These* (2015).

By 1989, thanks to Laura Medlock and Lynn Kramer, the Women's Skateboard Network had emerged, connecting 250 females across several countries. This international effort was aided by the *Equal Time* 'zine, featuring the likes of Kramer, Burnside and Tessensohn as well as Saecha Clarke, Lisa Foreman, Nathalie Richter, Patty Segovia, Christy Jordahl, Vicky Voughn, Joanna Gillespie and Chris Reis.[158] Clarke, Jordahl and Tessensohn were now recognized street-skaters, with Clarke performing a boardslide for a Venture advertisement and Jaime Reyes (Real) securing a *Thrasher* cover with a 360 flip.[159] *Sk8hers* (Ethan Fox, 1992) also promoted the female scene.

Towards the end of the decade women's skating emerged even stronger. In 1996 Thump produced Tasty decks for females, and Catherine Lyons and Elska Sandor set up Rookie. Other female-managed companies like Cherry skateboards and Nikita clothing followed, while Volcom introduced female-targeted clothing.[160] In 1997, ten per cent of *Thrasher* readers were female, and Patty Segovia-Krause's inaugural All Girl Skate Jam (AGSJ) drew competitors from the United States and internationally.[161] Burnside became the first female to gain a pro shoe (Vans) and appeared in Hurley's *Hallowed Ground* (2001). Around 2000, Kim Peterson, Candy Hiler-Kramer, Jodi MacDonald, Holly Lyons and Mimi Knoop were all noted transition skaters.[162]

As this suggests, the 1990s had witnessed the emergence of a new breed of women skaters, often arriving from snowboarding.[163] Many also compared favourably with males, as demonstrated by Burnside's considerable achievements and Jen O'Brien's pro model and multiple sponsorships. Elissa Steamer was a particular tour de force; a Floridian who joined Toy Machine in 1995 and turned pro in 1998, Steamer was interviewed in *Big Brother* and *TransWorld*, appeared in *Tony Hawk's Pro Skater* game, won X Games titles and scored a *Thrasher* back cover.[164] After her appearances in Toy Machine's *Welcome to Hell* (1996) and *Jump Off a Building* (1998) (Figure 3.10), *Sidewalk* noted that the exclusive 'boys club' of skateboarding had now departed.[165]

Despite *Sidewalk*'s comments, Burnside, O'Brien and Steamer were still perceived by many as exceptions to the notion that only males could be excellent riders. And as Beal and Wilson stated in 2004, 'skateboarding is a rarely a site for females' empowerment', noting that 'the core value of traditional masculinity and its resultant power relations has not significantly changed.'[166] Nonetheless, during the early 2000s, things continued to improve when the X Games and Gravity Games introduced female street and vert skating, Vanessa Torres featured in

Figure 3.10
Elissa Steamer in *Jump Off a Building* (Toy Machine, 1998).
www.bit.ly/Steamer-Jump

Girls get radical too... on ACS trucks

Skateboarding is for everyone. Knowing you've got the best equipment gives you the confidence to go for it with the rest of the guys. Whoever you are, you can count on ACS. 5 models to choose from — one is right for you.

SUSPENSION KIT

Here's a unique suspension kit in an exciting pocket soft-pak. Three color-coded sets — FIRM, FIRMER, FIRMEST. Carry it with you and choose just the right rubber for specific skating conditions and rider weights.

Ellen Oneal, 19, Gordon & Smith Team, Pepsi Team. Champion freestylist, Guinn World Record holder. Ellen is one of the most widely respected, well kno skaters in the wo

Logan, 19, Logan Earth Ski Team. World-renowned stylist, winning slalom racer, radical bank rider. Robin beat the boys in the Challenge of Sexes!

Deanna Calkins, 18, Hobie Team. Champion downhill slalom racer. Deanna is a serious skateboarder with results to prove it.

MODELS

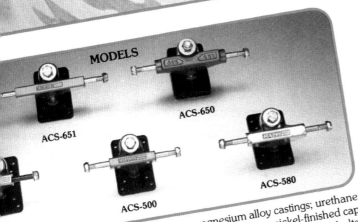

ACS-651

ACS-650

ACS-500

ACS-580

CS-430

Featuring 356 T-6 aluminum-magnesium alloy castings; urethane tips, natural rubbers; aircraft locknuts; alloy steel axles; nickel-finished cap washers, adjusting nuts and action bolts.

STAR TRUCK
Skateboard trucks by AC

ORDER NOW!

- Two decals and brochure $1.00
- Poster and headband $2.00
- Star Truck T-Shirt $4.00
  (Specify size S, M, L, XL)
  (Cal. residents add 6% sales tax) Mail to: ACS T-Shirts
- P.O. Box 306 • West Covina, CA 91793

ACS
TRUCKS

DIRECTOR INTERNATIONAL SKATEBOARD ASSN.

American Cycle Systems

1449 Industrial Park Street, Covina, CA 91722
Phone: 213-331-0582

All metal parts of ACS trucks are 100% guaranteed.
Send damaged parts to factory for free replacement.

Elementality (2005) and in 2006 the All Girl Skate Jam joined the Vans Warped Tour to reach fifty cities; by 2009, after pressure from the Action Sports Alliance, the X Games offered prize parity across genders.[167]

Media coverage also picked up, with magazines like *Check It Out*, *Wahine* and *Second Wind* and websites like *Skirtboarders*, *The Side Project* and *Girls Skate Better*. *Live and Let Ride* (Tara Copper, 1999) was the first female skate film documentary, followed by the *AKA*: *Girl Skater* video (Mike Hill, 2002) documenting Gallaz riders Jaime Reyes, Vanessa Torres, Amy Caron and Monica Shaw on an Australian road trip, as well as *Getting Nowhere Faster* (Villa Villa Cola, 2004).

The All Girl Skate Jam (AGSJ) has been particularly influential. Founded as an annual event, AGSJ provides a community-oriented atmosphere for 'all ages, all abilities, all girls', and has inspired events like Girl Skate Out (UK), Gallaz Jam (Australia and France) and Ride Like a Girl (Canada).[168] In 2016, over 170 skaters competed at Exposure Skate in Encinitas, California.[169] As Atencio, Beal and Wilson report, such events offer women of varied femininity, ability, age, ethnicity, class and sexuality the chance to skate without male intimidation. They have countered male dominance, particularly in street-skateboarding, as well as helping lead to men's and women's events being given equal weighting in the 2020 Tokyo Olympics.[170]

Aided by these kinds of developments, from the early 2000s onwards Burnside and Steamer were joined by newcomers like Heidi Fitzgerald, Vanessa Torres (in 2003 the first female to win an X Games gold) and Jen O'Brien (the first female to skate the X Games and join the Skateboarding Hall of Fame).[171] Alexis Sablone had a burly street-skating part in *P.J. Ladd's Wonderful, Horrible, Life* (2002), as did Marisa Dal Santo in Zero's *Strange World* (2009). Similarly, Lyndsey Adams Hawkins (Lyn-Z) became the first female skater to jump the DC MegaRamp (2004) and complete a 540° McTwist (2009), her considerable reputation being aided by appearances in *Tony Hawk's Project 8* game and the Nitro Circus Tour.[172] Other top females have included Lucy Adams, Lizzie Armanto (Figure 3.3), Lacey Baker, Evelien Bouilliart, Samarria Brevard, Amelia Brodka (Figure 3.12), Letícia Bufoni, Arianna Carmona, Nicole Hause, Karen Jonz, Allysha Le Bergado, Mimi Knoop, Hunter Long, Julz Lynn, Sarah Meurle, Kisa Nakamura, Poppy Starr Olsen, Gaby Ponce, Pamela Rosa, Alana Smith, Eliana Sosco, Nora Vasconcellos,

Brighton Zeuner and Abby Zsarnay; in 2017 Jordyn Barratt competed directly against male skaters in the Dew Tour. And while women have not enjoyed male levels of skate industry support – seventy-seven companies researched by Abulhawa sponsored over a thousand males, but just fourteen sponsored thirty-eight females – new female-focused or female-owned companies have emerged, including Cheers (Sabrina Göggel), Hoopla (Cara-Beth Burnside and Mimi Knoop), Gnarhunters (Elissa Steamer), Meow (Lisa Whitaker), Rogue (Jenna Selby) and Pink Widow Distribution/Silly Girl (Matt Gaudio).[173]

But what of everyday female skaters? By 2007, around twenty-six per cent of skaters were female, nearing the thirty to thirty-four per cent range or snowboarding, surfing and mountain biking.[174] Two years later, Atencio, Beal and Wilson noted the increasing female participation in skateboarding, snowboarding and surfing, with one industry executive seeing women as a crucial factor in expanding markets.[175] In 2010, Australians were also noting increased female participation.[176] Today, social and mainstream media regularly promote advanced female skaters; in 2014, YouTube showed eight-year-old Minna Stress dropping into the Woodward MegaRamp and Japanese females performing mind-blowing street tricks.[177] Even mainstream women's magazines recommend skateboarding as expressive and stylish; 'whether you love surfing pavements, cruising beach promenades or hitting hills,' enthused *Marie Claire* in 2015, 'skateboarding is all about letting go of your worries and living in the moment.'[178]

Numerous websites and social media have also promoted female skateboarding. During the mid-2000s, active female-centred initiatives included the US Girls Skate Network (2003), Skateboard Moms (2004), Action Sports Alliance (2005) and Girl Riders Organization (2006).[179] Segovia and Heller's *Skater Girl* (2007) guide included skateboarding history from a female perspective and tips on dealing with males at skateparks, and since 2010 the Spanish Longboard Girls Crew has developed into a high-profile international network (Figure 13.7).

Many of these carry powerful messages. Since 2002, the Skirtboarders website and documentary *Skirtboarders: le Film* (Mathilde Pigeon, 2004) have depicted Montreal and Ottawa communities as knowing rejections of male/female binaries; these 'polygendered' Skirtboarders fart, spit and wear T-shirts

Figure 3.11
ACS advertisement with Ellen O'Neal, Robin Logan and Deanna Calkins. *SkateBoarder* (August 1978). Courtesy ACS.

Figure 3.12
Amelia Brodka in *Underexposed: A Women's Skateboarding Documentary* (dir. Amelia Brodka and Brian Lynch, 2013). www.bit.ly/Underexposed-Skate

without bra-straps, while bikinis and painted nails may also appear, and so are fluidly female and/or male, hinting at new subjectivities.[180] Significantly, Mackay emphasizes, Skirtboarders go beyond media, confronting male-domination by actually skateboarding.[181] Kelly, Pomerantz and Currie have similarly shown how Vancouver women have rejected 'emphasized femininities' and instead appropriated male bravado, male clothing, Goth, hip-hop and punk subcultures; as these 'alternative', non-sexualized and androgynous femininities realize, 'you can't land an ollie properly in heels.'[182]

These are far from being isolated tactics. Many 1980s and 1990s females were masculine in style and appearance – Steamer was adamantly not a 'girl skater', while the 'Gayskullz' Australian, New Zealand and UK skaters also played with ambiguous sexuality.[183] Bäckström similarly recounts how some female Swedish skaters deploy gender manoeuvring, using tomboy or lesbian behaviours to disrupt male dominance, while Young and Dallaire note how risk-taking empowered Ottawa females to consciously challenge conventional notions of femininity.[184]

By the mid-2010s, many female skaters have become ever more comfortable in their skating identities. As Porter asserts, the sheer number of competent female riders means that 'skateboarding does the talking, and the rest is superfluous.'[185] Cindy Whitehead and Ian Logan's *It's Not About Pretty* and Julian Bleecker's *Hello Skater Girl* publications both bear this out, showing skaters in varied terrains, emphasizing their style, skill and determination rather than fashion, appearance or sexuality.

Today, blogs, websites and Facebook groups such as Brodka's Brodkasting Balderdash, Mexico's Chica Rider, Danni Gallacher's Girl Skate UK, Girls Skate Australia, Lisa Whitaker's Girls Skate Network and Cindy Whitehead's Girl is NOT a 4 Letter Word all foster female scenes,

as do films like *Underexposed: A Women's Skateboarding Documentary* (Amelia Brodka and Brian Lynch, 2013) (Figure 3.12), *Days Like These* (Jenna Selby, 2015) and *That One Day* (Crystal Moselle, 2016).[186] Similarly, notes Hannah Bailey, girl-only sessions like Brighton's She Shredders are 'pushing the scene to new heights', as are girls-only sessions at Malmö's Bryggeriet, while Cuban skaters challenge machista patriarchy through hill-bombing and skatepark-riding.[187] One skatepark in the US Bay Area runs female-only sessions, safety days and family-friendly events, and consequently, note Atencio and Beal, welcomes 'females and people of all abilities, backgrounds, and ages', thus challenging the stereotype of skaters being only independent, risk-taking males.[188] Some female groups like New York's Brujas have even extended beyond skateboarding to support LGBT, racial and ethnic minorities, including a free-access alternative camp (Figure 3.13).[189]

In the digital and media sphere, in 2014 Letícia Bufoni and Karen Jonz both garnered more social media interactions than famous male skaters like Daewon Song, Curren Caples, Mike Vallely and Eric Koston, while in *The Lovenskate Video* (Samuel Smith, 2012) Lucy Adams takes equal billing alongside other riders.[190] The female sections of the annual Vans Pool Party (USA) and Vert Attack (Sweden) competitions have proved to be increasingly popular, particularly as expertise has increased exponentially. In 2013 Women's Park riding was added to the Barcelona X Games, and three years later Lizzie Armanto gained both the first female *TransWorld* cover and a double-page Bones wheels advertisement.[191] This exposure is hugely encouraging for other females, explains black Skateistan skater-worker Niki Williams in *Underexposed*, for 'everyone needs to see an example of someone who looks like them.' Or as pro Lacey Baker asserts, 'It's important for us to create a platform ourselves. Instead of relying on this male dominated skate industry, let's create

Figure 3.13
New York's Brujas collective
(2016). Clockwise from top left:
Arianna Gil, Anne Adames, Nesa
Guzman, Ashley Luciano, Kayla
Morricona and Sam Olivieri.
© Ben Grieme.

our own fucking space.'[192]

As Atencio, Beal and Wilson conclude, rather than just high-profile initiatives like AGSJ, local events and niche media also help women to counter male skateboarding in general and masculinist street-skateboarding in particular. Whatever the exact context, female skaters in street and skateparks alike, who 'fluidly construct femininities which reflect a diverse and even contradictory range of personal and social identities,' will help reconstruct skateboarding's white, male, middle-class and heterosexual landscape.[193]

Female skaters are still comparatively less numerous, and still routinely gain less media coverage than male riders; frustratingly, Vans's *Propeller*, for example, does not include Armanto, despite her being on the Vans roster. And much skateboarding media, remarks Williams, continues to indicate that 'skateboarding is just for white males who have tattoos.' Nonetheless, in most skateparks females are commonly welcomed as equals; seventeen-year-old Emma Lindgren notes that, because of the social scene at Bryggeriet and other Malmö spots, 'it's not like they see me as a girl, more as a skater.'[194] And so, concludes Porter, it seems like we have perhaps finally arrived at the tipping point when skateboarders are no longer distinguished by gender, and 'the novelty of girls skateboarding has begun to wear off.'[195]

Polycultural Practices

For some practitioners, and especially during the 1990s, skateboarding has been a totalizing lifestyle. As Bob Burnquist recalled San Francisco life with Joey Tershay, Julien Stranger, John Cardiel and Jake Phelps, 'You *always* had your board, everywhere. They lived skateboarding.'[196] Nor is this tough-rider breed disappearing. 'Hardcore skateboarders are still there,' Glen Friedman informed the *New York Times*. 'As a percentage, are they as much as they used to be? Absolutely not. But overall, there are more.'[197]

Yet for most skaters, skateboarding is undoubtedly a central part of self-understanding, but without being all-encompassing or insurgent. As Sedo relates, for skaters like Tian Ju in 1990s Lanzhou, skateboarding was neither a heroic counter-cultural exploit nor a search for foreignness, as might have been expected in China's reform period, but rather was a 'youthful desire for fun and personal meaning.'[198]

Similarly, in 2009, Liu Qing of the Chinese Extreme Sports Association was noting that, where skateboarding had originally promoted teenage rebellion, by now it was simply 'a means for young people to challenge themselves.'[199]

In part this is generational, with skateboarding going beyond 1990s Generation X-ers – 'slackers' disgruntled with commercialization and embracing counter-culture – to include Generation Y-ers, that is, those who are born post-1982, affluently 'hooked-up' with merchandise, educated and ethnically diverse, and who embrace teamwork, achievement, modesty and good conduct.[200] For example, Nyjah Huston learned skateboarding less from urban peers in Los Angeles streets and more from training with his father Adeyemi at California skateparks and a skate-focused Puerto Rico family farm.[201] Consider also the clean and respectable skatepark riders of Osiris's *Children of the Revolution* (Tony Magnusson, 2008), or how one youngster in Curitiba explained that he skated because 'my dad is a skateboarder and always encouraged me.'[202] Young skaters at Kona skatepark, interviewed by Lorr in 2014, similarly viewed skateboarding as a mainstream sport like baseball, supported by parents and teachers; one fourteen-year-old reckoned that skateboarding was 'not rebellion or resistance' but 'just fun.'[203] Skateboarding here mirrors the path of other subcultures, no longer a unique channel of identity, but becoming part of the panoply of available style, consumer and entertainment options; for example, in the early 2000s, skateboarding was already being used to promote everything from 'Ollie Pop' bubble gum (Figure 3.14) to a clothing company called, without any apparent sense of irony, Counter Culture.[204]

Older skaters, too, engage in these polycultural practices. For example, one San Francisco company incorporates skatepark hire into employee benefits, a Johannesburg bank has constructed an on-site ramp, while the people I currently skate with include an accountant, architect, art dealer, graphic designer, lawyer, police officer, quantity surveyor, realtor and software developer, all of whom integrate their 'respectable' careers with 'alternative' skateboarding sensibilities.[205] 'No one should even be discussing if things are mainstream,' asserts Rob Brink. 'Just stop acting like it hasn't happened or that you're cooler or more "legit" because you're pointing it out.'[206]

From this perspective, skateboarding is simply another of those action, alternative, extreme, lifestyle or postmodern sports (such as BMX, mountain biking, kiteboarding, parkour, snowboarding, surfing, windsurfing etc.) that, according to Wheaton, emphasize newness, grassroots participation, lifestyle commitment, adrenalin, individualism and risk.[207] As Lorr notes, mid-2010s skaters are also more varied in age and less antagonistic than their 1990s and 2000s counterparts, seeing skateboarding as sporting, commercial and mainstream as well as subcultural, oppositional and anti-corporate.[208] In 2015, for many young riders skateboarding, far from being baseball's opposite, was now its natural friend: 'riding your board to a Little League game is not only commonplace, it's a necessity'.[209]

These changing attitudes are accompanied by new social possibilities, for, according to Giroux, popular culture is a rare 'site for negotiation' where youth can 'produce alternative public spheres and represent their own interests'.[210] For example, Sander Hölsgens has shown how in Seoul skateboarding can provide a way to address or compensate for South Korea's overbearing social strictures and pressures, while Rinehart even suggests that Generation Y's brand identifications are a substitute for democracy.[211]

This move to the mainstream is not necessarily a bad thing; in a post-industrial world where consumers individualize themselves and power favours segregation, contends Thornton, it is difficult to always think of difference in itself as being positive.[212] Skateboarding's increasing integration rather than isolationism is then constructive, at once formulating collaborative dialogues and mounting acerbic critiques. Hosoi consequently reflects on how far skateboarding has come since the 1970s: 'It's not like when we started, all rebels without a cause. All obstacles have been hurdled and the mainstream is falling in love with skateboarding'.[213] Or as Hawk argues,
A lot of people feel very strongly that skating shouldn't be shared with the general public. I never felt like that. It's amazing that a kid who chooses to skate now literally has career opportunities.'[214]

Johnny Pop, frontside noseblunt revert, Burnside.

GRIND SOME

WWW.OLLIEPOP.COM
1-800-446-1787

Skateboarding today is a way to engage with the world. It is neither wholly rebellious rejection nor fully acquiescent consumerism, but rather a means to cope, to construct meanings and to find pleasure. For older riders, skateboarding sits alongside money, career, relationships, play and travel – bleeding across boundaries, but not dominating. And for younger skaters, it means discovering values, building identities and forming friendships. Skateboarding is typically an intrinsic part of a skater's lifestyle, but not the only determinant, and each skater undertakes their own formulation of these equations

Figure 3.14
'Johnny Pop' does a frontside noseblunt to revert at Burnside. Courtesy Ollie Pop Bubble Gum Co.

Figure 3.15
Generation Y skaters Sky Brown and Ocean Brown. Kijo, Miyazaki prefecture (2018). © Behrouz Mehri/ AFP/Getty Images.

Chapter 4 Affiliate Worlds

Youth cultural styles may begin by issuing symbolic challenges, but they must inevitably end by establishing new sets of conventions; by creating new commodities, new industries or rejuvenating old ones.[1]
Dick Hebdige

Yochim and Meckiffe both point out that skateboarding's core-and-subcultural and mainstream-and-commercial sides are interconnected.[2] 'The standard co-optation model of a dominant industry raiding and diluting sub-cultural styles does not seem to hold up,' explains Meckiffe. 'The two contradictory traditions of representing skateboarding are locked together in a continuing and unstable relationship. Both tendencies are dependent upon each other.'[3] Correspondingly, contend Beal and Wilson, skater identities no longer uniformly oppose the mainstream, but are partly created through commercialism. Dinces takes this further, seeing skaters as the kind of neoliberal individuals who, following urban geographer David Harvey, are integral to late capitalism's strategy of flexible accumulation. From these kinds of perspectives, skateboarding's relationship to the commercial industries is not simply about conflict (opposing commercialism), resistance (refuting commercialism) or co-optation (commercialism changes skateboarding), but is more subtly articulated.[4]

That skateboarding has never been purely counter-cultural or oppositional is evident from its 1960s origins onwards, from the sale of skateboards, skate-branded clothing and shoes, to television shows, movies, videos and DVDs, and pay-to-access skateparks. 'The business side of skateboarding,' notes O'Connor, 'is a legitimate part of skate culture.'[5] As Bob Biniak explained, even the supposedly über-

rebellious 1970s Z-Boy skaters were quick to accept sponsorship – 'Money! We don't have a dime, we come from Dogtown. I want this, I want that.'[6] Similarly, many Z-Boy skaters – including Jay Adams, Tony Alva, Bob Biniak, Paul Constantineau, Shogo Kubo and Jim Muir – readily participated in the Hollywood teen-flick *Skateboard – the Movie*, along with other professionals like Ellen O'Neal (Figure 4.1). Within skateboarding, then, a series of attitudes, practices, organizations, discourses, brands and competitions together constitute a complex mainstream through which skateboarding is enacted and even regulated.

Although often thought to be less 'core' than skateboarding's subculturalist tendencies, these affiliate worlds are just as pervasive. Notably, and in contrast to the 'skate and destroy' stance of *Thrasher* and many other publications, *TransWorld Skateboarding* has tried to promote a more respectable 'skate and create' role for skateboarding. Hence, as Tony Hawk has viewed it, counter-cultural and post-punk skaters do not represent all of skateboarding such that, and particularly from the 2000s onwards, skaters are more diverse in nature. 'Now it's not about being rebellious, it's about pushing limits.'[7] What then are these affiliate worlds, and how do they operate?

Being Professional
Rick Blackhart, among other skaters, has been lauded by for 'not whoring himself

Figure 4.1
Ellen O'Neal freestyles as Jenny Bradshaw in *Skateboard – the Movie* (dir. George Gage, 1977).
www.bit.ly/ONeal-Skateboard

out to sponsors', while fellow 1970s skater Jay Adams similarly rejected a lucrative Band-Aid television advertisement, avowedly preferring self-respect over commercialism.[8] Such attitudes have prevailed through skateboarding, as in *Menikmati* (Fred Mortagne, 2000) when Geoff Rowley praises Tom Penny for riding for fun 'and not for magazines, fame, money or any of that stuff.' Professionals indeed commonly emphasize, like Steve Caballero in *We Are Skateboarders* (Ben Duffy, 2012), that the 'amazing feeling' of skating itself far 'outweighs all the fame, the fortune, the status, having a pro model'. And as Lombard explains, academic writing has also often colluded with this viewpoint, emphasizing skateboarding's subversive and oppositional nature over its corporate, money-oriented and mainstream dimensions.[9]

Yet despite evident anti-commercialist and anti-institutionalist tendencies, it is clear that sponsorship, salaries, competitions and status have always been established and indeed essential parts of skateboarding. For example, nearly all renowned skaters have joined a professional team, variously benefitting from increased media exposure, free equipment (flow), travel, royalties and salaries. Nor is this new. Already by 1975, US skater Russ Howell was being paid by Golden Breed sportswear to undertake promotional tours to places like Australia; by late 1976 Howell had earned over $50,000 from demonstrations and other deals, including those with Levi's, Coke and GMC-Holden.[10] Equally well known at this time was surf-skater Ty Page from the San Diego and La Costa scene. Known as Mr. Incredible for tricks like the Ty-Hop and Ty-Slide, Page was managed by sports promoter Bill Riordan as an American hero: 'His image is apple pie and ice cream', Riordan informed the *New York Times*. 'He's clean-cut, wears proper safety equipment, and everyone wants to mother him.' By 1976 Page was already putting his name to skateboards advertised in *SkateBoarder*; a year later, he earned $100,000 through endorsing Free Former mass-market skateboards and performing at mass events like the Cal Jam II rock festival (Figure 4.2).[11] Stacy Peralta, just before leaving G&S for Powell-Peralta in 1978, was earning similar sums, having sold 110,000 pro model decks and generating an annual salary of $55,000.[12] At this time even skaters like Ernie Martin – holder of the high jump world record, but today almost forgotten – could land a $15,000 contract and a Corvette sports car.[13]

From the touring Pepsi team of the late 1970s to the Swatch-sponsored 'Impact' rock-style events of the 1980s and 1990s, and through to the Dew-, Nike- and Vans-sponsored events of the 2010s, major international companies have been keen to associate with skateboarding. As a result, skaters like Christian Hosoi and Tony Hawk earned hundreds of thousands of dollars from product endorsements. Having turned professional in 1980 at age thirteen, Hosoi's career into the early 1990s generated around $350,000 per year, funding extravagant limousines, Harley-Davidsons, Hawaiian trips and a grand Echo Park house with its own half-pipe.[14]

Hawk's income has been even more stratospheric. In the 1980s Hawk progressed from royalty checks of eighty-five cents to earning over $100,000 annually. After lean times during the early 1990s (reduced to sleeping five to a motel room during demo tours), the 1995 Extreme Games (later X Games) resurrected Hawk as an action sports star. Having signed with the William Morris Agency and endorsement agent Peter Hess in 1998, four years later he was negotiating with video game makers Activision for a $20 million advance and use of a private plane, and by 2003 was selling over $300 million of branded sales (clothes, video games, demo tours etc.), while earning over $9 million annually.[15]

By 2002 there were around 380 to 430 pro skaters, and although few of these came even close to Hawk's income, even the less well-known earned $1,350 for a single demo on the Hawk-EPSN 'Gigantic Skatepark Tour' (2000–2002), while by 2012 top professionals like Chris Cole were earning up to $500,000 per year, with a handful exceeding $1 million.[16]

Significantly, although a few skaters have earned large sums of money from competitions – Nyjah Huston turned pro when aged eleven in 2005 and six years later had already garnered over $600,000 from his wins – most professional skaters do not make their living this way; despite Andy Macdonald winning innumerable 1990s contests, it was only after gaining commercial support with Powell-Peralta and other companies that his finances lifted above survival level.[17] Instead, high-profile competitions serve mainly to increase reputation and fame, and so help skaters gain advantageous sponsorships. When Hawk, for example, was earning around $10 million per year in the early 2000s, as much as seventy-five per cent came from video game royalties and the remainder from other business and sponsorship activities. At this time a single deal with a brand like Gillette could earn a top professional over $100,000, while even a middle-ranker like Danny Supa, sponsored by Nike, Independent, Zoo York and Von Zipper, earned around $100,000, with additional bonuses for any magazine coverage featuring his sponsors' logos.

For these skaters, their Generation X suspicion of corporatism and commercialism meant that sponsorship typically signified simply a contractual relationship, with little personal commitment to the products they helped advertise. Nonetheless, the money looked good, and royalties on pro model shoe sales were becoming particularly lucrative; in the early 2000s a single DC model made between $60,000 and $80,000 per month for its endorsing skater, and Geoff Rowley sold over 600,000 pairs of his $65 Vans model, generating, with a typical royalty of $1.50 per pair, close to $1 million.[18]

Given the allure of such deals, in the early 2000s some of the most successful skaters followed Hawk and started using agents like Steve Astephen of Familie (later Wasserman Media) to negotiate contracts and safeguard reputations; in 2011, Astephen represented Ryan Sheckler, Bob Burnquist, Bucky Lasek and Jen O'Brien.[19] In a world where serious injury could spell immediate loss of livelihood, the increased income was particularly welcomed by older skaters (many now with young families) and was often re-invested in skate shops, property and other business opportunities.[20]

As the use of agents suggests, in the new millennium skaters were no longer seeking just to maximize income, but were increasingly concerned with the reputations of their sponsoring businesses and products. By 2001, notes Dinces, video magazine *411* was intercutting street-skating footage with highlights of sponsor logos on boards, clothing and even as tattoos, hence suggesting a close affiliation between the skaters and their commercial supporters.[21]

If such tactics might appear somewhat contradictory to the supposed anti-commercial ideology of 1990s skateboarding, a decade or so later such concerns have all but disappeared; during the 2010s websites and forums have consistently discussed the coolest brands, such as one 2013 article entitled '10 Brands That Have Defined Skateboarding,' which also asserted that 'skateboarding has progressed thanks to the companies that push it forward.'[22] As Vans

marketing chief Jay Wilson remarked in 2002, 'there's no such thing as selling out anymore'; a decade later, a company like Palace, which channels 1990s street-level authenticity via VHS-tape videos and 'Skate Gang Shit' idiom, will happily sell football-style limited editions with the likes of Adidas and Reebok, open pop-up shops in London's touristic Covent Garden, do interviews for *GQ* and retail shoes for £180. 'I like the fact it crosses over to other people,' states Palace operator Lev Tanju. 'When mad-pretty fashion girls wear the T-shirts it totally stokes me out.'[23] The Adidas video *Away Days* (Matt Irving, 2016), similarly shows Palace skaters like Benny Fairfax, Chewy Cannon and Tom 'Blondey' McCoy prominently attired in Adidas-Palace clothing.

As this suggests, pro skaters today typically display relaxed Generation Y attitudes to branding and corporatism; they sign contracts with 'anti-offensiveness' and 'no disparagement' clauses, and, rather than being 'sponsored by' companies, look to 'represent' brands that correlate with their own outlook and that commonly spring from lifestyle markets, such as Adidas, Ethika, Leatherman, Levi's, Mountain Dew, Nike, Nixon, Oakley, Red Bull and Sprite.[24] For example, Bob Burnquist's New Age predilections and Christian Spiritism lead him to refuse sponsorship from energy drinks Red Bull and Monster ('I hate that stuff') but accept deals with Sambazon açaí-based drinks and Toyota, which paired Burnquist with its environmentally conscious hybrid-powered Prius car.[25]

Skateboarding, then, is not just an activity but also a potential career. As a result, many skaters aspire to join manufacturer and shop teams as professional or sponsored riders. Even the supposedly hyper-individualistic Dogtown skaters of the mid-1970s were keen to join the Zephyr shop team, readily wearing its uniformed shirts and standard issue Vans shoes, while in the same period Australian skaters like Cheyne Horan and Rob Bain accepted similar conditions when joining teams sponsored by Coca-Cola and Golden Breed.[26] Two decades later, as Jake Anderson recalled, when growing up in mid-1990s Canada all he wanted was to get sponsored and turn professional; today, guides like *Sponsored Life* show skaters how to attain this revered status.[27]

Similarly, ever since the 1990s emergence of camcorders, companies have been inundated with 'sponsor me' recordings sent by ambitious skaters – for example, in the early 1990s Jamie Thomas mailed a video every month in the hope

Figure 4.2
Ty Page stars for Free Former at Skatopia, Buena Park, California. *SkateBoarder* (November 1977). © Mike McIntire.

of becoming team rider. 'I was the nightmare kid who'd never leave you alone. I'd be calling up asking to see if they got it and what they thought of it.' After moving from Alabama to California, Thomas did eventually sign for Experience, Invisible and then Toy Machine, including directing and starring in the latter's *Welcome to Hell* (1996).[28]

Attitude, Image, Training

Many professionals have followed the path of skating, partying and living fast and high. By the late 1970s Tony Alva was taking chauffeur-driven limousines to pools and reservoirs and wearing a bespoke one-piece gold suit made by Elvis Presley's tailor, while a few years later Mark 'Gator' Rogowski gained massive popularity from his electrifying riding style, fashion-suicide day-glo clothing and rock-star persona. Changing his name to Gator Mark Anthony, appearing on MTV and building a demi-god self-image, Gator wholly bought into the world of glamour, parties and monetary gratification.[29] However, another stream within skateboarding balanced this kind of superstar immediacy with a more future-looking, industry-, media- and career-savvy perspective. Or as Tony Hawk concludes his autobiography, 'skateboarding is not a crime – it's my career.'[30]

In the 1970s, this position was typified by Stacy Peralta, an original Z-Boy who avoided the weed-smoking excesses of many teammates, joined the Pepsi demonstration team and, as the main character in *Freewheelin'* (1976), played a professional joining a sponsored Australian tour. Having realized his personal competitive skating career was likely to be short-lived (as it indeed it was, by wrist fractures), Peralta sought to maximize his income, media exposure, long-term reputation and financial stability.[31]

Indeed, this outlook was far from uncommon, particularly among 1970s professionals, the majority of whom were keen to see skateboarding develop as a full-blown sport.[32] A competitor such as Henry Hester – who like Peralta was renowned for his all-American image – was also a ruthless contestant in slalom and downhill disciplines, deploying psychological, technological and performance-enhancing techniques to win races. Contemporary Russ Howell took a similar approach, training for contests for ten hours a day, making mental maps of tricks and lines and setting routines to music. For Howell, this was less about winning and more a way to 'accelerate typical life experiences', magnifying physical and mental expression to audiences and to himself. 'Being the best skater is never more important than being the best person you can be.'[33]

Later in the 1970s, as Snyder relates, Alan Gelfand, in contrast to stereotypically boisterous skaters, was always 'humble, polite, respectful, and easy to approach' as well as being 'fearless' and 'insane' during his actual skating. Gelfand also understood the need to practice hard, avoiding drugs, remaining loyal to sponsors Powell-Peralta, entertaining crowds with sticker tosses and unusual music and choosing eye-catching moves that he could reliably complete. 'In professional settings, I never fell', Gelfand later recalled. 'I felt it was the professional thing to do.'[34]

Among other 1970s pros, Steve Alba adopted a similar attitude, attributing his success in the two-minute runs of the 1978 Hester contests to his sports stamina and training as much as to his repertoire of tricks.[35] As this suggests, while Bäckström has argued that the kinaesthetic skater's body 'unknowingly knows how to perform', and skaters generally tend to engage in self-taught processes rather than follow rules, professionals have nonetheless often utilized advanced training techniques.[36] For example, Eddie Elguera employed coach Dale 'Sausage Man' Smith to develop high-difficulty bowl-riding moves (Figure 9.13), a young Steve Caballero prepared for competitions by studiously pre-visualizing both venues and routines and Christian Hosoi studied the breathing patterns and discipline of martial arts expert Bruce Lee in order to boost his aerials.[37] Around the same time, the fast-developing Rodney Mullen adopted an even more analytic approach, understanding the physics of each stage of a move rather than trying to complete it in one go, a process that Schaffer has even compared with the philosophies of Spinoza and Deleuze and their emphasis on the relational interaction between things. 'Every motion would be taken apart and cycled over in my mind', explained Mullen, 'from foot plant and weight distribution to where I held my shoulders and eyes.' When taken on by Walker Skateboards, Mullen utilized two coaches, Bruce Walker and Barry Zaritsky, and quickly became obsessive about his competition preparation, meticulous timing, notebooks and self-assessment.[38]

Moving on a few years, Andy Macdonald's childhood jock-like focus on gymnastics in the 1970s and 1980s was matched by his later 1990s dedication to skateboarding, including a hard-

Figure 4.3 Tony Hawk celebrating the first ever 900° aerial. San Francisco X Games (X Games, 1999). www.bit.ly/Hawk900-XGames

skating (rather than party-going) attitude and an alcohol-, nicotine- and drug-free lifestyle.[39] And in the 2000s, skaters like Ryan Sheckler have taken a similar approach, working on competition runs for months before a contest, while many advanced skaters today use a range of mental techniques – such as visualizing moves or a run – to progress their expertise.[40]

As this all suggests, besides abundant natural talent, much expert training is required to operate professionally, and numerous skaters mix the persona of the anti-establishment rebel with the overall demeanour of a performance-focused athlete. For example, in the late 1970s, a hard-skating individual like Mike McGill (Figure 9.3) was also respected for appearing 'polished and presentable', showing sponsors' stickers on his board and generally playing the 'consummate professional'.[41] Even Alva, who was encouraged by mentor Bunker Spreckels to play up his 'Mad Dog' rebellious outlaw reputation, and who by his own admission had an ego-driven appetite for power, glory and girls, was in fact, according to Jim Goodrich, 'one of the coolest and nicest guys'.[42]

No skater, however, has better represented the consummate professional than Tony Hawk. Unlike contemporary vert-riding rivals Hosoi and Rogowski, who went to prison for, respectively, drug trafficking and rape-murder, or Jeff Phillips, whose notorious drug-taking ended with his 1993 suicide, Hawk is renowned as a hard-working professional with a responsible attitude to business, fans and life in general. As a result of his achievements – including numerous X Games victories, the completion of the first 900° aerial (Figure 4.3) and the global success of *Tony Hawk's Pro Skater* video games – by 2000 Hawk ranked as the second most popular athlete among US teenagers, beaten only by basketball superstar Michael Jordan. And unlike the stereotypical

skater who rebels against parents and schooling, Hawk maintained a close relationship with his father, Frank, who not only supported his son's career but also developed America's National Skateboarding Association.[43]

In terms of sponsorship, Hawk maintains that he has declined sponsorship from non-skater companies like Nike and Gap, with which he has no personal connection, while accepting it from brands like McDonald's because this is a place he and other skaters often visit, and that also donated large sums to the Tony Hawk Foundation and hence public skateparks. After a bad 1998 experience with Froot Loops, he has also refused to relinquish control of his name and image to outsiders, although this has not prevented Hawk from endorsing everything from skateboards and BMX bikes to clothing, chocolate drinks, electronic gadgets, roller coasters, shoes, soft drinks and waterpark rides. Hawk's related Boom Boom HuckJam brand has also been used on school and party supplies, bedding, bicycles, cartoons, fast food toys and vitamins.[44]

Hawk's undoubted willingness to seek both commercial gain and personal success has been occasionally contentious, for example when some skaters chose to believe the disingenuous portrayal of Hawk in *All This Mayhem* (2014) as a corporate sell-out who connived to restrict the career of Australian skater Tas Pappas. Nonetheless, Hawk's attitude of skate hard, try hard, be respectable and make money (rather than the, say, Jay Adams stance – skate hard, live for the moment, break laws, don't worry about money) is pervasive among many professional skateboarders, and one that many everyday skaters also consequently accept, respect or even admire.

Companies and Brands

> Truth is, the ultimate outlaw road sport is now about as countercultural as yoga. It's bad-boy past no longer defines it, except as a marketing hook for the $17 T-shirts and $66 skate shoes that bring in eight times as much money as skateboards.[45]
> *New York Times*

Skateboard culture is commercialized in a myriad of ways, involving everything from skateboards and safety equipment to publications, video games, DVDs, shoes, clothes and watches, as well as cultural outputs like art, music and photography. In the mid-1960s, *SkateBoarder* was including advertisements for skateboard manufacturers plus Randy 720 shoes ('the official sneaker of the National Skateboard Championships'), Nash helmets and Jantzen clothing.[46] The annual equipment business alone has been variously estimated as worth between $300 and $500 million in the late 1980s; Powell-Peralta was turning over between $30 million and $40 million per year during the 1980s, selling 2,000 decks every day and employing 150 staff, while Tracker and NHS were respectively selling over one million trucks and 400,000 decks.[47] Between 2004 and 2008, the skateboard industry as a whole (equipment, clothing etc.) was estimated at around $5 billion to $6 billion annually and by 2011, $7.3 billion in the United States.[48] Many core skate brands have also passed into corporate ownership, such as Zoo York to Iconix in 2009, while conversely in 2015 mainstream brands such as Eidos, OAMC, John Elliott and Noah were all producing heavily skate-influenced clothing.[49] And when *Tony Hawk's Pro Skater 5* was released in 2015, this sequence had already sold over forty million copies, making it the third best-selling sports-based video game series of all time.[50]

How does this equate with skateboarding's avowedly anti-commercial stance? As Rinehart points out, one significant tactic has been for skaters themselves to produce equipment, graphics, magazines and videos; in doing so they became the first action sports practitioners to take charge of their own cultural and technical goods.[51] It is to these practices that we now turn.

Retail

With retail, skaters have often operated neighbourhood skate shops. Skateboarding is of course by no means the first to attempt such tasks, for as Angela McRobbie points out the 'entrepreneurial dynamic' often lies within niche metropolitan practices.[52] In particular, shops such as Coliseum (Melrose and Boston), Rip City (Los Angeles), Uprise (Chicago), Bastard (Milan), BFD (Hong Kong), Fly (Shanghai), Skate City (Dublin), Slam City Skates (London), Snake Pit (Fitzroy), Sumo (Sheffield), ss20 (Oxford), Tour (Beijing) and Jimi (Taipei) through to outfits like Sean Goff's Todd Twist (Oxford), Chris Ward's Big Woody's (Blackpool) and Nic Powley's Skate Pharmacy (Kent) in the UK, plus Chris Nieratko and Steve Lenardo's NJ Skateshop (New Jersey) in the United States have all been skater-owned and run. Sponsoring skaters and events, organizing film screenings and exhibitions and creating videos, books and magazines are all ways these shops re-invest in skateboarding. Despite ever-increasing challenges from larger online operations, such mechanisms have often proven successful; in the early 2000s, the United States had around 2,000 local skater-owned shops, each typically offering a cave-like space packed with decks, clothes, shoes and other paraphernalia, with sticker-plastered walls creating an atmosphere more like an obsessive's hoard than a glossy retail environment.[53] Today, shops like Kit Lau's HKIT and Brian Siswojo's 8Five2 (Figure 4.4) in Hong Kong are perhaps more slick in style, but still act as important hubs for the local skate scene; in 2014 some seventy-seven per cent of US skaters had attended a demo at their local shop.[54]

For skaters, these kinds of stores have often provided a social space where they can watch videos and generally hang out. For example, Clive Rowen's Hill Street shop has been a central element of the Dublin skate community from the 1980s onwards, with Rowen acting like a surrogate father to many riders, providing jump ramps and grind rails in the road outside (Figure 4.5). 'Second or third time in there', recalled local skater John Heerey, 'and you felt it was home.'[55] Similarly, Bill Murray's Inland Surf Shop in Gainesville, Florida, was not only where Rodney Mullen bought his first skateboard in 1976 but where this young freestyler could escape his domineering father.[56] As Dupont explains, such shops also frequently employ the 'skate nerd', providing insider knowledge, teaching techniques, forging personal introductions and generally instilling 'authentic' skate values.[57]

As a result, many skaters still make purchases at local outlets rather than via large retailers like the United States's Zumiez, Tactics and Skatewarehouse or the UK's Route One and Skate Hut; in 2015, sixty-five per cent of US skaters purchased their most recent board from their local skate shop. 'I don't shop at Zumiez',

commented Chicago skater Jack Spanos. 'It's a sin.' Correspondingly, skate companies gain authenticity by distributing through these localized outlets. When launched in 2002, for example, the Nike SB sub-brand targeted 'core' shops to help it become, in 2014, the United States's best-selling skate brand.[58] 'Although Nike SB is not skater-owned', commented one skater, 'I respect that they sell shoes to "core" shops only.'[59] Conversely, selling via large chains such as Walmart often leads to disgrace; this happened to World Industries and Airwalk in the 1990s, and in 2015 Kryptonics were ridiculed on Facebook for selling cheaper equipment via K-Mart. Even über-fashionable brands like Palace can be slated for targeting wider markets. 'Palace was amazing when it started', commented one skater, 'but it's getting more and more wank as it makes more and more money out of all this faux chav hipster grime hype fashion shite.'[60]

New Paint on Old Wood?

More important than skate shops, however, are the various skater-owned companies. This is not a new phenomenon, with 1960s companies like Makaha and Hobie being operated by surfers with close affinities to skateboarding. And skaters such as Tony Alva (Alva Skates), Stacy Peralta (Powell-Peralta), Jim Muir (Dogtown) and others in the mid- to late-1970s quickly set up their own skater-run companies. Aided by local entrepreneur Pete Zehnder, Alva Skates began with decks in late 1977, with Alva describing other professionals as being mere 'puppets' who were simply 'getting burnt'. Instead, argued Alva, 'we gotta start our own companies, quit making boards and wheels and money for other people.'[61]

Many skateboarders have followed suit with an extraordinary list of skateboard, shoe, clothing and other enterprises. A caveat here, for it is not always clear who has owned or funded what and when, this situation being further complicated by later changes in proprietorship. For example, Tommy Guerrero is often cited as an owner of Real, yet although Guerrero helped start the company he is in fact merely a shareholder in Real's distributor Deluxe.[62] Nonetheless, many skate companies were either initially founded or co-founded by skaters, and/or with substantial skater ownership, from Acme (Jim Gray, 1991) to Zoo York (Eli Morgan Gesner, Adam Schatz and Rodney Smith, 1993).

Many of these are relatively small, but others have become global enterprises. As the buy-outs of World Industries (acquired by Globe in 2002 as part of a $46 million purchase of Kubic Marketing, and by i.e. Distribution in 2007), DC Shoes (to Quiksilver in 2004 for $87 million) and Vans (to McCown De Leeuw in 1988 for $74.4 million, and again in 2004 to VF Corporation for around $400 million) all suggest, this is a huge industry with some equally large figures attached.

Other companies, however, are regionally based, such as Magenta in Paris and Strasbourg, with a growing reputation for being wholly skater-owned and producing a large range of decks, wheels, clothes and videos.[63] A myriad of other companies are highly local, typically producing just a few decks and T-shirts that are sold by word of mouth and low-key online presence. To name but two of these – and there are hundreds if not thousands worldwide – in Johannesburg, Wandile Msomi founded Funisu in 2010 as South Africa's first black-owned skate company, while Dean Clarke's London-based R3V3R3NT operation offers a small range of decks and beanies, the sales of which may not generate significant income, but nonetheless represent the owner's commitment to building a skate brand from scratch.[64]

How then did this situation arise, and how much do companies operate independently? One cautionary note is the realization that the 1980s 'Big Five' – Powell-Peralta (George Powell and Stacey Peralta), SIMS and Vision (Brad Dorfman), Santa Cruz (Rich Novak), *Thrasher* (Fausto Vitello) and *TransWorld Skateboarding* (Larry Balma) – had by the early 1990s morphed into three pre-eminent Californian personalities and groupings: Fausto Vitello of Deluxe Distribution, High Speed Productions,

Figure 4.5
Clive Rowen's Dublin skateshop
in the late 1980s. *Hill Street* (dir. J.J.
Rolfe, 2014).
www.bit.ly/Owen-HillStreet

Santa Cruz/NHS and *Thrasher* in Northern California; Steve Rocco of World Industries and *Big Brother* in Los Angeles; and Larry Balma of Tracker Trucks and *TransWorld Skateboarding* in Torrance. Each represented multitudinous internationally distributed companies making decks, trucks, wheels, clothes, shoes, magazines and videos. Complex ownership and structures masked their direct involvement, but by 1994 these three individuals and their partners probably accounted for around seventy per cent of US skateboarding sales.[65] The role of *Thrasher* and *TransWorld* especially should not be underestimated; although in today's complex media world their influence has undoubtedly declined, during the 1980s and 1990s these magazines massively promoted particular opinions, products and skaters, even at times approaching the 'disciplinary power' theorized by Michel Foucault, in which everyday skaters felt a strong allegiance and even responsibility towards these publications' distinct values.[66]

Despite this dominance, the image of an industry of small-scale, skater-run outfits prevailed in the 1990s. In particular, a few younger manufacturers, and notably Rocco, highlighted skateboarding's more anarchic tendencies. Disillusioned with corporatized companies like Vision and Powell-Peralta (whose team rider manual included dress and behaviour codes), Rocco established World Industries (1987) and *Big Brother* (1992) to 'turn up the heat on everything', positioning himself as an ex pro who let riders act freely, abusing established manufacturers and generally 'taking the other guy's rules and breaking every one of them.'[67] In particular, Rocco used pro riders to head apparently independent brands that were actually just 'new paint on old wood' (Figure 13.9). 'Rocco', conjectured *Skateboard!*'s Steve Kane, 'will soon have set up every skater in the world with his own company.'[68]

Although a very different kind of business person, Balma also deployed this kind of corporate tactic. 'There's a consumer out there who in his early teens really wants to identify with a product,' figured Balma. 'If it's part of one corporation, then maybe it's not so neat.' Balma thus kept hidden his ownership of skate companies like Tracker, A-1 and House of Kasai, while Vitello similarly deployed pro riders to front purportedly independent companies like Think, Hubba, Spitfire, Venture and Thunder. All this allowed Vitello's *Thrasher* to disingenuously proclaim that there were 'so many, small skater-run companies out there.'[69]

Much of this was carefully masked from skaters, often through provocative advertisements replicating the self-deprecating nature of street-level skate culture, and even spoofing the whole company-skater relationship. As Rocco wrote in one advertisement, 'Yes, it's the mindless dolts which make it possible for new swindling corporations like us to stay in business. So, from the bottom of our Swiss bank accounts, thank you.' By 1991, World Industries was turning over $5 million per year.[70]

The control Rocco, Balma and Vitello exercised over the three major magazines was particularly instrumental. For example, in the early 1990s Balma's *TransWorld Skateboarding* carried no advertisements from Vitello's NHS companies, while in the May 1994 issue of Vitello's *Thrasher* thirty-five per cent of advertising was for Vitello-associated companies, even not including the numerous 'manufacturers' who re-badged equipment from Vitello-owned companies (such as Santa Monica Airlines decks, which were actually made by Santa Cruz). Preference was also given to skaters on Vitello-associated teams, and even in the 2010s some contend that 'if you ride Indy, Thunder or Venture, you're going to get coverage in *Thrasher*.'[71] Conversely, skaters like Jeremy Wray, who rode for the non-Vitello

Color Skateboards, were excluded from *Thrasher*. Some have even claimed that street-skating was either invented or at least very heavily promoted by these magazines, keen to stimulate new markets for their parent owners. 'Rocco was out in some ways to kill vert skating,' explained Mike Vallely. 'He understood that street-skating was accessible, and you'd sell a lot more skateboards to kids if they're out riding streets.'[72]

Although the skateboard industry can only influence what is essentially a grassroots community of skateboarders, certainly when street-skating emerged in the 1980s and 1990s it required smaller and lighter boards. This equipment also wore out faster as diminutive wheels flat-spotted and lighter decks broke quickly, while the 1990s trend for 'focusing' (deliberately breaking) boards further exacerbated the situation. First depicted in *Rubbish Heap* (World Industries, 1989) when Jeremy Klein stamps on Rodney Mullen's board, many skaters believe this was part of Rocco's plans to increase deck sales.[73] As one shop owner admitted, 'we love it because kids go through the shit even faster,' and by 2010 many street-skaters were complaining that wheels lasted only a month, decks three weeks and a pair of skate shoes even less. In 2014, forty-six per cent of US skaters were buying at least five decks per year. As Steve Olson has concluded, 'So we're going to make skateboards that fucking break, so the kids have to buy them again? Skateboarders running skateboard companies – well you're still a bunch of capitalist fucking pigs.'[74]

From Pepsi to Virgin Money

If the ownership and other tactics of commercial skateboard companies has sometimes been kept hidden from everyday skaters, more explicit has been the entry of non-skate companies. That such corporations would be interested in a supposedly 'marginal' activity like skateboarding is in fact unsurprising given that, according to *Forbes*, skateboarding offers an identifiable audience centred around the seventeen-year-old male demographic and commanding, even in 1999, a staggering $650 billion in sales power.[75]

By 1977, soft drink manufacturers like Orange Plus, Pepsi, RC Cola and Sunny Delight, alongside MG cars, Master Charge credit card and hamburger chain Wendy's, were already using skateboarding in their advertising. In the 1990s, this activity took off. Mountain Dew, for example, successfully connected their soft drink's sugar-caffeine surge with the adrenaline-fuelled rush of action sports, building a regional product from Knoxville, Tennessee into a $3 billion brand. Gillette similarly used action sports to market grooming products to teenagers and young men in the early 2000s, while others with skateboarding ties included travel company Club Med, health-hygiene Colgate-Palmolive and snack foods Doritos and Bagel Bites – the latter enjoying a twenty per cent sales rise after sponsoring the 2000 Winter X Games.[76] All this meant that into the 2000s many pro skaters might not even be connected to skateboard manufacturers, but could still made a good living from their energy drink, skate shoe or clothes sponsors.[77] Most recently, companies as diverse as Axe Body Spray, Dior, Hermes, Nissan, *Vogue* and Virgin have all used skateboarding in their marketing; in 2015 the helipad of Dubai's Burj Al Arab, the world's only seven-star hotel, saw Paul Rodriguez and others film a skateboarding sequence for *We Are Blood* and the hotel's global marketing programme (Figure 4.6).

Authenticity

Skateboarding has always been associated with the sales of skateboards, clothes and other paraphernalia. The first issue of *The Quarterly SkateBoarder* (1964) advertised the Hobie team wearing Jantzen 'Big J' sweaters and surf-shirts, while the 1970s and 1980s saw the arrival of specialist shoes from manufacturers such as Vans and Vision, protective pads from Rector, helmets from Kanoa, Protec and Norton, plus a plethora of branded socks, shorts, T-shirts and headgear. Furthermore, as skateboarding became fashionable in the late 1980s and 1990s, skateboard clothing entered mainstream culture. By 1989, Vision Street Wear clothing generated a turnover of $89 million, while by the late 1990s skateboard shoes by Vans, Airwalk, Converse, DC and Etnies were being sold in mass-market stores worldwide. In 1996, Airwalk, whose founder George Yohn deliberately targeted skateboarding with a specially designed high-protection shoe, boasted an annual turnover of $200 million.[78] Globe, started in 1984 by Melbourne skater brothers Matt, Peter and Stephen Hill, was by 2015 valued at over $150 million. Vans in particular successfully shifted into global non-skate markets, by 2000 becoming a NASDAQ-traded company with extensive overseas manufacturing. Clothes like Stüssy, originally marketed to skateboarders in the 1980s, similarly became standard high-street fare.[79] More recently, skate brands like Supreme, Palace and Thrasher have all had their clothes 'appropriated' by celebrities, pop stars and models, as well as by non-skaters generally.[80]

Figure 4.6
Skateboarding on the Burj Al Arab
helipad, Dubai. *We Are Blood*
(dir. Ty Evans, 2015).
www.bit.ly/Dubai-WeAreBlood

This has not always gone down well with skaters, who as early as 1975 had become suspicious of 'outsiders' copying their style. 'Just owning a skateboard doesn't qualify one as a skater' declared Craig Stecyk.[81] As a result, products from Vision – who had gone from sponsoring renowned skaters like Mark Gonzales, Mark Rogowski and Duane Peters to marketing cut-price mass-market gear – were being rejected by many skaters, while new company Blind was named by Mark Gonzales in mockery of his former employer (Figure 4.7). A decade later, World Industries also found themselves losing supporters after targeting juvenile markets and licensing their Devil Man figure to toys and other non-skate products.[82] Airwalk similarly suffered dramatic 1990s sales losses after extending into high-street outlets like Foot Locker.[83] In particular, Nike met with considerable hostility when it first attempted to enter the skateboarding market in the mid-1990s. This was despite Nike's products having been endorsed in the 1970s by Alva as his 'favorite safety equipment', and appearing on the first *Thrasher* cover and in the renowned skate video *The Search for Animal Chin* (1987). Nonetheless, considering Nike to be muscling in on skateboarding culture, skater anger was channelled by the independent company Consolidated, and notably through its 'Don't Do It' campaign.[84]

More skate-aware clothing companies have had greater success in their relationships with 'core' skaters. DC and Vans shoes, in particular, while not skater-owned, have kept close to skateboarding. DC Shoes was originally founded as part of Circus Distribution by snowboarder Ken Block and Damon Way (brother of pro skater Danny Way). After launching its high-tech pro models in 1995, by 2000 DC had annual revenues of $60 million before attaining $542 million in 2013.[85] Even more spectacular has been Vans. Founded in Anaheim in 1966 by non-skater

Paul Van Doren as a direct-selling operation to the general public, in the 1970s Vans found its grippy and lightweight shoes being adopted by skateboarders and surfers, and consequently targeted these markets with its 'Off the Wall' offerings, first advertised in a 1977 *SkateBoarder*. Demand exploded after slacker youth Jeff Spicoli (played by Sean Penn) wore checkered slip-on Vans in *Fast Times at Ridgemont High* (Amy Heckerling, 1982), and from this point Vans actively pursued leisure markets. After some major setbacks in the mid-1980s, by 1996 Vans's revenues had reached $100 million, by 2002 $341.2 million and by 2014 over $2 billion, with a target of $2.9 billion by 2017. In 2014, no less than sixty-one per cent of US skaters identified Vans as their most likely shoe purchase.[86]

The enormous scale of these earnings – along with its Disney collaborations, Asian manufacturing and a global outlet chain – could easily have lead Vans to face Nike-style accusations of corporatization. Nor did Vans until the mid-1970s even invent a shoe specifically for skateboarding. Like the Randy 720 shoes of the mid-1960s, Vans early skate shoes were essentially lightly modified from pre-existing models; 'it was because Vans shoes were thought of as skateboarding shoes', notes Turner, 'that they became skateboarding shoes.'[87]

Unlike the supposedly 'inauthentic' Nike, however, Vans has followed the advice of 1990s public relations firm Weber Shandwick, carefully maintaining the appearance of an organization which, according to Paul Van Doren's son Steve, 'has always been the underdog, the smaller company that scrapped and worked harder.'[88] This is sound advice in action sports, where from the early 2000s onwards marketing companies like Weber Shandwick and Fuse have constantly reminded corporate brands that they must treat skateboarders with enormous sensitivity. Skaters, warns Fuse founder Bill Carter, 'don't want to

Figure 4.7
Blind advertisement with Lavar McBride. *Thrasher* (September 1995).

see a brand coming with no grassroots support and just slapping a logo onto a high-profile event.'[89] In short, companies have to demonstrate what Giannoulakis has called 'authenticitude' ('authenticity' and 'attitude'), not just creating cool imagery but acting in 'legitimate', 'self-expressive', 'individualistic', 'anti-establishment' and 'anti-materialist' manners.[90]

In practice, such authentic behaviour means supporting a slew of skateparks, competitions, art projects, books, films and other initiatives, as with Levi's funding several DIY skateparks. For Vans, this has involved providing $400,000 for *Dogtown and Z-Boys* (2001) and sponsoring eleven US 'mega-skate parks' (2002), through to the recent Vans Custom Culture project to inspire art and design in high schools (2015), as well as its House of Vans free-access skateparks in places like London (2014) and Hong Kong (2017) – all demonstrating how Vans 'gives back' to skateboarding (Figure 8.18). Hence also Vans's myriad other initiatives, ranging from DIY installations, the Vans Shop Riot and other competitions to the Offthewall.tv channel and *Living Off the Wall* documentary series. A folksy family image is also nurtured, a rotund, aproned Steve Van Doren frequently manning the barbecue at Vans competitions. The focus here is less on marketing products and more on constructing the idea of Vans as an individualist, generous, spontaneous and, above all, authentic brand.[91]

As long as companies like Vans are seen to invest in skateboarding rather than change skateboarding into a spectacularized entity, then most skaters are seemingly content. Indeed, Tod Swank, founder of the Foundation and Tum Yeto companies, wishes that skateboarding could better emulate hip-hop culture in maintaining values and fan bases while also selling music and other products worldwide. 'How can hip-hop do it and still do cool things and still be edgy?', ponders Swank. 'When everybody's making money, the pie just gets huge and everybody's doing better. That's what I'd like to see.'[92]

Other parts of the skate industry and media are, however, less happy with the emerging corporatization of skateboarding. *Jenkem* in particular has railed against this trend, fearing a displacement of skateboarding from city streets into enclosed arenas, the replacement of street-based skate videos with spectacular SLS-style contests (Figure 4.8), the decline of smaller brands and skate shops, the polarization of pro skaters between highly remunerated superstars and journeyman workers, and the general commodification of skateboarding as an organized sport.[93]

Brand Identification

Today, skateboarding's commercial landscape is quite different to the 1980s and 1990s. Although Vitello's NHS certainly continues as a major force with brands like Bullet, Creature, Flip, Independent, OJ, Krux, Ricta and Santa Cruz, while also enjoying *Thrasher*'s support, the operations lead by Balma and in particular Rocco have gradually diminished. Instead, the wide range of manufacturers, media, clothing and shoe companies worldwide means that no single organization dominates. In the US, by 2013 large-scale distributors and/or manufacturer groupings such as Antics, Bakerboys, Blackbox, Blitz, Crailtap, Deluxe, DNA, Dwindle, High Grade, NHS Fun Factory, PS Stix, Pure, Quezon, Resource, Sole Technology, Strange Bird, Skate One, Syndrome and Tum Yeto each typically encompassed between five and fifteen brands, while in Europe distribution today is undertaken by the likes of Form, FORTrate, Go Europe, Havoc, iFive, Keen, Power and Shiner.

Given the context of this more dispersed and complex network of skateboarding companies, many professionals now earn their main income from a portfolio of sponsors rather than as a team rider for one particular manufacturer. In addition, explain Wheaton and Beal, since the early 2000s many extreme sports practitioners have desired sponsorship for reasons of status and reputation as well as financial income; which companies skaters have as their sponsors directly impacts on their identity, and hence also on their perceived cultural value and popularity among social media followers.[94] For this reason, many skaters now describe how they 'represent' brands rather than being 'sponsored' by them, indicating a personal affiliation based on style and ethos rather than on purely commercial transactions. As Rinehart remarks, this 'deep identification with corporate interests has, in effect, become synonymous with identity status within an action-sport subculture', to the point where interviews with professionals typically include opening statements about the brands they represent.[95]

Lastly, for many everyday skaters as well, brands can also be meaningful identity referents. This is unsurprising given that, as Yochim notes, current skaters are part of the millennial Generation Y who find themselves totally

Figure 4.8
Shane O'Neill at the Street League
Skateboarding series (SLS, 2013).
www.bit.ly/ONeill-SLS

immersed in branding not just as advertising but as a general life attitude.[96] Hence, explains Fuse's Carter, although skaters are often very cynical of non-skate brands in particular, once skaters form a relationship with a particular company they are often 'tremendously loyal'.[97] For example, over more than thirty-five years NHS's Independent truck company has gained an extraordinary following, many skaters identifying with the company's 'unruly and unkempt' and 'punk and disorderly' persona. According to Brad Bowman, Independent is 'totally fucking rock and roll, outrageous, out of control and perfect.' Or as Eric Dressen has commented, 'being hardcore is Independent. It's a lifestyle and everyone adopted it.' As this indicates, for many of the eighty-nine per cent of US skaters who have purchased at least one set of Independent trucks, this is an important part of their 'core, time-proven' commitment to skateboarding, visible not only from riding the trucks but from a myriad of Independent-branded stickers, clothes and even tattoos. And as Independent claims of this symbology, 'Independent's cross logo has become a cultural totem, representing individuality and pride in self-sufficiency.'[98]

Organizations and Control

Despite a fierce focus on independent individuals, skateboarding has always had representative and organizing groups. In the 1970s and early 1980s, such US organizations included the World Skateboard Association, International Skateboard Association, Pacific Skateboard Association and Professional Skateboard Association. The Australian Skateboard Association and Australian Pro/Am Skateboard Racing Association were already operating by 1975, while soon to follow were the British Skateboarding Association, Scottish Skateboard Association and innumerable others worldwide.[99] In East Germany, authorities even undertook state surveillance of the 'unorganized

rollersports scene' before trying to regiment skateboarding as a competitive sport, centred on the Greiz national sports academy.[100] Today, national associations operate in most countries, such as the Česká Asociace Skateboardingu (Czech Republic), Confederação Brasileira de Skate (Brazil), Indonesian Skateboarder Association, National Skateboarding Association of South Africa, Norsk Organisasjon for Rullebrett (Norway), Skateboard England, Skateboarding Turkey, Suomen Rullalautaliito (Finland) and Sveriges Skateboardförbund (Sweden). In a slightly different vein, the International Association of Skateboard Companies (IASC), founded by Jim Fitzpatrick in 1995, approaches skateboarding from a trade and business perspective, while companies like ActionWatch, Board-Trac and TransWorld Business all provide action sports–related market and industry intelligence.[101]

At a global level, the US-based National Skateboard Association (founded 1981) mutated in 1993 into the globally facing World Cup Skateboarding (WCS), offering a points and rankings system for professionals competing in street- and vert-based disciplines, with further divisions for females, youth, amateur and masters. Having grown to over twenty events in eleven countries in 2014, WCS events are in turn recognized by the 'world governing body' for skateboarding, the International Skateboarding Federation (ISF, founded 2002, lead by Gary Ream) with member organizations from fifty-eight countries, and that helped steer skateboarding into the 2020 Olympics.[102] A competing organization, the World Skateboarding Federation (WSF, led by Tim McFerran), has also sanctioned championships in Cuba and Africa (Figure 5.20).[103] Groups like the International Downhill Federation (IDF), International Gravity Sports Association (IGSA), International Slalom Skateboarding Association (ISSA) and World Freestyle Skateboard

Association (WFSA) play similar roles for downhill, freestyle, luge and slalom disciplines.

All of this, however, operates quite separately from most skateboarders. While professionals, brands and companies may be interested in such organizations, these tend, as Batuev and Robinson show, to be fairly informal networks rather than bureaucratic hierarchies.[104] Furthermore, everyday skaters tend to disregard these groups as an irrelevance or even a barrier to the perceived free-spirited nature of skateboarding. Such skaters often adopt an anti-competition and anti-regulation attitude that dismisses disciplined codes and organizations for not being authentic, 'legit' or 'core'.

However, the achievements of organizations should not be dismissed out of hand. Sometimes their actions are local, as when the IASC helped set up the Skateboard Hall of Fame in California, or when Frank Hawk as NSA president arranged for the Boy Scouts organization to run the Del Mar Skate Ranch skatepark, rescuing it from closure.[105] At other times their influence has been far more pervasive, particularly concerning matters of policy. For example, Fitzpatrick and the IASC were the main driving force behind California's AB1296 legislation, which from January 1998 allowed skateparks to operate free from liability issues. Five years later, the IASC inaugurated 'Go Skateboarding Day', held on 21 June annually, and now established as a popular worldwide event (Figure 1.1).[106]

Although many skateboarders themselves remain hugely suspicious that such organizations might try to control skateboarding, in reality many help promote the activity and provide funding for skateparks and other initiatives. As John Magnusson explains of Malmö's Bryggeriet club and national Sveriges Skateboardförbund, these entities unlock government revenue for skateparks; 'We don't want to become a sport, but it allows us more money, and that comes back to the skaters.'[107]

Boom Boom HuckJam

The most obvious way for skateboarding organizations and companies to directly impact on skateboarding is through events and training facilities, ranging from camps and competitions to entertainment-focused extravaganzas.

Skater-Campers

One early example of a skateboarding training facility was the Eurocana Summer Camp in Rättvik, Sweden, which between 1979 and 1985 attracted many European and US skaters. The high standard of Eurocana is affirmed by Mike McGill and Tony Hawk inventing their McTwist 540° (Figure 9.3), stalefish and 720° aerials here, while the 400 skaters attending annually benefitted from instruction from the likes of Mike Weed, Bob Skoldberg, Stacy Peralta, Per Welinder, Hans Göthberg and Alan Gelfand. Participants were even presented with a graduating diploma.[108]

Even more famous are the Woodward Camps, originally started in 1970s Pennsylvania for gymnastics, before BMX (1982), skateboarding (1987) and rollerblading (1992) were added, along with other locations in California, Wisconsin, Colorado and Beijing. These are elaborate facilities. Camp Woodward in Beijing – subsidized by the Chinese government with $12 million, and officially known as the Beijing Fashion Sports Park – opened in 2010 with a 3,000 m² plaza and 3,700 m² indoor arena.109 More extravagantly still, by 2017 the facilities at Woodward West in California included the 1,600 m² concrete Junction skatepark, Target Plaza and Art Park street courses, Crater flow-bowl, Animal Chin ramp replica, and even a MegaRamp.[110]

As this suggests, these are high-cost endeavours, with camp fees of between $1,100 and $1,450 per week in 2017, and generating millions of dollars in income. Days are structured, typically starting with two hours of formal instruction. Full safety equipment must be worn and is accompanied by warm-up sessions, on-site medical facilities, liability disclaimers and behaviour codes for swearing, alcohol and drugs. Staff cruise around on golf carts looking for bad behaviour.[111] Although Woodward might seem contrary to skateboarding's 1990s counter-cultural ideology, to many kids from the self-disciplined and motivated Generation Y, this is fully acceptable (Figure 4.9). 'Every time they succeed', explains Woodward co-founder Ed Isabelle, 'they're building confidence for the rest of their lives.' Or as psychologist Rich Luker explains, 'In team sports, there are rules. In action sports, your reward is doing things differently. It's less about direct competition and more about the ascension of excellence in expression.' For these reasons, Woodward even supplements its sports with other forms of creativity, such as video, photography and music recording, including advice from professionals like Grant Brittain and Ty Evans.[112]

Nonetheless, while for many skaters Woodward is about personal development, for others it is

Figure 4.9
Skate campers at
Woodward Camp,
Pennsylvania (2016).
Photograph Mike
Thomas/Courtesy
Woodward.

undoubtedly about pursuing a lucrative actions sports career. By 2004 some camp participants were increasingly competition-focused, thinking of themselves as athletes as much as skaters, and it is to these arenas we now turn.[113]

Competitions

Competitions have featured throughout skateboarding history. Early contests included a 1963 event organized by Larry Stevenson in Hermosa Beach, plus the 1965 national championships in Anaheim.[114] A decade later, as skateboarding enjoyed its urethane-propelled expansion, many new events arose, including the National Bahne-Cadillac Skateboard Championships in Del Mar. First held in April 1975, these Del Mar Nationals attracted hundreds of competitors (mostly Californians), boasted a slalom starting ramp costing $20,000 and attracted extensive national media coverage.[115] It was also here that the Z-Boys arrived on the skateboard scene (as depicted in *Dogtown and Z-Boys*), their ground-hugging and fast-moving surf-style clashing with the technical gymnasticism of other competitors (Figure 5.12).

Contests also occurred in places like Florida, New York, Japan and Australia, including the 1975 Victorian Skateboard Championships in Flinders Park and a Coke-sponsored 1975 event in Sydney, plus the 1976 World Invitational at New York's Nassau Coliseum.[116] In the UK, popular 1977 competitions were organized by the BBC's *Nationwide* and in London's Crystal Palace by the *London Evening News*.[117] In Canada, the BC Skateboard Championship was held annually from 1975, while in Caracas, Venezuela, the 1979 five-day Super Skate Show featured Pepsi-sponsored demonstrations. Skaters including Alan Gelfand, Tony Alva, Mike McGill, Ellen O'Neal, Tim Scroggs and Steve Rocco performed in the 13,000-seat Poliedro stadium, wore iridescent superhero capes and appeared on national television, while staying in five-star hotels and receiving a full VIP treatment.[118]

Back in the US, the 1977 and 1978 World Skateboard Championships organized by Jim O'Mahoney and Free Former were held at Derby Downs, Ohio. A two-day event broadcast by CBS, it included female and male competitions in downhill, slalom, freestyle and ramp-riding.[119] At the same time, the Pro-Am Race series for downhill and slalom was also popular, touring the Rocky Mountain area.[120] In 1978, 40,000 spectators attended Boston's Skate'78, including competitions and Pepsi team demos.[121] Most high-profile of all was the Hester Pro Bowl Series, inaugurated by Henry Hester in March 1978 with a Spring Valley event in Skateboard Heaven's pool. This series quickly gained a substantial reputation for advanced skateboarding through rapidly developing, innovative moves and extensive *SkateBoarder* coverage.[122]

During the 1980s, competitions were an important social lynchpin for a precarious skateboarding scene, often taking place on skaters' own ramps, like that of Joe Lopes in San Leandro or at special demos, like Australia's Moomba Ramp Jam in Melbourne and Ramp Riot events in Torquay; 'it was skaters trying to help out other skaters', recalled Sean Goff of similar events in Europe.[123] Big competitions like Prague's Euroskate '88 even had geopolitical dimensions, where East Germans met western counterparts, and so gained a sense of new horizons. 'We were on our way back to the country you couldn't leave', explained one East German skater. 'But we knew now. We had understood the scope of things. Understood that they locked us up out of fear that all their lies would be discovered.'[124]

Despite these qualities, the rise of street-oriented videos meant that into the 1990s competitions became much less important; Frankie Hill, for example, turned pro for Powell-Peralta strictly through his video appearances. 'Contests didn't matter anymore', realized Lance Mountain. 'It was all about capturing insane progression and shooting something that hadn't been done.'[125]

The main exception to this has been ESPN's X Games. When launched in 1993, the ESPN2 channel had already used action sports to attract audiences under twenty-five years old, who were often left cold by traditional team sports. Then one of its programmers, Ron Semiao, proposed a single event covering all extreme sports and that, crucially, ESPN2 could itself own, thus avoiding rights costs while also generating spin-off income. Originally launched in 1995 as the Extreme Games before 200,000 Rhode Island spectators, the event was swiftly renamed the X Games, and by 2011 was being beamed into 382 million homes worldwide.[126]

From the beginning, these 'psycho Olympics' staged skaters as being, on the one hand, 'on the edge' and 'from the streets', and, on the other hand, 'true athletes' with elevated competition standards and serious injury risks. Financial winners included both the riders (from the late 1990s each skate event boasted $70,000 in prizes) and the hosting cities; the first two X Games generated $30 million for the local Rhode Island economy. Advertisers were also delighted, reaching precisely those twelve to twenty-four and twenty-five to thirty-four year-old markets that other sports often missed out on. The likes of Miller Lite, Taco Bell, Mountain Dew, Nike and AT&T were consequently all willing to pay over $1 million in sponsorship.[127]

For some skaters, enhanced public status also ensued. At the San Francisco 1999 vert-ramp event, Tony Hawk successfully completed the first ever 900° (two-and-a-half rotations) aerial (Figure 4.3); this achievement launched a tidal wave of national media coverage. During the 1990s, other vert and ramp-riding professionals who benefitted from X Games competitions included Bob Burnquist, Cara-Beth Burnside, Jason Ellis, Mike Frazier, Rune Glifberg, Peter Hewitt, Neil Hendrix, Bucky Lasek, Andy Macdonald, Jodi MacDonald, Colin McKay, Jen O'Brien, Ben Pappas, Tas Pappas, Sluggo, Wade Speyer, Danny Way and Giorgio Zattoni.[128]

Yet despite the undoubted potential for financial and reputational reward, there were also, as Browne notes, significant presentational and bodily costs. In order to keep its young audience attentive, the X Games deployed an Olympics-style medals system, and until 2004 was broadcast only in edited formats so as to heighten the apparent intensity of action, further boosted by wild camera angles, brash graphics, excited crowds, punk and rock music and extended slam footage. Commentaries could be particularly excruciating: 'Bob Burnquist has a rocket in his pocket and who knows when it'll go off!'[129]

Even more significant has been the spectacularization of risk and injury, and it is no coincidence that one of the most replayed X Games incidents is Jake Brown's infamous 2007 14 m fall, with (as of 2018) over 3.4 million YouTube viewings. As Rinehart notes, by 2007, there was a 'growing acceptance and glorification of pain and injury' in the X Games, which helped bolster the 'angst-filled market of pre-teens and teenagers'. Risk of severe injury is indeed considerable; although no X Games skateboarders have actually died, (unlike snowmobile rider Caleb Moore and half-pipe skier Sarah Burke), serious accidents do occur. For example, Brown was hospitalized after his 2007 fall, and then knocked out on the 2013 Munich MegaRamp. Consequently some commentators, like Orpana, have interpreted these near-death experiences as a necessary X Games component, comparing their victims with philosopher Giorgio Agamben's figure of the *homo sacer*, the expendable subject whose misfortune is never due to corporate negligence but only caused by voluntary participation.[130]

Numerous other criticisms are also possible, including a lack of participation rates (only forty of over a thousand potential professionals competed at the 2002 Philadelphia X Games), a tendency to create false rivalries (such as Macdonald vs. Hawk), and, above all, a focus on 'winning' rather than on self-expression; as a *Concrete Disciples* blogger put it, the 'canned stunt show' X Games is the 'bastardization of skateboarding to meet the goals of a boardroom full of executive butf@#$s'.[131] Even competing pros have expressed dissatisfaction, as with disputes during 2001 and 2002 over image rights and pay, while in 2005 the Action Sports Alliance sought equal pay and greater television coverage for female skaters – a demand that was eventually met in 2009.[132]

The X Games have occasionally been rivalled by competitions like NBC's Gravity Games (1999–2006), the Maloof Money Cup (2008–2012) and the more recent WSF Skateboarding World Championship in South Africa. Its main rival, however, emerged in 2010, when Rob Dyrdek launched the Street League Skateboarding (SLS) world tour, with financial backing from sports agency IMG and offering revenue sharing to its invite-only competitors. After major investment from Causeway Media in 2014, in 2016 SLS was globally broadcast by Fox Sports/FS1 television, sponsored by Nike SB and GoPro, and toured five US and European cities. In SLS competition arenas, the ledges, rails and stairs associated with everyday urbanism are reduced to videodrome aesthetics, typically with colour-brightened elements contrasting against a grey floor, high-intensity lighting, advertising hoardings and digital scoreboards. The competition itself consists of individually scored tricks and runs, overlaid with commentaries and sponsor endorsements (Figure 4.8). Merchandise includes clothing, calendars and action figures. Clearly, this is far removed from the complex grittiness of real city street-skating, and other forms of reductive control are also in place; invited skaters have to sign exclusive contracts, frequently forbidding them from entering rival competitions.[133]

Significantly for skateboarding culture as a whole, although the X Games and SLS have undoubtedly promoted skateboarding worldwide, and some youngsters do emulate their spectacular content, they have actually done very little to change predominant skateboarding practices and viewpoints; as Beal and Wilson report, many everyday skaters are remarkably ambivalent about the X Games. Hence, notes Rinehart, although the X Games utilizes 'invented traditions' like medal winners to align skateboarding with mainstream sports, everyday skaters prefer to recall actions over standings or results; for example, skaters frequently refer to Hawk's 900° aerial as an impressive achievement (Figure 4.3), but rarely if ever mention his ten X Games gold medals. What matters for skaters most are not wins or rankings, but deeds and achievements, and so while the X Games and SLS may appropriate media images of skateboarding, they do not appropriate skateboarding itself.[134]

Olympics
Although as early as 1964 *The Quarterly SkateBoarder* predicted skateboarding's appearance in the Olympics, and 1970s pros like Russ Howell similarly argued for Olympic inclusion, many skaters have been wary of globally televised and ultra-competitive competitions.[135] Indeed, in the 1980s and 2010s, and no doubt with one eye on the spectacularized X Games and SLS, skaters have actively campaigned for skateboarding *not* to be included in the Olympics. 'Skateboarding is not a "sport",' asserted a 2010 petition. 'We do not want skateboarding exploited and transformed to fit the Olympic program.'[136] Chinese skaters have been particularly opposed, fearing that Olympic inclusion might strengthen the country's Tiwei skateboarding organization, and so lead to regimented leagues and training centres.[137]

More recently, however, such sentiments have diminished. In 2014 skateboarding was included as an exhibition event in the Nanjing Youth Olympic Games, and two years later the ISF and the International Federation of Roller Sports (FIRS), and who subsequently joined forces as the World Skate organization, successfully argued for street- and park-riding competitions to be held at the 2020 Tokyo Olympics. Notably, while there have been a few opposing petitions, the general mood among skateboarders has been much more guardedly affirmative. 'I want kids to skate because they love it, not for money,' explained Chris Cole. 'But the growth of the sport and letting this treasure get out to masses of people is more important.' Notably, of the professionals interviewed by *Thrasher* and by Batuev and Robinson, most were in favour of Olympics skateboarding. Many everyday skaters also now accept the development, often with the hope that greater female participation rates and more local skateparks will be constructed as a result.[138]

Competition Sociology

While skaters like Caballero, Hawk and Guerrero recognize the addictiveness of peer approval through competition victories, most skaters see skateboarding as competitive only in the most informal of terms, and prefer challenging self-progression over 'winning'; 'Soccer is a lot of pressure, you have to be as good if not better than everybody else', explained eighteen-year-old Pamela. 'Skating, you just push yourself harder and harder.' Or as pro Jaime Reyes described her attitude, 'I don't really care about contests. I'm just psyched to show up and do what I do.'[139] How then do regulated competitions square with the avowedly independent nature of skateboarding? How is it that, by 2014, over fifty-three per cent of US skaters had entered at least one contest?[140]

Chief here is what Beal and Weidman call 'participant control', where skaters create their own social space without recourse to formalized organization.[141] In the first place, notes Donnelly, skaters care less about competitions per se and more about specific formats and atmospheres.[142] For example, one reason that the tricks-based game of SKATE is popular, and despite its confrontational duelling format, is because its format and tenor are set by skaters themselves rather than by codified regulations. Similarly Beal and Petrone show how skaters typically eschew outright competitive behaviour in favour of self-definition; 'You don't want to do better than them', explained one rider, 'but you want to do better because they're doing better.'[143] Even professionals frequently express indifference to winning. Colin McKay, for example, despite topping many 1990s vert contests, was reputedly unconcerned if he missed the cut into the final.[144] Through such actions, it is clear that attitude, pleasure and commitment are rated as highly as technical achievement; even Hawk's X Games 900° air is remembered as much for his twelve unsuccessful attempts – and hence for Hawk's determination – as for its final completion (Figure 4.3). As the adage goes, the best skater is the one having the most fun.

For Beal and Weidman, this attitude can be understood through Goffman's conceptualizations of front-stage (conscious performance for a specific audience) and back-stage (performing for no audience, being candid and authentic) behaviours; skaters then perform in a back-stage manner but in a front-stage setting, such that a skater's authenticity is rendered through a 'public display of the norms and values of skateboard culture' that are 'recognizable only to other experienced skateboarders'.[145] This is demonstrated in numerous ways, as Petrone and others record, including loaning equipment, applauding fellow competitors, performing slapstick manoeuvres or generally behaving in a friendly manner – behaviours that are not normally associated with sports competition.[146] For example, at a Colorado event observed by Beal, many skaters practised out of turn, skated even though not entered as competitors, and generally transformed the tournament into a loose jam session.[147] Similarly skaters will often make fun of regulations, as with Ben Raybourn at the 2014 Van Doren Invitational, deliberately spinning a banned 540° aerial followed by a defiant one-fingered salute.[148] Events themselves also often replicate these free-form attitudes, typically offering only token prizes – at one 1980s Eagle Rock contest it was five dollars – and operating in open jam formats.[149] Today, even high-profile competitions like the Vans Park Series offer multi-rider formats, semi-chaotic prize-givings and ad hoc awards for unusual moves.

Similar behaviours pervade everyday skate sessions. While skaters may occasionally heckle those who break skatepark etiquette, such as by 'snaking' or riding out of turn, the general attitude is of friendly cooperation and implicit skills transferral; Engeström calls this 'transformative learning', absorbing knowledge through skateboarding's 'very operating principles and everyday social textures', while Petrone, Ma and Munster similarly note how skaters avoid formal instruction but nonetheless benefit from an 'embodied learning' via occasional advice and conversations.[150] For example, Ken Wormhoudt recalls a skater attempting a new trick until it 'nearly killed him', and yet also then helping another skater to learn it.[151] In a related code, it is often considered inappropriate for one skater to attempt the same trick as another skater, lest a successful completion be perceived as one-upmanship. As Doug, one of the skaters interviewed by Beal, commented, 'we don't skate *against* somebody, we skate *with* them.'[152]

Figure 4.10
Spontaneous carnival or media staging? Pedro Barros transfers over the Combi-Pool at the Vans Pool Party (Volcom, 2015).
www.bit.ly/Barros-Vans

Media and industry attitudes also play their part. As Beal and Weidman note, magazine advertisements rarely depict competitions, while YouTube clips decontextualize competition runs by emphasizing dynamism over formal adjudication.[153] As a result, from Christian Hosoi, Natas Kaupas (Figure 10.2) and Mark Gonzales (Figure 10.1) in the 1980s through to Ben Raybourn, Greyson Fletcher and Pedro Barros (Figure 4.10) today, it is generally recognized that a skater's style, attitude and ability matter most, all of this being reflected largely through peer respect, social media, video parts and online sequences, and rarely through competition wins or event standings.

Spectaculars
Although not necessarily competitions per se, orchestrated tours provide spectacular skateboarding displays. The Tony Hawk-ESPN Gigantic Skatepark Tour, for example, was popular enough for Wrangler, Nokia and others to front $1.8 million in sponsorship. Around the same time, Hawk's Boom Boom HuckJam skate, BMX, motocross and punk rock extravaganza grossed over $300,0000 per night, with an average crowd of 10,000. The arena event was a substantial undertaking; the demountable half-pipes, launch ramps and loop cost over $1 million, and required a sixty-person and fourteen-truck crew.[154]

Then there is the hugely popular and rambunctious annual Vans Pool Party, held at the recreated Combi-Pool in Orange County, livestreamed and fed via YouTube to hundreds of thousands of skaters worldwide (Figure 4.10), as well as the Vans Warped Tour. By 2010 the latter attracted over 600,000 visitors to its eclectic mixture of action sports, rock, reggae, punk and hip-hop. As to be expected, this is a multi-million dollar spectacular, which also welcomes sponsors ranging from Domino's Pizza to Snapple drinks. Critics like

Daniel Sinker have consequently noted how the Warped Tour co-opts punk values into mainstream capitalism, with Jeff Howe calling it 'a Wagnerian Opera for Kapital X' and a 'conflation of counter-cultural symbols swept clean of messy by-products'. Rinehart similarly notes how the Warped Tour, along with other 'mega-events' like the X Games and Vans Pool Party, supposedly create Bakhtinian carnivals of inverted and spontaneous behaviours, but are actually largely illusory stagings for both immediate and media audiences.[155]

Yet despite these undoubtedly warranted critiques, the Warped Tour and Vans Pool Party are somewhat different from many other skateboarding packagings, especially the pure-gloss SLS and X Games spectaculars. Vans has even undertaken some risky social innovations, such as incorporating the All Girl Skate Jam competition into the Warped Tour and sending 'shock waves through the male dominated skateboard industry'. Also notably evident at the Warped Tour and Vans Pool Party is an anti-establishment atmosphere, where both 'freedom and chaos' co-exist.[156] As a result, these are sophisticated deliveries of rebellious skate subculture, simultaneously rendered as commodified pleasure.

Skateboard Scenes
Chapter 5 Media Worlds

A multiplicity of micro-, niche- and increasingly mass-media depictions have played an integral part not only in skateboarding's dissemination but also in the development of its values. And as Willard points out, these media worlds have contributed massively to skateboarding's global presence, forming 'translocal' communities that escape the confines of the immediate neighbourhood to create connections and networks of much wider scales.[1] It is to these media channels and constructs that we now turn.

Truth and Screw the Consequences

Of skateboarding's massive array of media channels, perhaps the most well-known are printed magazines, a few of which – notably the US *SkateBoarder*, *Thrasher* and *TransWorld Skateboarding* – have had an extraordinary influence. Other major US titles have included *Big Brother*, *Confusion*, *Focus*, *Heckler*, *Juice*, *Poweredge*, *The Skateboard Mag*, *Slap*, *Strength* and *Warp*, plus a myriad of lesser-known titles like *North*, *Steez* and *Step Dad*. Equally important for their own regional and national scenes are the skateboard print and online magazines that have been produced worldwide, with titles as diverse as *Buenos Muchachos* (Argentina), *Five40* (Australia), *Last Try* (Austria), *Overall* (Brazil), *Color* (Canada), *Demolicion* (Chile), *Whatsup* (China), *SkateBoards* (Colombia), *Strictly Skateboarding* (Denmark), *Radical Skateboard* (Ecuador), *Soma* and *Sugar* (France), *Monster* and *Place Skateboard Culture* (Germany), *Happen* (Indonesia), *XXX* (Italy), *Lovely* (Japan), *Skate* (Mexico), *Manual* (New Zealand), *Dank* (Norway), *Barrier* (Poland), *Surge* (Portugal), *Skeit Novosti* (Russia), *Session* (South Africa), *Unsung* (South Korea), *Erosion* (Spain), *Väggarna* (Sweden), *Blackout* (Switzerland) and *Document*, *Free*, *Grey*, *Huck*, *Kingpin*, *R.A.D.*, *Sidewalk*, *Skateboard!* and *Skateboard Scene* (UK). Today, specialist magazines like *Confusion* (DIY), *Broken Fingers* (freestyle) and *Concrete Wave* (longboarding) also thrive.

Practical issues and factional politics are often at work in these publications, with titles inevitably favouring certain riders, manufacturers and regions. For example, in the late 1970s *SkateBoarder* became extraordinarily influential, at one point reaching a million readers. '*SkateBoarder* is our Bible,' recalled Christian Hosoi. 'We live on every word, photo and ad.'[2] Yet *SkateBoarder* largely favoured the Los Angeles scene, while reportedly blacklisting many skaters who appeared in the rival magazine *Skateboard World* or came from San Diego. Thus despite *Wild World of Skateboarding* arguing that San Diego was actually the first 'home of modern skateboarding,' much of California skating, along with vibrant New York and East Coast scenes, was left largely uncovered.[3]

Particularly important here was Craig Stecyk in creating the Dogtown mythology in *SkateBoarder* and as later co-writer for *Dogtown and Z-Boys*. Stacy Peralta calls Stecyk a 'political pyrotechnician' and Jocko Weyland eulogizes about his 'singular voice'. Conversely, Louison and others criticize Stecyk's 'collegiate and masturbatory' tone, 'made-for-TV adventure-screenplay' stories, dubious accuracy and covert marketing agenda. Either way, Stecyk's photo-text reportage-style essays crackle with a take-it-or-leave-it attitude, artistic sensibility and insider knowledge. Here is a world of fact and myth, everyday and the arcane, present and the future – a world where skaters in general and Dogtowners in particular are portrayed as restless innovators battling against routine normality. As Henry Rollins recollected, Stecyk transmitted a full-blown lifestyle, with a dramatic effect on thousands of readers worldwide, and as Jay Adams concluded, 'there would have been no Dogtown if it weren't for Stecyk.'[4]

Perhaps inspired by such manoeuvrings, some skateboard publications have embedded themselves deep within local and counter-cultural practices. Since the early 1980s, this has been evident in the large number of 'zines (low-cost and self-produced magazines) that have occasionally appeared. To begin with, these 'zines focused mainly on skateboarding itself,

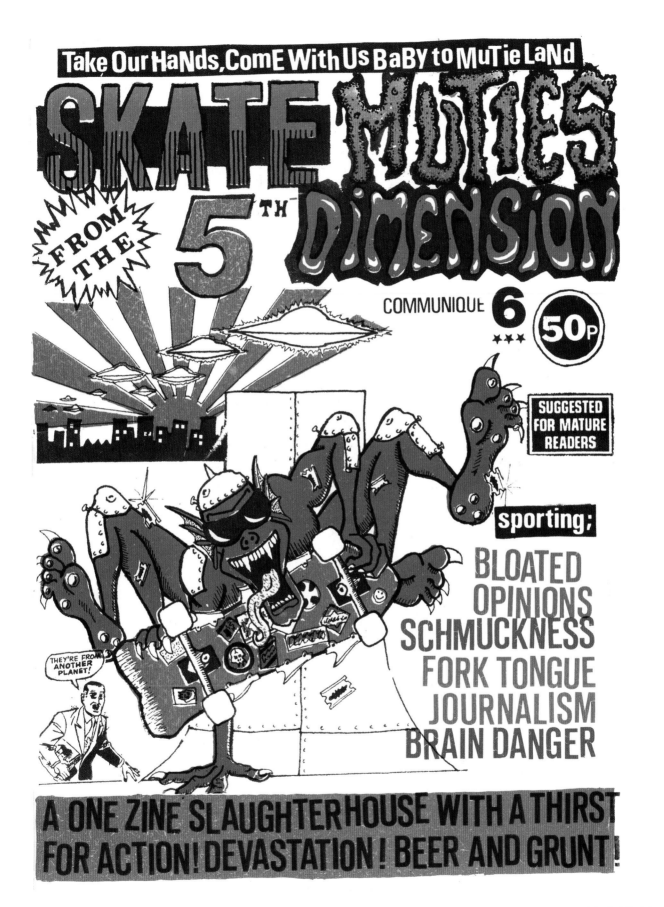

and in particular the more hardcore elements of its subculture. Filled with mottos like 'Skate or Die', 'Skate Tough or Go Home', 'Live to Skate and Skate to Live' and 'Slam the Rules', typical titles have included *Apathetic Injection*, *Body Slam*, *Death Skate*, *Equal Time* (originally *Girls Who Grind*), *Gut Feel'n*, *Mutant King Roller*, *Naughty Nomads*, *No Pedestrians*, *Revenge Against Boredom*, *Skate Punk* and *Swank* (US), *Skate On* and *Street Noise* (Australia), *Death Zone* and *Scum* (Germany), *Vertikaal* (Sweden) and *Go for It*, *Whiplash* and *Skate Muties from the 5th Dimension* (UK) (Figure 5.1).

As Duncombe has shown, these 'zines exude an 'angry idealism', letting readers ignore mainstream society and instead offering an authentic and supportive community. In 1990s China, for example, Karl Gao's *Ollie Newsletter* 'brought all the skaters in the country together and made them feel like members of a big family'.[5] Interestingly, despite or perhaps because of social media, during the 2000s many more 'zines have emerged, with recent examples ranging from *Lowcard*, *Sauce*, *Skate Jawn* and *Torture Chamber* (US) to *Cruysberghs* (Germany), *Over Plywood* (UK), *Patinho Feio* (Portugal) and *Ratz Art* (Slovakia). Others, like *Brash* (London), *Escape Route* (Seattle), *Check It Out* (Brazil), *Push* (Canada) and *Villa Villa Cola/VVC* (San Diego), have been aimed at female skaters, some even evolving into high-production-value products.[6]

The most consistent rejection of normative society has, however, come from *Thrasher*, probably the world's longest-running skateboard magazine, which, according to Weyland, can claim to 'define and be skateboarding' (Figure 5.2).[7] *Thrasher* has been a hugely influential mouthpiece for that young generation that displays, in Lefebvre's words, a 'hatred – blind or conscious – for the pressures exerted by authority' and that is 'no longer seduced, satisfied or overwhelmed by refrigerators and automobiles'.[8] As one Michigan skater (clearly unaware of *Thrasher*'s commercial Vitello connections) saw it, *Thrasher* was the best skateboarding magazine 'because it's raw skateboarding' and 'not a bunch of industry propaganda'. Particularly in its 1980s issues, *Thrasher* also acted as a global bulletin board, allowing committed skaters to connect with other local scenes; as Weyland recalls, 'it was about your far-flung tribe recognizing your will to exist and skate under the toughest of circumstances.'[9]

Founded in San Francisco in January 1981 with ex-Tunnel pro Kevin Thatcher as editor, *Thrasher* has offered a complete guide to skateboard subculture including articles on rock, punk and junk food ('skarfing material') alongside skatespot information, reader photographs and pro-rider interviews. Published in the spirit of the low budget 'zines with (at least in the early years) black-and-white punkish graphics accompanied by terse bylines like '100% Aggression', 'Burnout', 'Firing Line' and 'Truth and Screw the Consequences', *Thrasher*'s 'skate and destroy' street ethos contrasted starkly with *SkateBoarder*'s glossy authority. Inspired by the gonzo New Journalism of Hunter S. Thompson and Charles Bukowski, contributors MoFo, Stecyk and others wrote as much about the activities around skateboarding as skateboarding itself, from beer-fuelled misdemeanours to weird anecdotes and strange happenings. *Thrasher* might proclaim 'shut up and skate', but its content was like a manifesto, presenting skateboarding as a waywardly boisterous alternative to more decorous modes of living. The approach was highly successful, and by 1989 *Thrasher* had a global circulation of around 250,000.[10]

Thrasher mocks those in power as a form of vengeance and subversion, and so fulfils one of Lefebvre's expectations of young people, namely ridiculing virtues of decency, respect and good health.[11] In turn, skaters' own subculture – particularly in the 1980s and 1990s – has often been based on a nihilistic anti-order of bad taste, scatological humour, swearing and poor diets – anything that might be antagonistic to others. *Big Brother* of the 1990s perhaps best fulfilled this role, with articles variously combining sex, drugs, dwarves, pornography, suicide, rock music, alcohol and bodily fluids. Although supposedly a skateboard magazine, ultimately *Big Brother* was more about teenage skaters' wider lives and interests; as Ed Templeton explained 'it was a closer map to what skaters were really like'.[12]

In deliberate contrast to *Thrasher* and *Big Brother* sits *TransWorld Skateboarding* (and its later offshoot *The Skateboard Mag*, founded 2004). Launched in 1983 by Larry Balma, *TransWorld* countered *Thrasher*'s punk-fuelled 'skate and destroy' mantra with its own 'skate and create' persona, intended to signify a more 'positive' version of skateboarding as a wholesome, accessible and creative activity that could also incorporate high-achieving performances (Figure 5.3). Unlike *Thrasher*'s appeal to misfits and miscreants, *TransWorld* targeted not only skaters but parents, companies, authorities and others with an interest in skateboarding. According to its first editorial – signed by Balma, Neil Blender, Grant Brittain, Garry Scott Davis and Per Holknekt among others – a 'United Skate Front' had been formed from 'skate greats, uninhibited artists, radical skaters, old-timers, newcomers, and even moms and dads' to cover every aspect of 'our awesome sport'. To underline this new position, Peggy Cozens's article 'Skate and Create' argued against portraying skaters as low-life degenerates ('destruction requires no creativity, intelligence, sensitivity or skill'), and recognizing instead their 'magnificent talent, creativity, guts and expression of individuality'. Other *TransWorld* articles gave helpful advice on how to keep skatespots open, detailed reports on competitions and Powell-Peralta's Bones Brigade team, and notes on events in Sweden, Canada, Italy and Germany. Ramp-, skatepark- and street-based riding all made an appearance, as did freestyle and slalom. This formulation has also proved enduringly popular, and as recently as 2013 *TransWorld* had over 600,000 readers.[13]

Wide-Angled Viewing

Even in the 1960s issues of *SkateBoarder*, photographs played a key role, with renowned surf photographers like Ron Stoner (Figure 6.9) and Bev Morgan experimenting with neo-abstraction, blurs, fish-eyes, pixilation and smoke flares to convey dynamism. But it was in the 1970s that photographs truly became skateboarding's lifeblood, globally disseminating innovative moves and fantastic terrains. Among the most prolific of these 1970s US photographers were *SkateBoarder*'s Warren Bolster, Art Brewer, Craig Fineman (Figure 5.6), James Cassimus, Wynn Miller, Craig Stecyk and Ted Terrebonne, as well as freelancers Boyd Harnell and Glen Friedman (Figures 6.1, 6.11 and 9.14), plus William (Bill) and Stan Sharp of *Skateboard World*. Also important was *SkateBoarder*'s Jim Goodrich, who covered places like Florida, Utah, Canada, Mexico and Venezuela (Figures 6.8, 7.7, 7.8, 7.12, 7.17, 9.6, and 9.13). In recent years the work of Kent Sherwood, Spot and Hugh Holland has surfaced, while among 1970s UK photographers were *Skateboard!*'s Robert Vente, Jerry Young and Ian Dobbie, and *Skateboard Scene*'s Gregg Haythorpe.

In the 1980s and 1990s, other prominent photographers included *TransWorld*'s Grant Brittain, Thomas Campbell, Geoff Kula, Spike

Jonze (Adam Spiegel), Skin Phillips and Miki Vuckovich, *Thrasher*'s Mörizen Föche (MoFo), Jeff Newton, Bryce Kanights and Chris Ortiz, *Slap*'s Lance Dawes, *R.A.D.*'s Jay Podesta (Vernon Adams), Tim Leighton-Boyce (Figures 5.5, 7.14, 7.15, 7.16, 10.7, 10.17 and 10.24), Mike John, Dobie Campbell, Paul Sunman and Wig Worland, and *Skateboard!*'s (second series) Steve Kane and Paul Duffy. In the 1990s and 2000s UK skateboard photographers also included *Sidewalk*'s Richie Hopson, Andy Horsley, Andy Shaw, Leo Sharp and Worland (Figures 8.8, 9.4, 10.12, 10.13, 10.14, 11.9, 11.13, 12.14, 12.23, 12.24, 13.2 and 13.3).

Over the last three decades, myriad other photographers have emerged, including Anthony Acosta, Ryan Allan, Sam Ashley, Mike Blabac, Joe Brook, Michael Burnett, Thomas Campbell, Fred Mortagne (French Fred), Brian Gaberman (Figure 5.7), Jon Humphries (Figure 3.6), Atiba Jefferson, Chris Johnson, Reece Leung, Sam McGuire, Jonathan Mehring, Gabe Morford, Jody Morris, Nikwen (Figure 10.19), Patrick O'Dell, Luke Ogden, Mike O'Meally, Andrew Peters, Giovanni Reda, Chris 'Rhino' Rooney, Sem Rubio, Rob Shaw (Figures 6.13 and 11.6), Dan Sparagna, J. Strickland, Daniel Sturt, Helge Tscharn (Figures 6.15 and 12.26), Dave Van Laere (Figures 3.2, 6.12, 10.18 and 11.1) and Tobin Yelland, with hundreds of others also creating equally exemplary images. Mike Blabac's book *Blabac Photo* provides clear evidence of the skill and scope involved, ranging from dramatic action, artful form and light, insightful portraits and expressive landscapes, to poignant social commentaries, behind-the-scenes reportage and eccentric miscellanea.[14] Similarly, Fred Mortagne's images artfully amalgamate lines, compositions, light, colour/monochromy, post-shot manipulation, textures, layerings and film/digital media.[15] As this suggests, photographers look for more than just amazing tricks; for Bryce Kanights this might be 'killer portraits', 'killer spots' or the 'unexpected', for Anthony Costa unusual spots and an overall passion, for Jonathan Mehring 'culturally different places', for Michael Burnett 'oddballs and weirdos', for Mike O'Meally 'a sense of mystery', and for Jody Morris 'that pit in the stomach you get going over the edge in a roller coaster'.[16]

How then were these images created, and to what effect? In *SkateBoarder* around 1975 and 1976, conventional stills dominated, with Bolster recommending wide-angled views of skaters wearing brightly coloured clothes, often shot from below to contrast with a perfect blue sky,

Figure 5.3
Launch issue
of *TransWorld
Skateboarding*
(May–June 1983).
Courtesy *TransWorld*.

TRANS-WORLD SKATEBOARDING

MAY/JUNE 1983
VOL. 1 NO. 1
$1.75

SKATE AND CREATE

THE GREAT DESERT
☆ ★ RAMP BATTLE ☆ ★

DEL MAR REVISITED
RUSTY HARRIS SERIES WRAP-UP 1982

COLLECTOR'S EDITION

TWO RAD CENTERFOLDS!

Figure 5.4
Wide-angle motor
drive sequence
of Tom Inouye at
SkaterCross, Reseda.
SkateBoarder
(July 1977).
Photographer
unidentified.

pure pipe form or glistening white pool (Figure 6.8).[17] As Willard notes, the rider's tanned body and focused concentration here perfectly aligned with surfing's abstract idea of freedom, personal expression and nature.[18]

But after pool-riding emerged and the first skateparks appeared, motor drives were frequently deployed to capture rapid-fire sequences, a disclosure of human movement that reached back to the 1870s movement studies by Eadweard Muybridge, and that now allowed skaters to emulate the moves being depicted. For example, *SkateBoarder* used a three-frame sequence to show an early backside air by Tom 'Wally' Inouye at SkaterCross (Figure 5.4), while *Skateboard!* deployed a full-page six-frame sequence to explain Alan Gelfand's ollie innovation to its UK readers (Figure 9.2). Such images particularly helped skaters in distant locations to understand the new moves being depicted; 'when photo sequences became standard fare,' explained Ola Sixtensson from the remote Swedish north, 'that was a true blessing.'[19]

Photographers were also now shooting from above, including the context of a pool or skatepark, and so, notes Willard, underlining qualities of danger, innovation and aggression. Other tactics involved emphasizing qualities of decay (cracked, graffitied or abandoned terrains), self-realization (faces with calm confidence, grimaced concentration or confrontational snarls) or personal presence (the photographer's own feet or shadow caught in shot) (Figure 9.14).[20] Furthermore, and in contrast to sports photography's long lenses, skate photographers have typically used 15 to 18 mm wide-angles to get close up, emphasizing locational context, and so simultaneously documenting, analyzing and exaggerating the event. Other advantages of wide-angles have been a dramatization of bodily moves ('15 mm fisheyes distort everything just right' declared MoFo) and possibly, as such lenses are expensive, making shots appear noticeably 'professional'.[21]

Other innovations have included experimentation with combinations of flash, filters, slower shutter speeds and even stroboscopic effects (Figure 5.5), while Angus Leadley Brown's mid-2000s 'synchroballistic' images (where film stock is motorized behind an open lens), disclose moves as a distorted continuum of body and skateboard (Figure 5.23).[22] Equally experimental are Sebastian Denz's stereoscopic three-dimensional images,

exploring tensions between skaters, the technical means of representation and viewer perceptions.[23] More common techniques have encompassed multi-image frames or combining flash with slow shutter speeds to portray a sharp skater overlaid onto blurred background movement (Figure 5.6). Fire, dry ice and flint sparks have also occasionally been used to add dynamism. Most significant technically was the mid-1990s arrival of digital cameras, whose high-resolution images and avoidance of costly film stock meant that more complex tricks – often completed only after numerous attempts – could be more readily captured. Conversely, the various bodies, lenses and other paraphernalia could easily cost a professional like Shad Lambert around $25,000 in 2008.[24] Street-skating photographers had additional concerns, including aggravating authorities; 'You're basically a glorified criminal,' explains Atiba Jefferson, 'documenting trespassing destruction of property.'[25]

Most notable of all, however, has been the elucidation of new meanings and cultures. Examples here are both varied and legion, and include the plaintive depictions of the DIY scene by Nils Svensson and Richard Gilligan (Figure 8.16), or Marc Vallée's understated documentation of anti-skateboarding devices.[26] Daniel Månsson, Nikki Toole and Mark Whiteley have adopted a portrait approach to significant skateboarding figures, while *Full Bleed* and *Long Live Southbank* provide extended studies of New York and London skate scenes.[27] Brian Gaberman combines skateboarding, landscape, form, colour and contrast, all reflecting large-format photography (Figure 5.7), while other photographic projects include Charlotte Thomas's and Julian Bleecker's focus on female skaters, Tom Caron-Delion's documentation of post-earthquake Nepal skateboarding, Renato Custodio's studies of street-skating reflected in glass, Jessica Fulford-Dobson's portraits of Kabul females, James A. Hudson's recordings of skatepark social life, Jonathan Mehring's travelogues, Mike Paproski's downhill close-ups, Tino Razo's pool-riding studies, William Sharp and Ozzie Ausband's 1970s collection, Arthur Tress's explorations of body and skatepark form and Sergej Vutuc's manipulated surfaces. Such photography, in Mortagne's words, is 'not what we see in reality,' but extends into far richer and far wider skateboarding worlds.[28]

Hudson's images, for example, contrast with the context-free dynamism typical of much sports-related imagery. In one Malmö scene, a women

Figure 5.5
Stroboscopic image
of Neil Harding at
Rolling Thunder,
London (1979).
© Tim Leighton-
Boyce/R.A.D. Archive.

Figure 5.6
Vicki Vickers at
Marina del Rey,
Venice Beach, caught
by a combination of
slow shutter speed
and flash.
Photograph
Craig Fineman,
SkateBoarder (May
1979).

reads a paper, a boy stares at the floor, two
skaters peer across the skatepark and four girls
chat; meanwhile a skater shoots a double-axle
carve in a tough-looking pool. Bags and water
bottles lie unattended, deep shadows are sharply
cast. Each sub-scene has equal weighting,
bringing together engaged communication,
gentle speculation and energetic action within a
distinctly human world. This is an idyllic scene,
a near perfect co-existence of doing, conversing
and thinking, and such photography radically
expands skateboarding's centre far beyond
spectacular moves (Figure 5.8).

Still other approaches are disclosed by books
like the *Dirt Ollies*, the *Vans 1966 Photobook*
or the Fluff/Nike SB collaboration *1826*, which
variously use travelogue-, magazine- or diary-
like formats to display a myriad of scenes
from Morocco, Brazil, China and Thailand
to Iceland, Mongolia, Dubai and Peru. Here,
photographs are valuable less individually and

more in series, with the snapshot quality of the
images suggesting accidental exploration and
incidental pleasures as skaters encounter the
world around them.

Local photographs may also have equivalent
ambitions. For example, besides documenting
tricks, the Tyneside skaters studied by Jeffries,
Messer and Swords portrayed their local context,
analyzed urban space and challenged sexist
and homophobic tendencies.[29] Jones similarly
shows how photographs and videos allowed
Hong Kong skaters to learn moves, document
personal development, set values, build
belonging and even imagine idealized futures.
Indeed, so important is photography that simply
introducing a camera at a session can intensify
both performances and the attention that
skaters pay to what is occurring, while social
media postings help individuals to integrate
within social groups.[30]

Figure 5.7
Nick Garcia, rock fakie
in Santiago (2011).
© Brian Gaberman.

These are important practices, revealing how photography is an essential component of skateboarding, helping riders to establish friendships and develop life views. Indeed, for professionals, imagery is the most essential mode of communication and promotion; as Ryan Sheckler commented, 'Getting pictures is what it's all about,' while Chris Miller similarly explains that 'You really can't be a pro skater without documenting what you do.'[31]

As this brief account suggests, photography (and, later, video) has been an essential component of skateboarding, from professionals to beginners alike. Indeed, so integral is photography to skateboarding that images frequently include other image-makers in order to demonstrate the authenticity of the scene being depicted. Photography here doubles-up skateboarding, becoming not just a recording of its actions, but also an integral part of its everyday content.

Skateboarding at the Movies
Like still photography, moving images have always been part of skateboarding history,

reaching back to *America's Newest Sport* (1964) (Figure 2.4), ABC coverage of the National Skateboard Championships (1965), *Skaterdater* (1965) and *The Devil's Toy* (1966) (Figure 2.7). By the mid-1970s surf-inspired filmmakers were active, with shooting for Chris Carmichael's *Spinn'in Wheels* (1975) starting in 1973, capturing the likes of Skitch Hitchcock, Russ Howell, Roy Jamieson, Bruce Logan, Ty Page and Mike Weed (Figure 6.3). Over 10,000 people turned up for the Santa Monica premiere, causing a near riot.[32] Also popular was *Super Session* (1976) by Hal Jepsen, which repeatedly intercuts surfing and skateboarding. *Freewheelin'* (Scott Dittrich, 1976) also yields genuine depictions of most kinds of pre-skatepark skateboarding, with Stacy Peralta as its focus. In Australia, *The Ultimate Flex Machine* (Jason Cameron) was released in 1975 (Figure 6.4).

Other well-known 1970s documentaries included *Downhill Motion* (Greg Weaver and Spyder Wills, 1975), *Magic Rolling Board* (Jim Freeman and Greg MacGillivray, 1976, included in *Five Summer Stories*) (Figure 6.6), *Go For It*

Figure 5.8
An idyllic Malmö
skatepark scene
(2010).
© James A. Hudson.

(Paul Rapp, 1976) (Figure 6.2), *Hard Waves, Soft Wheels* (Jim Plimpton, 1977) (Figure 9.1) and *Skateboard Fever* (NBC, 1977), which variously set skateboarding alongside surfing, skiing and hang-gliding, plus typical 1970s themes of personal discovery, sunshine and bikini-clad girls. *Blaze On* (Al Benner, 1978) was shot largely at Lakewood's Skateboard World, thus providing rare footage of 1970s skatepark-riding (Figure 5.9). In the UK, *Hot Wheels* (Richard Gayer, 1978) recorded skateboarding at London's Skate City, Meanwhile Gardens and Southbank, plus in various streets and parks (Figure 5.10).[33]

For fiction films, skateboard scenes in *Kenny & Co* (Don Coscarelli, 1976) inspired young skaters worldwide. The French *Trocadero Bleu Citron* (Michael Schock, 1978) continued the *Skaterdater* tradition, weaving skateboarding into the life of a girl-struck boy. Another fictional release was *Skateboard – the Movie* (George Gage, 1977), boasting Tony Alva (Tony Bluetile), Ellen O'Neal (Jenny Bradshaw) and other well-known skaters alongside actor Leif Garret (Figure 4.1). Despite a corny plotline, *Skateboard* provides authentic insight

into 1970s skateboarding, indicating how commercialism, professionalism, ambition and even cynicism might accompany youthful exhilaration. Most comprehensive of these 1970s films is *Skateboard Madness* (Julian Pena, 1979), shot between 1977 and 1979. Caught between documentary, comedy and adventure, this movie was, according to starring rider Peralta, a valiant experiment in capturing the diverse activity, fast development and essential spirit of contemporary skateboarding (Figures 6.7, 7.9 and 7.18).[34]

Skateboarding also appeared in various television series, most memorably *Charlie's Angels*, where Farrah Fawcett escaped through Los Angeles's Griffith Park and Peralta later made a cameo appearance.[35] Indeed, in the 1970s and 1980s skateboarding continued to receive sporadic television coverage; from early 1980 onwards Ray Allen hosted a weekly skateboarding programme, while in mid-1981 *Action Now* (successor to the 1970s run of *SkateBoarder*) foreshadowed today's multi-channel initiatives by launching a television offshoot. In 1987, Australian viewers enjoyed

Figure 5.9
Teri Lawrence and others at
Skateboard World, Lakewood.
Blaze On (dir. Al Benner, 1978).
www.bit.ly/Lawrence-BlazeOn

Figure 5.10
John Sablosky at Skate City,
London. *Hot Wheels*
(dir. Richard Gayer, 1978).
www.bit.ly/HotWheels-Skate

the 'Easy Riders' short by Nine Network's
'60 Minutes' news. Skaters with early video
recorders might even have captured *Skateboard
Madness* or the other documentaries
occasionally televised worldwide.[36]

Other welcome coverage came through
mainstream movies like *Back to the Future*
(Robert Zemeckis, 1985), where Marty McFly
(played by Michael J. Fox) escapes pursuing
bullies on a skateboard, this Hollywood
treatment aiding a mid-1980s resurgence in
skateboarding. Similarly helpful was *Thrashin'*
(David Winters, 1986), with acting by Alva,
Hawk and Hosoi among others. Both *Police
Academy 4* (Jim Drake, 1987) and *Gleaming
the Cube* (Graeme Clifford, 1988) included
footage directed by Peralta and featuring the
Bones Brigade team, while Caballero and
McGill also featured in the B-movie *Escape
from El Diablo* (Gordon Hessler, 1983). In
a post-apocalyptic New Romantic world of
its own was Seattle-based skate-rock opera
Shredder Orpheus (Robert McGinley, 1989),
while only slightly more believable were the
Jackie Chan skateboard chase sequences in
City Hunter (1993). As *City Hunter*'s Hong Kong
location suggests, these films disseminated
skateboarding worldwide; for example, having

taped *Gleaming the Cube* from Chinese
television in 1992, Lanzhou skateboarders
Tian Jun and Zhang Jie excitedly copied Bones
Brigade moves on their imported Powell-Peralta
boards.[37] From the early 1990s, family movies
like *The Skateboard Kid* (Larry Swerdlove,
1993), *The Skateboard Kid 2* (Andrew Stevens,
1995), *MVP: Most Valuable Primate* (Robert
Vince, 2000) and *MVP 2: Most Vertical Primate*
(Robert Vince, 2001) achieved commercial
success with skateboarding-themed stories,
although less successful was *Grind* (Casey La
Scala, 2003), 'one of the worst skate movies of all
time' according to Tony Hawk, despite including
content from his own 900 Films operation.[38]

More recent films such as *Dishdogz* (Mikey Hilb,
2006), *Deck Dogz* (Steve Pasvolsky, 2005) and
Paranoid Park (Gus Van Sant, 2007) similarly
integrate skateboarding within coming-of-
age storylines, as does the Serbian *Tilva Roš*
featuring the Kolos skate team (Nikola Ležaić
and Kiselo Dete, 2010). More adult themes are
provided by the French *Skate or Die* (Miguel
Courtois, 2008) where late-teen skaters are
pursued by murderous police, and by the
skateboarding vampire of the Iranian *A Girl
Walks Home Alone at Night* (Ana Lily Amirpour,
2014), while Larry Clark's *Kids* (1995) and

Figure 5.11
Guinness World Record for the largest-ever skateboard. 'Fantasy Factory'/Guinness World Records (2009).
www.bit.ly/LargestSkateboard

Figure 5.12
Peggy Oki winning the women's freestyle event at the National Bahne-Cadillac Skateboard Championships, Del Mar (1975). *Dogtown and Z-Boys* (dir. Stacy Peralta, 2001).
www.bit.ly/DelMar-Dogtown

Wassup Rockers (2005) more realistically depict the sexual and street-set experiences of US teenage skaters. As professional Javier Nunez commented of *Kids*, it 'documented our life'.[39] The more mainstream *Street Dreams* (Chris Zamoscianyk, 2008) follows fictional skater Derrick Cabrera (played by Paul Rodriguez) as he finally lands a tre-flip crooked grind to gain fame and sponsorship. Skate-based cartoons have also appeared. Millions of children worldwide have enjoyed the animated skater-reptiles of the *Teenage Mutant Ninja Turtles* television series (1987) and movie (1990), as well as the misdemeanours of skate-rebel Bart Simpson (1989 onwards).

Television exposure of street-skating also became more common in the 1990s. In the US, Nickelodeon launched its youth-targeted 'SK8-TV' programme in 1990, co-produced by Z-Boy Nathan Pratt and directed by Peralta, and using the famous Pink Motel pool as its setting. A few years later, ESPN's X Games reached worldwide audiences, and from 2003 more commercial coverage was provided by Fox's Fuel TV channel (later Fox Sports 2). In China, in 1991 CCTV began repackaging western footage for its 'The Melody of Athletics' health and education programmes.[40]

Significantly, 1990s television frequently placed skateboarding within snowboarding, music and youth culture. A new twist on youth-oriented programming also arrived with MTV's 'Jackass' series (2000–2002), featuring Bam Margera, Johnny Knoxville, Chris Pontius, Jason 'Wee Man' Acuña and Steve-O, and whose hazing rituals and juvenile pranks successfully built on *Big Brother* and Margera's *Camp Kill Yourself/ CKY* (1999–2002) videos. Three Jackass movie spin-offs and videos like *American Misfits* (Cain Angelle, 2003) with Wee Man and Laban Pheidias followed, as did Margera's 'Viva La Bam' (2003–2005) television series. As interpreted by Tourino, Yochim and Brayton, much of this material obsesses with risk, pain and bodily fluids (what Brayton calls 'reflexive sadomasochism' and Andrin terms 'darker slapstick') both to mock participants as marginalized antiheroes and to display their pre-eminence over those of a different sexuality, gender or ethnicity. 'We sincerely apologize for hurting anyone's feelings,' states the DVD cover of *American Misfits*, 'now shut up and stop being a wuss.'[41]

Less coarse subsequent MTV productions have included 'Rob & Big' (2006–2008) and 'Fantasy Factory' (2009–2015), both starring pro Rob Dyrdek, as well as its pseudo-reality 'Life of Ryan' (2007–2008) mixing the life of Ryan Sheckler with stunts, skits and street-skating. Another Dyrdek production is the cartoon 'Wild Grinders' (2012–2015), whose main character, Lil Rob, is loosely based on Dyrdek himself. Although far less concerned with pain and overt offense than the 'Jackass' milieu, these programmes still integrate skateboarding within a predictable diet of stunts, celebrities and goofish ridicule. Typical is the Guinness World Record for the largest-ever skateboard, measuring 11 m long, and unveiled by Dyrdek in a 2009 'Fantasy Factory' episode (Figure 5.11).[42]

As Steiler and Shanken note, these programmes have proved immensely popular, with skateboarders and other action sports figures increasingly replacing older fictional characters like the Fonz from 'Happy Days' in the affections of youthful viewers, and have so engendered a community of suburban watchers who share viewing experiences via social media. They are also good vehicles for brand promotion; 'It's impossible to watch "Rob & Big" without seeing a DC Shoes logo', remarks Stiler.[43]

In the 2000s, however, a more serious communication of skate values also emerged, beginning with *Dogtown and Z-Boys* (2001), Peralta's acclaimed account of 1970s skateboarding in the dilapidated Dogtown area of Los Angeles. So successful has this documentary been that it is commonly used as the go-to source for anyone seeking to identify skateboarding's key history, original players and core values. As Petrone discovered at a Michigan skatepark, skaters themselves also typically use the film as their main historical grounding, helping to legitimize their own practices by connecting with their predecessors.[44]

As a documentary alternative to a feature film being prepared from Michael Brooke's *The Concrete Wave* and an article by Greg Beato, which would later appear as *Lords of Dogtown*, Peralta's *Dogtown and Z-Boys* skilfully weaves interviews, archival footage and still photographs alongside a Sean Penn narration. Using unconventional camera techniques and artful Paul Crowder editing, the result is a fast-paced account of the captivating personalities, inventive tactics and uncompromising attitudes of Dogtown skaters. After two awards at the 2001 Sundance festival, *Dogtown and Z-Boys* was released by Sony with a $5 million promotional budget, and was immediately acclaimed for radiating grit, authenticity and exuberance; the *New York Times* lauded its

'taut, viscerally propulsive' and 'hard-edged' qualities, while the skate media welcomed its portrayal of skateboarding's anti-authority history and rebel riders (Figure 5.12).[45]

One obvious criticism, however, is how the film centres on the Z-Boys and so promotes the myth that these skaters alone somehow created core skateboarding values. 'That was the beginning of the revolution', states Alva in the film. 'There wouldn't be any X Games, there wouldn't be any vert skating, there wouldn't be anything at all. That's where it all started.' Consequently, as film critic Robert Ebert remarked, the film describes skateboarding almost entirely from the perspective of Peralta and his friends. 'It's like the vet who thinks World War II centered around his platoon.'[46]

In addition, academics like Meckliffe, Sueyoshi, Yochim and Kusz have discerned some gender and racial bias in the way that Asian-Americans like Peggy Oki, Jeff Ho and Shogo Kubo are frequently sidelined, while the violent behaviour of riders like Adams is left unexplored, thus strengthening 1970s skateboarding's marketability as 'working-class teen rebellion'. Some contributors were also unhappy with seemingly commercialized scenes, such as linking Vans shoes with Z-Boy innovations, while the *New York Times* simply concluded that *Dogtown and Z-Boys* is 'at heart a promotional film'.[47]

Similar critiques have been made of *Lords of Dogtown* (Catherine Hardwicke, 2005), particularly how its simulations of skateboarding can readily lead to what Dixon calls a 'global youth imaginary', and in which cultural differences are extracted, tamed and internationally transferred. As Dixon described a *Lords of Dogtown*–themed photo shoot for Japanese pop star Takahiro, the result was 'a fantastic and globalized tangle of trans-Pacific imitation, nostalgia, appropriated style and mimetic performance'.[48] *Lords of Dogtown* was, of course, far from the first or last film to repackage skateboarding for consumerist markets, but such episodes demonstrate the danger of moving away from skateboarding as a real act, and into worlds of heightened simulation and fictionalized narrative.

Perhaps more successful than *Lords of Dogtown*, then, have been documentaries that adhere more closely to the *Dogtown and Z-Boys* method, namely charting particular skaters and scenes without recourse to actors or plot

Figure 5.13
Rollin' through the Decades (dir. Winstan Whitter, 2005), DVD and inner sleeve.
© Winstan Whitter.

lines. Notable here is *Deathbowl to Downtown: The Evolution of Skateboarding in New York City* (Coan Nichols and Rick Charnoski, 2009), whose Jocko Weyland script counters the 'frontier tale' and 'care-free mystique' of Californian skateboarding with an account of skateboarding as a 'bona fide son of the city'. Skateboarding here is born from New York's de-industrialization and middle-class white flight, where crime-infused, drug-ridden and graffiti-coated city territories encouraged graffiti artists, skateboarders and other space-appropriating creatives. At first copying Californian pool-riders in their own Deathbowl pool in the Bronx, by the 1980s these skaters had progressed to homemade ramps and full-blown street-skating. Locations like Washington Square Park became a 'democracy of derelicts, drug-dealers and buyers, street performers, buskers and skaters', while in 1986 Shut Skates, led by Bruno Musso and Rodney Smith, became the first street-only skate team. Legendary skatespots like the Brooklyn Banks emerged, many sited in the urban plazas created from New York's zoning policy, by which tall skyscrapers were permitted in return for providing more public space. In the mid-1990s, the Supreme store was established,

ghetto skaters like Harold Hunter hit the international stage, and Larry Clark's hard-hitting *Kids* promoted the city's street-skating scene worldwide. New York was no longer an addendum to Californian skateboarding, but firmly established as a premier world skate city.

More prosaic than *Deathbowl to Downtown* is Winstan Whitter's epic UK-based *Rollin' Through the Decades* (2004), which nonetheless details a vibrant skate scene both connected to and divergent from its US counterparts. This documentary charts British skateboarding development, including its migration from surf-inspired beginnings to 1970s skatepark mania, post-punk 1980s ramps, 'zines and English Skateboard Association competitions and into later street and slalom scenes (Figure 5.13). A slew of other documentaries have given important insights into various other skateboard developments, notably the two accounts of Australian skateboarding provided by *Canvas* (Mick Erausquin and Matt Hill, 1987) and *Tic Tac 2 Heelflip* (Mike Hill, 2001), plus, to cite but a few, Coan Nichols and Rick Charnoski's *Fruit of the Vine* (2002) (Figure 5.14) and *Northwest* (2003), Milan Spasic's *Chlorine* (2003), Mike

Figure 5.14
Baltimore pool-riding. *Fruit of the Vine* (dir. Coan Nichols and Rick Charnoski, 2002).
www.bit.ly/Baltimore-FruitVine

Hill's *The Man Who Souled the World* (2007), Jono Atkinson's *Over Plywood* (2015) and Charlie Samuels's *Virgin Blacktop* (2018), which variously explore pool-riding, new skateparks, commercialization and regional scenes. While much debate surrounding *All This Mayhem* (Eddie Martin, 2014) focused on its accusation that Tony Hawk somehow 'stole' the 900° aerial, this film nonetheless provides a cautionary and candid account of the lives of Australian pros Tas and Ben Pappas. More nuanced is *Freeling* (Andrew Lovgren, 2012), which interviews Sean Malto and others in Kansas City about their perceptions of urban architecture, friendships, commitment, travel and independence.

Video Worlds

Perhaps even more significant than movies and documentaries for skateboarding are company videos, which generate revenue for their makers, provide a key marketing tool and aid in the establishment and dissemination of core skateboarding values. For example, between 2002 and 2012, Nike SB released one promotional, two tour and three full-length videos, with a strong impact upon skaters' purchases and opinions of this oft-contentious industry player.[49] Videos are important for professionals too; a good video 'part' (typically three minutes of moves by a single rider, edited after several months of shooting) can be immediately positive for their career.

Yet despite this evident commercial role, skaters still perceive videos as authentic cultural definitions. In particular, Brayton and Yochim argue that some videos both critique middle-class whiteness and revel in its privileges: the skaters depicted typically engage in eternal adolescence, individualized collectivity and homosocial heterosexuality, a world where spontaneity, attitude and rough-and-ready skatespots are valued more than success, achievement or spectacular settings. Including

the film crew in shots also connects with viewers, suggesting that video-makers and video-viewers constitute the same community. The result, contends Yochim, is to depict skaters together as 'oppressed individuals' negotiating 'a hostile world'.[50] How, then do these two apparently contrasting worlds – commercial marketing and collective ideology – combine in skate videos?

Company Videos

Often cited as the earliest skate videos – that is, single-company productions released on VHS rather than documentaries or fiction films screened in movie theatres – are Powell-Peralta's mid-1980s productions, which 'blew open' skateboarding.[51] Building on Stacy Peralta's earlier experimentations with Super 8 and consumer video cameras, the first of these new creations, *The Bones Brigade Video Show* (1984), took six months to make using three-quarter inch tape, a Sony camera and a wide-angle adapter (Figure 5.15). The company originally thought only 300 VHS tapes would sell and that the $18,000 costs would be simply written off as marketing expenses. In fact, 30,000 copies sold rapidly at between twenty and thirty dollars, helping to deliver Powell-Peralta from some tough financial circumstances.[52]

How did this work? From Peralta's perspective, the 'random access' VHS format had five advantages: skaters could repeatedly watch videos at home or skate shops, without having to pay for single theatre screenings; each VHS purchased was typically viewed by between thirty and fifty skaters, hence extending the Powell-Peralta brand; *Thrasher*'s privileging of certain skaters could be sidestepped, instead placing skaters like Hawk centre stage; skaters could see how moves were performed, helping skateboarding develop; and the combination of technical achievements by Hawk and Rodney Mullen, goofy skating by Lance Mountain, and numerous falls and comedy skits together

Figure 5.15
Stacy Peralta starts the skate video revolution. *The Bones Brigade Video Show* (Powell-Peralta, dir. Stacy Peralta, 1984).
www.bit.ly/BonesBrigadeVideoShow

rendered skateboarding attractive and accessible to younger audiences.[53]

Nonetheless, Powell-Peralta was keen to downplay its videos' marketing function. Hence *The Search for Animal Chin* (1987) thematically recoiled from increasing corporatization and commercialization, including fears that Taiwanese producers would flood markets with cheap boards, and that skaters were chasing sponsorship rather than pleasurable fun. Indeed, so influential has been *Animal Chin* that, despite some like Colberg seeing it as a 'scripted, phony exercise in branding,' for the majority the video is still viewed as an 'authentic' and 'essential' part of skateboarding culture.[54] Yet *Animal Chin* was itself part of skateboarding's spectacularization, taking over a year to make, and concluding with a fantastical ramp sequence, where a complex ramp and multiple-skater routines are elaborately shot using mobile cameras and even helicopter-borne angles (Figure 7.19). Powell-Peralta's later *Ban This* (1989) similarly deploys skateboard-mounted cameras, special lighting, overlays, montages, film stock and high-design graphics.

Videos like these had a huge impact. As Mike Vallely recalled, directly after watching *Future Primitive* with his New Jersey friends, 'we tore into the streets and had one of the most insane sessions.'[55] Other manufacturers also made their own videos, including Vision-SIMS's *Skatevisions* (Don Hoffman, 1984), G&S's *The '84 Gordon and Smith Skateboard Team* (Greg Thompson, 1984), Schmitt Stix's *Let's Go Skate* (Gary Langenheim, 1987), Alva's *Backyard Annihilation* (Kiki, 1988), Gullwing's *Skateboarding Inside Out* (1988), Santa Cruz's *Wheels of Fire* (Howard Dittrich, 1987), *Speed Freaks* (Tony Roberts, 1989) and *Streets on Fire* (Howard Dittrich, 1989) (Figures 3.1 and 10.2) and New Deal's *Useless Wooden Toys* (1990) (Figure 10.4). In particular, the increasingly

standardized use of video parts helped to construct a panoply of pro stars and so pushed board sales; *Future Primitive* (1985) helped Powell-Peralta's professionals to sell 7,000 decks each per month.

Not all early videos were so obviously marketing-conscious. In particular, the Mike Ternasky–managed H-Street created *Shackle Me Not* (1988) and *Hokus Pokus* (1989) by giving low-cost camcorders to team riders in order to shoot tricks; these videos suffered from poor editing and production values but, as Danny Way reflected, what mattered was their revelation of 'new progressive skateboarding that nobody had seen', and particularly through the speedy and innovative technicity of Matt Hensley.[56] In addition, notes Griffin, these projects encouraged the emergence of skate-specific 'filmers' like Daniel Sturt and Dave Schlossbach, who often shot while riding their own boards. Thus, while *Ban This* staged cop chases and other capers, H-Street videos showed the real thing: skaters confronting security guards, being ejected from skatespots, slamming hard and generally being anarchic, all enhanced by authentic shaky imagery. And as a result of this street-based realism, as Matt Hensley noted, 'kids everywhere said, yes, we can do this.'[57]

Artist Nam June Paik has described the potential of camcorders as a liberatory agent. 'Television has been attacking us all our lives. Now we can attack it back.'[58] Through this route, companies like H-Street disseminated their moves within weeks, suggesting they were ahead of larger outfits like Powell-Peralta, G&S or Vision. This was more than just promotional trickery, for camcorders also encouraged new street-skating moves. For *Useless Wooden Toys*, New Deal professionals filmed alongside amateurs, including only the most innovative tricks in the final edit (Figure 10.4); such was the rate of progression at this time that magazines often

Figure 5.16
Rudy Johnson in *Video Days*
(Blind, dir. Spike Jonze, 1991).
www.bit.ly/Johnson-VideoDays

Figure 5.17
Invisible skateboards in *Yeah Right!* (Girl, dir. Ty Evans and Spike Jonze, 2003).
www.bit.ly/Invisible-YeahRight

published lists of tricks invented since the previous issue. They also printed grainy video grab sequences to display technical moves; for example, some of 101's advertisements consisted entirely of Daewon Song and Eric Koston being captured this way.[59]

Blind's *Video Days* (Spike Jonze, 1991) in particular inspired a slew of street-skating videos, with scenes set across parking lots, plazas, gas stations and traffic. In distinct contrast to the massive ollies and high production values of, say, the Frankie Hill sequences in Powell-Peralta's *Propaganda* (1990), *Video Days* skaters Guy Mariano, Jason Lee, Mark Gonzales (Figure 10.1), Jordan Richter and Rudy Johnson effectively redefined street-skating, with Spike Jonze's apparently artless direction capturing switch-stance moves, kinked-rail boardslides, dark slides and freestyle adaptations set against everyday architecture (Figure 5.16).

Plan B's *Questionable* (Mike Ternasky, 1992) extended this approach, mixing advanced technical tricks from Sal Barber, Mike Carroll, Matt Hensley, Rick Howard, Rodney Mullen and Sean Sheffey with high-risk moves by Pat Duffy and Danny Way (Figure 10.3). Like *Video Days* and other precursors, *Questionable*

emphasized skaters as oppositional figures – appropriating skatespots, confronting guards, focusing (breaking) boards and having equipment confiscated – and quickly inspired new street-skaters. 'We had no idea this was possible', recalled Kyle Leeper. '*Questionable* changed my life.'[60]

New regional variations also emerged. Toy Machine's *Welcome to Hell* (Jamie Thomas, 1996), for example, foregrounds East Coast interests in fast-moving riding, showing Mike Maldonado, Brian Anderson, Satva Leung, Donny Barley, Elissa Steamer, Ed Templeton and Jamie Thomas dealing with handrails, no-complys and wall-rides. The same year, Dan Wolfe's *Underachievers: Eastern Exposure 3* (1996) preferred Philadelphia, Tampa and New York over California, and speed, consistency and style over ultra-technical tricks. More artistically, Stereo's *A Visual Sound* (1994) and *Tincan Folklore* (1996), plus Alien Workshop's *Memory Screen* (1991) and *Timecode* (1997), emphasized aesthetics by mixing camcorder and Super 8 footage, inserting random clips and altering film speeds.

Alternative modes of representations were also employed. The Spike Jonze and Ty Evans *Yeah Right!* (2003) for Girl and Chocolate built on Jonze's earlier work (notably the illusory

Figure 5.18
Jamie Thomas and the infamous
'Leap of Faith'. *Thrill of It All* (Zero,
dir. Jamie Thomas, 1997).
www.bit.ly/Thomas-Thrill

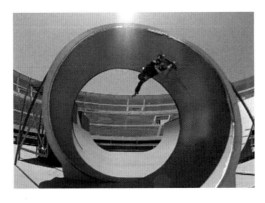

Figure 5.19
Tony Hawk loops the loop in a
Mexican bull-fighting arena.
The End (Birdhouse, dir. Jamie
Mosberg, 1998).
www.bit.ly/Hawk-End

forest-skating scenes of his 1996 *Mouse*), enhancing film quality with mini-DV and adding surreal visual trickery. In the *Yeah Right!* 'Magic Board' sequences, a neon-pink board rolls under its own power, before being thrown between impossibly distant skaters, while in the 'Invisible Board' sequences, green paint technology enables skaters to seemingly ride on dematerialized hoverboards (Figure 5.17). Two videos directed by Ty Evans, Spike Jonze and Cory Weincheque further progressed advanced cinematography. In *Fully Flared* (Lakai, 2007) skaters ride across exploding streets, Anthony Pappalardo shatters like a broken vase and multi-frame montages show synchronized skaters in different cities. *Pretty Sweet* (Girl and Chocolate, 2012) combines ultra-slow motion footage with flares, pyrotechnics, three-dimensional graphics, time collapse sequences and advanced tracking, plus appearances from A-list actors Jack Black and Will Arnett.

Besides technology, spectacles can be created through other means, most notably through the slams, transgressions and dangerous moves that many skate videos foreground. For example, Zero's *Thrill of It All* (Jamie Thomas, 1997) centres on extremely risky 'hammer' tricks, including Jamie Thomas's now infamous 'Leap of Faith' ollie into a 6 m drop (Figure

5.18), while *Dying to Live* (2002) includes many scenes in illicit venues. In addition, a certain kind of reciprocity is at work here, with technologically sophisticated creations like *Yeah Right!*, *Fully Flared* and *Pretty Sweet* using risky moves and slam scenes to puncture their more sensationalist tendencies, showing how their skaters face the same challenges as everyday street-skaters. Such processes also help build a collective sense of liberal masculinity, in Baker's terms showing skaters as heroic individuals achieving success through 'determination, self-reliance, and hard work.'[61] Nonetheless, and despite these attempts at relevance and connectivity, the technological fantasia of these skate videos, as Dince interprets *Yeah Right!*, removes them from everyday street-skateboarding, and so, like Harvey's characterization of postmodernism, displays 'instability and fleeting qualities' while emphasizing ephemerality and spectacle.[62]

These are just a few of the most significant videos, and along with those discussed later in this chapter, similarly influential have been Alien Workshop's *Mind Field* (Greg Hunt, 2009), Girl and Chocolate's *Goldfish* (Spike Jonze, 1993), éS's *Menikmati* (Fred Mortagne, 2000) (Figure 11.5), *TransWorld*'s *Sight Unseen* (Jon Holland and Greg Hunt, 2001), *Hallelujah* (Jon

Figure 5.20
Multiple cameras and split-screens. Luan Oliveira and Nyjah Huston at the Skateboarding World Championships, Kimberley (2015). www.bit.ly /OliveiraHuston-Kimberley

Figure 5.21
Javier Mendizabal in Thomas Campbell's dream vision *Cuatro Sueños Pequeños* (2013). www.bit.ly/Mendizabal-Cuatro

Figure 5.22
Colin Read's animalist interpretation of skateboarding in *Spirit Quest* (2017). www.bit.ly/SpiritQuest-Skate

Figure 5.23
Greg Finch transformed by the synchroballistic imagery of Angus Leadley Brown. *Passenger* (2004). www.bit.ly/Finch-Passenger

Figure 5.24
Cory Juneau caught by the time-collapse experimentation of Cy Kuckenbaker (2014). www.bit.ly/Juneau-TimeCollapse

Holland and Chris Ray, 2010) and *Perpetual Motion* (Jon Holland and Chris Thiessen, 2013), Tilt Mode Army's *Man Down* (Chris Avery and Matt Eversole, 2001), Flip's *Sorry* (Fred Mortagne, 2002), Coliseum's *P.J. Ladd's Wonderful Horrible Life* (Arty Vagianos and Matt Roman, 2002), DC's *The DC Video* (Greg Hunt, 2003), Antihero's *Cash Money Vagrant* (Dan Velucci and Julien Stranger, 2003), Emerica's *This Is Skateboarding* (Mike Manzoori and Jon Miner, 2003), *Stay Gold* (Jon Miner, 2010) and *Made* (Jon Miner, 2013), The Firm's *Can't Stop* (Jon Humphries, 2003), Cliché's *Bon Appétit* (Fred Mortagne, 2004), Almost's *Round Three* (Mike Hill, 2004), Baker's *Baker 3* (2005), DVS's *Skate More* (Colin Kennedy, 2005), Blind's *What If* (William Weiss, 2005), Real's *Since Day One* (Dan Wolfe, 2011), Plan B's *True* (Erik Bragg, 2014), Isle's *Vase* (Jacob Harris, 2015), Vans's *Propeller* (Greg Hunt, 2015), and Adidas's *Away Days* (Matt Irving, 2016), plus *Holy Stokes!* (Russell Houghten, 2016) and *I Like It Here Inside My Mind* (Pontus Alv, 2016).

All these videos catalogued and progressed skateboarding, and generated significant revenue. During the 1990s and early 2000s up to 800 videos per year were produced with total sales of $50 million annually; *Dying to Live* sold nearly 100,000 copies in its first year alone.[63] Some are also expensive and elaborate creations. Birdhouse's $160,000 *The End* (Jamie Mosberg, 1998) involved 16 mm and 35 mm film stock, bribes, porno actresses, orangutans, stuntmen and exploding cars. Jeremy Klein and Heath Kirchart set $1,500 suits on fire, while the massive half-pipe and loop – built by Tim Payne inside a Mexican bullfighting arena – cost $40,000 (Figure 5.19). Street-format competition footage often uses multiple cameras and split-screens (Figure 5.20). Zero's *Dying to Live* (2002) involved 920 shooting days, 253 mini-DV tapes, 60,000 air miles, 66,000 van miles and 1,500 rolls of film, plus heavy promotion.[64] Even more extreme is Ty Evans's high-budget *We Are Blood* (2015), using gyro-stabilized mounts, RED ultra-high resolution cameras, drones and full-size helicopters.[65]

New Approaches
Not all videos, however, have mixed the commercial and spectacular with the dangerous and the outrageous. In particular, camcorders like the infamous $3,500 Sony VX1000 (1995), Adobe Premiere (1991), Apple's Final Cut software (1999) and other advancements created what Fuel TV's C.J. Olivares calls a 'democratization of technology', facilitating a plethora of new genres and approaches, from

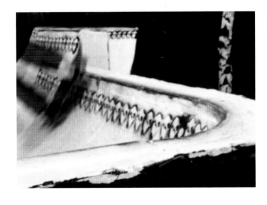

Figure 5.25
The DIY Steppe Side, Malmö, in
the Dadaist *Strongest of the Strange*
(dir. Pontus Alv, 2005).
www.bit.ly/SteppeSide-
StrongestStrange

1990s video magazines like *411* and *Video-Log*
to eclectic twenty-first-century treatments.[66]
The latter have included Krooked's lo-fi *Gnar
Gnar* (2007) and Josh Stewart's VX1000-based
and street vibe *Static* (1999–2014), along with
the meditative qualities of Hurley's *Hallowed
Ground* (Scott Soens, 2001), experimental
engagement with White Mountain Apache
culture in Dustinn Craig's *4wheelwarpony*
(2007), madcap tomfoolery in Chris Atherton's
Avit (2007), the localities of Dublin, Bristol,
Amsterdam and Stockholm in Philip Evans's
Super 8 *The Scrum Tilly Lush* (2009), the
dream narrative of Thomas Campbell's *Cuatro
Sueños Pequeños* (2013) (Figure 5.21), Franco-
Japanese hybridity in Magenta's *Soleil Levant*
(Yoan Taillandier and Vivien Feil, 2013), the
silhouetted bodies of Colin Kennedy's *Form*
(2014), the multi-screen New York montages
in William Strobeck's *Cherry* (Supreme, 2014),
the reimaginations of *The Devil's Toy Redux*
(various directors, 2014), the multimedia
formulations of Philip Evans's *Lightbox* (2015)
and the bizarre animalizations of Colin Read's
Spirit Quest (2017) (Figure 5.22). Such videos
propose skateboarding as an enriching activity,
helping to fuse cultures and connect personal
mores with art, philosophy and tradition.
Skateboarding here abounds with allegiances
and meanings.

Equally innovative, this time in their
cinematographic approaches, are the
synchroballistic distortions of Angus Leadley
Brown's extraordinary *Passenger* (2004) (Figure
5.23) and Steven Sebring's 360° video for *Vogue*
(2016) with bewitching space alterations centred
on Rodney Mullen's freestyling, while similar
concerns lie behind Cy Kuckenbaker's time-
collapse of Cory Juneau (2014), where multiple
Juneau skaters traverse in otherworldly train-
like sequences (Figure 5.24).[67]

Other experimentations abound. *TransWorld*'s
The Cinematographer Project (2012), for
example, showcases the work of Torsten Frank,
William Strobeck, Mike Manzoori, Chris Ray,
Brennan Conroy, Dan Wolfe, R.B. Umali,
Beagle, Lee Dupont (Figure 8.15), Christopher
Middlebrook, Jon Holland and Russell
Houghten, disclosing sophisticated techniques
that range from moving cameras and shifting
speeds to advanced angles and soundscapes.
Houghten's contribution renders skateboarders
temporally distinct from their context, moving at
normal speed while cars, clouds and stars whirl
by at accelerated rates. Houghten's later RED
short *Urban Isolation* (2014) extends this theme,
an astounding post-production technique
allowing a skater to traverse eerily empty Los
Angeles freeways and bridges.

In a more theoretical mode, Sangam Sharma's
Hacking the Streets (2009) intersects found
footage with Lefebvrian considerations
(including interviews with myself), while
Jeremy Knickerbocker's *Space for Rent* (2012)
pursues similar ideas in relation to Michigan
street-skating. More prosaically, *The Rebirth
of Skateparks* (Mike Salinger and Mike Hirsch,
2005) documents 1970s and 2000s skateparks,
mostly in California.

Particularly noteworthy are Pontus Alv's *In
Search of the Miraculous* (2010) and *Strongest
of the Strange* (2005). The latter constructs
skateboarding as a lo-fi montage of small ramps,
Scandinavian skatespots and DIY venues mixed
with the spoken words of Charles Bukowski
and an eclectic soundtrack encompassing
jazz, fairground music and Joy Division (Figure
5.25). 'Skateboarding is so much deeper and
complex than just tricks', explained Alv. 'We
are dealing with so many different subjects,
friendships, architecture, searching for spots

Figure 5.26 Jet-set skateboarding. *Bon Voyage* (Cliché, dir. Boris Proust, 2013). www.bit.ly/BonVoyage-Skate

dealing with people, ups and downs in life and so on. I want to show everything in life.'[68] Consequently, *Strongest of the Strange* shows skateboarding amid ruptured surfaces, home movies, wastelands, public art, snatched memories and statements like 'life itself is still beautiful.' A Dadaist vision, the video – for which Alv deliberately restricted distribution – moves skateboarding into an anti-bourgeois, anti-formal world of local skaters, sketchy riding, collaborative actions and personal thoughts. Above all, it turns everyday worlds into places far stranger and more fantastical than we might have ever realized; home turf is rendered strange, uncanny, *unheimlich*.

Other Places

Other videos have made equally distinct contributions to skateboarding, notably through different geographies. *RIDE*'s *Skate* and Satva Leung's *Streets* (2003–2008) series both provide local skatespot knowledge of places like Los Angeles, Barcelona, Toronto and Atlanta. In the 2006 Melbourne edition of *Streets*, for example, the Flinders Street, Melbourne Museum, Drains and Lincoln Square locations are introduced, complete with insider tips on the best steps, ledges and access times. These videos also encourage travelling to new destinations, and since the 2000s this has been a burgeoning genre. Fallen's *Road Less Travelled* (Mike Gilbert, 2013), for example, visits Croatia, South Africa and Thailand, with Jamie Thomas extolling the virtues of 'getting outside your comfort zone' and 'going to new cities, meeting new people'.

Despite Thomas's well-meaning intentions, however, Yochim and others have equated skateboarding's ideology of rebellion with white-skinned explorers who courageously ventured to perilous foreign lands, and it would be easy to interpret travelogue videos

in this light, as with Cliché's *Bon Voyage* (Boris Proust, 2013), where international skaters jet between skatespots worldwide (Figure 5.26).[69] Although skateboarding has never overtly advanced US imperialism in the way that Laderman identifies for surfing, a politics of globalization is nonetheless discernible.[70] Sedo identifies an 'incipient imperialist imperative' when visiting (usually US) professionals seek out new terrains. In the 1990s, Tokyo was a favoured destination, before Barcelona in the early 2000s and then China, the latter being highly visible in Plan B's *True*; indeed, guides like Jay Wu and Anthony Claravall have taken over 200 US pros to Shenzhen and Guangzhou skatespots. With their attendant spectators and film crews, these famous skaters can 'blow out' skatespots – attracting attention from authorities and so rendering them unskateable for neighbourhood riders. Alternatively, as O'Connor explains in relation to the Hong Kong skate scene, and seen in YouTube videos like *RIDE*'s 'Skate Hong Kong with Chris Bradley' (Figure 10.9), both globetrotting pro riders and regionally renowned individuals can together constitute substantial networks of contacts and exchange, building up their own 'network capital' and furthering their status and future career opportunities.[71]

Many travelling skaters also pay only lip service to the immediate skate scene they visit; *We Are Blood*, for example, shows pros landing in unnamed cities, skating 'a never-ending supply of skatespots' while antagonizing security guards and being watched by local crowds who had supposedly 'never seen a skateboard'. In a Red Bull video of Michael Mackrodt and Walker Ryan discovering 'untouched street features' in Cuba, the accompanying YouTube description informs us that this Caribbean island is a place where 'time stands still', and 'old US cars

Figure 5.27
Skateboarding in Ulaanbaatar.
Mongolian Tyres
(dir. Henrik Edelbo, 2007).
www.bit.ly/MongolianTyres

and vast colonial mansions' form a 'beautiful background' for skateboarding. In this kind of video, where the true complexity of a local situation is hidden beneath an aestheticized and reductive presentation, we can identify what Sedo calls an 'almost colonial relationship' where 'a new land of abundant raw resources (spots)' is exploited by travelling pros 'to advance their careers where it really matters', namely 'back in the US skateboard core'.[72]

Seasoned filmer-skaters like Patrik Wallner – who has skateboarded in countries like Afghanistan, Cambodia, Kazakhstan, Kyrgyzstan, Mongolia, Myanmar, Uzbekistan and Vietnam – accepts that 'we are modern day conquistadors, going eastwards seeking new treasures'.[73] Yet, as demonstrated by Wallner's *10,000 Kilometers* (2010), *Meet the Stans* (2012) and *Under the African Capricorn* (2016), plus other videos like the Australian road trip *Tent City* (Rick Charnoski and Coan Nichols, 2004), such journeys can be undertaken with genuine care and respect. For example, when, between 2007 and 2009, Rob Thomson rode 7,555 miles in eleven countries within Asia, Europe and North America, he realized how skateboarding provided 'the opportunity to experience life in foreign countries as a grass-roots level', along with the realization that affluent western ways were not universal, that media stories of dangerous foreign lands were far from accurate, and that China could offer 'the simple unforced rhythms of a life free from continuous stimulation and entertainment'.[74] In *Drive*, Mike Vallely argues that travel-based skateboarding can transcend barriers like class, ethnicity and religion: 'It's amazing how skateboarding can knock down walls. Travelling around is one of the most incredible experiences'.[75] Similarly, *Mongolian Tyres* (Henrik Edelbo, 2007) charts the journey by Alv and other westerners to Mongolia in order to fix up an Ulaanbaatar skatepark and provide equipment (Figure 5.27).[76]

Other values may also be at work when travelling. In particular, many skaters perceive journeying to far-flung skatespots as evidence of their commitment. Voyaging between California and Vancouver in a 1970s motorhome, as documented in *The Weenabago Projekt* (Kristian McCue and Tosh Townend, 2005), is neither cheap nor easy, while, as one Canadian interviewed by Harris put it, 'a hardcore skater is somebody who goes on road trips for four hours to skate a location'[77] Alternatively, videos like *Hot Chocolate* (Spike Jonze, Ty Evans and Cory Weincheque, 2004) portray journeys as sharing brotherhood and forging deeper friendships; 'it was a great experience to be with all those guys' reflected Gino Ianucci at the end of *Hot Chocolate*, 'because these are some great memories.'

Self-Documentation

When new camera and production technologies arrived in the 1980s and 1990s, these relatively affordable ways of creating and disseminating videos allowed skaters to document their local scenes. In 1985, *Thrasher* was already exhorting readers to make their own recordings – 'Go get your camera, point, shoot and the rest is up to you' – while this process has today become so ubiquitous that, as one skater admitted, 'I don't remember skateboarding without a video camera'.[78] The results are sold for minimal cost, posted on YouTube or simply relayed by Instagram.

Early UK examples included *Renaissance* (Wayne Fenlon, 1996–1997) from Edinburgh and *Network Neighbourhood* (1997) from Chelmsford, these low-budget productions being the filmic equivalents of contemporary 'zines. 'News of modern moves, the tricky tricks and the flippity kicks,' reported *Thrasher*, 'spread like wildfire via phone, fax, Xerox and mini-cams'.[79] Innumerable later versions include the documentations of Fredericksburg in *City*

Figure 5.28
Documenting the Cornwall downhill scene. *The Art of Going Sideways* (Faltown, 2007). www.bit.ly/ArtGoingSideways

by the Battlefield (2007), Miami in *Incognito* (Mike Atwood, 2013), Manchester in *Snake Eyes Die* (Joe Gavin, 2013), Bordeaux in *Bordeaux Exposure* (Julien Januszkiewicz, 2013) and Cornwall's downhill Castle Hill Mob in *The Art of Going Sideways* (Faltown, 2007) (Figure 5.28).

Most recently, internet forums like *SkatePerception* provide evidence of ever-increasing interest in filmmaking and photography, with over 26,000 members and three million posts in 2015. Videos made here, as Buckingham relates, are often a form of symbolic action and not just records, and thus concentrate on capturing style, local knowledge and confrontations. Their creators are typically highly adept, spending hours filming, editing, post-producing and disseminating their creations, and, notes Harris, the resulting video quality is often as important as tricks for constructing shared values.[80]

Despite the typical use of a standardized structure, with each skater introduced in turn and culminating in a best trick, videographers pay considerable attention to what and how they film. Low- and wide-angle shots dramatize bodily and architectural shapes, while also building community through capturing onlooking skaters. Tracking shots further bring viewers into the scene. Alternatively, mobile GoPro cameras collapse complex bodily rhythms into a highly scopic rendition, while drones can create unusual overhead and fly-through shots (Figures 8.3 and 13.6).

Editing and, in particular, music, further create specific moods and attitudes, although the original grinds, rumbles and other skateboarding sounds are also normally preserved. These amateur productions, remarks Buckingham, also overlap with professional videos, showing how global trends in fashion, music and riding styles are played out in

specific neighbourhoods. And they often have an idealizing function, with most failed attempts being edited out, so that a skater apparently proceeds effortlessly from one successful move to another. 'I'm really not that good, you know', admitted one Hong Kong skater, 'but if I'm good at editing, I can make myself look like a pro.'[81]

While Jones notes how amateur video-making allows for 'legitimate peripheral participation', by which new skaters integrate within groups, and Hollett has identified a symbiotic learning process and social intimacy between riders and filmers, others note a more exclusionary process. According to Dupont, filmer-skaters can be 'gatekeepers' of local scenes by determining which skaters are seen, while a filmer-skater's typical middle-class status provides them with the significant time resources and capital expenditure required. In 2003, for example, the Century Optics ultra-fisheye 'death lens' favoured by serious filmers cost £850 in the UK.[82] Similarly, Encheva and colleagues see video-making as a route to job opportunities and commercial projects. For those who successfully follow this path, the rewards can be significant, including, for example, a yearly salary from Zoo York and Red Bull for a renowned videographer like R.B. Umali.[83]

Social Media

By 2010, US teenagers were spending nearly every free minute using television, smartphones, tablets or computers.[84] With brands now releasing videos online for free – as Nike SB did with *Debacle* (2009) – and skaters also accessing video clips online, the sales of skateboarding DVDs plummeted. In response, companies started producing films for websites and social media. Particularly successful was *RIDE*'s website and YouTube channel, created by Hawk's 900 Films and Complex as 'the digital embodiment of every conversation you've ever heard in a skateboard shop.'[85]

This was not, however, a wholly new phenomenon, and indeed websites, blogs and internet sources have abounded in skateboarding history. From the mid-1980s, through ventures like *Thrasher*'s bulletin board, the English Skateboard Association's *Skate News* newsletter (possibly the first-ever Mac-typeset publication) and *R.A.D.*'s e-mail address, skateboarders have often been early adopters of new technologies, and by 1997 alt. skateboard was increasingly active. By this date over 130 websites ranged from manufacturers and shops to magazines like *Influx, Heckler* and *Dansworld*, plus the UK *Project*, Dutch *Hupthur*, Melbourne female-skater *b-grrrl* and country-specific sites from Finland to Canada. Through such channels, and by using texts, ASCII-based choreographic codes, photographs and clips, skaters could now disseminate skateboarding much easier than via full-blown commercial magazines and videos.

Ever since the late 1990s, skate websites have proliferated, and today include, to cite but a few of the most well-known, *Cemporcento Skate* (Brazil), *Protest* (Canada), *Freemind* (Eastern Europe), *La Tabla* (Chile), *China Skateboards, Kicker Club, Made in China* and *SkateHere* (China), *SkateRojo* (Central America), *Elcubocr* (Costa Rica), *SkateRock* (Czech Republic), *Wunderbaum* (Denmark), *Limited* and *Playboard* (Germany), *SkateboardingJapan* and *VHS* (Japan), *Skater* (Russia), *Dogway Media* (Spain), *Info* (Poland), *Giftorm* (Sweden) and *Blue Tile Obsession, Bulldog Skates, Muckmouth* and *Skatopia* (USA). More globally facing are *The Berrics, Crailtap, Crossfire, Chromeball Incident, I Skate Therefore I Am, Juice, Rubicon Girl, SkateAndAnnoy, SkateDaily, Skatevideosite* and *TackyWorld*. Yet more digital sources include *Thrasher*'s website, *Skateboard.tv* and *Vans.tv*. Many of these, such as Ian Michna's Brooklyn-based *Jenkem* (2011), have exploited low-cost internet portals. 'Pay $4.99 a month to start a website, or magically find a couple of thousand dollars and print one issue of a magazine?', reflected Michna.[86] Other channels are multi-platform affairs, with, for example, Fuel TV already by 2010 dicing up its shows into YouTube and podcast variants.

But perhaps the biggest change has come from social media, particularly Facebook, Instagram and Twitter, with feeds focused on everything from collectors, professionals and locals to pool-riding, downhill and slalom. After YouTube's 2005 launch, skaters quickly realized this was an ideal way to watch and disseminate videos. The launch of smartphones, like Apple's iPhone in 2007 (which included the YouTube app), also changed the way skaters made, distributed and consumed skate media. By 2008, Giannoulakis observed how Denver skaters were already using smartphones for image-making, and four years later sponsor-me smartphone footage had increased tenfold. In 2014, forty-three per cent of US skaters used smartphones to document skating, while Instagram was now facilitating instant dissemination of ultra-short clips.[87] With these new channels also came new centres of attention. While companies like Independent, Powell, Vans, Girl and Polar command loyal supporters, as do smaller brands like ReVive, individual skaters also garner huge followings by sharing as-it-happens clips, behind-the-scenes insights and personal comment. Instagram feeds from skaters like Justin Figueroa (@killerpizza), Grant Taylor (@downsouthinhell) and Richie Jackson (@thefeatch) provide a continual drip of skateboarding, lifestyle and product information. Spectacularized stunts are also popular; a two-minute 2015 YouTube video, showing Hawk complete a 'vertical spiral' for Sony Action Cam, drew 200,000 hits within twenty-four hours, while a 2016 Sony episode with Hawk and Aaron Homoki in a zero gravity airplane ride attracted 375,000 views in one week.[88]

This effects of this are substantial. In 2014, sixty-seven per cent of US skaters used Instagram, fifty-eight per cent Facebook, forty-six per cent YouTube and seventeen per cent Twitter, with seventy-four per cent consulting at least one channel every week. Tony Hawk had 12.3 million social media followers, Ryan Sheckler 7.6 million, Nyjah Huston 3.3 million, Paul Rodriguez 3.3 million, Karen Jonz 1.6 million and Letícia Bufoni 1.2 million.[89] Consequently, skaters now connect with their favourite pros on a daily basis. 'The best way to get the ten to twenty-five year group,' explained Quiksilver's Bob McKnight, 'is through media like YouTube.' Or as *Jenkem* reckoned, for pro riders 'Instagram followers and a steady flow of content will keep your name buzzing much longer than a print ad.'[90]

Skateboarding media content has also changed according. While *Kingpin* castigated the onslaught of video clips for 'desensitizing' skaters and diminishing full-length videos, *Jenkem* argues that they expose all kinds of skateboarding 'from the jockish and "Xtreme", to the creative and inspiring, to the raw and just plain weird.'[91] For example, Brett Novak's short

Figure 5.29
Hyojoo Ko longboarding in
South Korea (2016).
www.bit.ly/HyojooKo

Freestyle Skateboarding (2009) and *Searching Sirocco* (2015), showing dance-like freestyler Kilian Martin, have become internationally famous through YouTube, as have the oddball inventions of the Japanese Gou Miyagi (Figure 11.3), the rock-star-meets-Dali demeanour of Richie Jackson, the demonic Deer Man of Dark Woods and 'world's weirdest skateboarder' Slovenian Almir Jusovic. The dance-inspired movements of South Korean longboarder Hyojoo Ko have also gained international attention via *Vogue* and YouTube, and by 2018 she had over 461,000 Instagram followers (Figure 5.29).[92] As this suggests, just as early websites like *WiSkate.com* (Wisconsin), *50-50.com* (Hawaii), *HoustonSkateScene.com* (Texas), *PacificSkateboarding.com* (Vancouver), *Conform.tv* (New England), *Eboarding.net* (later *SkateNC.com*) and *Metrospective.com* (New York) propelled what *Quartersnacks* has called the 1990s 'de-California-ization of skateboard media', so social media has made skateboarding more geographically democratic, releasing many pros and aspiring amateurs from the US West Coast.[93] 'You no longer need to be skating in SoCal with the "right filmer", the "right photographer" and schmoozing with big magazine editors,' explained *Jenkem*. 'Instead, you can upload a trick from Bumfuck, Nowhere, that can go viral way before that mag could even get to press.'[94] By 2015, having left California for New York, established pros Mark Gonzales, Brian Anderson, Alex Olson and Stefan Janoski were being joined by the upcoming Yonnie Cruz, Aaron Herrington and Gavin Nolan. Skaters like Malmö's Pontus Alv even see virtues in being distanced from California. 'If everything is coming from the same place, it gets hard to come up with new perspectives. Sometimes it's good to be far away from everything.'[95]

Social media can also have other benefits. As Thorpe, Williams and Copes note, 'expressing subcultural identities online is part of the identity work individuals perform', and so real-life skateboarding is now constantly reinforced by social media manifestations. For example, at Michigan's Franklin skatepark, the contest-riding of local skater Derrick was rapidly disseminated. 'Within twenty-four hours,' marvelled Petrone, 'many who were not at the park to witness Derrick's feats were explaining how they saw them on his Myspace page.'[96] And as Thorpe reports, such processes are true not only of affluent western skate scenes but also of places like Palestine, where skaters use YouTube to develop tricks, jargon and English language, while simultaneously producing Arabic videos to develop their regional scene.[97] As these episodes suggest, social media allow skateboarders to rapidly communicate at local as well as global scales, and with considerable cultural effect.

Section Two
Skateboarding

Skateboarding
Chapter 6 Found Space

That's what's so cool about pool skating. We're tapping into something like architecture that is art, and we are using it for a completely different thing than the original artist created that surface for. [1]
Tony Alva

Asphalt and Concrete Waves

The earliest skateboarders rattled along neighbourhood sidewalks. 'Seems like you always had your skateboard with you,' recalled Jay Adams, 'that was your main way of getting around.'[2] Today, skateboarding still provides local transportation, particularly for youngsters on Penny boards or those cruising or longboarding. *The New York Times*, for example, has reported on how Andrei Hippix longboards four miles between his Brooklyn apartment and real estate job due to skateboarding's ease of use, cardio exercise and pleasurable experience.[3] However, apart from simply getting from A to B, skaters have responded to urban space in a more unusual manner. Where capitalism sub-divides land into a homogeneous commodity – producing what Lefebvre terms 'abstract space' – skaters create their own spaces in cities worldwide.[4] This is a central characteristic of skateboarding,

enacting distinctive new uses and so changing urban terrains.

During the 1960s and 1970s, many Californian suburbs offered gently curving roads that were remarkably devoid of cars. One such area, recorded in *Downhill Motion*, was San Diego County's La Costa, where the Teamsters Union Pension Fund had invested in road infrastructure but had yet to build many houses. Places like this consequently became, according to Larry Balma, a 'Mecca for skateboarders from all over Southern California,' allowing frustrated surfers to roll down car-free asphalted roads as if these were ocean waves, while even steeper descents like Signal Hill in San Diego were similarly compared with the massive surfing swells of California's Mavericks and Hawaii's Waimea Bay. 'We used to skate when the surf was no good,' recalled John Milius, 'imitate a surf style or perfect a move.'[5] In short, skaters

Figure 6.1
Chuck Askerneese and Marty Grimes at Kenter Canyon Elementary school (1977). © Glen E. Friedman.

Figure 6.2
Escondido, school banks and
tube-ride skateboarding.
Go for It (dir. Paul Rapp, 1976).
www.bit.ly/Escondido-GoForIt

adopted what Lefebvre calls the artificial 'second nature' of the built environment, and reimagined it as if it were the 'first nature' of land and water.[6] 'Every surface becomes a dance floor', announced *The Magic Rolling Board.*

This kind of skateboarding closely tracked the asphalt's curves and undulations. Skateboarders frequently rode barefoot and upright or, conversely, crouched with arms parallel to the ground. Sensuous movement was key, with the skater floating a few inches above the road, reflecting back its planar smoothness, scanning for minute irregularities and dynamically mapping contours, all of which replicated a surfer's traversal of changing waves.

Besides roads and sidewalks, skateboarders encountered more exciting terrains, in particular the gentle asphalt banks of Los Angeles schoolyards like Mar Vista Elementary, Bellagio Elementary in Bel Air, Paul Revere Junior High in Pacific Palisades and Kenter Canyon Elementary in Brentwood (Figure 6.1). In the mid-1960s surf-skaters like Jim Fitzpatrick, George Trafton, Dave Hilton, Steve Hilton, Torger Johnson, Tommy Ryan, Scotty Archer, John Freis, Woody Woodward and Danny Bearer traversed these banks just as surfers carve waves, as documented in historic footage included in *Public Domain*. Later mid-1970s skaters did the same, emulating surfing moves by touching asphalt as if trailing a hand in watery spray, hanging five toes over the board nose, or even replicating a surfer's tube-ride by skating through a hooped blue-cloth tunnel (Figure 6.2). 'Banks', explained Paul Constantineau, 'are really just cement waves.'[7] Or as renowned surfer Larry Bertlemann recounted in *Go for It*, 'the take-off is the same in surfing, you climb up one wall like a roller coaster, then drop back down.'

Later in the 1970s, skaters like Stacy Peralta, Tony Alva, Jay Adams and Marty Grimes (Figure

6.1) further extended the surf-skate bank-riding experience by creating new turns and slides – 'we were always touching the pavement', described Peralta, 'feeling your wheels grinding and pivoting around your hands.'[8] As *Super Session* shows, similar bank moves were explored at Hawaiian skatespots like Uluwatu, Wallos (aka Wallows) and Stoker Hill. Wallos, an extended rainwater ditch in the Niu Valley, was especially challenging and was later described by Tommy Guerrero as 'fuckin' gnarly, rough and brutal'. Here steep banks, bowl-like stages, over-grown vegetation and graffiti created a primeval skateboarding terrain. Skating Wallos, recalls Weyland, was 'akin to surfing consecutive big waves, a downhill run and a half-pipe combined. It was insane.' *Spinn'in Wheels* portrays a barefooted Roy Jamieson enacting surf-style kickturns and hand-down turns (Figure 6.3), while a decade later riders in *The Search for Animal Chin* treated Wallos as a perpetual half-pipe by carving banks, jumping hips, throwing slides and boosting footplants.[9]

Besides banks, skateboarders discovered other variants of what I term 'found space', including concrete drainage ditches and other large-scale water-management projects. LA County alone boasted over 2,000 miles of tunnels and 150 basins and canals, which skaters quickly exploited. Favoured locations included the Toilet Bowl in the Hollywood Hills – a shallow-sided and irregularly shaped reservoir measuring 23 m across and 11 m deep.[10] Similar locations included the San Fernando Valley's Sepulveda Dam and LA County's Vermont Drop/The Funnel, which featured in *Spinn'in Wheels*. Even more popular was the abandoned Escondido reservoir in San Diego County, whose owner James Malero was happy for skaters to ride, until authorities enforced closure. With its rounded-off rectangular shape and angled flat banks, Escondido was described in *Go for It* as 'an almost ideal location', in *Freewheelin'* as 'one

Figure 6.3
Roy Jamieson at Wallos, Hawaii.
Spinn'in Wheels (dir. Chris
Carmichael, 1975).
www.bit.ly/Jamieson-
SpinninWheels

Figure 6.4
The Spillway in Victoria. *The
Ultimate Flex Machine* (dir. Jason
Cameron, 1975).
www.bit.ly/Spillway-UltimateFlex

of the ultimate rides' and in *SkateBoarder* as 'a magic place' that 'everyone silently considered their own' (Figures 6.2 and 6.5).[11]

Around Santa Cruz, favoured spots included The Pit (aka The Dip), Lipton Bowl and Uvas Spillway. Further north, places like the Yuvis Dam spillway were favoured, while spots in other states included Texas's Lipps and EZ-7 ditches and Albuquerque's Jefferson, Ventura, Commanche, Four Hills and Indian School ditches, some of which allow twenty minutes of continuous downhill rolling.[12]

Among other hot spots, Florida's favoured locations included Palm Beach County's Hypoluxo and other ditches, as well as banks beneath the Haulover Inlet overpass and Miramar's Toilet Bowl sewer pond. As Snyder details, an intense Florida scene was created by skaters like Jeff Duerr, Mike Folmer, Rick Furness, Alan Gelfand, Scott Goodman, Pat Love, Jeannie Narducci, Dave Nicks, Bert Parkerson, Kevin Peterson, Bill Reilly, Karen Snyder, Bobby Summers, Bruce Walker and Chris West.[13] In Australia, places like Tullamarine Drains, Bloodbath and Eltham Fish Pond in Melbourne and the Boat Ramp in Sydney were popular, while *The Ultimate Flex Machine* shows locals like Steve Platt, Cheyne

Horan, John Sanderson, Anthony Moxson, Rob Bain and Wedge Francis performing handstands, slides and carves across Victoria's monumental The Spillway and roadside banks in Sydney's Bellevue Hill (Figure 6.4).[14]

This surf-inspired skateboarding was also transposed to Europe, inserting mobile euphoria into mundane urbanism. Ben Powell's experience was typical – 'I started off by rolling down a hill with a pair of sunglasses on, pretending to be Californian' – while as early as 1973 the area below the Southbank Centre's Queen Elizabeth Hall (later known as the Undercroft) in London proved ideal for surf-related moves. 'A seemingly endless stream of kids were hurtling up to the bank, riding it, and turning back down,' reported an excited *Time Out*. 'Others were riding along the top edge, crouched down holding on to their boards ("carving").'[15] In similar ways, skaters discovered innumerable banks and other inclines in hundreds of cities worldwide, while one of the very first skateboarding books – Russ Howell's *Skateboard* (1975) – was published in Sydney and featured Australian skateboarders negotiating flat-grounds, banks and roads.[16]

On one level these skateboarders might appear to be simply escapists, just as Lefebvre describes

Figure 6.5
'One of the ultimate
rides.' Escondido
reservoir in San
Diego County.
SkateBoarder (August
1976). Photographer
unidentified.

Figure 6.6
Waldo Autry at the notorious Mount Baldy. *The Magic Rolling Board* (dir. Jim Freeman and Greg MacGillivray, 1976).
www.bit.ly/Autry-MagicRolling

Figure 6.7
The Promised Land of Arizona pipe-riding (1977). *Skateboard Madness* (Hal Jepsen Films, dir. Julian Pena, 1979).
www.bit.ly/ArizonaPipes-SkateboardMadness

Figure 6.8
Steve Cathey rides an otherworldly Arizona pipe (1977).
© Jim Goodrich.

surfers and mountaineers as fleeing cities in order to 'really' live.[17] However, skateboarding was less about avoiding and more about reimagining the urban realm. Through their surf-related moves, skaters recombined body, board and terrain. They copied one activity (surfing), initiated a second (skateboarding) and consequently transfigured everyday urban spaces into pleasurable asphalt and concrete waves; 'hillside housing tracts', declared Stephen Cline, 'lost their hideous urban negativity and emerged from the metamorphosis as smooth uncrowded ribbons of winding joy.'[18] This kind of transformation lies at the very heart of skateboarding, and is a process to which I frequently return in the rest of this book.

Forevers

Even more extreme variants of found spaces were the fully circular concrete full-pipes, typically fabricated for water infrastructure projects, which *SkateBoarder* covered from 1976 onwards. Most famous is the 150-m-long Mount Baldy pipe north-east of Los Angeles, constructed for the San Antonio Dam in 1955. First ridden around 1970 when discovered by Pat 'Muckus' Mullis, this now-infamous pipe featured in many of the 1970s skate documentaries, which showed skaters like Waldo Autry oscillating within its 5 m girth (Figure 6.6).[19]

In Southern California, similar pipes were skated at the US Marines Camp Pendleton and the San Onofre power station, while to the north skaters found the 4.25 m diameter Ameron pipes near Palo Alto, the 4.25 m diameter and 75 m long Bombora pipeline and the enormous 8.5 m diameter Glory Hole spillway for the Monticello Dam (Lake Berryessa).[20] In Florida, skaters enjoyed the 3.65 m full-pipe shown in *Hard Waves, Soft Wheels*, plus the 6 m pipes constructed for the Saint Lucie power station. In 1979, *SkateBoarder* even featured massive 7.3 m underground cooling pipes, possibly sited in Mexico as part of the US Atlas intercontinental ballistic missile network.[21] Australian skaters discovered Melbourne's Rocla and Hawthorn pipes, plus the 7.6 m sections of the City Loop rail system then under construction; later in the mid-1980s, the smooth surfaces of the 4.9 m Werribee pipes in Victoria were another favourite.[22]

Most epic of all were the free-standing pipes discovered in the Arizona desert, fabricated by Ameron for a $1.7 billion federal canal project (Figures 6.7 and 6.8). Here, the flat terrain and an expansive sky contrasted with the striking pipe forms – each immense section typically measured 6.4 m diameter, 6.7 m long and weighed 225 tons – the whole fantastical scene

being memorably captured in 'Skateboard Kings' (1978), *Skateboard Madness* (1979) (Figure 6.7) and the pages of *SkateBoarder*. 'Still three miles away, we could barely see some giant structures. "What are those?" Laura asked. Everyone started hooting as we moved closer. Pipe sections littered the desert floor as far as the eye could see.'[23] Photographs taken here remain some of the most evocative of all skateboarding images, the otherworldly qualities of the pipes, desert and sunlight being redolent, notes Zarka, of Nancy Holt's land art 'Sun Tunnels' (1973–1976).[24]

Within these pipes, skaters instigated unique spatial explorations. At Baldy's long section, Chris Miller described 'riding all the way through, doing frontside thrusters as high as you could go, skimming your hand along the wall.'[25] In the shorter single-section Arizona pipes a more rhythmical side-to-side riding ensued, where the overhang zone pushed the skater into highly compressed manoeuvres. 'The wall is just so clean,' enthused Alva to the BBC, 'that you feel weightless, and when you're high you feel totally upside down.' Here, in this singular moment, 'the skater defies the laws of gravity and floats in space.'[26]

On completing their over-vertical turn, the skater falls down the pipe surface, feeling the wall move away until the nine o'clock position is regained, before the wall returns to the body on descent to ground. Furthermore, the skater immediately encounters the opposite wall, for the full-pipe has no flat-bottom; consequently pipe-riders undertake seemingly perpetual moves on opposite walls – 'forevers' – using bodily compression-decompression techniques akin to children on playground swings. These forevers are a magically rhythmic performance, rendered even more unworldly by the lunar-landscape setting of desert pipes, or the bunker-like quality of spillway pipes. As a result, eulogizes Hamm, the flowing trajectory of pipe-riding yields a 'spiritual experience', the skater 'rushing in slow motion through the Promised Land.'[27]

The mystique of the forever has been further emphasized by the 'unconquered frontier' – the seemingly impossible idea of passing over twelve o'clock and completing a full revolution. Possibly Skitch Hitchcock and Duane Peters in the 'Skateboard Mania' show (1978) completed full rotations on a specially looped track, while in Birdhouse's *The End* Tony Hawk definitely navigates a loop constructed inside a Mexican

bull ring (Figure 5.19). In later years only twenty or so skaters have achieved this feat, including Al Partanen and Bob Burnquist (switch-stance) at Skatepark of Tampa in 2001, while Josh Borden, Dave Hackett Aaron Homoki and Josh Stafford were among the very few to complete the 'Loops of Death' commissioned by Hawk in 2008 and 2013.[28]

Some skaters have also managed to perform near-full loops in skatepark cradles and the Turningpoint ramp (Figure 7.18), as well as complete rotations by using high-speed run-ups; for example, in Lifeblood's *Service for the Sick* (2014) Kevin Kowalski carves a bowl to segue into a full-pipe, loop over, and then sliding 180° to emerge switch-stance, while in 2016 Chris Cope similarly used an extended charge to encircle a small full-pipe.[29] Most dramatically and against all logic, in 2003, and after an infamous failed attempt to loop Mount Baldy a year earlier, Bob Burnquist did complete a full rotation of a 'natural' (not made for skateboarding) full-pipe *without* any run-up. Burnquist achieved this by simply working higher up the sides of a 4 m diameter metal pipe before thrusting his body over the top.[30] A decade later, Jimmy Carlin completed the same manoeuvre in another small pipe, as shown in *Perpetual Motion* (2013).

Despite being largely eclipsed by skateparks, full-pipes have consistently fascinated skateboarders. One explanation for this compelling attraction is that, because they have frequently been found in remote deserts or hidden wastelands, these constructions often appeared to be primeval yet forgotten elements of infrastructure. As such, skaters act like urban explorers, 'place-hackers' uncovering our industrial past and who, writes Bradley Garrett, 'take back what we didn't know we'd lost' and so 'give life back to a building after it has been abandoned.'[31] And through such urban explorations, other even more demanding found spaces were also being unearthed.

Into the Deep End

> Just when you get to thinking you've finally found the limits of what can be done on a skateboard, or of what places are left to be found, something new turns up to broaden the imagination and boggle the mind.[32]
> Warren Bolster

Although full-pipes were iconic and challenging, 1970s skateboarding found an ever better location for its found space appropriations in

Figure 6.9
Early pool-riding at the Foxtail
Pool, Santa Monica (1965).
SkateBoarder (May 1980).
Photograph Ron Stoner.

Figure 6.10
'No socio-economic level of neighbourhood is taboo in the search for locations.' *Go for It* (dir. Paul Rapp, 1976).
www.bit.ly/Pools-GoForIt

the form of swimming pools, whose typically eye-catching keyhole-, kidney- or organically-shaped forms were derived from the pool at the famous 1948 Donnell Garden house in Sonoma County, California, itself based on the 1939 Alvar Aalto-designed kidney pool at the Villa Mairea in Noormarkku, Finland.[33]

Taking advantage of this architectural lineage, somewhere between 1963 and 1965, Gary Swanson drained his Santa Monica backyard pool and, noting the curved transition from base to wall, rode up the rounded deep end. Alternatively, the first pool skated may have been a burnt-out house in Orange County's Stanton by Herbie Fletcher, or the Foxtail pool at a vacant Santa Monica house, carved by George Trafton, Dave Hilton, Steve Hilton and Torger Johnson around 1965 (Figure 6.9). Or it may have been Roy Diederichsen's pool in Menlo Park near San Francisco, featured in the first 1965 *SkateBoarder*, offering the 'big thrill' of 'banking off the deep end wall'.[34] In yet another variant, it may have happened first in Canada, where Wee Willi Winkels skated the family pool while it was emptied for cleaning.[35]

Whatever the founding event, these kinds of pools were skated occasionally after 1965 and more intensively from around 1973; by 1976, documentaries like *Downhill Motion*, S*pinn'in Wheels*, *Freewheelin'* and *Super Session* were all including significant pool-riding sequences, frequently at a San Juan Capistrano version with square coping, wall extension and idiosyncratic overhanging boulder. Fed by neighbourhood rumour, inspired by images in *SkateBoarder*, *Skateboard World* and other magazines and further excited by a nationwide 1976 Beach Boys television special featuring Lonnie Toft and Gordy Lienemann, skaters identified backyard locations all over California, sometimes in the grounds of abandoned residences or illegally, without the permission

of temporarily absent owners. Although pools were undoubtedly skated in many other US states and cities, Los Angeles lays best claim to being skateboarding's 'pool capital' at this time, particularly in the moneyed Hollywood Hills, Beverly Hills, Malibu, Pacific Palisades and San Fernando Valley, where luxurious private pools abounded.[36] *Go for It* and the BBC's 'Skateboard Kings' consequently followed Alva and others searching for the perfect Los Angeles backyard pool (Figure 6.10).

Other pools across the state were also being discovered, often only ridden for short periods of time and known by idiosyncratic labels, such as Adolph's, Dog Bowl (Figure 6.11), Fruit Bowl, Gonzales, Kona, L-pool, Manhole, Massage Bowl, Pearl Pool, Rabbit Hole, Sewers, Skipper's and Soul Bowl. By Peralta's reckoning, he skated over one hundred of these pools over a two-year period.[37] Northern California offered the Arab Pool, Dolphin Pool, Gilroy Brocerios Bowl and Los Altos pool. In Florida the Rat Hole in Pensacola, Oaks Pool in Daytona Beach, Duncan's Pool/Fruit Bowl in Highland Beach and the Miramar pool proved especially skateable, while Dead Cat and Work a Bowl were popular Arizona locations, as were the Rathole in Texas and another pool at Long Island's East Hampton. Australia had pools like Dolphin, Greene's, Pymble and Vanda's, and even the UK had its Croydon Dustbowl.[38] Mostly, however, pool-hunting was a Californian endeavour, certainly as represented in *SkateBoarder*. 'We found as many pools as we could', explained Alva, 'and just skated the hell out of them.'[39]

Sensory Space

What was the particular attraction of these pools, and what kinds of skateboarding did they inspire? In the beginning, skaters undertook surf-derived carves, attacking the wall at a low-angled sweeping trajectory while prevented

Figure 6.11
Tony Alva, frontside
air at the Dog Bowl,
Los Angeles (1977).
© Glen E. Friedman

from falling by centrifugal force. However, skaters soon realized that carving alone was not enough, and more complex manoeuvres quickly emerged.

The 'kickturn' was an especially empathetic engagement with the pool, having been executed in pools by skaters like Autry and Alva in the early 1970s.[40] Here, the skater ascends the wall in a near vertical path, before, as speed drops, lifting the front wheels, pivoting 180° around the rear wheels and riding back down. Through this kickturn, skaters encounter how the pool's wallness morphs from horizontal to vertical under their feet; the higher the ride, the more wall-like that surface becomes. This involves a quadripartite sequence of body, board and surface. Initially comes sudden compression as skateboard and body encounter the lower transition, where the pool presses back and translates forward momentum into upward trajectory; next comes tense body-compression, the rider feeling concave curvature give way to vertical flatness and spatial expansivity. Third is the stall near the top of the trajectory where the skater begins the kickturn, a dream-like experience where space-time is conflated into a dynamic-yet-stable moment. Fourth is the return to floor, the rider experiencing in reverse the compression of curvature and body as a mirrored rhythm of the first two stages. This complex sequence is then repeated, the skater composing carves, kickturns and other moves within the same run.

Another engagement with the pool is via surface, and particularly smoothness as silky texture and continuous curve. The micro-architecture of surface grain, cracks and rippling all become evident, translated – via wheels, trucks, deck and feet – into grip, judder and slides. Noise is also key, the traverse over the pool wall creating a mono-tonal hum, a near silent yet clearly audible interlude to the machine gun rapid-fire rasped out by wheels passing over blue tile and to the industrial bray of metal trucks grinding along the upper stone coping. In pool skating, contends Rick Blackhart, 'the way everything sounds is different' so that 'every grind has a strange resonating howl'.[41] Such noises are further enriched by appreciative onlookers: 'Snarls and growls rise from the deep end as skaters get down and out. Shouts and howls rise from the crowded shallow end full of screaming skaters-in-waiting.'[42] Additionally, since Dave Allen initiated the gesture in the 1990s, skaters often express appreciation by noisily smacking their board tail against the pool coping or other hard objects.[43]

These aural salvos recall Lefebvre's contention that 'space is listened for as much as seen, and heard before it comes into view', and that hearing is part of our encounter with space. Indeed, when I first witnessed pool-riding at the UK's Solid Surf skatepark at Harrow in 1978, I heard exactly the sounds described by Blackhart even before seeing the pool, and my auditory memory of the explosive juddering of skaters carving the as-yet-unseen blue-tiled pool remains with me forty years later. Skateboarding hence creates Rodaway's 'sensuous geography' and Lefebvre's 'sensory space', made up from the subconscious interplay of 'reflections, references, mirrors and echoes'.[44]

On one level, pool-riding was an extension of surf-related experiences, and the summer 1975 cover of the re-published *SkateBoarder* consequently showed Gregg Weaver carving surf-style and barefoot in the San Marcos pool, clearly being inspired by surfers' tactile reading of waves.[45] And three years later, *SkateBoarder* still described skaters as 'adapting from waves to walls', while according to Peralta, 'riding the right pool feels just like being weightless in the tube'.[46] Today, films like *I Had Too Much to Dream Last Night* (Dustin Humphrey, 2014), charting Harrison Roach and Bryce Young surfing and skateboarding across Indonesia, continue to emphasize the inter-relation between watery waves and concrete walls.

However, pool skateboarding is far more than just emulating surfing, particularly as many up-and-coming skaters like Steve Alba, Steve Olson and Rick Blackhart had never been surfers. 'I hated that Fluid Floyd Aquanoid crap,' declared Blackhart, 'I lived in Santa Cruz for five years, and I got in the water twice'.[47] Fuelled by these new attitudes, around 1976 and 1977 skaters' relationship to the pool changed, noting that 'when you fly up into the air and land on concrete – that's not water'.[48] Peralta, for example, understood that skaters were beginning 'to use the terrain as a force, to gain speed from the vertical' and to 'work the surface'.[49] This meant thinking less about the pool as a wave, and more as an element to be encountered in new ways. 'Round pools with fat coping and wide-open shallow-ends. The faster the better,' wrote Hamm. 'Go over the light, then the love-seat, through the shallow, carve-grind the deep-end pocket and ride that hip that tips past vert. Are you scared to frontside grind over the death-box? Haul ass!'[50]

So how exactly did this migration from surf-style skateboarding progress? During the mid-1970s, San Diego and Los Angeles area skaters took a whole new approach to skateboarding. These pioneers famously included the Z-Boy team of the Zephyr surf shop (owned by Jeff Ho, Skip Engblom and Craig Stecyk), as promulgated in *Dogtown and Z-Boys* and *Lords of Dogtown*. Under the influence of a recent Australian and Hawaiian trend for aggressive short-board

surfing, skaters like Jay Adams, Tony Alva, Bob Biniak, Chris Cahill, Paul Constantineau, Shogo Kubo, Jim Muir, Peggy Oki, Stacy Peralta, Nathan Pratt, Wentzle Ruml, Alan Sarlo, Billy Yeron and many others began to explore the boundaries of the surface and the space beyond, aiming, as Peralta explained, 'to project yourself through the bowl continuously, forever doing off-the-lips, from one wall to another'.[51]

Initially, as seen in a *SkateBoarder* feature on the San Juan Capistrano pool, skaters like Mike Weed, Craig Chastney and Peralta simply carved walls, occasionally passing over blue tile.[52] A few months later, they concentrated on the very top of the wall, shuddering over blue tiles to grind the rear truck against the coping blocks, while riders like Biniak were emphasizing 'how long you can ride at the top, how fast you go at the top – frontside off-the-lips at speed'.[53]

This also often involved a particularly belligerent attitude. 'Back then,' recalled Peralta, 'Alva, Adams, Yeron, all those guys. It was 100% aggression'.[54] Skaters consequently confronted pools as dangerous terrains to be conquered and redefined. 'You're tapping in to something that was made for people to enjoy filled with water,' stated Alva, 'and you're taking it to this aggressive, artistic, creative level'.[55]

Within this aggression, the skater addresses the precise inter-relation of the very limits of the wall with their wheels and trucks (Figure 7.12). In Rodney Jesse's words, 'It's just unreal, because you feel everything lifting off, then you feel the edge on the coping while you're turning'.[56] Furthermore, *Thrasher* later described these kinds of 'edger' as the 'slim difference between yes and no, between light and dark, genius and insanity'.[57] The edger was precisely physical, dynamically experiential and personally profound, a way to confront oneself and the external world – 'You can't be on the edge if there is no edge'.[58]

The edger, however, was not the final limit. New moves like the fakie – where skaters climb the wall, stall and ride down backwards – were evidently unlike surfing. More spectacular still is the aerial, where the skater passes over the wall edge, torques in mid-air (grasping the board with one hand) and returns to the side-wall. Tony Alva is usually credited as the first to achieve this astonishing invention in the summer of 1977, and in January 1978 *SkateBoarder* showed Glen Friedman's classic image of an Alva aerial at the Dog Bowl, which has had a massive impact on skateboarding worldwide (Figure 6.11). Whatever the precise origin, the aerial was a move of unreal fantasy. As Friedman recalled after seeing Alva first air the Dog Bowl: 'I went to school the next day and had a tough time just describing it to my friends, let alone getting them to believe it.'[59]

Moves like the aerial initiated a new skateboarding experience, space being produced centrifugally as a spiralling field thrown out from the body, and then centripetally, pulling terrain back into the realm of body space. As a result, pool skateboarding opened up an incomparable kind of found space. 'Sure,' explained Hamm, 'I still bomb hills, skate ramps and ditches, and cruise the streets after hours, but pools rule.'[60] Indeed, even before aerials, pool-riding was seen as skateboarding's state-of-the-art expression. 'No other type of riding offers such radical departures from the past, and no other form progresses so swiftly towards the future,' declared *SkateBoarder* in 1976. 'Pool-riding has the juice.'[61]

Territory and Tactics

As a result of pipe- and pool-based skateboarding, skaters in places like Los Angeles and San Diego gained an international reputation. 'The parks and pools of California,' claimed Curtis Hesselgrave, 'are to skating what surf breaks like Sunset Beach, Laniakea or Pipeline are to surfing. It's the proving ground of the best skateboarders of the world.'[62]

In particular, the skaters of 1970s Santa Monica, Ocean Park and Venice Beach areas of Los Angeles adopted a new territorial moniker, Dogtown, probably invented by Craig Stecyk. Whatever its origins, Dogtown riders reacted against their neighbourhood's dilapidated housing and social impoverishment – Engblom called Venice Beach a 'seaside slum' – by skating in an ultra-aggressive manner.[63] In doing so they attained a mythic global status so strong that skaters wrote to *SkateBoarder* claiming that 'only God could have created Dogtown,'[64] and in emulation riders worldwide gave their locales similar titles such as Pig City (Brighton) and Dread City (Portsmouth).[65]

Others, however, have disputed the accuracy of this Dogtown-centricity, interpreting it as more the product of the Californian-based *SkateBoarder* than as accurate history. Snyder, for example, shows how 1970s Florida boasted a substantial ditch-, pool- and skatepark-riding community, while Browne similarly details

the 1970s exploits of Zoo York and other New York skaters, including riding the Death Bowl pool.[66] Other skateboarding hotspots were also emerging – particularly in South Africa, Australia and other surfing locations – where skaters were no doubt doing extraordinary things, but out of sight of the presiding California-based magazines. Cannon's Creek in New Zealand (1974) and Albany Skate Track in Australia (1976) (Figure 7.3), for example, both pre-date any of the US skateparks from skateboarding's 1970s phase. Nonetheless, whatever the veracity of the overall history, it was the Dogtown skaters who became most famous through *SkateBoarder, Skateboard – the Movie*, the BBC's 'Skateboard Kings' and other documentaries. Certainly among my fellow UK skaters, our paramount perception was that 1970s skateboarding was predominantly developing in California in general and Dogtown in particular.

To copy these innovations meant first finding and then transforming new locations. The banks, ditches, pipes and pools were already present in the urban realm, with pools being typically found on private land, hidden behind houses and obscured by fences and foliage. Drainage ditches were in interstitial zones away from residential areas and accessible only from obscure (and often gated) entrances. Pipes were mostly in distant deserts or mountains, away from the city and seemingly forgotten. Even schoolyard banks were 'discovered' through being rethought as ocean waves. All these terrains were there, awaiting disclosure and reimagination through skateboarding.

The urban tactics of found space skateboarding were, therefore, initially those of reconnaissance, with riders scouting districts to identify new terrains – 'no socio-economic level of neighbourhood is taboo in the search for locations' declared *Go for It* (Figure 6.10) – and for skaters like Adams this was an essential part the enjoyment: 'The most fun was stickin' with all the guys on the team and goin' out and finding pools and stuff.'[67] Journeys by bicycle, car and skateboard were used to survey neighbourhoods, keeping eyes, ears and noses tuned for telling signs like 'high pool fencing, pool sweeps, slides, the smell of chlorine, inflatable pool toys, solar-power panels, big hoses gushing for days or chlorine deposits'; committed pool-riders like Steve Alba considered this nuanced detective work to be 'an art form.'[68] Valuable intelligence could also be gained by consulting aerial maps in local City Halls, reviewing the federal Housing

Figure 6.12
Chris Pfanner goes over-vert somewhere in Greece.
@dvlphoto.

and Urban Development real estate list, impersonating house buyers, police and pool maintenance operatives or stationing binoculars atop canyon-high vantage points. Even aircraft were occasionally used to reconnoitre for empty white pools, as undertaken by San Jose skaters and Floridians like Jeff Duerr.[69]

As Hamm explains, prime targets were houses with pools that had been drained for maintenance or winter: 'From the alley we can tell which yards have pools, so we stop and peek over the wall. Forty-nine times out of fifty the pool is full of crystal-clear water. But that one smooth-walled, empty bowl is worth every unrewarding alley.'[70] Usefully, the California drought of 1976 to 1977 left many pools bone dry, while frequent fires in the Hollywood Hills and Santa Monica mountains also meant numerous abandoned homes; one major Santa Barbara fire led to twenty skateable pools being identified.[71] Other favoured targets were homes being remodelled, airport districts with homes vacated due to excessive noise, plus low-rental districts and schools where pools had been drained to reduce maintenance costs. Skaters even sometimes asked municipal authorities to enforce draining, as required by Californian safety codes for unsupervized pools.[72] Particularly welcome were larger motel pools, like the fish-shaped example at San Fernando Valley's Pink Motel and shown in *The Search for Animal Chin.*

Once located, different tactics kicked in. Often the favoured manoeuvre was a one-off 'barge', a single session until the irate owner or police arrived to throw skaters out. 'A common practice is the fifteen-minute rule,' explained Alba. 'It usually takes five minutes for the people to realize we're there, five minutes for them to call the cops, and five minutes for the cops to arrive.'[73] Here, the risk of being caught was part of the attraction. 'It's better to be ready for police, ready for the owner, for dogs, anything,' warned Alva. 'Part of pool-riding is the adventure of being ready for anything that's gonna come down.'[74]

This has been a long tradition in pool hunting, with pool-riders in the 1980s and beyond pursuing similar tactics and encountering similar problems. 'We staked it out, it was six in the morning. We got in and bailed it, waiting for the right time,' recounted Scott Smiley. 'We rode it for thirty-forty minutes, then all of a sudden this big fat dude comes running out. We just grabbed our shit and this guy was yelling out for

blood.'[75] Or as Hamm succinctly put it, 'it's all good fun until Johnny Law arrives.'[76]

Appropriation here is spontaneous and ephemeral. As a result, pool sessions were socially somewhere between guerrilla raids and what *Thrasher* celebrated in one lyrical text as a rowdy 'Pool Party' – 'We're going to have a dry pool party tonight! We've got nothing better to do than skate this pool, and pay some heavy dues. We've got nothing better to do than pump this pool, and have a couple of brews. It'll be dry for only two days, I don't wanna be late.'[77]

But not all found space skateboarding has relied on isolated raids. Wherever possible, skaters have returned to the same ditch or pool, and for which opaque naming and concealment processes often came into play. Photographers sometimes just invented names for ephemeral locations – like Barney Miller's pool – when submitting their shots to magazines, but others – such as Fruit Bowl, Kona Bowl and Soul Bowl – acquired established reputations. In part this naming aided identification, but, conversely, it helped hide pool locations from other skaters, and so discouraged overuse or unwanted attention. 'The less people you tell,' advised Brian Brannon, 'the longer you will skate. The lips of fools lose pools.'[78] Surfers had long deployed this tactic to protect favoured surf spots, and skaters have similarly pursued it for years. For example, Alva berated Alba for revealing pool-finding tips in *Thrasher*, 'I'm not digging your fucking over-exposure of pools. You're giving out the secrets dude.'[79] Similarly, in 2015 the Rash Bowl was unhelpfully described on the *Skatenorcal* website as 'Directions: Inland SoCal. If I told you more I'd have to kill you.'[80]

This mode of secrecy was also adopted for the desert pipes, whose exact Arizona location was a closely guarded secret. 'It's all strictly classified information,' warned *SkateBoarder*. 'Unless, of course, you know someone who knows someone who . . .'[81] For some locations, such as Santa Monica's Dog Bowl and Gonzales pool, select skaters had negotiated personal access, and here, particularly when accompanied by exotic magazine images, the names inferred a mystical sun-soaked paradise, clearly real yet frustratingly known only to an élite few.

Protected in this way, some found space pools lasted for months or even years; by the late 1980s, the Buena Vista pool near Santa Cruz had been ridden for over fifteen years.[82] Skateboarders here acted like anarchist communities, supplementing their spontaneous appropriation of pools with more established colonization procedures, such that established locations such as the Key-Hole, Canyon Pool and Soul Bowl gained their own names, boundaries, access conditions and internal culture. Graffiti was another occasional act of territorialization, helping to both claim the pool and warn off others. In such ways, pools gained what Lefebvre identifies as socio-spatial boundaries, becoming tightly defined places that excluded anyone outside the sanctioned group.[83]

But above all, skaters themselves – and not just the physical pool – defined the social space. 'If the boys are there, the competitive thing is really intense,' cautioned Peralta. 'I've seen outsiders who are pretty good skaters just walk away without riding; I guess it was too insane.'[84] As this suggests and as Lefebvre theorizes, people use space, and particularly boundary spaces of passage and encounter, to create their own identity, often doing so through ritual and induction.

> All 'subjects' are situated in a space in which they must either recognize themselves or lose themselves, a space which they may both enjoy and modify. In order to accede to this space, individuals (children, adolescents) who are, paradoxically, already within it, must pass tests. This has the effect of setting up reserved spaces, such as places of initiation, within social space.[85]

A pool, then, was often a 'reserved space' with rites of passage, where skaters proved themselves to peers, where 'you had to have big balls' and where skaters like 'master of disaster' Duane Peters took centre stage.[86] 'The brawl was in the pool,' declared Peters. 'You'd go in the pool and you'd tell the guy to fuck off by doing a better run than his last run. You'd stay in longer.'[87] Or as Dave Hackett recalled Orange County's famous Fruit Bowl, 'if you didn't have pool skills and couldn't rip, you sat in the shallow end. You watched. It was a gnarly scene.'[88] Such scenes therefore encouraged a particular form of masculinity as pugnacious and competitive behaviour. 'When the boys are together, you could never find a more aggressive, arrogant, rowdy, perhaps ignorant bunch of people,' advised Alva. 'That's the way we skateboard; that's the way we talk.'[89] Three decades later, long-time pool-riders like Pat Quirk were still talking in similar terms: 'This

shit's for real dude. You hit the fucking ground, man, and it hurts. You want to be in skate army? You'd better pay your fucking dues, dude. We got our own fucking gang, and you'd better not fuck with us.'[90]

Taken together, the tactics of appropriation, colonization and belligerent attitude helped skaters to redefine both the city and themselves. Through their reimagination of found spaces, skateboarders transformed California's sedate suburbs into dramatic concrete-and-body constructions, exploited under an air of espionage. This was no small achievement, especially as many 1970s residents perceived suburbia as, in Lefebvre's terms, the 'specially labelled, guaranteed place' of nature, liberty, privacy and escape. Disrupting this powerful ideology, conversely, skateboarders made suburbs more explicitly urban by disclosing its 'schizophrenic' spaces of play, exchange, politics and culture.[91] Above all, where suburbia typically divorces people from participatory creativity, skateboarders engaged directly with the physicality of this urbanism, recharging dead streets, empty reservoirs and unused pools, and so – conceptually at least – moving suburbia closer to complex city cores. These aspects of skateboarding are even more explicit in the street-skating of the 1980s and beyond, which are explored in Chapters 10 and 11.

Before moving on, however, there is one problem to consider. When colonizing 1970s pools, pipes and ditches, skaters implicitly treated found space as if it were a 'natural' or pre-existent thing. But space, as Lefebvre's *Production of Space* emphatically demonstrates, is not natural but a social product. What skaters thought to have 'found' was not 'already there,' but was actually a product of skateboarding and other non-skateboarding functions, and with inevitable conflicts. Thus the pools and pipes used by skaters were commonly reclaimed by others (police, owners, developers, authorities), and consequently relatively few of the appropriated or colonized spaces from the 1970s have continued to be skated today.

That skateboarders commonly lost out in these confrontations is because of an inherent contradiction within their tactics. On the one hand, they undertook what Lefebvre calls a 'primitive history', that is marking and traversing found spaces, such as by giving pools idiosyncratic names, adding graffiti and by simply riding.[92] On the other hand, these acts alone did not constitute social space. And conversely, when skateboarders did try to produce social space by colonizing and taking ownership of pools for longer periods, the longer duration (repeated visits over weeks or months) and 'ownership' (such as a pool reserved for specific riders) implied by this colonization was unacceptable to more powerful parties. Occasional appropriations might be tolerated, but permanence was not.

These 1970s skateboarders were in fact less appropriating and more engaging in what Lefebvre calls 'co-optation' – a practice that lies intermediate to domination and appropriation, that takes over without mastering and appropriates without ephemerality and that can be useful where control is guaranteed by political rule or law.[93] Except that skateboarders usually did not control the found spaces they co-opted, and, therefore, this strategy was unlikely to succeed except on the rarest of occasions.

If skateboarders were to skate with impunity, different locations and tactics were required. Above all, this meant realizing that true or full appropriation is not the simple reuse of cities, but must also involve its creative reworking.[94] As shown in Chapters 10 and 11, this eventually lead to skateboarding in city streets, and a new approach to the time as well as the space of architecture. Yet another approach, as explored in the next chapter, is a different form of control and production: purpose-built skateparks. 'If pool-riding is going to survive', realized Jim Muir, 'you're gonna have to build your own pool to do it.'[95]

Blue Tile Obsession

Before turning to skateparks, however, an ongoing history of found space skating is worth noting. Pipes continue to fascinate skaters, and some of those discovered in the 1970s are still subjected to military-style forages. Mount Baldy and the Glory Hole spillway at the Monticello Dam, for example, are still frequently skated and filmed (for example, Super 8 footage of Baldy by Coan Nichols and Rick Charnoski appears as a dream sequence in *Paranoid Park*), and have been joined by undercover spots like an Arizona 7.3 m diameter pipe and a Texas 8.5 m pipe, the latter originally built in 1968 for a dam and today accessible via raft.[96] Around 1987, a downtown Phoenix construction project created 3.65 m and 6.1 m pipes accessible to urban explorer–style adventurers.[97] In Australia, the enormous 9.75 m diameter Pot Hole in the Snowy Mountains of New South Wales continues to be skated, as seen in *Tent City*, as does the Huia pipe

near Auckland in New Zealand,[98] along with innumerable other pipes in undisclosed locations (Figure 6.12).

Other oddities have included the Love Bowl portrayed in *Wheels of Fire*, this being a massive pair of crescent-shaped walls in Carefree, Arizona, originally constructed in the late 1960s for CBS television's 'New Dick Van Dyke Show'.[99] In the early 1980s, the strange Sadlands mini-moonscape, located in Anaheim's Brookhurst Community Park, proved another favourite found space, while even natural landscapes have become occasional skatespots, as with the undulating sandstone of Slickrock, Utah, recorded by Jonathan Mehring.[100]

In particular, backyard pool-riding has developed into a distinct skateboarding sub-genre with its own geography, ideologies and history. Throughout the 1980s, magazines like *Thrasher* continued to cover pools (albeit less intensively than had *SkateBoarder*), while videos like *Shackle Me Not* and *Speed Freaks* also included pool-riding segments, as did *Gleaming the Cube*. *Sick Boys* (Michael McEntire, 1988) featured the Oakland's Blood Bowl, Larva Bowl and other Californian pools, while the Suicidal Tendencies 'Possessed to Skate' video (1986) depicted a middle-class suburban pool being transformed into a site of dynamic skateboarding, flying boards and loud punk. And throughout the 1990s pool-riding devotees like Alba persevered with their obsession, particularly after the 1994 Northridge earthquake left innumerable houses abandoned across the San Fernando Valley. 'In the *LA Times* they showed a map of devastated areas', recalled Alba. 'You could skate thirty pools in three blocks.'[101]

Into the early 2000s, encouraged by *Dogtown and Z-Boys*, pool-riding enjoyed a sharp resurgence; first came Nichols and Charnoski's poetic documentation *Fruit of the Vine* (2002) (Figure 5.14), swiftly followed by *Chlorine* (2003), which tracked pool-riding by the likes of Alba, Alva, Dave Reul and Darrel Delgado. Magazine advertisements started to show pools again, as did big budget productions like *The DC Video* (2003) amid its plethora of street, MegaRamp, half-pipe and skatepark scenes. A few years later, even teen-movie *Dishdogz* was including pool scenes with Alva, while in the 2010s the likes of *Dragonslayer* (Tristan Patterson, 2011), Bones's *New Ground* (Jared Lucas, 2013), *Smell the 'Crete 2* (Bart Saric, 2014), Volcom's *Holy Stokes!* (Russell Houghten,

Figure 6.13
Benson rides a rare UK pool (2011).
© Rob Shaw.

2016) and a Jeff Grosso feature on 'Empty Pools' have all positioned pool-riding as central to skate culture. 'You will never find the same exact pool,' enthused Chet Childress, 'the coping sticks out different, the tile, the hip, the love seat, the death box, the stairs, there's so many shapes of freaky pools.'[102]

Specific pool scenes here include Californian candidates based around pools such as the Chino, Convict, Sunset and Hesh or the countless examples logged in Ozzie Ausband's ever-informative *Blue Tile Obsession* blog, those in Arizona, Maryland, Oregon and Washington DC, plus the likes of New Jersey's Deal Lake pool in Asbury Park, New York's Albany and Cambridge's C-Pool.[103] Other notable pool-riding communities have developed in Canada and Australia (Figure 6.14), and even the UK throws up the odd opportunity (Figure 6.13). As with the 1970s, many of these locations are found during summer campaigns, when drought, fine weather, forest fires and absent homeowners often yield skateable pools. Here, pool-riders have continued with 1970s tactics of surveillance and appropriation ('good skating requires a little trespassing,' declared *Juice*), but now aided by Google Earth, online realtor sites and even helicopter-borne surveillance; in Washington State the DC Drain and Clean group (DCDC) employ satellite maps to track down unused pools.[104] The 2008 economic downturn and subsequent foreclosures also resulted in thousands of abandoned Californian houses ready to have their pools drained; 'There are more pools right now than I could possibly skate,' reported Los Angeles skater Adam Morgan.[105]

In part, nostalgia and tradition are at work here, as evoked by *Fruit of the Vine*'s grainy Super 8 footage, while in *Chlorine* Alva talks of pool-riders as honouring age-old codes of close secrecy, networked espionage, devoted labour

and neo-criminal activity. Yet this later pool scene is also in some ways quite different from its 1970s forebears, not least because of some distinctive new meanings.

As Hamm describes, for skaters like Adam 'Chili' Stern and fellow pool-skaters in early 2000s Santa Barbara, pool-riding has been an obsessive life filled with 'extensive exploration, addictive mystery, high risk, giddy anticipation, back-breaking labor, and, ultimately, unforgettable secret sessions shared among the best of friends.' For these kinds of skater, pool-riding represents something truly authentic, part of skateboarding's history of appropriating found spaces, and standing in complete opposition to more organized and mediated forms of skateboarding. As another of the Santa Barbara crew, Tony Capalby, remarked, 'I'd rather get shot in the head than check out the Warped Tour.'[106] In this world, getting a grind, skating over the death box (water outlet) or just carving during a 'barge' (illicitly accessed) pool is to connect with skateboarding's history, rituals and avowedly uncommercial origins, and so to forge a tight-knit neighbourhood community.

For another Santa Barbara skater, Kresky, pool-riding is even more profound, tapping into a 'deep inner drive acted out in a modern context,' undertaking a 'heroic search for the Holy Grail' and so linking with the 'primal world.'[107] Neo-religious associations aside, for many other skaters contemporary pool-riding is equally serious. Trippe and Butz, for example, interpret pool-skating as the punky 'safety pin' that pierces the pool's perfect symbolization of wealth, success and leisure, and so inserts disorder and chaos within suburbia's 'empty promise of utopia.'[108] Hence the portrayal in *Beers, Bowls & Barneys* and *Fruit of the Vine* of run-down pools where 'paradise has turned to shit' – no longer the white-walled pools of the 1970s in whose idyllic settings frizzy-haired and

Figure 6.15
Sandros Dias boosts
a stalefish at Pedro
Barros's RTMF bowl,
Florianapolis (2014).
© Helge Tscharn.

colourfully dressed riders rode beneath palm trees and perfect blue skies, but now graffitied and grime-stained bowls where short-cropped and black-clothed skaters ride amid constricted backyards, vacant houses and incomplete construction projects (Figure 3.5). In such seemingly post-apocalyptic landscapes, the new pool-riders remove filthy slime, chemicals and dead rats from abandoned pools, fight impossibly tight transitions and broken coping and perform physical heroics among decaying surroundings. In short, contemporary pool-riding is no longer just an appropriation for the purposes of pleasure or nostalgia, but has become an additionally political act; twenty-first-century skateboarding in empty pools bears witness to personal upheaval (absent owners), economic crisis (abandoned properties) and environmental distress (drought), and suggests an alternative world of ownerless occupation, open access and dynamic movement. DCDC skaters even forge friendships with elderly and impecunious homeowners, trading gardening and house-repair duties for pool-riding access.

One last and contrasting point on pools. While back in 1986 *Thrasher* mocked the idea of private residences having luxurious skateboarding facilities attached, this soon became a reality for a few fortunate souls. Notably, Barrett 'Chicken' Deck and Kelly Belmar, founders of deck-screeners Screaming Squeegies, both used their company profits to build backyard pools in 1991, this decision later being emulated by many other skaters, from Bucky Lasek's 4.1 m deep bowl in Encinitas, to skatepark builder Mark Hubbard in Seattle, Kevin Kowalski's Oregon facility, Steve 'Cholo' Ellis's amoeba-shaped pool on Oahu's North Shore (2004), Pedro Barros's RTMF bowl in Florianapolis (2008) (Figure 6.15), the Ashley Mott and Lindsey Kuhn pools in Colorado, Foster Huntingdon's elongated bowl in Skamania, Washington (2014), Fidi's pool in Austria (2002) and Dan Cates's pool in Margate (2016).[109] As these skaters have all realized, purpose-built skateboarding terrain can offer significant advantages, and it is to these kinds of ridable architecture that we now turn.

Skateboarding
Chapter 7 Skatopia

It's time to build.[1]
Action Now

Concrete Utopia

In 1975, Southern California reputedly had two million skateboarders. Fuelled by coverage in *People*, *Sports Illustrated* and *Newsweek*, plus specialist magazines like California's *SkateBoarder* and *Skateboard World*, Florida's *Skate Rider*, Australia's *Slicks* and the UK's *Skateboard!* and *Skateboard Scene*, skateboarding went global; the US alone had up to forty million skateboarders by 1979.[2]

First Generation Skateparks

Such massive markets unsurprisingly attracted commercial investors, including those proposing bespoke skateboarding terrains. There had, in fact, been skateparks even before the mid-1970s. The first boom years of 1963 to 1965 lead to facilities like Surf City skatepark in Tucson, Arizona (opened September 1965), offering a 42 m curving concrete track.[3] Nearby, the Pipeline track (opened 1965) at Phoenix's Legend City park boasted a 300 m twisting path.[4] Anaheim's flat-asphalt Surfer's World opened in 1966 and hosted several contests, while Oregon's Portland demarcated one of its streets for skateboarding.[5] Another early facility in Washington State's Kelso even appeared in *Popular Science*, with a narrow 180 m plywood track raised on low stilts; riding cost fifty cents during the daytime and seventy-five cents under evening floodlights (Figure 7.1).[6] Other primitive skateparks were constructed in Visalia (1964) and Orange County (1966).[7]

Figure 7.1
An early skatepark in Kelso, Washington State. *Popular Science* (April 1966). Photographer unidentified.

Figure 7.2
Taito Skateboard
Centre, Chiba.
SkateBoarder
(August 1976).
Photographer
unidentified.

and an innovative surfing scene, encouraged some of the country's earliest skateparks. Consequently the first US commercial skatepark was Florida's SkatBoard City (later Skateboard City), which officially opened on 21 February 1976. Located in Port Orange, Joe Quinn's $75,000 construction offered a large freestyle area, gentle concrete runs and a few banks.[13] By the end of 1976, Florida had at least two more skateparks in the form of the Paved Wave facilities at both Cocoa Beach and Pensacola, the former mimicking surfing waves by varying steepness within one banked run.[14] Other 1976 East Coast skateparks included South Carolina's 1,100 m² Fun Land at Myrtle Beach, sporting bizarrely blue-painted runs separated by red and white stripes. Texas's Corpus Christi was another early venture, while during 1976 and 1977 Wizard developed a chain of skateparks across South Carolina, North Carolina and New Hampshire.[15]

Today, the world's oldest surviving purpose-built skatepark is probably the free-access Cannon's Creek, publicly built in 1974 in Porirua, New Zealand, with around 200 m² of gentle asphalted banks.[8] A year later came the oval-shaped $4,420 facility in Ventura County's Camino Real Park, providing novices with a 85 m asphalt 'push track'.[9] More promisingly, December 1975 saw the Taito Skateboard Centre commercial skatepark open in Chiba, Japan, this $17,000 5,400 m² facility sporting a wide sloping asphalt surface bounded by two 45° and 1-m-high concrete banks, plus a central spine bank (Figure 7.2).[10]

Other early skateparks included two in Western Australia, at Geraldton (1975) and Albany (February–March 1976).[11] The latter, the influential shotcrete Albany Skate Track, documented in *The Snake Run* (Matt Zafir and Tim Zafir, 2016), exploited an existing hill and quarry for its 140 m undulating surf-inspired run (Figure 7.3). With one wall nearing vertical, it cost Aus$18,000 and over 1,200 people arrived on opening day, including Russ Howell who called it 'just outrageous'. Like Cannon's Creek, Albany endures today.[12]

However, these skateparks were somewhat rudimentary, and instead it was the US commercial sector that responded most dramatically to mid-1970s skateboarding, creating purpose-built venues that exaggerated the found space banks, pools and pipes. Florida offered far fewer spillways, pipes, pools and undulating terrains than did California, and this absence, along with a temperate climate

On the opposite coast, the first Californian commercial skatepark was Carlsbad in north San Diego County, opened on 13 March 1976. Developed by surfer-skater John O'Malley (design) and Jack Graham (construction) of Skatepark Constructors, this $50,000 1,200 m² enterprise gained significant *SkateBoarder* coverage. Although financially successful, Carlsbad's undulating contours – as shown in *Highway Star* (Brian Tissot, 1976) – proved rather unchallenging, and within eighteen months it was upgraded and re-branded as Sparks.[16]

Many other US skateparks also arrived in 1976, with Skatepark Constructors now advertising in *SkateBoarder* to potential investors; according to Snyder, by late 1976 there were at least three skateparks in Florida, three in California and one each in Rhode Island, Maryland, South Carolina, Texas and Arizona, while *SkateBoarder* reckoned there were thirteen worldwide. Some twenty had opened by July 1977.[17] Unfettered by clear precedent, a rapid design evolution ensued. Opened in summer 1976, Lou Peralta's SkaterCross (Reseda, California) (Figure 5.4) took inspiration from surfing and motocross for its lengthy continuous route (as seen in *Skateboard – the Movie*), the same linear approach as Michael Collins and John Kogler's Concrete Wave (Anaheim, California), where the four sinuous tracks and freestyle area included what Eddie Elguera called 'the best snake run ever', all separated by AstroTurf landscaping (Figure 7.5).[18] Also adopting a linear design was Aloha Skatetown in Agoura, California, with its 131 m

Figure 7.3
Albany Skate Track, Western
Australia (1976). *The Snake Run*
(dir. Matt and Tim Zafir, 2016).
www.bit.ly/Albany-Skate

Figure 7.4
Skatopia, Buena Park, California.
'Skateboard Kings' (BBC, prod.
Horace Ové, 1978).
www.bit.ly/Skatopia-
SkateboardingKings-BBC

Cobra, 38 m Spaghetti and 37 m Wallows runs.[19]
At Solid Surf (Fort Lauderdale, Florida), the
snake runs, ditches and banked walls attracted
over 3,200 skaters during a single weekend.[20]

Whatever their inventiveness and initial
popularity, however, these gentle gradients and
sinuous banks, as captured in documentaries
like *The Magic Rolling Board*, *Go for It* and *Hard
Waves, Soft Wheels* (Figure 9.1), could not rival
the challenges of desert pipes and backyard
pools. This is perhaps unsurprisingly, given that
many developers had never seen skateboarding
in action. Untested building techniques were
also problematic, resulting in the 'ripply, lumpy,
rough finish' that Kelly Lynn encountered at
SkatBoard City.[21]

Construction methods and design were,
however, both improving, including the
adoption of the swimming pool–derived gunite
process, where cement and sand are forced
along a pipe with compressed air before water
arrives at the nozzle. Alternatively, builders
deployed the 'wet process' shotcrete method,
where pre-mixed sand, cement and water are
piped together, with compressed air arriving
at the nozzle for spraying.[22] In another later
variant, an ultra-smooth finish was sometimes
achieved by filling a pool with water while the
concrete cured, a technique used by Wally

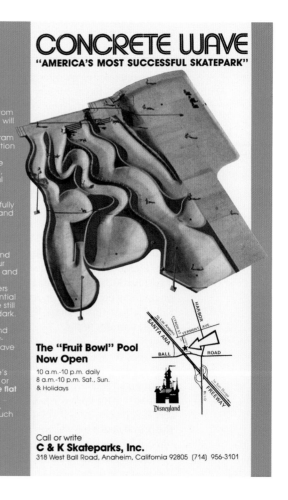

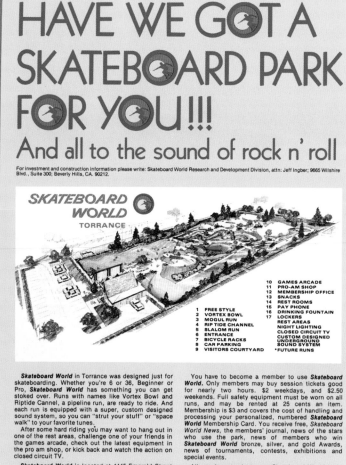

Figure 7.6
Skateboard World,
Torrance, California.
SkateBoarder
(August 1977).

Figure 7.5
Linear runs at
Concrete Wave,
Anaheim (1976).
C&K Skateparks
advertisement,
SkateBoarder
(October 1977).

Hollyday for various facilities and at Pipeline's Combi-Pool.[23]

Second Generation Skateparks

By early 1977 Graham and O'Malley had already published their $200 guide *Skatepark Development* and were touting skateparks as 'one of the 70's most profitable business opportunities', while a San Diego conference in December 1977 attracted 370 developers from thirty-five US states and eight other countries.[24] As design sophistication, construction prowess and market opportunities all advanced, numerous 'second generation' US parks opened during 1977 and 1978, with *Wild World of Skateboarding* listing no less than 101 completed projects in February 1978.[25] Here, continuously contoured landscapes gave way to discrete skateable elements in the form of

separate half-pipes, snake runs, freestyle areas, reservoir, bowls, pools, moguls and slalom runs. Some unbuilt projects were spectacularly ambitious. San Gabriel Valley's 2,975 m² $180,000 Skateboard Heaven proposed complex elements called things like Vortex, Whirlpool and Rip Tide, while its The Tube concrete-and-Plexiglas full-pipe would even have used swirling water and sound effects to simulate surfing. Another drawing-board project, Orlando's Sooper City, envisaged a massive indoor park with 4,460 m² spread over four floors, all interconnected by snake-like runs, return-journey elevators and CCTV.[26]

Of those skateparks actually constructed, among the most noteworthy was Warwick and Belinda Charlton's Skateboard World in Torrance, California, a $450,000 facility by theme park designer Randall Duell (Figure 7.6).[27] Equally elaborate was Buena Park's landscaped $500,000 Skatopia, designed and developed by Victor Peloquin and starring in the BBC's 'Skateboard Kings'; it featured the Escondido Bowl, derived from the found space Escondido reservoir, a four-bowl Whirlpool and a famous 53 m long half-pipe with bordering brick wall (Figures 4.2 and 7.4).[28] Carson's Runway offered a three-leafed 'superbowl' plus an element based on Vermont Drop, as did Jeff Spencer's $150,000 Skateboard Safari in West Palm Beach, Florida (Figure 9.1). Like many new skateparks, Skateboard Safari was approved by the American Skateboard Association.[29]

Florida welcomed Jacksonville's $225,000 Kona, Tampa's Rainbow Wave and Clearwater, with the state's first concrete half-pipe, Gainesville's $500,000 Sensation Basin and Orlando's Longwood Skateboard Track with the first skatepark full-pipe. Opened on 1 March 1977, the $220,000 gunite Skateboard USA in Hollywood claimed the first vertical skatepark walls for both Florida and the country as a whole, as well as a dramatic launch tower with traffic lights regulating skaters descending into two C-shaped bowls (Figure 9.1).[30] Other skateparks nationwide included the unusual Riding-the-Glass in Minnesota and Fyber Rider in Lakewood, New Jersey, where the flat-bottomed half-pipe, full-pipe, reservoir and other runs were composed from bright-blue fibreglass modules fabricated by the International Sports & Recreation Corporation.[31]

Most famous of all these second generation skateparks was the $125,000 Upland Pipeline,

Figure 7.9
'34,000 square feet of concrete poetry' at Cherry Hill, New Jersey (1978). *Skateboard Madness* (Hal Jepsen Films, dir. Julian Pena, 1979), DVD bonus extra.
www.bit.ly/CherryHill-SkateboardMadness

Figure 7.10
Dave Hackett and Tony Alva ride Marina del Rey's Dogbowl. 'Hot Shots' (Toby Keeler, 1981).
www.bit.ly/Hackett-Marina-HotShots

Figure 7.11
Steve Alba airs the Combi-Pool shortly before its demolition. *Streets on Fire* (Santa Cruz, dir. Howard Dittrich, 1989).
www.bit.ly/Alba-StreetsOnFire

Figure 7.7
Tom 'Wally' Inouye
in the 'first real pool
for skateboarding',
Skateboard Heaven,
Spring Valley, San
Diego (1977).
© Jim Goodrich

Figure 7.8
Hester competition in
the Capsule Bowl at
Big O, Orange (1978).
© Jim Goodrich.

located in the Los Angeles 'Badlands' area of San Bernardino Valley. Owned by Jean and Stan Hoffman with son Don, and dubbed the 'World's First Vertical Skatepark' when opened on 28 May 1977, Pipeline – aka Upland – boasted the first Californian full-pipe and truly vertical walls intended for skateboarding. A 6.1 m diameter and 12.2 m long full-pipe fed into a 3.65 m deep bowl, while the 67 m slalom run lead to another 4.6 m bowl with one side slightly over vertical. Other features accommodated more relaxed skating. Exaggerating California's found space pipes, ditches and pools (especially the nearby Mount Baldy full-pipe), Pipeline was generally considered the best skatepark so far, starring in *Skateboard Fever* (NBC Sports, 1977) and massively impacting on skateboarding's collective imaginary. 'How did they build that huge swimming pool thing out of cement?', wondered Eric Muss-Barnes. 'I was astonished and stoked and stunned.'[32]

From mid-1977 onwards, design and construction techniques underwent further refinement. Many skateparks still had flawed transitions, uneven surfaces and non-functional designs; in particular, even the best second-generation skateparks initially lacked the tiles and coping of authentic backyard pools; for example, Steve Evans realized that Pipeline 'needs coping really bad', while its pipe surfaces were also criticized.[33] As competition increased from other skateparks and skaters' moves became more advanced, many ventures incorporated pool-style elements. One of the first was the Fruit Bowl pool at Anaheim's Concrete Wave in mid-1977, along with Flow Motion in Richmond, Virginia. For Skateboard Heaven at Spring Valley, San Diego, the new pool took the design of the popular local backyard Soul Bowl (located in a vacant fraternity house), including its shallow-end coves and love seats, while offering more relaxed transitions, reduced amounts of vertical wall and new coping all precisely tuned for skateboarding; according to Peralta, it was the 'first real pool for skateboarding' (Figure 7.7). Some skateparks also added other distinctive features, such as the lunar mogul field at Carlsbad/Sparks.[34]

Figure 7.12
The ultimate
playground? Duane
Peters edges the
square section of
the Combi-Pool at
Pipeline, Upland
(1980).
© Jim Goodrich

Third Generation Skateparks
Competition between skateparks was now fierce, and consequently most 1978 ventures further emphasized pool-style tiles and coping. Two San Diego examples were Oasis, which included a white egg-shaped pool, and the renowned Del Mar Skate Ranch (Figures 9.3

and 9.6), designed by Curtis Hesselgrave, Chris Strople and Tom Inouye, managed by Grant Brittain, and incorporating the keyhole pool and kidney replica of the local Kona backyard pool.[35] Skateboard World in Lakewood, California, sported a snake run, banked slalom and freestyle areas, a long half-pipe and three-bowl cloverleaf, plus back-to-back keyhole pools and another pool with tile and coping, all of which featured heavily in *Blaze On* (Figure 5.9). Owned by Joel Vest and Glenn Smith, Skateboard World was designed by Vest and Wally Hollyday and constructed by swimming pool contractors Superior Gunite.[36] Whittier's Skate City (1979) boasted distinctively variegated tile colouring, plus a three-bowl cloverleaf, full-pipe and half-pipe; it even required skaters to use truck 'Coper' devices to preserve its coping blocks.[37]

Also significant were High Roller in Phoenix, Arizona (May 1978), with a tombstoned keyhole pool and 6.1 m diameter full-pipe; Skate in the Shade (Tempe, Arizona), with a keyhole pool constructed by swimming pool builder Duane Bigelow; Skatepark Victoria (Milpitas, California); Rancho Mediterrania aka Ranch (Colton, California); and Winchester (Campbell, San Jose, California). Frank Nasworthy's Cadillac Wheels Skateboard Concourse (Pompano Beach, Florida) included a formidable 4 m Monster Hole (Florida's first skatepark pool) and more relaxed Ditch Bowl and Egg Bowl.[38] Jerry Valdez and Marc Smith designed Endless Wave at Oxnard, which incorporated a conjoined pair of cement-coping pools, as featured in 'Skateboard Kings'.[39] Yet another favourite was Big O (Orange), opened June 1978, whose complex three-quarter pipes, three-bowl cloverleaf and other pools proved 'sick as shit' to Steve Alba; according to *Concrete Disciples*, the channelled capsule was 'one of the most famous pools in skateboarding history' (Figure 7.8).[40]

Pre-eminent among these third-generation pool-oriented skateparks was New Jersey's Cherry Hill (1978), described by *SkateBoarder* as '34,000 square feet of concrete poetry that flows, ebbs and rips' (Figure 7.9). Owned by Steve Durst and Bob Hurley, with design and construction by a combination of Hurley, Hollyday, Bigelow and local skaters, the indoor Cherry Hill cost just $300,000 yet boasted no less than four tile-and-coping pools of various configurations, together with a half-pipe, three-quarter pipe and two reservoirs; the preferred Egg Bowl pool was described by Glen Friedman as 'the masterpiece of all time'.[41]

Not to be outdone, in November 1978 Dogtown finally acquired its own skatepark at Marina del Rey, south of Venice Beach. Designed and managed by Ray Allen (later by Ivan Hosoi) and owned by Dennis Ogden, the skatepark sported speakers set into riding surfaces, shadow-free lighting and the superlative Dogbowl modelled after the famous local pool (Figure 5.6).[42] Cherry Hill and Marina del Rey rapidly acquired reputations as advanced pool-oriented destinations, the latter even featuring in Devo's 'Freedom of Choice' video (1980) and the 'Hot Shots' television programme (Toby Keeler, 1981) (Figure 7.10).

As Cherry Hill indicates, states beyond California were also further responding to the expanding skateboard scene. Other advanced facilities included Get-A-Way (Huntsville, Alabama), designed by Bill Underwood and described by Variflex pros as one of the best skateparks ever. Here, substantial New York backing funded a 4 m keyhole and other pools, extended snake run, special lighting, sound system, ultra-smooth finishing by Bigelow, and even a terrifying over-vertical cradle-like bowl – yet the park suffered from its Alabama location and consequently poor media coverage.[43] More

well-known was Apple (Columbus, Ohio), designed by Hollyday and Peter Drotlef and constructed by Bigelow. This 3,700 m² indoor skatepark had no fewer than eight pools, including egg-, kidney- and keyhole-shaped variants, plus a half-pipe with over-vertical extensions. Contrasting with the poor quality of even supposedly advanced facilities like Del Mar Skate Ranch, whose cheaply made keyhole pool suffered from mismatched walls, kinked transitions and lumpy surfaces, construction at Apple and other new skateparks was now finally attaining a high standard, through techniques like piano-wire shaping templates and grey-coat cement finishing.[44]

In response, many of the slightly older skateparks added distinctive pools. For Fort Lauderdale's Solid Surf and Whittier's Skate City these were relatively simple keyhole-shaped affairs,[45] but for Pipeline the freestyle area was replaced in 1979 with the hugely influential and infamous Combi-Pool – partly based on the local L-Pool, and effectively a 9.75 m wide and 3.65 m deep square pool with tightly rounded corners and a 9.1 m diameter and 3.35 m deep circular pool, joined together at a pronounced hip and shared shallow entrance, and sporting huge

Figure 7.13
James Parry in the marbelite pool of Rom skatepark (1979).
© Iain Borden.

Figure 7.14
Rodga Harvey tail-
blocks the formidable
P-Bowl at Solid Surf,
Harrow (1981).
© Tim Leighton-
Boyce/R.A.D. Archive.

hand-poured coping. Designed by Don Hoffman in collaboration with skateboarders like Steve Alba, Micke Alba, Tay Hunt, Chris Strople and Tom Inouye (some of whom donated towards costs), and constructed by Bigelow for around $30,000, the Combi-Pool was a backyard pool on steroids, with increased depth (and hence more danger), greater areas of wall (around 1 m of vertical), faster transitions from base to wall, a flat bottom between walls and a smoother surface. The shallow end, clenched square-pool corners and central hip presented further riding variations, and the overall result – evident in much 1980s footage, from the 1981 'Eye on LA' television programme to the 1989 *Streets on Fire* video – was 'unquestionably the finest, most demanding terrain ever developed for skating' and the 'ultimate playground' (Figures 7.11 and 7.12).[46]

The Combi-Pool consequently lays strong claim to being skateboarding's Parthenon, fusing severely attuned design, awe-inspiring appearance and a semi-mythic aura unmatched by any other skatepark architecture. In 1999 (and refreshed in 2010) Vans even replicated the pool inside their Orange County skatepark; indeed, the reborn Combi-Pool still 'dares even

the most experienced skater,' and since 2005 has hosted the Vans Pool Party event (Figure 4.10).[47]

Following the original Combi-Pool's success and substantial *SkateBoarder* reporting, other skateparks responded, notes Alba, with 'crazier pools to bring in the masses, attract pros and get magazine coverage'. For example, Solid Surf (Fort Lauderdale) commissioned a peanut bowl designed by Alan Gelfand and Kevin Peterson, Ranch (Colton) constructed a rose-tinted Hollyday-designed bowl for a 1980 Gold Cup competition and Skateboard World (Lakewood) opened a clam-shaped pool in July 1981.[48]

Skatepark development was now big business; during 1997 and 1978 Skatepark Constructors, California Skateboard Parks, Campo Construction, Wizard, International Sports & Recreation Corporation, Solid Surf and Hi-Flite all advertised design, construction and information services in *SkateBoarder*. Build costs averaged between $200,000 and $250,000 in the late 1970s (although smaller skateparks could require only $60,0000).[49] A few, however, were considerably more expensive, such as the $1.3 million Big O and $1 million Get-A-Way.[50] Whatever the expense, by 1982 between 200 and

400 skateparks had been built across thirty-five US states; at least forty-eight were in California, twenty-two in Florida and sixteen in Texas.[51] At one point, the San Diego area supported no less than nine ventures, including Del Mar Skate Ranch, Whirlin' Wheels (Escondido), Carlsbad, Skateboard Heaven (Spring Valley), Oasis, El Cajon, La Mesa, Moving-On (Home Avenue) and Surf de Earth (Vista). Many also attracted large memberships – 2,000 skateboarders joined Olympic skatepark in Washington State.[52]

Global Skateparks

Given skateboarding's global reach, this construction activity was unsurprisingly repeated throughout Europe, South America and Asia, where many ventures mimicked their US precedents. In the UK, skateboarding took off in the summer of 1976, with *Skateboard!* quickly championing skatepark construction. By late summer 1977, these already included the Skate-Escape (Portland Bill) facility, built by Lorne Edwards after visiting Anaheim's Concrete Wave, Stalybridge Bowl (near Manchester) and Watergate Bowl (near Newquay's surfing scene). However, as with early US skateparks these were unchallenging

terrains, leaving British skaters hungering for more advanced facilities.[53]

The UK's first commercial skatepark with vertical walls was the £100,000 Skate City, built by Skate Park Construction and designed by Richard Wrigley, which opened in London's Tooley Street in the summer of 1977; most famous of its three runs was the 'advanced pipeline' Black Bowl (Figure 5.10).[54] More complex skateparks appeared in 1978, including Malibu Dog Bowl (Nottingham) and Skateboard City (Bolton).[55] With many different investment (Tate & Lyle), swimming pool (Skate Park Construction, an offshoot of Rainbow Pools), tennis court (En-tout-cas) and building construction (Bovis) companies now entering the market, standards were unsurprisingly variable, while the Greater London Council, National Playing Fields Association and Sports Council all struggled to supply useful advice. The barely ridable Malibu Dog Bowl, for example, suffered from severe transitions, overly gentle descents, numerous obstructions and distracting spotlights.[56]

Somewhat improved were the mid-1978 'second generation' skateparks, including Southsea's

Figure 7.15
La Villette skatepark, Paris (1979).
© Tim Leighton-Boyce/R.A.D. Archive.

£50,000 En-tout-cas-designed mogul field and bowls.[57] The gunite Skateopia (Knebworth House, Hertfordshire), designed by High-Point Developments and constructed by Trant, offered a snake run, bowls and half-pipe, while the indoor Rolling Thunder (Brentford, London) contained numerous quirky bowls and an extended half-pipe, all designed by Wrigley (Figure 5.5).[58] Other notable skateparks included Skateworld (Wokingham), Earth'n'Ocean (Barnstaple), Kelvingrove Wheelies (Kelvingrove), Skateopia (Wolverhampton), Skatestar (Guildford), Spandrel Skate-Dome (Uxbridge), Arrow (Wolverhampton), Roxyskate (Doncaster) and others in Plymouth, Southport and Stevenage.[59] In 1979 the indoor Skateslalom (Colne) arrived, whose 3.65 m pool Shogo Kubo described as the best in England.[60] Another late arrival was the 1981 Rock 'n Roll (Livingston), where architect Iain Urquhart achieved near-perfect transitions via a template 'transition machine', and whose pool was based on Marina del Rey's keyhole.[61]

Other UK skateparks – principally the shotcrete projects designed by G-Force and Adrian Rolt and built by Skate Park Construction – also drew heavily on US precedents. This series included Barn (Brighton), Beachcomber (Hemsby), Black Lion (Gillingham), Kidderminster Safari Park (West Midlands), Locomotion (Hemel Hempstead), Mad Dog Bowl (London), Rom (Hornchurch), Skatecountry (Bristol) and Solid Surf (Harrow), with varying terrains drawn from a standardized repertoire of half-pipe, snake run, moguls, large concrete bowl, keyhole pool and reservoir. The centrepiece keyhole pool was derived from the Skateboard Heaven (Spring Valley) pool, itself based on the local Soul Bowl, meaning that a specific backyard pool had now been transplanted across the Atlantic (Figure 7.13). Kidderminster's version – a 'really heavy pool' – measured 3 m deep and 6.7 m across, its blue tiles, coping and white 'marbelite' surface loudly proclaiming its Californian origins; when I skated this pool bareback under a blue sky in 1979 alongside fellow British skaters, we imagined ourselves amid those Californian wonderlands we had so avidly devoured in *Skateboard!* and *SkateBoarder*. Footage of a blond-haired Mark Baker at Harrow's Solid Surf similarly captures these imitative scenes.[62] American associations were further strengthened by the large 4.6 m Performance Bowl (aka P-Bowl) at Rom and Harrow (Figure 7.14), which was based on the Autry-designed 4.9 m Vertibowl at California's Skatepark Paramount (1978), where the cavernous sunken

section was extended by 1.5 m of above-ground vertical.[63] In many ways, however, such deep designs were too challenging, even for professionals. Consequently Rom's P-Bowl quickly had its upper walls removed, while Solid Surf's version was later filled in.

British skateboarders also benefited from innumerable community facilities. These ranged from lone half-pipes, such as the steel-framed version in Barton (Oxford), where I learned to skate vertical, to the larger concrete Stockwell (Brixton, London). Other free-access facilities included a DIY venture in Hereford and Meanwhile Gardens in London's Westbourne Park, led by sculptor Jamie McCullough and partly designed by Marc Sinclair.[64] In the United States, community skateparks included Santa Cruz's Derby (1976, designed by Ken Wormhoudt), Maryland's Ocean Bowl (1976), San Francisco's Dish, Rhode Island's Yagoo Valley (1976), Irvine's University Community Park (1977) and Tampa's Bro Bowl (1978) (Figure 13.6). Although given infrequent magazine coverage, these open-access facilities were nonetheless fertile skateboarding grounds, particularly as they often survived longer than most commercial skateparks; the 'pads-optional, barbecue-friendly, go-to' Derby, for example, stars in *Sick Boys* (1988), *Goin' Off* (1989) and *Streets on Fire* (1989), where skaters fly gleefully over its sinuous banks.[65]

During this period, other skateparks constructed worldwide included those in Belgium, Germany, Guatemala, Ireland, Netherlands, Puerto Rico and Switzerland.[66] Stockholm's indoor New Sport House (1978), later seen in *I Like It Here Inside My Mind* (2016), offered not only an egg-shaped bowl and five ramps but what owner Alf Eriksson called a 'total human environment' with café, music, film screenings and street-aesthetic décor by artist Joakim Mansen.[67] In Canada, West Vancouver Park (August 1977) was the country's first concrete skatepark, quickly followed by the indoor Skateboard Palace in nearby Burnaby and Ontario Skateboard Park.[68] Fourteen months later Seylynn Bowl in north Vancouver – designed by Nelson Holland and today Canada's oldest skatepark – offered a surf-style snake run terminating in a bowl.[69] Among further significant ventures were Caracola Bowl (Argentina); West Hobart in Tasmania, Doveton, Northland, Nunawading, Parkdale, Ringwood, Skate City and Melton in Melbourne, Phillip in Canberra, and North Ryde and Manly Skate City in New South Wales (Australia); Campo Grande in Rio de Janeiro, Wave Park in São Paulo and

Anchieta Keyhole (refurbished 2015) in Belo Horizonte (Brazil); Béton Hurlant and La Villette (Figure 7.15) in Paris, and Skatepark Erromardie at St-Jean de Luz (France); Torino Roller Disco in Turin (Italy); California, Yoyogi and Hewajima in Tokyo and Matsudo Park (Japan); Skapistas de Mexico and Dogtown (Mexico); Marlborough Park in Takapuna (New Zealand); Camino Royal in Lima (Peru); Cresta Wave in Johannesburg (South Africa); and Syndicale in Madrid and Skate Club Catalunya near Barcelona (Spain).[70]

Most of these skateparks boasted features derived from US found spaces, hence the startling full-pipes that appeared in locations as diverse as Skateland in Gothenburg (Denmark), Skateside in Kettering (UK), Park de Carolina in Quito (Ecuador), New Lynn in Auckland (New Zealand) and Skatopistas del Sol in Guadalajara (Mexico). Many skatepark names were also derived from US precedents and/or surfing, as Earth'n'Ocean (UK), Surf News (South Africa) and Tiquius Skate and Surf (Mexico) all demonstrate.[71]

Closure, Dereliction, Destruction

By the late 1970s, skateparks were a global phenomenon, this new architectural type – all but unknown just a few years earlier – now being established in hundreds if not thousands of cities worldwide. Yet, with a handful of exceptions, the ambitious commercial ventures of the 1970s did not usually prove financially viable. Already in 1978 many US skateparks were insolvent after lavish costs had necessitated admission fees of between three and six dollars per two-hour session, and by 1980 most had closed.[72] A year later in Florida, only Sensation Basin, Bro Bowl and Kona still survived; today Kona is the United States's oldest privately run skatepark, owned by the Ramos family since 1979.[73] US skateboard sales tumbled from $166 million in 1977 to $64 million in 1978, while in the UK sales also plummeted after their Christmas 1977 peak.[74] Even renowned US skateparks faced problems: Cherry Hill and Apple resorted to weekend-only opening, and by 1982 Pipeline was lucky to attract fifteen customers each week.[75]

Declining magazine publicity and professional patronage added to the misery. After the 1979 disappearance of *Skateboard World*, *National Skateboard Review*, *Skates East*, *Skate*, *SkateRider* and *Wild World of Skateboarding*, only *SkateBoarder* remained among US magazines, only to transmogrify into the 'sports/lifestyle' *SkateBoarder's Action Now* (August 1980) and *Action Now* (May 1981), covering the 'new age sports' of snowboarding, windsurfing, bodyboarding and BMX.[76] The decline also affected skateboard companies and their team riders – of 175 pros in the 1980 US Gold Cup series, within a year only fifteen were left. In January 1982 *Action Now* published its last issue.

Insurance was yet another problem, particularly in the United States, where, despite skateparks maintaining low 1:200 injury-per-participant ratios, the inevitable accidents lead to entanglement with the prevalent US liability culture. 'Every parent of a kid with a broken wrist', recalled Big O's manager Gerry Hurtado, 'wanted to grab a lawyer and sue for the one-mil cash out.' As a result, by 1978 many skateparks found meaningful insurance difficult to obtain. Frank Nasworthy wound up Cadillac Wheels Skateboard Concourse after insurance costs rocketed five hundred per cent. Pipeline did without insurance altogether, while other skateparks resorted to legally dubious liability releases.[77] In 1998, California would eventually legislate for limited skatepark liability, so deterring riders from suing skateparks, but this was two decades away.[78] A further threat often emerged when a skatepark's lease ran out and developers spotted more profitable uses for the land.[79]

Faced with these commercial, publicity, legal and urban challenges, many early skateparks like Concrete Wave (Anaheim), Skatopia (Buena Park) and Whirlin' Wheels (Escondido) had already closed by 1980, while California's third generation facility Big O ceased operations in 1981, rapidly followed by Marina del Rey and Oasis. In 1982 Skateboard World (Lakewood) became a McDonald's, Skate City (Whittier) and Carlsbad closed a year later, Runway (Carson) turned into a motorhome showroom, Hi-Roller (Boulder, Colorado) condominiums and Ranch (Colton) a ploughed field.[80] Del Mar Skate Ranch and Pipeline struggled on, but in July 1987 Del Mar closed to be replaced by a hotel complex, while Pipeline's final demolition came in 1989, as later shown in *Bones Brigade: An Autobiography* (2012).[81] To the east, Cherry Hill perished in 1981.[82] In Florida, Skateboard USA disappeared in early 1978 and by 1980 some seventy-five per cent of its skateparks had already vanished.[83] Of around one hundred UK skateparks, during 1978 many closed almost as soon as they opened, and only twenty or so remained by the decade's end; by 1982 most had gone forever.[84] Many met an ignoble fate; the derelict Chester's Inner City Truckers filled

Figure 7.16
Crystal Palace half-
pipe, London (1982).
© Tim Leighton-
Boyce/R.A.D. Archive.

Figure 7.18
The Lexan and aluminium Turningpoint ramp. *Skateboard Madness* (Hal Jepsen Films, dir. Julian Pena, 1979).
www.bit.ly/TurningPoint-SkateboardMadness

Figure 7.17
Steve Caballero at the Mount Trashmore half-pipe, Virginia (1985).
© Jim Goodrich.

up with stagnant rain water while its owner languished in jail after embezzling membership fees.[85] France's Béton Hurlant and La Villette both died in 1979.[86]

Most of these skateparks were demolished or filled in, but some survived as ruins or semi-buried, such as the three-quarter pipe of Big O, while skaters recognized these archaeological treasures by scavenging coping and other fragments as mementoes or even for reuse on ramps. And although a handful of facilities like the American Kona and the British Rom, Harrow, Livingston, Stevenage and Southsea have endured, often through the patronage of BMX and scooter riders, by the early 1980s the first skatepark era was well and truly over.

Mutant Wood

Although the 1970s phase of concrete skateparks had finished, salvation was nonetheless at hand. From around 1976 onwards, skaters had increasingly explored homemade wooden ramps. At first these were typically mono-pitch surfaces, fabricated by riders in locations without any nearby skateparks or backyard pools. In 1976 *SkateBoarder* enthusiastically promoted makeshift wooden banks in Florida as a 'hot-wired reality' ready to be copied across the United States, while Skitch Hitchcock constructed his fibreglass transportable The Wave, replete with a porthole for photography.[87] Between 1976 and 1977, Ramp Rider advertised ramp plans in *SkateBoarder,* and *Skateboard!* published schematics for a 1.5 m high and 40° flat-angled construction.[88] More prosaically, many skaters 'lumber liberated' 8 x 4 ft wood sheets from building sites, tilting them up against ledges and benches to form a crude but enjoyable riding surface.[89]

As many skateparks closed in the late 1970s, skaters further exploited these improvised devices, and by 1980 Rampage had sold 4,000

blueprints across forty-six countries. 'The answer to these blues lies close at hand', proclaimed *SkateBoarder*. 'The answer is ramps.'[90]

Half-Pipes

Unlike the typical lean-to ramps of the mid-1970s, the versions developed in the late 1970s onwards were often independently standing, curved-profile structures. Typically of timber construction, the most common of these later ramps is the 'half-pipe', referring to the U-section profile and parallel side-walls. One of the first was Mark Lake's backyard version in Florida's Indialantic (1977), as featured in *Skateboard Madness*. Like most early half-pipes – including Tom Stewart's 6-m-diameter Rampage construction in Encinitas, California, heavily featured in *SkateBoarder*, the Nelson half-pipe in Vancouver and Patton's Ramp in Blackburn, Australia – Lake's was a classic half-circle, providing a compressed riding experience, like a scaled-down version of an Arizona desert full-pipe.[91]

From around 1979 ramps also subtly changed, with a flat bottom commonly being inserted between the two transitions, thus providing skaters with greater time between moves on the opposing walls. This invention featured at Sweden's Eurocana Summer Camp and was subsequently popularized in the United States via Powell-Peralta professionals in 1980, although many skaters worldwide were in fact already slotting flat bottoms into ramps during the late 1970s; for example, Florida's 1978 Hollywood ramp included a short flat insertion, as did Oxford's Barton ramp.[92] The overall height of these half-pipes has typically varied between 2 and 5 m, walls being topped by a narrow platform. Riding surfaces are usually plywood (often two layers of 9 mm birch ply) or Masonite (oil-tempered hardboard), and occasionally thin steel. Coping is also added as 40 to 60 mm steel tubing or even pool-

Figure 7.19
The famous Animal Chin ramp.
The *Search for Animal Chin*
(Powell-Peralta, dir. Stacy Peralta,
1987).
www.bit.ly/Ramp-AnimalChin

style stone. Although elliptical curves are sometimes used, the transitions are commonly a pure quarter-circle with a constant radius of between 2 and 5 m, which can be more easily fabricated. Other features can include wall-top modifications such as channels (cut-outs), escalators (sloping coping sections), extensions (tombstone-like additions) and spines (ramps joined back-to-back).

By the mid-1980s, half-pipes had become so popular that a 1983 *Thrasher* issue offering ramp-building plans sold out, followed by a stand-alone detailed guide on building 'a radical, wooden skateboard ramp'.[93] Some famous 1980s and early 1990s constructions included those at Eurocana, Skatemates ramp (Amsterdam), Parkhill Road (Melbourne), Bourges (France), Monza (Italy) and a series of government-funded half-pipes across Venezuela, plus British versions at places like Hastings, Swansea, Farnborough, Warrington's Empire State Building and London's Latimer Road and Crystal Palace (Figure 7.16).[94]

Significant US 1980s examples included those owned by John Grigley (St. Pete), Lance Mountain (Alhambra), Joe Lopes (San Leandro), Jay Moore (Eagle Rock) and Joe Johnson (Fort Collins), plus others like The Ark (Fresno), Blue Ramp and Clown Ramp (Dallas), Bran Ramp (Rochester), Cambodia III (Miami), Cedar Crest Country Club (Virginia), Farm Ramp (Raleigh), Hell Ramp (Chesapeake) and Mile High (Lake Tahoe). The 16.75 m wide Great Desert Ramp at Palmdale, documented in *Sierra Highway* (Jeff Ryckebosch, 2009), sported numerous extensions and a roll-in channel, while Debbie McAddo's 9.75 m wide and 3.2 m high Ramp Ranch (Atlanta) incorporated roll-out decks and a 1.2 m wide canyon jump. The Mount Trashmore (Virginia Beach) ramp later featured strongly in videos like *Future Primitive* (1985) and *Stoked* (2002) (Figure 7.17). Professionals

like Lance Mountain, Steve Caballero, Ken Park and Jeff Kendall also fabricated ramps; Kendall's had transitions emulating Apple skatepark, whereas Caballero's larger ramp transitions facilitated knee-slides when bailing.[95]

As this implies, ramps partly replicated skatepark half-pipes and bowls. More complicated versions, however, were also being built for demonstrations and competitions, hence encouraging advanced skateboarding and novel viewing opportunities. During 1977 and 1978, these included metal-framed devices surfaced in transparent acrylic (Plexiglas) or polycarbonate (Tuffac or Lexan), including the Hi-Flite/Firestone, Imperial Century/Pepsi and Tracker ramps, which proved extremely popular at American football games and similar spectacles.[96] Most famous of all was the aluminium-framed and Lexan-surfaced Turningpoint, a 6-m-diameter capsule-shaped device used for a 1979 US exhibition tour. Accompanied by a similar bowl, the $250,000 portable Turningpoint capsule was designed by Scott Senatore to be inclined at an angle, with riders climbing a ladder before dropping in from the upper open end and carving the hemispherical lower section – in effect, a see-through hybrid of full-pipes, bowls and later skatepark cradles. Turningpoint was an immediate media success, featuring in *SkateBoarder*, *Going for It* and the worldwide press, plus the *Skateboard Madness* film with which it shared investors (Figure 7.18).[97]

Although Turningpoint was an iconic invention, its capsule design restricted riding lines, and, according to Peralta, made skaters feel like hamsters in a wheel.[98] During the 1980s, more expansive multi-section ramps appeared, such as the Vision's 'Skate Escape' competition ramp (1988) where main and subsidiary half-pipes were linked by spine and roll-in transfers. In another variation, the massive 30-m-long

Figure 7.20
Daewon Song and Chris Haslam
have a mini-ramp skate-fest.
Cheese & Crackers (Almost, 2006).
www.bit.ly/SongHaslam-
CheeseCrackers

Boomer Ramp (1987), L-shaped in plan with a bowled-out corner, was constructed at San Jose's Raging Waters park, and featured extensively in *Wheels of Fire* and *Goin' Off*.[99] The same year, the most famous of all 1980s ramps was constructed by Tim Payne for *The Search for Animal Chin*, a fantastical fabrication with roll-ins, channels, extensions, escalators, spine, trap-door route and platform-level mini-ramp (Figure 7.19). Demolished immediately after filming, the Animal Chin ramp was subsequently re-created for a 2016 video shoot, before being moved to Woodward West skate camp.

No doubt inspired by *Animal Chin*, a year later Hawk's four-acre Fallbrook home sprouted a $30,000 Masonite half-pipe and bowl joined by a spine, which also became famous after starring in Powell-Peralta videos; in *Ban This*, slow-motion 35 mm footage, unusual angles, pink-hued night-time lighting and effects-laden music add to Hawk's otherworldly manoeuvres.[100] A later Hawk ramp, located in an Irvine warehouse, was a $15,000 Payne-constructed affair measuring 14.6 m wide and 3.65 m high, while his 2010s Vista-based indoor facility, with reconfigurable panels, cost a cool $600,000 to install.[101]

Mini-Ramps
Far removed from the 'Skate Escape', *Animal Chin* and Hawk ramp extravagances, mini-ramps became increasingly common during the 1980s, these being 1- to 2-m-high affairs fabricated relatively cheaply for everyday locations. Although full-size half-pipe riders sometimes dismissed mini-ramp skaters – 'Kids just want to do an ollie grab finger-flipple-kipple-thing', complained Gary Valentine – mini-ramps proved highly popular with both locals searching for ridable terrain and authorities keen on lower-risk facilities.[102] Significantly, while skateparks required substantial user-bases to survive, and so were often connected to larger

cities, leisure attractions and transport networks, mini-ramps popped up among thousands of smaller communities and private residences; in the early 1990s, UK manufacturers like Zebra, Rareunit and Freestyle installed mini-ramps in relatively minor places like Bootle, Chelmsford, Ilchester and Chesham.[103] By the mid-2000s, as displayed in Almost's 'snack-size mini-ramp video' *Cheese & Crackers* (2006), skaters worldwide used mini-ramps to perform intricate moves at innumerable accessible locations (Figure 7.20).

Even more diminutive ramps and obstacles were created for streetstyle courses and individual use, ranging from simple quarter-pipes, pyramids and snowplough shapes to handrails, ledges and other elements mimicking typical urban streets. Low (less than 1 m high), flat-angled jump ramps were especially popular in the late 1980s.[104]

Many of these half-pipes and mini-ramps also encouraged craft handiwork, with skateboarders as 'enterprising individuals with a few tools and a little wood' being actively involved in the design and construction of their own architecture, as when Southern Ute Indian Tribe skaters fabricated a 3 m half-pipe with $5,000 of municipal funds.[105] These ramps can also be ad hoc urban implants; to cite one example, in late 1980s Los Angeles, Lance Mountain fabricated a 1.5 m half-pipe for Stacy Peralta in the backyard of his Skolnik House, which had been designed by renowned modernist architect Rudolph Schindler in 1952.[106]

As disruptive architectural insertions, ramps also equate with other forms of skaterly disarray. 'In skating, nothing is defined, everything can be new,' proclaimed Dan Adams. 'There are no laws.'[107] For example, in 1986 the co-operative Tennessee Half-Pipe Company created the ramp-based World's Unfair on a

Figure 7.21
Bob Burnquist's Dreamland
MegaRamp. *Dreamland: A
Backyard Progression* (2013).
www.bit.ly/Burnquist-MegaRamp

former exposition site. Lasting only ten months, the World's Unfair was a perfect example of ramp adaptability, allowing temporary land appropriation to take place during an interlude between more legitimized uses.[108]

With appropriation, however, often comes conflict, the rumbling, thumps and grinds of ramp-riding often interfering noisily with quiet neighbourhoods. Some residents also objected to 'ugly' makeshift ramp materials. 'It's an obscene edifice, it should be chopped down this minute,' demanded one irate Californian of a neighbourhood ramp.[109] Indeed, where local ordinances allowed, some 1980s ramps were removed for creating 'visible nuisances'. With similar objections lodged across the United States, by 1990 it had become nearly impossible to build substantial ramps in, for example, the more populated areas of Los Angeles.[110] In Norway, where skateboarding was entirely banned in 1979, skaters like Lars Petter Lunder and Jason d'Ancona even resorted to camouflaging their ramps in isolated woods.[111]

MegaRamps

If the *Animal Chin* ramp seemed extraordinary, and in complete contrast to mini-ramps, far more dramatic constructions were still to come.

In 1999 Andy Macdonald was experimenting with a 91 m long and 11 m high ramp to break the long distance jump world record.[112] Similarly extreme were Danny Way's exploits, as documented in *Waiting for Lightning* (Jacob Rosenberg, 2012). Having undertaken some daring media stunts in 1997 – like dropping from a helicopter onto the DC Shoes 5.5 m high Super Ramp, plus setting the highest aerial world record at 5.03 m – Way began covertly testing still larger ramps in the Californian desert. In 2003 at the Point X skatepark camp in Temecula, Way used one of the earliest MegaRamps to set new world records for both distance jumping (22.86 m) and highest air (7.16 m).[113] Even more flamboyantly, *The DC Video* (Greg Hunt, 2003) showed Way performing heelflips, boardslides and nose-grinds on a rail atop the MegaRamp's quarter-pipe. Still not content, Way famously jumped the 21 m wide Great Wall of China in 2005, using a 30 m high launch ramp to make a 55 mph leap over the wall.[114] Most recently, at California's Cuyamaca mountains in 2015, Way set a highest air world of 7.77 m, a feat that necessitated the tallest-ever 25.9 m high ramp for Way's drop-in, plus a connecting run-in, launch quarter-pipe and 17 m landing section.[115] Even a 'basic' jump on a 'normal' MegaRamp is breath-taking deed, as described by Josh Dean.

Figure 7.22
Arto Saari and others at Radlands, Northampton. *Scorchin' Summer* (Thrasher, 1999).
www.bit.ly/Radlands-
ScorchinSummer

Figure 7.23
One of the numerous
sections of Adrenaline
Alley skatepark, Corby
(2017).
© Iain Borden.

You roll in from a platform the height of a five-storey building, reach 40 or 50 miles per hour on the 180-foot approach, then launch over a 50-foot gap, land on a downslope, and zip toward a 30-foot-high quarterpipe that propels you another 15 to 25 feet into the air. You'll need to land back on the near-vertical face of that quarterpipe, and not on the deck up top or the flat bottom below, either of which spells almost certain injury.[116]

Given the spectacular nature of such stunts, and tapping in to what Kotler identifies as 'the rise of superman' among action sports practitioners like Way, since 2004 the televisual X Games has unsurprisingly incorporated a MegaRamp event, on which skaters launch their staggering jumps.[117] At the 2014 Austin event, for example, Tom Schaar's gold-medal-winning run consisted of a backside 720° leap followed by a 900° air, completed despite wayward footing and fierce headwinds.[118]

Other skaters have also undertaken sensational exploits, notably Bob Burnquist at his private Dreamland facility (Figure 7.21) in San Diego County, including jumps from and onto

helicopters. Dreamland's $280,000 MegaRamp (2006) was funded by Oakley and Hurley, eating up 400 sheets of plywood.[119] In Flip's *Extremely Sorry* (2009), Burnquist even skated a rail extended over the Grand Canyon, before skydiving into the chasm below, while four years later, Norwegian Adil Dyani completed a world record 'bomb drop', leaping off a raised platform to plunge 9.39 m onto a quarter-pipe below.[120]

Wooden Skateparks

Apart from ramps as free-standing half-pipes, urban insertions or pumped-up MegaRamps, wood can also form entire skateparks. Although a few indoor skateparks had appeared in the 1970s – such as Skate-Away in Nanuet, New York, the 1,850 m² Zero Gravity in Cambridge, Massachusetts and Arrow in Wolverhampton, UK – this typology truly took off in the 1980s and 1990s.[121] Whereas rain eradicates wheel traction, low temperatures increase injury when falling and high temperatures can restrict skating to evenings, indoor skateparks typically allow for all-day, all-year-round skateboarding. Taking advantage of these benefits, significant mid-1980s ramp-based skateparks included Bike Haus (Arizona),

Charleston Hangar Bowl (South Carolina), Jeff Phillips Skatepark (Dallas), Rotation Station (Illinois), Mike McGill's Skatepark (Carlsbad), Skatepark of Houston (Houston), Eat Concrete (Omaha) and Kevin Harris's Richmond Skate Ranch (Vancouver). Others emerged all over the United States, including Skatehut (Rhode Island), Middle School and Ramp House (North Carolina), Ratz (Maine), Skate Zone (Atlanta) and another Mike McGill's Skatepark (Tampa). Powell-Peralta even constructed its own SkateZone private training facility.[122]

More than 120 skateparks across the United States were in operation in 1992, rising to over 165 in 1997, by which time nearly half were indoor wooden facilities.[123] Significantly, many of these new skateparks were also owned and managed by skaters, a factor that undoubtedly contributed to their success.[124] Alternatively, some – such as San Jose's Kennedy warehouse, the Powell-Peralta facility in Amsterdam and another warehouse in the UK's Dewsbury – were member-only affairs, this arrangement helping with finance and insurance.[125]

In other countries, indoor ramp-based skateparks in the 1980s and 1990s ranged from the elaborate, such as Ultra (São Paulo, Brazil), Thomas i. Punkt (Hamburg, Germany), Titus Warehouse (Münster, Germany), Fryshuset (Stockholm, Sweden) and Bryggeriet (Malmö, Sweden), to the moderate, such as Simon's Skatepark (Dublin, Ireland) and the extremely basic, such as Hobbies (Bandung, Indonesia).[126] In the UK, ramp skateparks included Skate Shack (Barrow-in-Furness), Skate & Ride (Bristol), Pioneer (St. Albans), Rock City (Hull), Fast Eddies (Whitley Bay), Fearless Ramp Base (Essex), Liverpark (Liverpool), Mount Hawke (Cornwall), Radlands (Northampton) (Figure 7.22), Re-Hab (Wakefield) and Ewer Street Arches, Spitalfields and Playstation (London), the latter being founded by music promoter Paul McDermott (1997) and later re-launched as the Nike-sponsored BaySixty6 (2012).[127]

Some of the significant advantages enjoyed by ramp-based skateparks over their 1970s concrete predecessors were fast and cheap above-ground construction, which in turn allowed for the exploitation of less expensive out-of-town warehouses; the original Radlands, spread over 880 m², was fabricated in just ten days by Payne using skateboarder labour.[128] Far more varied terrain was also possible. In 1997 Wakefield boasted a vert-ramp, mini-ramp with escalator and volcano features, vert-wall, jump boxes, free-standing spine, driveways, handrails, hips, wallie pole, banks and quarter-pipes. Even professionals were impressed. 'Wakefield's the best skatepark I've ever skated,' proclaimed Arron Bleasdale, 'There's shit everywhere.'[129]

The intimidating 1970s concrete skateparks had often been built, reflected *Thrasher*, with the idea that 'very radical structures are somehow challenging to skateboarders,' whereas, in fact, 'nothing could be further from the truth.' Instead of deep bowls, pro-standard pools and overhanging pipes, the wooden 1990s skateparks offered ramps in myriad sizes and combinations. 'Modern skatepark design is a mixture of the urban environment and suggestions of skateboarders,' concluded *Thrasher*. 'It is emphatically not the crazy, mogul-like fantasies of desk-bound architects. Skateparks are not like ballparks that have set rules regarding dimensions and playing surface.'[130] Consequently, skateparks like Radlands and Wakefield constantly modified their elements, creating ever-changing environments. Wakefield, remarked *Sidewalk*, 'breeds obstacles like the US government breeds genetic mutants.'[131] Metamorphosing terrains also encouraged new kinds of skateboarding, and generally kept skaters' interests alive; 'skating can't sustain,' argued *Thrasher*, 'if the terrain remains the same.'[132] In such a manner, skateparks had become low-cost, ever-morphing and occasionally ephemeral constructions specifically adapted to riders' preferences. Pro-design and anti-monumental, pro-creativity and anti-static, their forms and surfaces were skater-centred and subject to constant change.

In more recent years, some indoor wooden skateparks have continued to offer variable and makeshift constructions; Utah's aptly named Proving Grounds offered 3,000 m² of scattered quarter-pipes, wall-rides, rails and ledges, replete with harsh strip lighting and minimal ventilation.[133] Most others, however, have veered closer to concrete skateparks, often with bowl-like features and leisure-oriented facilities. For example, Skatepark of Tampa, initiated in 1993 with a vert-ramp, has evolved into a multi-purpose facility with an extensive street course, mini-ramps, elongated bowl, kids area and street courtyard, as well as skate shop, café, parents' lounge and art gallery. Similarly the 2,045 m² Adrenalin, Moscow's first indoor skatepark (2001), sported several bowls, vert-ramp, mini-ramp and other features, Eindhoven's 3,000 m² AreaFiftyOne (2002) today offers one of Europe's largest indoor wooden bowls, extensive

Figure 7.24
Rune Glifberg airs
over a Skatelite-
surfaced ramp at the
X Games, Los Angeles
(2007).
© Dustin Snipes/
Icon SMI/Icon Sport
Media/Getty Images.

street course, mini-ramp, skate shop, bar and music venue, and Mystic in Prague provides a similar range of ramps, bowls and club venue.[134] Australia's Monster skatepark in Sydney combines an indoor street course with outdoor vert- and mini-ramps, plus an iSkate Academy training programme.[135] In the UK, parks like Creation (Birmingham), Ramp City (Blackpool), Transition Extreme (Aberdeen), Adrenaline Alley (Corby) (Figure 7.23) and Better Extreme (Barking, London) (Figure 9.7) similarly offer substantial flow-bowls, spines, ramps, pipes, vert-walls and even foam pits for practising flip moves, and often sit alongside trampoline parks, climbing walls and other sports amenities.

Contemporary wooden construction techniques have also become more sophisticated, including specialist riding surface materials like Ramp Armor and SkateBlend; the popular paper-composite Skatelite can be printed with logos and graphics (Figure 7.24).[136] Mountain Dew's idiosyncratic Pinball skatepark (2011) in Auckland, New Zealand, even featured Plexiglas and wood fabrication, with elaborate pinball-style obstacles, graphics, sounds and scoring system.[137] These highly wrought designs, constructions and brandings also partly reflect a re-emergence of outdoor concrete skateparks during the twenty-first century, and this is where we now turn our attention.

Skateboarding
Chapter 8 Skatepark Renaissance

Comparatively few concrete skateparks were constructed during the 1980s. Rare exceptions included Spain's La Kantera in Algorta (1984, pool added 2001) and multi-bowl Alcobendas facility near Madrid (1980s), the narrow-channelled Death Bowl and snake run of Annaka (Japan), Pizzey on Australia's Gold Coast and Itagurá Country Club at Guaratinguetá (Brazil). For the municipal Berg Fidel at Münster (Germany, 1989), Claus Grabke and Titus Dittmann designed a snake run and prefabricated bowl. Breaking from US precedents, the latter was avowedly 'a pool for the nineties', with steel coping, narrow channel entry, 3 m transitions, 0.5 m of vertical wall and 3 m flat bottom – features that made it closer to wooden half-pipes than to backyard pools. In the US, occasional projects included Stone Edge (Daytona, Florida, 1989), a $750,000 'concrete paradise' designed by Bill Danforth, whose multiple pool-bowls, half-pipe and street arena featured briefly in *Ban This*.[1]

A few other skateparks also popped up in the 1990s, most notably Plage du Prado in Marseilles (1991), designed by architecture student Jean-Pierre Collinet, which quickly became a staple of European skateboarding tours (Figure 8.1).[2] Near Montpellier, Rooler Gab's one mile banked downhill course incorporated a ski lift for return transfers (1992), and the same year Livingston skatepark in Scotland was extended according to Kenny Omond designs. Around the same time, Slovenia enjoyed a new concrete pool at Kranj, Brazil's new ventures included Dominio with two half-pipes and reservoir and Macau gained a municipal facility in the Jardim Comendador Yo Hin.[3] In the United States, among smaller free-access facilities were the Frank Hawk–designed Dodge in Columbus, Ohio (1990), Northern California's Benicia, Palo Alto, Davis, Napa and San Francisco (1992), the Kevin Thatcher–designed Temecula (1996) and another in Yuba City (1997).[4]

A New Dawn

By the end of the 1990s onward, a veritable skatepark renaissance was underway. Fuelled by the popularity of street-skating, the X Games, *Tony Hawk's Pro Skater* video game (Activision, 1999), new legislation reducing liability claims, a slew of magazines worldwide and the emergent internet, skateboarding was on rise. In this new dawn, by the year 2000 over 180 skateparks of various sizes, complexity and ownership had already opened across the United States.[5]

Expert skatepark constructors like Airspeed, California Skateparks, Dreamland, Grindline, PTR/Placed To Ride, Purkiss Rose, SITE, Team Pain and Wormhoudt were also appearing. Today, similar expertise exists globally, from Convic in Australia, to Canvas, Freestyle, Gravity, Maverick and Wheelscape in the UK, or Constructo and The Edge in France, Mystic in the Czech Republic, G Ramps and LNDSKT in Germany and Beaver, Spectrum and New Line in Canada. Advanced construction and finishing processes are particular features of this new expertise, such as hand-finishing via specially shaped trowels and employing dedicated workers with personal skateboarding experience.[6] The results can be impressive. 'To say that Oregon's Newberg and Lincoln City skateparks are masterpieces is not an exaggeration', asserts Jocko Weyland. 'These works put their builders in league with artists like Richard Serra, Robert Smithson and James Turrell: the parks are beautiful environments, awesome to look at and, on some level, superior to sculpture because they combine aestheticism with athletic functionalism.'[7]

By 2004, there were nearly 200 skateparks in California alone, with more arriving every year; one guide listed thirty-nine of real substance in this state plus seventeen in Oregon and eleven each in Arizona and Washington.[8] Many were large, skilfully designed and carefully constructed endeavours, including Ocean Beach (San Diego, 2000), Coronado Island (San Diego County, 2001), Mission Valley YMCA (San Diego County, 2001), Fontana (San

Figure 8.1
Alex Chalmers and others ride
Marseilles skatepark. *Scorchin'*
Summer (Thrasher, 1999).
www.bit.ly/Marseille-
ScorchinSummer

Bernardino County, 2002), Etnies (Lake Forest, Orange County, 2003), Laguna Niguel (Orange County, 2003), Poway (San Diego County, 2003), Encinitas YMCA (San Diego County, 2004), Glendale (Los Angeles County, 2004) and Montclair (San Bernardino County, 2004).[9] After design input from Steve Alba, a 1,140 m² version of Pipeline was opened in San Bernardino County (2002), including a 6.1 m full-pipe.[10] In 2009 there were over 2,100 US skateparks, and around sixteen per cent of all Los Angeles neighbourhood parks included some kind of skateboarding facility; in 2014, some eighty-five per cent of US skaters lived within ten miles of a skatepark, skated at least once a week and had been skating for over five years.[11]

Some of these new skateparks were truly elaborate affairs. For example, the Vans skatepark (Orange County, 1999) has featured an enormous range of timber and concrete offerings, including in 2017 its version of the Combi-Pool plus a 1,850 m² indoor street course, warm-up section, 24 m wide mini-ramp and outdoor street course.[12] In 2002, the Orcas Island/Scott Stamnes Memorial Skatepark by Dreamland and Grindline in Washington State comprised complex intersections of flowing bowls, channels, walls, protrusions and bumps, creating a fluid 2,800 m² landscape (Figure 8.5). 'It's all about level changes,' explained Dreamland's Mark Hubbard, 'being on your board like it's a roller-coaster.'[13]

One year later, the Palm Springs skatepark incorporated a replica of the nearby Nude Bowl – a kidney-shaped desert-located swimming pool in the grounds of an abandoned Californian nudist colony that has been skated from the mid-1980s onwards. However, in sharp contrast to the original's rowdy parties and sporadic violence – offering a 'dirt-road approach, bathhouse ruins, blazing guns, all-night acid drops, Lucky Lager and generator-

powered mullet metal' – the Palm Springs version is highly regulated, replete with ultra-smooth transitions, shadow-free lighting, fenced enclosure, restrooms, refreshments and compulsory safety gear, and also hosts carefully staged competitions such as Eddie Elguera's annual El Gato Classic (Figure 8.2).[14]

As the Nude Bowl re-enactment suggests, for a few skaters some twenty-first century skateparks have become overly sanitized; 'too clean, too well-lit,' complained Mike Vallely.[15] Others facilities, however, were still robustly challenging in their designs, including those in Klamath Falls (Oregon), Carbondale (Colorado) and Hailey (Idaho). For example, Lincoln City (Oregon, 1999–2008) includes a cradle (bowled-out full-pipe section), while Dreamland's Hailey (2002) boasts a 4.9 m full-pipe that can be ridden both internally and externally, as does the 2,800 m² Goodyear Community (Phoenix, Arizona).[16] Dreamland's 2,700 m² Newberg skatepark (Oregon, 2000) sports intersecting bowls, channels and reservoirs, along with a volcano-shaped mound topped by a rotating metal drum.[17] Some skateparks have even resurrected features associated with 1970s skateparks, such as the snake runs at Lincoln City and Goodyear, while Winchester skatepark's distinctive 'washboard' feature reappeared in an elongated bowl in Monrovia and the Vans skatepark in Milpitas.[18]

Other significant US skateparks have included the nation's largest ever facility, the $6.5 million Spring/North Houston venture in Greenspoint (2014). This 7,250 m² Grindline-designed operation boasts a street course, 3.65 m vert-ramp, 3 m bowl, 'Texas-shaped' bowl and 'lazy river' pathway for novices (Figure 8.3).[19] Nearly as big is San Jose's 6,300 m² Lake Cunningham Regional Skatepark (2008). Designed by Wormhoudt and constructed by California Skateparks, Lake Cunningham claims the

Figure 8.2
El Gato Classic #3 in the Nude
Bowl re-creation, Palm Springs
skatepark (2017).
www.bit.ly/PalmSprings-ElGato

Figure 8.3
The $6.5 million Spring/North
Houston skatepark, Greenspoint,
Texas (Lance Childers, 2014).
www.bit.ly/SpringHouston

Figure 8.4
A timeless skatepark?
Stapelbäddsparken, Malmö. *Coping
Mechanism* (dir. Philip Evans, 2014).
www.bit.ly/Stapel-CopingMechanism

Figure 8.5
Skatepark as roller
coaster. Orcas Island,
Washington State
(2002).
© Dan Hughes.

world's largest vert-wall, plus a 6.1 m full-pipe
and 6.7 m cradle.[20] Also impressive is Grindline's
3,700 m² Volcom skatepark in Mammoth Lakes,
this time integrating skateable boulders into
its terrain. At 2,150 m², Oregon's Washington-
Jefferson skatepark (2014), nestled under
Interstate 105 in Eugene, is the largest outdoor
and under-cover facility in the United States,
built by Dreamland. The 2009 construction of
Venice Beach skatepark finally saw a significant
facility appear in the heart of Dogtown.[21]

Somewhat different in character are Evergreen's
designs, foregrounding flow over extreme
difficulty, challenging size or spectacular
features. Typifying this approach are Montana's
Thunder Park on the Blackfeet Reservation
(2014) and Mississippi's small Pidgeon Park in
Hernando (2015), the latter offering an ear-
shaped pattern of bowls, humps and curves
developed from a dirt-formed model.[22]

International Scene

This US activity has been paralleled by similar
developments worldwide. For example,
Canada's 7,000 m² Shaw Millennium Park
municipal venture opened in Calgary (2000),
offering a cloverleaf bowl, street courses
and full-pipe, and attracting 35,000 riders a
year.[23] Even more extravagant are some of
the skateparks in China, notably SMP in New
Jiangwan City, Shanghai (2005), designed by
Australia's Simon Oxenham and Convic. Named
after its backers, an action sports clothing
company, the $26 million SMP facility covers
13,700 m² of ridable terrain, making it at that
time the world's largest and most expensive
skatepark, including the world's widest vert-
ramp (52 m) and largest concrete skate bowl
(the 1,500 m² Mondo Bowl) (Figure 8.6). In 2015
came the even larger, 16,900 m² GMP skatepark
in Guangzhou (2015), constructed by Brad Shaw
and Eddie Liao of B&E Actionsports, where the

Figure 8.6
13,700 m² of ridable
terrain at SMP
skatepark,
Shanghai (2005).
Courtesy Convic
Pty Ltd.

vast terrain includes an international-standard combi-bowl, 79 m banked slalom run, full-pipe and street plaza.[24]

In Denmark, Copenhagen's 4,600 m² Faelledparken (2011), designed by skater-architect Søren Nordal Enevoldsen and Grindline, combines street areas with a vert-ramp and large bowl, including a famous overhanging section. In nearby Malmö, Sweden, the 3,000 m² Stapelbäddsparken (2005 onwards), according to project leader John Magnusson, is intended as 'a timeless skatepark, something that you never grow tired of'.[25] The complex arrangement of pool, flow-bowls, snake run, half-pipes and street course was laid out by Stefan Hauser of Placed To Ride along with local skaters, using their skaterly imaginations to drive the build process largely without blueprints or bureaucratic oversight (Figure 8.4).

In Australia, notable 2000s skateparks included Bondi (2004) and Five Dock (2007) in Sydney, Eaglehawk in Bendigo (2008), Cairns (2006), Frankston (2006), Nerang in Gold Coast (2009) and Victoria in Perth (2007).[26] Dreamland built the first modern skatepark cradle at Brixlegg, Austria (2001), while Wave House in Durban, South Africa, used design input from Tony Hawk and Andrew Morck to create 4,000 m² of terrain, including a 55 m snake run, kidney bowl, street course and vert-ramp.[27] Other notable skateparks built worldwide have included Strašnice in Prague (2001), Parque de Los Reyes in Santiago (2005), Switch Plaza in Shenzhen (2006), Cinecittà in Rome (2009), Pokhara in Nepal (2011), TKO in Hong Kong (2014), Terror in Tahoe in Tehran (2014), Skatepark Péitruss in Luxembourg (2016) and XDubai in Dubai (2016). Still others have appeared everywhere from Iceland, India and Singapore to Kenya, Peru and the Philippines. Perhaps the most surprising of all, given North Korea's anti-American ideology, is the large concrete skatepark (2013) in Pyongyang, constructed as part of the Ryugyong Health Complex.[28]

Municipalities and Social Enterprises

The majority of US and European skateparks in the 1970s were commercial enterprises, typically involving admission fees, membership cards, mandatory safety equipment and boundary fences. However, a few skateparks, like the US Derby and Bro Bowl (Figure 13.6) and the British Meanwhile Gardens, were free-spirited and open-access community affairs. Similarly, in the 1980s the Venezuelan and Swedish governments both backed skateboarding via funded ramps and skateboard clubs.[29] This enlightened attitude, however, did not truly take hold until the mid-2000s, when local politicians and charity workers increasingly realized that skateboarding in general and skateparks in particular offered significant social benefits. In the US, the Skaters for Public Skateparks organization, Tony Hawk Foundation and the International Association of Skatepark Companies (IASC) also combined to produce an extensive *Public Skatepark Development Guide* (2009), yielding detailed advice on how to conceive, advocate, fundraise, design, construct and manage local skateparks.

Apart from skaters doing something relatively healthy, affordable and accessible, skateboarding was now seen to encourage important qualities like creativity, entrepreneurship, resilience, confidence and independence, and so help develop self-directed, determined and innovative individuals. In addition, new laws and policies in many countries now enabled skateparks to operate relatively free from liability issues (although safety equipment regulations can sometimes remain problematic). Outdoor concrete skateparks were also now relatively cheap, with 2008 design-and-build rates being approximately \$400 per m^2 for street-based and \$500 per m^2 for transition skateparks, while also offering lower noise levels than wooden ramps; a 1,000 m^2 skatepark emits less constant noise than light automobile traffic and is no louder than a basketball court.[30] Design and construction standards had also progressed massively since the 1970s. 'People talk about how great all of these old parks were but in all reality they weren't. They were bumpy with fucked-up coping,' noted Allen Losi. 'Nowadays, skateparks are perfect.'[31]

All this supported a boom in free and subsidized skateparks, with providers ranging from city authorities to social enterprise initiatives such as the UK's GLE/Better and Transition Extreme, and the United States's YMCA, 4-H youth network, Rotary Club and Boys & Girls Clubs. California's Magdalena Ecke YMCA skatepark in Encinitas is particularly well known, and in 2015 offered concrete pools, transitioned reservoir, street course and vert-ramp. Churches have also

joined in, including the UK's twelfth-century Malmesbury Abbey, which since 2009 has annually inserted a temporary skatepark into its nave.[32] In the United States, by 2005 American Presbyterians and evangelical churches, as well as a Mennonite congregation in Bowmansville, Pennsylvania, had all built skate parks as community endeavours. Today, organizations like Process Skateboard Ministry in Colorado hold weekly Skate Church meetings, combining Grace & Peace skatepark sessions with Bible study.[33]

One principal benefit of this proliferation of skatepark providers is the sheer number of local communities who now have ready access to skateparks. Rather than having to travel large distances, or to rely on family and friends for transport, many skaters can now reach a purpose-built skate space in their own neighbourhood. For example, in 1990 there were probably only three municipal skateparks in the entire United States; by 2005, the *New York Times* was reporting 2,000 skateparks across the country, with another 1,000 in development, the majority of these being open-access facilities.[34] Indeed, so successful have municipally funded skateparks become that many commercially operated skateparks closed down, including many Vans- and ESPN/X Games-branded facilities in the United States.

Several of these municipal skateparks have incorporated inventive landscaping. For example, as shown in *Second Nature* (2012), many of the Finnish skateparks designed by skater and landscape architect Janne Saario exploit existing site features and recycled materials, as with the understated Micropolis (2006) in Helsinki and Grani (2007) in Kaunianen. Saario's terraced Olari skatepark in Espoo curls around a bedrock outcrop (Figure 8.7), while Steel Park (2011) in Luleå, Sweden, includes massive steel elements retrieved from the SSAB factory. Similarly, at the Hyttgardsparken (2013) in Falun, Sweden, designer Johan Berglund of 42 Architects took an archaeological approach to a UNESCO World Heritage site, generating angled banks and folded surfaces, while at London's Crystal Palace (2017), a historic park setting led to a design by myself, local skaters, Canvas and KLA for a curvilinear arrangement of transitions and cloverleaf pool.[35] For Peitruss Skatepark in Luxembourg, Constructo used geometric patchworked forms to acknowledge the adjacent seventeenth century Vauban Fortress. In Tokyo, the Miyashita Park skatepark (2011), designed in conjunction with renowned architects Atelier

Bow-Wow and located over a car park, weaves around numerous pre-existing trees and rests gently alongside other leisure facilities.[36] In such projects, sophisticated design processes are at work. 'I look for not separate recognizable special features,' explains Saario, 'but comprehensive concepts that make the whole park whisper the same story.' Skaters also benefit from such attitudes. 'The park fits to its landscape and becomes unique and recognizable,' continues Saario. 'This way it's easier for the skaters to bond a personal and deeper relationship to the place where they hang out and skate.'[37]

Other innovative designs have included the glow-in-the-dark Otro (2012) at Vassivière, France, and Evertro (2015) in Everton, UK, both created by Korean artist Koo Jeong A, who was inspired by everything from dripping paint, to the wilderness and Kant's notion of perpetual peace.[38] Skatepark bowls have also been painted to look like everything from breaking waves and watermelons to a giant octopus. The Moscow-based Zuk Club art group even transformed a Lugano flow-bowl into a functioning sundial and a Moscow skatepark into a giant fish, while in Llanera, Spain, the disused church of Santa Barbara was repurposed into an indoor skatepark, complete with highly coloured wall and roof decorations by artist Okuda San Miguel.[39]

Smooth Space

Before moving on, it also worth noting how innovative design approaches have also encouraged different kinds of riding and riders. Late 1970s skateparks were typically based around individual features such as a showcase keyhole pool or full-pipe, and so can be equated with Deleuze and Guattari's 'striated space', where lines are subordinate to points, which produces 'an order and succession of distinct forms'. In skateparks, striated space is produced when skaters are restricted to a choice between discrete elements, and to taking relatively simple lines. By contrast with such ordered hierarchies and discrete forms, a key feature of many recent skateparks has been the introduction of open flow-bowls or even seascapes of wave-like ridable terrain. These new fluid landscapes correlated with Deleuze and Guattari's 'smooth space', where points are subordinate to trajectories, priority is given to 'vectors', space is 'constructed by local operators involving changes in direction'

Figure 8.7
Andreas Eklund
at Olari skatepark,
Espoo.
© Janne Saario.

Figure 8.8
Stealth skateable
space or skatepark?
Urban simulation
at the Buszy, Milton
Keynes (2005).
© Wig Worland.

and 'the smooth' is 'the continuous variation, continuous development of form' and the 'fusion of harmony and melody'.[40] In skateparks, smooth space is consequently produced when skaters take multiple lines, speeds, vectors and rhythms across landscapes of variable and interconnecting shapes. 'The way I skate', explains Ben Schroeder in *We Are Skateboarders* (Ben Duffy, 2012), 'is one long continuous drawing activity, like a song.'

These new smooth-space and landscape-oriented forms have proved extremely popular with young and old skaters alike. In particular, many street-skaters have turned to the multiplex transitions and lines of these skateparks, sometimes to mitigate the impact-related knee injuries associated with street-skateboarding (jumping a stair, for example, can generate a landing force twenty-two times the skater's body weight), and sometimes simply to enjoy the new riding opportunities on offer; in 2014, nearly as many US skaters rode skateparks (seventy-five per cent) as street-located skatespots (seventy-seven per cent).[41] One challenge here is to bring street techniques to skatepark-like terrains, and in this vein

skaters like John Cardiel, Tony Trujillo, Greyson Fletcher, Kevin Kowalski, Ben Raybourn and Chris Russell among many others have helped re-shape transition skateboarding, in the words of *The Skateboard Mag* 'mixing old-school fun with new-school progression'.[42] For example, *Service for the Sick* (2014) montages street, DIY, pool and skatepark riding into a single heterogeneous mix, with skaters like Cody Lockwood and Dalton Dern transferring seamlessly between variable terrains. And while purpose-built skateparks can potentially run against 'core' skateboarding values of danger and subversion, these kinds of riding – often while skating 'padless' (without protective gear), as shown in O'Connor's Hong Kong study – help return skateparks to the realm of the overtly risky. All this has encouraged, since around 2000, a massive resurgence in skatepark-, vert-, bowl- and pool-riding – or what is often now simply referred to as 'transition' skateboarding.[43]

Plazas and Paths
Alongside this growing interest in transition-riding, many 1990s and 2000s skateparks have also looked for ways to accommodate

Figure 8.9
Tommy Sandoval rides
scenographic simulation at The
Berrics, Los Angeles (2017).
www.bit.ly/Sandoval-Berrics

street-skateboarders, and so have turned for
inspiration to ordinary urban features, as found
in typical streets and squares worldwide.

Skate Plazas

A few 1990s skateparks had included some
street-derived elements, but skate plazas as
full-blown simulations of everyday urbanism
properly emerged in the early 2000s. In 2002,
I suggested to Andrew Armes of the Milton
Keynes architecture and planning department,
UK, that they might construct a skate facility that
looked less like a skatepark and more like typical
streets. Landscape architect Richard Ferrington
and skater Rob Selley subsequently designed
the £100,000 Buszy facility (2005), consisting of
stone ledges, grind box, flat-ground and hubba
(a stairway with adjacent inclined ledge, named
after San Francisco's Hubba Hideout skatespot),
none of which was announced as being
deliberately for skateboarding (Figure 8.8).[44]

Also using some of this logic is the 3,700 m² DC
Skate Plaza in Kettering, Ohio, (2005), where Rob
Dyrdek and SITE Design copied San Francisco's
Pier 7, Philadelphia's Love Park and other
skatespots to create idealized street-skating
terrain.[45] However, where Buszy is deliberately
stealthy and low-key, the public-private
partnership DC Skate Plaza is far less ambiguous
in its intentions, with its DC Shoe logos and
symmetrical array of ledges, rails and hubbas
all loudly proclaiming their street-skating
purpose. At a smaller scale, Dyrdek's 'Safe Spot,
Skatespot' (2009) concept – effectively cheaper,
miniaturized versions of the DC Skate Plaza –
encourages authorities to scatter facilities across
neighbourhoods without extensive costs and
time-consuming planning.[46]

These showy Dyrdek facilities are skateboarding
equivalents of Disneyland's Main Street,
correlating with Umberto Eco's notion of the
'hyperreal' as 'improved' versions of reality, or

even Jean Baudrillard's simulacrum as an entity
'without origin or reality'.[47] Some have even
been designated 'SLS Certified Skate Plazas' in
support of Dyrdek's Street League Skateboarding
competitions and brand. Academics Atencio
and Beal also argue that these 'entrepreneurial
and non-activist' amenities predominantly
target SLS competitors and select young males
who 'inhabit street-skate spaces at the expense
of others'. As they conclude, this strategy can
privilege 'legitimate' male skateboarders, and so
hinder more socially inclusive public spaces.[48]

Nonetheless, skate plazas have undoubtedly
proven popular, and since 2005 similar terrains
worldwide have included both stand-alone
skate plazas and street-course elements within
transitioned skateparks. In the UK, Stoke's 3,150
m² Skateboard Plaza (2005) cost £500,000, its
circular composition of urban features sitting
somewhat incongruously within Central Forest
Park, while a year later Middlesbrough's Prissick
Plaza offered a similarly aesthetic arrangement
of hubbas, ledges and rails.[49] Particularly
grandiose is Canada's The Forks in Winnipeg
(2007). Designed by New Line with 800 m² of
bowls alongside a 3,000 m² skate plaza, elements
derived from San Francisco, Barcelona and
Tokyo skatespots are joined by a public art-style
Magic Carpet steel ribbon, plus heavily greened
landscaping. The $2.5 million bill was footed
largely by local businesses and philanthropic
interests.[50]

Perhaps most well-known of all plazas is The
Berrics, originated in Los Angeles (2007) by
Steve Berra and Eric Koston, where painted
steps, rails and flat banks are surrounded
by scenographic simulations of stores and
billboards (Figure 8.9). Although open only
to invited guests, the renown of this private
indoor warehouse has been propelled by the
'Battle at the Berrics' contest, filming sessions
and other online initiatives, and in 2017 The

Berrics had over 1.3 million Instagram followers. In a similar manner, DC Shoes constructed its Embassy indoor plaza in Barcelona (2011) as a private training facility and generator of internet footage.[51] Also behind closed doors, although often well-known through social media disseminations, are the indoor training facilities belonging to pro street-skaters like Paul Rodriquez, Sean Malto, Ryan Sheckler and Chaz Ortiz, typically resembling skate plazas with their steps, rails, ledges, angled banks, quarter-pipes and hubbas.[52]

Paths, Pumps and Dots

Other skateparks have taken different approaches to conventional skateparks and skate plazas. For example, at Denmark's Lemvig (2013), designed by Glifberg+Lykke and Effekt, an undulating route snakes amid a basketball area, sandpit and other park features, thus weaving skateboarding amid other pursuits.[53] Also in Denmark, Roskilde's Rabalder (2012) was extended by Søren Nordal Enevoldsen out of a 440 m storm water system, accommodating skateboarding alongside BMX-riding, trampolining, barbecues and other leisure activities.[54]

Equally inventive is New Zealand's Omokoroa skate path (2016), where Rich Landscapes designed a loop and figure-of-eight circuit around a local park, along which sit various ledges, banks, taco corners and pump bumps.[55] As with Lemvig and Roskilde, skateboarding is integrated within a park-like setting, while meeting community and environmental goals. Omokoroa's partial aim of accommodating longboarding is more directly addressed by the world's first longboard track at Kamloops, Canada (2014). This Can$100,000 facility offers a 380 m downhill path with fourteen bends and hairpins attuned to sliding and drifting.[56] Yet another variation are 'skatercross' or 'skateboard supercross' facilities plus the related genre of pump tracks and pump parks, such as the asphalted Lake Hayes at Queenstown, New Zealand (2014) and the Velosolutions examples in Aranyaprathet (Thailand), Oklahoma City (USA), Pretoria (South Africa) and Sils (Switzerland), where skaters charge round a dense series of bumps, hillocks, jumps and banks (Figure 8.10).[57] Smaller versions can also be created from modular transportable sections. Indeed, these inventive fluid-track skateparks have even inspired non-skate playgrounds, as with, for example, the immersive wooden undulations and bends of Korogaru Park (2015) in Sapporo, Japan designed by architect Jun Igarashi and YCAM Interlab.[58]

Yet another skatepark manifestation is the skate dot or 'integrated skateable terrain', as promoted by Matt Johnson in 2005 and introduced by Seattle in 2007.[59] Typically comprising small pieces of skateable terrain (compact flat areas plus a bank, ledge, sculpture, hump, rail etc.), skate dots are dispersed within parks and neighbourhoods. Although seemingly similar to street-skateboarding skatespots – skateable pieces of random urban terrain – skate dots are actually purposefully designed and located. Saario's 'Street Unit' project – transportable pads, ledges, tables, bins and kicker ramps deployed to make public spaces more skateable – correlates strongly with the skate dot concept, as does the zig-zag green path of obstacles inserted by artist Raphaël Zarka and Constructo into Rue Cladel, Paris (2012).[60]

Terrain Vague

The transitioned sides and ledges of Singapore's Henderson Waves Bridge, the white marble surroundings of Sofia's National Palace of Culture, the sinuous pathways and continuous rails of Hong Kong's Morrison Hill, the tiled moonscape at Palma de Mallorca's Plaza Bellver and the whole Chinese 'ghost city' of Ordos are all perfectly attuned for skateboarding, albeit with the unwitting collusion of their designers. In particular, cities like Guanzhou, Shenzhen, Chongqing and Shanghai (Figure 10.19) offer acres of smooth roads, open plazas and creamy pathways, dotted with glistening ledges, ramps, stairs and sculptures. 'Every time I come here,' commented Brian Dolle of Shanghai's marbled 'Black Banks', 'I think it's a dream.'[61]

As such places suggest, urban spaces should be able to accommodate skateboarding without being obviously designed for it, versions of what Ignasi de Solà-Morales terms 'terrain vague', where architecture acts with 'attention to continuity of the flows, the energies, the rhythms established by the passing of time and the loss of limits.'[62] Beyond being simply accommodated within urban realms, in return skateboarding can enhance our cities; 'Skateboarding contributes to the variety, vitality and security of outdoor public spaces,' states architect Anthony Bracali. 'Skateboarders are tourists, consumers and participants in the arts, culture and economy of cities. Skateboarders extend the hours of the use of public spaces. Many non-skateboarders are attracted to spaces where people skateboard, just to watch the activity.'[63]

Enacting these two themes of skateboarding's accommodation within, and positive

Figure 8.10 Adrien Loron negotiates Sils Pump Park, Switzerland (2014). Courtesy Velosolutions/ Hansueli Spitznagel.

contribution to, urban space is the Bracali-designed Paine's Park in Philadelphia (2013). Following skateboarding being banned from the Love Park downtown site, as documented in detail by Howell and Nemeth, this $4.5 million street-skateboarding facility was opened in a waterside park next to Philadelphia Museum of Art.[64] Designed with local skaters and financed by Franklin's Paine Skatepark Fund, the 10,000 m² site includes brick banks, handrails, stone ledges, stairs and blocks and even benches rescued from Love Park. As Bracali explains, the concept was for 'a great public space that just happened to be a skatepark', thus merging functions and making the site more usable and sustainable.[65] This is very different from normal mono-function and bounded skateparks. 'Bracali doesn't segregate the skateboard course from the park's other features, he weaves them together', comments architectural critic Inga Saffron. 'Granite ledges and benches double as skateboarding obstacles, and walking paths serve as skating areas. It's up to visitors to watch where they're going.'[66]

For some, Paine's Park seems too far removed from downtown – 'Paine's makes me feel', bemoaned Tracy Gee, 'like they built the park in that location to quarantine us' – but blogs like the influential *Quartersnacks* have praised it for attracting skateboarders, BMX-riders and the general public alike. Locals also appreciate the varied riders attracted to the site: 'I am a little heavier, and I still don't know how to kick flip', noted Michael Haeflinger. 'But at Paine's, everyone is so mellow and supportive and friendly.'[67]

Similar in concept to Paine's Park, although more urban in appearance, is the unrealized 2013 design for the Hungerford Bridge skateable space proposed by myself, Richard Holland and Søren Nordal Enevoldsen for London's Southbank Centre. Suggested as a fall-back replacement for the renowned adjacent Undercroft skate space then under threat of redevelopment, the £2–3 million Hungerford Bridge scheme envisaged seating, ledges, stairs, banks, rails and other features tuned for skateboarding, and so, like Paine's Park, welcomed skaters, BMX-riders, street artists and the general public within one inclusive space (Figure 8.11).

Although the Hungerford Bridge project was ultimately never required, the existing Undercroft thankfully being retained for skateboarding, there are numerous places worldwide where skateboard-friendly public space has been successfully implemented.

Not least here is the Undercroft itself, where the original 1960s designs deliberately accommodated indeterminate public activities (Figure 13.2). Furthermore, the Undercroft features used most extensively today – the skateable blocks first installed by Holland and The Side Effects of Urethane art collective in the mid-2000s (Figure 13.3), and more recently upgraded with a Nike-funded quarter-pipe, ledge and C-block – were expressly provided for skateboarding, hence turning the Undercroft into a complex amalgam of raw found space, accidental functionality and deliberately skate-focused interventions.[68]

Other such places include Barcelona's stealth-skateable Auditoria Park (2004), designed by Foreign Office Architects, where innumerable walls and banks tempt skaters, as do the curved banks and handrails of Wolfsburg's Phaeno Science Centre (2005) and Glasgow's Riverside Museum of Transport (2011), both designed by Zaha Hadid Architects. At Oslo's Opera House (2008), architects Snøhetta even consulted skateboarders regarding textures, materials and skateable areas (Figure 10.8). Parts of the building and surroundings are consequently arranged with stone ledges, kerbs, bench-like blocks and railings.[69]

As Snøhetta's actions suggest, public spaces can be purposed for skateboarding. Sometimes the results are skatepark-like, as at Paine's Park or Ursulines square in Brussels (2005), where skate collective Brusk have merged a bowl and other skateboarding elements with multi-purpose functions. More understated is Innsbruck's 2011 Landhausplatz (LHP) public plaza, designed by LAAC Architekten and Stiefel Kramer Architecture, where undulating banks, ledges, plateaus and blocks accommodate 'a new mélange of urban activities' for skaters, pedestrians and BMX-riders alike (Figure 8.12); the German *Playboard* magazine described LHP as providing 'obstacles of all kinds which are perfectly integrated into the cityscape.'[70] Subtle programming is also evident at SNE's experimental Concrete Plaza (2013) in Horsens, Denmark, and at Rotterdam's Benthemplein Water Plaza (2013), where urban designers De Urbanisten combined water storage with a multi-coloured public square, including ledges, steps and gutters for street-skating.[71] Designed by Metrobox Architekten, the linear Kap 686 skatepark (2011) in Cologne weaves skaterly lines and obstacles among pedestrians and geometric landscaping, as does Delaware's proposed 1,700 m² under-bridge skatepark in

Figure 8.11
Design for
Hungerford Bridge
skateable space,
London (2013).
Courtesy Søren
Nordal Enevoldsen/
SNE Architects.

Wilmington, where Grindline's design (2015) allows for criss-crossing skaters, cyclists and pedestrians.[72] In Italy, the Pietrasanta Skate Plaza (2012), designed by Marco Morigi, uses white marble donated by local businesses for its low-level banks, geometric ledges and curved shapes, creating, as *Land of Marble* (Simone Verona, 2014) shows, an artistic urban insertion. Similarly aesthetically attuned is Spain's Logroño project, designed by architect Daniel Yabar, where red-and-cream patterned flooring contrast with orthogonal slabs and ledges.[73]

DIY

Stop waiting for miracles. Make it happen.[74]

In Search of the Miraculous

Skateboarding has always had at its heart a do-it-yourself (DIY) ethos of self-reliance, inventive adaptation and unscripted adventure, which even stretches to the fabrication of ridable concrete. Back in 1977, for example, Ed DaRosa and friends constructed the 10 by 20 m Fish Bowl in Santa Cruz, using DaRosa's backyard and spending just $174. DaRosa then used similar techniques for the larger Skatepark Soquel, with a $65,000 budget and riders trading labour for skating hours.[75]

Even more distinctive is Ohio's eighty-eight acre Skatopia in Rutland, owned by Brewce Martin since 1995, and which, explains Rob Erickson, attracts skaters desiring 'bonfires, the bands, the bandits, the broads (political correctness is not an issue), the brew-ha-ha, the BOWL, and all the other b- words that blaze through the night.' This DIY wonderland, with its ever-evolving bowls, cradles and pipes, is far removed from both the pay-to-enter skateparks of the 1970s and the community-consensus endeavours of the 2000s. Instead, as documented in *Skatopia: 88 Acres of Anarchy* (Laurie House and Colin Powers, 2009), Skatopia operates as a Mad Max concoction of cooperative building, trashed cars, loaded guns, natural law, raucous pay-to-leave parties and frenzied skateboarding (Figure 8.13). 'The only competition at Skatopia is with yourself', concludes Erickson. 'Can you endure?' So intense is Skatopia that it infers a post-apocalyptic alternative existence. 'I am here to prove a point,' declares self-described skatepark-cult-leader Martin, 'that you can survive without immersing yourself in the system.'[76]

Most DIY terrains are more accessible than Skatopia's enclavism, offering alternative ways of sitting among, and even participating with, their

Figure 8.12
Cityscape as skateable terrain.
Landhausplatz, Innsbruck
(2011). *DC am Landhausplatz*
(dir. Martin Venier, 2013).
www.bit.ly/DC-LHP

surrounding city. Pre-eminent here is the hugely influential Burnside in Portland, Oregon, and it is worth considering this project in some detail (Figure 8.14).[77]

Burnside began on a disused parking lot beneath the Burnside Bridge in Portland. Already covered in asphalt and boasting a steeply angled skateable wall, this site provided a hassle-free terrain sheltered from inclement weather. In the summer of 1990, some of these skaters – who at various times have included Mark 'Monk' Hubbard, Mark 'Red' Scott, Sage Bolyard, Kent Dahlgren, Bret Taylor and Osage Buffalo, among many others – fabricated a small transition to soften the wall-floor junction. A second transition quickly followed, allowing wall-rides over the heads of crashed-out junkies, while further additions included more banks and a 1-m-high quarter-pipe.[78] This was basic DIY, where primitive additions modified found space, and construction was little more than detritus piled up into a rough shape, crudely layered with concrete. 'Imagine Kent Dahlgren', declared Hamm, 'cutting salvaged inch-thick rebar with a dull hacksaw before pounding it into place with a massive hunk of concrete.'[79]

Mark 'Red' Scott is often identified as Burnside's driving force and principal organizer. A long-time constructor of sketchy ramps, and later founder (with Hubbard) of Dreamland skatepark constructors, Scott pushed Burnside from a few raw features into an internationally famous landscape. However, as shown by FDR footage in *Under the Bridge* (Thrasher, 2009), DIY skatepark construction is always collaborative, requiring the time, blood, sweat and finances of many like-minded skaters, and whose participation implies collective ownership (Figure 11.4). As Hubbard explained, 'come to help, and you're in.' The physical exertion was particularly demanding, as Hamm has described. 'Concrete work is hard, heavy labor, and it takes its bodily toil in kinked muscles; in clattering lungs stuccoed with cement dust; and in throbbing, swollen burns that blister up when concrete splatter cures on exposed flesh.'[80]

By way of recompense, DIY skateparks can provide skater-builders with a friendship often missing from contemporary society, what Orpana calls 'a compensatory experience of un-alienated, collective, but also individualized and creative labor and sociality', and, in the face of anti-union policies, 'an alternative sense of solidarity'. Even non-skaters were involved in this Burnside camaraderie, including 'godmother of Burnside', Joanne Ferrero, a neighbouring business owner who helped garner support from businesses, police and politicians.[81]

Burnside has also evolved constantly. By 1997 the available land had been almost completely built upon, and most early features had been replaced by new ones, which included wall-rides, pillar-rides, bowls, a crow's nest and a pump-bump track, as well as quarter-pipes, hips, lips, pyramid, spine and 'punk wall' tombstone. Rather than the predetermined designs of typical skateparks, much was decided during construction itself, skaters responding to their excavations and formwork to adapt features before finalizing them in re-bar and concrete. As a New York DIY builder has described this process, 'everything was sorta designed, sorta accidental – we just started plopping things down and it just sorta worked itself out'.[82] This methodology has even been transferred to authorized skateparks, as when Burnside's Scott undertook Lincoln City skatepark, where his construction crew 'designed as they built, testing out hardened sections before voting on how to shape subsequent pours'.[83] An equally flexible approach to finance was also required at Burnside, including surplus-to-requirements concrete being gained from a local company, along with inevitable contributions from the skaters themselves.[84]

Significantly, much of Burnside was initially undertaken without official permission. Portland authorities have

Figure 8.13
Anarchic DIY wonderland at Skatopia, Rutland, Ohio. *Skatopia: 88 Acres of Anarchy* (dir. Laurie House and Colin Powers, 2009). www.bit.ly/Skatopia88

successively ignored the park, threatened closure, backed it and finally sanctioned the project as an experiment in community policing, accepting how Burnside has created a rich social space – and not just for skaters – from a previously derelict and dangerous site.

As this suggests, and as Carr notes for Seattle's later Ballard Bowl, these kinds of DIY facility typically deploy a 'build first, ask questions later' approach to abandoned property, in effect ignoring market logics and instead claiming land for social uses. Once built, DIY skateparks can then impact upon other urban projects, either preventing their construction or gaining compensation by way of replacement skate facilities; in Seattle, for example, DIY-based activism has led to a new $900,000 skatepark, helped to place skateparks in more favourable locations, gained philanthropic grants and created a city-wide skateboarding masterplan. As Carr concludes, these skaters have therefore worked 'both within and around the law to assert their continuing claims to the city.'[85]

Significantly, DIY projects have also encouraged new forms of skateboard culture and riding. In contrast to most other skateparks, which aim at smooth surfaces, Platonic forms, consistent transitions and hyperreal pipes and pools, Burnside was the bastard child of street-skating transgression, skatepark- and ramp-derived transitions and the decades-long skateboarding tradition of simply doing the unexpected. The result, particularly in the first years, was a quirky terrain that seduced and terrified in equal measure. 'It was kill', recalled Scott. 'A lot of that early shit had a lot of style and character cuz it was so ghetto.' Even after more advanced features have been added, the project has maintained a fearsome reputation for demanding terrain and anarchic attitude, celebrated at notorious Halloween parties with 'hard skating, hard drinking, hard drugs, and

hard rock dressed in a demented costume, set free with fireworks, firearms, and flying faeces.'[86] In Blake Nelson's literary novel *Paranoid Park*, Burnside possesses a 'dangerous, sketchy vibe' where 'nobody's ever ready' for its challenging and sometimes violent character.[87]

Most important of all is Burnside's riding experience, where skaters not so much encounter discrete elements as traverse a wayward landscape. In Hamm's words, this 'envelope-pushing' project offers a 'spectrum of challenges' and 'countless lines' where skaters can 'hit', 'carve', 'lunge', 'dive', 'take swipes', 'race' and 'speed'. The result is what *Thrasher* calls 'one of the fastest, scariest and punkest parks on the planet.'[88]

As a result, Burnside has been phenomenally successful, attracting skaters from all over the world, and enhancing its reputation through magazines and videos, plus appearances in the Tony Hawk video games series and *Paranoid Park* (2007). But perhaps even more important is how Burnside, along with other early DIY projects, has galvanized thousands of skaters worldwide to create similar projects, building simply for the joy of constructing their own domain. 'The outcome inspired a whole new era of skater-builders,' explained Hubbard, 'taking architecture to the next level, building whatever they wanted.' Or as one DIY skater-builder has argued, using this model of provision the best skatepark a city could offer would be 'a piece of land with nothing on it', then letting skaters design and produce it themselves.[89]

Similar to Burnside in its take-no-prisoners atmosphere is Philadelphia's FDR (Figure 11.4). Started in 1996 with a few authority-provided elements, FDR was rapidly extended as a DIY enterprise by local skaters, and is today recognized as a place of 'heroes, villains, triumph and tragedy', where the over-vert dome pocket, rough coping, transitioned bridge

Figure 8.14
Sparrow traverses Burnside at night (2011). © Pod.

piers, ever-changing graffiti and riotous 4th of July celebrations engender an unforgiving vibe and even barbaric world; FDR is a 'pirate world' where 'We don't fuck around. Don't come here if you don't know how to skate.' FDR is even seen as 'a completely different world' distinct geographically and socially from most other skateboarding scenes. 'It's that fucking hard man, and rough and shitty,' warns George Dragans. 'It's not like some silky smooth California lifestyle thing.'[90]

Despite these assertions, California also has significant DIY enterprises. Notable here is San Diego's Washington Street (1999), described by architect Teddy Cruz as an example of 'visualizing citizenship'. To complete this project, Washington Street's builders negotiated land ownership, fought courtroom battles, formed an NGO and arranged permits and insurance. Both conflict and legitimized organization were hence deployed to create an innovative kind of public space, characterized, in Cruz's terms, by new forms of democratic politics and social and economic justice.[91] The result is a barely intelligible landscape of morphing undulations and walls, while floor-set steel sleeves allow rails and other devices to be plugged in (Figure 8.15). 'Bring your slashing skills and an open mind,' declared *Thrasher*, 'to get the most out of this pit.'[92]

For Lombard, the Washington Street, Burnside and similar DIY skateparks are examples of 'indigenous governance', whereby skaters' everyday rules and conduct not only create new social spaces but also change official procedures and laws. Skateboarding's ambiguity is particularly effective here, being 'neither explicit protest nor quiet conformism', and can thus disrupt government without recourse to hostile conflict.[93] Indeed, this sense of alternative democracy even infuses riding experiences within DIY skateparks; as Mike Flint realized at Burnside, the skatepark not only had skateable 'crazy shit concrete' but also a discernible ethos, where 'the energy is, "you can't tell us what to fucking do." And you felt that when you were skating it.'[94]

Another Californian DIY enterprise is Channel Street in San Pedro, where, in 2002, Andy Harris, Robbie O'Connell and others appropriated disused land under the 110 freeway. Starting with a few banks before adding a bowl – all work being done by the skaters, some as young as twelve – they later formed the non-profit San Pedro Skatepark Association to unlock a $5,000 grant from the Tony Hawk Foundation

and gain official acceptance from authorities. By 2015, Channel Street boasted complex bowls, spines, walls and pillar-rides, as well as providing a notable community space for diverse local residents. In Seattle, Marginal Way (2004) similarly commandeered land under an overpass, contending with prostitutes, drug users, the homeless and authority concerns with liability before gaining official status as a non-profit organization. A Burnside-style facility has resulted, with a complex landscape of bowls, transitioned walls, extensions and column-rides.[95]

More low-key in character were the volcano, quarter-pipe and other features of New York's Shantytown, fabricated in the wastelands of Brooklyn Eastern District Terminal (1999). As Campo notes, two advantages of Shantytown, before its 2001 demise, were its re-use of deserted land and provision of a 'great place to hang out'. According to Steve Rodriguez, at Shantytown 'to see and be seen was vital to the activity, and spectators, even those not skating, were an important part of the experience.' Or as Weyland reflected, 'It was an antidote to the sterility and organization of society in general, a place to get away from rules and order.'[96]

Several European DIY projects have also been hugely influential. Sweden's Savannah Side in Malmö (2002) was initiated by Pontus Alv and others, and is depicted in *Strongest of the Strange* and *In Search of the Miraculous* as 'a process born out of frustration', a surreptitious 'paradise with its own rules and standards'. Over the course of two years, it provided an 'autonomous zone' for skaters, outlaws, junkies and other vagrants trying to sidestep 'strict society'. After running out of control, Savannah Side was erased by authorities in 2004.

Alv and company subsequently constructed Steppe Side, a bowled-out concrete mini-ramp modulated by erratic transitions, extensions and paint work (Figure 5.25). Yet another DIY creation, TBS (Train Bank Spot), offers a 100 m strip of ad hoc ledges, wall rides, banks and gaps. For such skatespots, *Coping Mechanism* (Philip Evans, 2014) provides in-depth insight into Alv and other Malmö DIY-builders like Mattias Hallén and Oskar Ristenfeldt; 'a DIY spot offers me much more freedom when I skate,' reflects Hallén, 'and I get to do things with my own hands too.' Or as Ristenfeldt explains, 'it's much more of a challenge to skate something that's not perfect', while also noting how the transitory nature of DIY spots further adds to their character, each session perhaps being the last.

Figure 8.15
Washington Street, San Diego. Lee Dupont for *The Cinematographer Project* (TransWorld, 2012). www.bit.ly/WashingtonSt-Cinematograher

Of the thousands of other DIY projects constructed globally, one of the best known is Berlin's Betonhausen, where Lennie Burmeister and others have filled the space between two buildings with a choppy sea of concrete (Figure 8.16). Finland's Suvilhati Spot in Helsinki offers more skatepark-like forms, while the UK's Sheafside in Sheffield occupies wasteland with bordering banks plus smaller ledges, pole jams and humps. Unusually, Italy's Creedence Park in Brescia began as a purpose-built skatepark, but after funding fell through the local skaters completed the facility themselves.[97] Latraac in Athens (2016) was constructed by architect Zachos Varfis as a garden, skatepark and 'an alternate proposal for ways to occupy and relate to derelict inner city space.' La Caverne, set in an abandoned Marseilles warehouse, was inspired by Washington Street, while other notable DIY constructions have included Tokyo's Felem in Sashima County, Portland's Brooklyn Street, Glacier's Coal Pad and Hamburg's Rote Flora.[98]

DIY skateparks have even started influencing professionally designed and constructed facilities. For example, the small Bloblands in London's Norwood Park (2014) was converted by Freestyle from an existing paddling pool by mixing quirky low-level transitions with existing obstacles. At a larger scale, Wisconsin's Central Park skatepark in Madison was constructed as a replica of the defunct local Slam Walls skatespot, while, as already noted, many Dreamline, Grindline and Evergreen skateparks also draw on ad hoc design and construction methodologies.[99]

As this suggests, all manner of cities worldwide are enjoying a DIY explosion, much of it documented in *Confusion* magazine. In La Paz, Bolivia, the 2,000 m² Pura Pura park was freeform designed and constructed in just five weeks during 2014 by a collaboration of over one hundred skaters from fifteen countries.

Documented in *Skateboarding in La Paz* (Simon Weyhe, 2014), those involved included Milton Arellano from Asociacion de Skateboard de La Paz, Make Life Skate Life, Skate-aid and 2er from Hanover (Figure 8.17).[100] Another DIY spot, HolyStoked in Bangalore, India, recorded in *Skateboarding in India* (Simon Weyhe and Mathias Nyholm Schmidt, 2013), similarly involved a collaborative team comprising Nick Smith from the UK, the 2er crew and many others.[101]

More idiosyncratically, teenager Anselmo Arruda turned his São Paulo home into a self-made skatepark, using the project to help overcome the death of his parents.[102] Still other projects consist of simple micro-transitions to render existing architecture (walls, fountains, highway barriers etc.) more skateable, or the assemblage of wood sheets, metal frames and other found objects into temporary obstacles. These incidental interventions, as recorded in Richard Gilligan's book *DIY* (2012), are all but invisible to the public, acting as secret markers discernible only to skaters.

As *Space for Rent* (2012) states, these kinds of creative acts impart industrial wastelands and out-of-the-way urban spaces with 'a new and soulful sense of value independent from any economic or materialistic value.' As such, and besides performing transgressive acts on sites of indeterminate ownership, DIY projects can also create new meanings and add social value. Recognizing these positive qualities, many DIY initiatives are founded as or have become partnerships, undertaken with the tacit acceptance or even endorsement of landowners, councillors and urban managers. This arrangement, as Orpana and Lombard recognize, provides the chance to engage in city politics and culture in a way denied to more oppositional or isolationist skaters.[103] Perhaps more problematic, however, is how many

DIY spots have been courted by commercial brands for their ability to represent 'authentic' values and supply raw urban aesthetics, as with Levi's backing of Pura Pura and HolyStoked in order to demonstrate its 'commitment' to skateboarding. Brooklyn's Shantytown, for example, was frequently used for fashion shoots, while London's partly-DIY Undercroft is often favoured by marketeers; even Burnside featured in Warner's *Free Willy* family movie (2007).[104]

Although places like Burnside and FDR may be dauntingly intimidating to newcomers, many DIY skateparks are accessible for skateboarders of varied backgrounds, riding styles and proficiency. Certainly Shantytown's dispersed low-level obstacles and implicit codes accommodated large numbers of skaters of different abilities; this was in sharp contrast to, for example, the nearby official Owl's Head skatepark, whose specialized California-influenced bowls suffered

from fewer opportunities for rides and long wait times, as well as innumerable regulations, opening restrictions and legal waivers. Despite their sometimes fearsome reputation, DIY spots typically have their own etiquette, often inculcating an increased sense of responsibility and care. At Shantytown, for example, the builder-skaters themselves dealt with typical skatepark issues with litter, repairs, destructive behaviour and relations with non-skaters. 'All the kids in the neighborhood had a hand in, and as a result no one really littered, no one was breaking bottles,' explained Nevitt. 'Everyone was real respectful, because it was something that everybody spent their own time, money and effort in building.'[105]

All of this adds up to a rich and distinctive DIY skateboarding scene, stretching from the projects noted above to innumerable other initiatives dotted around cities worldwide.

Figure 8.16
The compressed
site of the DIY
Betonhausen, Berlin.
© Richard Gilligan.

Figure 8.17
International collaborative
DIY construction at Pura Pura.
Skateboarding in La Paz (dir.
Simon Weyhe, 2014).
www.bit.ly/Pura-LaPaz

They have also proved highly popular with riders, and by 2014, some thirty-four per cent of US skaters regularly skated DIY spots, nearly half the figure for regular skateparks.[106] Today, even official skateboarding organizations like the IASC recognize the central importance of DIY skateparks, working with cities to support DIY skatepark creation and preservation, and emphasizing that 'DIY is the heart of skateboarding culture.'[107]

Skatepark Worlds

As DIY construction suggests, skateparks are for more than spectacular terrains. In particular, different kinds of users are also created in skateparks, whether from constructing, operating, riding or just hanging out. But this very characteristic can lead to occasional disquiet, particularly with non-skaters, some of whom exhibit what Taylor and Khan call a 'moral teenaphobic panic' over young people socializing together, and so perceive skateparks as having negative impacts through injuries, noise, graffiti and disorder.[108] Even liberal-minded champions of vernacular landscapes like J.B. Jackson have voiced concerns. 'Noisy, deliberately artificial in its man-made topography, used by a boisterous and undisciplined public, and dedicated to violent expenditure of energy', worried Jackson, for whom the skatepark 'repudiates and makes a mockery of everything the word *park* has stood for.'[109]

Given the unfortunate prevalence of such misguided opinions, skateparks are unsurprisingly often located in marginal sites. Too often a local council, fearing conflicts between skaters and other citizens (unsightly concrete, unwanted noise, graffiti, drugs or simply the gathering of youth are commonly cited as problems), will place its skatepark not in a popular park or central part of town but around the back of a warehouse or remote leisure centre, next to the recycling bins, car park or other low-quality sites. Yet concrete

skateparks actually produce similarly low levels of noise as playgrounds, one Australian study found no correlation with graffiti incidence, and still other New Zealand and UK studies have actually identified reductions in crime after skatepark construction; at the UK's Dorchester, elderly residents and police alike noted the huge community benefits of their centrally located skatepark, including a forty-five per cent fall in antisocial behaviour.[110] In short, skateparks typically offer distinct social, cultural, health and even economic advantages, and often stretching far beyond the act of skateboarding.

Community Scenes

As noted above, some claim that the unstructured nature of skateboarding (in contrast to the rules, training and supervision of regular sports) leads to antisocial violence, public nuisance, vandalism and substance abuse: 'If you let the skaters in', opined one Seattle objector, 'you are just opening our neighborhood to pushers, pimps, paedophiles, and prostitutes.'[111] Yet such outbursts are typically based on false perceptions rather than actual evidence. Indeed, to the contrary, and as numerous studies demonstrate, skateparks help build adolescents' autonomy, social skills, self-confidence, friendships and peer-group status. Encouraging skaters to learn about cooperation, design, negotiation and aiding others, plus gaining a sense of ownership, belonging and responsibility, are key features of skateparks.[112]

Problems do of course arise, for, as Turner and Carr have shown, like any public space skateparks are areas of negotiation, where 'noise, low-level mischief, and reproduction of patriarchy are often inseparable from developing community, the building of self-esteem, and the creation of positive life paths.' Very occasionally, conflicts are irresolvable, as when skaters who repeatedly transgress skatepark rules (typically ranging from helmet-

wearing, session times and entrance fees to bans on smoking, alcohol and abuse) are excluded or simply boycott the facility. In such instances, skateparks may lose some of the very people they were most intended to reach.[113]

Nonetheless, positive qualities are substantial, and indeed skateparks readily answer Robert Putnam's plea for less of the 'civic broccoli' which is 'good for you but unappealing' and more 'ingenious combinations of values and fun.'[114] For example, Pablo Sendra, following Deleuze, argues that less-regulated and free-access skateparks like London's Stockwell operate as urban 'unbound points', offering zones of creativity and resistance.[115] In more practical terms, as the Montreal-based study by Dumas and Laforest shows, skateparks not only lead to fewer injuries than street-skating or indeed mainstream sports, but also provide 'opportunity structures' for enhancing skaters' social, psychological and physical well-being; another Canadian research project by Shannon and Werner concluded that skateparks were more than just places to skate, being realms where riders were 'welcomed, accepted and encouraged.'[116] Similarly, Weller shows how British skateparks in rural and deprived locations help build social capital, as places where 'teenagers actively contribute to shaping their communities.'[117] Indeed, skateparks frequently accommodate not only riding but street art, fashion shoots, pop videos and impromptu gatherings. For local skaters, as with Kevin and Hollywood, two Michigan skaters interviewed by Petrone, these are important qualities. 'For some of these kids it's a second home', explained Kevin of his local Franklin skatepark. 'This is my way to get away from everything, from my home stress, work stress. I come up here every night. Meet up with my friends and skateboard a little.' Or as Hollywood simply stated, 'if I didn't have this skate park, I'd be in jail.'[118] For Casey Helseth in Santa Cruz, the community Derby skatepark has been a constant friend during his troubled life, offering a place to skate, party, meet friends and even periodically sleep.[119]

Clearly then, as Dumas and Laforest state, skateparks can be 'favourable spaces for attracting youth to safe and active lifestyles', and many local authorities worldwide have wisely concurred; for example, the city of Queensland, Australia, considers a skatepark to be 'a hub for community life' and 'a catalyst for healthy community life in which young and old socialize, have fun, develop new skills, make new friends, hang out and much more.'[120]

These beneficial effects are in part due to the act of skateboarding itself, and partly due to social groupings, but also due to changes in recent skatepark design. In 2000 Jones and Graves criticized six 1990s Oregon skateparks as being 'inside the bowl' designs rather than community spaces.[121] Similarly, Chiu noted skater criticisms of New York's Hudson River skatepark for being 'like a cage' and a 'forced environment' with strict opening hours, plus, when compared to street-skatespots, less authenticity.[122] But by around 2010, as Dumas, Laforest, Rinehart and Grenfell all indicate, skateparks had become less dangerous and more welcoming of skaters of different ages, genders and backgrounds than had many street-skateboarding environments.[123] Besides their more varied riding terrains, typically accommodating a wide range of riding styles and abilities, skateparks now also often include water fountains, lighting, seating, tables, barbecue and hang-out areas, while artful landscaping, avant-garde architecture and interior design, skate shops, cafés and even Wi-Fi are increasingly common. Integration within larger urban design and landscape projects can also occur. Chicago's substantial 2,000 m^2 Burnham skatepark nestles alongside a nature prairie, bird sanctuaries, water trail, bicycle paths, playground, marina and beach house, while New Zealand's Marine Parade skatepark in Napier (2017) is accompanied by a splash park and concert venue, creating 'a public space that belongs to all of Napier and beyond.'[124]

The best skateparks, then, are far more than just isolated and exclusive terrains accessible only by courageous males. For example, although undoubtedly some females have felt excluded from skateparks, this is not always the case; one Vancouver skatepark explored by Kelly, Pomerantz and Currie has offered a marginal space for its Park Gang riders to enact political expression, first challenging and then gaining respect from male counterparts, while also developing alternative female identities.[125] Harris uncovered similar qualities in 2010s Ontario, where newcomers frequented skateparks in order to gradually enter the skate scene, and Carr has reported on how community-oriented skateparks in public parks, which attract a wide range of rider abilities and ages, can prove more attractive to female skaters.[126]

Many skateparks worldwide today work hard at fostering this kind of atmosphere, using female-only and age-specific sessions along with numerous jams, Halloween evenings,

Figure 8.18
Daryl Dominguez at the hybrid economy House of Vans, London (2014). © Gorm Ashurst.

graffiti and DJ workshops, school-related projects and other events to encourage accessibility and sense of belonging. 'It's not just a skatepark', explains the manager of Dundee's Factory Skatepark, 'it's a twenty-first century community facility'.[127] Other places, such as the DIY Parasite skatepark in New Orleans, reflect transgressive behaviour through their semi-illegal construction but also, through their collaborative nature, encourage positive social behaviour and individual development.[128]

Age variety is another significant feature of many current skateparks, and besides the most commonplace teenagers, skaters under ten years old are also prevalent (typically accompanied by parents), and sometimes receive lessons. Much older skaters are also frequently drawn to skateparks; a 2015 survey by the Skaters Over 50 Facebook group showed that sixty-two per cent of these riders preferred skatepark and transition skate terrains, compared to just twenty-two per cent for street and sixteen per cent for freestyle, slalom and downhill.[129] For example, the $2.8 million, 6,000 m² Denver skatepark is situated near the city's downtown, offering early morning and flood-lit evening sessions to cater for working-age skaters. 'It turns out we had a huge unmet need for skating', acknowledged Parks & Recreation officer Leslie Roper, 'and we're very happy with the result.'[130]

Neoliberal Training and Hybrid Economies

Over the last decade, one common strain at skateparks has been the development of stewardship programmes, where young adults learn to procure, operate, monitor and maintain their facilities, as well as to teach those beginning to skate. Apart from the obvious benefits in maintaining terrain and encouraging skateboarding take-up, those involved gain a sense of pride, achievement and civic responsibility, and so become active and respected community members.[131] According to Peter Whitley of the Tony Hawk Foundation, the process of petitioning for a skatepark, for example, often builds substantial civic engagement, during which 'skateboarders go from getting tickets and having their boards confiscated to being on a first-name basis with city council members.'[132] Once a skatepark is constructed, even deeper community ties can be formed; at the tough working-class Franklin skatepark in Michigan, studied by Petrone, skaters self-police graffiti, weed-smoking, litter and loud music, and even organize measures against non-skater vandalism.[133]

As Turner, Howell and others highlight, through this kind of 'civilizing process' urban managers use skateparks to nurture certain character traits in youngsters, principally 'personal responsibility, self-sufficiency, and entrepreneurialism', all of these being qualities that equate directly with neoliberal values.[134] As such, skateparks can also be part of a larger process, in which the relationship between citizens and the state changes from one of 'entitlement' to 'contractualism' – skaters get skateparks not because they deserve them, but because they earn them through appropriate social behaviour and contributions.[135] Some Asian skateparks demonstrate a broadly similar rationale, for, as Striler shows, the Chinese government backed the Woodward facility in Beijing so that youth would have a place for creative expression and the development of western consumerist attitudes.[136]

The Woodward Beijing enterprise indicates how commerce and consumption can also be at play in contemporary skateparks, particularly as marketing. In Milan, the Bastard store and offices for parent company Comvert includes a 200 m² wooden bowl, spectacularly suspended above a distribution depot, and so acts both as a riding facility for staff and as a potent promotional symbol,[137] while the Beach Burrito restaurant in Fitzroy, Australia, similarly incorporates a kidney pool (2015) as an idiosyncratic publicity-generating device.[138]

Even heavier marketing benefits are apparent at the Nike SB Shelter (2014) in Berlin, and at Palace's Mwadlands (2017) and Vans's House of Vans (2014) in London. Occupying 2,500 m² of Victorian railway arches, House of Vans integrates free-access skateboarding (bowl and street course) alongside art, music and film facilities (Figure 8.18).[139] Operating as a continuous advertisement for its billion-dollar backer, the nuanced design (by Tim Greatorex, Pete Hellicar and Marc Churchill) and the wide programme of activities are far more generous than the kind of corporate annexation of skateboarding of which some international brands have been accused. It is also a step beyond the kind of corporate sponsorship (Mountain Dew, Pepsi, etc.) that, according to Tony Hawk, supports professionals yet still remains outside core skate values.[140]

House of Vans, then, marks a shift away from the outright opposition between, on the one hand, the 'authentic' realms of street-level, spontaneous and unfunded actions and, on the other hand, the 'inauthentic' world of spectacularized, controlled and commercial projects. Instead, House of Vans is what Lawrence Lessig has termed a 'hybrid' economy, operating simultaneously as a commercial economy for financial gain and as a sharing economy for collaborative and collective benefit.[141] In short, House of Vans shows how some skateparks might combine profit, media and control with credibility, performance and disorder.

Tourism and Regeneration

Beyond Vans-style marketing, wider skatepark ambitions may also include tourism and even urban regeneration. As Lee Bofkin notes, cities that support street artists like Banksy, SpY and Vhils find it easier to develop urban identities, engage with communities and attract visitors.[142] Skateboarding can also be part of this process. 'Skateparks are no longer seen as a grudging way to deal with the so-called problem of skateboarders', explains Kyle Duvall. 'Instead, cities have begun to see them as assets, even showpieces.'[143] Hence alongside neighbourhood facilities, some cities appreciate how skateparks appeal at wider regional, national or even international levels, and so nest within wider planning goals.

One of the first cities to understand this possibility was Louisville, Kentucky, whose Extreme Park (2002) was partly aimed at attracting new visitors. Costing $2 million, the Metro Government's 3,700 m² Wormhoudt-designed skatepark boasted a street course, 3.65 m vert-ramp, several bowls, 7.3 m full-pipe and flood-lit 24/7 opening. The booster intention was successful, and, explained Mayor David Armstrong, Louisville's reputation changed from 'a sleepy little southern town' to 'an exciting, youthful extreme town'. A $2.2 million reconfiguration (2015) replaced some of the original features with a new bowl, street course, flow-bowl and full-pipe with dramatic upper perforations.[144] Similarly, the SITE-designed 6,200 m² Black Pearl skatepark (2005) in the Cayman Islands was constructed both for locals and to boost tourism; Tony Hawk has described it as a 'monstrous' ridable landscape that takes over a week to explore.[145]

Also with an eye on tourism are many of China's large skateparks, including SMP, plus Denmark's $5.5 million indoor-outdoor 'Streetdome' in

Haderslev, designed by Rune Glifberg, Ebbe Lykke and CEBRA architects. Constructed by Grindline, the 4,500 m² facility contains a grass-domed weather-proof arena, as well as provision for kayaking, music, parkour and climbing. This 'cultural and experiential powerhouse' acts as a 'facilitator' where 'urban sport, street culture and youthful souls all meet together' (Figure 8.19).[146] A similar multi-arts programme drives Spain's Factoria Joven ('youth factory') in Merida, where in 2011 architects SelgasCano combined skateboarding, climbing and cycling functions, along with provisions for computing, dance, theatre, video and graffiti, all located amid brightly coloured architecture.[147]

More commercially, in 2017 Camp Woodward and the Hard Rock Hotel in Riviera Maya, Mexico, opened a five-star 'paradise' of skateboarding and fine cuisine.[148] And in 2018 California Skateparks opened the CA TF 'Elite Skateboarding Training Facility' in Vista to simulate athletic competition terrains, with membership costing $350–$850 per month.

As these projects suggest, skateboarding can generate significant revenues and attract new facilities to its host venues. For example, spectacular events like the X Games may not necessarily aid local skaters, but Los Angeles nonetheless benefitted to the tune of $50 million for its 2010 X Games, while, for hosting the final round of the Vans Park Series in 2016, Malmö successfully negotiated for Vans to provide the permanent Kroksbäck skatepark, which also acts as a social space for low-income housing residents.[149] On an even larger scale than Kroksbäck, and perhaps unique in skateboarding history, is the world's first multi-storey concrete skatepark, the F51 'urban sports centre' funded by the Roger de Haan Charitable Trust and in 2018 under construction in Folkestone, UK. Unlike typical out-of-town sites, this skatepark sits within a masterplan to transform a run-down yet central area into a sustainable creative quarter, and so will help to both encourage youth to stay in Folkestone and to attract new residents. The skatepark – designed by Guy Hollaway Architects and Maverick, with some advisory input from myself – is appropriately ambitious, intersecting innovative architectural design, three storeys of fluid ridable surfaces and substantial community facilities.[150] Here, skateboarding, design artistry, community engagement and urban regeneration are all at play.

Figure 8.19
Skatepark as urban
hub. Streetdome,
Haderslev (2014).
© Mikkel Frost/
CEBRA.

Skateboarding
Chapter 9 Super-Architectural Space

I am not in space and time, nor do I conceive space and time; I belong to them, my body combines with them and includes them.[1]
Maurice Merleau-Ponty

'Consciousness,' postulates existentialist philosopher Maurice Merleau-Ponty, 'is being-towards-the-thing through the intermediary of the body,' or put more simply, we know things not only with our minds but also through our physical bodies.[2] Nor do we just passively accept the world around us, for, argues Lefebvre, while our urban experiences often seem overwhelmingly constrained by external forces, nonetheless these experiences offer the prospect of 'recovering the world of differences – the natural, the sensory/sensual, sexuality and pleasure.'[3] In short, our bodies, experiences and actions can change the world around us.

For skateboarding, this means that skateparks and other riding terrains, despite their near unique appearance and forms, are not skateboarding's only or most important contribution to society. Instead, much of this significance lies in the performative aspects – the actions – of skateboarding, wherein skateboarders recreate both architectural space and themselves into what I call super-architectural space.

Body Space
The sinuous curves and rounded-lip walls of early skateparks encouraged surf-related skating; Bruce Walker, for example, described Florida's SkatBoard City as being 'just like surfing – you just get up on the wall and sock it through the lip a few times.'[4] Although undoubtedly exciting, this riding relied heavily on carving and kickturn variations, plus a few sliding, tail-block, hand-down and 'bunny-hop' moves (Figure 9.1). Freestyle was slightly more inventive, with various spins, wheelies, jumps and gymnastic manoeuvres, plus complex non-surfing moves like the kickflip, where the rider jumps while flipping the board 360° about its long axis. However, partly due to slight coverage in skate magazines, these freestyle moves featured little in skatepark riding experiences.

Extraordinary Terrain, Extraordinary Moves
In contrast to the simple topographies of their predecessors, the second generation of skateparks inspired more distinctive skateboarding styles – 'extraordinary terrain dictates extraordinary moves,' declared *SkateBoarder* – with backyard pool moves like the aerial, as pioneered by the likes of Tony Alva and George Orton, quickly evolving into manoeuvres such as the invert aerial and rock 'n roll.[5] Within two years skaters often had little to say about surf-skateboarding connections; 'They're related in some ways,' explained Micke Alba, 'but not too many. Surfing is like a whole different thing.'[6]

Pre-eminent of all these new tricks was the 'ollie,' first invented by Jeff Duerr and then perfected by Alan Gelfand during 1977 and 1978 in response to walls of Skateboard USA, Solid Surf and other Florida skateparks. In the ollie, the skater aerials without holding the board, balanced flight being achieved via a precise

Figure 9.2
Alan Gelfand's ollie is revealed to UK skaters by *Skateboard!* (February 1979). Photographer unidentified.

Figure 9.1
Early skatepark riding at Skateboard Safari and Skateboard USA, Florida. *Hard Waves, Soft Wheels* (dir. Jim Plimpton, 1977). www.bit.ly/HardWaves

THE NO-HANDED AERIAL

Alan Gelfand of the Powell/Peralta Team was the inventor of this outrageous new manoeuvre and in this month's *Going-for-It* we offer some words of advice on making it.

1 Take the line you would for a straight-forward frontside kickturn on the lip. Kick the tail of the board just as the back wheels start to edge. The action must be done gently in order to retain control over your stick. . . it's a critical movement. Foot positions should be as follows: front foot

to the rear of the leading truck, back foot close-up to the trailing truck.
2 & 3 Unweight immediately you start the board turning and hold your feet clear of it. Both stick and rider should prescribe the same circumference of arc, though of course

the torque generated by the arms and shoulders (to initiate the kickturn) will cause them to 'lead' the rest of the body.
4 & 5 Returning to solid vert, as your feet hit the grip tape, remember to stay in position over the board; also shoe to platform contact should again be made gently. Correct

tuning of these two factors is essential if rider and skateboard are to remain 'stuck' on landing, and on proper course.
6 All being well, you'll be back on line for an easy ride down.

Points of interest

It stands to reason that this is a very advanced manoeuvre — in fact, to the best of our knowledge, at the time of writing we know of no one in the UK capable of reliably pulling it off. Alan Gelfand strongly advises those attempting it to start on flatland and to build up through increasing angles of bank before finally making the vertical. Equipment should be light, though capable of taking fairly high levels of stress.

manipulation of body, board, terrain and gravity so magical that Brad Bowman called it 'utterly outrageous, futuristic, impossible, mystifying'.[7] Essentially the move involves a frontside air where, at the wall's top, the skater uses their rear foot to kick the board tail down on to the bowl surface and so makes it bounce or jump; the board is then gently guided through a 180° turn by the skater's feet (Figure 9.2). Requiring enormous skill and courage, most skaters took months or even years to copy Gelfand. But after the move was first published in September 1978 and was subsequently mastered by others, the ollie became the 'cornerstone of modern skateboarding', adapted into bewildering variations of direction, rotation and combinations. It's biomechanical procedures have even been subjected to scientific analysis.[8]

However seminal the ollie might prove to be, particularly after Mullen, Kaupas, Gonzales and others transformed it into a street-skating move in the 1980s (Figures 10.1 through 10.3), other moves were also significant. For between 1978 and 1979, during what Jeff Grosso calls a 'trick explosion', innumerable technical moves were also invented, collectively redefining what was possible on a skateboard. Such moves included the 'invert' (Bobby Valdez, mid-1978), a one-handed board-holding handstand first captured in *Blaze On*, which ushered in other upside-down moves (Andrecht air, sadplant, eggplant, frontside invert, etc.); the footplant, where the skater takes their rear foot off the board and boosts themself higher (Eric Grisham, 1978), leading to 'sweeper', 'boneless' and other variants; and the 'rock 'n roll' (Ed Womble/ Tim Marting/Richie De Losada, mid-1978), where the skateboard see-saws across the top of the wall.[9] Other advanced moves included the 'disaster' (Dan Murray, 1978), with the rear truck nearly hanging-up on the wall edge; 'layback' (late 1978), where the skater stretches back off the skateboard, with rear hand planted on the wall; 'Gunnair' backside aerial with the skater's rear hand grabbing the toe-side rail (Gunnar Haugo, 1978, later called 'Indy air'); 'alley-oop' backside aerial with a backwards trajectory (Chris Strople, 1977–1978); 'layback air' frontside aerial with the skater's rear hand grasping the coping (Kelly Lynn, 1978–1979); 'cess slide' combination of two 90° slides (Buddy Allred and Chris Strople, 1975–1978); and 'Lake Flip/Miller Flip' 360° frontside invert aerial (Mark Lake/Darrell Miller, 1978–9). The similarly exotic 'Elguerial' backwards invert and fakie ollie were made famous by Eddie Elguera and Allen Losi, respectively.[10]

By mid-1979, skaters were combining these complex moves within a single run. 'He had his rock 'n roll slides fully wired,' rhapsodized *SkateBoarder* of Doug 'Pineapple' Saladino at an Oasis contest. 'Couple this with long grinders, hand plants, inverts, frontside and backside airs at high speed, and you have an incredible run.'[11] At the 1980 King of the Mountain competition at Colorado's Hi-Roller, skaters like Duane Peters, Dave Andrecht, Allen Losi, Eric Grisham and Bert Lamar were doing roll-outs/roll-ins, inverts, frontside rock 'n rolls, layback airs, fakie ollies and Elguerials.[12] Such performances put great demands on professionals and advanced amateurs alike. 'Gone are the days where a skater could win with just one extraordinary trick,' explained *SkateBoarder*. 'Pro pool-riding has grown up into a sport that demands versatility, planning and precision execution.'[13]

By the early 1980s, skaters were developing 'bionic' versions of older moves, with aerials rising 2 m or more, or their bodies becoming strangely contorted. 'Unreal bio tricks, impossible variations and combinations of moves and perfection in style,' declared a dumbfounded Iain Urquhart, 'all make past efforts look decidedly tame.'[14] Variflex's Eddie Elguera in particular was creating new moves on a seemingly monthly basis, and his sequences at the Powell-Peralta Marina Cup (1980) included a fakie ollie 180 into a rock 'n roll and a varial layback air into a switch-stance fakie footplant.[15] Such feats shifted skateboarding from single tricks to combinatorial moves involving multiple body-board-terrain engagements. In addition, larger half-pipes let skaters investigate the space high above the wall; as Stacy Peralta explained, with generous ramp transitions and flat-bottoms 'you don't even need the ramp to do tricks *on* – you're using it to get into the air.'[16]

Pre-eminent of these composite moves was Mike McGill's 540° 'McTwist' aerial (1984), invented at the Eurocana Skate Camp, a manoeuvre immediately recognized as a seminal skateboarding event (Figure 9.3).[17] 'As he flew out four or five feet, he went upside down and spun – and kept spinning until he had turned 540°, completely inverted at the 360° point with his head three feet above the coping,' recalled Weyland. 'In that moment when he was flying with his top and bottom reversed, everyone who was watching the pool saw something so amazing as to be unbelievable.'[18] According to Hawk, McGill's move 'opened the direction to an entirely new

Most of the people who saw Bobby Valdez do the first hand-plants, had to wipe their eyes and watch again, because they couldn't believe what was going on. Then again it was the same case with the ollie, the vertical layback, channel-airs, the foot-plant and a variety of other tricks. All of these were new and clever tricks, but the one thing they had in common, was the fact that given some basic vertical ability, most seasoned skaters

were able to adapt quickly to these tricks, and today they comprise a novice's basic routine. But then, at the last Del Mar contest, Mike McGill unveiled the ultimate trick, the 540° McTwist. Word is, he makes 90% of his attempts at this trick. Kasai and Hawk are already attempting it, but, as of this time, have only succeeded a few times. Mike McGill's 540° McTwist, easily the trick of 1984.

540° McTWIST

Figure 9.3
Thrasher announces Mike McGill's mind-blowing 540° McTwist (October 1984). Courtesy High Speed Productions.

direction in vertical skating,' while raising the bar beyond the skill or comfort level of some professionals.[19]

Despite the McTwist seemingly setting a new limit, by the late 1980s Hawk was doing varial, flip and even ollie variants.[20] Around this time, Peralta was advising his team members to introduce a new move at every contest, while vert riders were performing ever more complex moves, refocusing on the wall's top edge (rather than the air above), as with Bod Boyle's ollie to front truck grind and Ben Schroeder's alley-oop 50-50 fakie. These were 'balance point' tricks, where the skater treats the wall lip, body and board as one entity.[21] Into the 1990s, Danny Way, Sluggo, Tas Pappas, Giorgio Zattoni and Hawk were even experimenting with 900° aerials, while by decade's the end, Bob Burnquist and others undertook many moves riding backwards (switch-stance).[22]

These intricate and dangerous moves were encouraged by wooden ramps, which were kinder to fall upon and offered more predictable transitions than did concrete skateparks. Furthermore, while curved pool walls let skaters change direction at high speed, this was not

possible on half-pipe parallel walls, making skaters focus on the ramp's top edge and air above. In short, half-pipes encouraged a more rhythmical, trick-oriented and gymnastic approach, in contrast to the discordant slashing lines of much skatepark and pool-riding.

Body-Centric Space

Beyond videos and photographic sequences – which in any case depict skateboarding from an external perspective – skaters' own descriptions of these experiences are both infrequent and largely descriptive. For example, Weyland described one ramp run with terms like 'drop in,' 'curving slope,' 'popping off the lip,' 'scraping the metal' and 'hurtling through space,' all of which metaphorically and lyrically describe skateboarding but without dissecting its spatial experience.[23]

How, then, is skateboarding space constituted as an integration of body, skateboard and terrain? At the heart of a skateboarder's actions lies a purely spatial composition, using a series of front-back, left-right, up-down reversals and rotations, in combination with precise relations of board, hands, body and terrain, all of which generates an extraordinarily dynamic body-centric space.

Figure 9.4
Moving with the
board. Tony Hawk
performs a heel
flip varial lien air
at Long Beach,
California (1995).
© Wig Worland.

'So technical, so precise, so balanced and light footed,' eulogized Christian Hosoi of Hawk. 'His body twists from one position to the other, then he goes in backwards.'[24]

This, then, is a space produced by skaters out of the dynamic intersection of body, board and terrain. Firstly, comes the body itself. Lefebvre describes space as having 'properties' (dualities, symmetries etc.) that derive not from the mind or conscious design, but from the occupation of space, and in which 'each living body *is* space and *has* its space.'[25] Here, skateboarding space is produced first from within the body (left-right, front-back, up-down, spinal rotation, etc., as when launching an aerial), then centrifugally outward from the body (in the middle of the aerial), and finally centripetally pulled back in (when landing the aerial). 'You must get the feeling that your mind is located in your center of gravity,' explained Curtis Hesselgrave. 'The rest of your body moves around this center point as a wheel moves around its hub.'[26]

On the one hand this is a primary space within and around the body. It can even mean a super-extended body, that, in Stephen Connor's descriptions of athletes, 'is always up against, and going beyond, itself.'[27] But there is also an outside to the body, for, as German sociologist Georg Simmel has described, 'man does not end with the limits of his body' but is 'constituted by the sum of effects emanating from him temporally and spatially.'[28] As this suggests, a skateboarder's spatiality goes beyond their body to be additionally produced in relation to two other physical entities: the skateboard and the terrain.

For someone learning to skate, a skateboard initially seems like a separate platform upon which to balance. By contrast, proficient skateboarders reconceive the skateboard as at once separate to, and part of, their body. 'As the rider gets more advanced,' wrote Hesselgrave, 'he begins to discover that the skateboard as a vehicle operates more as part of himself than as something he rides on.' For Hesselgrave, a frontside aerial exemplified this process, with rider and board moving as one unit around a common centre of gravity.[29] Alternatively, in a move like a frontside rock 'n roll, the board is intricately related to the skater's body in more complex ways. First the board is pushed away from the body and over the top of the wall, and then delicately brought back by the toe of the rear foot on the extreme corner of the kicktail, during which two fulcrum points – the deck on the wall

and the deck beneath the rear toe – interplay within a precise body-board combination.

In such acts, the skateboard is less the simple application of a device against a remote object (what German phenomenology philosopher Martin Heidegger calls the *Vorhandenheit*, or 'presentness-at-hand' of the object 'out there'), and more concurs with the notion of the tool-object as *Zuhandenheit*, or 'readiness-to-hand'. 'The less we just stare at the hammer-Thing, and the more we seize hold of it and use it,' states Heidegger, 'the more primordial does our relationship to it become.'[30] In skateboarding this relationship is rendered spatial and dynamic, as recognized by skaters like Peralta when saying that 'in the old days you moved *on* the board, while now you move *with* the board and the board moves with you' (Figure 9.4). Or as Haugo simply described Gelfand, 'It was like the board was part of his body.'[31]

For the skater, the skateboard is further related to the body through differing co-ordinates; Rodney Mullen described this process as thinking in categories 'like rolling forward, backward rail, stationary, 50/50 or aerial', or as combinations of movements.[32] These movements can be basic, such as whether the skater stands on the board with their left or right foot forward ('regular' or 'goofy'), moves backward ('fakie', 'switch-stance') or transfers to a backward direction ('revert', 'fakie'), or whether the move is slow or fast, ('slash grind', 'axle stall', 'fast plant') etc. Alternatively, move variations can be mind-bogglingly complex, for example body-board relations, referring to specific arm-leg-foot-board dynamics, such as a 'pop shove-it' (ollie with board kicked through 180° beneath the skater); forms of rotation, such as a 'varial heelflip' (heelflip combined with a frontside pop shove-it); body-terrain orientations, such as a 'boneless' (front foot taken off the board to enact a jump); and board-terrain combinations, such as a 'blunt' (board nose or tail blocked against the top of the wall). Indeed, *The Berrics*'s 'Trickipedia' classifies over 200 tricks, from the relatively simple '360 flip' to the artful 'nollie backside 180 switch backside 50-50'.[33] Similarly, in one duel-format run at the 2015 Skateboarding World Championships at Kimberley, South Africa, Luan Oliveira and Nyjah Huston completed such moves as a backspin nose grind, hardflip over the rail, frontside flip, fakie 5-0 grind, nollie 180 backside nose grind with 180 out, switch frontside flip manual, switch tailslide 270 out, cab backslide lipslide to fakie, switch 360 flip, half cab

backsmith 180 out, switch back flip, switch frontside feeble, backside flip over the rail and backside 270 noseblunt (Figure 5.20).[34]

Within such moves, the skateboard becomes a bodily augmentation, absorbed into the body-terrain encounter such that, according to *Thrasher*, 'making your board an extension of your body is control of your soul.'[35] As this suggests, such acts are mental as well as physical, skaters projecting themselves out into the board and space beyond. Some even remark on how their skateboard takes on their personality, and becomes 'almost an actual part' of themselves.[36] Mullen again provides intriguing insights, conceiving of the skateboard as being something both autonomous and brought within the body, a process where technical operations are secondary considerations. 'I kick my board around sometimes and watch its motions as it twirls around,' muses Mullen. 'I get an idea of what I want to do, then I think over it a lot, like where my feet have to be to press the board back. I think about the mechanics of it after the fact;'[37] all of this is evident in Mullen's freestyle skateboarding, as seen at Vancouver's 1986 Transworld Skateboard Championships recorded in *Radical Moves* (Larry Dean, 1988) (Figure 9.5), and in the later 360° footage for *Liminal* shot by Steven Sebring.[38]

In these interactions, skaters create what Heidegger calls *circumspection*, whereby an intimate knowledge of an instrument (skateboard) and a craft (skateboarding) leads to a heightened understanding of the inter-relation between skater and skateboard.[39] However, while this suggests the skateboard, skateboarding and the body are, in Heideggerean terms, linked solely as a tool-body relation, in fact the skater and skateboard are also engaged with the terrain underfoot. Furthermore, a skater is never alone, but always encounters other people and things. In short, skateboarding's production of space is not *purely* sensorial; instead, the skater's body produces its space as part of larger processes and contexts, that we will now investigate.

Ask the Coping

How does body-centric space relate to those terrains that are directed at skateboarding, such as skateparks? What is involved in the body-skateboard-terrain intersection?

Bodies and Terrains

While some skateparks were designed as highly visual affairs – like the $1 million *Star Wars*–based The Galaxy intended for the San Fernando Valley (1978) and the more recent Pinball skatepark in Auckland (2011) – most skateparks are intensely directed towards the skater's kinetic body.[40] Pre-eminent here is how the *curvature in plan* of many features, such as round pools and snake runs, provokes high-speed carving across walls, throwing the skater back against themselves through centrifugal and centripetal forces. 'In pools and on banks,' explained Peralta, 'I use the inherent power of the forms, working with the natural speed.'[41] For example, the tight hooks of Pipeline's Combi-Pool allowed skaters to gain speed, and so helped originate moves like corner boardslides. 'On a ramp you learn how to manipulate your board,' argued Chris Miller, 'but in a big pool you just ride it.'[42]

Second, different *transitions* – curvature in section – of floor-wall junctions also have varying effects. In particular, tighter transitions lead to greater speed and availability of flat wall above, thrusting skaters upwards both suddenly and forcefully. Again, this occurred at the Combi-Pool as, according to Bill Stinson, 'a sensation of weightlessness' and an 'ease in which the body would naturally surge.'[43] Alternatively, the more relaxed transitions of vert-ramps allow skaters to ascend more gently, and so concentrate on more complex moves.

Third, the *flat bottoms* added to bowls and half-pipes in the late 1970s allowed greater time between moves and stronger pumping through transitions. Riding across flat bottoms also contrasts with explosive efforts generated on the walls, forming a counter-rhythm within a skater's run.

Fourth, *drop-in points* forming the entrance to some pools and pipes help accelerate initial speed. They also provide orientation and directionality to otherwise continuous or symmetrical shapes.

Fifth, the *smoothness* of surface contributes dramatically to the skater's micro-experience, affecting speed, noise, grip and predictability. Smoothness may also encourage a heightened fluidity in the skater's own style, wherein surface is translated into gesture and attitude.

Sixth, the *harmony* (symmetry and balanced combinations) of walls excites a greater diversity of moves and dynamism of a run. The recent flow-bowls of the 2010s particularly emphasize these qualities, as with Georgia's Kenneshaw skatepark (2013). Kenneshaw's website proclaims:

> You want a bowl that starts at a depth of four-and-a-half feet, with waterfalls to a six-foot depth and then nine- to eight-foot transitions and a foot of vert. You want an area that has an oververt pocket with a one foot extension and a roll-in on the hip. And all this adds up to boat loads of fun, fast lines. Good times.[44]

Seventh, the *wall edge* provides a focus for a move and, particularly where projecting coping is used, suddenly throws skaters back onto themselves. Such events form contrapuntal moments within the continuity of a run generated from harmony and smoothness.

Eighth, a skatepark's *variegated range* of features allows skateboarders to combine diverse trajectories within one run. In particular, skate plazas and street course areas allow skaters to move between elements, such as the Huntington Beach Vans skatepark street course (2014) with 'hundreds of lines and options to choose from.'[45]

But this architecture does not entirely dictate skateboarding; for example, Del Mar Skate Ranch, asserted Garry Davis, was a 'drawing board' where new moves and routes constantly ensued (Figure 9.6).[46] Instead, the skatepark-skater relation is a process of response and re-creation, where architecture is no longer entirely separate to the skater, instead being absorbed into the body-board-terrain relation. Furthermore, enactments of this spatial process vary according to individual skaters' actions. 'The lines a skater takes,' declared Simon Napper, 'are like fingerprints.'[47]

This process all takes place through a precise bodily *questioning* of skatepark architecture by skateboarding. What is the purpose of these forms? What is the relation of curves, verticals, textures, surfaces? 'Ask the coping,' demanded Brian Brannon. 'It quivers at the sight of a pool-rider's bare trucks. But that's what it's for; its round edge protrudes to be pulverized, its cement cries to be ground to the bone, its fat lip exists as an earthly exit for sky-bound wheels.'[48] In short, the skater interrogates architecture as another body in relation to their own actions, and so correlates readily with Lefebvre's theorization of such processes.

> Objects touch one another, feel, smell and hear one another. Then they contemplate one another with eye and gaze. Within each body the rest of the world is reflected, and referred back to, in an ever-renewed to-and-fro of reciprocal reflection, an interplay of shifting colours, lights and forms.[49]

These questioning actions are highly significant. Where architectural modernism is often viewed by Lefebvre and others as emphasizing homogeneity, intellectualism, vision and geometry at the expense of richer bodily senses, pleasures and locality, the skater projects their body onto architecture, and so reproduces it on their own terms, a process in skateboarding that Glenney and Mull have called 're-wilding.'[50] Skateboarding thus accords with Lefebvre's contention that space 'does not consist in the projection of an intellectual representation, does not arise from the visible-readable realm' but rather space is 'first of all *heard* (listened to) and *enacted* (through physical gestures and movements).'[51]

These assertions correlate with what O'Connor and others refer to as skateboarding's embodied experience.[52] The range of senses is key here, for besides intense vision skateboarding is highly responsive in touch, balance, hearing, muscularity, agility and fluidity, thus concurring with philosopher Michel Serres's contention that the senses are not isolated channels but part of 'mingled bodies.'[53] 'You use your whole body and your whole mind,' revealed Peralta, 'You

Figure 9.7
Reformulation of
the body. Iain Borden,
frontside air at Better
Extreme, London
(2016).
© Andy Turner.

can't help but flow.'[54] *SkateBoarder* similarly referred to Ellen Berryman's 'incredible space-orientation (balance, timing, reflexes)' and to moves as being 'felt rather than seen.'[55] As this suggests, in skateboarding intense bodily and mental processes become as one.

Much of this stems from skateboarding's intrinsic dynamism; 'I've gotta be moving fast,' professed Napper.[56] As both Merleau-Ponty and aesthetician August Schmarsow note, we relate to space by envisaging that we are in motion by using terms like 'extension,' 'expanse' and 'direction,' and by measuring size through the movement of the body and eye. 'Because movement is not limited to submitting passively to space and time, it actively assumes them,' explains Merleau-Ponty.[57] Or as Schmarsow contends, we cannot express space 'in any other way than by imagining that we are in motion, measuring the length, width and depth, or by attributing to the static lines, surfaces, and volumes the movement that our eyes and our kinesthetic sensations suggest.'[58] This is a liberating process, particularly when, as with skateboarding, movement is inherent to the activity. 'Speed will set you free,' proclaimed Brannon. 'Catch it and then hang on for the glide. With speed, nothing is impossible.'[59]

Because skateboarding is both body-centric and mobile, space is projected from the whole body and not just the eye or intellect. Hesselgrave thus exhorts skaters to 'put your mind and

your body in tune.'[60] Alongside this mind-body construct, skaters also interpolate architecture as an equally significant projector of space. For example, Lefebvre notes that a pedestrian crossing a road consciously calculates distance and steps, the resulting space being composed of architecture (road), mind (calculation) and bodily action (steps).[61] Similarly, when a street-skater ollies between two ledges, their mental computation of architectural distance and direction is accompanied by bodily speed and jumping. Furthermore, both architectural *presence* (ledges) and *absence* (gap) are addressed, the ollie changing ledge-separation into ledge-coupling; the gap is at once stressed and removed, and architecture is transformed. In skateboarding, architecture, to borrow from Lefebvre, 'reproduces itself within those who use the space in question, within their lived experience. Of that experience the tourist, the passive spectator, can grasp but a pale shadow.'[62] Architecture is at once erased and reborn in the act of skateboarding.

Space, then, is produced outward from the body, with the skateboard and terrain underfoot both being transformed within in this process. 'The body, your body, my body,' advances architect Bernard Tschumi, are 'the starting point and point of arrival of architecture.'[63] But of course the body, too, is reformulated. To give one obvious example, my seated body as I type these words involves the smallest movements of hands, neck and eyes, and so is very different

Figure 9.8
Kyle Wester sets a new speed
record at 89.41 mph (Santa Cruz
Skateboards, 2016).
www.bit.ly/Wester-Fastest

to my dynamic body as constituted in, say, a frontside aerial (Figure 9.7). Through such processes, skateboarding, within a world dominated by passive and visual bodies, allows a glimpse of a more dynamic and complete body, what Lefebvre calls a 'fleshy' and 'spatial body' produced through 'rhythmanalysis' – going beyond vision or simple bodily actions like breathing, hungering, looking and sleeping, to include all senses, social life and thought.[64]

In the act of skateboarding, the skater's body is born from its complex distortions and engagements with skateboard and terrain. For example, when Hawk performs a 540° variation, his body becomes a 'twisted mass' unrecognizable though speed and contortion.[65] The names given to such moves are then merely attempts to classify otherwise incomprehensible entities; tellingly, *The Berrics*'s 'Trickipedia' does not try to explain moves in words, relying instead purely on moving images for elucidation. Beyond words is where skateboarding really occurs.

A different kind of time is also intrinsic to skateboarding space. Whereas time today is increasingly dominated by measured clock-time and economic rationales, time in skateboarding ranges from the duration of the session to the length of a skater's run, or the rhythmic pattern as the skater progresses from obstacle to obstacle. A street run, for example, is an undulating flow of glides and pushes, interspersed by sudden eruptions of energy. Calm periods, a few seconds long, are punctuated by even shorter engagements between board and terrain; intervals of serene efficiency contrast with massive concentrations of physical effort.

Within each move, time and energy are further differentiated; in a street ollie, for example, the moment when the skater leaves the ground is a

sudden departure, announced by the crack of the board tail striking the ground, followed by a suspended interval where board and body hover in space, waiting for gravity to complete the final and sudden landing. 'Everything slows down up there,' described Christian Hosoi of a large aerial. 'It takes forever because you're thinking of what you've got to do, calculating your projectile, your landing, everything.'[66] The most spectacular part of the move is thus often, contradictorily, where time seemingly stands still.

Dynamic Composition

In summary, skateboarding is a process wherein body, skateboard and architecture are all absorbed, destroyed and reborn in relation to each other. Consequently its mode of composition is very different to that of architecture, skateboarding being, according to Jerry Casale, 'beyond the normal balance of things.'[67] In place of architecture's serious arrangements, instilling cohesion and balance, hierarchies and order, logic and predictability, are skateboarding's playful oscillations, suggesting conflict and contradiction, chaos and confusion, emotion and spontaneity.

Correspondingly, skateboarding's engagement with architecture is dynamic, and as such is closer to the performance of music or the declaration of poetry than it is to the sights of the visual arts. Like music and dance, skateboarding creates what Lefebvre calls 'repetitions and redundancies of rhythms' and 'symmetries and asymmetries' irreducible to analytic thought, such that for *Thrasher* an 'insane trick' has 'nothing to do with the trick itself' but is instead a combination of 'terrain, the individual, the madness of the moment and the situation at hand'.[68] Skateboarding is like James Joyce's 'festival of language, a delirium of words' transposed into a festival of movements, a series of precise yet deranged bodily actions, that ultimately destroys and re-creates

Figure 9.9
Cliff Coleman control sliding in *Flow*
(Gravity, 2003).
www.bit.ly/Coleman-Flow

body, skateboard and architecture together. Skateboarding space is above, beyond and in excess of the space of objects or the space of the body.[69] This is super-architectural space.

Flow

While *The Quarterly SkateBoarder* encouraged readers to slow down and focus on other performance measures – 'this isn't a sport of speed, it's a sport of skill' – going fast has in fact always been an essential skateboarding thrill.[70] Indeed today, as noted in *Signal Hill Speed Run* (2014), stand-up and luge downhill riders are an international phenomenon, with speedsters like Kenny Anderson, Mauritz Armfelt, J.M. Duran, James Kelly, Matt Kienzle, Patrick Rizzo and Noah Sakamoto hitting velocities over 70 mph; in 2016, at an undisclosed location, Kyle Wester set an astounding stand-up world record of 89.41 mph (Figure 9.8).[71] Downhill has even come downtown, with an increased fashion in the 2010s for 'bombing' urban hills, often risking unpredictable asphalt, unsighted intersections and wayward traffic.

What then are the main spatial features of this high-speed skateboarding? What bodily and mental processes are involved, and how might they differ from other riding specialisms?

Continuity

During the early 1970s, semi-illegal road racing was taking place in Southern Californian mountains. 'It was highly underground,' recalled luge-skater Marcus Rietema. 'We would get thirty guys together and race nine miles down a road where cars were traveling at the same time. We kept going until the police stopped us.'[72] By 1975, *SkateBoarder* was actively promoting downhill, with Denis Shufeldt extolling the 'rush of adrenalin that excited me to the point of ignorant bliss,' while San Diego's famous annual Signal Hill event (1975–1978) provided speeds approaching 60 mph, as well as several near-fatal crashes.[73]

In subsequent years all manner of road-racing, downhill and velocity-intensive riding has taken place. Significantly, during the mid-1970s Northern Californian Cliff Coleman perfected the 'Coleman slide' to rapidly decelerate while speeding downwards. In this manoeuvre, the skater adopts a low-gravity stance, throwing a controlled sideways skid while leaning off the board and skimming a specially-gloved sliding hand along the road surface (Figure 9.9).

The Coleman slide and other variants (pendulum slides, drifts, pre-drifts, speed checks, etc.) have opened up a whole series of new terrains, allowing skaters to negotiate almost any mountainous gradients, twisting turns and even motorized traffic. Other tactics adopted include lookouts posted on blind corners, signalling with arm-movements or walkie-talkies. A sense of commitment and abandonment is, however, still required. Hamm, for example, describes Buena Vista Run in Coleman's San Francisco as having fifteen 'narrow, tight switchbacks' where 'bombing down on a skateboard requires something more. Call it insanity.'[74]

While Coleman-type slides allow downhillers to readily adjust their speed, just as important is the hyper-alert anticipation these skaters share with fast-moving cyclists and motorcyclists, who are constantly tuned to changes in direction, texture, grip, undulation and camber, as well as to straying vehicles. Here, the immediate sense of movement – speed, trajectory, adhesion – is constantly modulated with an anticipation of what is about to occur (a manhole cover just to the left, a right-hand turn in 50 m) and that which might occur (will that car pull out, what lies around the next bend?). Consequently, the absolutely immediate is always imbued with the soon-to-arrive, creating a mobile compression of time and space, of the here-and-now *with* the there-and-next, and so in a manner quite different to a street-skater's move *from* one

Figure 9.10
Byron Essert and Alex Tongue
rush along an extended Alpine
descent (2014).
www.bit.ly/EssertTongue-Alps

object to another, or a vert rider's transition *between* walls, or a slalom racer's focus on the *precise distance* between cones.

Rhythmic modulations further complicate this experience, such as tucked-in straights, decelerating speed checks, drifting bends and high-velocity curves. Different techniques and styles also occur; during the 1970s, downhillers like Chuy Madrigal, John Hutson, Dave Dillberg and Mike Goldman developed different forms of body-streamlining, with various body squats and tucks, and swept-back or stretched-forward arms, while other variations involve subtly attenuated crouches, slides, feet positions, hand gestures and visual road-tracking techniques.[75] The overall sense is of skateboarding as a single, unfolding trajectory, as a combination of road surface, board, body and time that makes most sense as an integrated run lasting minutes and not seconds. Accordingly, *Spinn'in Wheels* shows an extended La Costa descent as an unbroken trajectory, while today YouTube offers innumerable examples, such as Aera trucks riders Byron Essert and Alex Tongue during a two-minute Alpine descent in 2014 (Figure 9.10).[76]

Freedom in the Now

Because of this extended temporality, compared to other skateboarding specialisms downhill is more open to mental contemplation and what Wheaton calls the 'buzz' or 'the ecstasy of speed, being "at one" with the environment, the standing still of time.'[77] In particular, forms of skateboard racing like downhill, slalom and skatercross engender the positive sense of 'flow' articulated by psychologist Mihaly Csikszentmihalyi, who proposes that life's best moments occur 'when a person's body or mind is stretched to its limits in a voluntary effort to accomplish something difficult and worthwhile'. In short, flow as an optimal state of inner

experience occurs when our skills fully match opportunities, and we 'concentrate attention on the task at hand and momentarily forget everything else.'[78]

This sense of flow is not of course unique to downhill. For example, freestyler Daniel Gesmer has spoken of the 'magic of effortless gliding', James Pisano relates skateboarding to Taoist I Ching principles of being centred, aware, disciplined, authentic, positive, balanced, modest and in constant progress, and Peralta has described how skateboarding inculcates a sense of total peace within complete chaos, and consequently a feeling of being more relaxed than even when sitting down.[79] Similarly, in Seifert and Hedderson's explorations of flow, skatepark riders commented on feelings of euphoria, emancipation, transcendence, absorption, tranquillity and an altered sense of time. 'I feel like I am unstoppable', recounted Skater B, 'like a weight has been lifted off my shoulders and I am under no pressure whatsoever.' Similarly Skater M talked of being 'in the zone' and 'in a different world all together. You just feel away.'[80] The same is true for vert skaters like Andy Macdonald, who described his X Games riding as when 'my body just takes over and I don't think about the routine step-by-step. It all becomes one forty-five-second trick – one movement of the body.'[81]

But it is undoubtedly in gravity-oriented skateboarding that flow is foregrounded most, whether Justin Metcalf characterizing hill descents as simply 'bliss' or slalomer John Ravitch feeling that his body instinctively knows what to do – 'go hard, go fast and think about it later.'[82] More evocatively still, the yoga-trained Shufeldt described steep hills as the 'energy source' upon which 'mastering the moment' could lead to 'freedom in the now'.[83]

Figure 9.11
Informal hill bomb contest, San Francisco (Snack Skateboards, 2016).
www.bit.ly/HillBomb-SanFrancisco

Risk

In action sports like skateboarding, feelings of flow are heightened by an element of danger, which Orpana interprets in terms of Stephen Lyng's theory of 'edgework'. This edgework – a term originally coined by Hunter S. Thompson – is the heightened experience derived from negotiating the boundaries of control, chaos, life and death in situations that others would consider impossible, the result for actions sports practitioners being a 'hyperreal' focus on the immediate present. Significantly, and still following Lyng, Orpana sees edgework not as purely personal acts, but as being born from our shared experience of alienation and reification, the risk-taker being motivated by a 'sense of communal or public recognition' to pursue their death-defying feats. 'Only in the situation of death can the bare life of the subject', argues Orpana, 'be fully isolated and "freed" from biopolitical governance, thus performing the desire for escape (from precariousness and fragmentation) that drives these practices.'[84]

To some extent this, of course, occurs in all skateboarding, where, argues Langseth, risk-taking is either a compensatory escape from modern society or is a personal adaptation to the imperatives of late modernity.[85] Certainly some skateboarders are attracted to danger; vert skater Andy Macdonald was diagnosed by a psychologist studying X Games athletes as a 'natural-born risk taker' who only ever feels truly alive when close to dying.[86] Skate prankster Bam Margera has even extended this into non-skateboarding realms, including jumping from a six storey hotel balcony into a pool just 2.6 m deep, while Christian Hosoi has similarly described a life of death-defying incidents, from crawling along a roof while still a baby to standing on a twenty-storey penthouse ledge. 'I did enjoy the scent of danger,' reasoned Hosoi. 'I got the same kind of rush from tempting fate that I get from skating big ramps.'[87]

Yet it is during downhill skateboarding – whether full-on attacks on Alpine passes, bombing local hills or negotiating inner-city slopes – that skateboarders typically meet their most dangerous and sometimes life-threatening situations. Even organized hill bomb contests frequently involve high-speed spills, slides and scrapes (Figure 9.11), while for downhillers the results can be much worse; Justin Metcalf, for example, was in a coma following a 15 m mountain-side fall in Washington State in 2007, while Australian documentarian Anton Fricker died during the filming of *Skate Australia* (2010) after a collision with a fellow downhiller.[88] Any quick internet search will reveal a litany of accidents during downhill, hill bombing and fast cruising, including fatal collisions with other downhillers, trees or traffic. In 2013, there were twenty-one US skateboarding fatalities, all involving downhill, hill bombing or 'skitching' a ride from a moving vehicle. As a result, many US cities, including Los Angeles, Malibu, Laguna Beach, Rancho Palos Verdes and Newport Beach, have banned irresponsible downhill riding, issuing miscreants with fines up to $1,000. In Auckland, New Zealand, police have attempted to remove downhillers from suburban roads even though the activity is not in fact illegal.[89]

Acid Drops

One physiological explanation for the attraction of action sports practitioners to high-thrill activities is an addiction to dopamine, the compound secreted in the brain to signal pleasure.[90] While some academics dispute this theory, there is undoubtedly some kind of 'rush' inherent to skateboarding speed. Skateboarding, declares Tony Alva, is 'that thing that burns inside you – it's like the cleanest, purest form of high that you can get.'[91]

This might help explain how some riders have used drugs to heighten their awareness of body, board and skateboarding dynamism,

JEFF PHILLIPS

TRACKER
TRUCKS

while Davidson has argued that marijuana both increases oxygen intake for short periods and reduces fears of injury.[92] Certainly Hosoi considered marijuana to be a central feature of the Marina del Rey skatepark skate scene, where heavier drugs were also prevalent. 'Marijuana makes you focus more on your board,' explained one professional vert contestant. 'I can concentrate more when I'm high.'[93] According to Hamm, smoking pot also featured strongly in the 1970s Northern Californian downhill scene, as 'part of the sensory thrill and focused confidence and therapeutic catharsis' when negotiating high-speed hairpin turns.[94] Alternatively, for street-skater Almir Jusovic, the drug is integral to the expressive process. 'I usually smoke weed before I skate,' explains Jusovic. 'I was high the whole time filming my first skate part. I am most creative and get ideas when I take a break and don't smoke for a week or so. Then when I get high again I just start writing down stuff like crazy.'[95]

Other drugs have also featured. Supposedly, Mike Goldman took LSD before his 1977 Signal Hill downhill run, and in the 1980s Jeff Phillips (Figure 9.12) took hallucinogens during vert contests, including while winning the Vision Rock 'n Roll Jam (1986).[96] Around this time, drugs like acid, cocaine, ecstasy, heroin, marijuana and hallucinogenic mushrooms figured in some professionals' lives. 'We travel from contest to contest,' disclosed Hosoi, 'do a few practice runs, maybe score some mushrooms or acid and drop it for our entertainment at night.'[97] Tas Pappas later recalled how skating on acid at the Skatepark of Tampa made him feel as balanced as Leonardo da Vinci's 'Vitruvian Man,' while some famous video parts were also reputedly performed under the heavy influence of stimulants, including alcohol for Dustin Dollin in *Baker 3* (2005), pharmaceutical pills for Dylan Rieder in *Mind Field* (2009) and crack for James Kelch in *The Real Video* (1993).[98] As this all indicates, in skateboarding the lines between drug-induced sensations and adrenaline-fuelled highs of physical movement can sometimes become blurred, intermingling to form new performances and social scenes.

Projecting

So far we have considered skateboarding performance in relation to the skater's personal body, immediate terrain and speed. However, as Lefebvre argues, the space of the body is also the space of others, seeing 'my space' as 'first of all my body' but then also 'my body's counterpart or "other"', its mirror-image or shadow.'[99] For skateboarders, one important element in this process is the way representations of skateboarding are integrated into their practices. These are *lived images* – photographs, movies, names and other descriptions which are reborn through the acts of skateboarding and its wider networks.

Performing Images

From its earliest days, imagery has been central to skateboarding, as with the extensive photography of the first *SkateBoarder* issues or the way that skaters like Jay Adams and Russ Howell learned moves from the movie *Skaterdater*. Indeed, beginners, competent amateurs and professionals alike are highly influenced by photographs. 'We see a hot shot in the magazine,' reflected Jeremy Henderson, 'and we have to figure what went on before that.'[100] Or as *Sidewalk* concluded, 'Without photographs, there wouldn't be a global skate scene.'[101] But what is the process by which this occurs?

Obviously, imagery is often instructional, allowing skaters to learn skills and moves from each other. Imagery is also significant for how it documents, celebrates, interprets, postulates and communicates skateboarding, as discussed in Chapter 5. But there is also another and hugely significant aspect worth considering – the way skaters bodily incorporate images by re-enacting photographs and video clips through their own moves and gestures.

Pre-eminent here is the way skaters ride, for qualities of elegance, fluidity, speed and above all style are undoubtedly important in skateboarding. 'If a rider looks good, if he's got style, his tricks are going to look all the more healthy,' argued Danny Acton-Bond.[102] Steve Caballero agreed, 'It's not how many hard tricks you can do, it's the way you perform the trick. That's where style comes in.'[103] For these reasons the Variflex pros of the late 1970s and 1980s – including Allen Losi, Eric Grisham, Pattie Hoffman, Steve Hirsch and Eddie Elguera (Figure 9.13) – were sometimes castigated as 'Varibots' for their supposedly robotic emphasis on complicated moves rather than on aggression, grace or attitude. 'Instead of worrying about style,' admits Losi, 'we just did tricks.'[104] Hawk met with similar criticisms (Duane Peters attacked him for 'doing some shit that didn't make any sense'), as did street-skater Nate Sherwood, vert-rider Andy Macdonald and Rodney Mullen, whose minimal-style and trick-filled freestyling has even been termed 'skating degree zero' by Bill Schaffer (Figure 9.5).[105]

Style itself, however, is notoriously difficult to specify. Definitions have varied from Yochim's 'dialectic of grace and aggression' and Chris Miller's 'economy of motion' to Steve Kane's 'more an attitude than a technique'.[106] 'Style in skateboarding is the way you move and carry yourself on skateboard,' says Vivien Fell. 'It's what makes a skateboarder obviously unique and immediately recognisable, like the features of someone's face.'[107] More metaphorically, *Thrasher* suggests style as being not 'the full action-wear wardrobe' but 'the backspin on the quarters as you put them in the candy machine'.[108] Style can also be related to craftsmanship, which sociologist Richard Sennett's considers as being not what you do but how you do it.[109] Whatever the definition, in skateboarding style is commonly considered superior to expertise. The 1978 UK tour by Alva, for example, produced considerable debate on this matter, when it became clear that his technical ability fell below that of local skaters like Mark Baker. Nonetheless, as James Fraser elaborated, Alva's reputation was founded on 'force, grace and sheer fluidity' and going beyond 'mere accomplishment of tricks'.[110] In short, asserts downhill rider Sergio Yuppie, 'tricks deserve applause, but style deserves respect'.[111]

Nonetheless, while professionals as varied as Lizzie Armanto (Figure 3.3), Neil Blender, Mark Gonzales (Figure 10.1), Gou Miyagi (Figure 11.3), Tom Penny, Dylan Rieder (Figure 10.11), Ben Raybourn, Mark Suciu, Ishod Wair and Brandon Westgate have become renowned for their individual style, for many skaters the tricks they do are important measures of success and self-identity. This is most explicit in magazines, where photograph captions typically identify the skateboarder, move and location, such as one from *Thrasher* citing 'Brad Cromer, ollie up to impossible on the Challenger monument'.[112] The skater-move combination also comes together explicitly whenever a new move is named after its inventor, such as 'Bert' (Larry Bertlemann), 'Elguerial' (Eddie Elguera) 'Caballerial (Steve Caballero), 'Miller Flip' (Darrell Miller) and 'McTwist' (Mike McGill) (Figure 9.3).

The importance of moves is also evident in that skateboarders frequently spend inordinate amounts of time actually failing to do what they attempt; for example, while filming for *Stay Gold*, Andrew Reynolds repeatedly and obsessively attempted a kickflip ollie down some stairs.[113] Nor is this unusual behaviour; *The Onion* even jokingly claimed that US researchers had discovered that 'not one of the nation's

nineteen million amateur skateboarders has successfully landed a single trick since 2001'.[114] Furthermore, having spent hours, days or even weeks trying a new trick, once successfully completed (and, importantly, filmed) the skater will often progress immediately to an even more difficult manoeuvre. This is especially true of a highly technical tendency within street-skating – as displayed in videos like *Questionable* (1992) (Figure 10.3), *In Bloom* (2002) and *Round Three* (2004) – wherein, encouraged by camcorders, smartphones and social media, skaters attempt ever more intricate moves until just one 'make' is recorded and shown to others. 'In the 80s, you were trying to learn a trick to keep in your arsenal,' explains Hawk. 'Nowadays I'm striving to learn tricks that I know I'm only going to do one time, film it, document it, and it's over.'[115]

Innovation, then, is highly prized within skateboarding. 'From the very beginning,' declared *Sidewalk*, 'skateboarders have been obsessed with forging new directions, inventing new tricks and claiming new obstacles.'[116] This kind of attitude was unsurprisingly prevalent among freestyle skaters like Mullen, who claimed that 'originality is most important to me', or Ellen O'Neal, who described how 'every time I get on the board, I'm trying to figure out something new.'[117] Contemporary street-skaters often adopt similar attitudes, where the intricacy of ollie variations mastered, number of steps conquered and gap-distance flown all serve to project skateboarding as an increasingly difficult endeavour. As Dupont relates in his study of the Buffalo and Phoenix scenes, avoiding ABD ('already been done') tricks in favour of NBD ('never been done') variations is key to gaining legitimacy as a skater.[118]

Many moves are elaborate evolutions of older ones, such as the 'kickflip frontside crooked grind', where the skater ollies onto a ledge while rotating the board rotating 360° about its longitudinal axis, performs a frontside grind along the ledge and then ollies back to ground. The visual dissemination of such new moves is also accompanied by language, with a welter of terms constantly being devised. To cite but a few, in 1995 the *DansWORLD* website was already listing, among many others, 'boardslide', 'fakie', 'hardflip', 'heelflip', 'kickflip', 'nollie kickflip', '360 flip', 'varial', 'grind', 'crooked', 'feeble', '50-50', '5-0', 'nosegrind', 'Smith', 'lipslide', 'noseslide', 'switch-stance' and 'tailslide', while in 2015 the hundreds of variations on The Berrics's 'Trickipedia' included 'bigflip', 'bigspin', 'boneless', 'bluntslide', 'Caballerial', 'half cab',

Figure 9.13
Eddie Elguera at a
Hester competition,
Hi-Roller, Boulder
(1979).
© Jim Goodrich.

'hurricane', 'impossible', 'no comply', 'pole jam', 'pop shuvit', 'pressure flip' and 'sugarcane'.[119]

Whether a trick is ABD or NBD can also be a matter of geography and location. Again, magazines, camcorders and social media play an important role here, quickly disseminating new moves worldwide, leading to globally dispersed rivalries among local skaters to see who can become, if not a trick inventor, then at least the first in their neighbourhood to re-create a new trick, or to achieve it at a specific skatespot. Indeed, skaters typically view repeating a move less as emulation and more as rendering it new to themselves, regardless of how often they duplicate it. 'No matter how many times you do something on your board, you never truly repeat yourself,' asserted *Sidewalk*. 'Every single trick is absolutely unique.'[120]

If tricks measure status and achievement, they also act as units of exchange, with skaters spending hours poring over photographs and videos to understand and acquire them. 'First time I saw Caballero doing a frontside slide-and-roll in a magazine,' recalled Lucian Hendricks, 'I studied that thing for weeks.'[121] Through such processes, skateboarders acquire moves and stockpile them in their reservoir of capabilities, although to preserve this ownership skaters must also continually re-perform their moves. 'Every new transition in your pocket,' considered Bob Burnquist, 'makes you a better skater.'[122] Consequently, when skaters undertake a run they are not only performing a physical act but also bodily reproducing skateboarding as codified in moves and communicated as images. Skateboarding moves are performed images, being simultaneously representations and action.

Reflections
In these performed images, photographs and videos act as a mirror, reflecting skaters back to themselves and others. In short, depictions of skateboarding moves are displayed both to the skater themself and to other skaters. This is particularly true in collective and informally competitive skateboarding sessions. 'Sessioneering,' explained Stecyk, is where 'the action is always faster, always more furious, and limits are always pushed harder than ever before.'[123] This kind of situation takes place at skateparks worldwide, including, for example, the Solid Surf at Harrow, where some of the best-known London skaters and H-Boyz locals took over (Figure 7.14). 'We would terrorize everybody,' revealed Rodga Harvey. 'Nobody would skate with us, they would just watch.'[124]

Although most skate sessions are less aggressive than those described by Stecyk and Harvey, they nonetheless incorporate unspoken codes and tacit customs. A session thus typically involves a group of skaters standing on a ramp platform, beside a bowl or near a skatespot, waiting for their run. Although never a formal queue, there is an implicit understanding that skaters generally get one run in turn; jumping this sequence is disparaged as 'snaking'.[125] Further, this waiting-looking area forms the primary social space; although non-skaters may look on, skaters are the ones who most loudly bang their boards in appreciation, shout encouragement, voice astonishment or offer friendly abuse. The result is a collective assault on the terrain being skated, skateboarders making individual contributions to the session as a whole. As Oskar Ristenfeldt describes sessions at challenging DIY spots like Malmö's Steppe Side, 'you need friends there, anyone who can get the fire burning' (Figure 5.25).[126] The session is both an informal competition between individuals and a collective action against architecture, filled with social intensity.

In this context, completing a trick is to render the skater, at the same time, themself, someone different, and part of a collective group. The process by which this occurs is the skate trick as something performed, recorded and imagined. The skate move or trick is, therefore, neither physical action nor pure representation, but a *lived image*. As such, the skater's run is at once a communication, development and personal enactment of websites, photographs, videos and social media clips. Every time skaters make moves they are at once replaying visual material through their own bodies, and transforming this imagery and themselves into complex intersections of each other.

Skateboarding consequently accords with the view of cultural theorists Ella Shohat and Robert Stam that there is nothing inherently regressive about spectatorship and images, and that skateboarding individuals and communities alike can relate together through these processes.[127] 'Seeing is not only believing but actually more pedagogical for these participants,' contends Petrone, 'for it is in the visual representation of something that the practices of the culture are embodied and personified and imbued with a greater sense of authenticity, credibility, and integrity.'[128]

This has some significant effects in skateboarding. Spatially, skaters incessantly oscillate between the immediacy of their bodies and the global dispersion of the skate community. Given that there are skateboarders in just about every city worldwide, a skater from, say, Paris's Bercy skatepark and skatespot may feel more in common, and have more communication, with other skaters in Lima, Prague or Tokyo than they do with non-skaters in Paris. 'I could go to Czechoslovakia,' considered Bod Boyle, 'and meet someone, couldn't even speak to the guy, but because we skate, have something between us.'[129] This community is knitted together though a lexicon of skate moves that riders view and enact. The image is hence not only locally lived but globally reproduced and internationally exchanged, while a skater's social space is similarly at once sited in a specific neighbourhood and networked with other localities dispersed worldwide.

There are two other considerations of skateboarding imagery worth exploring here. The first concerns the role of the photographer, for, as discussed in Chapter 5, skate photography reaches far beyond the technical exaggeration of moves. Skateboard photographers' deployment of wide-angle lenses is extremely unusual, for in most sports photography the telephoto lens is more common. Wide-angles, by contrast, emphasize not only the dramatic shapes of skaters' bodies, but also the location and social context of a skatepark or skatespot, allowing the viewer to imagine their own participation. Using wide-angles also forces photographers closer to the action, often shooting very near the riders; 'If you're not getting hit,' explains Grant Brittain, 'you're probably not close enough.'[130] At times this immediacy is even evidenced in the photograph itself: in the very first roll of 35 mm film shot by the fourteen-year-old Glen Friedman, two black and white images of Jay Adams riding the Teardrop pool capture either the photographer's own foot or his shadow at the base of the frame (Figure 9.14).[131] Like the personal reportage of gonzo journalism, Friedman here is not recording action with an external gaze, but is an intimate participant engaging with the unfolding scene. Sometimes this intimacy is more subtle, as, for example, when a street-skater photographer is captured in an urban reflection by Hendrik Herzmann (Figure 10.22), or a famous shot by Brittain using a pole-mounted camera to capture Chris Miller in the Combi-Pool, and where a shadow cast by the skater, photographer and an onlooker is revealed in the background.[132]

The second aspect of imagery worth considering concerns how particular skateboarding terrains become globally renowned, principally through repeated photography and filming. This is particularly the case with acclaimed skatespots, such as Barcelona's MACBA (Figure 10.10), Berlin's Kulturforum (Figure 10.11), Los Angeles's ARCO Rails and San Francisco's Hubba Hideout. Significantly, many of these skatespots have gained their reputation from videos, such as Shenzhen's Deng Xiaoping Plaza, Bao'an ledges, Museum, Palace and other locales 'clocking footage', according to *TransWorld*, 'in every major video from Zoo York to Lakai.'[133] Some spots, like Los Angeles's Carlsbad Gap and Berlin's Warschauer Benches, have even been subjected to focused film studies, while video parts like Mike Carroll's in *Goldfish* helped propel San Francisco's Embarcadero scene to global prominence, as did Tom Penny's part in *Uno* (1996) for San Diego's Chain to Bank.[134]

Skatepark elements can also gain spectacular qualities, as with the pools at Münster, Marina del Rey (Figure 7.10) and Rom (Figure 7.13). The iconic forms of Pipeline's Combi-Pool, for example, made it instantly recognizable in photographs, which enhanced its global renown as somewhere 'designed to test and push the limits of skateboarding.'[135] Consequently, skaters may perceive themselves as much for skating the famous Combi-Pool as the physical Combi-Pool (Figures 7.11 and 7.12). Similarly a move like Heath Kirchart's lipslide at Orange County's El Toro in 1998 was remarkable for the audacious move itself, for being performed down a renowned twenty-stair handrail and for featuring in *The End*. In the same vein, Guy Mariano's switch pop shove-it nosegrind down the UC Irvine rail (1997), Andy Reynold's kickflip down the Hollywood sixteen-stair (2000) and Mike Vallely's ollie airwalk down the West Hollywood twelve-stair (2005), were all cited in a *TransWorld* survey as key moments in skateboard history, at least in part because of the specific places where they occurred.[136]

This may partly explain the occasional territorialization of skateparks or skatespots, when locals meet outsiders with disdain or aggression. 'The local kids won't even speak to us,' complained Gilbert Angol. 'They really resent us coming up to "their" park.'[137] In such instances, locals see the terrain as being invested with a character of their own making, and that outsiders are somehow threatening.

'It was good,' declared Harvey of Solid Surf, 'because it was OUR park and it was us.'[138]

This is similar to how sports fans often feel attachment to their local stadium. But for skateboarders, the process is more directly participatory, a bodily, painful and emotional familiarity to the extent that for some their skatepark becomes the only place they can imagine skating. 'I've been skating here for seven years and I've slammed a lot,' recounted Dan Cavaliero of Pipeline. 'When this place is torn down, I'll probably quit skating. It's the only place I have.'[139] Or as Hawk felt on frequenting Oasis and Del Mar, 'for the first in my life I actually felt content. The park was my family room.'[140]

Skaters give to the terrain, and terrain reflects back to them, meaning and identity. Consequently, the aura of danger associated with some skatespots and skateparks has helped riders to distinguish themselves through localized masculinity. For example, over many years local professionals like Steve Alba and Jim Gray built up an injury-strewn intimacy with the Combi-Pool. 'This place separates the men from the boys,' asserted Alba. 'The people here know how to deal with the pain.'[141] Or in Jeff Grosso's blunt provocation, 'come to Upland and ride the pool and show me you're a man.'[142] Indeed, this masculinity was even considered to extend much further afield. 'If you did good there in a contest,' recalled Alba, 'you were considered by many to have conquered all of skateboarding' (Figures 7.11 and 7.12).[143]

However, the spectacular nature of some skatepark pools, bowls and pipes can also lead to skaters becoming dissatisfied, bored or even scared. The intimidatingly deep Combi-Pool at Pipeline, the Performance Bowls at London's Solid Surf and Rom skateparks, Marina del Rey's Dogbowl and Münster's pool were often seen as 'proving ground' terrains, being too large, difficult or intimidating for all but the most expert or courageous.[144] Indeed, the Combi-Pool's tight transitions and expansive verticals were ill-suited to the more complex and risky moves developed in the 1980s; according to Hawk, other challenges included coping that 'protruded like a set of buckteeth' and flat-bottoms 'so rough that they resembled a gravel pit'. As co-owner Jean Hoffman explained, these were not endearing features, for 'kids found it was hard and they didn't look good here.'[145]

Indeed, even advanced skaters were wary of the Combi-Pool which, according to Gray, may have been a 'concrete wonderland' but was also a bumpy and unpredictable 'concrete nightmare' at which 'eighty per cent of pros are afraid to skate.'[146] In an infamous incident during the 1985 Rage at Badlands contest, Chris Miller rocketed a high-speed backside air before, on re-entry, hitting the square-pool coping with his rear truck. Diving straight to the tight transition, Miller thumped the back of his head before collapsing like a rag doll into an immobile, twitching heap.[147]

Whatever the challenges offered, because skateparks have self-evidently been deliberately provided for skateboarding, some skateboarders tire of them. 'That's the thing about skate parks,' complained Alva. 'The Dogtown guys have hit every skate park and ripped it; then they've split, cuz they've taken it to the limit and then get burned out on a spot.'[148] Dissatisfaction is often strongest when skateparks also impose strict regulations; for example, Del Mar Skate Ranch tried to establish rigid opening hours, safety rules, entrance charges and even behaviour codes.[149] More usually, skatepark regulations focus on session-based time periods or ask skaters to demonstrate competence. In the 1970s, for example, London's Skate City operated a coloured-badge proficiency system, while today Hong Kong's TKO skatepark opens its keyhole pool only for pre-booked training sessions and competitions. More frequently, many skateparks use ID cards to control access, which runs contrary to skateboarders' anti-institutional sensitivities.

* * *

If skateboarders dislike the way some skateparks implement fees, memberships, codes and standards, and can offer somewhat standardized and predictable terrains, they nonetheless resist these tendencies through their dynamic bodily actions. Lefebvre describes this process as 'a body facing another body' each having an 'accessible symmetry' through 'expenditures of energy, of aggression or desire.'[150] Architecture is therefore both separate from, yet brought within, the act of skateboarding, and so is dissolved, recast and rematerialized. In this sense, skateboarding is nothing less than a sensual, physical and emotional desire for one's own body in motion, and to engage with architecture and other people; skateboarding is a crash and rebirth of self, body and terrain.

Figure 9.14
Jay Adams with
Paul Constantineau
(background) and
Glen Friedman
(shadow) at the
Teardrop pool,
Los Angeles (1976).
© Glen E. Friedman.

Skateboarding
Chapter 10 Skate and Destroy

To play is to be in world. Playing is a form of understanding what surrounds us and who we are, and a way of engaging with others.[1]
Miguel Sicart

Skateboarding is most distinctive when placed in urban streets, a role predicted by Kevin Thatcher's first *Thrasher* editorial, when describing it as 'a fast-paced feeling to fit this modern world', a process of 'finding something' and 'taking it to the ultimate limit – not dwelling on it, but using it to the fullest and moving on.' And as Thatcher concluded, 'there are tons of asphalt and concrete being poured every day, so – Grab That Board!'[2]

Through an everyday activity, skateboarding suggests that pleasure rather than work, using space rather than paying for it, activity rather than passivity, performing rather than watching, and creativity rather than destruction, are all potential components of our cities. Or as Craig Stecyk has famously asserted, 'Two hundred years of American technology has unwittingly created a massive cement playground of unlimited potential. But it was the minds of 11-year-olds that could see that potential.'[3]

The City Is the Hardware

Skaters can exist on the essentials of what is out there. Any terrain. For urban skaters the city is the hardware on their trip.[4]
Stacy Peralta

The 1980s witnessed the near total closure of the first skateparks. Rather than disappearing, however, skateboarding simply returned to the streets. For *Thrasher*, this meant targeting the everyday 'concrete jungle' offering 'literally thousands of shreddable terrains' in the form of 'banks, ramps, pools, curbs, loading docks, steps, parking garages, your driveway, anything!'[5] Or as *Space for Rent* postulates, 'street-skateboarding is a unique way of interacting with spaces and architecture, using shapes and surfaces in an entirely different way than they were originally intended.'

Skateboarding in urban terrains, of course, extended back to 1960s sidewalks and 1970s found spaces, and even continued alongside skatepark riding. 'Somewhere beyond the formalized spectrum, street-skating remains

supreme,' wrote Stecyk in 1976. 'On the banks, drainage ditches and streets of the land it's coming down hard and heavy.'[6] This kind of skater, considered Stecyk, was an 'urban anarchist' who used car parks, streets, sidewalks and sewers 'in a thousand ways that the original architects could never even dream of.'[7] Despite these exhortations, truly inventive street-based skateboarding in the late 1970s was limited to oddities like Steve Rocco's curb-based inverts. By 1981, however, *SkateBoarder* was again promoting street-skating – partly as a return to skateboarding's surf-related roots and partly as a search for the 'new urban terrorist' – while flat-ground freestyle was being invigorated by the street-crossover developments of Jim McCall, Bob Schmelzer, Tim Scroggs and Rodney Mullen.[8] Particularly important was Mullen's flat-ground adaptation of the ollie, although other skaters worldwide were no doubt also undertaking similar developments.[9] The cornerstone of street-skateboarding, the ollie's seemingly magical flight, by which a skater can

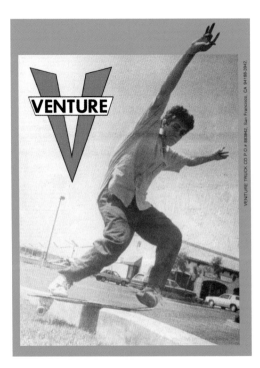

Figure 10.1
Mark Gonzales boardslides a ledge. Venture advertisement, *Thrasher* (October–November 1986).

make the board pop-up into the air, is nowadays enacted by millions of riders globally.

Commercial interests were also at play in the birth of street-skateboarding. Manufacturers such as Powell-Peralta anxiously sought post-skatepark terrains in order to stimulate consumer demand, and so in 1980 marketed back-to-basics 'Street Issue' decks, while Independent ran advertisements with lines like 'Free on the Streets'. A year later, Santa Cruz's advertisements focused exclusively on street-skating equipment.[10]

Action Now provided the first major coverage of street-skateboarding in 1981, but *Thrasher*'s April 1982 release was the first 'gnarly street issue' to concentrate on the new riding.[11] And although street-skating was occurring across the United States, the California-based magazines highlighted local riders. Pre-eminent through the 1980s were Natas Kaupas and Mark Gonzales (Figure 10.1), plus the likes of Ray Barbee, Eric Dressen and Tommy Guerrero, who exploited the ollie to ride up onto the walls, steps and street furniture of everyday urbanism.[12] 'I attempt to make everything skateable,' proclaimed Kaupas, 'walls, curbs, ramps, whatever', and his ability to negotiate the ninety degree junction between the ground and a wall, as shown in *Wheels of Fire* and *Streets on Fire*, emphatically proved his point (Figure 10.2).[13] Two years later, Gonzales famously ollied between a wave-shaped wall and platform at San Francisco's Embarcadero plaza, thus cementing the 'Gonz Gap' into skate folklore.[14] In 1987, *Thrasher* declared that skateboarding could engage with anything in the modern city, its seventy-two element list featuring everything from alleys, benches, curbs, dumpsters and hand rails to mail boxes, planters, sewer pipes, stairs and walls.[15] 'We're going to skate the whole city', declared Shiloh Greathouse in *First Love* (Jon Holland and Jason Hernandez, 2005). 'That's what street-skating is all about.'

Beyond finding new terrains, street-skating was also a new mode of engagement. Gonzales, for example, amazed visiting UK skaters in 1984

with his 1-m-high ollies onto walls, and later achieved the first boardslide on a handrail.[16] Around 1987, Gonz also introduced switch-stance riding – wrong-way-round riding, with the skater's normally leading leg placed at the rear – as later perfected by street-skaters like Stefan Janoski and Zered Bassett (Figures 10.16 and 11.12).[17] 'Mark Gonzales changed the way the world looks at a skateboard,' eulogized *Thrasher*. 'Handrails, stairs, benches and gaps are the canvas of his masterwork.' In a 2013 *TransWorld* survey, Gonzales was named the most influential skater of all time.[18]

Other early street-skaters also achieved extraordinary things. In *Streets on Fire*, Kaupas ollies into a spin on a fire hydrant and strings together wall-rides, board-slides, rail-slides, footplants and ollie variations (Figure 10.2). Mullen in particular pursued a highly technical version of streetstyle – *TransWorld* called him 'The Godfather of Tech' – including moves like heelflips, kickflip ollies and the 'impossible' ollie where the board is rolled 360° around a foot.[19] In *Questionable*, Mullen avoids the stunt-like jumps and boardslides of his fellow team Plan B team riders, instead kicking out a bewildering array of flips, spins, ollies, shoves, heels and slides, many of which require slow-motion to be properly appreciated; his concluding trick is a ollie half-kickflip into casper tailslide and backside shove-it half-kickflip (Figure 10.3). Following Mullen, skaters like Paul Rodriguez, Chris Haslam (Figure 7.20), Eric Koston (Figure 11.5), P.J. Ladd, Shane O'Neill (Figure 4.8), Daewon Song (Figure 7.20), Luan Oliveira (Figure 5.20) and Manolo Robles have become well known for their ability to enact similarly complex fusions of ollies, slides, flips, rotations and spins.

Street-based competitions also emerged, the first major event, won by Guerrero and later recalled as the birthplace of street-skateboarding, being held in April 1983 amid San Francisco's Golden Gate Park, using little more than a small pyramid and a scattering of launch ramps.[20] Slightly more elaborate events

Figure 10.2
Natas Kaupas in *Streets on Fire* (Santa Cruz, dir. Howard Dittrich, 1989). www.bit.ly/Kaupas-StreetsOnFire

Figure 10.3
Rodney Mullen in *Questionable* (Plan B, dir. Mike Ternasky, 1992). www.bit.ly/Mullen-Questionable-Skate

Figure 10.4
Ed Templeton in *Useless Wooden Toys* (New Deal, 1990). www.bit.ly/Templeton-Useless

Figure 10.5
East German skaters travel to West Berlin for the German Skateboard Championships (1989). *This Ain't California* (dir. Marten Persiel, 2013). www.bit.ly/Berlin-ThisAintCalifornia

with titles like Wake Up and Smell the Pavement, Terror in Tahoe and Slaughter in the Sierras were soon being organized across the country. At Georgia's Savannah Slamma (1987), skaters negotiated a car, walls, kerbs, quarter-pipes, launch ramps, rails, blocks and multiform obstacles, while similar contests were now being held in the UK and other countries worldwide.[21]

However, it was predominantly in the city streets themselves that the new skateboarding took place. Numerous videos, from *The Bones Brigade Video Show* (1984) (Figure 5.15) to *Useless Wooden Toys* (1990) (Figure 10.4), showed skaters jumping over automobiles, riding up buildings, ollieing over hydrants and planters, popping onto benches, flying over steps and sliding down handrails; 'these are just a few of the sick boys destroying the streets across America,' intoned *Sick Boys*, 'there are no limits anymore.' In parts of *Rubbish Heap* and *Future Primitive*, this included the gritty urbanism of Washington and New York, while *Wheels of Fire* featured Jeff Kendall skating downtown Indianapolis, all of which emphasized the geographic ubiquity of street-skating.

In July 1992, *Thrasher*'s front cover proclaimed the death of vert-riding; fuelled by the spread of litigation from skateparks to ramps, by new companies like World Industries, by the street-level reporting of *Thrasher*, *R.A.D.* and other magazines, and by its easy accessibility and everyday locations, street-skateboarding now dominated the skate scene. Renowned street-riding specialists now emerged, including 1990s professionals like Salman Agah, Brian Anderson, John Cardiel, Mike Carroll, Jason Dill, Pat Duffy, Matt Hensley, Heath Kirchart, Rudy Johnson (Figure 5.16), Eric Koston (Figure 11.5), Guy Mariano, Chad Muska, Tom Penny, Geoff Rowley (Figure 10.13), Daewon Song (Figure 7.20), Andrew Reynolds, Ed Templeton (Figure 10.4), Jamie Thomas (Figure 5.18) and Mike Vallely. During the 2000s, newcomers have included the likes of Mark Appleyard, Silas Baxter-Neal, Letícia Bufoni, Chris Cole, Chris Haslam (Figure 7.20), Nyjah Huston (Figure 5.20), Marc Johnson, P.J. Ladd, Sean Malto, Luan Oliveira (Figure 5.20), Shane O'Neill (Figure 4.8), Torey Pudwill, Paul Rodriguez, Alexis Sablone, Arto Saari (Figure 7.22), Ryan Sheckler, Rodrigo Teixeira, Vanessa Torres, Anthony van Engelen, Ishod Wair and Stevie Williams (Figure 13.1). And besides these western riders, in other countries, other skaters are just as well known to their peers, such as China's Jeff Han, Che Lin, Fu Ling Chao and Johnny Tang.

Despite these skilled professionals performing sensational moves at iconic skatespots, street-skateboarding is predominantly based on the everyday activities of millions of practitioners worldwide. 'Everybody, Everywhere!' proclaimed Santa Cruz.[22] The expansive geography of this phenomenon is impressive. In the early 1980s, Powell-Peralta was receiving correspondence from Australia, Brazil, Canada, Czechoslovakia, Germany, New Zealand, Poland, Sweden and Thailand, while *Pravda* reported a skateboarding boom in the USSR.[23] In East Germany, many skaters heard about skateboarding from Czech television, such that, as *This Ain't California* (Marten Persiel, 2013) explains, in their eyes skateboarding by now had 'nothing to do with America' and instead was more about freedom and exhilarating movement, and even united German skaters from both sides of the East-West divide (Figure 10.5). 'Feature it,' proclaimed Peralta, 'they're concrete carving on the Berlin wall.'[24] From 1985, skateboarding had undergone rapid growth and by 1988 had already attained pre-1980 levels.[25] By the 1990s, there were healthy skate scenes far beyond the established skateboarding countries of North America, Australasia and Europe, encompassing places as diverse as Chile, Greenland, Iceland, Indonesia, Iran, Iraq and Israel, plus Malaysia, Poland, Puerto Rico, Saudi Arabia, Slovenia, Tahiti and Turkey. Today, skateboarding has even reached such disparate locations as Costa Rica, Cuba, Ethiopia, India, Latvia, Myanmar and Morocco (Figure 10.6), along with Nepal, Nigeria, North Korea, Qatar, Vietnam, the United Arab Emirates and the Philippines (Figure 1.1).

Absolute numbers are notoriously difficult to gauge, but *TransWorld*, *American Sports Analysis* and *Wall Street Journal* have variously estimated there being around 10 million US skaters in 2000, rising to 11 million in 2006 and 13 million in 2008. Put a different way, these figures indicate that approximately nearly four per cent of the total US population, and no less than one in seven of youth, are skateboarders.[26] Numbers in other countries can be similarly prodigious; Brazil had around 3.85 million skaters in 2009.[27] The total number of skaters worldwide has been assessed as between 12 million and 18 million during the 2000s, although today these figures are almost certainly an underestimation. Some have even placed the global figure at 40 million in 2006 and 50 million in 2009.[28]

Figure 10.6 Determined young skaters in Morocco (2013). @dvlphoto.

Zero Degree Architecture

> One can escape from the commonplace only by manipulating it, controlling it, pushing it into our dreams, or giving it over to the pleasure of subjectivity.[29]
> Raoul Vaneigem.

Through street-skateboarding, skaters relocated from suburbia and fenced-off skateparks into the downtown cores and everyday spaces of cities worldwide. 'I would have to leave the hills and open countryside to progress in skating,' figured Ewan Bowman. 'Towards the urban jungle I headed. Bigger and more varied types of terrain were my driving force.'[30]

Furthermore, from the 1990s onwards they inhabited not only long-established skateboarding cities like London, New York, Philadelphia, San Francisco and Washington but also Beijing, Beirut, Istanbul, Melbourne, Mexico City, Prague, Reykjavik, Riyadh, Shanghai, São Paulo, Tehran, Vancouver and Wellington. Alongside major cities, skaters also arose in what Miki Vuckovich calls the 'average, suburban, dysfunctional, adolescent anonymity' of more everyday towns, or what *R.A.D.* called 'Anytown', such as the UK's Oxford, Wakefield and Cardiff.[31] A single issue of *Slap*, for example, covered not San Diego and Los Angeles but Sacramento, Fort Lauderdale and the urban backwaters of Nevada, Utah, Iowa, Kentucky, Connecticut and New Jersey.[32] Sean Young's experiences of the 'small boonfuck town' of Enterprise, Alabama, were typical. 'In this town I learned tic-tacs, early-grabs off launch-ramps, rode my first handrail and got laid for the first time,' recalls Young. 'I lived there with roasting rednecks in the unbearable heat. There was nothing to do. It was inevitable that I skate.'[33]

Within these disparate locations, the new skatespots favoured by street-skaters were no longer hidden away in private suburban backyards or detached communities, but highly visible in university campuses, national theatres and office plazas, as well as centrally located alleys, sidewalks and car parks. All these became sites of appropriation, where skateboarders answer cultural theorist Paul Virilio's call for a 'counter-habitation' of public 'critical spaces.'[34] But how does this occur, and what does it mean for the skateboarding and the city?

Spatial Degree Zero

Compared to the suburbs, Lefebvre explains, city cores are enlivened by monuments, chance encounters and everyday experiences.[35] They offer an abundance of easily accessible buildings and spaces. However, such architecture frequently suffers from hard materials and wilful shapes that triumph over social needs and pleasurable activities, in turn causing theorists like Michel de Certeau to seek alternative practices that are 'foreign to the "geometrical" or "geographical" space of visual, panoptic, or theoretical constructions' (Figure 10.7).[36] Skateboarding, then, is one of Certeau's 'foreign' practices, which has, according to architect Anthony Bracali, 'energized many of these poorly conceived and under-utilized spaces with a new activity.'[37] Such potential ranges from the 'unlimited possibilities' of Earn Beckinger's Baltimore and the 'sea of shapeless angles' at Wig Worland's Milton Keynes, to the 'powerful and strong' buildings of Chicago, which pro skater Jesse Neuhaus has said he could 'manipulate to my advantage.'[38]

How then are these possibilities exploited? Theorists like Henri Lefebvre and Michel Foucault have argued that spaces filled with symbols are most suited for appropriation, and skaters indeed frequently operate in high profile territories like Prague's national theatre, Madrid's Christopher Columbus monument, Porto's Casa da Música, Hong Kong's Central area (Figure 10.9), Oslo's town hall and opera house (Figure 10.8) and Barcelona's Museum of Contemporary Art (MACBA) (Figure 10.10).[39]

But, as Lefebvre also notes, because they are not explicitly occupied by institutions, public spaces like streets and squares are even more open to counter-cultural activities.[40] Correspondingly, street-skateboarders, asserts *Thrasher*, focus on 'forgotten no-man's land' and so thrive on the 'discarded, abandoned and generally disregarded portions' of cities.[41] Or as *R.A.D.* summarized, 'skaters take the spaces the others ignore', exemplified by the countless banks, blocks, gaps, ledges and other nondescript elements catalogued by Harry Bastard in *Spots*.[42] In Berlin this is typified by the open area besides the Kulturforum (Figure 10.11) and in London by the Southbank Centre's Undercroft, where flat-ground, angles and stairs are simultaneously hidden beneath the Brutalist Queen Elizabeth Hall and exposed to the millions of visitors enjoying the adjacent riverside walkway; here, explains Mike John, some 'shitty little banks' have been turned into the 'heart and mother of English skating' (Figures 13.2 and 13.3).[43] Thus rather than emblematic or monumental architecture, skateboarders frequently prefer

Figure 10.7
Manipulating
geometrical
space (1991).
© Tim Leighton-
Boyce/R.A.D.
Archive.

the relative meaninglessness of everyday yet accessible spaces – alleys, roundabouts, plazas etc. – just as graffiti artists tend to prefer out-of-the-way yet still-visible sites.

These spaces without any explicit meaning are typically either everyday terrains (like sidewalks and ledges), spaces leftover after planning ('SLOAP', like vacant land under bridges) or decision-making domains (like office plazas) that symbolize not through overt iconography but through their large size and expansivity (Figure 10.9). Lefebvre characterizes these, after literary theorist Roland Barthes, as a 'spatial degree zero' where everything has only a functional, predictable and organized quality, and where urban experience is reduced to the reading of signs.[44] Such places are where skaters see conventional urbanism as being 'fraught with boredom and frustration'; we live, argues Bowman, in a 'bland culture governed by the sacred principle of convenience' where everything is 'pre-planned, pre-arranged and pre-packaged.'[45]

Laboratories of the Possible

All, however, is not lost. Street-skateboarding demonstrates that passivity and ennui are not the only possible responses to zero degree architecture. *R.A.D.*, for example, recognized that while 'new towns feel like they're waiting' with their empty buildings, oversized car parks, deserted walkways and unused benches, skaters nonetheless bring these under-utilized spaces back to life.[46] Hence skaters are 'one step ahead of the pedestrian or static eye, the architects and the artists,' finding at Milton Keynes 'an infinite number of skatespots – hundreds of steps, banks, handrails, curbs, carparks, flowerbeds, gaps, benches, blocks, everything.'[47] *Thrasher* agreed, seeing how street 'skaters create their own fun on the periphery of mass culture. Sewers, streets, malls, curbs and a million other concrete constructions have been put to new uses.'[48]

As sociologist Thomas S. Henricks has noted, the activities of play are 'laboratories of the possible', sidestepping into another reality where 'things

Figure 10.8
Writing different lines
across Oslo's Opera
House (2013).
© Svein Nordrum.

Figure 10.9
Chris Bradley exploits the everyday
terrains of Hong Kong (*RIDE*
Channel, 2013).
www.bit.ly/HongKong-Skate

are dismantled and built anew.'[49] For skaters like Tom Hodgkinson, playful skateboarding is then 'a challenge to our everyday concepts of the functions of buildings.'[50] For example, a handrail is a simple signal that imparts an instructive message – 'use me and be safer.' But when a skateboarder ollies onto the rail and adroitly boardslides its length, something concerned with reassurance and safety is quickly transposed into a site of uncertainty and risk. The whole logic of the handrail is turned on its head (Figures 10.12 through 10.14). 'If some businessman puts his hand on a handrail, he's not going to think twice about it,' explains Austin Cosler in *Freeling* (2012). 'But if we look at that, it's like gold.'

Street-skateboarding creates unexpected eruptions of meaning, retranslating the objects of the city. As *Thrasher* explained, 'A curb is an obstacle until you grind across it. A cement bank is a useless slab of concrete until you shred it.'[51] Where handrails, curbs and banks are at first glance part of a system of mundane signals, skateboarding transforms these elements into sites of energetic pleasure. Skateboarding is a critique of the emptiness of meaning in zero degree architecture.

Urban Rhythms

How does skateboarding create this critique of architecture? Architectural theorist Steen Eiler Rasmussen called for buildings to be engaged with through scale, proportion, rhythm, texture and even sonic qualities, a request that skaters answer by acting through sensory rhythms.[52] In particular, skaters initially encounter cities as sets of objects, which they then negate by exploiting urban texture and by being, in Beal's words, 'keenly aware of rhythms, tempos and flows while navigating different spaces.'[53] It is this focus on texture, surface and tactility that gives skaters a different kind of urban and architectural knowledge. 'We grew up skating

Figure 10.10
Skateboarding
MACBA's space
of symbols,
Barcelona (2015).
© Emmi Holmer.

in New York City,' proclaimed a Zoo York advertisement. 'You better believe we know all there is to know about asphalt and concrete.'[54]

So how does this process operate? According to Lefebvre's conception of rhythmanalysis, all cities can be understood from rhythmic viewpoints, such as the stair architecture of Mediterranean cities providing a unique cadence for urban walking. The same applies to street-skaters, who insert what Lefebvre would call an alternating rhythm within the regularity of the city.[55] First, all urban elements are seen as being amenable to new patterns of use. 'Bumps, curbs and gaps,' explained Matt Rodriguez, 'the street is really universal.'[56] The street-skater's rhythm is here a run across city space, interspersed with momentary engagements with specific ledges and rails. To state the obvious, this could not happen in medieval or renaissance cities, as street-skateboarding requires the smooth asphalt and extensive paving of contemporary urbanism and, above all, the object-space-object-space pulse of fragmented objects disposed across homogeneous space. For example, in one of the world's most modernist cities, Chicago, the marble planes of Mies van der Rohe's plazas were 'Mecca' to the city's 1990s street-skaters, who celebrated its Federal, Amoco, Daley Center and Prudential buildings for offering innumerable stairs, benches, handrails and ledges.[57]

Secondly, new speeds, directions and tempos are introduced by the street-skater's run. In *Quik* (dir. Colin Kennedy, 2012), Austyn Gillette skates through Los Angeles's East Side and Downtown, his rolls, pushes, slides and ollies inserting new vectors amid pedestrians, drivers, cyclists, runners and street-sellers (Figure 10.15). Through such performances, skateboarders interweave their own compositions within conventional routines, such as by waging a fast assault on a plaza ledge, or by 'skating past all the business-suit lames that slog gloomily

down the sidewalk.[58] For Garry Scott Davis, this skateboarding takes place 'at such a rapid pace' that pedestrians 'have little chance of understanding what has transformed', while for street-riding pioneer Steve Rocco it was an entirely new rhythm. 'Weaving wildly amidst strand cruisers, roller skaters, skateboarders, and those that still prefer walking,' eulogized *SkateBoarder*, 'he terrorizes oncoming motion with precision kickflips and slides, always narrowly, but precisely missing, moving on to find vacant areas.'[59]

Thirdly, skateboarding's urban rhythms involve acute sensory experiences, riders relating through bodily motion to the physical minutiae of the city. 'Skaters have that kind of sensory connectedness with the ground through the nuances of force and feel,' considered Mullen. 'As though motion combined with the punctuated rhythms of tricks all harmonize into an unthinking somatic awareness – chords of knowing.'[60]

In part this 'sensory connectedness' is based on a hyper-sensitive vision, and, unlike the passive overdependence on the eye that Michel

Foucault, Richard Sennett, John Urry and others have castigated as typical conditions of our modern urban experience, it engenders the skater's body as a full-sensory construct and mobile interaction with architecture.[61] 'Most long-time skateboarders can read streets like lifelong surfers read wind and sea,' explains Hamm. 'It's simply a matter of paying attention – close attention – to the traffic's red, yellow and green, to the pedestrians' flashing crossing signals, to the reactions and intentions on the faces of drivers and walkers and bikers, to dripping garbage trucks.'[62] But this visual alertness is also enhanced by other senses, including feeling surfaces. 'You pay particular attention to the different textures of the streets and sidewalks as you roll,' describes Justin Hocking, ever alert to 'cracks, rows of brick, tile, asphalt, each with its own vibrational frequency.'[63] Or as *R.A.D.* commented, 'these things have purpose because we have movement as well as vision.'[64]

Acute hearing is another necessity, street-skaters being constantly attuned to vehicles accelerating, car doors opening, people talking

Figure 10.11
Dylan Rieder traverses the nondescript zero degree architecture of the Kulturforum, Berlin (2014).
© Erik Gross.

Figure 10.12
Joel Curtis transposes
safety into risk,
Sheffield (2003).
© Wig Worland.

Figure 10.13
Skating to the rhythm of the night. Geoff Rowley, frontside 50-50, Liverpool (1994). © Wig Worland.

Figure 10.14
Disrupting the logic of cities with play and pleasure. Paul Alexander boardslides in a Bristol laundromat (2001). © Wig Worland.

Figure 10.15
Austyn Gillette inserts new speeds
and directions into Los Angeles.
Quik (dir. Colin Kennedy, 2012).
www.bit.ly/Gillette-Quik

and footsteps nearing. In particular, the skateboard's rumbling over the ground beneath supplies information about surface speed, grip and predictability. 'Like a blind man, he had to rely on his other senses,' described Michael Gumkowski. 'He listened to the hum of his wheels, trying to detect if he was in gravel or water or cement or dust.'[65] Here the smoothness of tarmac or what *Slap* called the 'roaring sound' of wheels become bound into urban experience.[66] 'One thing was music to us all,' stated *Thrasher*, 'the sound of urethane rolling along the street or a truck grinding concrete,'[67] while Sean Wilsey described how skating down San Francisco's Market Street produced a rhythmical and trance-inducing 'clop–pssh–rraaoowwrr–reepp–rraaoowwrrpp' interspersed by moments of silence and talking. 'We'd push off for more speed, the decibels would spike, heads would whip around up ahead of us, conversation would go back and forth.'[68]

Given the importance of these sounds, it is perhaps surprising that most videos overlay a dominant music track. A few, however, do not; Zered Bassett's New York traversal for Converse (2014), for example, emphasizes the distinctive soundscape, which adds so much to skateboarding (Figure 10.16), and more generally to what geographer Matthew Gandy has described as the 'porous and disruptive' nature of the 'acoustic city.'[69] 'I have found my own fulfilment in the rumble clack soar rattle clatter of so many different directions,' reflected Aaron Bleasdale.[70]

Taken together, the various sound rhythms – the mono-tonal roar of wheels on tarmac, rasping of truck on concrete, slide of deck on metal rail and clicking of paving slabs, combined with intermittent silences during ollie flight and with sudden cracks as the skateboard returns to ground – are distinctive features of urban skateboarding. Skaters thus also add to the

non-skater's urban experience; the skateboard's noise-scape is unlike any other in the city, such that when street-skaters propel themselves along a sidewalk 'you can really hear it.'[71]

Vision and hearing are additionally complemented by touch, generated either from direct contact (hand on building, foot on wall) or from surface rhythms passed up through the skateboard into the skater's feet and body (Figure 10.17). El Zopilote's account of skating in a parking structure exemplifies this latter experience:

> I glide over a patch of textured concrete. The little grooves running perpendicular to my flight path pluck a note from my board that I can feel in my body. The noise echoes down the ramp then stops abruptly as I return to porcelain smooth concrete.[72]

T.J. Richter provides similar insights when describing how New York 'rumbles beneath my skate, like the wheels of so many subway trains – with vibrations that carry up through my legs – and remain like magic long after.'[73] What matters here are sensorial phenomena like 'the feeling of a raspy axle grind' and the 'sensation of wheels rolling along the pavement,' or what deaf pro Brandon White describes as 'the vibration, like an earthquake, through my board.'[74] Even smell can be significant, allowing Chris Carnel to speak of how 'feeling of rhythm and an aroma of sweat overcome my senses' and Vaj Potenza of how 'the walls have taken on my body's odour.'[75]

Fourthly, street-skaters construct different rhythms through time, as when commuters rush to their scheduled connections but riders dwell longer upon planters and benches. In contested terrains like shopping malls or privatized public spaces, a different temporal tactic is often deployed: out-of-sync timings (Figure 10.13). For example, skaters exploit London's financial

Figure 10.16
Zered Bassett's New York street-skating soundscape. *Converse Weapon Skate* (2014).
www.bit.ly/Bassett-NewYork

district during weekends and evenings, while skaters in Newcastle-upon-Tyne frequent the Monument shopping area and Law Courts during out-of-hours periods.[76] 'Everyone goes home, and then the skaters go out', commented Jeff Pang of New York. 'There's a lot of stuff going on in the middle of the night.'[77]

A different kind of approach to urban time is therefore at work here. Modern cities are commonly a mixture of production and speculation, alternatively sacrificing long-term social benefits for short-term profits, or, conversely, short-term social needs for programmed investments. Skateboarding time, by contrast, is more rhythmic, varying between seconds (single moves), minutes (runs), weeks and months (repeated visits) and a few years (long-term engagements). It is also discontinuous, composed of a few encounters here and there, spread over different parts of the city, and thus runs contrary to conventional arrangements. For example, the longer time of property ownership, the medium time of lease arrangements and the short time of parking meters are all avoided by street-skaters, whose skateboarding is more ephemeral than the appropriations and co-optations of 1970s found spaces, often taking over sites for just a few minutes or seconds; New York skaters, explained Kevin Wilkins, often considered twenty minutes to be a lengthy time at a skatespot, while *Thrasher* described how 'stagnating' at one skatespot means that 'the regular world will always know where to find us.'[78] The simple answer, according to *R.A.D.*, is 'always move on.'[79]

Fifthly, in its encounter with zero degree architecture, street-skateboarding creates what geographer John Urry calls kinaesthetics, the 'sixth sense that informs one what the body is doing in space through the sensations of movement', or what *Sidewalk* describes as 'a total focus of mind, body and environment to a level way beyond that

of the dead consumers'.[80] *Sidewalk* also emphasizes how street-skaters enjoy 'something rare in this synthetic world of plastic and concrete', namely an 'enhanced experience of life' where 'through the medium of a skateboard you actually interact with the world around you.'[81] Worland's account of Milton Keynes street-skating is again instructive, speaking of 'learning the properties of everyday life unwittingly' and how 'evolving into a higher state of urban awareness starts with doing and looking.'[82] Similarly Bowman characterized skating amid London traffic as a combination of speeds and emotions, with 'a mad rush' while 'over-taking the cars, being overtaken, going through a red light in a junction, dicing with big metal f**kers that would probably kill you.'[83] Or as Jesse Driggs attested, 'If you haven't dodged traffic in the urban jungle, then you haven't lived.'[84]

Through these kinds of experiences, a skater's elevated awareness of balance, speed, hearing, sight, touch and responsivity – and hence of *knowing* through bodily senses – can be viewed as products of the modern metropolis, a newly expanded sensory mapping (Figure 10.18); as Hamm argues, calling street-skaters 'an evolved hybrid of pedestrian and vehicle wouldn't be much of an exaggeration.'[85]

Writing the City

What meanings does skateboarding inscribe onto zero degree architecture, and how are such propositions stated? I consider exactly *what* skateboarding says in Chapter 11, and, so focus the rest of this chapter on *how* skateboarding says something – less through words, images and videos, and more through its city-based actions.

Above all, street-skateboarding does not escape urban spaces but works physically against them. For street-skaters like Eric Dressen, the scratches, grinds and paint traces left behind are an essential part of relating to the city, as when the wax applied to ledges and curbs deposits

Figure 10.18
Korahn Gayle, sensory
mapping in Ashdod,
Israel (2015).
@dvlphoto.

Figure 10.17
Wurzel touching and
feeling architecture
during a frontside
wall-ride (1988).
© Tim Leighton-
Boyce/R.A.D. Archive.

tell-tale smears.[86] 'Most would call it senseless vandalism,' argues Jake Phelps, 'but loafed curbs, dirty buildings, worked planter boxes and broken benches are true things of beauty.'[87] The constant planting of hands and feet gradually forms grubby reminders of skaters' presence. Urethane wheels and graphic decks leave technicolour streaks across ledges and benches. Grinding trucks produce gouges and striations.

But why mark objects in this way? Certainly architecture contains elements of power, making us obey barriers and routes, informing us that transgressions will be met by hostile response, or simply reminding us of the pervasive presence of public institutions, the state, corporations and urban managers. This is what Lefebvre terms architecture's 'phallic formant', symbolizing masculine force as image and threat.[88] In this context, skateboarders' assault is a small yet significant challenge to power, meeting like with like. Where owners and managers inscribe authority by 'writing on the ground' with signs, fences and other markers, traces like skateboarding marks and graffiti are forms of counter-inscription; both skateboarding and graffiti, notes Vivoni, 'claim space by drawing lines across the urban

landscape' and so 'challenge the prescribed order imposed through top-down planning processes.'[89] And in this light, the 'Skate and Destroy' motif – which first accompanied a Stecyk *Thrasher* article of that title – has understandably been one of the most persistent skateboard symbols and aphorisms.[90]

These urban inscriptions go far beyond the semantic urbanism favoured by semiologists like Umberto Eco and Françoise Choay, who treat architecture as a text and urban experience as passive decoding.[91] Instead, as August Schmarsow realized, 'reading' a building is a bodily act and an experienced understanding.[92] Furthermore, this 'reading' can be entirely different to the intentions of authors (architects, planners, urban managers), even being a new writing across the page. For example, when skaters encounter Oslo's prize-winning Opera House, designed by renowned architects Snøhetta, they are concerned with neither architecture-as-design nor architect-as-designer, but only with their own riding on that architecture (Figure 10.8). Skateboarders are in this sense *writing* the city, creating vectors, traces and furrows, and so concur with architectural theorists Chris Smith and Andrew

Ballantyne who argue that 'design is not about some transcendent "creation" of objects' but rather 'the territorialising of flow' that can 'articulate sensations,' and with Jill Stoner, who sees value in the 'minor architecture' of inhabitation and adaptation.[93]

Significantly, and despite its seeming aggression, the 'destroy' in 'Skate and Destroy' is predominantly conceptual, and skateboarding rarely modifies city form in any substantial manner. Its scratches and grinds are neither obvious nor remarkable. Instead of dominating city spaces, skateboarding appropriates and negates (denies or opposes) these spaces. This takes us back to skateboarding's dependence on the physicality of zero degree architecture, and forward to the question of skateboarding's meaning. If skateboarding is simultaneously predicated on the surface of modern urbanism, and yet acts differently to this urbanism's intended functions, what new things are created? In response to this question, as we shall now see, skateboarding is far more than urban writing, for it also involves critiques of objects (reinterpreting buildings and spaces), articulation (speaking and not just writing), consumption (consuming without owning), production (producing energies rather than things) and control (opposing urban managers). It is to these considerations that we now turn, for the rest of this chapter and the next.

Decentred Objects
To view cities only as objects is to miss their real character – and this is exactly an apparent 'failure' of skateboarding, which does little to understand urban processes, simply treating city spaces as physical grounds on which to ride, and effects little or no change. Skateboarding, we could then say, is ignorant and insubstantial.

Building Blocks for the Open Minded
Yet exactly within this failure lies a profound critique of the city. On the one hand, street-skaters focus purely on architecture as ridable artefacts. 'Look at a world full of skate shapes,' encouraged R.A.D., 'shapes left there by architects for you to skate.'[94] On the other hand, it is through this very focus on architecture-as-object that alterations are made. 'In a world of complex questions, the street strategist must become his own answer,' asserted Stecyk. 'Alleys, curbs, streets, pools, ramps, parking lots, hills, banks, and all other conceivable contours are the arenas of individual advancement. How and what you do with them are your own affair.'[95] More specifically, when skaters ride along a wall or ledge, they are

indifferent to the architect's intended meaning, function or aesthetic, and instead treat projects simply as sets of discrete physical elements. Thus, where architectural considerations of building users often implies subordinating bodies to designs (Deleuze and Guattari's 'striated space'), skaters, according to Stecyk, have the ability to take 'a set of pre-determined circumstances' and 'extract what you want and discard the rest.'[96] In this way, street-skating reproduces architecture in its own measure, re-editing it as an open landscape of surfaces and textures (Deleuze and Guattari's 'smooth space').[97] 'Buildings are building blocks for the open minded,' announced R.A.D., while Thrasher declared simply that 'skaters are the creators.'[98]

According to Lefebvre's Toward an Architecture of Enjoyment (2014), architecture is founded on habitation, characterized by translator Łukasz Stanek as the 'half-real, half-imaginary distribution of times and places of everyday life.' Instead of architects and monuments, architecture is that which 'reproduces itself within those who use the space in question, within their lived experience,' and, more specifically, is a 'genuine space' of 'moments, encounters, friendships,' 'exaltation, love, sensuality,' 'struggle, play' and, above all, 'no signs!'[99] Hence, through skateboarding, architecture is energetically engaged with in relation to measure (height, distance), texture (tactility, grip, roughness), curvature (transitions), drops (stairs, ramps), kinks (handrails), profiles (edges) and so on. Furthermore, only a relatively small section of architecture is used; the 'building' for street-skaters is only part of its whole. For example, in the UK's Ipswich, one school was known simply for its handrails, a college for its roof and ledges, a church for wooden benches and an entire air base for a single fire hydrant.[100] This process has been replicated in every city worldwide. In New York, for example, the postmodern Marriott Marquis Hotel (1985, architect John Portman) was reconceived as 'modern day skate architecture' with 'tight transitions,' 'black walls' and a street-level walkway and planters, while the gothic and neo-classical American Museum of Natural History (1877–1898, architects Vaux, Mould and Cady), became '100 yards of Italian marble, benches curbed for frontside and backside rails, six steps, and statues of famous dudes with marble bases.'[101]

Through this kind of 'urban transcendentalism,' as Ron Allen described street-skating, 'benches, banks and smooth pavement' are prioritized over famous historical landmarks and design

Figure 10.19
Exploiting everyday
architecture. Erik J.
Pettersson, backside
flip in Shanghai
(2014). © Nikwen.

classics, with a preference for barriers, curbs, fire hydrants, ledges, planters, porches, rails, salt bins, sidewalks, skips, steps, tables, walls, water tanks and so on.[102] Through such street-skating predilections, 1990s New York was not the Statue of Liberty, Times Square and Empire State Building but the Harlem banks (Malcolm X Avenue and 139th), Brooklyn banks (Manhattan end of the Brooklyn Bridge), Washington Square Park and Mullaly Park.[103] Other cities received similar treatments. Rotterdam was known for its Weena covered walkway, Beurs stairs, Blaak station, Oosterhof mall and Alexanderpolder station; Tallinn for its Linnahall, Kosmos cinema, hotel Olümpia and Coca-Cola Plaza; East Berlin for Alexanderplatz and the Fernsehturm; and Tokyo for Akihabara Park, Tokyo Station ledges, Yotsuya Station curbs and runs across the Aoyama-Omotesando-Harajuku-Shibuya area. Today, Shanghai's Pudong district has been known for its Black Banks, three-gap-three set and the Great Ledge of China in Love Park. As *R.A.D.* explained, 'to us these things are more.'[104]

Strategies Embracing Architecture

Tying these elements together are street-skaters' runs and moves, which 1990s magazines often tried to capture with long sequence shots, with

twenty-eight frames or more. The extended runs of street-skaters are, however, ultimately beyond the reach of photography, and are particularly evident when riders – likened by Steven Flusty to 'pavement commandos' – move rapidly between urban elements.[105] Deploying what Santa Cruz called 'strategies embracing architecture', and exemplified in videos like *A Visual Sound*, skaters select what in design terms are discontinuous walls, surfaces and steps, but that in skateboarding become fluid encounters between board, body and terrain.[106] For example, in *Cityscape* (Ryuichi Tanaka, 2012), Takahiro Morita takes a feverish six-minute circuit around Tokyo's Aoyama and Shibuya districts, where, to the tune of Yo La Tengo's hypnotic 'Nuclear War', he traverses car parks, playgrounds, sidewalks and squares, threads between cars, cyclists and pedestrians, and rides over art works, bollards, curbs, ledges, planters, rails and steps, while using fast slides, multiple ollies, powerful pushes, energetic jumps and weaving turns (Figure 10.21).

Ricky Oyola has similarly described how a skater 'can throw your board down and skate around for hours hitting anything that crosses your path', what Peralta called 'a total attack approach'

Figure 10.20
Reese Forbes
recomposes
the fragmented
city (2003).
© Pete Thompson.

Figure 10.21
A fluid encounter with Tokyo urbanism. Takahiro Morita in *Cityscape* (Strush, dir. Ryuichi Tanaka, 2012).
www.bit.ly/Morita-Cityscape

where, in contrast to the old suburban surf-skater's approach of slaloming *around* obstacles, the new urban street-skater *becomes* the terrain they encounter.[107] Numerous other videos emphasize this process, including the Osaka section of *Lenz* (Shinpei Ueno, 2012), where a multi-paced montage of charging skaters and fractured architecture is interspersed with locational information, dimensional data, maps and other graphics.

A somewhat different compositional process is evident in many recent high-budget videos like *True* and *We Are Blood*, which are frequently filmed in multiple international locations; *Away Days*, for example, was shot in ninety different cities.[108] Here, where skatespots from many different towns and even countries are juxtaposed within a single skater's video part, architecture is splintered and geography is flattened out, rendering urban space nameless and homogeneous.[109] In yet another reconfiguration, *Tony Hawk's Underground* video game (Activision, 2003) distributes renowned New York skatespots around a fictional core of generic buildings, as a psychogeographic reimagination of what a street-skater's Manhattan might be like. Consequently, when *Thrasher* supplies a pithy summation like 'find it, grind it, leave it behind', this means more than just linear movement; through street-skating, cities are spatially and temporally fragmented and are simultaneously recomposed through new rhythms of movements, sites and visualizations (Figure 10.20).[110]

Speaking the City
With a few notable exceptions, most everyday and professional skaters do not conceptualize their exploits; 'My skating comes from my heart, not my head,' states Mike Vallely. 'It is something I feel, not think.'[111] Skateboarding is nonetheless embedded with ideas, being a *lived* concept, speaking with actions as much as through

words. In this sense, skateboarding is what Lefebvre calls an aesthetic practice, functioning by 'making, saying and living', which goes beyond discourse and 'works upon a material' and transfigures the real world in order to create alternative realities.[112] How then does this aesthetic activity take place? What techniques are involved?

As we have seen, skaters analyze architecture not for historical or symbolic meaning but for its skateable surfaces or what Justin Hocking terms the 'possibility of motion'.[113] *Thrasher* describes this way of seeing as the 'skater's eye', where skaters constantly 'look at the world in a very different way' so that 'angles, spots, lurkers and cops all dot the landscape' (Figure 10.22).[114]

Furthermore, according to geographers Edward Soja and Steve Pile, cities are at once real-and-imagined, solid-and-intangible.[115] Skaters enact a specific version of this process, wherein objects, images and the skateboarder's lived experience are constantly remade. It is to this three-way production of things, representations and encounters that we now turn, showing how street-skaters' mode of composition is more than just maps, photographs or texts, and comes closer to performance as spatialized speech.

Situated Mapping
Skateboarders edit architecture and urban space, recomposing cities from different locations, elements, routes and times. Although not entirely unique to skaters, as *R.A.D.* argued this is largely 'a world the pedestrians and motorists cannot share', being 'an alternative reality, co-existing on a different plane', and certainly the otherworldly nature of this kind of urban experience is emphasized in videos like Brett Novak's short *Out of Line* (2013), where a skater jumps seamlessly from one area of Los Angeles to another.[116] In particular, where sightseers use cameras and smartphones to view tourist landmarks, skaters

Figure 10.22
The skater's eye.
Alex Ullmann and
photographer
Hendrik Herzmann in
Frankfurt (2013).
© Hendrik Herzmann.

use mobile bodies to focus upon mundane, forgotten and everyday spaces.

Occasionally, of course, skaters do use maps or other classifications, from 1970s skatepark guides and the 1990s *Knowhere* website, to *SkateBoarder*'s 'Cityscape' feature in the 2000s and today's innumerable internet listings of skateparks and skatespots.[117] Here, skaters find exhaustive inventories of local skatespots, not just as invitations to visit but also as demonstrations that similar locations are available in every city. 'Here are more pictures of Everyman skating in Everytown,' urged *R.A.D.* 'It could be your town. It could be you.'[118] Today, almost every skate magazine and Instagram feed shows skaters riding exactly these everyday spaces, available in large cities, middling towns, distant villages and forgotten wastelands worldwide. In contrast to the fantastical photographs of the 1970s, which tended to

show spectacular moves in distant and utopian settings, these depictions of more mundane settings foster empathy between skaters, helping them to share an everyday and accessible reality.

In their own neighbourhood, therefore, skaters think less in terms of spectacular images or abstract maps, and more in terms of a highly local knowledge about exactly what to look for, where to go and when to arrive. 'ALWAYS be on the alert for a possible spot', commanded Davis. 'Keep your eyes open and your head oscillating,' while Oyola concluded that simply 'adventuring around and finding new spots is without a doubt the best aspect of city skating.'[119] As *Thrasher* declared, searching for places is an integral part of skateboarding, from the very moment that a beginner first takes up a skateboard: 'somewhere between your board hitting the ground and that first push, the spot hunt has already begun.'[120]

Figure 10.23
Drifting trajectories in *A Guide to Cracks & Curbs: London* (dir. Shade Media, 2015).
www.bit.ly/London-CracksCurbs

When Swords and Jeffries asked Tyneside skaters to map their habitual 'skateworlds', they were presented with non-sequential shapes, strange proportions, narrative schematics, graphic cartoons and doodles – none of which bore much resemblance to traditional maps.[121] As such visualizations suggest, skaters' experiences are here close to the Situationist tactics of the dérive and détournement, where drifting journeys and psychogeographic maps are composed from the physical and emotional contours of the city, and, above all, enacted through riding across urban space.[122] 'We observe the cracks and the curbs, the absurdity that our city has an unadmired beauty', states video poem *A Guide to Cracks & Curbs* (2015). 'Our commute is from A to everywhere, it is your nothing and our everything' (Figure 10.23). Quentin Stevens, Kim Dovey and Hunter Fine have additionally related such drifting trajectories to Deleuze and Guattari's concept of the rhizome, by which non-organizational connections are made between multiple and non-hierarchical points.[123] 'I'm directed most to movements, the way I travel, the directions I move in', explained Mullen. 'I follow my feelings.'[124]

Skateboarders' 'maps' are thus always *situated* through a continual reliving of the city, using what *Sidewalk* called 'an open mind always seeking out new lines and possibilities', the skater 'twisting the environment' to 'fit their own needs and imagination'.[125] Caine Gayle described this street-skating mapping process as 'a continual search for the unknown'.[126]

Skaters' situated maps also treat time in a distinctive manner. In conventional maps, an entire city is understood as a frozen moment, whereas for street-skaters their cognitive mapping is derived from prolonged and discontinuous runs, whether this means skating objects in sequence (linear time), just once (isolated time), several times (repeated time), on varied occasions (cyclical time) or in different

combinations and speeds (differential time) (Figure 10.24). 'Riding from spot-to-spot, at high speed, during rush hour is the ultimate test for any urban street-skater', described Jesse Triggs of one such mapping run. 'On a good day, when all the stop lights are working in my favour, I feel like I've figured out where my place is in this fucked-up world.'[127] Through such journeys, street-skating time is not scheduled or measured, but lived, experienced and multiple.

Performative Critique
Despite the prevalence of skate-filmers and photographers, the vast majority of street-skating is unrecorded, and is simply reborn with every skater's run. Just as skateboarders rarely attempt to understand the city, so they seldom document it. Skateboarding leaves almost no texts to be read; although visible, its marks are barely discernible to others. We must then revise our earlier conception of skateboarding as a mode of *writing* to that of *speaking* the city – that 'speech doubling', to use Lefebvre's term, which interrogates and increases the meaning of the city, while leaving its original text intact. Above all, this urban speech requires active speakers, who are not 'cool' but 'hot'.[128] Speaking-skateboarding is not an oration of a pre-given text, but a performative critique in which expressive skaters forever form anew both themselves and the city. 'Act, don't react', demanded Stecyk, 'turn off the air conditioner, go outside and move.'[129]

It is, therefore, in skateboarding's continual performance that its meanings are most manifest; as one oft-repeated skateboard maxim puts it, 'shut up and skate'. Above all, through engaging bodily with the city as a set of places, times, rhythms and representations, skaters enact a kind of *lived* thought, rethinking the city through their actions. Thus, the question begs as to what thoughts and statements are made through such actions. What does skateboarding say about the city?

Figure 10.24
Cognitive mapping captured as a 35 mm contact sheet (1989).
© Tim Leighton-Boyce/R.A.D. Archive.

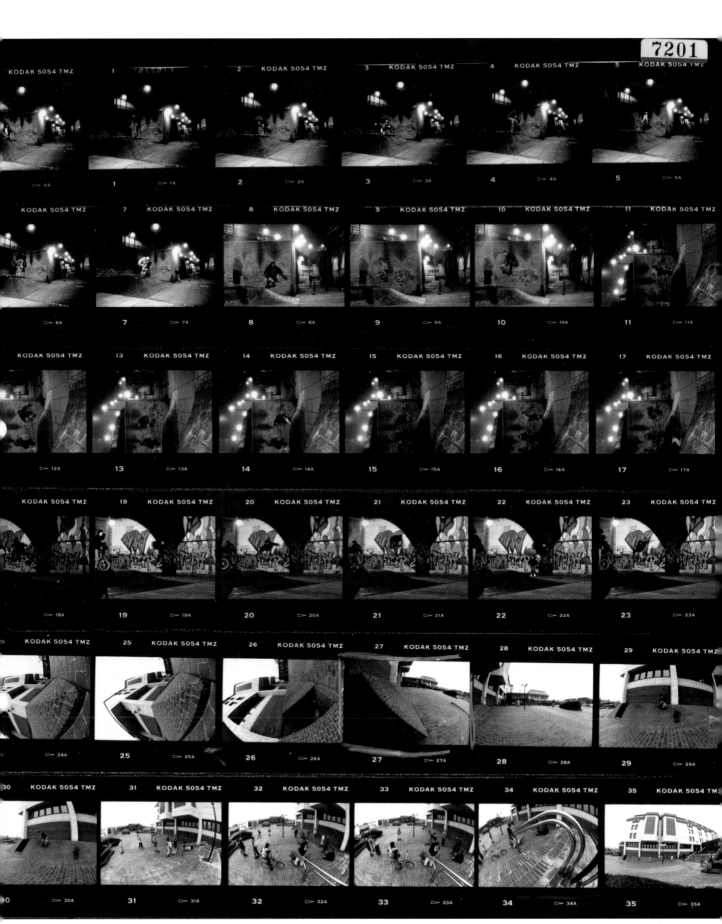

Skateboarding
Chapter 11 Movement Without Words

You self-righteous, blind, arseholes. You cannot control the use of public space.[1]
Sidewalk

Critical Citizens

Zero degree architecture is a field of warning signs and dogmatic instructions, recognizable in contemporary cities worldwide. Yet modern urbanism is not wholly constraining, for, explains Lefebvre, there is a contradiction between, on the hand, the homogenization of space for economic purposes, where 'abstract space' is treated as a uniform commodity, and, on the other hand, the varied uses of space, where cities are enjoyed in different ways.[2] It is this contradiction that skateboarding works within. 'The act of street-skating', states *Space for Rent*, 'is in direct conflict with the ideals of society that places its principal emphasis on economic growth and profit.' While advertisements, fences, gates and other controls contribute to what Lefebvre rather dramatically refers to as the 'terrorism' of everyday life, skateboarding helps to both confront this terrorism and provide an alternative or compensating way of living (Figure 11.1).[3] 'There are no more white lines to stay within, sidewalks to conform to or bases to tag,' asserted Peralta. 'It's all an open highway with hydrants, curbs, bumpers, shopping carts, door handles and pedestrians.'[4]

Skateboarding counters signs and signals, and so implicitly critiques their logic of efficiency, normalcy and predictability. This does not mean, however, that skateboarding opposes all aspects of society, and indeed, in contrast to the public confrontations of videos like *Baker 3*, many skaters act with respect towards their fellow citizens. As Stephen Hill points out in 'Easy Riders', while skaters may be energetic in their redefinition of the urban realm, they are very rarely violent.[5] Joe Penny, for example, records how Clermont-Ferrand street-skaters carefully replace café furniture, cease skating to avoid being annoying and banter good-humouredly with police officers; 'I pay attention to how I skate,' states local rider Joseph, 'I'm considerate of other people.'[6] Similarly, Magenta pros emphasize how city skating helps them communicate and connect with the 'soul of the place', while *1st & Hope* (2006) depicts the good-neighbourly vibe of

Brian Lotti and others in downtown Los Angeles, whose chilled urban drift incorporates friendly encounters with multi-ethnic fellow skaters, African-American pedestrians, white low-riders and Japanese restaurateurs.[7] In *Albion* (2014), despite a few run-ins with the British public, skaters shake hands with cyclists, converse with everyone from elderly pedestrians to religious oddballs, and repair a broken bollard. In videos like *All the Days Roll Into One* (2008), actual skateboarding even takes a backstage role when the Volcom team enjoy friendships and street encounters (Figure 11.2).

In another, relatively recent development, and here building upon the sometimes clown-like antics of 1980s skaters like Neil Blender, Mark Gonzales, Jeff Grosso and Lance Mountain, skaters like Richie Jackson and Gou Miyagi (Figure 11.3) have used intricate moves and eccentric styles to forge humorous relationships with the city. Similar approaches are taken by Tim Olson and Eric Risser, who, in *Secondhand Stoke* (Roger Skateboards, 2012), swing through gates, transfer across skateboards and knee-ride in what *Thrasher* called 'one of the most absurd, fun, creative parts ever.'[8]

All this invokes a sense of polite citizenship and friendly co-existence between skaters, fellow residents and their shared urban environment, a relationship not of antagonism or confrontation but affable respect and gentle belonging. Here, skaters stand not against the city per se, but as critical citizens who interweave a distinctive rhythm within the urban symphony.

It would be wrong, therefore, to simplistically portray skaters – as per *Thrasher*'s beer and barneys trope – as a bunch of screw-you rebels and self-centred outcasts. Yet, in its general operations, skateboarding nonetheless challenges the notion that cities must be obeyed, that we exist solely as passive citizens and that urban space is closed to negotiation and diversity. Furthermore, there are corresponding shifts in consumption, exchange and use, and it is to these areas that we now turn.

Figure 11.1 Compensatory and friendly skateboarding. Muki Rüstig at the Broiler Skate Jam, Dresden (2010). @dvlphoto.

Figure 11.2
The good neighbourly vibe of skateboarding in Brooklyn, New York. *All the Days Roll into One* (Volcom, dir. Ryan Thomas, 2008). www.bit.ly/AllDaysRoll

Figure 11.3
Gou Miyagi's humorous engagement with everyday architecture. *Video Nasty* (Heroin, 2013). www.bit.ly/Miyagi-VideoNasty

Beyond the Shiny Product

Cities make things and provide services – commodities in factories, knowledge in universities, accommodation in housing, management in offices etc. Street-skating, however, offers little such contribution, consuming buildings without engaging with their productive activity. Consequently, it implicitly denies both that architecture should always be directed toward that production and, more generally, that work should always be productive or 'useful' at all. This is clear in many skate magazines, as when a *Thrasher* photo caption declares that 'office politics mean nothing to Jamie Thomas as he rides the glass of a San Bernadino business complex.'[9] Skateboarding is a pleasure-driven activity of its own.

Furthermore, skateboarding disrupts the highly ordered districts and economic logic of cities by inserting an entirely different rationale. 'In a culture that measures progress in terms of cost per square foot', noted Stecyk, 'the streetstylist dictates his own terms and makes his own fun.'[10] This is particularly evident in city centres, those concentrations of decision-making, power and consumer spending, where skateboarding appears as an irrational eruption. Why would one devote so much time balancing on a piece of wood and four small

wheels? Why would one replace conventional urban practices of even-paced walking and distanced gazing with eccentric movement, heightened adrenalin, risky balance, sensuous touching and variable velocity?

This irrationality is particularly evident from the way street-skating takes place up to 1 m above the sidewalk, and especially through fantastical ollies and absurd wall-riding, the latter being described by *Thrasher* as 'the most nonsensical facet of skateboarding.'[11] Indeed, such wilful non-conformity pervades skateboarding, causing one critic to protest that skateboarding 'appears to serve no known purpose in life and does nothing to raise national productivity.'[12]

This, however, is to miss the point. Although, the dynamic act of skateboarding creates no immediate products, it nonetheless releases energies that create and modify space, thus generating a sense of everyday festival, or what Lefebvre calls Eros or the pleasure principle (Figure 10.14).[13] So when Gareth Catterick asserts that 'when they work, we'll skate', or Ben Powell describes skaters as having 'moved beyond shiny products and consumerism' and being able to 'rise above the repressive, hassle-filled, cess pit world', everyday street-skating is clearly directed not at the production of goods or services but at

Figure 11.4
Reviving the dead labour of urban
wastelands. FDR, Philadelphia, in
Under the Bridge (Thrasher, 2009).
www.bit.ly/FDR-UnderTheBridge

play and the ludic.[14] In doing so, skateboarding
correlates with Pat Kane's contention that
the work ethic should be accompanied by an
equivalent 'play ethic', in which play is not just
personally pleasurable but also collaborative,
creative, politicized and thoughtful.[15]

In addition, skateboarding can be seen, to
follow Karl Marx, as a revival of the past or
'dead' labour congealed in cities.[16] As *Space for
Rent* notes, many of the buildings and spaces
utilized by skateboarding are considered to be
useless or abandoned, into which street-skaters
'breathe new life'. Consider, for example, the
under-bridge territories, industrial wastelands
and other forgotten terrains taken up by street-
skaters and DIY interventions such as Burnside
(Figure 8.14), Channel Street, FDR (Figure 11.4)
and Washington Street (Figure 8.15), as well as
Berlin's Skatehalle, constructed within a disused
train repair facility, or Malmö's Bryggeriet
skateboarding-based school, sited in a former
brewery (Figure 13.10). Even more prevalent
is all of the everyday street-skating, which uses
buildings and spaces while they are still in
operation, and here skateboarding redirects
dead labour into new and unexpected purposes.

Gifts of Freedom

Just as skateboarding addresses production
and work, it also critiques exchange and
consumption. Above all, to borrow Lefebvre's
words, skateboarding creates 'spaces for play,
spaces for enjoyment' such that 'use value
may gain the upper hand over exchange value',
hence emphasizing meaning and pleasure over
ownership and profit.[17]

City space frequently exists for the purposes of
exchange, either as a commodity that can itself
be sold or rented, like housing and retail units, or
to facilitate the exchange of other goods, as with
markets and trading floors. Thus by the simple
act of reasserting use values – taking advantage

of space without paying for it – skateboarding
is indifferent to these purposes of exchange.
Skaters, argued *Sidewalk*, oppose 'the real
criminals, who despoil the world in their never
ending quest for capital.'[18] As Brad Erlandson
argued in *Slap*, skateboarding recognizes that
instead of private property rights, 'the streets
are owned by everyone. Streets give the gift of
freedom, so enjoy your possession.'[19]

Over the last thirty years or so, nearly all
city spaces, from shops and markets to
train stations and museums, have become
increasingly 'mallified' as opportunities for retail
expenditure, hence fulfilling Lefebvre's warning
that 'exchange value is so dominant over use and
use value that it more or less suppresses it.'[20] But
it is precisely this concentration on exchange
that skateboarding rejects; in occupying those
spaces outside stores and offices, skateboarders
refute such processes by substituting dynamic
new use values. For Marc Spiegler, skateboarders
are therefore far more than mere 'secondary
users' and instead 'essentially redefine business
and governmental spaces.'[21]

This kind of attitude is particularly evident in
street-skaters' dislike of commercial skatepark
entrance fees, preferring to skate in free-to-
access streets (Figure 11.6). As Aaron Bleasdale
observed, London skaters just 'aren't willing
to pay' and would rather skate 'sick spots
everywhere.'[22] As such, skateboarding is a small
fragment of that utopian conception of cities as
being places of rich and divergent uses, helping to
fulfil Lefebvre's contention that 'urban society has
a logic different from that of merchandise. It is
another world. The *urban* is based on use value.'[23]

Besides cities, and as neoliberal capitalism
intensifies into everyday life, society itself
is also becoming ever more organized for
consumerism, through the consumption
of either physical things (coffee, clothes,

Figure 11.5
Wealth through bodily and sensory engagement. Eric Koston in *Menikmati* (éS, dir. Fred Mortagne, 2000).
www.bit.ly/Koston-Menikmati

transportation) and, increasingly, less tangible entities (ideas, brands, signs). In architecture, the consumption of signs can be found whenever the appearance of buildings is emphasized, in the most extreme cases creating Las Vegas–style theme-park-like spaces. The result is an urbanism of competing advertisements, icons, logos and shapes that call out to citizens, including skateboarders. As skater CSTR recounted:

> I grabbed my skateboard and started rolling downtown. All around were billboards with new cars, cell phones, fast food, giant heads smoking six-foot-long cigarettes. Posters advertised movies and TV shows, clothes I couldn't afford being worn by people who looked too good to be human. Everyone wanted my attention.[24]

Street-skating, however, has an answer. Where signs clamour to be viewed, skateboarding both focuses on architecture's material qualities and makes the skater's whole body active, and hence supplements vision with other forms of encounter. 'There was craziness all over the city,' described CSTR, 'but I skimmed above it on my skateboard. Just gliding along, protected by my board.'[25] In short, skateboarding sidesteps the purely visual and passive consumption of cities. 'There are only a few routes to authentic happiness left that haven't been turned into theme parks for the brain dead,' argued Ewan Bowman. 'Thankfully, skateboarding is one of those alternative routes to fulfilment.'[26]

Skateboarding also inherently asserts that true social wealth comes not from exclusive possession or private ownership but from the ability to, in Lefebvre's words, 'have the most complex, the "richest" relationships of joy or happiness with the "object"'.[27] It is precisely this that street-skating addresses, asserting that, in

Tod Swank's words, 'just because you own it doesn't mean you're in charge.'[28]

So if the relation between skater and city is not one of production or exchange, what is it? As Paul Mulshine noted in Philadelphia, a street-skater's 'primary relationships are with the earth beneath his feet, concrete and all.'[29] In other words, skaters relate to cities via their bodily senses, something highly evident in street-skating video parts like Eric Koston's in *Menikmati* (Figure 11.5). This can also be a highly idiosyncratic process, as with the Vancouver-based Barrier Kult crew, who express dissatisfaction with the star-skater tendencies of some contemporary skateboarding by riding masked on 'Jersey' highway barriers.[30] As such, where cities control their inhabitants through building, boundaries, signs and other gestures – the kind of 'marketing orientation' that, according to psychologist Erich Fromm, encourages people to adopt a specific social role – by contrast, skaters like Koston or the Barrier Kult use their appropriation of cities to construct a specific self-identity.[31] Nor is this uncommon: 'If I ever stopped skateboarding,' professed Dan Cates, 'I would be no one.'[32] Rather than allowing cities to dictate who their identities, skaters ask 'who am I?', and answer through their own actions in city streets. This is an explicit dialectic of the social and the spatial, each being produced through the other.

In terms of the society this might indicate, evidently skateboarders, as what Bonnie Blouin called 'small bait in a sea of corporate sharks', rarely create substantial change.[33] Indeed, as Yochim notes, following historian Leerom Medovoi, skateboarding often correlates with the Cold War United States as both anti-authoritarian *and* democratic, welcoming rebels within its over-arching middle-class suburbia.[34] 'We're not out to fight the world,' declared *Thrasher*.[35]

Figure 11.6
Daryl Dominguez using without paying. Zoetermeer (2011). © Rob Shaw.

Instead, the act of skateboarding offers what Beal, following anthropologist James Scott, identifies as an 'infrapolitics' of resistance and a 'hidden transcript' intelligible only to other skaters.[36] Nonetheless, skaters do undertake an 'ironic' assault upon architecture and so, argues Joel Patterson, defiantly 'irritate giants'.[37] In particular, through highlighting the conflict between, on the one hand, private property and business efficiency, and, on the other hand, pleasurable uses of urban spaces, skaters irritate officialdom and convention, and so interrogate the city as a whole; as Patterson concludes, 'always question authority'.[38]

As such, skateboarding concurs with Lefebvre's idea that a new society might display a greater degree of uses than exchanges, qualities than quantities and local rather than centralized powers.[39] Above all, it shows that pre-existing functions are not the only possibilities, and that city spaces can filled with activities that are not immediately commodified. Urban space, we might then propose, should be simultaneously filled with functions and experiences, logic and love, objects and ideas. This is the most overt political space produced by skateboarders, a pleasure ground carved out of the city as a continuous reaffirmation of one of the central Situationist and Lefebvrian slogans of 1968, that 'sous les pavés, la plage' – that beneath the pavement lies the beach.[40]

Ban This

In redefining urban space for themselves, skateboarders challenge what other people understand by the city, and so can 'hammer the panic buttons' of those who do not skate.[41] For example, in mid-1980s Philadelphia there was, according to Brian Casey, a quiet garden near 37th Street where students conversed amid flowering trees. Here Casey advised fellow skaters to do some grinds and so unsettle those relaxing and contemplating. 'They're in a city. Don't let them forget it.' Or as Arianna Gil comments some thirty years later of her New York street-skating, 'we're here to add a little chaos'.[42] As this suggests, and as Lefebvre notes, urban rhythms are ever in negotiation, for polyrhythmy is always a conflict, and urban space accordingly always involves contestation and negotiation.[43] Inevitably, therefore, consequences similarly arise from skateboarding's distinctive activity for, notes Mark Gonzales, 'anytime something moves like water, they want to stop it.'[44]

Indeed, attempts to block skateboarding are as old as skateboarding itself, and the very first mention of skateboarding in the *Los Angeles Times*, on 14 June 1959, was a call to outlaw skaters from Pasadena.[45] In the mid-1960s, American skaters met protests from the California Medical Association and faced restrictions in twenty cities. Portland rescinded its previously skateboarding-allowed street, and Floridian skaters had their boards confiscated and received fines from Jacksonville police.[46] In *Skaterdater*, a disapproving office worker simply scatters gravel over the sidewalk. Negative press reporting featured in countless regional newspapers, plus publications like *Consumer Reports*, *Consumer Bulletin*, *Good Housekeeping*, *New York Times*, *Wall Street Journal* and *Washington Post*.[47] The Skateboard Association for Education (SAFE) sought to control skateboarding through safety equipment, supervision and responsible organizations, and, even more seriously, in 1964 fifteen-year-old Los Angeleno Chris Villalobos was shot dead by an irate neighbour annoyed by the sound of skateboarding.[48]

Beyond the United States, anti-roller-skate laws were used to ban skateboarders from the Champs-Elysées in Paris, while in Auckland a skater was fined for 'reckless skateboard riding'.[49] *The Devil's Toy* showed Montreal skaters having boards confiscated and being confined to a roller skate rink, while a deadpan voice-over compared skateboarding to the terrors of guns, bombs and the plague, 'a dread disease which needed only pavement in order to multiply and proliferate'. Later in the 1970s, Californian skaters were fined for riding pools and full-pipes and for being hazardous to pedestrians, while innumerable other riders encountered similar reactions nationwide. 'Every time someone managed to find a slight slant', complained Greg Meisched, 'the cops would erect a No Skateboarding sign.'[50]

At this time, city ordinances were mostly aimed at reducing collisions with pedestrians and were being implemented everywhere from Santa Monica to Zurich. In Australia, many favoured skatespots were shut down and sidewalks were hosed by shop owners, while local newspapers like the *Waverley Gazette* castigated the 'skateboard craze' as 'dangerous and lethal'.[51] Fuelled by reports about skateboarding hazards, similar actions were common in the UK: London's Kensington Gardens was gravelled, twenty Dudley skateboarders faced prosecution under by-laws and skaters found themselves

Figure 11.7
Sensible advice from
Captain Radical.
Skateboard Special,
n.22 (1978).

banned everywhere from Blackpool's promenade and Cardiff's roads to the inside of London's Royal Festival Hall.[52] While *The Times* still saw skateboarding as the 'best youthful antidote to urban boredom that has come along for years', more typical was the London's *Evening News* call to have skateboarding outlawed from all city streets.[53] Groups like Americans for Democratic Action, Consumer Product Safety Commission (CPSC) and Royal Society for the Prevention of Accidents (RoSPA) even proposed complete skateboarding prohibition.[54] Indeed, in 1979, Norway did ban skateboarding entirely, forcing skaters to smuggle in boards and ride in secret locations. Although this regulation was relaxed by 1985, street-skating was not legal in Norway until the early 1990s.[55]

A particular institutional concern, at least on the surface, was for skateboarders' physical well-being. Official advice addressed everything from safety gear to training and first aid, while pseudo-scientific equipment surveys were carried out by the UK's RoSPA and consumer organization Which?.[56] In the United States, in 1977 the National Safety Committee (NSC)

and CPSC discussed standards for skateboards, skateparks and safety equipment, while one survey estimated there were 325,000 skateboard-related accidents in 1978.[57] Leveraging these supposedly alarming statistics, many organizations tried to institutionalize skateboarding; for RoSPA, this meant public service announcements, training programmes, a national conference, the pocket-sized *Safe Skateboarding* book ('*never* skate on the streets – it's highly dangerous') and an accident-prevention code childishly titled *The Skatcats Quizbook*.[58] Safety films appeared in the United States for skaters and parents alike.[59] Even skateboard magazines ran safety-related features, such as *SkateBoarder*'s 'Skate Safe', *Skateboard!*'s 'Skateboarding Safety Code' and *Skateboard Special*'s 'Captain Radical' cartoon strip (Figure 11.7); US professional riders also often contributed to safety clinics during this decade, while every Pepsi team demo began with a speech about safety, followed by precautionary equipment inspections.[60]

Today, serious safety fears have largely retreated into the background, as people

Figure 11.8
A priest confronts street-skaters in
Welcome to Hell (Toy Machine, dir.
Jamie Thomas, 1996).
www.bit.ly/Priest-WelcomeToHell

have generally recognized that, although still deemed by epidemiologists to be 'an important source of injury for children and adolescents', skateboarding rarely leads to death or life-changing accidents.[61] Admittedly, street-skating in particular can lead to both acute and chronic conditions, and especially among advanced riders. In 1992, Frankie Hill's pro career was all but terminated by a buckled knee while attempting a handrail move; later that decade Jamie Thomas, a rider renowned for attempting high drops and other risky manoeuvres, suffered repeated testicular crushing and skull impacts. 'I hit my head two or three times a year,' recounted Thomas, 'where I was unconscious, drooling on the concrete.'[62] Similarly, by 2011 Ryan Sheckler had already broken his elbow ten times, by 2015 Chris Joslin was on his tenth knee brace, while Rodney Mullen endured severe scar tissue build-up on his femur and pelvis, a chronic condition that he chose to alleviate through painful self-inflicted procedures.[63]

Yet despite these tales of professional suffering, for everyday skaters, according to the American Academy of Orthopaedic Surgeons, skate-related injuries commonly involve only minor sprains, contusions, abrasions and breaks to wrists and ankles, a third being incurred by novices who have been skating for less than a week.[64] The US Consumer Product Safety Commission has also reported that just 0.77 per cent of skaters suffer serious injury each year, which is half the rate for baseball, basketball and football, with skaters over eighteen years old being most at risk.[65] The Tony Hawk Foundation reported in 2016 a total injury rate of only 20 per 1,000 skaters, far less than the 224 per 1,000 baseball players.[66] When major injury does occur, this is typically when skaters use inappropriate locations like high-level roofs or, more usually, are struck by traffic; of the thirty US skateboarding fatalities in 2012, twenty-four involved collisions with motorized

vehicles, while all others involved some kind of hill or longboarding descent. Another major US study reported that all skateboarding fatalities recorded over a nineteen-year period related to collisions with motor vehicles.[67] In 2012, no deaths occurred in US skateparks, where the greatest danger typically comes from wayward boards rather than from falling.[68]

Although, in the face of such statistics, safety-first concerns have now largely died away, street-skateboarding has nonetheless faced a more pervasive form of control and repression. By the late 1980s, street-skaters like those depicted in *Ban This* and *Wheels of Fire* regularly had to contend with the police, for by now many Californian cities – including San Diego, Sacramento, San Francisco and Santa Cruz – had placed curfews or banned skateboarding from public areas.[69] Throughout the 1980s and 1990s similar legislation was passed everywhere from Chicago, Denver and Fort Worth to New York, Portland and Savannah.[70] Even usually thoughtful newspapers like the *Washington Post* considered skateboarding as a destructive activity to be barred from public realms, while across the United States innumerable instances of harassment came from cops, security guards and the outraged public, including no-skateboarding tickets ranging from $25 in Philadelphia to $350 in Los Angeles.[71] This pattern was repeated in small towns like Dardanelle, Arkansas, where skaters were treated as 'common criminals', thrown out of parking lots, parks and driveways and threatened with violence. 'Any new spot you found,' protested David Thornton, 'chances were you'd be kicked out within the hour by someone screaming threats at you.'[72] Toy Machine's *Welcome to Hell* (Jamie Thomas, 1996) exemplifies 1990s videos by showing numerous instances of anti-skate attitudes, including a filmer being assaulted by a rather distressed priest (Figure 11.8).

Figure 11.9
A City of London
policeman issues
a fine for street-
skating (2001).
© Wig Worland.

In 1990s UK, skateboarding was banned
in sections of Chelmsford, Birmingham,
Manchester, Leeds and Plymouth, while Derby
instituted an entire skateboard no-go area in its
city centre.[73] Private citizens often 'confiscated'
skateboards, an action that is legally theft,
and in Sheffield riders were labelled 'public
enemy number one'.[74] This general pattern of
anti-skate legislation and behaviour has been
repeated worldwide, including Australia, Brazil,
Canada, Mexico, Netherlands, New Zealand and
Sweden.[75] Today, skateboarding in public spaces
is legislated against everywhere from Brisbane
and Manchester to Quebec and the Bronx; in
2018 Madrid even proposed banning street-
skateboarding throughout the city.[76] The general
effect is to embed in everyday street-skaters a
fear of arrest, penalties and even imprisonment.

Why is this? Although, as Woolley, Hazelwood
and Simkins explain, repairing the damage
caused by skateboarding can be costly, there are
also ideological and cultural factors at play.[77]
As a result, skaters encounter a targeted politics
of space, particularly in those areas hovering
between private and public domains. Because
they occupy cities without engaging in work or

consumerism, skaters frequently annoy building
managers; in sociologist Zygmunt Bauman's
terms, skaters appear to be 'flawed consumers',
being 'short of cash, credit cards and shopping
enthusiasm' and 'immune to the blandishments
of marketing'. 'The local business leaders',
noted Frank Hamlin of Santa Rosa, 'do not
want the kids interfering with their customers'
and consider that 'kids are only okay when
spending money'.[78] Besides not acting as regular
consumers, skaters also seemingly act without
any discernible ambition – there is no 'goal' or
'victory' to be gained from, say, boardsliding
a ledge – and so street-skaters simply madden
those who think they should be doing something
more productive or achievement-focused.

Consequently, many urban managers treat
skaters as trespassers and, using Bauman's
terms, as deficient members of society to be
'earmarked for exclusion' with 'no appeal
allowed'.[79] Additionally, the marks and wax
left by skateboarding are cited as criminal
damage, despite being only relatively minor
blemishes and discolourations that do little to
impede anyone else's enjoyment of cities. In
London's financial district, for example, 1990s

skateboarders chipped edges and deposited coloured streaks on the stone benches around the Broadgate and Liverpool Street district. The City Corporation, police and private security consequently began CCTV surveillance and implemented a £30 fine (Figure 11.9). Skaters were ejected from the area and prosecuted using legislation dating from 1839, while a further 1990 by-law banned skaters from all walkways. 'With the grinding sound of truck against marble', noted Tim Hoad, 'we are inevitably clocked by the notoriously petty Liverpool Street security brigade.'[80] Here, in the bastion of London's banking and trading centre, as Chris Long notes, 'the protection of money, wealth and property is the true spirit of skateboard laws.'[81]

Temporal control is also often deployed. In keeping with the age-related curfews of over 500 US cities – including Baltimore's 2014 legislation for all unaccompanied children under fourteen years old to be indoors by 9:00 p.m. – skateboarders have faced similar restrictions.[82] San Francisco City and County, for example, banned night-time skateboarding from all roads and sidewalks.[83] Somewhat contradictorily, therefore, skateboarding is often criminalized when taking place at night and treated as mere child's play during the day. Much of this accords with a common societal fear of teenagers in general, with skaters as young adults being regularly viewed as potential muggers, robbers or worse; as former US President George Bush once remarked of skateboarders, 'just thank God they don't have guns.'[84]

Yet another response has been similar to the treatment of the homeless. Where the homeless are routinely ejected from business and retail areas by odd-shaped benches, window-ledge spikes and doorway sprinklers, so skaters encounter rough-textured surfaces, obstructive blocks, restrictive chains and scatterings of gravel. Leicester Council spent £10,000 making the banks around its Crown Court unskateable, while in London in 1997 Broadgate managers hindered boardslides by adding vertical dividers to benches.[85] From around 1998 onwards, various metal spikes and bumps (aka 'skatestoppers', first invented by Chris Loarie in San Diego) have been added to handrails, ledges and other street furniture to frustrate skaters' slides and grinds. Vancouver's New Spot and Sydney's Chifley Square were among the first to be rendered unskateable in this way, while Perth's 2002 anti-skateboarding strategy used skatestoppers, grooved surfaces, rough materials, uneven pavements and exclusion zones to deter skateboarding from several sites.[86]

By 2000, these kinds of device were commonplace worldwide, and by 2015 Loarie's company Skatestoppers, after which they are generically known, claimed to have installed over one million examples at over 10,000 locations.[87] During the 2000s, Ravensforge similarly offered metal teardrops, bars and strips, while today SkateBlock offers eighteen different products which, it proudly announces, 'only require a one-time cost and are "on duty" 24 hours a day, 7 days a week, 365 days a year!'[88] Some cities have even played with skatestopper aesthetics, as with the snail, wallet and umbrella shapes at Budapest's Széll Kálmán square and the starfish, turtle and octopus-shaped devices at San Francisco's Fisherman's Wharf (Figure 11.10).[89] Skatestopper itself offers variations looking like leaves, animals, baseballs and even trolley buses, which it markets as 'beautiful, handcrafted skateboard deterrents' that supposedly add 'artistic flare to any application.'[90] In 2014, London witnessed the Camden bench, a complexly surfaced and specially coated object that provided somewhere to sit, but was also deliberately designed to repel those wishing to linger, lie down, paint or, of course, skate.[91] Here, as Lombard points out, skateboarding is caught up in a shift from the policing of specific individuals to the more general governance of 'crimogenic' spaces, such as those car parks, town squares, bus stops and late-night neighbourhoods where crime is considered to be more rife.[92]

Skateboarding Is Not a Crime

> When fun is outlawed, only the outlaws will have fun.[93]
> Warren Bolster

Skateboarding rarely mounts the kinds of explicit political critique offered by groups like Reclaim the Streets and Occupy, nor does it provoke much social disruption; rare exceptions include the 2006 Wild in the Streets event, when thousands of Chicago skaters briefly blocked downtown Michigan Avenue, seeking to assert their rights to public space and to highlight the need for skateparks. However, even this event was hardly a radical protest, as it was sponsored by Emerica shoes, included formal photographs with a banner thanking the mayor for supporting skateboarding, and took place as part of the annual Go Skateboarding Day.[94]

Nonetheless, street-skateboarding conceptually challenges city conventions, precisely because it neither explicitly protests nor quietly conforms. Perhaps because of this uncertainty as to exactly

Figure 11.10
Starfish skatestoppers
at San Francisco's
Fisherman's
Wharf (2010).
© Matt MacQueen.

what might be skateboarding's challenge to society, and despite the pervasiveness of skatestopper measures, the repression of skateboarding is rarely systematic, certainly when compared to laws against serious crimes; as Carr points out, Seattle skaters are far more likely to fall foul of the law of trespass than of anti-skate ordinances.[95] But there are undoubted and persistent tensions between more counter-cultural practices like skateboarding and more normative social practices like shopping and working. This is true whether in London, where Piers Woodford found that 'you always get grief from security guards, the police and drunk businessmen', or small-town United States, where skaters complained that 'we were the scapegoats of the whole town' and that 'every crime or act of vandalism was blamed on us'.[96] Very occasionally this can even spill over into acts of extreme violence; in 2015, a cab driver was convicted for the manslaughter of Ralph Bissonnette, a chef who had been longboarding in downtown Toronto, while two years later another driver ran down at least five skaters celebrating Go Skateboarding Day in São Paulo.[97]

In general, from the mid-1990s onward, skateboarding has been increasingly controlled through localized conventions and laws, and by 2011 was considered by the US Department of Justice as one of the 'problems' of 'disorderly youth' in public places, particularly when 'recklessly' practised.[98] As *Sidewalk* commented, 'hardly a session goes by these days without someone hurling threats of by-laws, cops or fines in our faces.'[99] Or as another skater commented after arriving in London, 'I hadn't counted on being moved on by the police every minute; had not expected to encounter so many skater-hating pedestrians and had not even begun to imagine that such ignorant gorillas could be employed as security guards.'[100]

Treating skateboarding as a crime verges on the ludicrous, and soon falls apart under cross-examination. Consider *Sidewalk*'s comparison between a car that 'runs on poisonous shit, pollutes the air and water, and causes the death of hundreds of thousands' and a skateboard that 'runs on leg power, causes chips and scratches', while society generally believes that 'cars are okay but skateboards are evil, objects of vandalism, a dangerous menace that *must* be stopped.'[101] Skateboard company Santa Monica Airlines made a similar juxtaposition. 'We live in a society where thieves, rapists and murderers enjoy the luxury of wandering the streets clueless, while skaters are constantly bombarded with signs, harassment and just about every type of brainwashing known to man.'[102]

If skateboarding is rendered criminal through petty-minded laws, why is this? Perhaps the fundamental answer here is found when reminding ourselves that skateboarding is aimed at the appropriation – and not domination – of city spaces, and so implicitly (in the act of skateboarding) and explicitly (in occasional texts and videos) opposes the principle of private or public ownership, which seeks to restrict access and enjoyments to certain sanctioned users. 'All space is public space', asserted *Sidewalk*.[103]

Hence, although skateboarding seldom stops property development – the Long Live Southbank campaign during 2013 and 2014 opposing the Southbank Centre redevelopment in London is a rare exception – it does, as we have seen, run contrary to the underlying rationale (business, retail, commuting, organized leisure, orderly behaviour) of urban space. Anti-skateboarding legislature is then less concerned with an actual 'crime' as finding new ways to validate conventional society. According to Derby's city centre manager, one main reason

Figure 11.11
'Skateboarding Is Not
a Crime' deck (2008).
Private collection.

for its skateboard ban was so councillors could avoid 'seeing untidy people skating', while in 1980s San Francisco skateboarding was prohibited only in business and not residential districts, thus highlighting the city's problem with skateboarding for opposing commercial logic, rather than with skateboarding per se.[104] In instances like this skateboarding evidently shares its supposed criminality with that of graffiti which, as geographer Tim Cresswell has noted, 'lies in its being seen, in its transgression of official appearances'.[105] Rather than any real offence, it is skateboarding's 'disorder' as 'untidiness' – what Long calls the 'cognitive dissonance' between skateboarding and social norms – that is targeted. In short, skateboarding is one of those 'false crimes' that Lefebvre identifies as being used to legitimize the business- and commodity-oriented city.[106]

The conflict between skateboarding and conventional urban practices can also be representational. Although some street-oriented videos depict skaters squaring up to irate police, security guards and shop owners, in everyday circumstances skaters' resistance to anti-skateboarding practices is rarely manifested as direct contestation. More common are campaigns like 'Skateboarding Is Not a Crime', as featured in Powell-Peralta's 1988 video *Public*

Domain, where stickers are plastered onto city surfaces and slogans are applied to decks and T-shirts (Figure 11.11). A myriad of similar tactics has included the 'Skateboarding Allowed' stencils applied to San Francisco's Pier 7, and the 'Go Skateboarding' kit produced by Yogi Proctor for Emerica, where a pre-printed letter 'G' can be strategically stickered over the 'N' of 'No Skateboarding' signs.[107] In 2015, artist The Wa even détourned skatestopper devices by removing and reassembling them as art-object skateboards.[108] Other actions include skaters simply removing 'No Skateboarding' signs (often displaying them at home), and participating in the annual Go Skateboarding Day, which celebrates the belief that skateboarding can and should take place anywhere (Figure 1.1). Such acts, contends sociologist Jeff Ferrell, are 'skirmishes in an ongoing battle to liberate public space from legal regulation' and so reinscribe the meaning of public space within skateboarding experiences.[109]

Minor direct action can also be undertaken, as what Ferrell calls instances of 'skatespot liberation'.[110] For example, at London's Undercroft anti-skate barriers were removed, in Los Angeles skaters like Kool Kutter removed skatestoppers using grinders, sanders or their own skateboard trucks, while around 2005 the Skatespot

Liberation Front variously détourned anti-skateboarding signs, hacked away skatestoppers, smoothed cracks with automotive filler and deployed concrete to fashion ad hoc transitions.[111] More commonly, skaters simply ollie over skatestoppers, while those like Jeremy Klein have gone the opposite route, dismantling and stealing bus benches and other street furniture.[112]

Ultimately, being banned from the public domain becomes simply another obstacle to be overcome. 'Skatestoppers', explained Brock Essick, 'only force us to find a new favorite spot.'[113] And as Flusty concluded his study of downtown Los Angeles skateboarding:

> No matter how restrictively space is programmed, no matter how many 'armed response' security patrols roam the streets, and no matter how many video cameras keep watch over the plazas, there remain blindspots that await and even invite inhabitation by unforeseen and potent alternative practices.[114]

The prevailing psychology here is proud defiance, as expressed by Homey when announcing that 'I, for one, like skate harassment and the rush you get kicking down the street from some raving shop owner, or even better, the police.'[115] Or as Ben Powell obdurately asserted, 'the point is f**ck 'em all, they can't touch us now.'[116] In more legalistic terms, according to Carr, skaters use both temporary appropriations and more permanent claims in order 'to find seams within the law that enable them to circumvent exclusionary efforts.'[117]

These attitudes have also gained a degree of wider support. Over the last three decades or so, public realms – as Mike Davis, Monica Degen, Anna Minton, Neil Smith and Michael Sorkin have all shown – have become increasingly privatized, unwelcoming and even hostile to citizens who are not directly engaged in shopping, tourism and work.[118] Significantly, many members of the public have disapproved of these worrisome trends; in the UK, the killjoy Camden bench met with widespread criticism, and an online petition opposing anti-homeless spikes attracted 130,000 supporters, while the 'Mosquito' high-frequency sound devices aimed at repelling teenagers, along with the removal of litter bins to reduce food sources for the homeless, were equally condemned.[119]

Amid these kinds of public concern, street-skaters have consequently gained some empathy from academics. 'Something active and free like skateboarding shouldn't be automatically disapproved of,' stated eminent planner Jane Jacobs in 2003. 'This is a healthy thing, that's part of freedom.'[120] In Australia, Elaine Stratford has called for 'geographies of generosity' that encourage street-skating, and in the United States Chris Giamarino proposes more skateboarding within multi-purpose uses of Los Angeles streets and squares, partly inspired by Leonie Sandercock's conception of 'Cosmopolis' as a place where 'people can cartwheel across pedestrian crossings without being arrested for playfulness.'[121]

These scholarly pleas have occasionally been recognized, as when the Brisbane public rued the disappearance of skaters cruising the city streets, and Newcastle city officials, while seeking to prevent 'bad' street-skaters in shopping areas, also let 'good' skaters use their boards for local transport and leisure.[122] Planning officers and academics like Stephen Lorimer and Stephen Marshall are increasingly considering how skateboarding might contribute to neighbourhood transportation, while by 2015 Montreal had legalized skateboarding on bike paths and in Peace Park, as had Grand Rapids City in Michigan and Victoria in Canada for their downtown streets.[123] In a similar mood, eighty-eight per cent of Coventry's public opposed a mooted city centre skateboarding ban, 150,000 people supported the campaign to prevent skateboarding being replaced by food and retail outlets at London's Undercroft, and in Wisconsin's Green Bay police officer Joel Zwicky longboards around his beat to allow greater interaction with his community.[124] Black and ethnic Bronx skaters, records White, are today less likely to attract police hassle when riding, for skateboarding provides them with a legitimate reason to be in public space; 'You're not looking to cause trouble,' remarked one skater, 'you're just looking to skate.'[125]

Whatever their solidarity with non-skaters, for skateboarders themselves legislation and authority are still there to be resisted, for, asserts Miki Vuckovich, 'reinterpretation and often downright subversion of such regulation is the skateboarder's creed.'[126] Or as *Thrasher* declares, every street-skater's mark is 'evidence of endurance and determination, a message to those who would try and deter us.'[127] In this respect, skateboarders are part of a long process in the history of cities, a fight by the disempowered and disenfranchised for distinctive spaces of their own. In this

Figure 11.12
Zered Bassett creates distinctive urban space in New York (2014).
© Giovanni Reda.

Figure 11.13
Mike Manzoori,
Southbank Centre,
London (2000).
© Wig Worland.

way, skaters engage city spaces, surfaces and buildings in a highly positive manner – they create not only a physical mobility but a shifting of ideas, a critique of the spaces around them. To borrow from Lefebvre, skateboarding is 'not only the space of "no", it is also the space of the body, and the space of "yes", of the affirmation of life'.[128] *R.A.D.* perhaps put it best of all: 'This is just a small dream. A dream of endless pure creation. A movement without words.'[129]

Section Three
Skate and Create

Skate and Create
Chapter 12 Artistry

There's something one-of-a-kind about the creative impulse and skateboarders,
The two seem to go together quite well, like soundwaves and air.[1]
Garry Scott Davies

In opposition to *Thrasher*'s 'skate and destroy' mantra, when *TransWorld Skateboarding* originated in 1983 it purposely offered a different direction for skateboarding, one determinedly centred around the motif of 'skate and create' (Figure 5.3). While *TransWorld*'s thematic was primarily concerned with act of skateboarding itself, the notion of skate and create can also be readily applied to other areas of expression within and around skateboarding. Photography and filmmaking have already been explored in Chapter 5. In this chapter, we look at other avenues, notably graphic design, art and architecture, along with how creativity might be inherent to skateboarding.

Graphic Design

Graphic design has always been integral to skateboarding, primarily through decks adorned with myriad symbols, patterns, motifs and scenes. Even early 1960s boards by the likes of Bauer, Bun Buster and Roller Derby typically sported designs on their upper surfaces (Figure 2.3). However, while *The Devil's Toy* movie portrays perhaps the first ever skateboard skull, and the likes of Nash, Mustang and Union Surfer occasionally used voodoo, snake, skull and cross-bones motifs, the vast majority of 1960s deck designs consisted simply of the manufacturer's name or a few coloured stripes.[2] Early 1970s graphic designs – such as the airbrush-style work by Jim Evans for Cadillac Wheels – extended into surf-related themes like waves, sunsets and palm trees, but was largely restricted to advertisements and T-shirts, and rarely featured on skateboards themselves.

Skulls and Screaming Hands

By the mid-1970s things started to change, particularly when graphics shifted to the undersides of decks. To begin with, these devices were confined to the names of companies, deck models and pro skaters, such as Caster, SIMS Superply, Variflex Eric Grisham etc. Meanwhile, more inventive designs were emerging, partly through connections between skateboarding and graffiti, such as New York's Soul Artists of Zoo York graffiti crew, which included skaters like Andy Kessler, Ricky Mujica and Jaime Affoumado.[3] Most influentially, Wes Humpston evolved his hand-embellished decks into the distinctive idiom of the Dogtown company's production boards, combining crosses, feathered wings, dragons and Hispanic gang-style lettering (Figure 12.1).[4]

Skaters like Steve Olson, Steve Alba (Figure 7.11) and Duane Peters (Figure 7.12) also helped lead skateboarding away from surfing to the world of punk and indie music, replacing Led Zeppelin, sunlight and waves with The Clash, brash colours and geometric patterns.[5] Particularly iconic was Jim Phillips's Maltese cross-derived logo for Independent, plus two decks for Santa Cruz: the Steve Olson pro model (1979) with a black, white and red checker-board pattern, and the Duane Peter's model (1980) with a red background, black stripes and calligraphic white letters drawn from punk clothing and Japanese samurai.[6]

Another significant change in the late 1970s and early 1980s was the rising popularity of goth-style skulls, swords and serpents. Skulls in particular were favoured by Vernon Courtland Johnson (VCJ) at Powell-Peralta (Figure 12.2), Brian 'Pushead' Schroeder at *Thrasher* and Zorlac and Peter Ducommun ('PD') at Skull Skates.[7] Other renowned designs from this period included the demonic faces and other maniacal graphics that Phillips created for Santa Cruz (Figure 12.3), as well as his iconic Screaming Hand motif, first used for Speed Wheels in 1985 (Figure 12.4).[8] Bernie Tostenson of SIMS similarly migrated from cool-tech logos to new wave designs, including a Superman-esque logo for a Brad Bowman model (1980), the splat design for a Lester Kasai model (1983) and the punk-photocopy Screamer (1983), as well as later Brand-X and Flip decks.[9] Skater-designers working in a similar vein included Neil Blender, Garry Scott Davis, Natas Kaupas and Lance Mountain. John Lucero created the creepy Jester (1985) for Madrid and Schmitt Stix, Steve Walker composed Walker's harrowing Mark Lake Nightmare deck (1986) and Vision, inspired by London-based *i-D* fashion magazine and

Figure 12.1
Wes Humpston designs for Dogtown. *SkateBoarder* (June 1979). Courtesy Dogtown Skateboards.

LET US TURN YOU ON

Plug into a strong new line of lightweight fiberglas and maple laminate glass-bottom beauties.

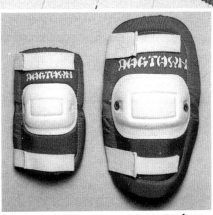

Dogtown Protective Equipment

DOGTOWN SKATES • THE ORIGINAL SKATES
133 Arena St., El Segundo, CA 90245 • (213) 322-9078

Seattle's punk culture, produced multiple-colour variants of its psychedelically geometric Gator (1984), Hippie Stick (1985), Mark Gonzales (1985) and Psycho Stick (1987) models, variously designed by Greg Evans, John Grigley and Andy Takakjian (Figure 12.5).[10]

Wonka-land

If this move from surfing themes of sun and ocean to those of death and primitive survival rendered skate symbology increasingly incomprehensible to outsiders, then all the better; skaters wanted to be noticed, but not understood. As Lefebvre explains, the symbols of 'partial groups' are deliberately 'equivocal and ambiguous,' expressing aspirations that remain secret to members, all of which was particularly relevant to skateboarding while it still remained largely outside the cultural mainstream.[11] Mike Hill even wanted his Ohio-based Alien Workshop, formed in 1990, to mutate into a non-human sect-like cult of art, music, skateboarding and self-sufficiency, and the company's graphics of alien cryogenics, mind control, clone technology and other enigmatic devices consequently helped to foster an aura of mysterious otherworldliness.[12]

Furthermore, as the Alien Workshop designs suggest, deck graphics were now changing again. In the G&S *Footage* video of 1990, skater-artist Neil Blender famously dismissed Santa Cruz's Corey O'Brien pro model with the comment 'it's 1990 boys, let's get rid of the skeletons.' This statement marked a rapid shift from the skulls and bones of the 1980s to more plural and lateral symbolisms (Figure 12.6), and decks were soon displaying everything from light bulbs in a field (Panic) and semi-naked women (Acme) to cartoon cows (New Deal), Escher-style geometric patterns (Consolidated), architects' drawing instruments (Blueprint) and cartoon characters like Blind Reaper, Devil Man, Flame Boy and Wet Willy (World Industries). These kinds of design share less a common subject matter and more a decidedly non-realist graphic style, ranging from the airbrushed imagery of heavy metal to children's comics and oriental illustration techniques, and so maintain the symbolism of Lefebvre's partial groups by curiously combining the old and modern, weird and wonderful, familiar and disturbing.[13]

Figure 12.2
VCJ skull and sword design for Powell-Peralta's Ray Rodriguez pro model. *SkateBoarder* (June 1979).

Figure 12.3
Jim Phillips designs for Santa Cruz. *R.A.D.* (November 1989). Courtesy NHS.

Figure 12.4
'Screaming Hand'
by Jim Phillips (1985).
Courtesy NHS and
Jim Phillips.

Figure 12.5
Vision Psycho
Stick (1987).
Courtesy Peter Joynt.

Despite this broad spectrum, some tendencies can be discerned. Notably, one deck design sub-genre targeted the younger demographic of X Games–watching skaters; hence, for example, the World Industries Stickerama decks with street scenes that could be modified by skater-applied sticker characters, as well as Christian Cooper's Magritte-inspired This Is a Burning Teddy Bear design for Stereo (1996).[14] As Sean Cliver's explains, such 'strange graphics' turned banality into art via a fusion of pop culture, pop art sensibilities and cartoon characters.[15] Another variant has been the deployment of sophisticated typographic and postmodern imagery (Figure 12.7), such as that used by Ged Wells for Insane, Evan Hecox for his coolly architectural City Series (1997) and other Chocolate graphics (many designed as panoramic multi-board sets), or by Tony Larson for Girl's Modern Chair series (2000). Again, the intention was not to explain skateboarding, but rather, as Rudy Vanderlans explains, these designs variously deployed 'consumer products, advertising, Japanese cartoons, instruction manuals, electronic gadgets, Blade Runner movies, and the Macintosh computer' in order to reflect the confusion and chaos of contemporary society.[16]

Other graphics have been more overtly challenging in nature, such as the anarcho-punk sensibility of the R.A.D. magazine page layouts created by art editor Nick Phillips and his successors Ian Lawson (later known as Ian Roxburgh) and Dan Adams.[17] Although rendered in a rather different idiom, political currents are also evident in the cartoon barnyard deck designed by Marc McKee for the World Industries Mike Vallely pro model (1990), which was both a reference to George Orwell's Animal Farm and to Vallely's own vegetarianism (Figure

2.12), and in such designs as the Hanging Klu Klux Klansman (Real's Jim Thiebaud model, 1990), Sean Cliver's substance-abusing Bad Babies (101 Skateboards, 1995), Ed Templeton's mind-washing Religion, Politics, Lies (Toy Machine, 1994) and Todd Francis's anti-religious McJesus – Over Fifty Million Killed (Antihero, 1997). World Industries also mocked the tobacco industry's marketing to kids via deck graphics showing crack pipes and cigarettes. Many of these were unflinching statements. Although he received death threats and hate mail after releasing his KKK deck, a defiant Thiebaud still asserted that 'Putting racial injustice under the spotlight is always possible, and needed. Skateboarding is always a great medium — our voices are loud as fuck!'[18]

In much of this work, deck designers have adopted the Situationist tactic of détournement, reusing corporate motifs and popular icons in order to destabilize their apparent legitimacy. Famous examples of this ruse include McKee's Winnie the Pooh figure for Santa Monica Airlines and World Industries Steve Rocco

models (1989), the Burger King–style Bun Halves motif for Blind's Jason Lee model (1991), the Scientology-style Colvinetics logo for a World Industries Randy Colvin model (1991) and the Sean Coons–designed Star Wars series for Plan B (1993) (Figure 12.8). Other usurpations of corporate imagery have involved Coca-Cola, Disney, Smurfs, Snoopy, Warner Brothers cartoons and David Bowie, while Erik Brunetti's Fuct company has made innumerable DIY-style reappropriations of the Ford logo, iconic movie stills, Rolling Stones albums and other famed motifs.[19] Most recently, DGK have adapted Disney, Burger King, MasterCard, McDonald's and NASA logos for pro models. Many of these decks have been manufactured in short production runs in order to sidestep the inevitable legal objections, a game at which World Industries became particularly adept: 'over the years,' recalled Mullen, 'we collected stacks of cease-and-desist letters from lawyers representing everybody from the Hell's Angels to Disney and the Church of Scientology.'[20] Whatever their legal standing, these graphic appropriations were

Figure 12.6
Plural and lateral symbolism. *Sidewalk* (March 1997).

Figure 12.7
Postmodern graphic design. Utility Board Supply, *TransWorld Skateboarding* (October 2000).

DECKS

GIRL - $47.99 with premium grip tape.
Build your own custom complete for just $104.99 (see above for details).

Koston	Mariano	Carroll	Howard	McKay
7.63 x 31.5	7.5 x 31.25	7.5 x 31.5	8 x 32	7.88 x 31.5

ELEMENT - $47.99 with premium grip tape. Build your own custom complete for just $104.99 (see above for details).

Bam	Barley	Wray	Ivy	Skate
8 x 32	7.86 x 31.86	7.86 x 31.75	7.86 x 31.75	8 x 31.75

SHORTY'S - $47.99 with premium grip tape. Build your own custom complete for just $104.99 (see above for details).

Muska	Muska	Team	Olsen	ODS-Dice
Medium	Silhouette	Medium	Eye	Medium
7.6 x 31.5	8 x 32	7.7 x 32	7.5 x 31	7.7 x 31.5

WORLD INDUSTRIES - $47.99 with premium grip tape. Build your own custom complete for just $104.99 (see above for details).

ACE	MATHIAS	TNT 2	HAMMER2	BRUCE
7.75 x 31.63	7.75 x 31.5	7.75 x 31.5	7.75 x 31.75	WIL-LEE
				7.63 x 31.38

ZERO - $47.99 with premium grip tape.
Build your own custom complete for just $104.99 (see above for details).

Ellington	Lopez	Mumford	Thomas	Eagle
8 x 32	7.88 x 31.5	7.63 x 31.5	8.13 x 32	7.88 x 31

REAL - $47.99 with premium grip tape.
Build your own custom complete for just $104.99 (see above for details).

Foster	Gonzales	Hufnagel	Star Sm.	Star Med.
7.56 x 31.38	7.56 x 31.38	7.63 x 31.25	7.63 x 31.38	7.75 x 31.5

Figure 12.8
The cease-and-desist and
boundary-testing tactics of Marc
McKee and World Industries. *The
Man Who Souled the World*
(dir. Mike Hill, 2007).
www.bit.ly/ManWhoSouled

deliberately intended as playful postmodern commentaries, and, mixed with rich graphic and cultural sources, they are consequently suggestive of the kind of 'cultural hybridity' that cultural theorist Homi Bhabha describes as 'entertaining difference without an assumed or imposed hierarchy'.[21]

Designer Marc McKee – according to Thomas Campbell 'probably the single most important artist of skateboards' who 'defined what a skateboard graphic was and subsequently is' – was, along with employer Steve Rocco and parent company World Industries, particularly willing to test legal, political and ethical boundaries.[22] After effectively torpedoing Powell-Peralta with a series of antagonistic advertisements and spoof Powell-Peralta graphics, World Industries introduced the notorious Napping Negro graphic (1992) for black skater Jovontae Turner, which, while acknowledging that 'negroes were bought, sold, enslaved, tortured, raped and killed', also promised to 'transport you back to a simpler time, when colored people knew their place'.[23] Other controversial McKee-designed graphics for World Industries included the dead pope and decapitated baby of the Devil Worship design (1991), the Roy Lichtenstein–style Boom! graphic depicting the exploding Challenger spacecraft for Natas Kaupas models (1992) and the explicit masturbating women featured on Randy Colvin decks (1990), the latter being distributed in black bags with stickers announcing 'Warning: Censorship Is Weak as Fuck.' Equally challenging were McKee's Accidental Gun Death (1992) for Guy Mariano pro models and the Fucked Up Blind Kids series (1992), as well as the ironic ethnic stereotyping of the Hot Dog on a Stick pro model for Daewon Song and Orange Vendor pro model for Chico Brenes (Figure 12.8). McKee admits that many of these were 'purely created for shock value' and to make fun at (or with) ethnically diverse

World Industries riders; as Sean Cliver has described these controversial graphics, in this 'delightfully twisted Wonka-land' absolutely nothing was 'unimaginable, unattainable, or incapable of being produced'.[24] Although more socially acceptable and targeted at younger skaters, the later McKee-designed Devil Man, Flame Boy and Wet Willy characters continued with typical World Industries themes of cartoon violence and general irreverence, and tripled the company's sales within one year.[25]

Nor has McKee been alone in this desire to produce graphics that are alternatively defiant, disturbing, provocative or offensive. To reference just a few examples, Alex Duke's I'm Soooo Gay (Consolidated 2007), Todd Bratrud's Skull Fuck (Roots, 2007), Cleon Peterson's Nick Merlino/Golden Vagina (Foundation, 2012), Wally Wood's Disneyland Memorial Orgy 1967 (Boom-Art/Holenite Pool, 2012), Paul Parker's Banfield (Witchcraft, 2012), Jason Moore's Don Nguyen/Gooks of Hazard (Baker, 2012), Ian Reid's Girl collaborations (2016) and Sean Cliver designs for Supreme deal with themes like child drug abuse, fetish photography, pornography, racial prejudice, religion, sex and sexuality, and with varying degrees of explicit detail, comic delight and po-faced ambiguity.[26]

Less overtly controversial but nonetheless substantial subjects have also been tackled. For example, the likes of Mike Hill's Exalt the New God (Alien Workshop, 2010), Alex Kramer's Giant Squid Kid (Yama, 2008), Todd Bratrud's Bradtrud GMO (Enjoi, 2007), Pete Panciera's Spencer Hamilton/Monsanto Kills (Expedition, 2013), Darren Young's Taliban This (Skate Mental, 2011), Brice Raysseguier's Fuck the World Trader (Trauma, 2011) and Ben Horton's Farewell ($lave, 2008) (Figure 12.11) have addressed issues like televisual culture, gene manipulation, agri-business, secret societies, geopolitics, financial greed and Republican

Figure 12.9
Douglas Miles and Apache
Skateboards in *I Paint What I Like*
(dir. Erin Gramzinski and Steve
Filmer, 2013).
www.bit.ly/Miles-Paint

politics.[27] Alex Olson's Bianca Chandôn
company (2014) has taken an anti-homophobic
line with its graphics and brand imagery, using
aesthetics derived from Fire Island gay culture
and 1970s New York disco, while according to
Soy Panday many Magenta boards address the
importance of travel and cultural differences.[28]

As recorded by Martinez, indigenous Americans
have similarly tackled issues of identity,
politics, oppression and resistance, including
Dustinn Craig (4WheelWarPony), Todd Harder
(Native Skates), Jim Murphy (Wounded Knee
Skateboards) and Liana Nelson and Tracy
Lee Nelson (Full Blood Skates). In particular,
artist Douglas Miles's designs for his Apache
Skateboards company draw parallels between
skateboarding and Apache warrior traditions,
creating a visual expression of a social
movement (Figure 12.9).[29]

The general effect of all this activity is of a
thoroughly eclectic hybridity, as a visit to any
skate shop today will quickly confirm. 'There's
tons of awesome shit going down right now',
comments Hardisty, 'skateboarding has never
been more visual.'[30] The sheer variety and
inventiveness on display suggests an alternative
reality, parallel to the everyday world of work,
leisure, shopping and realism.

There is also something of a contradiction
at work, with these much revered graphics
often being swiftly erased through the act of
skateboarding; 'a graphic on a skateboard goes
the full cycle from creation to destruction,'
explains Powell designer, John Keester. 'It's
created specifically for someone to go grind it
back into the elements it was made from.'[31] Or as
Brian Kerezel, art director at Maple skateboards
sees it, 'skateboard graphics are almost
disposable' and a skater's new deck graphic 'will
be gone in a couple of weeks.'[32] The fast turnover
of designs (in the early 1990s World Industries

often produced only 300 units of any single
graphic) attenuates this situation still further,
meaning that once worn out a particular deck is
almost impossible to replace.[33]

Collecting, Collaborating and Branding

If decks often last only a few months, and are
frequently produced in small numbers, this
means they can quickly become rare objects.
Predictably perhaps, an entire sub-genre of
skateboard acquisition and museology has now
emerged, including thousands of collectors
communicating via specialist Facebook groups
and internet forums. Some collections are
substantial, such as Brewce Martin's Skatopia,
Jack Smith's Morro Bay Skateboard Museum,
Todd Huber's Skatelab in Simi Valley, the
NHS Skate Museum in Santa Cruz, the Pulp
68 Skateboard Museum in Geneva and the
Skateboard Museum in Stuttgart. So expensive
have some of these decks become – for example,
in the mid-2010s a mint condition SIMS deck
from the late 1970s might well command $5,000
– that many famous decks have been reissued
as replica or homage versions in order to satisfy
demand from less wealthy enthusiasts, such
as the H-Street tribute (2016) to a SIMS Dave
Andrecht pro model (1979) (Figure 9.7) and
a G&S reissue (2017) of a Doug 'Pineapple'
Saladino pro model (Figure 12.10).

In addition, several significant exhibitions
have explored decks and skate culture, and
often with a marked post-colonial emphasis,
including 'Remix: New Modernities in a Post-
Indian World' at the Smithsonian's National
Museum of the American Indian, (2007), 'The
Rise of Rad: The Influence of Skate Culture on
Contemporary Art' at Torrance Art Museum,
California (2010), 'Sidewalk Surfing: the Art
and Culture of Skateboarding' at the Everhart
Museum, Scranton, Pennsylvania (2013), 'How
We Roll' at the California African American
Museum (2010), 'Ramp It Up: Skateboard

Culture in Native America' at the Smithsonian's National Museum of the American Indian (2014) and 'Landskating Anywhere' at the Arc en rêve centre d'architecture, Bordeaux (2017). Some of these displays have been hugely popular; when skateboarding was connected with graffiti and street art in the 'Art in the Streets' exhibition in Los Angeles (2011), it drew over 200,000 visitors.[34] As all this indicates, not all skateboarding decks are fated to an ephemeral life of destruction and disposal, with a few passing into more curatorial futures.

Cultural values have also been heightened through collaborations with renowned artists, designers and brands. Following the art decks offered by Keith Haring, Kenny Scharf and Jean-Michel Basquiat in the mid-1980s, the Supreme skate boutique, for example, has undertaken numerous collaborations with artists like John Baldessari, Larry Clark, Sean Cliver, George Condo, Damien Hirst, KAWS, Jeff Koons, Harmony Korine, Marilyn Minter, Takashi Murakami, Richard Prince and Terry Richardson. In the twenty-first century, Natas Kaupas's Designarium Skateboards has worked with Thomas Campbell, Shepard Fairey, Jim Houser, Don Pendleton and Ed Templeton, Alien Workshop with graphics from Keith Haring and Andy Warhol, Santa Cruz with Robert Williams and Krooked with the Clayton Brothers. Tie-ins with non-skate brands have also become fashionable, such as those between Girl and Hello Kitty, Black Label and Jägermeister and Santa Cruz with Pabst, Star Wars and The Simpsons.

Even high-end brands have produced decks. While Marc Jacobs and Commes des Garcons, do seem, notes Brandt, somewhat aligned to youth and subcultural values, other brands, such as Chanel, Gucci, Ferrari, Prada, Polo and Ralph Lauren, are less likely candidates for skateboard design; in 2011 the leather decks by Greg Hervieux with Domeau & Pérès were priced at €900, while in 2014 Louis Vuitton's complete board and case cost $8,250. Even more rarefied creations have included two more from 2014, and each priced at $15,000 – a Rick Owens board made of petrified wood, and a fully-functioning gold-plated mirror-finish device, designed by Matthew Willet and offered by New York's skate shop Shut.[35]

Not all art decks, however, are purely about brand development or eye-catching bling. The Skateroom project in Brussels, for example, uses artist boards to support non-profit projects like

Skateistan (Figure 12.12). Under the strapline of 'Skating Beyond Skating – Art You've Never Seen on a Board – Helping Youth a Skateboard at a Time', an extensive range of limited edition decks from the likes of Nobuyoshi Araki, Banksy, Jean-Michel Basquiat, Andy Hope, Jeff Koons, Paul McCarthy, Takasi Murakami, Neckface, José Parla, ROA, Ai Weiwei and Christopher Wool are sold for anywhere from €300 to €5,000, with a percentage going to charity.[36] Similar ventures are now common. For example, Goodhood's 'Art of Skateboarding' exhibition in London (2014) charity-auctioned decks by artists Jake and Dinos Chapman, Will Sweeney, James Jarvis, Russell Maurice, Daniel Sparkes, Ged Wells and Trevor Jackson.[37]

Art

Skateboarding, argues Brandt, has always contained DIY impulses, nihilism, romance and sardonic humour, creating a 'brilliantly stupid' combination of intellect and anarchic sensitivity.[38] Along with mental tenacity and a readiness to embrace failure and imperfection,

Figure 12.10
G&S Pine Design II reissue (2017) of a Doug 'Pineapple' Saladino pro model (*c.* 1979).
Private collection.

Figure 12.11
Ben Horton's Farewell design for $lave (2008).
© Ben Horton/ Courtesy $lave Skateboards.

Figure 12.12
Paul McCarthy decks for The Skateroom (2015).
www.bit.ly/McCarthy-Skateroom

Figure 12.13
'Beautiful Losers' exhibition at Yerba Buena Center for the Arts, San Francisco (2004). *Beautiful Losers* (dir. Aaron Rose and Joshua Leonard, 2008).
www.bit.ly/BeautifulLosers-Yerba

these qualities infuse skateboarding's preference for pursuing expression and experimentation over competition or profit. 'Skateboarding is performance art to me', stated Christian Hosoi, 'and while it's about winning, I'm even more interested in expressing myself to the crowd.'[39]

Beautiful Losers

From the mid-1980s onwards, skaters like Neil Blender, Bill Danforth, Mark Gonzales, Lance Mountain and Sean Sheffey adorned their decks with self-created embellishments. Marker pens, scalpels, stencils and spray paint were used for splintered patterns, curving shapes, fragmentary words and other idiosyncratic decorations.[40] From here, it was but a small step to more formal displays of expression. By 1987 *TransWorld* was reviewing examples of fine art created by skaters, while the first show of skater art was possibly Dan Field's 'Degenerates' in 1992, including work by Gonzales, Mountain, Garry Scott Davis, Andy Jenkins and Tod Swank.[41] Other early exhibitions of skate graphics included 'Dysfunctional' at London's Blue Note in 1995, and two years later 'Uncut' at London's Institute of Contemporary Arts (ICA). Also in 1997, Aaron Rose's 'Shred Sled Symposium' was held at New York's Thread Waxing Space and Glen Friedman's 'Fuck You All' photography went on display at the ICA.

'Stationary Motion' (1998) at Sheffield's Sumo skate shop showcased photographic work by Skin Phillips, Wig Worland and Tim Leighton-Boyce, while 'Modart 98' in San Diego featured art by Ed Templeton and Marc McKee.[42]

As these events suggest, skate-related artists have found considerable renown beyond the skateboard world, reaching far more public venues and audiences. A particularly seminal event for the art-skateboarding scene was 'Beautiful Losers', held at various US venues (2004–2005) (Figure 12.13). Curated by Aaron Rose and Christian Strike, this exhibition combined established figures like Keith Haring, Robert Crum and Andy Warhol with other artists who were either skaters or were closely connected to skateboarding, including Thomas Campbell, Larry Clark, Garry Scott Davis, Shepard Fairey, Glen Friedman, Phil Frost, Mark Gonzales, Tommy Guerrero, Evan Hecox, Chris Johanson, Spike Jonze, Margaret Kilgallen, Harmony Korine, Geoff McFetridge, Barry McGee, Ryan McGinley, Ari Marcopoulos, Mike Mills, Pushead, Terry Richardson, Craig Stecyk, Ed Templeton and Tobin Yelland. Given the disparate range of artists involved, the work was inevitably highly varied, but was nonetheless united by concerns with DIY ethics, urban streets, 'low' culture (graffiti, skateboarding,

indie music etc.), and, frequently, by an absence of formal art training.[43]

Despite, however, the curatorial concern to position these artists as art world outsiders, and even as being from the fringes of society, such exhibitions also raise some cultural and political questions. In particular, 'Beautiful Losers', argue Atencio and Beal, is based mainly on middle-class and white-male perspectives, creating an idealized image of US cities, espousing a DIY ethos over state support and largely ignoring the urban plight of minority citizens. Conversely, the exhibitors, as valued 'street' and 'outsider' artists, gained elevation within the post-industrial creative classes, while brands like Pepsi, VW, Gap, Nike, TMobile and Levi's also benefitted from associating with this kind of 'authentic', 'cool' and 'hip' art.[44]

The key neoliberal worker skills of autonomy, flexibility and self-reflexivity are also readily apparent, particularly in the later film *Beautiful Losers* (dir. Aaron Rose and Joshua Leonard, 2008) (Figure 12.13). Here, argue Atencio and Beal, the project's idealization of DIY art displays the American 'myth of upward social mobility', where citizens work hard and submit to 'regulated freedom' in order to achieve individual success and happiness.[45] Nor is this confined to US skaters. Even someone like Pontus Alv, the respected street-skater, DIY-fabricator, filmmaker and owner of Polar, can sound disconcertingly neoliberal when saying that 'If you want something in life make it happen. Work hard and all the things you dream of can be yours.'[46]

Nonetheless, these criticisms can also be levelled at the art world in general, and so should be balanced against the particular

Figure 12.14
'Units Moved'
exhibition at
the Architecture
Foundation, London
(2006), with work by
Toby Paterson in the
foreground.
© Wig Worland.

Figure 12.15
Ed Templeton
'Religion' collage
at 'The Cemetery of
Reason' exhibition,
SMAK, Ghent (2010).
@dvlphoto.

qualities of skate-related art. On the one hand, notes Brandt, there are many new skate-related galleries, such as Alleged and BLK/MRKT Gallery in Los Angeles, Deitch Projects and KCDC in New York, Space 1026 in Philadelphia, China Heights and Monster Children in Sydney, Collette in Paris, AntiSocial in Vancouver and Fifty 24 in San Francisco and Portland.[47] More importantly, argues Thornton, skateboarding's movement and appropriations of terrains can encourage new ways of creating art, including forming an 'entryway into the concept of non-representational art.'[48] Representational art, of course, has also benefitted from associations with skateboarding, and examples of both tendencies are legion. For example, the 'Units Moved' exhibition at London's Architecture Foundation (2006), curated by Richard Holland, Wig Worland and myself, incorporated painting, sculpture, video, photography, mixed media and installation pieces from the likes of Alex Hartley, Kathy Barber, Nic Clear, Richard Gilligan, Sam Griffin, Toby Paterson, Sem Rubio, Toby Shuall, Wig Worland, Richard Holland and Peter Evans (Figure 12.14). Of these, Paterson's work is perhaps most renowned, frequently involving – just as street-skaters reimagine

buildings as discontinuous ledges, walls and rails – abstracted compositions of architectural elements, shapes and colours.

Besides those individuals mentioned elsewhere in this chapter, other notable skate-related artists and artworks include Angela Boatwright's photographic and video recordings of subcultures, Erik Brunetti's assemblage of lost-animal flyers, Glen Fox's neo-cubist paintings, Mike Giant's graffiti- and tattoo-inspired drawings, Andy Howell's spray-painted canvases, Stefan Janoski's bronze and ceramic sculptures, Andrew Lewicki's anti-consumerist sculptures, Lance Mountain's paintings and skate-pool tables, Kris Markovich's deck-based paintings, Peggy Oki's activist environmentalism, Chad Muska's graffiti and wheat-paste creations, Brian Lotti's paintings of Californian urban landscapes and Steve Olson's multimedia sculptures.

With even greater reputations are Neil Blender, Ed Templeton and Mark Gonzales, each of whom extends a unique sensibility across both their skateboarding and artistic practices. For example, the skateboarding of Neil Blender –

in Weyland's words a 'self-invented Dadaist' – combined immense concentration with inventive board and body manipulations, these qualities being equally apparent in his strangely obsessive and childlike drawings of people, animals, insects and everyday objects. 'Skateboarding was an obsession with me,' explained Blender to *Thrasher*, 'now it's just an art expression.'[49]

In a similar way, street-skater Ed Templeton has become one of skateboarding's most celebrated artists through his close observations and recordings of everyday life (Figure 12.15). After the *Teenage Smokers* photographic collection (2000) first brought Templeton to the attention of the art world, further acclaimed projects followed, such as *Deformer* (2008) and *Wayward Cognitions* (2014). The autobiographical *Deformer* publication, for example, incorporates photographs and sketches of bodily, sexual, landscape, religious and gun-toting themes from California's 'suburban domestic incubators'. Poignant, messy and mildly disturbing, it offers frank insights into real teenage life, far removed from the idyllic sun-soaked life typically associated with this state.

Performance
The most celebrated of all skater-artists has been Mark Gonzales, less for individual works and more for his continual life performance – the way that idiosyncratic energy pervades everything he does, from how he skates and speaks to how he makes and draws. Famously, Gonzales has always been an unpredictable rider, such as grabbing a mid-1960s skateboard (with no grip tape or kicktail and sporting slippery clay wheels) to perform an ollie air on an intimidating vert-ramp. As Sem Rubio has described him, Gonzales is relatively unconditioned by skateboarding tricks and images, and so truly improvises his engagement with board and immediate surroundings. Furthermore, explains Brian Gaberman, Gonzales 'doesn't differentiate between animate and inanimate objects' but 'has the same relationship with all of them.'[50] Such attitudes readily transfer to other practices, and Gonzales's outputs have consequently encompassed innumerable paintings, drawings, text-daubings and graphic designs, plus idiosyncratic publications like *Instead of Eros Avenged* (2011), a collection of mobile-phone images inspired by Jerry Chadwick poetry. Other pieces include the 'Circle Board' (2009) – a giant wheel-shaped sculpture-as-skateboard comprising nine boards connected

end-to-end – in which Gonzales has skated around Paris and New York (Figure 12.16). A decade earlier, he even turned skateboarding directly into performance art. Collaborating with artist Johannes Wohnseifer and filmmaker Cheryl Dunn, Gonzales, while eccentrically clad in a white fencing outfit, sliced around the galleries of Mönchengladbach's Städtisches Museum Abteiberg.[51]

Recalling Gonzales's Mönchengladbach performance is the *Ratsrepus* (2015) video by Fabiano Rodrigues and Akira Shiroma, which shows two headless bodies skating around Rio de Janeiro's Cidade das Artes complex (Figure 12.17). Part of a series curated by Lucas Ribeiro for Adidas, the malfunctioning movements of the neo-surrealist figures operate in 'a parallel universe where everything is inverted, strange and pointless', and so critique the concept of 'superstar' skateboarders.[52] Other photographic works by Rodrigues explore the relation of the human body to the designs of architect Oscar Niemeyer and to other pieces of modern architecture.

As these works testify, performance can be a rich territory for art-skateboarding exploration. Hence skateboarding's inclusion in many other recent cultural events, including a skate bowl as part of 'Finding a Line: Skateboarding, Music, and Media' (2015) at Washington's Kennedy Center for the Performing Arts, which explored improvisation, movement and interaction, and also 'Grind' (2014), an Aberdeen, Glasgow and London collaboration between skateboarders, the Tête à Tête opera and composer Samuel Bordoli, which drew on skatepark resonant acoustics and skateboarding's percussive noises (Figure 12.18).[53] Similarly, 'Transit Space' (2012) by Los Angeles dance company Diavolo was inspired by *Dogtown and Z-Boys* and skate culture in general, involving a shuttling set of ramps and bridges against which dancers skittered and leapt.[54]

Alternative Journeys
Skateboards as objects can also be incorporated within artworks, as with Jeremy Fish's cut-out and painted boards and Silke Wagner's cut-up decks from the mid-2000s.[55] Best known here is the work of Tokyo-based artist Haroshi, who produces sculptures from discarded decks by combining laminates, colours and contours before sculpting and polishing. The final creations range from small fingers and feet to oversized busts, monumental vultures and giant hands. Influenced by the Great Buddhas

Figure 12.16
Mark Gonzalez, *Circle Board in Paris* (dir. Ludovic Azemar, 2009).
www.bit.ly/Gonzales-CircleBoard

Figure 12.17
Critiquing 'Superstar' skaters.
Ratsrepus (dir. Fabiano Rodrigues and Akira Shiroma, 2015).
www.bit.ly/Ratsrepus-Skate

Figure 12.18
Samuel Bordoli's 'Grind' composition of choral singing and skateboarding acoustics (Tête à Tête, 2014).
www.bit.ly/Bordoli-Grind

Figure 12.19
Haroshi sculptures using recycled skateboard decks. (Monster Children, 2015).
www.bit.ly/Haroshi-MonsterChildren

Figure 12.20
Raphaël Zarka's 'Riding Schönflies'.
Paving Space (dir. Dan Magee, 2016).
www.bit.ly/Zarka-PavingSpace

Figure 12.21
Jesus Esteban negotiates art
by Donald Judd in Shaun
Gladwell's 'Skateboarders vs
Minimalism' (2015).
www.bit.ly/Gladwell-Minimalism

of Japanese sculptors like Unkei, Haroshi conceals a damaged skateboard fragment in each of his pieces, thus referencing these precedents and symbolizing the 'soul' of his work (Figure 12.19).[56]

On an even larger scale, in 2013 the wood left over after 3,000 skate decks had been cut from timber sheets was recycled for a temporary pavilion at the MoMA PS1 facility in New York. The result was the perforated 'Partywall', a giant steel-framed and negative-deck construction anchored to the ground by water-filled balloons.[57]

The French artist and skateboarding essayist Raphaël Zarka has undertaken a range of skate-influenced works, including sculptures and the film *Species of Spaces in Skateboarding* (2008). With reference to artists like Kurt Schwitters, Robert Morris, Simone Forti and Carl Andre, Zarka is highly influenced by skatepark and ramp forms, while also using the street-skater's methodology of exploiting pre-existing architecture.[58] His 'Paving Space' installations (2016) at the Palais de Tokyo in Paris, Institute of Contemporary Art of Singapore, Sainte-Croix Museum in Poitiers and EAAC in Castellón de la Plana included the 'Riding Schönflies'

geometric skateable sculptures, transforming the galleries into a 'hybrid space where skaters and spectators establish their own frameworks of cohabitation' (Figure 12.20).[59] Zarka's 'Riding Modern Art' photographs and video (2010) likewise show skaters riding on public art, where they 'prioritize a relationship with the work' and explore 'the variety of movements that it recommends.'[60]

One of the most successful of skateboarding artists has been Shaun Gladwell, who sees direct affinities between skateboarders and artists in their mutual interests in redefining space, pushing language and taking risks. Gladwell's early tri-partite video installation 'Kickflipping Flâneur' (Artspace, Sydney, 2000) explored the poetic and urban qualities of skateboarding, as did the 'Storm Sequence' video (2000) depicting Gladwell freestyling before a turbulent ocean. Later works include 'Mini Ramp Intersection' at the De La Warr Pavilion in Bexhill-on-Sea, UK (2013), where skaters and BMX-riders engage in battling conflicts and near misses, and the 'Skateboarders vs Minimalism' videowork (2015), where Jesus Esteban, Hillary Thompson and Rodney Mullen slow-motion skateboard across sculptures by Donald Judd, Dan Flavin and Carl Andre (Figure 12.21).[61]

Indeed, Gladwell's work has been a particular fascination of mine. Since 2000, a still from 'Linework: a Road Movie' (2000) has been my desktop image, showing a skater's foot, an infinity sign on the board nose and a meandering road surface – all of which hypnotically track a line demarcating the route of the Sydney Olympics marathon. Here, and in the contemporaneous *Sydney: A Guide to Recent Architecture* (2000), political connotations are evident when, as skaterly re-enactions of Debord's dérive and Certeau's call for street-level tactics, Gladwell's skaters creatively misuse architecture and so forge their own urban realm. Hence Gladwell's acts, according to Croggon and Green, symbolize the 'infinite, inescapable loop of resistance and appropriation that characterizes global capitalism'.[62]

Similar interests with skateboarding motion are apparent in D*Face's intervention at the Ridiculous pool in California (2011) and in Matt Reilly's 'Wide Ride' (2014), both of which used moving skateboards to create dynamic artworks reminiscent of Aaron Young and Jackson Pollock's action paintings.[63] While less embodied, Kirill Savchenkov's mixed media 'Museum of Skateboarding' installed in London (2016) explored alternative spatial manoeuvres, portraying skateboarding as a reconnoitre of urban space with affinities to martial arts, cartography and paramilitary tactics.[64] Florian Rivière's 'hactivist' art adopts other precise spatial tactics, including using skateboards to alter the functionality of mundane public spaces, such as adding a shelf to a bench or a coat hanger to a bus shelter.[65]

Above all, in such works we find alternative journeys into the unknown possibilities of ourselves. Because so many of the pieces described here incorporate skateboards and bodies in everyday places, then, the suggestion is, we too could journey to as-yet-unknown experiences, traverse cities with only the simplest of equipment, create coloured traces across pool surfaces or construct meanings from discarded decks. All these things are, or might be, possible.

Skateable Sculpture

We have already seen in Chapter 8 instances of 'terrain vague', which accommodate and even stimulate skateboarding in parks, concourses and plazas. Yet another rich possibility here has been the emergence of 'skateable sculptures' or similar interventions into galleries, streets and parks. Sometimes these are high art conceptualizations, as with Zarka and Gladwell's work, while others remained as purely theoretical proposals, as with the twisted sculptures, curved benches and melted cars of Rotterdam's 'Reclaiming the Street' exhibition (2010), or Dan Graham's unrealized 'Skateboard Pavilion' (1989), where a graffitied concrete bowl surmounted by a glass pyramidal roof would have provided skaters with kaleidoscopic reflections.[66]

Still other projects have been more openly accessible and realizable. In 1992, Mowry Baden added the 'Toy Amenity' railside bar to Embarcadero, while three years later New York artist Maura Sheehan formed a ridable sculpture within the base of the Brooklyn Bridge, although this was essentially a 3 m half-pipe.[67] More interesting sculpturally was 'Free Basin' (2000), at Chicago's Hyde Park Art Center by Simparch, including designers Steve Badgett and Matt Lynch, and later installed at other German, UK and United States venues. In Chicago, the steel and timber pool-shaped bowl was inserted into a 1920s ornamental ballroom and incorporated music, discussions and skate performances. Notably, visitors first accessed the bowl from below, thus emphasizing skateboarding's terrain construction and sonic qualities over its visual representations.[68] Another Simparch project, 'Drum', similarly placed a skateable pipe within the industrial spaces of the A Foundation in Liverpool (2007). Other installations have included a 32-m-long mini-ramp at Seville's Bienal Internacional de Arte Contemporáneo (2004), covered in projected graphics proclaiming that 'The Intentions of Artists Are Overvalued' and 'Fuck the Intention of the Artist', plus a similar skatepark-as-canvas project in an abandoned garment factory in Puerto Rico (late 1990s).[69]

In 2005, Jeppe Hein's 'Modified Social Benches 1–10' installation reconfigured park benches to encourage active uses like skateboarding (Figure 12.22).[70] Around the same time, in Robert Bajac Square, Paris, an eccentric 6-m-diameter bowl-cradle replete with world map graphic was created by Peter Kogler and the Département de l'Art dans la Ville. Although the concrete 'Skate Park' (2006) looks like public sculpture, it is actually, as a sombre notice declares, reserved for skateboarding, BMX and rollerblading.[71] The same year, another skateable sculpture – this time a semi-circular Plexiglas half-pipe with slash-angled sides – was installed at Copenhagen's Kongens Have.[72] Other recent projects have included Stefan Marx's quirky

narrow half-pipe in the 'Egyptian Loneliness' exhibition at Sydney's Monster Children gallery (2007), Janne Saario's 30-m-long and 2-m-wide 'Striiti' installation (2011) at Finland's Fiskars art gallery, Jonathan Monk's Sol LeWitt–inspired 'Steps and Pyramid' (2015) installation at Philadelphia's Paine's Park and the Zenga Brothers 'Skate Heads' sculpture contraptions (2015), including an invertible skateable boat and a blue-painted ramp-shack that can be propelled along train tracks.[73]

A particularly noteworthy stream of projects has been produced by the UK-based collective The Side Effects of Urethane (TSEOU), including Richard 'Badger' Holland and

Toby Shuall. Early installations like 'A Surface In-Between' (London, 2003) were geometric insertions into existing buildings (Figure 12.23), while 'Moving Units' (2004) created a series of bespoke sculptural concrete blocks, distributed (sometimes without permission) across the Southbank and other London skatespots. More curvilinear was 'Aalto' at Helsinki's Kiasma, (2005), where a wave-like wooden form snaked across the floor, creating both a complex modulation to the Stephen Holl–designed gallery space and a challenging performance space for invited skaters (Figure 12.24). For 'Interstices' (2006) at Lille's La Tri Postale, a 1,500 m² landscape of ledges, banks, curved walls and attenuated blocks formed an

Figure 12.22
Jeppe Hein's 'Modified Social Bench #7', Copenhagen (2005). Courtesy König Gallerie, Berlin, 303 Gallery, New York and Galleri Nicolai Wallner, Copenhagen. Photograph Henrik Edelbo.

Figure 12.23
Fos negotiates 'A
Surface In-Between'
by The Side Effects
of Urethane,
London (2003).
© Wig Worland.

abstracted version of everyday urban spaces.
Photographs and videos by the likes of Fred
Mortagne and Winstan Whitter completed the
cultural environment.[74]

More recently, Holland produced a simulated
streetscape for Converse's CONS Project
(2014) in Peckham, London, accompanied
by music and art workshops, while the same
year in Seattle, the large metal 'Red Bull Skate
Space' was designed by skater Torey Pudwill
and artist C.J. Rench as a permanent skateable
addition to Jefferson Park. 'Architects, designers
and city planners are devising measures to
exclude skateboarding from the public domain,'
commented Rench. 'It's about time we embrace

skateboarding as an art form by creating
unique multi-use art where the innovation of
the skateboarders can truly flourish.'[75] Another
Red Bull-sponsored installation, this time a
transformable 'no skateboarding' logo entitled
'Icon', was created by Philipp Schuster in 2016.[76]

Skateboardable residences have also been
attempted, most dramatic being the PAS House
by architect Francois Perrin and skater-designer
Gil Le Bon Delapointe, intended for their client
Pierre André Senizergues and a site in Malibu.
Although unrealized as a residence, a full-sized
prototype living area – shown in 2011 at the
Public Domaine exhibition, La Gaîté Lyrique –
included continuous-surface walls matched

by ledged benches and kitchen equipment, all of which accommodated skateboarding trajectories (Figure 12.25).[77]

More permanent residences have included Tokyo's Skate Park House (2011) by Level Architects, where a shallow bowl accompanies a piano room, and the Ramp House (2006) penthouse in Athens, where the client's desire for a 'skateable habitat' is translated across all her living areas. Concrete and wood here allude to street-skating and, according to designers Archivirus, the everyday atmosphere assumes skateboarding's inherent 'feeling of acceleration'.[78] More whimsical is the DIY-adapted Skate Villa in Salzburg (2012), where Philipp Schuster, with the help of some friends and eight tons of concrete, transformed a hunting lodge into an indoor skatepark. After constructing banks, quarter-pipes and bumps, skaters could ride onto walls, beneath windows and over the fireplace.[79]

Figure 12.24
'Aalto' by Richard Holland/The Side Effects of Urethane, Helsinki (2005).
© Wig Worland.

Figure 12.25
Prototype of the PAS house by
Francois Perrin and Gil Le Bon
Delapointe for Pierre André
Senizergues, Paris (Etnies, 2011).
www.bit.ly/PAS-Skate

The projects by Pudwill, Rench and Schuster were all funded by Red Bull, and, as this suggests, many skateable sculptures have complex relationships with commerce and property. For example, some TSEOU installations were facilitated by London property developers keen to promote empty buildings and edgy locations to affluent audiences. In 2001, when TSEOU created a skate-and-art exhibition at the Jam Factory in London's Bermondsey, the neighbourhood was considered an undesirable backwater. By 2016, the same building contained loft-style apartments selling for up to £1.75 million and was surrounded by hipster bars and galleries like the White Cube.

Creativity

Renowned artist Shepard Fairey has noted how, when aged fourteen, skateboarding and street culture opened his eyes to art and design, extending beyond aesthetics into ideology and attitude. 'I am who I am today largely because of the impact skateboarding, punk rock and hip-hop have had on my life', reflects Fairey. 'I credit them for my belief in creativity, provocation, defiance of orthodoxy, and living on my own terms.'[80] These are powerful claims, and it is therefore worth reflecting briefly on the links that Fairey sets up between skateboarding and creativity. How are such connections formed and strengthened?

At its simplest, many people have been inspired by the independent attitude of many professional skateboarders. 'The reason I'm a success,' explains script-writer Phil Beauman, 'is because those were my heroes and their attitude was pushing the extreme.'[81] But there is more to skateboarders' creativity than simply pro riders inspiring others with their determination. One answer is that skateboarding satisfies the need for personal development, as with Doug,

a teacher interviewed by Beal. 'Skating reflects your mood at the time and how you're skating,' he considered. 'It's definitely a way to express yourself.'[82] With such attitudes being highly prevalent, it is unsurprising that many riders are first attracted to skateboarding simply because its eccentricity and experimentation mirrors their own life story; for example, for Rodney Mullen, the innovative yet technically disciplined realm of freestyle (Figure 9.5) tallied with his personal combination of economic privilege, paternal stricture, polymath intelligence and oddball obsessions. Indeed, according to Mullen, until he encountered skateboarding when aged ten, nothing had allowed him such total creativity: 'My father always said skateboarding would ruin my life. Instead, it gave me freedom.'[83] Similarly Ryan Sheckler's early adoption of skateboarding at age four was partially due to his attention deficit disorder (ADD) and what Mullen referred to as Sheckler's special kind of mental 'wiring'.[84]

If eccentric and innovative people are frequently drawn by affinity to skateboarding, then it follows that this scene will be filled with people who possess, at the very least, the potential to develop in creative ways. Certainly skateboarding's history bears this out, as this chapter has already shown. Such people in turn attract others of a similar outlook and social positioning. In part this is because skateboarding attracts outsiders who do not easily fit within more conventional groupings. According to Korine, skateboarding was therefore 'almost like a real lifestyle choice' where 'you were going to hang out with people that were on the fringe of their community.' Nor, then, is skateboarding about loners, but rather, as Andy Jenkins has reasoned, provides a creative milieu where it is easy to discover like-minded people with whom to collaborate and experiment.[85]

Key here is the notion of experimentation, for one of skateboarding's central attributes is that it is rarely concerned with finite goals like winning or perfection. Indeed, Korine's 'Mistakist Declaration' declares that 'there is no such thing as a true mistake', and that only in randomness and error can one express what is otherwise ineffable.[86] Leaving aside Korine's belief in the profound meaning of mistakes, most skaters do consistently fail when performing tricks and moves, and so learn their craft through determination, trial-and-error exploration, self-reliance and self-exploration. 'Falling in skateboarding is not a sign of defeat,' explains Gregory Shewchuk, 'it is a sign that you are challenging yourself, learning and progressing.'[87] Or as Kevin Eason states, 'There are no short cuts in skateboarding. It's the long hard less-travelled road that leads to personal experience, creative focus, depth and inclusion.'[88]

These kinds of attitude then readily transfer to other creative activities. 'Discipline is a great way to get things done,' reasons skater, musician, writer and publisher Henry Rollins. 'Performing solo, owning my own publishing company; it was the discipline and the focus and the tenacity that got me through.'[89] Former pro skater and now acclaimed novelist Michael Christie also sees parallels between skateboarding and writing, for both feature pain, constant failure, independence, obsessive devotion and high risk. 'In both skateboarding and literature,' describes Christie, 'there is that sublime moment when someone pulls something off that is clearly at the very outer limits of their ability — this is where the true magic happens. Art is risk. That's why it captivates us.'[90]

Indeed, these qualities even transfer to non-artistic fields of endeavour. For cricketer Dale Steyn, for example, coping with skateboarding pain taught him to persevere through injuries and to focus on personal goals.[91] Toy company Lego even credits skateboarding with its successful turnaround in the 2000s, after learning from a young skater's beaten-up shoes that perseverance and the mastery of difficult tasks are desirable aspects of play, and consequently concentrating these attributes into their commercial products.[92]

Skateboarding's engagement with the physical qualities of skateparks and urban streets has been another cause for artistic connection. For Jeremy Henderson, 'art and skateboarding go together' because 'they're both reacting to the space of architecture.'[93] Hence, and particularly in street-skating, skaters rethink the possibilities of things, such as transforming public art into a skateable object to be appreciated for its form, texture and openness to interaction (Figure 12.26). 'The second you started riding down the sidewalk on your skateboard,' figured skater-turned-actor Jason Lee, 'that opens up your perspective. This is my thing that I've created.' Or as Samuli 'Hessu' Heino comments in *Second Nature* (Yves Marchon, 2012), 'skateboarding is such a creative thing that you think and feel the city and landscape in a completely different way.' Yet another suggestion around street-skating is that motivation and illumination can be found in the most ordinary and accessible of locations: 'You don't have to go places to find inspiration,' asserts Ed Templeton. 'It's all right in your backyard.'[94]

In a form of creative negation, the anti-skate legislation and harassment faced by many street-skaters have also been sources of inspiration. Such things lead comedian Tom Green, for example, to confront some of the 'petty and ridiculous rules' in society. 'That's why I'm critical of the media and critical of the sorts of things that we do as human beings,' explains Green. 'That all comes from being a skateboarder.'[95]

Finally, and particularly when practised outside of professional, industry and media spheres, everyday skateboarding is rarely undertaken for reasons of money or profit. Skateboarding's authentic mode of engagement – where ordinary skateboarders skate because they find it enjoyable and meaningful – thus concurs readily with those artists, architects, designers and musicians who do not consider themselves to be pursuing their work, at least primarily, for financial reasons, and who instead seek satisfaction in every aspect of their personal and working lives. 'Make things because you want to make things,' states Korine. 'All that stuff about deals and money, that's bullshit.'[96]

Figure 12.26
Skateboarding, creativity and the city. Mirco Suzuki reimagines public art in Rio de Janeiro (2005). © Helge Tscharn.

Skate and Create
Chapter 13 Do It for Others

A do-it-yourself ethic has been consistently present within skateboarding, from independent riding to backyard ramp-building, local DIY skateparks and personal art projects. But before concluding that skateboarders act solely for themselves, whether as individuals or as groups, we should also note the emergence of a highly substantial do-it-for-others movement. Here, all kinds of skateboard-centred projects and organizations have been established to help build communities, enrich individual lives and create cultural capital, and so nurture qualities of trust, independence, confidence and hope. Such initiatives have been undertaken in some of the most deprived and challenging parts of our world.

Furthermore, the same attitude has been applied within more privileged cities, where skateboarding today is contributing to issues of public space, historic preservation, health and economic activity. Taking all of this together, and considered alongside the creative art, community skateparks and wider cultural resonances explored in previous chapters, it is now quite clear that skateboarding, far from being a marginal activity practised by alienated riders, is now emerging as an integral and vital part of our urban world.

Public Space
We have already seen how skaters take over public space physically and conceptually,

enacting a performative critique of the city. But what of this public space itself? How might skateboarding help affect how other people value and design our public places?

One notorious example, as detailed by Howell and Nemeth, of how skaters can use but then lose public space under controversial circumstances is Philadelphia's John F. Kennedy Plaza, aka Love Park.[1] Originally devised by architect Edmund Bacon and Vincent Kling as a civic space, Love Park was opened in 1965, and during the 1990s and early 2000s became internationally renowned for offering, in *Jenkem*'s words, 'ledges of all sizes, rails, big steps and small steps, all designed in a round on perfect granite ground'.[2] Frequented by local amateurs and professionals like Brian Wenning, Stevie Williams and Josh Kalis, the lively scene is captured by such videos as Alien Workshop's *Photosynthesis* (Joe Castrucci, 2000), *The DC Video* (Greg Hunt, 2003) and *TransWorld*'s *The Reason* (dir. Ty Evans and Jon Holland, 1999) (Figure 13.1). The presence of skaters also reduced drug dealing and crime, and was consequently welcomed by many business leaders; according to banker Andrew Hohns, the site was 'an international symbol of youth and vitality' that provided 'generous free publicity for the city' and so generated 'a significant amount of tourism'. In addition, Love Park's reputation helped attract the 2001 and 2002 X Games, benefitting Philadelphia to the tune of around $80 million.[3]

Figure 13.1
Stevie Williams at Love Park in *The Reason* (TransWorld, dir. Ty Evans and Jon Holland, 1999).
www.bit.ly/Williams-Reason

Nonetheless, citing $60,000 of damaged ledges and perceived dangers to other users, in 2000 a city ordinance banned skateboarding, and two years later the park was reconfigured with intrusive benches, planters and other anti-skate measures. Police patrols were reinforced by the threat of $300 fines and imprisonment. Despite the local skaters' counter-proposal to enhance the square's multi-use characteristics, supported by architect Bacon and by a $1 million offer from DC Shoes, Love Park has remained closed to skaters ever since.

Significantly, much of the debate concerned the consequent loss not only to skaters but to Philadelphia as a whole. Howell cites Richard Florida's influential text *The Rise of the Creative Class*, which argues that favouring short-term business risks ignoring the younger creative generation, that is, the workers and future leaders of the very companies that modern cities are so keen to attract. 'Skate parks are very important to young people, an intrinsic part of their creative culture, part of their identity', contended Florida about Love Park. 'To take the park away is to tell them they are not valid. Big mistake.'[4] Significantly, Florida was here considering younger workers as well as school-age skaters, thus placing skateboarding as an integral part of wider urban culture. Correspondingly, in a 2003 *Philadelphia Daily News* poll, sixty-nine per cent of respondents favoured returning skateboarding to Love Park.[5]

Similarly, as Jenson, Swords and Jeffries have shown, the public viewed street-skateboarders as a positive presence in the UK's Newcastle and Gateshead, through making the elderly feel safe and helping to reduce crime and anti-social behaviour.[6] Back in the United States, 2003 plans to demolish skateparks in Seattle's Ballard area were successfully countered by large-scale protests from both skaters and non-skaters (including many thirty-something media and technology professionals), whose advocacy in turn lead to a 2007 masterplan for skateparks across the city.[7]

One reason why the general public often support skaters is because of the way riders can aid urban development. For example, Howell notes how Love Park skaters acted as the 'shock troops of gentrification', part of a 'creative class' that 'produces marketable "street culture" imagery' and so 'reclaims space'. According to Howell, 'in the public eye, the skateboarders were tempering the activities of the homeless population, injecting skateboard

industry capital into the plaza, and generating a hip image for the city'.[8] Or as skater Ricky Oyola bluntly asserted, 'It was just fucking drug dealers, dudes chilling up there, fighting each other all the time. We came here and we gave it life.'[9] Orpana similarly notes how Canadian skaters in Hamilton unwittingly acted as gentrifiers, rendering run-down neighbourhoods more attractive to artists, professionals and the affluent classes, and so helped turn a working-class steel town into a creative and cultural hub.[10]

Moving History

When the Hayward Gallery, Queen Elizabeth Hall and Purcell Room (aka Festival Wing) complex opened at London's Southbank Centre in 1967, and in accordance with its architects' experimental theories, the meandering walkways and ground-level spaces – the latter being known today as the Undercroft – were left open for unpredictable uses. Consequently, when skateboarding arrived a few years later, the Undercroft yielded exactly the eruption of creativity for which its designers had hoped. Where others saw only boring flat spaces surrounded by uselessly angled banks, skateboarders saw a free-access version of the commercial skateparks then being constructed. The Undercroft roof was another bonus, under which up to a thousand skateboarders at a time emulated the surf-style skateboarding then being promoted in *Skateboard!* and *SkateBoarder*.

Skateboarding, therefore, has been an essential part of the Southbank Centre, turning architecture as high design into a place of youthful energy and joy (Figure 13.2). Nor has skateboarding been a short-lived visitor. As Winstan Whitter's *Rollin' through the Decades* (2004) and *Save Southbank* (with Toby Shuall, 2007) ably demonstrate, skateboarding has been in the Undercroft for nigh on forty years, making it very probably the oldest place in the world that has been subjected to skateboarding in a continuously intensive manner.

Skateboarders' determined usage of the Undercroft was particularly evident during the 1980s and 1990s. In these years, the new street-based skateboarding emerged, with skateboarders ollieing over ledges, stairs and handrails. The Undercroft changed too, becoming less like a free skatepark and more like a city street, somewhere appropriated both by skateboarders and the homeless, whose 2,000 or more shelters constituted Southbank's

'Cardboard City'; according to *The Spectator*, amid this otherwise 'godforsaken waste-land' the skateboarders provided 'one of the few rational purposes' and 'some small evidence of human life'.[11]

The Undercroft changed again in 2004 and in 2006, when several skateable concrete and stone blocks were installed by Holland and The Side Effects of Urethane, with financial support from Sony Playstation, Nike, Casio G-Shock and Olympus (Figure 13.3). This initiative rendered the space particularly suited to street-skateboarding. 'At a time when a good ledge spot was the holy grail', enthused Jake Sawyer, 'this really was a godsend.'[12] At the same time, the Southbank Centre organized lighting and CCTV, while new railings and yellow lines demarcated a skateboardable space for the centre's liability insurance, and so legally allowed skateboarding to occur.

Murals and graffiti also started to appear in the Undercroft, again with Southbank Centre permission, marking it as a centre for varied urban arts. BMX-riders, photographers, filmmakers, poets, dancers and musicians were now being increasingly drawn to the spot. As photographer Wig Worland noted, the Undercroft facilitated a 'studio in the street', while skater-artist Nick Jensen similarly credits the Southbank with informing the style and aesthetics of his work. Conversely, for Karim Bakthouai, it was the social space that mattered most, the Undercroft allowing an escape from gangland crime and other council estate constraints: 'All the people I know like, they all fucking in jail, I didn't want that, I ain't about that, I'd rather be skating.'[13] Southbank slalom-skater Dobie Campbell similarly commented that 'if I didn't skate, I don't know where I would have ended up. I wasn't just stuck on my block pissing around. I had something to focus on.'[14]

Despite these positive attributes and while recognizing the Undercroft was, according to the Southbank Centre's Mike McCart, 'the Mecca of skating in the world', during 2004 and 2005 the Centre still reduced by two-thirds the amount of skate space available. This assertive action recalled past episodes when skateboarding had been deliberately discouraged, such as the mid-1980s when security teams scattered stones, prised-up paving slabs and generally made skaters feel uncomfortable.[15]

Despite these challenges, or perhaps because of them, the Undercroft achieved near mythic status as the epicentre of UK skateboarding, where tens of thousands learned their craft, from novices to professionals, and from hardcore locals to occasional visitors. Consequently, the Undercroft lays strong claim to being British skateboarding's most precious home, its original Garden of Eden, oldest sparring partner and most famous Wembley arena – all rolled into one. It is also a place of pilgrimage for skateboarders worldwide, travelling long distances to roll across one of skateboarding's most hallowed grounds.

Given all this, it is unsurprising that large numbers of skaters and the general public alike reacted extremely unfavourably to the Southbank Centre's suggestion in 2013 that, to help pay for a £100 million package of improvements to the Festival Wing while simultaneously facing massive cuts in public funding, the Undercroft should be turned into retail units, with skaters being relocated to the adjacent Hungerford Bridge site.[16] United mostly under the Long Live Southbank (LLSB) banner, and enjoying financial backing from the father of local rider Tom 'Blondey' McCoy, these objectors mounted a skilful campaign under the headings of 'You Can't Move History', 'Preservation and Not Relocation' and 'Construction Without Destruction'.

Widespread backing came from the skateboard community, musicians, artists, the general public and British MPs Kate Hoey and Ben Bradshaw. Academics like Oli Mould and myself supported the campaign with texts and videos.[17] Most importantly, after 150,000 people had signed a petition supporting the Undercroft and over 27,000 opposed the planning application, the Conservative party Mayor of London, Boris Johnson, seized the political opportunity to back the skaters, calling the Undercroft 'the epicentre of UK skateboarding' and 'part of the cultural fabric of London'. As Johnson saw it, this 'much-loved community space' also 'attracts tourists from across the world and undoubtedly adds to the vibrancy of the area'. Effectively vetoing the centre's planning application, Johnson's declaration was a decisive moment in skateboarding's eventual victory.[18]

Moreover, legal factors were at play. Planning lawyer Simon Ricketts helped to have the Undercroft designated an 'Asset of Community Value' (ACV) under the Localism Act 2011, and also sought to have it designated as a 'Town or Village Green' under the Commons Act 2006.[19] Faced with this public, political and legal

Figure 13.2
Benny Fairfax and friends, Undercroft, London (2003).
© Wig Worland.

turmoil, the Southbank Centre leadership – artistic director Jude Kelly, chief executive Alan Bishop and chairman Rick Haythornthwaite – capitulated in January 2014, signing a section 106 planning agreement with Lambeth borough council that effectively secured the Undercroft for skateboarding in perpetuity.[20]

I have described these episodes in some detail, partly because they represent a rare and substantial victory of skateboarding in the face of wider forces, but partly because of their significance for our understanding of public space in general, and for what everyone – skaters and non-skaters alike – values in cities. Thus, however important the place is for skateboarding, it is also worth remembering why so many non-skateboarders enjoy the Undercroft. Above all, people find pleasure in the Undercroft's unique combination of skateboarding-against-concrete, in street-level spontaneity amidst increasing sanitization and in witnessing a truly public space in action. Skateboarding at the Undercroft is 'inspiring and uplifting', commented one member of the public. 'It promotes all kinds of values that we need in society.' Or as another noted, 'take away the diversity of the Southbank and you will kill the charm.' Even the conservatively minded *The Times* proclaimed that destroying the skate space to provide retail outlets would amount to 'cultural vandalism.'[21]

This is serious stuff, and transcends skateboarding to speak to larger questions concerning the value of public spaces today. As David Harvey has noted, the right to the city is not about accessing what property speculators and planners provide, but is 'an active right to make the city different' and 'to re-make ourselves thereby in a different image.'[22] In concert with Harvey, skateboarding at the Undercroft suggests that public spaces can be richer than typical shopping malls or high streets, where coffee outlets, branded shops and chain restaurants dominate. It suggests that different people doing different things perceive and enjoy city spaces in different ways. It suggests that we would like our cities to be similarly varied, being at once loud and quiet, rough and smooth, monochrome and colourful, flat and angled. And, above all, it suggests that we most enjoy cities and buildings when they both comfort and challenge us, when they provide us with things that we both expect and cannot anticipate, when their history is not just factual and physical but also emotional and changing. The kind of moving

history demonstrated by skateboarding at the Southbank Centre is one small yet vital part of this process.

Somewhat different, although just as telling with regard to public attitudes towards skateboarding architecture, is the recent history of Rom skatepark in Essex. First constructed in 1978 (Figure 7.13), it was Rom that I recommended in 2013 to English Heritage (now Historic England), the official body for the historic preservation of architecture. After Simon Inglis and English Heritage subsequently underlined Rom's historic significance as the best preserved of 1970s UK skateparks and an icon of skateboarding and youth culture, Rom was granted Grade II listing status on 11 September 2014 – the first European skatepark to be accorded this grading.[23]

Rom's preservation order met with considerable media attention, including substantial news coverage by the BBC (Figure 13.4), ITV and *The Times*, plus an article by myself in *The Guardian* extolling the skatepark's beguiling charms and obdurate survival.[24] Indeed, just how embedded Rom and skateboarding in general has become within national and cultural identity can be seen in Historic England's *Welcome to Historic England* video (2015), which includes Rom skatepark and street-skating alongside St. Pauls, the countryside and other archetypal English icons.[25] As government minister Ed Vaizey commented of Rom's listing, this 'highlights how the UK's unique heritage reflects all parts of our culture and history', and clearly skateboarding was now an integral part of that official, pluralistic narrative.[26]

The acceptance of skateboarding as an intrinsic part of urban culture and heritage has also extended internationally, including the 2016 granting of historic preservation status to the Albany Skate Track, Australia (Figure 7.3). In Canada, a similar victory was gained after a concrete oval tunnel within the 1976 Montreal Olympics complex had been appropriated by local skaters, and the Big O, as this tunnel was now known, became the city's most revered skatespot, where tight transitions, punctured roof and truncated walls form an idiosyncratic and challenging terrain. By 2006, the commemorative *Pipe Fiends* publication was describing the tunnel's graffiti-strewn walls not only as a 'skateboarding sanctuary' and a piece of 'true punk essence' but as a 'heritage landmark' with a worldwide reputation.[27]

Figure 13.3
Skateable blocks
at the Undercroft
designed and
installed by Richard
Holland (in red) and
The Side Effects of
Urethane (2006).
© Wig Worland.

Consequently, when in 2011 the pipe faced demolition due to construction work on Montreal Impact's soccer stadium, the skateboarders decided not to mount outright opposition but instead worked with the authorities to move the tunnel some 30 m. Re-opened in 2013, the relocation of the Big O was celebrated as a victory for local skateboarders, Montreal Impact and the city alike, and as a new chapter in the ongoing history of skateboarding in the city (Figure 13.5).[28] In 2016, Team Pain

even constructed a faithful replica in a skatepark in the Colorado town of Golden.

In Tampa, Florida, the skatepark in the Perry Harvey Sr. Park, commonly known as the Bro Bowl, has also been subject to complex challenges and resolution. Originally constructed in 1978 to designs by municipal employee Joel Jackson, the Bro Bowl consisted of a gentle snake run leading to a dish-like bowl and low-level bumps.[29] Although less innovative

Figure 13.4
Historic preservation
of Rom skatepark
announced on the
BBC news.

than the commercial skateparks then being built, the open-access Bro Bowl was devoid of safety-gear regulations, entrance charges or other constraints. Indeed, over subsequent decades the Bro Bowl became renowned for its relaxed skateboarding in a community-based environment, what Snyder has described as a 'common ground where people of different backgrounds, gender, and ethnicity could coexist through brotherhood.' It even acquired wider recognition through appearing in Birdhouse's *The End* and the *Tony Hawk's Underground* video game.[30]

In 2013, however, the city proposed demolishing the skatepark as part of larger modifications to the surrounding park and providing a replacement facility nearby. After years of contestation, during which locals like Shannon Bruffett and Craig Snyder succeeded in getting the Bro Bowl placed on the National Register of Historic Places, the bowl was indeed eventually demolished, but not before being three-dimensionally laser-scanned and cloned in another part of Perry Harvey Sr. Park (Figure 13.6).[31] Although this result is somewhat different to the Undercroft, Rom and Big O pipe, the Bro Bowl has raised similar issues regarding the heritage value of early skateparks and the authenticity of original skatepark materials, as well as the community value of skateboarding to skaters and non-skaters alike. Although cloning and relocation rather than outright preservation may not be everyone's preferred solution, the very fact that Tampa accepted the need for a skatepark, as well as replicating the original facility at considerable cost, shows that

skateboarding and skateparks are now firmly established within architectural heritage, social history and community values.

Healthy Living

By 2011, skate commentators like Chris Lundry and academics like Dumas, Laforest, Taylor and Khan were all recognizing that skateboarding, as the fastest-growing activity among US youth, could help address a potentially devastating problem with increasing childhood obesity. As Lundry noted, the social costs of reduced self-esteem and limited friendship, the health costs from obesity and lack of exercise, and the financial costs from associated work inefficiency and health care – all of which are exacerbated by ever-rising rates of indoor digital play – might be mitigated by skateboarding. 'Skateboarding is the perfect antidote to apathy and laziness; potential healthful benefits abound.'[32]

Furthermore, argues Ben Wixon, skateboarding, as a relatively cheap and accessible practice, offers practitioners increased physical fitness and enhanced risk-taking skills alongside learning the benefits of dedication, discipline and practice. As Turner's work in Scotland shows, skateboarding can also reach those youth who are otherwise not attracted to team sports and traditional forms of physical education. 'The PE curriculum has, for many years, been stuck around football, basketball, rugby, netball, swimming', explained one Dundee education officer. 'But we're finding that some kids who will just not take part in PE, will go to the skateboarding park.'[33] Similarly in 2009, Ofsted – the UK government body that oversees schools –

Figure 13.5
Barry Walsh at the re-opening of
the Big O, Montreal (Vans, 2013).
www.bit.ly/BigO-Skate

Figure 13.6
The 3-D laser-scanned replica of
the Bro Bowl, Tampa Bay (Vantage
Point UAS, 2016).
www.bit.ly/BroBowl

found that skateboarding (plus other non-team activities like archery, cheerleading, cycling, Frisbee, golf, parkour, martial arts and yoga) was being increasingly requested by youth, and so helped to improve participation rates, particularly among vulnerable groups.[34] The overall effect of skateboarding is then not only enhanced bodily health and vigour among more varied participants, but greater goal-setting, confidence, self-esteem and creativity – all of which can be readily continued throughout a skater's adult life, unrestricted by the schedules and strictures of many team sports.[35]

As this last point suggests, the health benefits of skateboarding can extend beyond skateparks and school-age riders to city streets, parks and a wider range of participants. Here, for all its preoccupation with an immediate experience of rushing speed, skateboarders, as with cyclists, can be easily seen to correlate with the CittàSlow ('slow cities') movement, and particularly its emphasis on the slower rhythms of neighbourhoods, reductions in machinic noise, lower environmental pollution, minimal visual clutter and avoidance of fast-paced technologies.[36] By 2005, records Ducommun, longboards for cruising, commuting and downhill-riding were already enjoying a resurgence, these forms of skateboarding, and

again like cycling, providing a more sustainable and healthy alternative to motorized vehicles.[37] Electric skateboards in various formats, capacities and costs were also beginning to emerge, and today include devices by the likes of Blink, Boosted, Evolve, Inboard, Luoov, Marbel, Maverix, Yuneec and ZBoard, facilitating longer travelling distances with minimal environmental impact.

Skateboarding using longboards, cruisers and shorter boards like the plastic Penny has become especially popular in the 2010s, being moderately vigorous in intensity yet metabolically efficient, plus offering a combination of functionality, fun, exhilaration and decent speed.[38] Such boards are also often easier to ride and are often seen as more socially inclusive than the popsicle-shaped set-ups typically associated with teenage male street-skaters. As such, they frequently appeal to riders who might otherwise be discouraged by skateboarding's media-lead image of youth, masculinity and heterosexuality. 'Uniformity and conformity,' argues Brooke, 'that mould is being broken by the world of longboarding.'[39] Or as Justin Metcalf describes his pleasurable rediscovery of longboarding during his adult years, 'The realization that there were different types of skating that didn't involve ollies and

Figure 13.7
The Longboard Girls Crew
explore the good life. *Endless
Roads* (dir. Juan Rayos, 2014).
www.bit.ly/Endless-Skate

ramps took me by surprise. I got my first longboard and I felt like I was re-learning how to skate.'[40] Similarly, the Madrid-based Longboard Girls Crew, founded in 2010, encourages more women skateboarding and without recourse to sexualized imagery; aided by videos like *Endless Roads* (Juan Rayos, 2014), today it is possibly the world's largest longboard community, with representative groups in over seventy countries (Figure 13.7).[41] In all these cases, skateboarding is widening its social reach, and hence further contributing to levels of health among urban communities.

Extending the reach of public transport systems is another possibility, particularly where, as Fang has shown, skateboards are frequently ridden on the 'first and last mile' of complex urban journeys, helping to connect places of residence and work with bus stops and train stations.[42] Small boards like the Penny are particularly useful here, their diminutive size facilitating easy carriage and storage. As a result, the health and environmental benefits skateboarding as urban transportation are starting to be recognized and accommodated; in 2015, California legalized electric skateboards for sidewalks, bike tracks and lower-speed roads, while Hawaiian university Mānoa provided students with specially designed racks to lock up their boards.[43] Academics like Lorimer and Marshall have even speculated on the possibility of making designs changes to cities, either with futuristic 'rollerblade arcades' and 'skating skyways' or with more traditional short blocks and multi-functional streets, and so reducing congestion, noise and air pollution, while raising health levels, economic competitiveness and social inclusivity.[44]

The design and construction of skateparks, too, can enhance sustainability and health. For example, Vivoni records how some builders, inspired by the LEED environmental rating system for construction, have located

skateparks outside of conservation and preservation areas, while also exploiting recycled materials and managing water run-off through natural surface infiltration.[45] Perhaps even more effectively, building skate plazas and skateparks on brownfield sites can revitalize abandoned wastelands, while simultaneously producing, as Vivoni also notes, an 'ethic of care' through the collaboration of skaters, developers and authorities, and so challenging the prevailing logic of market-rate private property development.[46] The rising trend for DIY-constructed skateparks has a similar undercurrent of urban upcycling, here exploiting unused land, discarded timber and even concrete left over from other construction projects in order to create new skateable terrains and skateboarding communities.

Finally, some skateboard companies have recognized that their environmental initiatives and standards may well affect consumer decisions and brand perceptions.[47] In 2005 the Element video *Elementality* (2005), for example, began with founder Andy Howell expounding the necessity of embracing ethics, the environment and nature, while one year later Sector 9's sales of bamboo longboard decks topped $1 million.[48] In 2008, Comet Skateboards, in collaboration with e2e Materials, introduced its Bio-Whip skateboards, made from a patented biodegradable composite of soy resin, North American-grown bamboo and hemp.[49] More recently Pierre André Senizergues's Sole Technology group has foregrounded its environmental initiatives, including corporate installations of solar panel systems, company-wide recycling, water-free urinals, audits for water usage and carbon emissions, and the intention of becoming carbon-neutral by 2020.[50]

Numerous start-up brands have also made much of their environmental credentials; for example, Uitto in Finland offers non-toxic and recyclable decks manufactured from a

Figure 13.8
Bureo Ahi Cruiser
deck, fabricated
from recycled fishing
nets (2017).
Courtesy Bureo.

polypropylene and Nordic timber biocomposite, and Bureo fabricates skateboard decks from Chilean recycled fishing nets (Figure 13.8).[51] Further into their product lifecycle, worn-out skateboards have been utilized for everything from furniture and staircases to handbags and decorative objects. Focused in Rotterdam, for example, reuse European boards for its striped 'DecksTop' table, Peter Urbacz offers everything from jewellery to Easter eggs, George Rocha makes skateboards decks and furniture, Jacob Ryder constructs chairs, benches and tables, while Art of Board's 'I Ride, I Recycle' series includes floor mats, wall hangings and decorative tiles.[52]

Building Business

> To learn to do a skateboard trick, how many times do you have to do something wrong until you get it right? You learn to do that trick, now you got a life lesson. Whenever I see those skateboard kids, I think, those kids will be all right.[53]
> Jerry Seinfeld

Most skateboarders rightly consider that their personal skateboarding is largely devoid of

economic motivation. Certainly bombing down a hill, carving a pool or sliding a ledge are not acts that will make any money, unless of course the rider is one of skateboarding's comparatively rare professionals. Yet skateboarding has always been part physical pleasure and part commercial enterprise. Even during the early 1960s, as Turner notes, skaters collaborated with manufacturers to help make skateboarding flourish, and indeed were often the inventers, makers, marketeers and financial beneficiaries of commercial enterprises.[54] The rise of skater-owned companies and brands has already been considered in Chapter 4, so here we focus briefly on entrepreneurship and building business in general, and in particular the degree to which these endeavours might form one of skateboarding's attendant attributes.

Skateboarding, asserts graphic artist and filmmaker Mike Mills, 'makes you feel totally entitled like you should go start your own company. Do it yourself – you don't have to wait for someone else to come along.'[55] Such statements are perhaps unsurprisingly given that skateboarding's independence, risk-taking and embracing of failure readily equate with neoliberal society's expectation of its active citizens, namely, as Lombard has identified, that they should act as entrepreneurs of their own skills and talents.[56] As a result, many skaters have been entrepreneurial both generally – taking charge of their own capabilities and opportunities – and in the stricter sense of this term, building up business empires that generate significant revenue, jobs and cultural capital. For example, some of the most successful skaters of the 1970s and 1980s – notably Tony Alva, Stacy Peralta and Christian Hosoi – were quick to develop their business acumen, such as developing their own companies and negotiating advantageous sponsorship deals. Much of this was also done at a precociously early age; Alva started Alva Skates when just nineteen, while the similarly-aged Hosoi pre-researched all business arrangements in order to maximize his gainful contracts.[57]

In particular, a comparatively large proportion of freestyle skaters – mostly from the 1980s and including Rodney Mullen, Steve Rocco, Pierre André Senizergues, Kevin Harris and Per Welinder – went on to found successful companies, their combination of precision, experimentation and determination providing the key qualities needed for commercial leadership.[58] Indeed, so great has their domination of the skateboard industry sometimes seemed, that some skaters even speak of a 'freestyle conspiracy'. 'What does an unemployable freak that rides a skateboard do?', asked Jeff Grosso. 'They go and they work for skateboard companies and they end up inheriting the industry.'[59] Senizergues, for example, was a leading freestyler during the 1980s, winning twelve French Championships, nine European Cup Titles, five European Championships and three world titles, before setting up the éS, Emerica, Etnies, ThirtyTwo and Altamont brands, all of which now operate under the Sole Technology corporate umbrella.[60]

Of all these freestylers, though, Steve Rocco has been the most notorious figure. In particular, Rocco innovated less through any advances in equipment and more by attitudinal marketing, setting up apparently small skater-owned companies and controversial devices like offensive graphics and the puerile *Big Brother* magazine. Shrewd business deals that recognized the short-termism of skate trends were another Rocco tactic, such as demanding cash-on-delivery terms with retailers and refusing to supply World Industries products to any skate shop that took less than twelve copies of *Big Brother*.[61]

Rocco was also willing to take risks. Despite being jobless, sponsor-less and homeless, at the age of twenty-seven he started his first skateboard business with a $6,000 credit card purchase of stock and a highly dubious $20,000 loan; as Rocco later commented, 'nothing motivates like fear.' Despite setbacks and minimal income, Rocco quickly introduced new deck designs and marketing techniques. Above all, as Rodney Mullen recalled, Rocco had 'an intuitive perspective on the skating industries that the old guards didn't. His ear was to the ground.' Particularly transformational, as seen in Chapter 12, was Rocco's decision for World Industries to move away from conventional skull-based deck graphics to more innovative cartoons and illustrations, including many designs by Marc McKee.[62]

According to Jim Fitzpatrick, despite his chaotic financial practices, Rocco targeted business success rather than the good of skateboarding – as when Rocco extracted a punitively large sum from skate funster Simon Woodstock and Rich Metiver for their spoofing of the World Industries 'Devil Man' character, despite Rocco having himself been doing exactly this kind of thing for a decade. Or as World Industries team rider Mike Vallely later reflected, Rocco 'got what he needed out of me, now it was time to throw me away.'[63]

These criticisms aside, Rocco did much to encourage a sense of entrepreneurialism in skateboarding, not least in quickly turning talented amateurs into professionals and paying his team riders two dollars per board royalties (double the industry standard), thus offering instant rewards rather than the management-controlled exposure and top-down team hierarchy that featured at more heavily structured companies like Powell-Peralta.[64] 'Skate now, get paid now, succeed now' were the new watchwords, and following Rocco's lead many skaters were quick to join the World Industries deal as pro riders or to head up affiliate brands (including Gonzales's Blind, Kaupas's 101, Ternasky's Plan B and Mullen's A-Team). Other skaters just set up companies independent of World Industries (such as Alien Workshop, Birdhouse, Chocolate, Girl and New Deal among many others), but nonetheless shared its run-by-skaters ethic and free-spirited approach to design, marketing and promotion (Figure 13.9). Indeed, many started their own

The Rocco Seed

The World Industries Family Tree
Words and Diagram by Mackenzie Eisenhour

In 1987, an unemployed/unsponsored freestyler known as Steve Rocco bought 500 blank boards off Skip Engblom of Santa Monica Airlines and subsequently launched SMA's Rocco Division, the pre-cursor to World Industries. At the time, three major corporations, conveniently titled here the Big Three (Powell Peralta, Santa Cruz, and Vision) held everything from Park Place to the Utility Companies on the Monopoly Board that is the skateboard industry. Since then, Steve Rocco's "little" company single-handedly collapsed the Big Three and rebuilt the industry from the ground up. Like it or not, Steve Rocco opened the door for skater-owned companies, shifted focus away from skulls, hammerheads, and launch ramps, and made many a teenage boy giggle. He provided direct financial backing of projects ranging from Big Brother to Plan B, and indirectly laid the groundwork for separate entities from Tum-Yeto to MTV's Jackass. This convenient color-coded diagram attempts to document the scope of Steve Rocco's direct and indirect influences on the present day skateboard industry. For the sake of simplicity and sanity, this diagram does not include bearing, griptape, or hardware companies. Flameboy and Wet Willy sold separately.

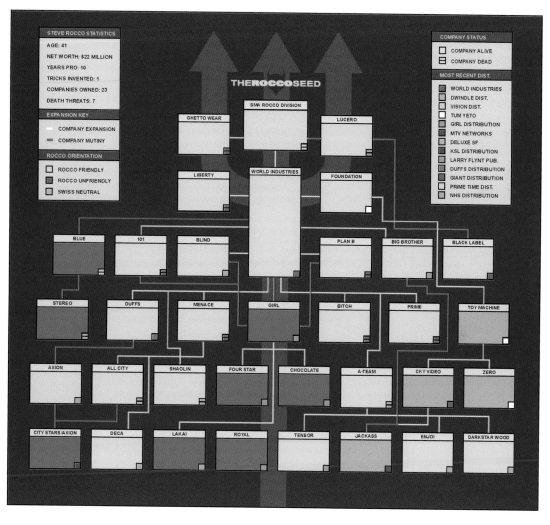

Figure 13.9
'The Rocco Seed'. Mackenzie Eisenhour's diagram
showing Steve Rocco's impact on the skateboard industry,
SkateBoarder (May 2001).
© Mackenzie Eisenhour.

companies, explained Vallely, 'because Rocco showed them that you could be a skateboarder and do your own thing, create your own brand, and make it happen.'[65]

Although very different in character and business approach to Rocco, Tony Hawk has also developed an extensive business empire. By 2010, Tony Hawk Inc. comprised a state-of-the-art facility near San Diego, incorporating Birdhouse Skateboards, Hawk Clothing, Tony Hawk Foundation, 900 Films and other initiatives, along with a skatepark, HuckJam half-pipe, radio studio, two film production studios, climate-controlled film library and extensive computer system. So large have the extensive licensing, production, events, media and other operations become, that an annual 'Tony Hawk Brand Summit' is held for all the various international partners – from global players like Jeep, Nixon and Quiksilver to local street-level sponsors – in order to coordinate brand strategy across disparate markets.[66]

Not all skateboard entrepreneurs are as well-known or wealthy as Rocco or Hawk, but the kind of creativity, independent-mindedness and self-discipline associated with skateboarding seems to regularly throw up other successful innovators. Typical is someone like Daniel Gesmer. Born in Illinois in 1964, by the mid-1980s Gesmer had become a highly rated freestyle skater, while also graduating from Yale. In stark contrast to Mullen's trick-based and relatively static performances (Figure 9.5), Gesmer developed a highly idiosyncratic gliding- and dance-based approach to freestyle, which he combined with diverse interests in philosophy, psychology, modernist dance, ice skating and human body mechanics. All of this has informed some highly inventive new equipment. Principal here are Gesmer's metal-coiled Seismic trucks (1994), which benefitted from a development programme involving precise video, kinematic and force-vector analysis, a four-year enhancement period with German manufacturers, collaborations with university engineers and modelling with Wolfram Research's Mathematica software. This eventually led to a range of spring-loaded trucks with different spring-rates, geometries and widths, all of which have helped Seismic gain a strong position in the truck marketplace and particularly for downhill, longboarding and slalom specialisms.[67]

Building Lives
Skateboarding's sharing culture, as explored by O'Connor, has an intrinsic rhythm of inclusivity.

This ranges from a simple gesture like catching a skater's wayward board, to passing on equipment to impoverished riders, and, as we shall see, acts of charity and benevolence. In addition, skateboarding offers a 'prefigurative' politics that, in its practices and ethos, embodies the world its wishes to create. This is a significant extension to my previous emphasis on skateboarding's critique of capitalism, namely that, alongside skateboarding as a *performative* critique of capitalism's values and tenets, so skateboarding culture suggests participation and inclusion as ways to live in the world. This *prefigurative* politics, stresses O'Connor, is therefore not focused solely on appropriating urban space, but also contains a 'transformative edge' that seeks to preserve 'the values, attitudes, and knowledge' of skateboarding.[68]

How then might this occur? We have already noted how skateboarding can potentially challenge barriers of class, race, age and gender. Its qualities of friendship, sharing and independence, as well as its non-hierarchical organization, opposition to rules, cynicism towards commercial exploitation, and embracing of both failure and achievement, all impart skateboarding with a different attitude to urban living than one of anonymized, self-centred society. But if this is skateboarding's internal social logic, how might it move outside of itself, and so influence or aid others?

Skateboarders have often sought to raise funds for charities and special causes. Thousands of such acts have been undertaken, and to cite but a few, Jack Smith has crossed the United States several times to generate funds for medical charities, David Cornthwaite's 3,621 mile expedition from Perth to Brisbane during 2006 and 2007 generated £20,000, in 1994 *TransWorld* launched Board AID to focus on teenagers with AIDS and in 2005 the Lords of Dogtown Art Collection exhibition supported Boarding for Breast Cancer.[69] Let It Flow, a non-profit organization founded by Nyjah Huston and his mother Kelle, provides clean water in countries like Chad, Ethiopia, Kenya and Haiti.[70] Beyond these substantial acts of fundraising, yet another benefit of skateboarding rests in its relationship to education, learning and wider social enterprise, and it is these areas that we now turn.

Education and Learning
As Petrone's study of Michigan skateparks demonstrates, learning to skate is simultaneously collaborative

Figure 13.10
Skateboarding-based Bryggeriet
school, Malmö. *Bryggeriet #2* (dir.
Philip Evans, 2016).
www.bit.ly/Bryggeriet

and individualized, anti-competitive and aspirational, and trans-generational and embodied, and so is often apprentice-like in its procedures. It is also dependent on the skater actually wishing to participate and on a range of teaching modes. In particular, skaters can be both mentors and learners, thus allowing every participant to make original contributions to communities.[71] This suggests that skateboarding's mode of learning is inherently flexible and open, consequently extending opportunities for assimilation, acquisition and understanding. Similarly, Jim Fitzpatrick describes the key tenets of skateboarding as being independence, persistence, self-reliance, creativity and learning, and clearly these attributes also have the potential to be highly relevant for education.[72]

How might this work in practice? Sometimes, as Russ Howell and Ben Wixon have both argued, this can mean skateboard riding itself being directly inserted into school curricula.[73] Indeed, Maine's Gould Academy and Malmö's Bryggeriet Gymnasium both boast indoor skateparks that 'blur the boundaries between school and leisure', with Bryggeriet even extending across its curriculum the formative assessment educational approach of Dylan William and the equivalent skateboarding ethos of constantly checking one's own development (Figure 13.10).[74]

Nor is this just about a few individual schools. In the 2010s, New Zealand's OnBoard Skate has promoted skateboarding within schools' physical education programmes, while the 'New PE' – including skateboarding, snowboarding and land paddling – has been actively promoted across North America.[75] For example, Tony Hawk's high school – San Dieguito in California – had a complete ban on skateboards during the 1970s and 1980s, but by 2000 had a substantial skate-based

physical education component.[76] Also in the United States, the Skate Pass company's system has been developed by snowboarder Eric Klassen, PE teacher Richard Cendali and Eva Mullen to stimulate not only child health but personal expression, cooperation and friendship. Skate Pass's curriculum development and teacher training, backed by ready-made packages of skateboards and safety equipment, have consequently been taken up across the United States, as well as in Canada, Germany, Singapore and the Dominican Republic.[77] In a more competitive vein, US organizations like the National Scholastic Skateboarding League (founded 2010) and the National High School Skateboard Association (founded 2008) facilitate inter-school skateboard contests with scheduled fixtures and league tables.[78]

Many of these initiatives have particularly connected with hard-to-reach kids, with those suffering from obesity and with those many children who dislike the combative, stressful and regulated nature of traditional school sports such as football, tennis, gymnastics and athletics. For example, in 2004, Stevie Williams and his father Steven Lassiter set up Philadelphia's Educate to Skate Foundation, with the express aim of running after-school programmes for at-risk youth. The impact of these kinds of project on participants can be immediate and significant; as one father commented of his kids after a Skateboarding Australia session in Brisbane, 'because their bodies are all excited, they're really positive about their homework. I've seen my boys just gain so much confidence.'[79]

Since the mid-2000s, CreateaSkate, a non-profit initiative set up by skateboard manufacturer Paul Schmitt, has offered a different kind of school programme, this time focusing on skateboard decks and encouraging pupils to deploy their mathematics, science, language,

Figure 13.11
Building skills while designing
and fabricating decks. The FAR
Academy, Kent (2017)
www.bit.ly/FAR-Academy

design and engineering skills.[80] Similar thematics lie behind other projects, such as the Action Science programme of science, technology, engineering and mathematics offered by Bill Robertson (aka Dr Skateboard), the Skatepark Mathematics Extravaganza (2014), which engaged Texan high school students in real-world explorations of data-gathering, physics, geometry and algebra, a Brazilian-Portuguese project using the ollie move to teach Newton's laws of physics and the UK's FAR Academy syllabus for designing and building decks (Figure 13.11).[81] For the humanities, Badoni has shown how classroom-based study of skateboards designed by Native Americans can yield unique insights into historical events, personal stories, cultural beliefs and traditions, while the Colonialism Board Company uses skateboards enhanced with historical documents to educate Canadians about their country's colonialist past.[82] Entrepreneurialism too can be addressed: at Toronto's Oasis Skateboard Factory, students work on developing skate brands and managing a design business.[83]

Skateboarding can also be a route into wider social issues and life stories. Former professional Doug Brown now focuses on his Skate Straight and Dream Big programmes, addressing anti-drug activities, bullying and the importance of meaningful friendships. 'It was imperative that my journey with skateboarding have more purpose than just entertainment', explains Brown. 'I was able to encourage people to stay clear from drugs and alcohol and believe in themselves and their dreams. My skateboard became my microphone.'[84]

Finally, university-level education and research is another active territory for exploring skateboarding and its related cultural and social dimensions, as shown by all the research cited in this book and at Pushing Boarders, the first

international conference on skateboarding, hosted at University College London (UCL) and the House of Vans in London in 2018. A few academic departments have concentrations of PhD researchers focused on skateboarding, including UCL's Bartlett School of Architecture and Waikato University's Sport and Leisure Studies. Zachary Sanford offers a course on action sports management at the University of Dayton, Ohio, covering authenticity, criminality, the X Games, the Olympics and representations of athletes, and Neftalie Williams runs a programme on skate business and culture at the University of Southern California.[85]

Social Enterprise

Skaters often articulate how skateboarding has saved them from a life of drugs, gangs and crime. 'All the people I know like, they all fucking in jail', remarked London rider Karim Bakthouai. 'I didn't want that, I ain't about that, I'd rather be skating.'[86] As White reports, skateboarding shields black and ethnic Bronx riders from police harassment, provides an affirmative community and helps skaters avoid gang membership.[87] Beyond the actual riding of skateboards, providing skateparks is another way to engage with at-risk members of society, while even more can be done via those social enterprises that deploy skateboarding to engage with youth, the disempowered and the disadvantaged.

However, before exploring some of these programmes in more detail, it is worth noting a few doubts and queries. In particular, commercial, legal and financial complexities can arise, as when the Rob Dyrdek Foundation (founded 2003) allegedly funded some skate plazas on the condition of these facilities being constructed by California Skateparks, a company owned by Dyrdek's business associate Joe Ciaglia, and that also in 2013 became embroiled

Figure 13.12
A global citizen of Skateistan
(2016).
www.bit.ly/Skateistan-Skate

in alleged contract bidding improprieties.[88] Furthermore, observes Louison, entities like the Sheckler Foundation may act as tax-efficient vehicles while providing exposure for sponsors, just as philanthropy helps corporations like Levi's and Nike to associate with skateboarding's authentic cultural capital, and so increase their sales.[89] On the other hand, considers O'Connor, those projects that fail to match skateboarding values will not be supported by skaters and so will not enhance brand values.[90]

Despite these concerns, the vast majority of skateboarding charities, educational initiatives and social enterprises make considerable contributions to wider society, from developing specific individual skills to building wider personal and cultural qualities. It is to these positive initiatives that we now turn.

Perhaps the most successful and well known of skateboarding social enterprises is Skateistan (Figure 13.12). Oliver Percovich, the Australian skater who in 2008 founded Skateistan in Kabul, Afghanistan, and is now its executive director, explains how, after many decades of civil war and fluctuating ruling powers, the children who make up seventy per cent of the Afghanistan Muslim population have only roadsides in which to play. Girls are banned from riding bicycles or flying kites, but they are allowed to skateboard, and so Skateistan teaches girls and boys alike to ride alongside an arts-based curriculum ranging from world cultures, human rights and environmental studies to nutrition, hygiene and storytelling.[91]

The aim here is to break the cycles of violence, desperation and poverty to which Kabul youth are commonly accustomed, and instead to build confidence and other skills. 'When it comes down to it, kids just want to be kids,' explains Percovich. 'Skateboarding provides that because it's fun and challenging. It lets them forget their

problems for a moment. Once kids are hooked on skateboarding, so much more is possible. Skateboarding itself teaches important life skills, like creativity and problem solving.'[92]

Through this approach, and aided by key workers such as Max Henninger, Shams Razi, Sharna Nolan and many others, Skateistan's achievements have been considerable, even when measured simply in terms of skateboarding. By 2012, some 500 Afghan kids were skaters, of which forty per cent were female; a year later, it reached 850 youth weekly with between forty and fifty per cent female participation in all activities. Skaters like Noorzai Ibrahimi and Merza reached an advanced level, joining the DC Shoes Europe pro team on a visit to the United Arab Emirates, while disabled skaters like Mohammad Bilal Mirbat Zai also won competitions. Two skateparks, one in Kabul and another in Mazar-e-Sharif, were built.

Skateistan's most significant achievements, however, lie beyond skateboarding itself. Keen to avoid charges of cultural imperialism and imposing western skateboarding on Kabul children, Skateistan provides wider knowledge and social skills; as O'Connor notes, change at Skateistan ultimately comes not from skateboarding per se but from the bodies of the riders, such that 'skateboarding is in multiple ways a vehicle for transformation but not the driving force.' In short, at Skateistan skateboarding is the method, and not the destination.[93]

In this context, Skateistan's 'Skate and Create', 'Back to School' and 'Youth Leadership' programmes variously teach the kids about health and nutrition, operate workshops on arts, computing and environmental issues and hold sessions on Dari language, mathematics and Qur'anic study, as well as helping children to build confidence, courage, self-esteem and trust.

Working, learning and playing with each other, the kids develop friendships across Pashtun, Hazara, Tajik and Uzbek ethnicities, as well as recognizing gender-based equality; one of the first things the boys learn is that the girls have equal rights to skate. As Lukas Feireiss notes:

> Even in the most desolate of situations skateboarding, as a performative instrument for transformation, teaches the children of Skateistan not to accept the city and therefore society as it is, but to create their own city, their own spaces and their own futures. In its essence, the power of skateboarding in Afghanistan is about what it symbolizes: the freedom of movement and the empowerment of the individual beyond all restrictions and conventions.

Or as the fourteen-year-old Afghan girl Negina simply states, 'skateboarding lets me feel like I'm flying.'[94]

These achievements are substantial and profound, helping to do no less than, according to Skateistan volunteer Sophie Friedel, 'build peace', and in 2013 Skateistan was included in *The Global Journal*'s list of one hundred top NGOs.[95] Many professionals have visited and supported Skateistan, including Cairo Foster, Maysam Faraj, Tony Hawk, Louisa Menke, Kenny Reed and Jamie Thomas, while Black Box, Fallen, IOU Ramps, Route One, Skateroom, Spitfire, Theeve, TSG and Zero are among the skate companies to have provided support, as have Architecture for Humanity, the Canadian, Danish, Finnish, German, Norwegian, Swiss and US governments, the Kabul municipality and the Afghan National Olympic Committee.[96] As a result of this kind of worldwide backing, by 2015 Skateistan was able to spread its operations beyond Kabul, setting up facilities in northern Afghanistan, Vietnam, Cambodia and Johannesburg.

Numerous other social enterprises are also using skateboarding for community aims. Thorpe has identified how skateboarding and other alternative sports have helped form 'therapeutic landscapes' in post-disaster zones caused by war, earthquakes and hurricanes, and so allow youth to 'redefine physical and emotional

Figure 13.13
A.Skate instructor Peter Karvonen helps a child with autism to skate in Paris (2013).
© Nathan Gallagher/ Courtesy A.Skate.

Figure 13.14
Going from alienated to empowered. Opening of a skatepark supported by the Tony Hawk Foundation (2016). www.bit.ly/THF-Skate

disaster geographies and rebuild social networks and connections.[97] Since 2008 Board Rescue has provided equipment to low-income kids and at-risk youth in the United States, showing children how exercise, determination, practice and commitment can lead to positive results.[98] During the 2010s, large numbers of other community-oriented projects – like Stoked Mentoring in the United States, Cuba Skate in Cuba, Ethiopia Skate and Megabiskate in Ethiopia, Janwaar Castle in Madhya Pradesh, India, Skate-aid, SkateQilya and SkatePal in Palestine, 7Hills skatepark in Amman, Jordan, Engineers Without Boarders and Outlangish in Cape Town, Latraac in Athens, Skate Style in Cambodia, Bedouins in Tunisia and the international chapters of Skate for Change – have all deployed skateboarding to counter deep-rooted issues like alcohol and drug abuse, unemployment, poverty, violence, religious intolerance, ethnic and gender prejudices and access to education.[99] Amid abandoned properties in Detroit, for example, the Ride-It Sculpture Park (2012) uses art and greenspace to form a youth-oriented skatepark and community hub, while, as *I Am Thalente* (Natalie Johns, 2015) shows, South Africa's Indigo Skate Camp project has enriched the lives of Thalente Biyela and other local Durban kids.[100]

Even more projects are also active. A.Skate provides skate lessons for those with autism and raises awareness about this condition, thus addressing related problems with self-esteem, anxiety, truancy, depression and suicide (Figure 13.13).[101] Also in the United States, the All Nations Skate Project, Stronghold Society and Wounded Knee 4-Directions skateparks have addressed violence, drugs, alcohol and suicide among Native youth; some support has come here from Jeff Ament of rock band Pearl Jam, who has also helped fund several skateparks in less-privileged neighbourhoods.[102] Canada's

The Forks skatepark in Winnipeg runs skate camps plus film and photography workshops for under-privileged youth, and is co-located with the world's first Human Rights Museum.[103] In all these projects, skateboarding is part of an answer to complex social conditions, where both the act of skateboarding itself, and the avenues it opens up, are of equal value.

Complementary to many of these initiatives is the Tony Hawk Foundation, which supports disadvantaged communities and at-risk children through skatepark provision (Figure 13.14). Started in 2001 by Hawk and his sponsors, the Foundation supports public skateparks and related projects, partly by giving design and construction advice and partly by supplying funding. By 2018, the foundation had helped 596 US skateparks to the tune of over $5.8 million, provided over 1,000 skateparks worldwide with guidance and assistance, donated $100,000 to Skateistan and reached over 6 million skaters per year. As with Skateistan and other community initiatives, the benefits often go far beyond skateboarding itself. 'A skatepark project can teach young people a lifelong lesson in the power of perseverance,' explains Hawk. 'Kids discover they can accomplish something by working within the system rather than beating their heads against it. They learn how to communicate in a way that will encourage adults to listen, and they go from feeling alienated to empowered.'[104]

Skate and Create
Chapter 14 Skateboarding – A Magnificent Life?

Skateboarding is inherently plural and contradictory, being at once authentic and corporate, playful and serious, rebellious and conformist, street-based and skatepark-bound. If offering no singular definition seems like a strange kind of conclusion for this book, then this is simply a reflection of how skateboarding operates, for skateboarders act between categories, disrupt conventional codes and produce new spaces – mental, physical, creative and social – to inhabit. In this sense, skateboarding's contradictory character contributes to what Chantal Mouffe has postulated as an agonistic society, where conflicts and oppositions are an essential part of the democratic arena.[1]

As we have seen, there are many positive outcomes from skateboarding, for skaters and non-skaters alike. In its urban actions, skateboarding rethinks architecture and cities according to its own dynamic demands. Through appropriation – taking over space without dominating or physically changing it – skaters reimagine space for themselves, provide new functions and uses, critique underlying logics of consumerism, work and leisure and propose new values for our public spaces, buildings and heritage. At times subcultural, territorial, masculine and age-bound, skateboarding can also be artistic, polycultural, gender-fluid, transnational and life-encompassing, as well as commercial, corporate, entrepreneurial, professional, regulated and spectacular. Activated primarily through energetic performances, and so forming healthy bodies and environments, skateboarding can also be visual, mediated and theorized. The material objects of skateboarding are also sophisticated entities, either as attuned skateboard designs, or, and more significantly, as the skatepark typology, whose unique and varied forms, construction methods and arrangements are appreciated not only as challenging riding terrains but as generators of cultural, heritage and social values. Finally, skateboarding is increasingly contributing to the visual and plastic arts, and, perhaps most importantly of all, to the lives of thousands of disadvantaged and at-risk members of our society, and often situated in the world's most challenging locations.

Geographically, and despite what some sections of the media may suggest, skateboarding as an everyday activity is no longer centred on California. For example, as Tim Sedo notes, for many Chinese riders skateboarding may have originated in America but is today a transglobal practice that 'belongs to the world'.[2] And for their own riders, the skate scenes in Barcelona, London, Melbourne, São Paulo and Shanghai are as developed as those as Los Angeles, New York or Philadelphia.

Indeed, one could even argue that it is Malmö in Sweden that today boasts the world's most progressive skateboarding environment, from lively DIY constructions and street-skating to the Bryggeriet school and skate organization, which helps activate the city's skateparks, and the city-funded Skate Malmö partnership, which coordinates local activities, hosts events and even employs Gustav Edén as full-time director. Here, authorities, organizations and riders alike co-create a vibrant street-skatespot, DIY, skatepark, female-friendly, competition and educational scene.[3] As a result, and apart from huge benefits to its own local riders and residents, Malmö is now an international centre for skateboarding, with numerous professionals and other skate visitors, plus a major Vans-run World Championship final. Other cities, too, seem to be taking note. In 2016, the UK's Hull declared a similar intention of becoming a centre for skateboarding, by hosting an annual festival and incorporating skate-friendly areas within its public building projects,[4] while in Australia the city of Melbourne launched a major public consultation to help foster 'healthy and inclusive skate culture for all people'.[5]

Beyond this rich history and these promising trends, what else lies around the corner? Of the recent world-stage developments in skateboarding – notably the rise of Street

League competitions and the inclusion of skateboarding in the 2020 Tokyo Olympics – the spectacular, scheduled, win-focused version of skateboarding proposed by such events is certainly not many skaters' preferred model of skateboarding. Nonetheless, considerable good may come from the Olympics, including female skaters gaining the same exposure as their male counterparts, encouraging the take-up of skateboarding by wider sections of society and heightening the perceived value of skateboarding among those who provide skateparks, formulate city legislation, design city spaces and develop school curricula.

So will skateboarding being included in the Olympics as a competition of highly trained athletes mean the end of transgressive street-skating, informal skatepark sessions or speeding crews of downhill riders? Surely not, for, just as cycling's significant Olympic profile has not lead to its confinement within competitive tours and velodromes but conversely has encouraged everyday participation, skateboarding's fundamentally quotidian, participant and diverse character is far too established to be overtaken by a single event held but once every four years. Similarly, while skateboarding will always appeal to trend-conscious riders attracted by its insurgent style, kids seduced by skate video games, or what the Chinese call a *hua shou* – someone who owns a skateboard but rarely skates – such people do not stop 'real' skaters from skating.[6] Indeed, the important thing here is to realize that no single form of skateboarding is 'superior' to or dominates over any other, for just as every human has, within the confines of law, the right to believe and act as they will, so skaters should express themselves through whatever skateboarding variant they might prefer.

Indeed, if there is any hierarchy of the most 'authentic' or 'core' attributes of skateboarding, then I rate the qualities of openness, inclusivity, accessibility and freedom of interpretation over those of cool-bound exclusivity, essentialist dogmatism and constant aggression. Personally, I prefer Patti McGee's pioneering spirit, Tony Alva's riding style, Stacy Peralta's industry, Hillary Thompson's bravery, Mark Gonzales's artistry, Sean Goff's dedication, Mike Vallely's determination, Rodney Mullen's scientism, Jeff Grosso's passion, Tony Hawk's professionalism, Skateistan's engagement, Daewon Song's technicity, Gou Miyagi's eccentricity, Lizzie Armanto's resolution, Pontus Alv's lateralism, Tired's wit, Pedro Barros's commitment and

Ben Raybourn's invention over spectacular packaging, team uniforms, bad-boy posturing, blood-and-fracture horror shows, turf rivalries, frat-boy humour, casual misogyny, bullish heteronormativity, rock-star personas, hyper-cool vibing, or the habitual slagging-off of other skaters. Skateboarding is best when it openly questions, challenges, explores, surprises and welcomes rather than when it is narrowly comfortable, judgmental, predictable, stable or exclusionary.

Is this a weak position, in which we risk losing the 'core' values of counter-cultural skateboarding beneath a tsunami of dilutions, commercialism and bastardizations? But who defines what is 'core' about skateboarding? Who are the 'owners' of these values, and how are they maintained? If skateboarding teaches us anything, it is that skateboarding is whatever skateboarders do, and that skateboarding means whatever is explicitly and implicitly spoken through its activity. There is, then, no singular immutable heart to skateboarding, only a number of similar-yet-different trajectories, as pursued by people who are female, male and gender-fluid, who are old and young, street and vert, commercial and subcultural, hipster and grungy, fast and slow.

Consequently, diversity is not a weakness for skateboarding, but conversely is its very strength. Skateboarding has not been and will not be ruined by dominant commercial media or spectacular international events, for its dispersed and participant-based nature means its future does not lie in the hands of worldwide federations. Fox and the Olympics may believe skateboarding should be beamed worldwide to millions of passive spectators, but this is, in the end, only a bunch of images; and if you don't like this particular packaging, you can always go outside and skate.

There are, of course, problems within skateboarding, not least those to do with the frequent promotion, at least in some sections of its practitioners and media, of exclusionary attitudes with regard to gender, race and sexuality, or even towards certain skateboarding specialisms.[7] In the twenty-first century, dismissing, for example, metropolitan longboarders as gay wrong-boarders is tiresome, inappropriate and frankly indefensible. Nonetheless, in its general attitudes and disposition, skateboarding normally transcends its failings and flaws more than it is constrained by them. As Raphaël Zarka notes, in *Mythologies*

the literary theorist and philosopher Roland
Barthes regretted how play-with-me wooden
toys, which encouraged children to be creators,
had been increasingly replaced by look-at-me
plastic toys, which have conditioned children as
owner-users.[8] The skateboard helps to reverse
this process, turning all skaters, whether children,
youth or adults, into creators, that is, into people
who typically act not in order to win, master or
collect but to create, explore and innovate. The
skateboard, then, is a tool, but it is skateboarding
that is the action, and that consequently is open
to so much more; skateboarding may provide
us with few answers, but it certainly offers
challenging questions and tantalizing suggestions
as to the way we live in cities today.

Traditional sports are, in part, a way for young
people to be trained in the ways of democratic
capitalism, where, this ideology proposes,
unequal social benefits (money, power,
property, status etc.) are acquired through
fairly regulated competition (the 'game' of life).
Sport's rules, victories and rewards are thus
a proxy for how neoliberal society distributes
its spoils. So what of the 'alternative' sport of
skateboarding, in which 'rules' are few and far
between, 'victories' are rarely offered or sought
and 'rewards' are apparently more to do with
respect and renown than with hierarchical
status or financial wealth? Skateboarding in
effect embeds in its practitioners a different
life perspective, one in which participation,

Figure 14.1
Vasco De Gama
bridge, Lisbon (2003).
© Alberto Polo.

expression, satisfaction and community are
more highly valued than scores, fame, riches or
power. In Paul O'Connor's terms, skateboarding
is therefore prefigurative, offering us not just a
glimpse but a partially enacted vision of what a
different world might be like.[9] In this sense, as
an entity born out of contemporary urbanism,
both indicating but not yet fully portraying
new potentials, skateboarding concurs
with Henri Lefebvre's enigmatic contention
regarding the potential of cities. 'Here, in the
new town, boredom is pregnant with desires,
frustrated frenzies, unrealized possibilities.
A magnificent life is waiting just around the
corner, and far, far away.'[10]

References, Bibliography and Index

References

Chapter 1 Introduction

1   Michele K. Donnelly, 'Alternative *and* Mainstream: Revisiting the Sociological Analysis of Skateboarding', Michael Atkinson and Kevin Young, (eds), *Tribal Play* (Bingley: JAI Press, 2008), p. 211.
2   'Unknown Feature', *R.A.D.*, n.97 (June 1991), p. 25.

Chapter 2 Skateboards

1   Ben J. Davidson, *The Skateboard Book* (New York: Grosset & Dunlap, 1976) pp. 13–14; Ben Marcus and Lucia Daniella Griggi, *The Skateboard* (Minneapolis: MVP Books, 2011), pp. 16–23; Rhyn Noll, *Skateboard Retrospective* (Atglen: Schiffer, 2000), pp. 11–13; www.flexy-racer.com; and Peter Ducommun, *Skateboarding Vancouver* (Toronto: Concrete Wave, 2005), pp. 10–14.
2   Bruce Logan, interview, *SkateBoarder*, v.3 n.4 (April 1977), p. 48; Mary Horowitz, 'Skateboard Decks: Design Symposium', *SkateBoarder*, v.4 n.6 (January 1978), p. 98; Low E. Thompson, letter, *Thrasher*, v.12 n.1 (January 1992), p. 8; Powell-Peralta, advertisement, *Thrasher*, v.12 n.9 (September 1992), p. 24; Larry Balma, *Tracker* (Oceanside: Foundry Press, 2015), p. 197; and Daniel Gesmer, (ed.), *The Legacy of Warren Bolster* (Thornhill: Concrete Wave, 2004), p. 83.
3   Denis Shufeldt, interview, *SkateBoarder*, v.3 n.2 (December 1976), p. 41.
4   Marcus and Griggi, *Skateboard*, p. 54.
5   Bob Schmidt, 'The Day They Invented the Skateboard', *Dansworld*, www. web.cps.msu.edu.
6   Adam, 'A British Skate Story', *Skate Geezer*, www.interlog.net; and Schmidt, 'Day They Invented.'
7   Cole Louison, *The Impossible* (Guilford: Lyons Press, 2011), p. 15; Sean Mortimer, *Stalefish* (San Francisco: Chronicle Books, 2008), p. 17; Marcus and Griggi, *Skateboard*, p. 45–7; Noll, *Skateboard Retrospective*, pp. 26–7, 36–7; and Ducommun, *Skateboarding Vancouver*, pp. 24–7.
8   Pete Pan, 'The Third Strike', *Thrasher*, v.6 n.6 (June 1986), pp. 50–1.
9   Nick Ford and David Brown, *Surfing and Social Theory* (London: Routledge, 2006), pp. 25–30, 93–4.
10 Marcus and Griggi, *Skateboard*, pp. 71, 138.
11 Brian Gillogly, 'Trucks', *SkateBoarder*, v.3 n.5 (June 1977), pp. 38–9; Davidson, *Skateboard*, pp. 14–15; and Marilyn Gould, *Skateboarding* (Mankato, Capstone: 1991), pp. 10–11.
12 *Thrasher*, v.4 n.5 (May 1984), p. 28.
13 Pahl Dixon and Peter Dixon, *Your Complete Guide to Hot Skateboarding* (New York: Warner Books, 1977), pp. 40–2; Ben Marcus and Griggi, *Skateboard*, pp. 62–3; Keith David Hamm, *Scarred for Life* (San Francisco: Chronicle, 2004), pp. 42–4; and Louison, *Impossible*, p. 11.
14 Gordon & Smith, *One Long Ride* (San Diego: Gordon & Smith, 2014), pp. 44–7.
15 LaVada Weir, *Skateboards and Skateboarding* (New York: Julian Messner, 1977), pp. 13–14; Michael Brooke, *The Concrete Wave* (Toronto: Warwick, 1999), pp. 27–31; Marcus and Griggi, *Skateboard*, pp. 54–5, 69; and *America's Newest Sport* (Bruce Brown, 1964).
16 Sean Cliver, *The Disposable Skateboard Bible* (Berkeley: Gingko Press, 2009), pp. 34–63.
17 Marcus and Griggi, *Skateboard*, p. 63.
18 Louison, *Impossible*, p. 12.
19 Mortimer, *Stalefish*, p. 21; and Dr Skaterock, *Vintage Skaterock* (Wuerzburg: Skaterock, 2012), pp. 17–33.
20 John Severson, 'Editorial: Skateboarding Comes of Age', *SkateBoarder*, v.1 n.3 (August 1965), p. 9; and Robert E. Dallos, 'Skateboards Roll Up Dizzying Sales', *Wall Street Journal* (24 March 1965).
21 'International Skateboard Championships', *SkateBoarder*, v.1 n.3 (August 1965), pp. 15–37; and '1965 American Skateboard Slalom Championships' (1965), www.youtube.com/watch?v=ADtgbABmG18.
22 Nick Green, 'Cast of Acclaimed 1965 Skateboarding Film "Skaterdater" Reunite', *Daily Breeze* (28 June 2015), www.dailybreeze.com.
23 *Life* (14 May 1965); John Boykin and Bob Grant, 'Skateboard Acrobatics', *Popular Mechanics* (July 1965), pp. 81–5; Dallos, 'Skateboards Roll Up Dizzying Sales'; Charles Schulz, 'Peanuts' cartoon (29 March 1965); and 'Charlie Brown's All-Stars', TV Special (CBS, 8 June 1966).
24 Don Hoffman, 'Dale "Sausage Man" Smith', *SkateBoarder*, v.6 n.10 (May 1980), pp. 70–1; Keller, 'Skateboarding's First Wave: a Palisades Story', *Palisadian Post* (21 November 2013), 'Lifestyle' section, p. 9; Brian Gillogly, 'Torger Johnson', *SkateBoarder*, v.2 n.5 (June 1976), pp. 46–51; and Louison, *Impossible*, p. 12.
25 British Pathé, 'Gremlins and Sandies in New Craze' (1964), www.britishpathe.com; '1965 Australian Skateboarding Midget Farrelly' (1965), www.youtube.com/watch?v=yPoXPC8VbmQ; 'Skateboarding Around the World', *The Quarterly SkateBoarder*, v.1 n.2 (Spring 1965), pp. 38–9; and Over *Plywood* (Jono Atkinson, 2015).
26 Claude Queyrel, 'Jim Fitzpatrick:

Exclusive Interview 2011', *Endless Lines*, (November 2010–January 2011), www.endlesslines.free.fr; and *The Quarterly SkateBoarder*, v.1 n.2 (Spring 1965), p. 41.

27   'The Devil's Toy', www.nfb.ca; and Hazel Pennell, *Skateboarding* (London: GLC Intelligence Unit, London Topics n.24, 1978), p. 1.

28   'Le Roll' Surf: un Sport Acrobatique', *Pilote*, n.316 (11 November 1965), pp, 46–7; 'Le Roll' Surf: Acrobaties Pour une Planche à Roulettes', *Tintin*, n.916 (12 May 1966), pp. 12–13; Raphaël Zarka, *On a Day with No Waves*, (Paris: Editions B42, 2011), pp. 17, 80; www.endlesslines.free.fr; and Joel DeRosnay, 'Skateboarding France', *SkateBoarder*, v.1 n.4 (October 1965), pp. 15–21.

29   'Tory Leader, Mr Heath Off Duty', ITN, (13 March 1966), www.itnsource. com; Katharine Hepburn, *Me: Stories of My Life* (London: Viking, 1991); and 'The Unseen 1960s-Era Beatles Photos by Henry Grossman', www. shootingfilm.net.

30   Julien Glauser, *Tokyo-Skate* (Gollion: Infolio, 2016), p. 43.

31   Ducommun, *Skateboarding Vancouver*, pp. 23, 28–35; and *Tic Tac 2 Heelflip* (dir. Mike Hill, 2001).

32   Marcus and Griggi, *Skateboard*, pp. 55, 93; and Louison, *Impossible*, p. 51.

33   Marcus and Griggi, *Skateboard*, p. 99.

34   Logan, interview, p. 51; Ty Page, interview, *SkateBoarder*, v.4 n.2 (September 1977), p. 108; Tony Roberts, 'Santa Cruz', *Thrasher*, v.8 n.7 (July 1988), p. 79; John Smythe, 'The History of the World and Other Short Subjects', *SkateBoarder*, v.6 n.10 (May 1980), pp. 28–51; and Marcus and Griggi, *Skateboard*, pp. 12, 103.

35   Marcus and Griggi, *Skateboard*, p. 93; Brooke, *Concrete Wave*, pp. 30–1; and Balma, *Tracker*, pp. 12–13.

36   Brian Gillogly, 'Wheels', *SkateBoarder*, v.3 n.3, (February 1977), pp. 94–5; Brooke, *Concrete Wave*, pp. 30–1, 46–7; Marcus and Griggi, *Skateboard*, pp. 108–113; Eric M. Weiss, 'A Reinvention of the Wheel', *Washington Post* (17 August 2004), B01; Craig B. Snyder, *A Secret History of the Ollie* (Delray Beach: Black Salt Press, 2015), pp. 20–3; Frank Nasworthy, 'Breakthrough – the Urethane Wheel', *SkateBoarder*, v.2 n.1 (Summer 1975), pp. 22–3; and Ben Marcus, 'Plastics Explosive', *The Skateboarder's Journal* (Winter 2012), pp. 18–29.

37   Noel Wanner, 'Wheels: Where the Rubber Meets the Road', www. exploratorium.edu.

38   *Rollin' through the Decades* (Winstan Whitter, 2004).

39   'Who's Hot! Peter Boronski', *SkateBoarder*, v.4 n.11 (June 1978), p. 108; and Marcus and Griggi, *Skateboard*, p. 12.

40   Snyder, *Secret History*, p. 22.

41   Nasworthy, 'Breakthrough', pp. 22–3; and Metaflex, advertisement, *SkateBoarder*, v.2 n.3 (Winter 1975), p. 28.

42   Road Rider Wheels, advertisement, *SkateBoarder*, v.2 n.3 (Winter 1975), p. 8.

43   Snyder, *Secret History*, p. 44.

44   Brooke, *Concrete Wave*, pp. 22–5; Marcus and Griggi, *Skateboard*, pp. 62–3, 99, 104–5; and Noll, *Skateboard Retrospective*, pp. 64–5.

45   Cliver, *Disposable Skateboard Bible*, p. 248; and Snyder, *Secret History*, pp. 47–9.

46   Denike, *Built to Grind*, p. 18; Snyder, *Secret History*, p. 37; Balma, *Tracker*, pp. 43–5; and Gillogly, 'Trucks', pp. 38–9.

47   Leland Ware, 'The Smithsonian Just Recognized One of the Oldest Skate Companies Around', *Ride* (4 September 2015), www.

theridechannel.com.

48   Balma, *Tracker*, pp. 31–51, 64–71, 92–7.

49   'The History of Gullwing', www. gullwingtruckco.com.

50   Marcus and Griggi, *Skateboard*, p. 120–3; Jim Phillips, *Surf, Skate & Rock Art of Jim Phillips* (Atglen: Schiffer, 2004), p. 69; Jim Phillips, *The Skateboard Art of Jim Phillips* (Atglen: Schiffer, 2007), pp. 12–15; Snyder, *Secret History*, pp. 28–9, 34, 43; and Jonathan Harms and Jack Smith, (eds), *The Skateboarder's Journal* (Morro Bay: Morro Skateboard Group, 2009), pp. 87–9.

51   Bob Denike, (ed.), *Built to Grind* (San Francisco: High Speed Productions, 2004), p. 14.

52   Magnum, advertisement, *SkateBoarder*, v.3 n.5 (June 1977), pp. 31–4; and 'Skateboarding Comes of Age', *Skateboard World*, v.1 n.3 (September 1977), pp. 74–9.

53   Marcus and Griggi, *Skateboard*, p. 120–3; and Snyder, *Secret History*, pp. 28–9, 34, 43.

54   *Skateboard Industry News*, v.1 n.2 (1977).

55   'The Man Who Spotted the Skateboard Trend', *Skateboard Special*, n.1 (September 1977), p. 8.

56   Gordon & Smith, *The Gordon & Smith Skateboard Team Book* (San Diego: MLP, 2010), pp. 77–8; and Gordon & Smith, *One Long Ride*, p. 135.

57   Balma, *Tracker*, p. 47.

58   'Skateboard Kings' (BBC, prod. Horace Ové, 1978).

59   Louison, *Impossible*, p. 64; and G&S, advertisement, *SkateBoarder*, v.4 n.4, (November 1977), p. 14.

60   'Skate Extra', *SkateBoarder*, v.3 n.2 (December 1976), p. 127; 'Who's Hot! Lonnie Toft', *SkateBoarder*, v.4 n.1 (August 1977), p. 90; Lonnie Toft, interview, *SkateBoarder*, v.5 n.9 (April 1979), p. 35; Lonnie Toft, letter,

SkateBoarder, v.5 n.6 (January 1979), p. 15; and Don Sheridan, 'Evolution of the Pig', *SkateBoarder*, v.5 n.4 (November 1978).

61 SIMS advertisement, *SkateBoarder*, v.4 n.11 (June 1978), back cover; and Wes Humpston, *Bulldog's Art by Wes Humpston* (Thornhill: Concrete Wave, 2013), pp. 6–8.

62 Balma, *Tracker*, pp. 14, 86–90; and G&S, advertisement, *SkateBoarder*, v.4 n.2 (September 1977), p. 32.

63 Colin Field, 'Wee Wonder: the Legend of Wee Willi Winkels', *Mountain Life* (16 July 2014), www.mountainlifemag.ca; Snyder, *Secret History*, pp. 250–7; and *Brooke, Concrete Wave*, pp. 60–3.

64 Sheridan, 'Evolution of the Pig', pp. 88–93; and SIMS advertisement, *SkateBoarder*, v.5 n.3 (October 1978), p. 43 and rear cover.

65 John Sablosky, interview, *Skateboard!*, n.10 (June 1978), p. 52; and Ducommun, *Skateboarding Vancouver*, p. 83.

66 Scott Peck, 'A Brief Window of Skateboard History: Boulder Boards and the Kryptonics K Beam', reproduced in Sean Cliver, 'Disposable: a history of Boulder Boards', www.skateandannoy.com, (11 March 2010); Dave Goldsmith, 'The Kryptonics Deck', *Skateboard!*, n.14 (October 1978), pp. 60–3; Sam Fernando, 'Lite Board Symposium', *SkateBoarder*, v.6 n.7 (February 1980), pp. 46–53; and Ducommun, *Skateboarding Vancouver*, pp. 79–81.

67 Marcus and Griggi, *Skateboard*, p. 200.

68 Rick Blackhart, interview, *SkateBoarder*, v.5 n.3 (October 1978), p. 73; Rick Blackhart, 'Ask the Doctor', *Thrasher*, v.2 n.5 (May–June 1982), p. 10; Denike, *Built to Grind*, pp. 7–37, 58–9; and Balma, *Tracker*, p. 104.

69 'Bringing Back Kryptonics: Episode #4 Formula', www.kryptonics.com; Kailee Bradsheet, 'Kryptonics Wheels Re-emerge', *TransWorld Business* (3 October 2013), www.business.transworld.net; 'Kryptonics', Skateboard Zoo, www.skateboardzoo.com; and The Longboard Consortium, 'It's the Secret Sauce', www.silverfishlongboarding.com.

70 Dave Goldsmith, 'Skata Data: Lime Green and Beyond', *Skateboard!*, n.11 (July 1978), pp. 44–7.

71 Powell-Peralta, advertisement, *Thrasher*, v.7 n.2 (February 1987), p. 69; Santa Cruz, advertisement, *Thrasher*, v.6 n.8 (August 1986), p. 32; and Ducommun, *Skateboarding Vancouver*, p. 125.

72 Balma, *Tracker*, pp. 201–3.

73 Powell-Peralta, advertisement, *Thrasher*, v.12 n.9 (September 1992), p. 24.

74 'Trash', *Thrasher*, v.7 n.7 (July 1987), p. 97.

75 Editorial, *Thrasher*, v.12 n.3 (March 1992), p. 4.

76 Tim Sedo, 'Dead-Stock Boards, Blown-out Spots, and the Olympic Games', Petra Rethmann, Imre Szeman and William D. Coleman, (eds), *Cultural Autonomy* (Vancouver: University of British Columbia Press, 2010), pp. 265–9.

77 Rodney Mullen with Sean Mortimer, *The Mutt* (New York: HarperCollins, 2004), p. 185.

78 Mullen, *Mutt*, p. 187.

79 Snyder, *Secret History*, p. 732.

80 Dirk Vogel, 'What If Skateboarding Looked Like the Video Game Industry?', *Jenkem* (2014), www.jenkemmag.com.

81 *Stuntwood* (Jeff Roe, 2006).

82 Blind, advertisement, *The Skateboard Mag*, n.42 (September 2007), back cover.

83 Cliver, *Disposable Skateboard Bible*, pp. 124–5; Rhyn Noll, *Skateboards That Rock* (Atglen: Schiffer, 2003), pp. 68–88; and Gordon & Smith, *One Long Ride*, p. 194.

84 Balma, *Tracker*, p. 267; and TransWorld Business, 'The State of Skate', (2015), p. 6.

85 Patrick Burgoyne and Jeremy Leslie, *Bored* (London: Lawrence King and Creative Review, 1997).

86 Rodney Mullen, interview, *Warp*, v.6 n.3 (August 1997), p. 106; and David S. Wisenthal, alt.skateboard, 'Subject. Re. Toy Machine Question (About the trucks)' (posted 1 July 1996).

87 Editor's response to letter, *Slap*, v.6 n.1 (January 1997), p. 16; '2000 Stuntwood' post on www.fairwaysandflips.blogspot.co.uk (29 August 2008); and 'Deck Manufacturing Locations List', www.

skateboard-city.com (27 March 2009).

88 *Stuntwood*.

89 Sedo, 'Dead-Stock Boards', p. 271; and Austin Li, 'China's Skateboarding Youth Culture as an Emerging Cultural Industry' (PhD thesis, Loughborough University, 2018).

90 Quoted in Noel Wanner, 'So What the Heck is a "Truck", Anyway?', www.exploratorium.edu.

91 Mullen, *Mutt*, p. 266; and James Boulter, *Unemployable* (Sydney: Thames & Hudson, 2015), pp. 597–8

92 Telephone conversation with Brad Horn (5 August 2014); 'Revenge Trucks for Longboards' (2011), www.youtube.com/watch?v=7fV6uU4shiI; and www.koastal.com.

93 Kailee Bradstreet, 'The Board Room', *TransWorld Business* (26 September 2012), www.business.transworld.net.

94 Powell, advertisement, *SkateBoarder*, v.6 n.2 (September 1979), p. 23.

95 Horowitz, 'Skateboard Decks', pp. 94–9; Fernando, 'Lite Board Symposium', pp. 46–53; Goldsmith, 'Skata Data', (July 1978), pp. 44–7; and Mickey Wisternoff, 'Techno Talk', *Skateboard!*, n.16 (December 1978), p. 46.

96 Jake Shaft, 'Life, Liberty, and the Pursuit of Longboarding', *Thrasher*, v.6 n.3 (March 1986), p. 59.

Chapter 3 Living by the Board

1 'NDIIIPP Special Event: Ian MacKaye', Library of Congress (7 May 2013), www.youtube.com/watch?v=AvqtY_7Q7hI.

2 Paula M. L. Moya and Michael Roy Hames-Garcia, *Reclaiming Identity* (Berkeley: University of California Press, 2000).

3 Steve Pile, *The Body and the City* (London: Routledge, 1996), p. 74.

4 Pierre Bourdieu, *Distinction* (Cambridge, Mass.: Harvard University Press, 1984).

5 Dick Hebdige, *Subculture* (London: Methuen, 1979), especially pp. 1–19.

6 Stacy Peralta, interview, *Thrasher*, v.2 n.5 (May–June 1982), p. 17; Steve Rocco, interview, *TransWorld Skateboarding*, v.6 n.1 (February 1988), p. 85.

7   Julie Angel, *Ciné Parkour* (CreateSpace, 2011).

8   wwwguanmu.name.

9   Andy Bennett, 'Subcultures or Neo-Tribes?', *Sociology*, v.33 n.3 (1999), pp. 599–617; Steve Redhead, *The End of the Century Party* (Manchester: Manchester University Press, 1990); and David Muggleton and Rupert Weinzierl, (eds), *The Post-Subcultures Reader* (Oxford: Berg, 2003).

10   Sarah Thornton, 'General Introduction', Ken Gelder and Sarah Thornton, *The Subcultures Reader* (London: Routledge, 1997), pp. 1–7.

11   Henri Lefebvre, *Introduction to Modernity* (London: Verso, 1995), pp. 239–388.

12   Mullen, *Mutt*, p. 144.

13   'Jeff Grosso's Loveletters to Skateboarding – Freaks and Geeks' (2015), www.youtube.com/watch?v=d1M3dx2o-A4.

14   Peter Whitley, *Public Skatepark Development Guide* (Portland: Skaters for Public Skateparks, 2009), p. 87.

15   Henri Lefebvre, *The Explosion* (New York: Monthly Review, 1969), pp. 106–7.

16   Kevin Thatcher, in Trip Gabriel, 'Rolling Thunder' *Rolling Stone* (16–30 July 1987), pp. 73–6.

17   Harms and Smith, *Skateboarder's Journal*, p. 49.

18   Becky Beal, 'Symbolic Inversion in the Subculture of Skateboarding', Margaret Duncan, Garry Chick and Alan Aycock, (eds), *Diversions and Divergences in Fields of Play* (Greenwich: Ablex, 1998), p. 213.

19   Gary Davis, 'Steep Slopes', *Thrasher*, v.3 n.5 (May 1983), p. 8.

20   *The Skateboard Mag*, n.132 (March 2015), p. 68.

21   Christian Hosoi, interview, *Skateboard!* (second series), n.39 (January 1990), p. 45.

22   Skatemaster Tate, in David Grogan and Carl Arrington 'He's Not Lean but His Rap Is Mean, So the *Thrasher*s Relate to Skatemaster Tate', *People Weekly*, v.27 (8 June 1987), p. 156.

23   Editor's response to letter, *Thrasher*, v.8 n.7 (July 1988), p. 16.

24   Kyle Kusz, 'The Cultural Politics of Extreme Sports in America', Belinda Wheaton, (ed.), *Understanding Lifestyle Sports* (London: Routledge, 2004), pp. 197–213.

25   Emily Chivers Yochim, *Skate Life* (Ann Arbor: University of Michigan, 2010); and Annika Amelie Hellman, 'Skateboarding is Like Dancing: Masculinity as a Performative Visual Culture in Art Education', *International Journal of Education Through Art*, v.12 n.3 (2016), pp. 327–44.

26   Konstantin Butz, *Grinding California* (Bielefeld: Transcript Verlag, 2012), pp. 190–7.

27   David Leonard, 'To the White Extreme in the Mainstream: Manhood and White Youth Culture in a Virtual Sports World', Michael Giardina and Michele Donnelly, (eds) *Youth Culture and Sport* (Abingdon: Routledge, 2008), pp. 91–112.

28   Sean Brayton, 'Black-Lash: Revisiting the "White Negro" through Skateboarding', *Sociology of Sport Journal*, v.22 n.3 (2005), pp. 356–72.

29   Belinda Wheaton and Becky Beal, '"Keeping It Real": Subcultural Media and the Discourses of Authenticity in Alternative Sport", *International Review for the Sociology of Sport*, v.38 n.2 (2003), p. 171; and Becky Beal and Charlene Wilson, '"Chicks Dig Scars": Commercialisation and the Transformations of Skateboarders' Identities', Wheaton, *Understanding Lifestyle Sports*, p. 39.

30   Simon Orpana, 'Steep Transitions: Spatial-temporal Incorporation, Beasley Skate Park, and Subcultural Politics in the Gentrifying City', Lombard, *Skateboarding*, p. 160; Matthew Atencio, Becky Beal and Charlene Wilson, 'The Distinction of Risk: Urban Skateboarding, Street Habitus and the Construction of Hierarchical Gender Relations', *Qualitative Research in Sport & Exercise*, v.1 n.1 (2009), pp. 3–20; Becky Beal, 'Alternative Masculinity and Its Effects on Gender Relations in the Subculture of Skateboarding', *Journal of Sport Behaviour*, v.19 n.3 (1996), pp. 204–20; Beal and Wilson, 'Chicks Dig Scars', pp. 31–54; and Becky Beal, Matthew Atencio, E. Missy Wright and Zánean McClain, 'Skateboarding, Community and Urban Politics: Shifting Practices and Challenges', *International Journal of Sport Policy and Politics* (online 7 November 2016), pp. 1–13.

31   Yochim, *Skate Life*, pp. 4, 21–3, *passim.*

32   Jeremy Henderson, interview, *SkateBoarder*, v.6 n.2 (September 1979), p. 35; Andy Macdonald with Theresa Foy Digeronimo, *Dropping In with Andy Mac* (New York: Simon Pulse, 2003), p. 36; and *The Reality of Bob Burnquist* (dir. Jamie Mosberg, 2006).

33   Stuart Thomas and Jason Potts, 'How Industry Competition Ruined Windsurfing', Sport, *Business and Management*, v.6 n.5 (2016), pp. 565–78.

34   Sean Dinces, '"Flexible Opposition": Skateboarding Subcultures under the Rubric of Late Capitalism', *International Journal of the History of Sport*, v.28 n.11 (2011), pp. 1512–35.

35   David Drissel, 'Skateboarding Spaces of Youth in Belfast', *Spaces & Flows*, v.2 n.4 (2012), pp. 115–38.

36   Peggy Fletcher Stack, 'Utah's Skateboarding Rabbi', Salt Lake Tribune (27 August 2015), www.sltrib.com; and Lucas Wisenthal, 'The Greatest Jewish Skateboarders Ever', *Ride* (17 December 2014), www.theridechannel.com.

37   Dan Wener, 'Ultra-Orthodox Skateboarder in Jerusalem', *United with Israel* (29 September 2014), www.unitedwithisrael.org.

38   Karl Watson, Pushing Boarders conference, Bartlett School of Architecture, UCL (Saturday 2 June 2018).

39   *TransWorld Skateboarding*, v.6 n.1 (February 1988), p. 38.

40   Sean Cliver, *Disposable* (Corte Madera: Gingko Press, 2004), pp. 106–7; Grind King, advertisement, *Thrasher*, v.11 n.12 (December 1991), p. 25; Eric Blehm, (ed.), *Agents of Change* (New York: ReganBooks, 2003), p. 18; and Armando Barajas, 'My Pro Spotlight', *TransWorld Skateboarding*, v.13 n.5 (May 1995), p. 83.

41   Ben Detrick, 'Skateboarding Rolls Out the Suburbs', *New York Times* (11 November 2007), www.nytimes.com.

42   Matthew Atencio, Becky Beal and Emily Chivers Yochim, '"It Ain't Just Black Kids and White Kids": the

Representation and Reproduction of Authentic "Skurban" Masculinities', *Sociology of Sport Journal*, v.30 n.2 (2013), p. 169.

43 bell hooks, 'Eating the Other', *Black Looks: Race and Representation* (Boston: South End Press, 1992), pp. 21–39.

44 Atencio, Beal and Yochim, 'It Ain't Just Black Kids and White Kids', pp. 153–72.

45 Brayton, 'Black-Lash', p. 367.

46 Billy Miller, interview, *Heckler*.

47 *Tic Tac 2 Heelflip*.

48 Amy Sueyoshi, 'Skate and Create: Skateboarding, Asian Pacific America, and Masculinity', *Amerasia*, v.41 n.2 (2015), p. 9.

49 Detrick, 'Skateboarding Rolls Out'.

50 Katherine White, '"We Out Here": Skateboarding, Segregation and Resistance in the Bronx' (MA dissertation, Fordham University, 2015), p. 6, *passim*.

51 Jane Forsyth, 'Aboriginal Sport in the City', *Aboriginal Policy Studies*, v.3 n.1 & 2 (2014), pp. 214–22.

52 Aubrey Edwards, 'Swamp Suburbia and Rebellion against a Culture of Crime: the Birth of Black Skateboarding in the Big Easy' (MSc Urban Studies dissertation, University of New Orleans, 2015).

53 Detrick, 'Skateboarding Rolls Out'; *TransWorld*, 'State of Skate', p. 8; and Michael White, 'U.S. Percentage of Non-Hispanic Whites Hits All-Time Low of 63%', *Daily News* (13 June 2013), www.nydailynews.com.

54 Aaron Barksdale, 'How Skateboarding Became More Than a White Dude's Sport', *Huffington Post* (4 December 2015), www.huffingtonpost.com.

55 Blehm, *Agents of Change*, p. 155; and Brian Ridgeway, interview, www.copingblock.blogspot.co.uk.

56 Sueyoshi, 'Skate and Create', p. 9.

57 Belinda Wheaton, *The Cultural Politics of Lifestyle Sports* (London: Routledge, 2013), pp. 100–12.

58 Tony Alva, interview, *Thrasher*, v.4 n.5 (May 1984), p. 29.

59 *SkateBoarder*, v.3 n.5 (June 1977), p. 18.

60 *Tic Tac 2 Heelflip*.

61 '10 Not-So-Great Things About Skateboarding in the Nineties', www.kingpin.mpora.com (11 February 2014); and '15 Things You Didn't Know About Embarcadero', *SkateBoarder* (29 April 2003), p. 33.

62 Dirk Vogel, 'The Skateboard as a Medium of Experiencing Urban Space and Appropriating American Public Sites' (Masters dissertation, Johannes Gutenberg University, 2002), pp. 85–6.

63 Daniel Campo, *The Accidental Playground* (New York: Empire State, 2013), p. 57; and Davie Browne, 'Dogtown East', *New York Magazine* (2005), www.nymag.com.

64 Sedo, 'Dead-Stock Boards', p. 276.

65 Fran Tonkiss, *Space, the City and Social Theory* (Cambridge: Polity, 2005), p. 14.

66 Yochim, *Skate Life*, p. 21.

67 *Who Cares: the Duane Peters Story* (dir. John Lucero, 2005).

68 Judith Butler, *Gender Trouble* (London: Routledge, 1990), p. 24.

69 Raewyn Connell, *Masculinities* (Cambridge: Polity, second edition, 2005); and Brayton, 'Black-Lash', pp. 356–72.

70 Asphalt advertisement, *Thrasher*, n.405 (April 2014), pp. 42–3.

71 Brian Brannon, 'Working the Street Beat', *Thrasher*, v.6 n.2 (February 1986), p. 56.

72 'Vancouver Contest', *Big Brother*, n.17 (undated, ca. Summer 1995), np.

73 Becky Beal, 'The Subculture of Skateboarding: Beyond Social Resistance' (EdD thesis, University of Northern Colorado, 1992), p. 167; and Joe Brook, *15 Years of Gonz and Adidas* (dir. Juice Design, 2014), www.youtube.com/watch?v=i67Xbvc8IfM.

74 Marcia Clemmit, 'Extreme Sports: Are They Too Dangerous?', *CQ Researcher Blog* (3 April 2009), www.cqresearcherblog.blogspot.co.uk; and Charles Hackenheimer, 'Risk-Taking Behavior of Skateboarders and Traditional Sport Participants in Students Ages 13-16 Years' (MSc Sports Education Leadership dissertation, University of Nevada, 2007), p. 33.

75 Mackenzie Eisenhour, 'Flesh Wounds', *SkateBoarder*, v.10 n.9 (August 2001), p. 62.

76 Jake Phelps, (ed.), *Skate and Destroy* (New York: Universe, 2006), p. 238–9.

77 *Thrasher, Maximum Rad* (New York: Universe, 2012), np.

78 Natalie Porter, 'Female Skateboarders and their Negotiation of Space and Identity' (PhD thesis, Concordia University, 2003), p. 42.

79 Andy Roy, 'Raney Beres', *Thrasher* (26 May 2016), www.*Thrasher*magazine.com.

80 Chops, 'The Chrome Ball Incident for ABD #1: Jeremy Wray', www.alreadybeendone.com.

81 Mortimer, *Stalefish*, p. 100.

82 Andrew Norton, 'The Photographer Series: Ryan Allan' (2013), www.vimeo.com/49205150.

83 Templeton Elliot, 'The Most Dangerous Tricks Ever Done', *Ride* (11 November 2014), www.theridechannel.com.

84 'Jaws vs. the Lyon 25' (2016), www.youtube.com/watch?v=4GFIXrybfKg; and B. David Zarley, 'Jaws vs. the Lyon 25', *Vice Sports* (19 February 2016), www.sports.vice.com.

85 Alva, advertisement, *Best of Thrasher*, v.1 n.1 (Winter 1988), p. 11.; and Brer Mortimer, 'Stacy Peralta', *TransWorld Skateboarding*, v.15 n.11 (November 1997), p. 90.

86 Mackenzie Eisenhour, 'Alva Posse Chronicles 1985-1989', *SkateBoarder*, v.11 n.10 (August 2002), pp. 82–7.

87 *All This Mayhem* (dir. Eddie Martin, 2014); Jake Anderson, *Relapse* (Dublin, Ohio: Coventry House, 2014); Louison, *Impossible*, p. 122; 'Skateboarder Gets 6 Years in Son's Killing', *Los Angeles Times* (14 January 2006), www.articles.latimes.com; Christian Hosoi and Chris Ahrens, *Hosoi* (New York: HarperOne, 2012); *D.O.P.E. (Death or Prison Eventually* (dir. Chris Ahrens, 2008); www.jeremywalker.com; Harms and Smith, *Skateboarder's Journal*, p. 233; Eric Hendrikx, 'Andrew Reynolds', *Rolling Stone* (9 November 2016), www.rollingstone.com; Browne, 'Dogtown East'; Sean Mortimer, 'How Skateboarding Shaped Matt Hensley's Life', *Ride* (30 January 2015), www.theridechannel.com; and Brandon Novak with Joseph Frantz, *Dreamseller* (New York: Citadel Press, 2008).

88 Hamm, *Scarred*, pp. 88–9; and Jonathan Smith, 'Maybe We Shouldn't Be So Quick to Idolise a

Gay-Bashing Skateboarder', *Vice*, (19 August 2014), www.vice.com.

89 'Bringing Back Kryptonics. Episode #6', www.kryptonics.com; and Jocko Weyland, *The Answer Is Never* (London: Century, 2002), pp. 68–9.

90 www.mikevallely.com; and Hunter Charlton, 'Lizard King Wants to Keep Skating Forever', *Vice* (17 July 2014), www.vice.com.

91 Beal, 'Alternative Masculinity', pp. 204–20.

92 Louison, *Impossible*, pp. 18–19.

93 Mike Sinclair, 'Auby Taylor Xposed' (5 December 2012), www.xgames.espn.go.com; *Epicly Later'd*, 'The Madness of Andrew Reynolds' (2012), www.youtube.com/watch?v=sF_ApPgZCmc; 'Skateboarding Is Therapy for Billy Rohan', *Vice*, (June 2016), www.vice.com; Rhino, 'Steven "Lefty" Breeding', *Thrasher*, n.430 (May 2016), pp. 124–5; 'A Pro Skateboarder with No Legs' (2015), www.youtube.com/watch?v=qGJdY5yV-KM; Louison, *Impossible*, p. 25; and *Stoked* (dir. Helen Stickler, 2002).

94 Balma, *Tracker*, p. 110; Kevin, 'Monty Nolder 1986 Pro Spot Light', *Skately* (29 November 2013), www.skately.com; and Mario Solis, 'Deaf Professional Skateboarder Aims to Inspire Others', *NBC Los Angeles* (22 August 2015), www.nbclosangeles.com.

95 www.crutchdoc.com; www.aaronfotheringham.com.

96 Sarah Carty, 'Meet the Man Born with Spina Bifida', *Daily Mail* (2 July 2015), www.dailymail.co.uk; 'For All The Good Times – an Army Veteran's Return to Skateboarding' (2015), www.youtube.com/watch?v=Wr6DhLKYol4; Jack Blocker, 'Meet the One-Legged Skateboarder who Can Seriously Shred', *Metro* (26 October 2014), www.metro.co.uk; 'Kanya Sesser Skates Without Legs', *TransWorld Skateboarding* (24 September 2015), www.skateboarding.transworld.net; and Lisa Dowd, 'No Legs But Rosie Can Still Skateboard', *Sky News* (3 January 2015), www.news.sky.com.

97 Blind Skateboarder Launches Video', *CBC News* (20 May 2015), www.cbc.ca; Ryan Brower, 'Skateboarder Dan Mancina Talks About Being Blind and Still Skating', *Grind TV* (23 March 2017), www.grindtv.com; Chase Scheinbaum, 'This Spanish Skateboarder Rips. He's Also Blind', *The Inertia* (22 December 2016), www.theinertia.com; 'This Blind American Skateboarder Is Riding High', *Star 2* (25 February 2017), www.star2.com; and Tyrone Marshall, 'Man Who Broke His Back Learns How to Ride a Skateboard on His Wheelchair', *Daily Mirror* (21 August 2014), www.mirror.co.uk.

98 Ben Falconer, 'Skatepark Has No Barriers to Disability', Stroud Life (25 September 2015), www.stroudlife.co.uk; B.R. Thomas, M. Lafasakis and V. Spector, 'Using Behavioral Skills Training to Teach Skateboarding Skills to a Child with Autism Spectrum Disorder', *Journal of Autism and Developmental Disorders* (2016); and Paula Ebben, 'Skateboard Therapy Helps Whitman Boy Soar', WBZ-TV (10 June 2015), www.boston.cbslocal.com.

99 Warren Bolster, 'Gregg Weaver', *SkateBoarder*, v.2 n.6 (August 1976), pp. 40–7; and Tony Hawk with Sean Mortimer, *Hawk: Occupation Skateboarder* (London: ReganBooks, 2000), p. 75.

100 Macdonald, *Dropping In*, pp. 19, 41–2, 68-70.

101 Pete Davidson, *Reforming a Counter Culture* (Charleston: BookSurge, second edition, 2009); and Yochim, *Skate Life*, pp. 89–110.

102 Becky Beal and Lisa Weidman, 'Authenticity in the Skateboard World', Robert Rinehart and Synthia Sydnor, (eds) *To the Extreme* (New York: SUNY Press, 2003), p. 342.

103 Judith A. Johns, 'The Relationship between Involvement in Unstructured Unsupervised Leisure and Substance Use in a Cohort of Adolescent Male Skateboarders' (PhD thesis, Kent State University, 2011); and Israel Márquez and Ruben Diez García, 'La Cultura Skate en las Sociedades Contemporáneas', *EMPIRIA*, n.30 (2015), pp. 133–58.

104 Holly Thorpe, *Snowboarding Bodies in Theory and Practice* (Houndmills: Palgrave Macmillan, 2011), pp. 169–91.

105 Patrick Welch, 'Gay Skaters: the Last Taboo', *Huck* (5 September 2011), www.huckmagazine.com.

106 Plan B, advertisement, *Thrasher*, v.3 n.5 (May 1992), p. 13; and Nicholas Nolan, 'The Ins and Outs of Skateboarding and Transgression in Public Space in Newcastle, Australia', *Australian Geographer*, v.34 n.3 (2003), p. 325.

107 Hawk, *Hawk*, pp. 82–4.

108 Greg Hernandez, 'Skateboard Legend Tony Hawk Is Speaking Out in Favor of Gay Marriage', *Gay Star News* (31 July 2014), www.gaystarnews.com.

109 'Brian Anderson on Being a Gay Professional Skateboarder', *Vice Sports* (27 September 2016), www.sports.vice.com; and Welch, 'Gay Skaters'.

110 Indigo Willing and Scott Shearer, 'Skateboarding Activism', Kara-Jane Lombard, (ed.), *Skateboarding* (Abingdon: Routledge, 2016), pp. 44–56.

111 'The Insider Scoop with Rob Brink', *Jenkem* (24 January 2012), www.jenkemmag.com; Stefan Schwinghammer, 'No Homo', *Monster Skateboard*, n.334 (June 2014), pp. 66–71; Ian Michna, 'An Interview With Skateboarding's Gayest Photographer, Sam McGuire', *Jenkem* (17 June 2014), www.jenkemmag.com; and Sam McGuire, 'Is Skateboarding Ready to Openly Embrace a Transgender Skater?', *Jenkem* (18 March 2013), www.jenkemmag.com.

112 Nick Schager, 'Dragonslayer', *Slant* (7 November 2011), www.slantmagazine.com.

113 Séan Kirkegaard, 'The XXX Files', *The Guardian*, 'Education' section (24 June 1997), p. iv; and J. Patrick Williams and Heith Copes, 'How Edge Are You? Constructing Authentic Identities and Subcultural Boundaries in Straightedge Internet Forums', *Symbolic Interaction*, v.28 n.1 (2005), p. 69.

114 Lance Mountain, interview, *Thrasher*, v.3 n.1 (January 1983), p. 28.

115 Tait Colberg, *The Skateboarding Art* (Lulu, 2012), p. 77; and 'Steve Caballero', *TransWorld Skateboarding*, 25th anniversary issue (2007), p. 36.

116 David Browne, *Amped* (London: Bloomsbury, 2004), pp. 87–8; and Hamm, *Scarred for Life*, pp. 191–4.

117 Hamm, *Scarred for Life*, p. 195.

118 'Christian Hosoi, Outreach Pastor', www.mysanctuarychurch.com; and Hosoi and Ahrens, *Hosoi*, pp. 225–304.

119 Gordon & Smith, *Gordon & Smith Skateboard Team Book*, pp. 56–76; and Stephen Baldwin, *Livin It* (Nashville: B&H, 2006), p. 37.

120 Alice Truong, 'An 8-Year-Old Skateboarder Became the Youngest Girl to Compete Against Adults at Vans' Pro-Competition', *Quartz* (17 September 2016), www.qz.com; 'Watch 8-Year-Old Skater Crush This 16-Step Rail at Hollywood High School' (1 June 2017), www.theinertia.com; 'CJ Collins – CJ Sucks!!!' (2013), www.youtube.com/watch?v=4hUNHk9e4ls; '9 Year Old Girl Lands 540!' (2014), www.youtube.com/watch?v=mD_yjW64buU; Niall Neeson, 'Red Bull Skate Generation 2014' (4 April 2014), www.redbull.com; 'Nyjah Huston's Growing Pains – ESPN X Games' (2013), www.youtube.com/watch?v=dWekjaR0PMw; 'Tom Schaar Stomps First-Ever Skateboarding 1080' (2012), www.youtube.com/watch?v=tbjzZHuGTng; and '12 Year Old Alana Smith Makes History at X Games Barcelona' (2013), www.youtube.com/watch?v=5KdhFyBgXSk.

121 Patsy Eubanks Owens, 'Recreation and Restrictions: Community Skateboard Parks in the United States', *Urban Geography*, v.22 n.8 (2001), p. 790; Lucy Holden, 'Skate Ramps Buzz with Old City Rollers', *The Times* (23 August 2014), www.thetimes.co.uk; and Kate Youde, 'Skateboarding for Adults', *Independent* (7 September 2014), www.independent.co.uk.

122 Vincent Aviani, 'Skateboarding from Fad to Profit', *Liberty Voice* (15 June 2014), www.guardianlv.com.

123 *TransWorld*, 'State of Skate', p. 8.

124 'The Tired Video' (2014), www.youtube.com/watch?v=5BRZoqUTD5M.

125 L. Ruocco, letter, *Skateboard!*, n.4 (December 1977), p. 35.

126 Peralta, interview, *Thrasher*, p. 17.

127 *Oldog* (dir. Tyrell Mills, 2014).

128 'Neal Unger – 60 Year Old Skateboarder' (2014), www.youtube.com/watch?v=lM4FQ_FqEhQ; and Neal A. Unger and Mary Earhart, *Dude Logic* (eBook/Kindle, 2013).

129 Julien Laurent, *Le Skateboard* (Paris: L'Harmattan, 2012); and Paul O'Connor, 'Beyond the Youth Culture: Understanding Middle Aged Skateboarders through Temporal Capital' (Lingnan University Staff Publication, 2017).

130 Damien Cave, 'Dogtown USA', *New York Times* (12 June 2005), www.nytimes.com.

131 Meany, 'The XX Factor', *Skateboard!* (second series), n.6 (November 1989), p. 14; and Nyjah Huston, interview, *Thrasher* (July 2013), pp. 165–77.

132 *Underexposed* (dir. Amelia Brodka and Brian Lynch, 2013).

133 Shauna Pomerantz, Dawn H. Currie and Deirdre A. Kelly, 'Sk8er Girls: Skateboarders, Girlhood and Feminism in Motion', *Women's Studies International Forum*, v.27 n.5–6 (2004), p. 550; Deirdre M. Kelly, Shauna Pomerantz and Dawn Currie, 'Skater Girlhood and Emphasized Femininity', *Gender and Education*, v.17 n.3 (2005), p. 239; and Deirdre M. Kelly, Shauna Pomerantz and Dawn H. Currie, 'You Can Break So Many More Rules', Giardina and Donnelly, *Youth Culture and Sport*, p. 122.

134 Katherine Timpf, 'Feminists Blame the Patriarchy for Not Being Able to Skateboard', *National Review Online* (5 September 2015), www.nationalreview.com; and Noah Remnick, 'Sisterhood of the Skateboard', *New York Times* (29 July 2016), www.nytimes.com.

135 Beal, 'Alternative Masculinity', pp. 204–20; and Pomerantz, Currie and Kelly, 'Sk8er Girls', p. 550.

136 Jasmine Y. Ma and Charles Munter, 'The Spatial Production of Learning Opportunities in Skateboard Parks', *Mind, Culture and Activity*, v.21 n.3 (2014), pp. 238–58; and *Coping Mechanism* (dir. Phil Evans, 2014).

137 Powell-Peralta, advertisement, *Thrasher*, v.8 n.3 (March 1988), p. 110.

138 Holly Thorpe, 'Media Representations of Women in Actions Sports: More Than "Sexy Bad Girls" on Boards', Clarissa Smith, Feona Attwood and Brian McNair, (eds), *The Routledge Companion to Media, Sex and Sexuality* (Abingdon: Routledge, 2017), chapter 26.

139 Sean Cliver, (ed.), *Jackass* (New York: MTV Press, 2010), pp. 5–35, *passim*; Sean Cliver and Dave Carnie, (eds), *Shit: the Big Brother Book* (Berkeley: Gingko Press, 2016); and *Big Brother*, n.19 (undated, ca. late 1995), np.

140 Tara Aquino, 'The Ten Sexiest Female Skateboarders', *Complex Sports* (21 June 2012), www.complex.com.

141 Leonard, 'White Extreme', p. 93.

142 Michele Donnelly, '"Take the Slam and Get Back Up": Hardcore Candy and the Politics of Representation in Girl's and Women's Skateboarding and Snowboarding on Television', Giardina and Donnelly, *Youth Culture and Sport*, pp. 127–43; and Michele Donnelly, 'Extreme Sports Lite? Representations of Women's Skateboarding and Snowboarding on Television' (MA dissertation, Queen's University, Kingston, 2004).

143 Becky Beal, 'Skateboarding: an Alternative to Mainstreams Sports', J. Croakley and P. Donnelly, (eds), *Inside Sport* (London: Routledge, 1999), p. 144; and Tyler Dupont, 'From Core to Consumer: the Informal Hierarchy of the Skateboard Scene', *Journal of Contemporary Ethnography*, v.43 n.5 (2014), pp. 556–81.

144 Steph MacKay, 'Spreading the Skirtboarder Stoke: Reflexively Blogging Fluid Femininities and Constructing New Female Skateboarding Identities', Lombard, *Skateboarding*, p. 121; and Beal and Wilson, 'Chicks Dig Scars', pp. 31–54.

145 Patty Segovia and Rebecca Heller, *Skater Girl* (Berkeley: Ulysses, 2007), p. 117; and Natalie Porter, *The History of Women in Skateboarding* (eBook/Kindle, 2014), loc. 63.

146 Becky Beal, *Skateboarding* (Santa Barbara: Greenwood, 2013), pp. 10–11, 61–2; Harms and Smith, *Skateboarder's Journal*, pp. 323–4; and 'Profile: Pat McGee', *SkateBoarder*, v.1 n.4 (October 1965), pp. 10–13.

147 Pennell, Skateboarding, p. 1; and Cindy Berryman, 'Let's Hear It for the Ladies', SkateBoarder, v.2 n.6 (August 1976), pp. 58–63.

148 LaVada Weir, Advanced Skateboarding (New York: Julian Messner, 1979).

149 Snyder, Secret History, p. 35.

150 'Who's Hot! Brenda Devine', SkateBoarder, v.6 n.6 (January 1980), pp. 68–9; 'Who's Hot! Ellen Berryman', pp. 90–1; Ellen O'Neal, interview, SkateBoarder, v.4 n.6 (January 1978), pp. 64–73; Laura Thornhill and Ellen O'Neal, interview, Skateboard!, n.2 (October 1977), pp. 24–7; Sue Hazel, interview, Skateboard! (second series), n.6 (November 1989), pp. 20–1; 'Starshot: Sheenagh Burdell', Skateboard!, n.16 (December 1978), p. 54; 'Profile: Patti Hoffman', SkateBoarder, v.6 n.12 (July 1980), pp. 49–52; Vicki Vickers, interview, Skateboarder, v.6 n.5 (December 1979), pp. 46–51; 'Profile: Gale Webb', SkateBoarder, v.6 n.11 (June 1980), pp. 64–5; Segovia and Heller, Skater Girl, pp. 118–19; and Porter, History of Women in Skateboarding, locs. 100 and 158.

151 Signal Hill Speed Run (dir. Mike Horelick and Jon Carnoy, 2014).

152 O'Neal, interview, SkateBoarder, pp. 64–73.

153 Porter, History of Women in Skateboarding, loc. 138; Berryman, 'Let's Hear it for the Ladies', pp. 58–63.

154 Stan Sharp, 'Profile: a Look at Kim Cespedes', Skateboard World, v.1 n.2 (August 1977), pp. 80–5; and Warren Bolster, 'SkateBoarder Interview: Laura Thornhill', SkateBoarder, v.3 n.5 (June 1977), pp. 50–7.

155 ACS, advertisement, SkateBoarder, v.5 n.1 (August 1978), p. 46–7.

156 Porter, History of Women in Skateboarding, loc. 256; Sue Hazel and Michelle Picktin, interviews, Skateboard! (second series), n.6 (November 1989), pp. 20–3; Big Brother, n.27 (August 1997), pp. 62–9; and Spirit of the Blitz (dir. Dave Evans, 1991).

157 Powell-Peralta, advertisement, TransWorld Skateboarding, v.6 n.1 (February 1988), p. 26; and Bonnie Blouin, 'Sugar and Spice?', Thrasher, v.6 n.4 (April 1986), pp. 56–61.

158 Segovia and Heller, Skater Girl, pp. 121–2.

159 Porter, History of Women in Skateboarding, loc. 317; and Thrasher, n.158 (April 1994), front cover.

160 Slap, v.5 n.2 (February 1996), pp. 20, 24; and Porter, History of Women in Skateboarding, locs. 433–453.

161 'Thrasher Magazine Market Profile', www.prm.nau.edu; and Segovia and Heller, Skater Girl, p. 125.

162 Porter, History of Women in Skateboarding, locs. 352 and 594–615.

163 Hamm, Scarred for Life, p. 155.

164 Clyde Singleton, 'Elissa Steamer', Big Brother, n.27 (August 1997), np; Porter, History of Women in Skateboarding, locs. 373–413; and Bootleg Skateboard Co., advertisement, Thrasher, n.263 (December 2002), back cover.

165 Ryan Gray, '"Crashing The Boys Club" – Elissa Steamer interview', Sidewalk (11 June 2012) www.sidewalkmag.com.

166 Beal and Wilson, 'Chicks Dig Scars', p. 51.

167 Segovia and Heller, Skater Girl, pp. 123, 136; and Alex Striler, X Play Nation (San Diego: Striler Publishing, 2011), p. 258.

168 Porter, 'Female Skateboarders', pp. 64–5.

169 Mirin Fader, 'Voices of Exposure Skate 2016', ESPNW (17 November 2016), www.espn.com.

170 Atencio, Beal and Wilson, 'Distinction of Risk', pp. 3–20.

171 Segovia and Heller, Skater Girl, p. 123; and Striler, X Play Nation, p. 50.

172 Beal, Skateboarding, p. 87.

173 Dani Abulhawa, 'Female Skateboarding: Re-Writing Gender', Platform, v.3 n.1 (2008), pp. 56–72.

174 Douglas Booth, (ed.), Berkshire Encyclopedia of Extreme Sports (Great Barrington: Berkshire, 2007), p. 106.

175 Atencio, Beal and Wilson, 'Distinction of Risk', p. 2.

176 Graham L. Bradley, 'Skate Parks as a Context for Adolescent Development', Journal of Adolescent Research, v.25 n.2 (2010), p. 297.

177 'Minna Stess: Not Your Typical 8 Year Old Girl – Woodward West' (2014), www.youtube.com/watch?v=xNn0XIWfa2k.

178 Corinne Redfern, '10 Reasons to Get into Skateboarding as An Adult', Marie Claire (13 August 2015), www.marieclaire.co.uk.

179 www.girlsskatenetwork.com; www.facebook.com/girlsskatenetwork; www.skateboardmoms.wordpress.com; www.girlsriders.org; www.actionsportsalliance.com; and Striler, X Play Nation, pp. 257–9.

180 www.skirtboarders.com.

181 MacKay, 'Skirtboarder Stoke', pp. 121–35; Steph MacKay, 'Skirtboarder Net-a-Narratives: a Socio-Cultural Analysis of a Women's Skateboarding Blog' (PhD thesis, University of Ottawa, 2012); Steph MacKay and Christine Dallaire, 'Skirtboarder Net-a-Narratives: Young Women Creating Their Own Skateboarding (Re) Presentations', International Review for the Sociology of Sport, v.48 n.2 (2013), pp. 171–95; Steph Mackay and Christine Dallaire, 'Skirtboarders.com: Skateboarding Women and Self-Formation as Ethical Subjects', Sociology of Sport Journal, v.30 n.2 (2013), pp. 173–96; and Steph Mackay and Christine Dallaire, 'Skateboarding Women: Building Collective Identity in Cyberspace', Journal of Sport & Social Issues, v.38 n.548 (2014), pp. 548–66.

182 Kelly, Pomerantz and Currie, 'You Can Break', pp. 113–25; and Kelly, Pomerantz and Currie, 'Skater Girlhood', pp. 229–48.

183 Underexposed; and Porter, 'Female Skateboarders', p. 50.

184 Åsa Bäckström, 'Gender Manoeuvring in Swedish Skateboarding: Negotiations of Femininities and the Hierarchical Gender Structure', Young, v.21 n.1 (2013), pp. 29–53; and Alana Young and Christine Dallaire, 'Beware*#! Sk8 at Your Own Risk', Atkinson and Young, Tribal Play, pp. 235–54.

185 Porter, History of Women in Skateboarding, loc. 473.

186 www.ameliabrodka.com; www.facebook.com/proyectochicarider; www.girlskateuk.com; www.facebook.com/girlsskateoz; girlsskatenetwork.com; and www.girlisnota4letterword.com.

187 Hannah Bailey, 'Girls' Skateboarding in the UK Is Popping Off: the

Evolution of a Subculture', *Huck* (12 May 2015), www.huckmagazine. com; *Coping Mechanism*; and Jessica Weiss, 'Cuba's Female Skaters Ride for a More Open Future on the Island', *Miami New Times* (9 February 2016), www.miaminewtimes.com.

188 Matthew Atencio and Becky Beal, 'The "Legitimate" Skateboarder: Politics of Private-Public Skateboarding Spaces', Lombard, *Skateboarding*, pp. 115–17.

189 Remnick, 'Sisterhood of the Skateboard'.

190 *TransWorld*, 'State of Skate', p. 49.

191 Bones, advertisement, *Thrasher*, n.437 (December 2016), pp. 86–7.

192 Hannah Bailey, 'This Pro Skateboarder Wants the Skate Industry's Views on Women to 180', *Broadly* (17 December 2015), www. broadly.vice.com.

193 Atencio, Beal and Wilson, 'Distinction of Risk', p. 18.

194 *Coping Mechanism*.

195 Porter, *History of Women in Skateboarding*, loc. 756.

196 Hamm, *Scarred for Life*, p. 195.

197 Cave, 'Dogtown USA'.

198 Sedo, 'Dead-Stock Boards', p. 264.

199 He Bolin, 'Skateboarding Out of the Shadows', *China Daily* (22 June 2009), www.chinadaily.com.

200 Neil Howe and William Strauss, *Millennials Rising* (New York: Vintage Books, 2000), p. 4; and Beal and Wilson, 'Chicks Dig Scars', p. 42.

201 'Nyjah Huston's Growing Pains – ESPN X Games' (2013), www.youtube.com/ watch?v=dWekjaR0PMw.

202 Leandro Wille Pereira, João Egdoberto Siqueira and Adriana Maria Wan Stadnik, 'Motivational Factors for Skateboard Adhesion', *International Journal of Science Culture and Sport*, v.2 n.3 (2014), pp. 69–78.

203 Michael J. Lorr, 'Skateboarding as a Technology of the Collective: Kona Skatepark, Jacksonville, Florida, USA', Lombard, *Skateboarding*, p. 146.

204 *TransWorld Skateboarding* (Winter 2002) and v.21 n.4 (April 2003), p. 144.

205 Adam Oxford, 'Why Has Standard Bank Built a Skate Park in its Basement?', *HTXT Africa* (28 January 2015), www.htxt.co.za; and Sara Ashley O'Brien, 'Forget Six Figures. We Skateboard at Lunch', *KSPR 33* (4 August 2014), www.kspr.com.

206 'Insider Scoop with Rob Brink'.

207 Belinda Wheaton, 'Introduction: Mapping the Lifestyle Sport-Scape', Wheaton, *Understanding Lifestyle Sports*, pp. 1–28.

208 Lorr, 'Skateboarding as a Technology', p. 148; and Michael J. Lorr, 'Skateboarding and the X Gamer Phenomenon: a Case of Subcultural Cooptation', *Humanity & Society*, v.29 n.2 (2005), pp. 140–7.

209 Doug Padilla, 'Tyler Saladino's Connection to the Skateboarding World', *ESPN* (17 September 2015), www.espn.go.com.

210 Henry A. Giroux, *Stealing Innocence* (New York: St. Martin's Press, 2000), p. 13.

211 Sander Hölsgens, 'A Phenomenology of Skateboarding in Seoul, S. Korea: Experiential and Filmic Observations' (PhD thesis, University College London, Bartlett School of Architecture, 2018); and Robert Rinehart, 'Exploiting a New Generation: Corporate Branding and the Co-optation of Action Sport', Giardina and Donnelly, *Youth Culture and Sport*, p. 74.

212 Sarah Thornton, *Club Cultures* (Cambridge: Polity, 1995), p. 166.

213 Dave Duncan, 'Interview with Christian Hosoi', *Juice* (1 June 2007), www.juicemagazine.com.

214 *Off Camera with Sam Jones: Episode 6 with Tony Hawk* (Sam Jones, 2013), www.offcamera.com.

Chapter 4 Affiliate Worlds

1 Hebdige, *Subculture*, p. 96.

2 Yochim, *Skate Life*, p. 18.

3 Donald Meckiffe, 'Mainstreams and Subcultures: the Hidden Histories of Female Bodybuilding, Muhammad Ali, Skateboarding and Black Divas' (PhD thesis, University of Wisconsin, 2003), p. 278.

4 Dinces, 'Flexible Opposition', pp. 1512–35; and Beal and Wilson, 'Chicks Dig Scars', pp. 32–3.

5 Paul O'Connor, 'Skateboard Philanthropy: Inclusion and Prefigurative Politics', Lombard, *Skateboarding*, p. 30.

6 Steve Olson, 'Bob Biniak Interview', *Juice* (1 February 2001), www. juicemagazine.com.

7 Browne, *Amped*, p. 75.

8 Hosoi and Ahrens, *Hosoi*, pp. 77, 152.

9 Kara-Jane Lombard, 'Skate and Create/Skate and Destroy: the Commercial and Governmental Incorporation of Skateboarding', *Continuum*, v.24 n.4 (2010), p. 480.

10 *The Ultimate Flex Machine* (dir. Jason Cameron, 1975); Snyder, *Secret History*, p. 87; and Brian Gillogly, 'Russ Howell', *SkateBoarder*, v.2 n.4 (April 1976), p. 44.

11 Yochim, *Skate Life*, p. 26.

12 Snyder, *Secret History*, p. 407.

13 Snyder, *Secret History*, pp. 333–4.

14 Hosoi and Ahrens, *Hosoi*, pp. 95–9, 118–43, 148, 165.

15 Hawk, *Hawk*, pp. 77, 147, 174–5, 188–91, 225; and Lea Goldman, 'From Ramp to Riches', *Forbes* (5 July 2004), www.forbes.com.

16 Tim Layden, 'What Is This 34-Year-Old Man Doing On A Skateboard?', *Sports Illustrated* (10 June 2002); and Browne, *Amped*, p. 79.

17 Beal, *Skateboarding*, pp. 88–9; Louison, *Impossible*, p. 2; and Macdonald, *Dropping In*, pp. 128–35.

18 Browne, *Amped*, pp. 72–3, 107, 112, 191.

19 Louison, *Impossible*, p. 229.

20 Browne, *Amped*, pp. 193–9.

21 Dinces, 'Flexible Opposition', pp. 1525–6.

22 Hannah Ustel, '10 Brands That Have Defined Skateboarding' (2013), www. mpora.com.

23 Maria Hampton, 'How Nike Conquered Skateboard Culture', *Adbusters* (13 July 2006), www. adbusters.org; Jake Woolf, 'Lev Tanju on Palace Skateboards x Adidas', *GQ* (29 September 2014), www. gq.com; Alastair McLellan, *Palace* (London: Idea, 2016); and 'Lev talks Palace', *Grey* (9 February 2011), www. greyskatemag.com.

24 Ocean Howell, 'Extreme Market Research: Tales from the Underbelly of Skater-Cool', *Topic Magazine* (2004), www.webdelsol.com; Lurp Lurpington, 'How Corporations Are Changing Skateboarding and Why

It Matters', *Jenkem* (2012), www.
jenkemmag.com; and Hampton,
'How Nike Conquered'.

25   Josh Dean, 'Skateboarder Bob
Burnquist's Far-out Dreams', *Outside*
(29 July 2009), www.outsideonline.
com.

26   Greg Beato, 'The Lords of Dogtown',
Arielle Greenberg, (ed.), *Youth
Subcultures* (New York: Pearson
Longman, 2007), pp. 21–36; and *Tic
Tac 2 Heelflip*.

27   Anderson, *Relapse*, pp. 1–32; and
Matt Dawson, *Sponsored Life* (San
Juan Capistrano: Luma Publications,
2008).

28   Tom Peacock, *Skateboarding*
(Montreal: OverTime Books, 2006),
pp. 137–8.

29   Tony Alva, 'Dog Tails', *Thrasher*
(October 1995), www.angelfire.com;
Skatevisions (dir. Don Hoffman,
1984); and *Stoked*.

30   Hawk, *Hawk*, p. 256.

31   *Bones Brigade: an Autobiography* (dir.
Stacy Peralta, 2012); and *Dogtown
and Z-Boys* (dir. Stacy Peralta, 2001).

32   O'Neal, interview, *SkateBoarder*,
pp. 70–2; Bob Biniak, interview,
SkateBoarder, v.4 n.5 (December
1977), p. 70; Brian Gillogly, 'The Pepsi
Team', *SkateBoarder*, v.4 n.3 (October
1977), pp. 84-93; and Marc Sinclair
and Jeremy Henderson, interview,
SkateBoarder, v.6 n.2 (September
1979), p. 35.

33   Warren Bolster, '*SkateBoarder*
Interview: Henry Hester',
SkateBoarder, v.3 n.6 (July 1977), pp.
52–59; Brooke, *Concrete Wave*, p. 83;
and Harms and Smith, *Skateboarder's
Journal*, p. 227.

34   George Powell, 'Alan Gelfand
Interview', *Powell Skateboards Team
Zine* (Spring 1999); and Snyder, *Secret
History*, pp. 538–64.

35   Snyder, *Secret History*, p. 433.

36   Åsa Bäckström, 'Knowing and
Teaching Kinaesthetic Experience
in Skateboarding', *Sport, Education
and Society*, v.19 n.6 (2014), pp.
752–72; and Signe Højbjerre Larsen,
'What Can the Parkour Craftsmen
Tell Us About Bodily Expertise and
Skilled Movement?', *Sport, Ethics
and Philosophy*, v.10 n.3 (2016), pp.
295–309.

37   Phelps, *Skate and Destroy*, p. 62; and

Balma, *Tracker*, p. 161.

38   Bill Schaffer, 'No One Standing Above
You: Rodney Mullen and the Ethics of
Innovation', Lombard, *Skateboarding*,
pp. 17–29; Louison, *Impossible*, p. 39;
and Mullen, *Mutt*, pp. 54–77.

39   Macdonald, *Dropping In*, pp. 23,
30–3, 68–70, 120.

40   Louison, *Impossible*, p. 191; and
Doug Werner and Steve Badillo,
Skateboarding (San Diego: Tracks,
2002), pp. 18–21.

41   Snyder, *Secret History*, pp. 578–81.

42   Snyder, *Secret History*, pp. 674–5;
Art Brewer and C.R. Stecyk, *Bunker
Spreckels* (Los Angeles: Taschen,
2007), p. 7; and Glen E. Friedman, *My
Rules* (New York: Rizzoli, 2014), np.

43   Tony Hawk with Pat Hawk, *How Did I
Get Here?* (Hoboken: Wiley, 2010), p.
7; and Hawk, *Hawk, passim*.

44   Hawk, *How Did I Get Here?*, pp. 4,
60–1; and 'Tony Hawk: Who You
Callin' a Sell Out?', *The Berrics* (23
January 2015), www.theberrics.com.

45   Cave, 'Dogtown USA'.

46   Randolph Rubber Co., advertisement,
SkateBoarder, v.1 n.3 (August
1965), p. 3; Nash, 'The Official Nash
Skateboard Helmet', advertisement,
SkateBoarder, v.1 n.3 (August 1965),
p. 2; and Jantzen, advertisement,
SkateBoarder, v.1 n.4 (October 1965),
back cover.

47   Gabriel, 'Rolling Thunder', p. 76; K
Armen Keteyian, 'Chairman of the
Board', *Sports Illustrated*, v.65 n.23
(24 November 1986), p. 47; Barbara
Manning, 'Teenager Tony Hawk
Soars Above Everybody', *People
Weekly*, v.27 (23 March 1987), p. 49;
Jay Cocks, 'The Irresistible Air of
Grabbing Air', *Time*, v.131 (6 June
1988), p. 90; Marcus and Griggi,
Skateboard, pp. 121, 194; *Bones
Brigade: an Autobiography*; and
Cliver, *Disposable Skateboard Bible*,
p. 12.

48   Goldman, 'Ramp to Riches'; and
Stuntwood.

49   Sara Fruman, 'Iconix to Increase Zoo
York Ownership to 100%', *Transworld
Business* (27 July 2011), www.
business.transworld.net; and Jacob
Gallager, 'The New Board Meeting',
Wall Street Journal, 'Off Duty' section
(Saturday/Sunday 25–26 July 2015),
pp. D1–D2.

50   Gamescom, 'Tony Hawk's Pro Skater
5' factsheet, (2015).

51   Rinehart, 'Exploiting a New
Generation', p. 84.

52   Angela McRobbie, 'Second-Hand
Dresses and the Ragmarket', Gelder
and Thornton, *Subcultures Reader*,
pp. 191–99.

53   Browne, *Amped*, p. 114.

54   TransWorld, 'State of Skate', p. 12;
and Paul O'Connor, 'Skateboarding
Networks in East Asia: the View from
Hong Kong' (draft paper, 2017).

55   *Hill Street* (dir. J.J. Rolfe, 2014);
and Katie Roche, 'Meet Clive: the
Godfather of Irish Skateboarding' (13
December 2013), www.redbull.com.

56   Mullen, *Mutt*, pp. 32–3.

57   Dupont, 'From Core to Consumer',
pp. 556–81.

58   TransWorld, 'State of Skate', pp. 3, 30,
41, 52.

59   Brandon Gomez, 'How Did Nike Get
the Swoosh into Skateboarding?' (MA
Media Studies dissertation, Syracuse
University, 2012), pp. 1, 57; and
Hampton, 'How Nike Conquered'.

60   hoorayforthecornet, 'Re: Palace
welcome Shawn Powers' (3 March
2016), www.forums.sidewalkmag.
com.

61   Beato, 'Lords of Dogtown', p. 32; Alva,
interview, *Thrasher*, p. 33.

62   Chris Nieratko, 'Tommy Guerrero',
Vice (17 July 2014), www.vice.com.

63   'Interview with Magenta Skateboards
Founder & Brand Manager:
Vivien Feil', www.triadskate.com
(2 March 2014); and Benjamin
Deberdt, 'Meeting Vivien Fell!',
www.liveskateboardmedia.com (11
January 2013).

64   Robynne Raye and Michael
Strassburger, *Inside the World of
Board Graphics* (Beverly: Rockport,
2011), pp. 50–2.

65   'Hell On Wheels', *Bay Guardian*, San
Francisco (May 1994).

66   Michel Foucault, *Discipline and
Punish* (London: Allen Lane, 1977).

67   Mullen, *Mutt*, p. 184; James Lee,
'Uncovering the Mythical Powell
Rider Guide from the 80's', *Jenkem*
(31 May 2017), www.jenkemmag.
com; Bones Brigade, 'Operation
Motherhood Field Manual' (Powell-
Peralta Skateboards, *Intelligence
Report*, March 1989); and *The Man*

Who Souled the World (dir. Mike Hill, 2007).

68 Steve Kane, 'ZonaSkane', *Skateboard!* (second series), n.45 (August 1990), p. 64.

69 Editorial, *Thrasher*, v.11 n.9 (September 1991), p. 4.

70 Mullen, *Mutt*, pp. 191, 208.

71 Jim Gray in Balma, *Tracker*, p. 137.

72 Ian Michna, 'The Stuff You Want to Know About: Jeremy Wray', *Jenkem* (28 December 2011), www.jenkemmag.com; Beal, *Skateboarding*, pp. xix, 33; 'Jeff Grosso's Loveletters to Skateboarding – the Freestyle Conspiracy' (2015), www.youtube.com/watch?v=JNFn2mPDhr4; and '30th Anniversary Interviews: Mike Vallely Part 1', *TransWorld Skateboarding*, www.skateboarding.transworld.net.

73 '10 Not-So-Great Things About Skateboarding in the Nineties'; and 'Postscript: Mike Daher', www.chromeballincident.blogspot.co.uk (28 November 2013).

74 'Hell On Wheels'; Garth Harris, 'The Belonging Paradox: the Belonging Experience of Committed Uncertain Members' (PhD thesis, Queen's University Kingston, 2011), p. 333; TransWorld, 'State of Skate', p. 16; and *Chlorine* (dir. Milan Spasic, 2003).

75 Paul Hochman, 'Street Lugers, Stunt Bikers, and Colgate-Palmolive!', *Forbes* (22 November 1999), www.archive.fortune.com.

76 Browne, *Amped*, pp. 176–88; and Yochim, *Skate Life*, p. 8.

77 Sean Mortimer, 'The Evolution of the Pro Skater's Job According to Lance Mountain', *Jenkem* (6 January 2016), www.jenkemmag.com.

78 Jürgen Blümlein and Dirk Vogel, *Skateboarding Is Not a Fashion* (Berkeley: Gingko Press, 2018); Louison, *Impossible*, p. 107; 'Mandatory Information', *TransWorld Skateboarding*, v.14 n.5 (May 1996), p. 46; and Brooke, *Concrete Wave*, pp. 124–5.

79 Blanche Clark, 'Globe International', *Herald Sun* (27 November 2015), www.heraldsun.com.au.

80 Alexis Castro, 'How Skaters Really Feel About Fashion's Appropriation of Their Culture', *Fashionista* (12 July 2016), www.fashionista.com.

81 Carlos Izan, 'Aspects of the Downhill Slide', *SkateBoarder*, v.2 n.2 (Fall 1975), p. 32.

82 Winston Tseng and Marc McKee, *Warning* (New York: Mark Batty, 2011), p. 96.

83 Browne, *Amped*, p. 105.

84 Doug Schneider, 'Skate Shoes', *SkateBoarder*, v.6 n.3, (October 1979), p. 21; Thomas Turner, 'Transformative Improvisation: the Creation of the Commercial Skateboard Shoe, 1960–1979', Lombard, *Skateboarding*, pp. 191–2; Sebastien Carayol, *Agents Provocateurs* (Berkeley: Gingko Press, 2014), pp. 188–91; and Mark Munson and Steve Cardwell, *Skateboard Stickers* (London: Laurence King, 2004), pp. 110–11.

85 Brian Slattery, 'Brand Management: DC Shoe Co USA' (May 2010); Quiksilver, 'Press Release: Quiksilver Reports Fiscal 2013 Full-Year, Fourth Quarter Financial Results' (12 December 2013), www.ir.quiksilver.com; and Blehm, *Agents of Change*, pp. 9–47.

86 Vans, advertisement, *SkateBoarder*, v.3 n.6 (July 1977), p. 135; Cody Bay, 'Cinemode: Fast Times at Ridgemont High', www.onthisdayinfashion.com (13 August 2010); Striler, *X Play Nation*, p. 76; 'Mandatory Information', p. 46; www.fundinguniverse.com; www.reporting.vfc.com; VF Corporation press release, 'VF Reports 2014 Fourth Quarter and Full Year Results', www.vfc.com; Browne, *Amped*, p. 9; and *TransWorld*, 'State of Skate', p. 3.

87 Turner, 'Transformative Improvisation', pp. 182–94.

88 Browne, *Amped*, p. 103; and Doug Palladini, *Vans* (New York: Harry N. Abrams, 2009), p. 6.

89 Browne, *Amped*, p. 173.

90 Chrysostomos Giannoulakis, 'A Framework for Marketing Implementation to Surfing, Skateboarding, and Snowboarding' (PhD thesis, University of Northern Colorado, 2008), pp. 89–91.

91 Steve Olson, 'Interview with Stacy Peralta', *Juice* (1 September 2001), www.juicemagazine.com; and Beal and Wilson, 'Chicks Dig Scars', p. 43.

92 Roy Christopher, *Follow for Now* (Seattle: Well-Red Bear, 2007), p. 274.

93 Lurpington, 'How Corporations'.

94 Wheaton and Beal, 'Keeping It Real', pp. 155–76.

95 Robert Rinehart, 'ESPN's X Games: Contests of Opposition, Resistance, Co-option, and Negotiation', Atkinson and Young, *Tribal Play*, p. 181.

96 Yochim, *Skate Life*, p. 14.

97 Browne, *Amped*, p. 174.

98 TransWorld, 'State of Skate', p. 19; and Denike, *Built to Grind*, pp. 73, 124, 148, 177, 272.

99 *SkateBoarder*, *Skateboard Scene*, *Skateboard!* and *Thrasher*, passim; Becky Beal, 'Disqualifying the Official: an Exploration of Social Resistance Through the Subculture of Skateboarding', *Sociology of Sport Journal*, v.12 n.3 (1995), p. 257; Thor Svenson, 'Foreword', Russ Howell, *Skateboard* (Sydney: Ure Smith, 1975); and Pennell, *Skateboarding*, p. 7.

100 *This Ain't California* (dir. Marten Persiel, 2013).

101 *Stuntwood*.

102 www.wcsk8.com; www.internationalskateboardingfederation.com; and Beal, *Skateboarding*, pp. 36–7.

103 'World Skateboarding Federation Sanctions 10 National Championships in Africa' (29 May 2016), www.marketwired.com.

104 Mikhail Batuev and Leigh Robinson, 'How Skateboarding Made It to the Olympics: an Institutional Perspective', *International Journal of Sport Management and Marketing* (2018).

105 Nancy Ray, 'Scouts to Save Skateboard Park', *Los Angeles Times* (27 October 1985), Metro section, p.1.

106 Beal, *Skateboarding*, pp. xix, 33; Marcus and Griggi, *Skateboard*, pp. 224–5; and Hamm, *Scarred*, pp. 46–7.

107 *Coping Mechanism*.

108 Stacy Peralta, 'Eurocana Summer Camp', *SkateBoarder's Action Now*, v.7 n.8 (March 1981), pp. 52–5; Snyder, *Secret History*, pp. 776–83, 794; and Hawk, *Hawk*, p. 108.

109 Beal, *Skateboarding*, pp. 39, 52; Hawk, *How Did I Get Here?*, p. 147; Striler, *X Play Nation*, p. 272; and Li, 'China's Skateboarding Youth Culture'.

110 www.woodwardwest.com.

111 Browne, *Amped*, pp. 125, 136–7, 144.

112 Browne, *Amped*, pp. 138–9; and 'Woodward Digital Media Camp', www.theberrics.com (9 September 2011).

113 Browne, *Amped*, p. 142.

114 Mortimer, *Stalefish*, p. 126; and Kevin Brooker, *Way Inside ESPN's X Games* (New York: Hyperion/ESPN Books, 1998), p. 32.

115 Snyder, *Secret History*, pp. 54–7.

116 Oldog; Snyder, *Secret History*, pp. 57, 66–8, 94–9; Bruce Channon, 'The Coca-Cola Skateboarding Contest', *SkateBoarder*, v.2 n.4 (April 1976), pp. 108–9; and Mortimer, *Stalefish*, p. 144.

117 'Reports on the 1st National Championships', *Skateboard Special*, n.1 (September 1977), pp. 10–11; and 'Lip Torque', *Skateboard!*, n.6 (February 1978), pp. 32–3.

118 Ducommun, *Skateboarding Vancouver*, pp. 48–9; and Harms and Smith, *Skateboarder's Journal*, p. 178.

119 *Signal Hill Speed Run*.

120 Brooke, *Concrete Wave*, p. 121.

121 Snyder, *Secret History*, p. 497.

122 Curtis Hesselgrave, 'The First Hester/ISA Pro Bowl Contest', *SkateBoarder*, v.4 n.11 (June 1978), pp. 126–31.

123 *Rising Son* (dir. Cesario 'Block' Montano, 2006); Boulter, *Unemployable*, pp. 52, 60–3; and *Rollin' through the Decades*.

124 *This Ain't California*.

125 Mortimer, 'Evolution of the Pro Skater's Job'.

126 Browne, *Amped*, pp. 238–40; and Louison, *Impossible*, p. 1.

127 *X Games: Evolution of Skate* (Monarch, 2005); *X Games: the Movie* (dir. Steve Lawrence, 2009); Yochim, *Skate Life*, p. 62; and Browne, *Amped*, p. 239–47.

128 Hawk, *Hawk*, p. 4; Beal, *Skateboarding*, p. 33; and Blehm, *Agents of Change*, pp. 76–91.

129 Browne, *Amped*, pp. 243–7.

130 'Jake Brown Crash X Games 13 Mega Ramp' (2007), www.youtube.com/watch?v=1Q3PNj3tRW4; Rinehart, 'Exploiting a New Generation', pp. 82–3; Brent Rose, 'It's Only A Matter Of Time Before Someone Dies At The X Games' (31 January 2013), www.deadspin.com; 'Sarah Burke Dies From Injuries' (20 January 2012),

www.xgames.espn.go.com; 'X Games 2007 Skate Big Air – Jake Brown Crash' (2007), www.youtube.com/watch?v=ciCUCag5HjA; Colin Blake, 'Jake Brown Knocked Out in Fall' (29 June 2013), www.xgames.espn.go.com; Giorgio Agamben, *Homo Sacer* (Stanford: Stanford University Press, 1998); and Simon Orpana, 'Radical Gestures: Symbolism, Symptom and Skateboarding' (PhD thesis, McMaster University 2014), pp. 96–103.

131 Browne, *Amped*, pp. 249–50; and Marcus and Griggi, *Skateboard*, p. 227.

132 Macdonald, *Dropping In*, pp. 149–52; and Beal, *Skateboarding*, p. 40.

133 Elise Amendola, 'Boston Celtics Owners Invest in Skateboard League', *Washington Post* (17 May 2014), www.washingtonpost.com; Adam Salo, 'A League of Their Own', *ESPN Action Sports* (21 June 2010), www.espn.go.com; and Beal, *Skateboarding*, p. 40.

134 Beal and Wilson, 'Chicks Dig Scars', pp. 31–54; and Rinehart, 'ESPN's X Games', pp. 178–9.

135 Editorial, *The Quarterly SkateBoarder*, v.1 n.1 (Winter 1964), p. 7; and Gillogly, 'Russ Howell', p. 42.

136 Wheaton, *Cultural Politics*, p. 38.

137 Sedo, 'Dead-Stock Boards', pp. 276–80.

138 Paul Battison, 'Skateboarding: Could It Succeed as an Olympic Sport?' (15 May 2014), www.bbc.co.uk; 'What Do You Think About Skateboarding Being in the Olympics?', *Thrasher*, n.436 (November 2016), pp. 68–9; Batuev and Robinson, 'How Skateboarding Made It to the Olympics'; and Iain Borden, 'Ollies at the Olympics: Why Having Skateboarding at Tokyo 2020 is a Winning Move', *The Conversation* (4 August 2016), www.theconversation.com.

139 *Bones Brigade: an Autobiography*; Beal and Weidman, 'Authenticity', p. 339; and *AKA: Skater Girl* (dir. Mike Hill, 2003).

140 TransWorld, 'State of Skate', p. 12.

141 Beal and Weidman, 'Authenticity', pp. 337–52.

142 Donnelly, 'Alternative *and* Mainstream', pp. 197–214.

143 Beal, 'Disqualifying the Official', pp. 252–67; and Robert Petrone, 'Shreddin' It Up: Re-Thinking "Youth" through the Logics of Learning and Literacy in a Skateboarding Community' (PhD thesis, Michigan State University, 2008), p. 129.

144 Hawk, *Hawk*, p. 230.

145 Beal and Weidman, 'Authenticity', pp. 350–1; and Erving Goffman, *The Presentation of the Self in Everyday Life* (Edinburgh: University of Edinburgh Social Sciences Research Centre, 1956), pp. 66–86.

146 Petrone, 'Shreddin' It Up', pp. 127–30; and Weyland, *Answer Is Never*, p. 246.

147 Beal, 'Symbolic Inversion', pp. 215–16; and Beal, 'Disqualifying the Official', pp. 252–67.

148 'A Different Perspective: Vans US Open Van Doren Invitational 2014' (6 August 2014), www.theberrics.com.

149 Weyland, *Answer Is Never*, p. 236.

150 Yrjö Engeström, 'Wildfire Activities: New Patterns of Mobility and Learning', *International Journal of Mobile and Blended Learning*, v.1 n.2 (2009), p. 5; Petrone, 'Shreddin' It Up', pp. 156–66; and Ma and Munter, 'Spatial Production of Learning Opportunities', pp. 238–58.

151 Michael Nevin Willard, 'Seance, Tricknowlogy, Skateboarding, and the Space of Youth', J. Austin and M.N. Willard, (eds), *Generations of Youth* (New York: New York University Press, 1998), p. 335.

152 Beal, 'Symbolic Inversion', p. 217.

153 Beal and Weidman, 'Authenticity', p. 347.

154 Browne, *Amped*, pp. 60–1 and 95; Hawk, *How Did I Get Here?*, pp. 47–61; and Adam Salo, 'The 5 Most Lavish Tours of All Time', *SkateBoarder*, v.15 n.12 (August 2006), p. 36.

155 Palladini, *Vans*, pp. 6, 73–85; www.vanswarpedtour.com; Browne, *Amped*, p. 164; Jeff Howe, 'Drawing Lines: a Report from the Extreme World'; Rinehart and Sydnor, *To the Extreme*, p. 354; and Rinehart, 'ESPN's X Games', pp. 183–6.

156 Beal, *Skateboarding*, p. xviii; www.allgirlskatejam.com; 'Interview with Patty Segovia', www.istia.com (2 November 2011); and Palladini, Vans, p. 74.

Chapter 5 Media Worlds

1   Willard, 'Seance, Tricknowlogy, Skateboarding', pp. 326–46.

2   Marcus and Griggi, *Skateboard*, p. 134; and Hosoi and Ahrens, *Hosoi*, p. 34.

3   Neill Britt, 'Model City Skateboarding', *Wild World of Skateboarding*, v.2 n.4 (April 1978), pp. 30–1.

4   Weyland, A*nswer Is Never*, pp. 87–95; Dogtown and Z-Boys; and Snyder, *Secret History*, p. 674; and *The Original SkateBoarder* (dir. Coan Nichols and Rick Charnoski, 2018).

5   Stephen Duncombe, *Notes from Underground* (London: Verso, 1997), p. 3; and Sedo, 'Dead-Stock Boards', p. 270.

6   Porter, *History of Women in Skateboarding*, locs. 533–75; and Kimmy Pletting, 'Have You Zine Me? A Study of Zines as Empowerment for Women within Skateboarding' (BA dissertation, Utrecht University, 2014).

7   Weyland, *Answer Is Never*, p. 159.

8   Lefebvre, *Explosion*, pp. 98–9.

9   Petrone, 'Shreddin' It Up', p. 195; and Weyland, *Answer Is Never*, p. 162.

10   'Statement of Ownership, Management and Circulation', *Thrasher*, v.9 n.2 (February 1989), p. 108.

11   Lefebvre, *Introduction to Modernity*, pp. 243–4.

12   *The Man Who Souled the World.*

13   'A Letter from the Publisher', *TransWorld Skateboarding*, v.1 n.1 (May/June 1983), p. 4; Tracker Peggy, 'Skate and Create', *TransWorld Skateboarding*, v.1 n.1 (May/June 1983), pp. 13–15; and TransWorld Skateboarding, *2013 Media Portfolio*, v.31 (2013) p. 7.

14   Michael Blabac, *Blabac Photo* (Brooklyn: PowerHouse Books, 2009).

15   'Black and White Photography in Skateboarding' (2014), www.youtube.com/watch?v=Xegn2d6s-FY; and Fred Mortagne, *Attraper au vol* (Davenport: Um Yeah Arts, 2016).

16   Andrew Norton, 'The Photographer Series', www.vimeo.com/49205150.

17   Warren Bolster, 'Basic Skateboard Photography', *SkateBoarder*, v.2 n.6 (August 1976), pp. 32–4.

18   Michael Nevin Willard, 'Skate and Punk at the Far End of the American Century', Beth L. Bailey and David R. Farber, (eds), *America in the Seventies* (Lawrence: University Press of Kansas, 2004), p. 189.

19   'Extra', *SkateBoarder*, v.3 n.6 (July 1977), p. 141; 'Going-For-It', *Skateboard!*, n.18 (February 1979), p. 38; and Snyder, *Secret History*, p. 774.

20   Willard, 'Skate and Punk', pp. 190–2.

21   Morizen Föche, 'Pipes', *Thrasher*, v.4 n.6 (June 1984), p. 26; and Steve Kane, 'ZonaSkane', *Skateboard!* (second series), n.42 (May 1990), p. 64.

22   www.albphoto.com.

23   Sebastian Denz, *Skateboarding*. 3D (Munich: Prestel, 2009).

24   Gregory J. Snyder, 'The City and the Subculture Career: Professional Street Skateboarding in LA', *Ethnography*, v.13 n.3 (2012), pp. 305–6.

25   Arby Li, 'The Lonely Wanderer: Atiba Jefferson on the Evolution of Photography Through Skateboarding', *Hypebeast* (31 March 2015), www.hypebeast.com.

26   Richard Gilligan, *DIY* (Paris: 19/80 Éditions, 2012); *Format Perspective* (dir. Philip Evans, 2012); and Marc Vallée, *Anti-Skateboarding Devices* (London: Marc Vallée, 2012).

27   Nikki Toole, *Skater* (Heidelberg: Kehrer Verlag, 2015); Mark Whiteley, *This Is Not a Photo Opportunity* (Berkeley: Gingko Press, 2009); Daniel Månsson, *Faces of Skateboarding* (Stockholm: DDMN, 2006); Alex Corporan, Andre Razo and Ivory Serra, (eds), *Full Bleed* (Brooklyn, New York: Vice Books, 2010); and Long Live Southbank, *Long Live Southbank* (London: Long Live Southbank, 2014).

28   Brian Gaberman, *A Life in Transition* (USA: Element, 2013); Julian Bleecker, *Hello Skater Girl* (Pasadena: helloskatergirl.com, 2012); Gaurab Thakali and Tom Caron-Delion, *Thik Cha* (London: Our Place, 2016); Sylwia Grzegórzko, 'Renato Custodio', *Croco*, www.crocomag.com; Jessica Fulford-Dobson, *Skate Girls of Kabul* (London: Morland Tate, 2015; www.jamesahudson.info; Jonathan Mehring, *Skate the World*, (Washington: National Geographic, 2015); Tino Razo, *Party in the Back* (New York: Anthology, 2017); William Sharp and Ozzie Ausband, *Back in the Day* (Berkeley: Gingko Press, 2017); Arthur Tress, *Skate Park* (New York: Birch Books, 2010); Sergej Vutuc, *Something in Between* (Ghent: Snoeck, 2011); 'Black and White Photography in Skateboarding' (2014), www.youtube.com/watch?v=Xegn2d6s-FY; and Mortagne, *Attraper au vol*.

29   Michael Jeffries, Sebastian Messer, and Jon Swords, 'He Catches Things in Flight: Scopic Regimes, Visuality, and Skateboarding in Tyneside, England', Lombard, *Skateboarding*, pp. 57–72.

30   Rodney H. Jones, 'Sport and Re/Creation: What Skateboarders Can Teach Us About Learning', *Sport Education and Society*, v.16 n.5 (2011), pp. 593–611.

31   'Firsthand', *Fuel TV* (2005), www.youtube.com/watch?v=SZaAhKNyLKw; and *J. Grant Brittain* (dir. David Fokos and Barbarella Fokos, 2017).

32   Snyder, *Secret History*, p. 51–4.

33   Iain Borden, 'Skateboard City: London in Skateboarding Films', Pam Hirsch and Chris O'Rourke (eds), *London on Film* (London: Palgrave Macmillan, 2017).

34   'Interview with Stacy Peralta', *Skateboard Madness* (Hal Jepsen Films, dir. Julian Pena, 1979), DVD extra.

35   'Farrah Fawcett's Skateboard Chase', www.youtube.com/watch?v=wJTBs24szWo; and 'Stacy Peralta on Charlie's Angels', www.youtube.com/watch?v=g5IWFPWu7l0.

36   Borden, 'Skateboard City'; and Snyder, *Secret History*, p. 744–67.

37   Sedo, 'Dead-Stock Boards', pp. 262–3.

38   Hawk, *How Did I Get Here?*, p. 92.

39   *Concrete Jungle* (dir. Eli Morgan Gesner, 2009).

40   Sedo, 'Dead-Stock Boards', p. 262.

41   Yochim, *Skate Life*, pp. 111–38; Sean Brayton, 'MTV's Jackass: Transgression, Abjection and the Economy of White Masculinity', *Journal of Gender Studies*, v.16 n.1 (2007), pp. 57–72; Muriel Andrin,

'Back to the Slap', Tom Paulis and Rob King, (eds), *Slapstick Comedy* (Abingdon: Routledge, 2010), pp. 226–35; and Christina Tourino, 'The Leisured Testes: White Ball-Breaking as Surplus Masculinity in Jackass', *Journal of Popular Culture*, v.48 n.4 (2015), pp. 691–702;

42   'World's Largest Skateboard. Meet The Record Breakers. Guinness World Records' (2012), www.youtube.com/watch?v=sNAGxsIjvqk&spfreload=10.

43   Striler, *X Play Nation*, pp. 160, 162; and Andrew M. Shanken, 'The Sublime "Jackass": Transgression and Play in the Inner Suburbs', *Places: Forum of Design for the Public Realm*, v.19 n.3 (2007), pp. 50–5.

44   Petrone, 'Shreddin' It Up', p. 187.

45   Meckiffe, 'Mainstreams and Subcultures', pp. 245–6; Beato, 'Lords of Dogtown', pp. 21–36; *Off Camera with Sam Jones: Episode 10 with Stacy Peralta* (Sam Jones, 2013); and Stephen Holden, 'Dogtown and Z Boys', *New York Times* (26 April 2002), www.nytimes.com.

46   Roger Ebert, 'Dogtown and Z-Boys' (10 May 2002), www.rogerebert.com.

47   Meckiffe, 'Mainstreams and Subcultures', pp. 262–71; Sueyoshi, 'Skate and Create', p. 15; Yochim, *Skate Life*, pp. 69–71; Kyle Kusz, *Revolt of the White Athlete* (New York: Peter Lang, 2007); and Holden, 'Dogtown and Z Boys'.

48   Dwayne Dixon, 'Posing LA, Performing Tokyo: Photography and Race in Skateboarding's Global Imaginary', Lombard, *Skateboarding*, pp. 74–5.

49   Gomez, 'How Did Nike Get the Swoosh?', pp. 62–3.

50   Beal and Wilson, 'Chicks Dig Scars', pp. 35–6; and Yochim, *Skate Life*, pp. 140–2, 150–1.

51   Mortimer, 'Stacy Peralta', p. 90; and 'The Day Powell Set London on Fire', *R.A.D.*, n.71 (January 1989), pp. 26–35.

52   'Skating in the 80s', *The Bones Brigade Video Show* (1984), DVD extra; *Off Camera with Sam Jones: Episode 10*; Browne, *Amped*, pp. 104–5; *Bones Brigade: an Autobiography*; and Mortimer, *Stalefish*, pp. 118–9.

53   Hawk, *How Did I Get Here?*, pp. 86–7; *Off Camera with Sam Jones:*

Episode 10; and *Bones Brigade: an Autobiography*.

54   Hawk, *Hawk*, pp. 122–3; Jack Erwin, 'The Oral History of the Making of *The Search for Animal Chin*', *Complex* (13 June 2013), www.ca.complex.com; Colberg, *Skateboarding* Art, p. 158; and Kevin W. Bicknell, 'Examining Perceptions of Authenticity in Museum Exhibits About Skateboarding' (Masters dissertation, University of Washington, 2014), pp. 44–6.

55   Browne, *Amped*, 119.

56   '30th Anniversary Interviews: Danny Way Part 2', *TransWorld Skateboarding* (9 July 2013), www.skateboarding.transworld.net; and Colberg, Skateboarding Art, pp. 247–64.

57   Sam Griffin, 'Skateboarding in the Age of Mechanical Image Reproduction', Chiara Santini Parducci, (ed.), *Do Not Think* (Berlin: Oxylane Art Foundation, 2015), pp. 121–40; and 'Matt Hensley on Skateboarding and Joining Flogging Molly' (2012), www.youtube.com/watch?v=RU0gZ410Kp4.

58   Catherine Elwes, *Video Art* (London: IB Tauris, 2005), p. 5.

59   101, advertisements, *Thrasher*, v.12 n.6 (June 1992), p. 81, v.12 n.7 (July 1992), p. 81.

60   Peacock, *Skateboarding*, p. 125.

61   Aaron Baker, *Contesting Identities* (Urbana, University of Illinois Press, 2003), p. 49.

62   David Harvey, *The Condition of Postmodernity* (Oxford: Basil Blackwell, 1990), p. 156; and Dinces, 'Flexible Opposition', p. 1526.

63   Browne, *Amped*, pp. 120–2.

64   'Behind the Video', *TransWorld Skateboarding*, v.21 n.3 (March 2003), pp. 217–37.

65   Hawk, *How Did I Get Here?*, pp. 94–5; Hawk, *Hawk*, pp. 211–20; and 'Process: the Technology Behind "We Are Blood"', www.theberrics.com (2015).

66   Striler, *X Play Nation*, p. 154.

67   'Rodney Mullen Debuts New Tricks, Captured in 360 Degrees' (2016), www.youtube.com/watch?v=-3tDvMG87Ro; and 'Skateboarding Time Collapse: Shot with the Lumia 930' (Cy Kuckenbaker, 2014), www.

vimeo.com/101557016.

68   'Pontus Alv Interview', *Theories of Atlantis* (30 July 2014), www.theoriesofatlantis.com.

69   Yochim, *Skate Life*, p. 67.

70   Scott Laderman, *Empire in Waves* (Berkeley: University of California, 2014).

71   O'Connor, 'Skateboarding Networks'.

72   'China's Skateboarding Revolution', *Vice* (20 May 2015), www.vice.com; 'Skating Untouched Street Features in Cuba' (2014), www.youtube.com/watch?v=TdN4NRsFwl4; and Sedo, 'Dead-Stock Boards', pp. 259–60, 273–6.

73   Lurper, 'Skateboarding from China to Afghanistan with Patrik Wallner', *Jenkem* (11 December 2012), www.jenkemmag.com.

74   Harms and Smith, *Skateboarder's Journal*, pp. 56, 74–6

75   *Drive: My Life in Skateboarding* (dir. Mark Jeremias, 2002).

76   Edwin Faeh and Oliver Drewes, *Dirt Ollies* (Berlin: Verlag für Bildschöne Bücher, 2007).

77   Harris, 'Belonging Paradox', p. 226.

78   Butz, *Grinding California*, p. 164.

79   'Major Moves', *Thrasher*, v.11 n.9 (September 1991), p. 48.

80   www.skateperception.com; David Buckingham, 'Skate Perception: Self-Representation, Identity and Visual Style in a Youth Subculture', David Buckingham and Rebekah Willett, (eds), *Video Cultures* (Basingstoke: Palgrave, 2009), pp. 133–51; and Harris, 'Belonging Paradox', pp. 171–2.

81   Jones, 'Sport and Re/Creation', p. 605.

82   Jones, 'Sport and Re/Creation', p. 603; Ty Hollett, 'Symbiotic Learning Partnerships in Youth Action Sports', *Convergence* (2017), pp. 1–14; and Dupont, 'From Core to Consumer', pp. 556–81.

83   Kameliya Encheva, Olivier Driessens and Hans Verstraeten, 'The Mediatization of Deviant Subcultures: an Analysis of the Media-Related Practices of Graffiti Writers and Skaters', *MedieKultur*, n.54 (2013), pp. 8–25; and Snyder, 'City and the Subculture Career', p. 323.

84   Striler, *X Play Nation*, p. 138.

85   Hawk, *How Did I Get Here?*, pp. 96–111.

86 Stefan, 'Jenkem Magazine Interview', *Monster Skateboard Magazine* (27 October 2014).

87 Giannoulakis, 'Framework for Marketing', p. 125; Balma, *Tracker*, p. 318; and TransWorld, 'State of Skate', p. 13.

88 'Tony Hawk Skates First Downward Spiral Loop' (2015), www.youtube.com/watch?v=gaf8zHp-iaY; and 'ZeroG | Tony Hawk and Aaron "Jaws" Homoki | Sony' (2016), www.youtube.com/watch?v=Z0nHSMM_69w.

89 TransWorld, 'State of Skate', pp. 13, 49.

90 Striler, *X Play Nation*, p. 218; and Anthony Pappalardo, 'The Decentralization of the Pro Skateboard Career?', *Jenkem* (23 February 2015), www.jenkemmag.com.

91 Arthur Derrien, 'How Is the Internet Changing the Way We Appreciate Skate Videos?', *Kingpin* (2013), www.kingpin.mpora.com; and Rick Kaminski, 'Is the Internet Really Ruining How We Appreciate Skate Videos?', *Jenkem* (30 April 2013), www.jenkemmag.com.

92 Marjon Carlos, 'Meet Ko Hyojoo, the South Korean Longboarding Sensation', *Vogue* (27 June 2016), www.vogue.com.

93 Quartersnacks, *TF at 1* (Brooklyn: PowerHouse Books, 2015), p. 9.

94 Pappalardo, 'Decentralization'.

95 Oswaldo Sanchez, 'Pontus Alv: the Last Interview', *TransWorld Skateboarding* (28 February 2015), www.skateboarding.transworld.net.

96 Petrone, 'Shreddin' It Up', p. 119.

97 J. Patrick Williams and Heith Copes, 'How Edge Are You?', *Symbolic Interaction*, v.28 n.1 (2005), pp. 67–89; Holly Thorpe, 'Action Sports, Social Media, and New Technologies', *Communication & Sport* (2017); and Petrone, 'Shreddin' It Up' p. 19.

Chapter 6 Found Space

1 'Jeff Grosso's Loveletters to Skateboarding –Ben Schroeder' (2011), www.youtube.com/watch?v=PoL3ej7qMts.

2 Jay Adams, interview, *SkateBoarder*, v.6 n.4 (November 1979), p. 52.

3 Shivani Vora, 'Skateboards for Work and Working Out', *New York Times* (22 August 2013), www.nytimes.com.

4 Henri Lefebvre, *The Production of Space* (Oxford: Blackwell, 1991), pp. 49–53, 285–92, 306–21, 352–67.

5 *Signal Hill Speed Run*; Balma, Tracker, pp. 13, 31; Page, interview, p. 108; and Smythe, 'History', pp. 28–51.

6 Lefebvre, *Production of Space*, p. 109; and Henri Lefebvre, *The Survival of Capitalism* (New York: St. Martin's, 1976), pp. 14–15.

7 'Who's Hot! Paul Constantineau', *SkateBoarder*, v.3 n.2 (December 1976), p. 85.

8 *Dogtown and Z-Boys*.

9 *Thrasher*, *Maximum Rad*, np; and Weyland, *Answer Is Never*, p. 221.

10 Louison, *Impossible*, p. 58; and Skip Smith, 'The Toilet Bowl', *SkateBoarder*, v.2 n.2 (Fall 1975), pp. 42–5.

11 Sam Fernando, 'Things Are Hot in the Valley', *SkateBoarder*, v.4 n.1 (August 1977), p. 67; Brian Gillogly, 'Skate Parks: Part X', *SkateBoarder*, v.4 n.1 (August 1977), p. 94; Smythe, 'History', p. 37; and Warren Bolster, 'The Reservoir', *SkateBoarder*, v.2 n.6 (August 1976), pp. 104–11.

12 Marcus and Griggi, *Skateboard*, p. 12; Molly Roache, 'Straight from God's Land of Ditches', *Thrasher*, v.7 n.8 (August 1987), pp. 47–53; and *Thrasher*, Epic Spots (New York: Universe, 2008), pp. 116–7.

13 Snyder, *Secret History*, pp. 29, 121, 125, 155–6, *passim*.

14 Boulter, *Unemployable*, pp. 9–10; *Tic Tac 2 Heelflip*; and www.vicskatehistory.com.

15 Siân Liz Evans, 'Young, Gifted and Board Stupid', *Big Issue*, n.126 (17–23 April 1995), p. 18; Long Live Southbank, 'Southbank Undercroft: Cultural & Heritage Assessment Report' (London: Long Live Southbank, September 2014), pp. 20, 49; and Stan Hey, 'Wheelers and Dealers', *Time Out*, n.381 (15–21 July 1977), p. 13.

16 Howell, *Skateboard*.

17 Lefebvre, *Introduction to Modernity*, pp. 72–3; and Henri Lefebvre, *Writings on Cities* (Oxford: Blackwell, 1996), pp. 80, 158.

18 Stephen Cline, 'Skateboarding in the Dark Ages', *SkateBoarder*, v.2 n.2 (Fall 1975), p. 38.

19 Brian Gillogly, 'The Badlands Story', *SkateBoarder*, v.5 n.1 (August 1978), pp. 78–95; Mellow Cat, 'Ballad Through the Badlands', *SkateBoarder*, v.2 n.5 (June 1976), pp. 123–9; Chris Miller, interview, *Thrasher*, v.9 n.10 (May 1989), pp. 62–9, 102; and 'Baldy Pipeline', *Thrasher*, v.1 n.8 (August 1981), pp. 20–1.

20 Alva, 'Dog Tails'; 'Jeff Grosso's Loveletters to Skateboarding – Full Pipes' (2013), www.youtube.com/watch?v=qI-XR_3j0wE; 'Who's Hot! Rick Blackhart', *SkateBoarder*, v.4 n.4, (November 1977), pp. 114–15; and Joe Brook, 'Epic Spots: the Glory Hole', *Thrasher* (April 2014), pp. 50–1.

21 Sam Fernando, 'In Search of Giant Pipes', *SkateBoarder*, v.5 n.10 (May 1979), pp. 60–8; Grant C. Reynolds, letter, S*kateBoarder's Action Now*, v.7 n.5 (December 1980), p. 12; and Snyder, *Secret History*, p. 624.

22 Boulter, *Unemployable*, p. 8; and www.vicskatehistory.com.

23 Jim Cassimus, 'Pipe Dreams', *SkateBoarder*, v.3 n.3, (February 1977), pp. 90–3; Warren Bolster, 'Desert Discovery', *SkateBoarder*, v.3 n.6 (July 1977), pp. 72–83; Smythe, 'History', pp. 38, 44; Stan Sharp, 'Biscuit Flats', *Skateboard World*, v.1 n.4 (October 1977), pp. 94–101; *Desert Pipes* (dir. Steve Pingleton, 2010); Ameron map of projects, www.desertpipes.com; and Ameron International, 'Ameron Prestressed Concrete Cylinder Pipe' (2002), www.nov.com.

24 Zarka, *On a Day with No Waves*, p. 28; and Nancy Holt, 'Sun Tunnels', *Artforum* (April 1977), www.artforum.com.

25 Miller, interview, *Thrasher*, p. 102.

26 'Skateboard Kings'; and Kevin Thatcher and Brian Brannon, *Thrasher* (New York: Random House, 1992), p. 10.

27 Hamm, *Scarred*, p. 109.

28 'Extra', *SkateBoarder*, v.5 n.4 (November 1978), p. 157; Vickie Chang, 'Skitch Hitchcock and the Rest of the Salt Creek Beach Crew', *OC Weekly* (15 January 2009), www.ocweekly.com; Ian MacKaye, 'Interview with Duane Peters', *Juice* (1 March 2005), www.juicemagazine.

com; Don Redondo, 'The Last Ride', *Thrasher*, v.6 n.2 (February 1986), p. 49; Tony Hawk, interview, *TransWorld Skateboarding*, v.15 n.10 (October 1997), pp. 112, 240; 'SPoT History, Loop Knockouts and Mike Frazier' (2012), www.youtube.com/watch?v=H2RkXqCtVAI; Hamm, *Scarred for Life*, pp. 182–5; Sean Mortimer, 'Pipe Dream', *SkateBoarder*, v.16 n.4 (December 2006), p. 40; 'Tony Hawk Invites Friends to Try the Loop for the First Time – 2008', www.youtube.com/watch?v=TkeCZfG_KaI; and 'Tony Hawk's Loop of Death' (2013), www.youtube.com/watch?v=Y8dIIRCBuOI.

29 'Chris Cope's "Route 44" Part' (2016), www.youtube.com/watch?v=L90KBKlp7o4.

30 *Reality of Bob Burnquist*; 'Bob Burnquist Loop' (2006), www.youtube.com/watch?v=BDla-x-l4Hc; and 'Bob Burnquist Makes Skateboarding History', www.skateboarding.transworld.net (12 December 2003).

31 Bradley Garrett, *Explore Everything* (London: Verso, 2013), pp. 8, 33.

32 Bolster, 'Desert Discovery', pp. 72–83.

33 TWS, 'The First Kidney-Shaped Pool (1939)', *TransWorld Skateboarding* (27 September 2016), www.skateboarding.transworld.net.

34 Lowboy, 'Truth and Screw the Consequences', *Thrasher*, v.9 n.6 (June 1989), pp. 42–3; Brooke, *Concrete Wave*, p. 38; Smythe, 'History', pp. 28–51; 'Getting Around', *The Quarterly SkateBoarder*, v.1 n.1 (Winter 1964), p. 37; Marcus and Griggi, *Skateboard*, pp. 50–1, 80; Hamm, *Scarred for Life*, pp. 51–2; and Gillogly, 'Torger Johnson', pp. 46–51.

35 Snyder, *Secret History*, p. 142.

36 'Pools', *Thrasher*, v.4 n.6 (June 1984), p. 22.

37 *Off Camera with Sam Jones: Episode 10*.

38 Will Edler, 'Radical Northern Realities', *SkateBoarder*, v.6 n.11 (June 1980), pp. 47–51; 'Who's Hot! Rick Blackhart', pp. 114–15; Snyder, *Secret History*, pp. 107, 142–5, 159, 334–6; *The Legendary Dead Cat Pool* (dir. Steve Pingleton, 2010); www.desertpipes.com; 'Tres Amigos de Texas', *Thrasher*, v.10 n.3 (March 1990), pp. 60–3; Glen

E. Friedman, *Fuck You Too* (Los Angeles: Burning Flags, 1996), np; Boulter, *Unemployable*, pp. 21–2; Tim Dawe, 'The Early History of Ozi Skate' (2015), www.timdawe.com.au; Tim Lewis, interview, *Skateboard!*, n.9 (May 1978), p. 62.

39 Alva, interview, *Thrasher*, p. 29.

40 Waldo Autry, interview, *SkateBoarder*, v.4 n.1 (August 1977), p. 109.

41 Rick Blackhart, 'Ask the Doctor', *Thrasher*, v.5 n.1 (January 1985), p. 8.

42 Thatcher and Brannon, *Thrasher*, p. 10.

43 *Rollin' through the Decades*.

44 Paul Rodaway, *Sensuous Geographies* (London: Routledge, 1994); and Lefebvre, *Production of Space*, pp. 199–200, 210, 225.

45 *SkateBoarder*, v.1 n.1 (Summer 1975), front cover.

46 *SkateBoarder*, v.4 n.6 (January 1978), p. 100; and Stacy Peralta, interview, *SkateBoarder*, v.3 n.1 (October 1976), p. 58.

47 Marcus and Griggi, *Skateboard*, p. 181.

48 Cocks, 'Irresistible Air', p. 91.

49 Peralta, interview, *Thrasher*, p. 16.

50 Keith Hamm, 'Coping Conquistadors', *Slap*, v.4 n.9 (September 1995), p. 48.

51 Weyland, *Answer Is Never*, p. 47; '30th Anniversary Interviews: Tony Alva Part 1', *TransWorld Skateboarding*, www.skateboarding.transworld.net; Beato, 'Lords of Dogtown', p. 24; and 'Pool Riding Symposium', *SkateBoarder*, v.3 n.1 (October 1976), p. 74.

52 Kurt Ledterman, 'Bowls, Bongos and Other Riffs', *SkateBoarder*, v.2 n.4 (April 1976), pp. 117–21.

53 'Pool Riding Symposium', p. 74.

54 Micke Alba, interview, *Thrasher*, v.2 n.6 (July 1982), p. 32.

55 'Jeff Grosso's Loveletters to Skateboarding – Empty Pools' (2014), www.youtube.com/watch?v=6CWBnCA91Qg.

56 Rodney Jesse, interview, *SkateBoarder*, v.4 n.10 (May 1978), p. 59.

57 'Edge!', *Thrasher*, v.6 n.5 (May 1986), pp. 35–6.

58 'How to Build a Skatepark', *Thrasher*, v.17 n.9 (September 1997), p. 74.

59 Glen E. Friedman, *Fuck You Heroes* (New York: Burning Flags, 1994),

np; 'Air', *Thrasher*, v.4 n.4 (April 1984), p. 30; Nicolas Malinowski, 'L'Evolution d'une Espace', *Noway*, n.13 (November 1990), p. 10; Cliver, *Disposable Skateboard Bible*, p. 250; Hamm, *Scarred for Life*, p. 146; Snyder, *Secret History*, pp. 260–85; 'Extra', *SkateBoarder*, v.3 n.6 (July 1977), p. 141; and *SkateBoarder*, v.4 n.6 (January 1978), p. 75.

60 Hamm, 'Coping', p. 48.

61 'Pool Riding Symposium', p. 62.

62 Curtis Hesselgrave, 'Krypto Ball', *SkateBoarder*, v.4 n.11 (June 1978), p. 108.

63 *Dogtown and Z-Boys*.

64 Fido, letter, *SkateBoarder*, v.3 n.6 (July 1977), p. 18.

65 Kent Schiffman, letter, *Thrasher*, v.17 n.9 (September 1997), p. 12.

66 Snyder, *Secret History, passim*; and Browne, 'Dogtown East'.

67 Adams, interview, p. 53.

68 'On Being a Pool Mercenary', *Thrasher*, v.1 n.11 (November 1981), p. 21; and Steve Alba, 'Prime Evil', *Thrasher*, v.12 n.1 (January 1992), p. 49.

69 Weyland, *Answer Is Never*, p. 51; Hamm, *Scarred for Life*, pp. 121–4; and Snyder, *Secret History*, pp. 143–5.

70 Hamm, 'Coping', p. 48.

71 'The 1976–1977 California Drought: a Review' (State of California, The Resources Agency: Department of Water Resources, May 1978); and 'Trash', *Thrasher*, v.10 n.10 (October 1990), p. 106.

72 'Pool Mercenary', pp. 21–2; Steve Alba, 'Walk Through the Valley of Death', *Thrasher*, v.10 n.6 (June 1990), p. 50; and Hamm, *Scarred for Life*, p. 68.

73 Alba, 'Valley of Death', p. 50.

74 Tony Alva, interview, *SkateBoarder*, v.4 n.12, (July 1978), p. 80.

75 Scott Smiley, interview, *Thrasher*, v.16 n.2 (February 1996), p. 77.

76 Hamm, 'Coping', p. 48.

77 'Pool Party', *Thrasher*, v.2 n.11 (December 1982), p. 35.

78 Brian Brannon, 'Pool Jones', *Thrasher*, v.7 n.11 (November 1987), p. 87.

79 Hamm, *Scarred for Life*, p. 69.

80 www.skatenorcal.com.

81 Mick Angiulo, 'Rampage', *SkateBoarder*, v.4 n.3 (October 1977), p. 61.

82 'Somethin' Else', *Thrasher*, v.6 n.3

(March 1986), p. 95; and Marcus and Griggi, *Skateboard*, p. 12.

83 Lefebvre, *Production of Space*, p. 193.

84 Peralta, interview, *SkateBoarder*, p. 58.

85 Lefebvre, *Production of Space*, pp. 35, 193.

86 Joe Hartline, 'The Killer Pool', *Thrasher*, v.6 n.3 (March 1986), p. 50.

87 Duane Peters, interview, *Thrasher*, v.9 n.6 (June 1989), p. 94.

88 'Fruit Bowl Revisited', *Blue Tile Obsession*, www.ozzieausband. wordpress.com (28 March 2015).

89 John Smythe, 'SkateBoarder Interview: Tony Alva', *SkateBoarder*, v.3 n.3 (February 1977), pp. 34–41.

90 *Fruit of the Vine* (dir. Coan Nichols and Rick Charnoski, 2002).

91 Henri Lefebvre, *Everyday Life in the Modern World* (London: Transaction Publishers, 1984), pp. 121–2; Lefebvre, *Production of Space*, p. 309; and Lefebvre, *Writings on Cities*, pp. 75–7, 171–2.

92 Lefebvre, *Production of Space*, p. 142.

93 Lefebvre, *Production of Space*, pp. 368–9.

94 Lefebvre, *Production of Space*, pp. 166–8.

95 'Pool Riding Symposium', p. 75.

96 Steve Alba, 'The Biggest Skate Bust Ever', www.salbaland.com; and Hamm, *Scarred for Life*, pp. 92-109.

97 *Desert Pipes*.

98 Steve Gourlay, 'The Man From Snowy River', *TransWorld Skateboarding*, v.20 n.11 (November 2002), pp. 174–9; Don Balch, 'Kiwis on Wheels', *SkateBoarder*, v.4 n.3 (October 1977), pp. 70–1; and *Thrasher, Epic Spots*, p. 128.

99 Brian Brannon, 'Tall Tales', *Thrasher* (April 1987), pp. 54–62; and 'The Legend of the Love Bowls' (14 June 2010), www.saucepolicy.com.

100 Neil Blender, 'Sadlands', *TransWorld Skateboarding*, v.1 n.2 (July/August 1983), pp. 45–7; 'Jeff Grosso's Loveletters to Skateboarding – Sadlands' (2012), www.youtube.com/ watch?v=puy9NSUlJuQ; 'Darkside of the Moon' (2011), www.vimeo. com/21119024; and Andrew Norton, 'The Photographer Series: Jonathan Mehring' (2013), www.vimeo. com/67500403.

101 Mortimer, *Stalefish*, pp. 89–90.

102 'Jeff Grosso's Loveletters to Skateboarding – Empty Pools'.

103 Dave Swift, 'Pool Stories', *TransWorld Skateboarding*, v.20 n.11 (November 2002), pp. 260–311; www. ozzieausband.wordpress.com; Denike, *Built to Grind*, pp. 274–5; 'The Session at the Deal Lake Skate Pool', www.asburyanchor.com (15 October 2012); and *Fruit of the Vine*.

104 Dan Levy, 'Sonny Rodriguez', Juice, v.22 n.1 (2015), pp. 22–5; 'Helicopter Recon: Bob Burnquist's "Dreamland"' (2013), www.youtube.com/watch?v =6Jw3akxiVYg; Nadine Ajaka, 'How to Turn an Old Pool Into a Skate Park', *The Atlantic* (20 September 2015), www.theatlantic.com; DCDC (Chris Russ, 2015), www.vimeo.com /136870148.

105 Jesse McKinley and Malia Wollan, 'Skaters Jump In as Foreclosures Drain the Pool', *New York Times* (28 December 2008), www.nytimes.com.

106 Hamm, *Scarred for Life*, pp. 51, 58–9.

107 Hamm, *Scarred for Life*, p. 66.

108 Micah Trippe, 'Appropriating Pools', *Architecture Media Politics Society*, v.10 n.3 (2016), pp. 1–11; and Butz, *Grinding California*, pp. 222–3.

109 'Ads (We're Not Sure) We'd Like to See', *Thrasher* (March 1986), p. 26; 'Jeff Grosso's Loveletters to Skateboarding – Belmar's Bowl' (2011), www.youtube.com/watch?v=-TyDCa1LKAI; *Thrasher, Epic Spots*, pp. 166–7; 'Kevin Kowalski's Backyard DIY' (2013), www.youtube.com/ watch?v=VQ8MsFbvEgo; Ben Kelly, 'North Shore Bowl Jam', *TransWorld Skateboarding* (11 December 2006), www.skateboarding.transworld.net; Dave Swift, 'Cholo's North Shore Bowl Jam', *The Skateboard Mag*, n.37 (April 2007), pp. 32–7; 'Self-Built Cinder Cone Treehouse Perches Above a Skate Bowl' (3 June 2015), *DesignBoom*, www.designboom.com; Markus Suchanek, *Concrete Wave*, v.7 n.4 (Winter 2009), pp. 48–51; and 'Dan Cates Pool Party – September 2016' (2016), www.youtube.com/ watch?v=K5fbBlFKMh0

Chapter 7 Skatopia

1 Editors response to letter, *Action Now*, v.7 n.10 (May 1981), p.14.

2 Sarah Pileggi, 'Wheeling and Dealing', *Sports Illustrated* (1 September 1975); and Phillip M. Wishon and Marcia L. Oreskovich, 'Bicycles, Roller Skates and Skateboards: Safety Promotion and Accident Prevention', *Children Today*, v.15 n.3 (May–June 1986), pp. 11–15.

3 'Surfing – Tucson Style', *Tucson Daily Citizen* (2 September 1965), reproduced in Marcus and Griggi, *Skateboard*, pp. 89–91.

4 Ann Lucart, 'Arizona's Park', letter, *SkateBoarder*, v.1 n.4 (October 1965), p. 7.

5 Louison, *Impossible*, p. 12; and *Rebirth of Skateparks*.

6 'Outdoor Plywood Rink Built For Skateboards', *Popular Science* (April 1966), p. 127.

7 Gillogly, 'Skateparks: Part X', pp. 94–9; Brooke, *Concrete Wave*, p. 32; and Noll, *Skateboard Retrospective*, p. 86.

8 Snyder, *Secret History*, pp. 73–5; and Google Maps.

9 Davidson, *Skateboard Book*, p. 46; Howell, *Skateboard*, pp. 12, 36; and Brian Gillogly, 'Skate Parks: Fantasy or Reality?', *SkateBoarder*, v.2 n.4 (April 1976), pp. 68–77.

10 'Taito Skateboard Center', *SkateBoarder*, v.2 n.6 (August 1976), pp. 55–6; and *Revers de Tokyo* (dir. Julien Glauser, 2012).

11 Snyder, *Secret History*, p. 77.

12 Gillogly, 'Russ Howell', p. 44; 'Techniques – Skateboard Track', *Constructional Review* (November 1976), pp. 58–9, www. concreteconstruction.net; 'Albany Skate Track', *SkateBoarder*, v.2 n.6 (August 1976), p. 53; and Heritage Council of Western Australia, 'Register of Heritage Places Assessment Documentation: Albany Snake Run Skateboard Park' (15 December 2015).

13 Bruce Walker, letter, *SkateBoarder's Action Now*, v.7 n.1 (August 1980), p. 15; 'Skateboard Park Rescued by Florida Family at Suggestion of Jen O'Brien', www.skateboarddirectory. com; Snyder, *Secret History*, pp. 63–71; Balma, *Tracker*, p. 14; and Brian Gillogly, 'Skate Parks: Kickin' an' a Slidin' in Valleys of Cement At Last', *SkateBoarder*, v.2 n.6 (August 1976), pp. 48–57.

14 Gillogly, 'Kickin' an' a Slidin'', pp. 48–57; and Brian Gillogly, 'Skate Parks: Part V', *SkateBoarder*, v.3 n.2 (December 1976), pp. 48–55.

15 'Skate Parks: Part IV', *SkateBoarder*, v.3 n.1 (October 1976), pp. 46–53; and Gillogly, 'Skate Parks: Part V', pp. 48–55; Brian Gillogly, 'Skate Parks: Part XV', *SkateBoarder*, v.4 n.6 (January 1978), pp. 52–63.

16 www.carlsbadskatepark.org; Snyder, *Secret History*, pp. 69–71; Gillogly, 'Fantasy or Reality?', pp. 68–77; Warren Bolster, 'Skateparks: Reality!', *SkateBoarder*, v.2 n.5 (June 1976), pp. 84–9; Gillogly, 'Kickin' an' a Slidin'', pp. 48–57; 'Skate Parks: Part IV', pp. 46–53; Brian Gillogly, 'Skate Parks: Part VI. Perspective and Preview', *SkateBoarder*, v.3 n.3 (February 1977), pp. 44–9; Warren Bolster, '*SkateBoarder* Interview: John O'Malley', *SkateBoarder*, v.3 n.6 (July 1977), pp. 105–10; and Sparks, advertisement, *SkateBoarder*, v.4 n.4 (November 1977), p. 141.

17 Snyder, *Secret History*, p. 71; and Bolster, 'John O'Malley', pp. 105–10.

18 'SkaterCross', advertisement, *SkateBoarder*, v.3 n.1 (October 1976), p. 30; 'Skate Parks: Part IV', pp. 46–53; *Rebirth of Skateparks*; Gillogly, 'Skate Parks: Part VI', pp. 44–9; and Brian Gillogly, 'Skateparks: Part VII. Current Directions in Skate Environments', *SkateBoarder*, v.3 n.3 (February 1977), pp. 36–45.

19 Aloha Skatetown, advertisement, *Skateboard World*, v.1 n.5 (November 1977), p. 54.

20 Gillogly, 'Skateparks: Part VII', pp. 36–45.

21 Mary Horowitz, 'Radical Energy Infiltrates Big Business', *SkateBoarder*, v.4 n.8 (March 1978), pp. 120–1; Wally Inouye, interview, *SkateBoarder*, v.4 n.3 (October 1977), pp. 52–3; and Snyder, *Secret History*, p. 64.

22 Gregg Haythorpe, 'Gunite vs. Shotcrete', *Skateboard Scene*, v.1 n.4 (*c.* February 1978), pp. 46–7.

23 'Ears', *R.A.D.*, n.80 (October 1989), p. 11; and Terri Craft, 'Interview with Chris Miller', *Juice* (1 September 2006), www.juicemagazine.com.

24 Skatepark Publications, advertisements, *SkateBoarder*, v.3 n.3 (February 1977), p. 28, v.3 n.5 (June 1978), p. 21; The 1978 Skatepark Conference and Exposition, advertisement, *SkateBoarder*, v.4 n.5 (December 1977), p. 30; and Horowitz, 'Radical Energy', p. 120.

25 'Where to Skateboard', *Wild World of Skateboarding*, v.2 n.2 (February 1978), pp. 60–2.

26 Gillogly, 'Fantasy or Reality?', pp. 68–77; and R. Rice Gettings, 'Sooper City', *SkateBoarder*, v.2 n.6 (August 1976), p. 56.

27 'Off the Wall', *SkateBoarder*, v.3 n.6 (July 1977), p. 128; 'Skateboard World', advertisement, *SkateBoarder*, v.4 n.1 (August 1977), p. 42; and Gillogly, 'Skateparks: Part X', pp. 94–9.

28 Gillogly, 'Skateparks: Part X', pp. 94–9; and Stan Sharp, 'Skatepark Bonanza', *Skateboard World*, v.1 n.3 (September 1977), pp. 82–93.

29 Brian Gillogly, 'Skateparks: Part XIII', *SkateBoarder*, v.4 n.4 (November 1977), pp. 92–107; and Gillogly, 'Skateparks: Part X', pp. 94–9.

30 'Kona – America's Oldest Skatepark on SPOTS – Part 1 of 2' (2012), www.youtube.com/watch?v=PCDZnH8NRYo; Brian Gillogly, 'Skate Parks: Part IX', *SkateBoarder*, v.3 n.6 (July 1977), pp. 84–9; Gillogly, 'Skateparks: Part X', pp. 94–9; Brian Gillogly, 'Skate Parks: Part XI', *SkateBoarder*, v.4 n.2 (September 1977), pp. 90–8; Gillogly, 'Skate Parks: Part XIII', pp. 92–107; 'Off the Wall' (July 1977), p. 128; 'World News', *Skateboard!*, n.2 (October 1977), p. 22; Dudley Counts, 'L.A. Skatepark Paradise: Part I', *Thrasher*, v.1 n.3 (March 1981), pp. 10–15; and Snyder, *Secret History*, pp. 106–17, 162–3, 322, 367, 395, 423–5, 622.

31 Brian Gillogly, 'Skateparks: Part Sixteen', *SkateBoarder*, v.4 n.7 (February 1978), pp. 52–79; and Brian Gillogly, 'The Ramp Rage: a Perspective', *SkateBoarder*, v.4 n.8 (March 1978), pp. 76–93.

32 Sharp, 'Skatepark Bonanza', pp. 82–93; Gillogly, 'Skate Parks: Part XI', pp. 90–8; Gillogly, 'Skate Parks: Part XIII', pp. 92–107; Dudley Counts, 'Upland Gold Cup Finale', *Thrasher*, v.1 n.1 (January 1981), p. 11; 'Upland Pipeline: Closing Comments', *TransWorld Skateboarding*, v.7 n.2 (April 1989), pp. 64–72; Dudley Counts, 'L.A. Skatepark Paradise: Part II', *Thrasher*, v.1 n.4 (April 1981), pp. 9–15; Gerry Hurtado, 'A Radical Decade at the Upland Pipeline', *Thrasher*, v.7 n.6 (June 1987), pp. 77–9; and Harms and Smith, *Skateboarder's Journal*, pp. 7, 89–92.

33 Brian Gillogly, 'Interview: Steve Evans and Charlie Ransom', *SkateBoarder*, v.5 n.6 (January 1979), p. 52; and Gillogly, 'Skate Parks: Part XI', pp. 90–8.

34 Concrete Wave, advertisement, *SkateBoarder*, v.4 n.3 (October 1977), p. 32; Gillogly, 'Skate Parks: Part XIII', pp. 92–107; Snyder, *Secret History*, p. 326; Steve Olson, 'Doug Saladino', *Juice*, v.22 n.1 (2015), pp. 126–33; Harms and Smith, *Skateboarder's Journal*, p. 174; and Brian Gillogly, 'Skate Parks: Part XIV', *SkateBoarder*, v.4 n.5 (December 1977), pp. 78–83.

35 Garry Davis, 'Del Mar Was', *TransWorld Skateboarding*, v.6 n.1 (February 1988), pp. 106–11; 'Del Mar Skate Ranch on SPOTS – Part 1' (2012), www.youtube.com/watch?v=oXpQ7zpLH0A; Dave Swift, 'History: the Del Mar Skate Ranch', www.delmarskateranch.com; and Grant Brittain, 'Long Live Del Mar Skate Ranch!', *TransWorld Skateboarding*, v.21 n.1 (January 2003), pp. 286–91.

36 www.lakewoodskatepark.net.

37 Curtis Hesselgrave, 'Whittier Knights: Skate City – Hester Pro Bowl #4', *SkateBoarder*, v.6 n.5 (December 1979), pp. 24–33.

38 Duane Bigelow and Wally Hollyday, interview, *SkateBoarder*, v.6 n.8 (March 1980), p. 61; and Snyder, *Secret History*, pp. 325–31.

39 Gillogly, 'Skateparks: Part Sixteen', pp. 52–79; Counts, 'Paradise: Part I', pp. 10–15; Counts, 'Paradise: Part II', pp. 9–15; Stan Sharp, 'Riding the New Wave', *Skateboard World*, v.2 n.2 (February 1978), pp. 76–81; and Jerry Valdez, interview with Steve Olson, *Juice*, n.71 (1 June 2013), www.juicemagazine.com.

40 Steve Alba, 'Big O', www.salbaland.com; and Jeff Greenwood, 'Big-O Skatepark – Orange', www.concretedisciples.com.

41 'Cherry Hill: Not Just Another Skatepark', *SkateBoarder*, v.5 n.8

(March 1979), pp. 72–8; Shogo Kubo, interview, *SkateBoarder*, v.5 n.10 (May 1979), p. 36; 'The History of New Jersey's Most Beloved SkatePark', www.cherryhillskatepark. com; Snyder, *Secret History*, pp. 661–5; and Glen Friedman, interview with Matt Suchodolski, www. cherryhillskatepark.com.

42 Gregg Ayres, 'Ramps 79: a Discussion with Ramp Pioneer Ray Allen', *SkateBoarder*, v.5 n.9 (April 1979), p. 54; Counts, 'Paradise: Part I', p. 10; Snyder, *Secret History*, p. 441; and Dennis Ogden, 'History of Marina del Rey Skate Park: the Short Story', www. marinadelreyskatepark.com.

43 'Get-A-Way Skatepark!' (2014), www. youtube.com/watch?v=k6HT7PI-PNw; and Snyder, *Secret History*, pp. 800–1.

44 'Del Mar Skate Ranch on SPOTS – Part 1'; Swift, 'Del Mar Skate Ranch'; Ted Terrebonne, 'Apple Skatepark', *SkateBoarder*, v.6 n.11 (June 1980), p. 32; Wally Hollyday, letter, *SkateBoarder*, v.6 n.5 (December 1979), p. 17; Michael Musgrave, letter, *SkateBoarder*, v.6 n.7 (February 1980), p. 17; and Bigelow and Hollyday, interview, pp. 64–6.

45 Hesselgrave, 'Whittier Knights', p. 25; and Snyder, *Secret History*, p. 620.

46 Steve Alba, 'Give Till It Hurts', www. salbaland.com; Palladini, *Vans*, p. 99; Curtis Hesselgrave, 'Hester Finale: Battling in the Badlands, Again', *SkateBoarder*, v.6 n.6 (January 1980), p. 23; Bigelow and Hollyday, interview, p. 61; 'Upland Pipeline', pp. 64–72; Dee Urquhart and Iain Urquhart, 'A Look at America', *Skateline*, n.8 (Spring 1982), p. 18; Hurtado, 'Radical Decade', p. 78; *Thrasher*, v.9 n.6 (June 1989), pp. 53–8, 127; 'Jeff Grosso's Loveletters to Skateboarding – Badlands Part 1' (2011), www.youtube.com/ watch?v=ONSjPSEqgrM; Gillogly, 'Badlands Story', pp. 78–95; Hesselgrave, 'Hester Finale', p. 23; and Miller, interview, *Thrasher*, p. 102.

47 www.vans.com; and 'Vans Combi Pool Construction w/ Lance Mountain and Grosso' (2010), www.youtube.com/ watch?v=ZaqvVMZdlo0.

48 Alba, 'Give Till It Hurts'; Snyder,

Secret History, pp. 740–4; Curtis Hesselgrave, 'The Ranch/Variflex Cup', *SkateBoarder's Action Now*, v.7 n.4 (November 1980), pp. 19–20; Counts, 'Paradise: Part II', pp. 12–13; and Urquhart and Urquhart, 'America', p. 16.

49 'Skate Parks: Part IV', pp. 46–53; and Hollyday, letter.

50 Snyder, *Secret History*, p. 748; 'World News', (October 1977), p. 22; and Bigelow and Hollyday, interview, p. 65.

51 Iain Borden, 'Appendix A: Skateparks', in 'A Theorised History of Skateboarding, with Particular Reference to the Ideas of Henri Lefebvre' (PhD thesis, University of London/University College London, 1998); *Skateboard Industry News* (October/November 1978); and Marcus and Griggi, *Skateboard*, pp. 152, 171.

52 D. David Morin, 'Survival Revival', *SkateBoarder's Action Now*, v.7 n.8 (March 1981), pp. 70–1.

53 'Welcome to Skateboard Escape!', *Skateboard!*, n.1 (August 1977), pp. 48–51; 'UK News', *Skateboard!*, n.4 (December 1977), p. 19; 'Wheels Roll Out West', *Skateboard!*, n.2 (October 1977), pp. 31–5; and 'Watergate Bay Skate Bowl Cornwall 1970s' (Neil Watson, 1977), www.youtube.com/ watch?v=94XACcwryjg.

54 Skate Park Construction, advertisement, *Skateboard!*, n.4 (December 1977), p. 51; 'The Sun Rises on Skate City', *Skateboard!*, n.2 (October 1977), pp. 28–30; 'UK News', *Skateboard!*, n.3 (November 1977), p. 8; François Brown de Colstoun, 'Skate City, London', *Skate* (France), n.2 (Mars–Avril 1978), pp. 23–5; Lawrie Gatehouse, 'London, England's First Skatepark!', *Wild World of Skateboarding*, v.2 n.3 (March 1978), pp. 72–3; and *Rollin' through the Decades*.

55 'Lip Torque', *Skateboard!*, n.8 (April 1978), p. 50; 'New Parks and Bowls', *Skateboard!*, n.8 (April 1978), p. 65; and 'Nationwide', *Skateboard Scene*, v.1 n.4 (undated, ca. February 1978), p. 39.

56 'Lip Torque', *Skateboard!*, n.10 (June 1978), p. 37; En-tout-cas, advertisement, *Skateboard!*, n.8

(April 1978), p. 3; Skate City Bovis, advertisement, *Skateboard!*, n.6 (February 1978), p. 79; Neil Heayes, 'All Aboard for the Skateboard Take-Off', *Contract Journal* (19 January 1978), pp. 22–3; and 'New Parks and Bowls', *Skateboard!*, n.9 (May 1978), p. 48.

57 'Lip Torque', *Skateboard!*, n.12 (August 1978), p. 30; and *Reel Life: Saturdays in Film and Sound* (SEMLAC, University of Brighton, SEFVA, *c.* 1978–1985).

58 'New Parks and Bowls', *Skateboard!*, n.12 (August 1978), p. 41; 'Skatepark Supertest: Rolling Thunder, Brentford', *Skateboard!*, n.16 (December 1978), pp. 50–2; and Benito S., 'Travels with the King, Part III', *SkateBoarder*, v.6 n.5 (December 1979), p. 64.

59 'New Parks and Bowls', *Skateboard!*, n.13 (September 1978), pp. 42-3; 'New Parks and Bowls', *Skateboard!*, n.14 (October 1978), pp. 33–5; and Trawler, *Snakes and Moguls: a Scrapbook of Britain's Seventies Concrete Skateparks* (United Kingdom: Mark Lawer, 2016).

60 'Colne', *Alpine Sports Newsletter*, n.4 (undated, ca. January 1980), p. 8; and Kenny Omond, 'Up North: Colne Classic', *Alpine Sports Newsletter*, n.4 (undated, ca. January 1980), p. 3.

61 *Skateline*, n.8 (Spring 1982), p. 8; 'Global Skate '82', *Thrasher*, v.2 n.10 (November 1982), pp. 24–6; Louise Fyfe, 'Street Legal?', *Sport and Leisure* (Sports Council) (May–June 1989), p. 33; and Urquhart and Urquhart, 'America', p. 18.

62 'Lip Torque', *Skateboard!*, n.7 (March 1978), p. 36; 'Lip Torque', (April 1978), p. 49; 'Lip Torque' (June 1978), p. 37; 'Lip Torque', *Skateboard!*, n.11 (July 1978), p. 38; 'Lip Torque' (August 1978), p. 30; 'New Parks and Bowls', *Skateboard!*, n.10 (June 1978), pp. 61-2; 'New Parks and Bowls', *Skateboard!*, n.11 (July 1978), pp. 78–80; 'New Parks and Bowls' (September 1978), p. 41; 'New Parks and Bowls' (October 1978), p. 34; *Skateboard!*, n.9 (May 1978), p. 38; Skatepark Construction, advertisement, *Skateboard!*, n.10 (June 1978), p. 92; *Skateboard!*, n.16 (December 1978), p. 50; 'Skatepark Supertest: the Rom',

Skateboard!, n.15 (November 1978), pp. 33–5; 'Skatepark Supertest: Black Lion, Gillingham', Skateboard!, n.17 (January 1979), pp. 26–8; Iain Borden, 'Pipe Dreams: Rom Skatepark', The Guardian (1 November 2014), pp. 36–7, published online as 'Concrete Playgrounds', www.gu.com/p/43vyb/tw; and 'Baker Skates' (2012), www.youtube.com/watch?v=ZNQ6NTSsRQ8.

63 Gillogly, 'Skateparks: Part Sixteen', pp. 52–79; and 'Power of London', p. 61.

64 Pete Christopherson, 'Hereford Helps Itself', Skateboard!, n.16 (December 1978), pp. 25–7; 'Power of London', p. 60; 'Skate News', Skateboard!, n.1 (August 1977), p. 13; Meany, 'Concrete', Skateboard! (second series), n.43 (June 1990), pp. 44–6; and Jamie McCullough, Meanwhile Gardens (London: Calouste Gulbenkian Foundation, 1978).

65 J.R. Black, 'The Ocean Bowl', SkateBoarder, v.3 n.3, (February 1977), pp. 42–3; Gillogly, 'Skate Parks: Part VI', pp. 44–9; Snyder, Secret History, pp. 10–11; www.brobowl.org; Wesley Higgins, 'Bro Bowl Controversy Brings in USF for Compromise', Oracle (16 June 2014), www.usforacle.com; Cathy Kelley, 'Derby Park Skate Park Flap Calms with Design Changes' (2 May 2012), www.mercurynews.com; Wormhoudt, www.skateparks.com; and Keith Hamm, 'Changing the Derby Skatepark' (1 May 2012), www.xgames.espn.go.com.

66 Javier Alejandro Bianco, letter, Thrasher, v.3 n.12 (December 1983), p. 26; Dan Bourqui, 'Photograffiti: the Brazilian Skate Scene', Thrasher, v.3 n.7 (July 1983), pp. 28–9; Mic-E Reyes, 'Viva Ecuador', Thrasher, v.17 n.1 (January 1997), pp. 78–81; 'Photograffiti', Thrasher, v.4 n.5 (May 1984), p. 21; 'McRad', Thrasher, v.4 n.4 (April 1984), p. 42; 'Somethin' Else', Thrasher, v.3 n.5 (May 1983), p. 47; Brooke, Concrete Wave, p. 87; Scott Edwards, 'Photograffiti', Thrasher, v.3 n.7 (July 1983), p. 35; Skate Rampas, 'Reforma do Bowl', Facebook, www.facebook.com; and 'Beton Hurlant et skaters contents', Skate Magazine, n.5 (1978), pp. 6–7.

67 Benito S., 'Travels with the King: Part

1', SkateBoarder, v.6. n.3 (October 1979), pp. 59–67; and Snyder, Secret History, pp. 786–5.

68 Gillogly, 'Skateparks: Part Sixteen', pp. 52–79; Ducommun, Skateboarding Vancouver, pp. 202–3; 'Burnaby, British Columbia, Canada Old Indoor Park (1978)', www.northwestskater.com; Wee Ming Wong, 'A Blast From the Past', www.surfingvancouverisland.com; and Robert Muckle and Bruce Emmett, 'Never Say Last Run: Skateboarders Challenging the Terrain and Becoming Involved in Archaeology', Theoretical Archaeology Group Annual Meeting, Southampton University (19 December 2016).

69 The Seylynn Story (dir. George Faulkner, 2012).

70 Corbin Harris, Ultimate Guide to Skateboarding (Sydney: HarperCollins, 2009), pp. 98–9; Boulter, Unemployable, p. 10; 'La Villette Story', Skate Magazine, n.5 (1978), pp. 6–7, 38–41; 'Skatepark Saint Jean de Luz' (2013), www.youtube.com/watch?v=LVZAQ7uFk-s; Revers de Tokyo; Burr Jerger, 'Skate Junket to Japan', SkateBoarder, v.6 n.6 (January 1980), pp. 54–7; Brian Gillogly, 'Skate Parks: Part Eighteen', SkateBoarder, v.4 n.10 (May 1978), pp. 68–85; Don Balch, 'Kiwis on Wheels', SkateBoarder, v.4 n.3 (October 1977), pp. 70–1; Skate World: Spain (Vice, 2010); 'Skateboard Park at Doveton', www.caseycardinialinkstoourpast.blogspot.co.uk; and www.vicskatehistory.com.

71 'Skatepark Directory', Skateboard!, n.16 (December 1978), pp. 20–3; and 'Info', TransWorld Skateboarding, v.9 n.11 (November 1991), pp. 92–6.

72 Heayes, 'All Aboard, pp. 22–3; 'Sun Rises', Skateboard!, p. 29; Urquhart and Urquhart, 'America', p. 20; Bigelow and Hollyday, interview, p. 66.

73 Snyder, Secret History, p. 822; and 'Kona – America's Oldest Skatepark on SPOTS'.

74 Snyder, Secret History, p. 619.

75 'Upland Pipeline', pp. 64–72; and 'Last Session' (2007), www.youtube.com/watch?v=hEsaCFwJCZk.

76 Snyder, Secret History, pp. 806–7; and Action Now, v.7 n.11 (June 1981), p. 5.

77 Snyder, Secret History, p. 806; Marcus and Griggi, Skateboard, pp. 171–3; Marcus, 'Plastics Explosive', pp. 18–29; Jim Levy, 'Skate Park Insurance Discussion', interview, SkateBoarder, v.4 n.10 (May 1978), p. 124; and 'Upland Pipeline', pp. 64–72.

78 'AB 1296: Public Entity Hazardous Recreational Activity Immunity: Skateboarding', www.leginfo.ca.gov; Brigette Sheils and Joel Patterson, 'Filling the Void', TransWorld Skateboarding, v.14 n.1 (January 1996), p. 164; Simple Skateboards/International Association of Skateboard Companies, advertisement, Thrasher, v.16 n.11 (November 1996), p. 35; and 'WE WIN!!! ab 1296 Is Yours!!! Skateboarding Liability Law', www.skateboard.com/iasc.

79 Peralta, interview, Thrasher, p. 21.

80 Rebirth of Skateparks; and Redondo, 'Last Ride', pp. 49–51.

81 Urquhart and Urquhart, 'America', p. 18; and 'Tony Hawk vs Christian Hosoi & the Bulldozing of Del Mar Skate Ranch Part 2' (2012), www.youtube.com/watch?v=qXKY73GkeE0.

82 Cheryl Moskovitz, 'Cherry Hill Skatepark Drew Skateboarders From Across U.S.', Courier-Post (27 June 2003), www.cherryhillskatepark.com.

83 Mike Folmer, interview, SkateBoarder's Action Now, v.7 n.4 (November 1980), p. 48; and Snyder, Secret History, p. 380.

84 Schwartz, 'Travels', p. 64; Borden, 'Appendix A'; and Michael Brooman and Colin White, letter, SkateBoarder's Action Now, v.7 n.6 (January 1981), p. 12.

85 'Concrete: Chester Skatepark', Skateboard! (second series), n.41 (April 1990), pp. 32–3, 36–7, 41; and Pete Grant, letter, Skateboard News, n.17 (May 1982), p. 2.

86 Zarka, On a Day with No Waves, p. 35.

87 Lewis Graves, 'The Florida Ramps', SkateBoarder, v.2 n.6 (August 1976), pp. 96–7; and 'The Wave', SkateBoarder, v.2 n.6 (August 1976), pp. 105–11.

88 Ramp Rider, advertisements, SkateBoarder, v.3 n.2 (December 1976), p. 19, v.4 n.2 (September 1977),

p. 120; and Pete Kristopherson, 'Build Your Own Ramp', *Skateboard!*, n.3 (November 1977), pp. 28–31.

89 Tony Magnusson, interview, *Thrasher*, v.9 n.8 (August 1989), p. 46; Weyland, *Answer Is Never*, p. 120; and Macdonald, *Dropping In*, p. 50.

90 Rampage, advertisement, *SkateBoarder*, v.6 n.9 (April 1980), p. 16; and Morin, 'Survival', p. 71.

91 Ducommun, *Skateboarding Vancouver*, p. 81; Mick Angiulo, 'On the Rampage', *SkateBoarder*, v.4 n.3 (October 1977), pp. 60–9; Snyder, *Secret History*, p. 235; and Boulter, *Unemployable*, p. 2.

92 Snyder, *Secret History*, pp. 494–7; 'Off the Wall', *SkateBoarder*, v.6 n.10 (May 1980), p. 73; and Peralta, 'Eurocana Summer Camp', pp. 52–5.

93 *Thrasher*, v.9 n.6 (June 1989), p. 54; and *Thrasher*, *Ramps* (Berkeley: High Speed Productions, 1985).

94 Boulter, *Unemployable*, pp. 11–12, 37–43; 'Lost in France', *R.A.D.*, n.137 (February–March 1995), np; *Skate World: Italy* (Vice, 2010); Snyder, *Secret History*, p. 712; 'A Ramp with a View', *R.A.D.*, n.80 (October 1989), pp. 16–17; 'More Coke and No Stickers', *R.A.D.*, n.79 (September 1989), pp. 29–31; *Over Plywood*; Tim Leighton-Boyce, 'Goodbye to All That: Ten Years of British Skating', *R.A.D.*, n.83 (January 1990), p. 45; Rodga Harvey, interview, *R.A.D.*, n.83 (January 1990), p. 50; and Hugh 'Bod' Boyle, interview, *Thrasher*, v.10 n.5 (May 1990), p. 42.

95 Debbie McAdoo, 'Ramp Ranch', *Thrasher*, (October 1981), pp. 22–5.

96 Balma, *Tracker*, pp. 144–9; Brian Gillogly, 'The Pepsi Ramp Perspective', *SkateBoarder*, v.4 n.5 (December 1977), pp. 100–9; and Gillogly, 'Ramp Rage', pp. 76–93.

97 Rick Blackhart, 'Ask the Doctor', *Thrasher*, v.5 n.3 (March 1985), p. 10; Gregg Ayres, 'Turning Point Ramp', *SkateBoarder*, v.5 n.12 (July 1979), pp. 70–3; Snyder, *Secret History*, pp. 527–8, 621–9; and interview with Hal Jepsen, *Skateboard Madness*, DVD extra.

98 Interview with Stacy Peralta, *Skateboard Madness*, DVD extra.

99 '10 Killer Ramps', *Thrasher*, v.4 n.11 (November 1984), pp. 32–7; and

Weyland, *Answer Is Never*, p. 236.

100 Tony Hawk, interview, *R.A.D.*, n.88 (June 1990), pp. 26–35; Hawk, *Hawk*, pp. 135–4; and *Bones Brigade: an Autobiography*.

101 Hawk, *Hawk*, pp. 195–6; and 'Tony Hawk: Who You Callin' a Sell Out?'

102 Gary Valentine, interview, *Skateboard!* (second series), n.46 (September 1990), p. 44.

103 'Ears', *R.A.D.*, n.88 (June 1990), p. 88; 'Terrain', *Skateboard!* (second series), n.41 (April 1990), p. 6; and Steve Kane, 'Ramp Lust', *Skateboard!* (second series), n.41 (April 1990), pp. 12–16.

104 Craig Ramsay, 'The Ramp Page: Street Ramps Part 1', *Thrasher*, v.5 n.2 (February 1985), p. 14; Craig Ramsay, 'The Ramp Page: Street Ramps Part 2', *Thrasher*, v.5 n.3 (March 1985), p. 14; and 'One Hit', *Thrasher*, v.7 n.2 (January 1987), pp. 55–61.

105 Morin, 'Survival', p. 72; 'In Praise of Ply', *R.A.D.*, n.86 (April 1990), pp. 16–17; and 'Pay Your Dues', *Thrasher*, v.10 n.5 (May 1990), p. 53.

106 'Trash', (November 1987), p. 102.

107 Tom Hodgkinson, 'Rad, Mad and Dangerous to Know?', *Midweek* (18 January 1990), p. 11.

108 Brian Beauchene, 'Unfair, Tennessee', *Thrasher*, v.7 n.3 (March 1987), pp. 53–7.

109 Craig Ramsay, 'The Ramp Page', *Thrasher*, v.4 n.6 (June 1984), p. 46; 'Mount Frostmore', *Speed Wheels*, n.2 (c. August 1988), pp. 22–3; and 'Off the Wall', (May 1980), p. 72.

110 Harry, letter, *Thrasher*, v.5 n.8 (August 1985), p. 4; and Christian Hosoi, interview, *Thrasher* (June 1989), p. 60.

111 Snyder, *Secret History*, p. 781.

112 Macdonald, *Dropping In*, pp. 138–40; and Adam Sullivan, 'The Mega Ramp', *SkateBoarder*, v.16 n.10 (April 2007), p. 36.

113 Blehm, *Agents of Change*, pp. 39–40, 246–55.

114 Marcus and Griggi, *Skateboard*, pp. 235, 242.

115 'Danny Way: World Record High Air' (14 October 2015), www.dcshoes.com.

116 Dean, 'Burnquist's Far-out Dreams'.

117 Steven Kotler, *The Rise of Superman* (London: Quercus Editions, 2014).

118 'Tom Schaar Big Air Winning Run

2014 X Games Austin' (2014), www.youtube.com/watch?v=XlOQN_XRias.

119 'Bob Burnquist's "Dreamland" – a Backyard Progression' (Oakley, 2013), www.youtube.com/watch?v=tSnfO15cAHE; 'Bob Burnquist's "Dreamland" – Hip Dream' (Oakley, 2013), www.youtube.com/watch?v=WmgZfQxwtNk; and Dean, 'Skateboarder Bob Burnquist'.

120 *Extremely Sorry* (dir. Ewan Bowman, 2009); 'Bob Burnquist Grand Canyon Jump' (2009), www.youtube.com/watch?v=3DQLDLLBzok; and Zac, 'Adil Dyani's World Record 30.8ft Foot Bomb Drop', *Caught in the Crossfire* (19 March 2015), www.caughtinthecrossfire.com.

121 Gillogly, 'Skate Parks: Part Eighteen', pp. 68–85; and Gillogly, 'Ramp Rage', pp. 76–93.

122 'Pay Your Dues', pp. 48–54, 95; Kevin Wilkins, 'New England Hot Spots', *TransWorld Skateboarding*, v.9 n.11 (November 1991), pp. 38–9, 43; *TransWorld Skateboarding*, v.14 n.1 (January 1996), p. 113; Paul Duffy, 'Texas: a State of Mind', *Skateboard!*, (second series), n.46 (September 1990), p. 38; Jeff Phillips, interview, *Five 40* (February 1990), pp. 29–35; Don Fisher, 'Pay to Play', *Thrasher*, v.11 n.9 (September 1991), p. 37; 'Lost Coast of the Carolinas', *Thrasher*, v.10 n.10 (October 1990), pp. 51–4; Don Fisher, 'Rampage', *Thrasher*, v.9 n.8 (August 1989), p. 30; and John Oliver, *Anti Gravity Device Company* (Anti Gravity Device Company, 2017).

123 Borden, 'Appendix A'; 'The Skatepark List'; and *TransWorld Skateboarding*, v.15 n.10 (October 1997), p. 78, v.15 n.11 (November 1997), p. 274.

124 'Pay Your Dues', p. 52.

125 Jeff Kendall, interview, *Thrasher*, v.6 n.12 (December 1989), p. 74; 'Where?', *R.A.D.*, n.88 (June 1990), p. 40; and 'Where? Dewsbury', *R.A.D.*, n.83 (January 1990), pp. 38–9.

126 Lance Mountain, 'Ramp Locals', *TransWorld Skateboarding*, v.6 n.1 (February 1988), pp. 94–5; Blehm, *Agents of Change*; Brooke, *Concrete Wave*, p. 166; *Onboard, The Annual*, n.1 (1997), np; Søren Aaby, 'European Meltdown', *Thrasher*, v.12 n.3 (March

1992), pp. 26–7; Bryggeriet Malmö Skatepark, www.skatemalmo. se; 'Simply Simon's', *R.A.D.*, n.117 (February 1993), pp. 16–20; and Wez Lundry, 'Jumpin' in Java', *Thrasher*, v.17 n.7 (July 1997), pp. 42–3.

127 Meany, 'Barrow Boys', *Skateboard!* (second series), n.42 (May 1990), pp. 44–5; 'Undercover: a Nearly Comprehensive Indoor Skatepark Guide', *Sidewalk Surfer*, n.14 (March 1997), np; *Rollin' through the Decades*; Ben, 'Sleepless in Wakefield', *R.A.D.*, n.137 (February–March 1995), np; 'King Rad!', *R.A.D.*, n.116 (January 1993), pp. 16–20; 'Five Years On', *Sidewalk Surfer*, n.23 (January–February, 1998), np; England, 'What Goes Around', pp. 28–9; 'New Wood Mount Hawke', *Sidewalk Surfer*, n.20 (September 1997), np; and 'Nike Bay Sixty6 – the Founder' (2012), www.youtube.com/ watch?v=4VuKgbmAjsM.

128 'King Rad!', p. 20.

129 'Undercover', np; and Arron Bleasdale, interview, *Sidewalk Surfer*, n.9 (August 1996), np.

130 'How to Build a Skatepark', *Thrasher*, v.17 n.9 (September 1997), p. 71.

131 Dan Joyce, 'Strange Deaths in Wakefield', *Sidewalk Surfer*, n.15 (April 1997), np; 'Radiation', *R.A.D.*, n.118 (March 1993), pp. 8–9; and 'Highlights', *Sidewalk Surfer*, n.13 (January–February 1997), np.

132 *Thrasher, Maximum Rad*, np.

133 Browne, *Amped*, p. 90; and 'Proving Grounds Skatepark Footage from '00 to '01' (2013), www.youtube.com/ watch?v=cbJdLKLVkpw.

134 Kirill Korobkov, 'Boarders Winning Global Recognition as Russian Skateboarding Comes of Age' (3 November 2014), www.rbth.co.uk; www.area51skatepark.nl; and www. mysticskates.cz.

135 www.monsterpark.com.au.

136 www.renewresources.com; www. ramparmor.com; and www.skatelite. com.

137 David Kiefaber, 'Mountain Dew Designs Skate Park to Look Like Giant Pinball Machine', *AdWeek* (9 June 2011), www.adweek.com; and 'Mountain Dew Skate Pinball Making Of' (2011), www.youtube.com/ watch?v=G5WGgvGrANw

Chapter 8 Skatepark Renaissance

1 Jon Amiano, Fernando Elvira and Javier Mendizabal, *La Kantera 1987-2015* (Gipuzkoa, Euskal Herria: Sugarcane, 2015); 'The Story of the Park', *R.A.D.*, n.63 (May 1988), p. 31; *Skate World: Spain*; Denike, *Built to Grind*, pp. 242, 286; www.ajsa. jp; 'Pizzey Park Complex', www. skateboard.com; Cesár Chaves, 'Brazil', *TransWorld Skateboarding*, v.2 n.1 (February 1984), pp. 42–3; 'Bowl e Banks do Itaguará' (2010), www.skateparksdobrasil.com; Marco Contati, 'Münster Mösh', *Thrasher*, v.6 n.12 (December 1989), p. 46; 'A Touch of the Hard Stuff', *R.A.D.*, n.80 (October 1989), pp. 54–5; and Duffy, 'Texas', p. 34.

2 Jean-Pierre Blanc, (ed.), *Landskating* (Hyères: Villa Noailles, 2016), p. 50; and 'Conférence Landskating 6/6 Jean-Pierre Collinet' (2016), www. vimeo.com/158981683.

3 Zarka, *On a Day with No Waves*, p. 62; 'Skate With Skilift' (2013), www.youtube.com/ watch?v=AWZI07mV618.1; Pin, 'Pin Goes to Livingston', *Jenkem*, n.9 (August 1996), np; Marjorie Kerr, 'Project to Refurbish Livingston Skatepark Completed', *Daily Record* (1 July 2015), www.dailyrecord.co.uk; Mitja Borko 'Scene Slovenia', *Thrasher*, v.11 n.12 (December 1991), pp. 32–3; 'Terrain', *Skateboard!* (second series), n.46 (September 1990), p. 6; and Thomas Campbell, 'Europe Summer Part 2', *TransWorld Skateboarding*, v.14 n.1 (January 1996), pp. 124–9.

4 Wes Flexner, 'Donnie Humes Discusses Smelly Curb, Skateparks and More', *Columbus Free Press* (22 October 2014), www. columbusfreepress.com; Editorial, *Thrasher*, v.12 n.7 (July 1992), p. 4; Craig Stecyk, 'Episodic Discontrol', Aaron Rose, Ben Weaver and Andrew Holmes, *Dysfunctional* (London: Booth-Clibborn, 1999), p. 17; 'Temecula Skatepark', www. nosewheelie.com; 'Parks, City of Temecula', www.temelink.com; Captain Beefheart, 'Yuba City, CA', *Thrasher*, v.17 n.7 (July 1997), pp. 74–5; and *A Need for Speed* (*Thrasher*, 1993).

5 'Skatepark List', *TransWorld Skateboarding*, v.18 n.10 (October 2000), pp. 92–100.

6 Justin Hocking, *Dream Builders* (New York: Rosen Publishing, 2005), p. 10.

7 Weyland, *Answer Is Never*, p. 318.

8 Hamm, *Scarred*, p. 47; and Matt Hensley, *Best of the West: Skatepark Guide* (Thornhill: Concrete Wave, c. 2005).

9 Tony Hawk, *Between Boardslides and Burnout* (New York: HarperCollins, 2002), p. 9; and *Rebirth of Skateparks*.

10 Sean Sowell, 'Bringing Back Pipeline', *Landscape Online*, www. landscapeonline.com; and 'Upland Comes Full Circle', *TransWorld Skateboarding* (14 October 2002), www.skateboarding.transworld.net.

11 Clemmit, 'Extreme Sports'; Deborah A. Cohen et al., 'City of Los Angeles Neighborhood Parks' (Rand Corporation, Research Report, 2016); and TransWorld, 'State of Skate', p. 10.

12 www.vans.com.

13 'Orcas Island Skate Park', www. awesome-skateboard.com; 'Orcas Skatepark', www.orcasparkandrec.org; and Northwest (2003).

14 'TWS 10: Legendary Swimming Pools', *TransWorld Skateboarding* (5 May 2009), www.skateboarding. transworld.net; Ozzie, 'Return to the Nude Bowl', *Blue Tile Obsession* (16 June 2013), www.ozzieausband. wordpress.com; Ozzie, 'Nude Bowl, a Retrospective', *Juice* (1 September 1999), www.juicemagazine. com; 'Nude Bowl skateboarding 1986' (2012), www.youtube.com/ watch?v=zVa8_ct-NIk; 'Nude Bowl Skateboarding 1997' (2011), www. youtube.com/watch?v=I2r9Kmo Q1v0; 'Palm Springs Skate Park', www.ci.palm-springs.ca; and 'Nude Bowl Skateboarding 1997' (2011), www.youtube.com/ watch?v=I2r9KmoQ1v0.

15 Browne, *Amped*, p. 90.

16 Justin Hocking, *The World's Greatest Skate Parks* (New York: Rosen, 2009), pp. 16–23.

17 'Newberg, Chehalem Skate Park', www.skateoregon.com.

18 'Monrovia skatepark', www. socalskateparks.com; and 'Vans Skatepark in Milpitas, California Opens', *TransWorld Skateboarding*

(27 June 2000), www.skateboarding.transworld.net.

19 Syd Kearney, 'Largest Skatepark in North America Opens in Greenspoint', *Houston Chronicle* (14 August 2014), www.chron.com; and 'Largest Public Skatepark in the USA – Flyover Preview' (Lance Childers, 2014), www.youtube.com/watch?v=PJcigTu6UZs.

20 'Lake Cunningham Skatepark', www.californiaskateparks.com; and 'Lake Cunningham Skatepark/Vert Wall Session' (2008), www.youtube.com/watch?v=MvEDsFVd2jg.

21 *Bridge to Bridge* (dir. Elias Parias, 2014); 'Largest Covered U.S. Skatepark Revealed!' (2014), www.youtube.com/watch?v=WmlaaYbs8k8; and *Made in Venice* (dir. Jonathan Penson, 2016).

22 *Pidgeon Park* (dir. Buddy Pendergast, 2015), www.vimeo.com/143072005.

23 'Shaw Millennium Park', www.calgary.ca.

24 Alexandra Cain, 'Aussie Builds World's Largest Skateboard Park', *Sydney Morning Herald* (23 September 2013), www.smh.com.au; 'Brad Shaw Interview', *Whatsup* (4 December 2015), www.chinaskateboards.cn; 'The Biggest GMP Skate Park in the World in Guangzhou (China)' (2015), www.youtube.com/watch?v=BhHCsPQC_cw; and Li, 'China's Skateboarding Youth Culture'.

25 'Stapelbäddsparken', www.skatemalmo.se; and Nils Svensson, 'The Making of Stapelbäddsparken', *Kingpin*, reproduced at www.skatemalmo.se.

26 Harris, *Ultimate Guide to Skateboarding*, pp. 84–99.

27 'Cradle Skatepark: History', www.skatethecradle.com.

28 Andrew Guan, 'Switch Plaza in Shenzhen' (21 October 2007), www.kickerclub.com; Kilwag 'Additions to Lakeside, Pokhara Skate Park in Nepal', www.skateandannoy.com (8 January 2015); Bernd Debusmann, 'Largest GCC Skateboarding Park Opens in Dubai', *Khaleej Times* (16 January 2016), www.khaleejtimes.com; Kilwag 'Terror in Tahoe/Tehran', www.skateandannoy.com (4 November 2014); and 'Why Is North Korea Adopting Skateboarding?', *Jenkem* (3 September 2013), www.jenkemmag.com.

29 Snyder, *Secret History*, pp. 700–13, 782–3.

30 www.spausa.org; Whitley, *Public Skatepark Development Guide*, pp. 37–52; and Ben Wixon, *Skateboarding* (Champaign: Human Kinetics, 2009), p. 134.

31 Jim Murphy, 'Allen Losi Interview', *Juice* (1 June 2013), www.juicemagazine.com.

32 Callum Chaplin, 'Skateboarders Descend on Malmesbury Abbey Again', *Wilts and Gloucestershire Standard* (4 February 2016), www.wiltsglosstandard.co.uk.

33 Cave, 'Dogtown USA'; and Will Jarvis, 'Skateboarding, Religion Mixed in Unique Grouping in Colorado Springs', *The Gazette* (30 June 2016), www.gazette.com.

34 Cave, 'Dogtown USA'.

35 Cate St Hill, '42 Architects Complete First Phase of Park in Sweden', *Building Design* (14 January 2013), www.bdonline.co.uk.

36 Blanc, *Landskating*, pp. 66–9.

37 Daryl Mersom, 'Discussing Skate Park Design With Janne Saario', *The Green Skateboard Zine* (6 December 2015), www.thegreenzine.co.uk.

38 'Glow in the Dark Skateparks with South Korean Artist Koo Jeong-A', *Fakie Hill Bomb* (19 October 2015), www.fakiehillbomb.wordpress.com.

39 Graffuturism, 'Zuk Club Skatepark Mural Installation', *Graffuturism* (22 May 2014), www.graffuturism.com; 'A Bit Fishy', *DesignBoom* (25 August 2016), www.designboom.com; and Kristin Hohenadel, 'A Spanish Artist Transforms an Old Church Into a "Sistine Chapel" of Skateboarding', *Slate* (8 March 2016), www.slate.com.

40 Gilles Deleuze and Félix Guattari, *A Thousand Plateaus* (London: Athlone, 1988), p. 478.

41 *Stuntwood*; and TransWorld, 'State of Skate', p. 11.

42 *The Skateboard Mag*, n.132 (March 2015), p. 42.

43 Paul O'Connor, 'Skateboarders, Helmet Use and Control: Observations from Skateboard Media and a Hong Kong Skatepark', *Journal of Sport and Social Issues*, v.40 n.6 (2016), pp. 477–98.

44 'Milton Keynes Evolution', *Sidewalk*, n.104 (May 2005), pp. 64–9.

45 Claudine Heizer, 'Street Smarts', *Parks & Recreation*, v.39 n.11 (November 2004), pp. 74–9; Francisco Vivoni, 'Spots of Spatial Desire: Skateparks, Skateplazas, and Urban Politics', *Journal of Sport and Social Issues*, v.33 n.2 (2009), pp. 139–40; Paul Zitzer, 'Scene Building: the Rob Dyrdek/DC Shoes Skate Plaza', *The Skateboard Mag*, n.18 (September 2005), pp. 74–5; and 'DC Skate Plaza Grand Opening' (2007), www.youtube.com/watch?v=qBhtbgndOh4.

46 Peter Whitley, 'Dyrdek's Los Angeles Vision', *Skaters For Public Skateparks* (28 June 2010), www.skatepark.org.

47 Umberto Eco, *Travels in Hyper Reality* (San Diego: Harcourt Brace Jovanovich, 1986); and Jean Baudrillard, 'Simulacra and Simulations', in Mark Poster, *Jean Baudrillard* (Cambridge: Polity, 1988), p. 166.

48 Atencio and Beal, 'Legitimate Skateboarder', pp. 112, 118.

49 www.visitstoke.co.uk.

50 www.theforks.com; and Frank Daniello, 'The Plaza at the Forks, Winnipeg', *Concrete Skateboarding* (March 2007), pp. 53–63.

51 Zac, 'The DC Embassy Closes', *Caught in the Crossfire* (26 March 2014), www.caughtinthecrossfire.com.

52 www.skatelite.com.

53 'Lemvig Skatepark', www.skateparks.dk; www.glifberglykke.com; and www.effekt.dk.

54 'Roskilde: Storm Water Skate Park', www.dac.dk; 'Rabalder Park', www.skateparks.dk; Liz Stinson, 'Ingenious Architecture: a Skatepark that Prevents Flooding', *Wired* (25 June 2013), www.wired.com; and www.snearchitects.com.

55 'Omokoroa Skatepath Opening' (2016), www.youtube.com/watch?v=uuLWbwrAKFY.

56 Andrea Klassen, 'Longing to Board: a Canadian First in Kamloops', *Kamloops This Week* (4 September 2014), www.kamloopsthisweek.com; and Kade Krichko, 'Introducing the World's First Longboard Park', *GrindTV* (30 October 2014), www.grindtv.com.

57 'Go Skate – Lake Hayes Pump Track, Queenstown, NZ' (2014), www.vimeo.com/97737371; and www.velosolutions.com.

58 Philip Stevens, 'Wooden Playground by Jun Igarashi + YCAM Interlab Undulates through Sapporo Park', *DesignBoom* (18 February 2016), www.designboom.com.

59 Skatepark Advisory Task Force, *City of Seattle Citywide Skatepark Plan* (31 January 2007); and Paul O'Connor, interview with Aaron McGowen, 'Sk8 O'Clock' podcast (2015).

60 Blanc, *Landskating*, pp. 60–73.

61 Sedo, 'Dead-Stock Boards', p. 272; and 'SKATE Shanghai, China with Brian Dolle' (2013), www.youtube.com/watch?v=Rrjc16FGmCo.

62 Ignasi de Solà-Morales, 'Terrain Vague', Dean Almy, (ed.), *Center 14* (Austin: Centre for American Architecture and Design, 2007), pp. 104–13.

63 Anthony Bracali, 'Thanks, Le Corbusier', www.anthonybracali.com.

64 Ocean Howell, 'The "Creative Class" and the Gentrifying City: Skateboarding in Philadelphia's Love Park', *Journal of Architectural Education*, v.59 n.2 (2005), pp. 32–42; Jeremy Nemeth, 'Conflict, Exclusion, Relocation: Skateboarding and Public Space', *Journal of Urban Design*, v.11 n.3 (2006), pp. 297–318; and Sari Soffer, 'Franklin's Paine Skatepark' (2013), www.vimeo.com/72469036.

65 Katie Clark and Tim Hyland, 'Q&A With Drexel Alum Tony Bracali', *Drexel Now* (21 May 2013), www.drexel.edu.

66 Inga Saffron, 'Changing Skyline: Finding Common Ground for Skateboarders and Picnickers' (18 May 2013), www.philly.com.

67 Christian Kerr, 'The Death and Life of Great American Skate Plazas', *Jenkem* (11 March 2016), www.jenkemmag.com; 'Wow, Philadelphia Did Something Smart!', www.quartersnacks.com (22 May 2013); Cassie Owens, 'Skateboard Urbanism Could Change Park Planning', *Next City* (1 October 2014), www.nextcity.org; and 'The One Place Michael Haeflinger Loves?' (22 October 2013), www.phillylovenotes.com.

68 Iain Borden, 'Southbank Skateboarding, London and Urban Culture: the Undercroft, Hungerford Bridge and House of Vans', Lombard, *Skateboarding*, pp. 91–107.

69 Andrew Blum, 'New Oslo Opera House Is Really a Stealth Skate Park', *Wired*, v.16 n.12 (24 November 2008), www.wired.com; and Iain Borden, 'The Spaces of Skateboarding', *Architects' Journal* (28 November 2014), pp. 56–9.

70 Arnon Ritter, Marina Treichl and Claudia Wedekind, (eds), *Auszeichnung Des Landes Tirol Für Neues Bauen 2012* (Innsbruck: Culture Department, Tyrol, 2012); 'Landhausplatz by LAAC Architeken and Stiefel Kramer Architecture', *Dezeen* (2 June 2011), www.dezeen.com; LHP – Landhausplatz (Stefan Huber, 2012), www.vimeo.com/36787035; and 'City Skateboarding Guide – #5 Innsbruck', www.playboard.de.

71 'Water Square Benthemplein', www.urbanisten.nl.

72 'Kap 686 Skate Park/Metrobox Architekten', *Arch Daily* (1 September 2011), www.archdaily.com.

73 'Logroño Estrena una Nueva Street Plaza Insipirada en El Espolón', *Eplatín.com* (27 September 2016); Jan, 'Skatepark Design with Daniel Yabar', *Kingpin* (9 November 2016), www.kingpinmag.com; and www.danielyabar.com.

74 *In Search of the Miraculous* (dir. Pontus Alv, 2010).

75 Gillogly, 'Skateparks: Part Sixteen', pp. 52–79; and Roberts, 'Santa Cruz', p. 80.

76 Rob Erickson, 'Skatopia', *Juice* (1 December 1999), www.juicemagazine.com; and *Skatopia: 88 Acres of Anarchy* (dir. Laurie House and Colin Powers, 2009).

77 Roy the Barbecue Man, 'Portland Project', *Thrasher*, v.11 n.11 (November 1991), pp. 34–5, 80; Noah Martineau, 'A Piss Drenched Bert on the First Day of Spring', *Thrasher*, v.17 n.7 (July 1997), pp. 76–83; 'The Great North West Invaded', *Slap*, v.4 n.9 (September 1995), pp. 34–41; Paul Fujita, 'Burnside', *TransWorld Skateboarding*, v.15 n.11 (November 1997), pp. 140–57; www.burnsideproject.blogspot.co.uk; and Kara-Jane Lombard, 'Trucks, Tricks, and Technologies of Government: Analyzing the Productive Encounter between Governance and Resistance in Skateboarding', Lombard, *Skateboarding*, pp. 169–81.

78 Hamm, *Scarred for Life*, pp. 217–19; Stanton Jones and Arthur Graves, 'Power Plays in Public Space: Skateboard Parks as Battlegrounds, Gifts, and Expressions of Self', *Landscape Journal*, v.19 n.1-2 (2000), pp. 136–48; *Full Tilt Boogie* (dir. Chris Bredesen, Brenna Duffy and Julie Gerlach, 2003); and *Under the Bridge* (dir. Lucas Chemotti, 2015).

79 Hamm, *Scarred for Life*, p. 226.

80 Phelps, *Skate and Destroy*, p. 191; and Hamm, *Scarred for Life*, p. 217.

81 Orpana, 'Steep Transitions', p. 162; and Hamm, *Scarred for Life*, pp. 221–3.

82 Nels Gravstad, 'Bowl Builders Busted', *Thrasher*, v.12 n.7 (July 1992), pp. 14, 22; and Campo, *Accidental Playground*, p. 46.

83 Hamm, *Scarred for Life*, p. 230.

84 *Full Tilt Boogie*.

85 John Carr, 'Legal Geographies: Skating around the Edges of the Law: Urban Skateboarding and the Role of Law in Determining Young Peoples' Place in the City', *Urban Geography*, v.31 n.7 (2010), pp. 999–1000.

86 Hamm, *Scarred for Life*, pp. 219, 229.

87 Blake Nelson, *Paranoid Park* (London: Penguin, 2006), pp. 7–8; and *Paranoid Park* (dir. Gus Van Sant, 2007).

88 Hamm, *Scarred for Life*, p. 229; and *Thrasher*, *Epic Spots*, p. 154.

89 Phelps, *Skate and Destroy*, p. 191; and Gravstad, 'Bowl Builders', p. 22.

90 Phil Jackson, Scott Kmiec and Nicholas Orso, *FDR Skatepark* (Atglen: Schiffer, 2012), np.

91 Teddy Cruz, 'How Architectural Innovations Migrate Across Borders', *TED Global*, Edinburgh (June 2013), www.ted.com.

92 *Thrasher*, *Epic Spots*, p. 157.

93 Lombard, 'Trucks, Tricks, and Technologies', pp. 169–81.

94 Jackson, Kmiec and Orso, *FDR Skatepark*, np.

95 Hocking, *World's Greatest Skate Parks*, pp. 9–10; El Beardo 'The Never Ending Story', *Thrasher*, n.297, (August 2005), pp. 68–73; and 'Marginal Way DIY Skatepark', *Skaters for Public Skateparks* (2 December 2010), www.skatepark.org.

96 Campo, *Accidental Playground*, pp. 33–65.

97   Curtis O'Dell, 'Top DIY Spots in Europe', *Kingpin* (13 December 2013), www.kingpinmag.com.

98   Kashmira Gander, 'Greek Architect Builds Haven for Adult Skaters in Wake of Financial Crisis', *Independent* (4 January 2017), www.independent.co.uk; *Skate World: France* (Vice, 2011); www.skatedaily.net; www.skateboarding.transworld.net; and www.confuzine.com.

99   Kyle Duvall, 'What is the Future of Skateparks?', *Ride* (24 August 2016), www.theridechannel.com.

100 Chris Nieratko, 'Bolivia Has a Fancy New Skatepark', *Vice* (11 July 2014), www.vice.com; Mehring, *Skate the World*; and www.makelifeskatelife.org and www.skate-aid.com.

101 Robin Fleming, 'India's DIY Skatepark' (18 July 2013), www.xgames.espn.go.com.

102 'Man Beats Hardship by Turning Home to Skate Park', *Daily Telegraph* (28 May 2015), www.telegraph.co.uk.

103 Orpana, 'Steep Transitions', p. 162; and Lombard, 'Skate and Create/ Skate and Destroy', pp. 475–88.

104 Campo, *Accidental Playground*, p. 43.

105 Campo, *Accidental Playground*, pp. 49–56.

106 TransWorld, 'State of Skate', p. 11.

107 www.theiasc.org.

108 Myra Taylor and Umneea Khan, 'Skate-Park Builds, Teenaphobia and the Adolescent Need for Hang-out Spaces', *Journal of Urban Design*, v.16 n.4 (2011), pp. 489–510; and Helen Woolley and Ralph Johns, 'Skateboarding: the City as a Playground', *Journal of Urban Design*, v.6 n.2 (2001), pp. 211–30.

109 J.B. Jackson, *Discovering the Vernacular Landscape* (New Haven: Yale University Press, 1984), p. 130.

110 Myra Taylor and Ida Marais, 'Not in My Back Schoolyard', *Australian Planner*, v.48 n.2 (2011), pp. 84–95; Jo McFadyen & Glynis Longhurst, 'Parks for Sport and Recreation' (Hamilton City Council, research report, 28 March 2014); Dan Goater, 'Skate Respect: Anti-social Behaviour Down Thanks to Park', *Dorset Echo* (7 October 2010), www.dorsetecho.co.uk; and 'Street Patrol UK', BBC (17 September 2014), www.youtube.com/watch?v=BZlkjWEtaU8.

111 John Carr, 'Activist Research and City Politics: Ethical Lessons from Youth-Based Public Scholarship', *Action Research*, v.10 n.1 (2012), p. 71.

112 Bradley, 'Skate Parks', pp. 288–323; Carr, 'Activist Research', pp. 61–78; Jones and Graves, 'Power Plays', pp. 136–48; Taylor and Khan, 'Skate-Park Builds', pp. 489–510; and Marni Goldenberg and Wynn Shooter, 'Skateboard Park Participation: a Means-End Analysis', *Journal of Youth Development*, v.4 n.4 (2007), pp. 1–12.

113 Daniel Turner, 'The Civilised Skateboarder: a Figurational Analysis of the Provision of Adventure Recreation Facilities' (PhD thesis, Glasgow Caledonian University, 2013), pp. 189–90, 211–14; and Carr, 'Activist Research', p. 72.

114 Robert D. Putnam, *Bowling Alone* (New York: Simon & Schuster, 2000), p. 406.

115 Pablo Sendra, 'Rethinking Urban Public Space', *City*, v.19 n.6 (2015), pp. 820–36.

116 Charlene S. Shannon and Tara L. Werner, 'The Opening of a Municipal Skate Park', *Journal of Park and Recreation Administration*, v.26 n.3 (Fall 2008), pp. 39–58.

117 Susie Weller, 'Skateboarding Alone? Making Social Capital Discourse Relevant to Teenagers' Lives', *Journal of Youth Studies*, v.9 n.5 (2006), pp. 557–74.

118 Petrone, 'Shreddin' It Up', p. 94.

119 *Raising Helseth* (dir. Josh Becker and Mike Oliphant, 2013).

120 Alex Dumas and Sophie Laforest, 'Skateparks as a Health-Resource', *Leisure Studies*, v.28 n.1 (2009), pp. 19-34; and Bradley, 'Skate Parks as a Context', p. 290.

121 Jones and Graves, 'Power Plays', p. 147.

122 Chihsin Chiu, 'Contestation and Conformity: Street and Park Skateboarding in New York City Public Space', *Space and Culture*, v.12 n.1 (2009), p. 389.

123 Dumas and Laforest, 'Skateparks', pp. 19–34; and Robert Rinehart and Chris Grenfell, 'BMX Spaces: Children's Grass Roots Courses and Corporate-Sponsored Tracks', *Sociology of Sport Journal*, v.19 n.3 (2002), pp. 302–14.

124 Francisco Vivoni, 'Contesting Public Space: Skateboarding, Urban Development, and the Politics of Play' (PhD thesis, University of Illinois at Urbana-Champaign, 2010), pp. 55–60; 'Burnham Park', www.chicagoparkdistrict.com; and 'Marine Parade Redevelopment', www.napier.govt.nz.

125 Kelly, Pomerantz and Currie, 'You Can Break So Many More Rules', pp. 547–57.

126 Harris, 'Belonging Paradox', pp. 117–32; and John Carr, 'Skateboarding in Dude Space: the Roles of Space and Sport in Constructing Gender among Adult Skateboarders', *Sociology of Sport Journal*, v.34 n.1 (2016), pp. 25–34.

127 Daniel Turner, 'The Civilized Skateboarder and the Sports Funding Hegemony: a Case Study of Alternative Sport', *Sport in Society*, v.16 n.10 (2013), p. 1254.

128 Edwards, 'Swamp Suburbia', p. 45.

129 www.facebook.com/groups/skatersover50/permalink/756733984435970/.

130 Peter Harnik and Coleen Gentles, 'Coming to a City near You', *Parks & Recreation* (May 2009), pp. 34-8.

131 Wixon, *Skateboarding*, pp. 170–1.

132 Bethany Rodgers, 'Park Projects turn Skateboarders from Rebellion to Advocacy', *Seminole County News* (21 January 2016), www.orlandosentinel.com.

133 Petrone, 'Shreddin' It Up', pp. 98, 118.

134 Turner, 'Civilized Skateboarder and the Sports Funding Hegemony', p. 1527; Turner, 'The Civilised Skateboarder: a Figurational Analysis'; Daniel Turner, 'Performing Citizenship: Skateboarding and the Formalisation of Informal Spaces', Daniel Turner and Sandro Carnicelli, (eds), *Lifestyle Sports and Public Policy* (Abingdon: Routledge, 2017), pp. 13–26; Ocean Howell, 'Skatepark as Neoliberal Playground: Urban Governance, Recreation Space, and the Cultivation of Personal Responsibility', *Space and Culture*, v.11 n.4 (2008), p. 476; and Beal et al., 'Skateboarding, Community and Urban Politics', pp. 1–13.

135 Howell, 'Skatepark as Neoliberal Playground', p. 475.

136 Hawk, *How Did I Get Here?*, p. 147; and Striler, *X Play Nation*, pp. 272–3.

137 'Bastard Store/Studiometrico', *ArchDaily* (10 May 2009), www.archdaily.com; and Skate World: Italy (Vice, 2010).

138 www.beachburritocompany.com.

139 Borden, 'Southbank Skateboarding', pp. 91–107.

140 'Tony Hawk: Who You Callin' a Sell Out?'

141 Lawrence Lessig, *Remix* (New York: Penguin Press, 2008).

142 Lee Bofkin, *Concrete Canvas* (London: Cassell, 2014), pp. 6–8.

143 Duvall, 'What Is the Future of Skateparks?'.

144 'Final Designs on Louisville Extreme Park Being Fine-tuned', *Courier-Journal* (29 October 2013), www.courier-journal.com; Sali Baba, 'Louisville Skatepark', *TransWorld Skateboarding*, v.20 n.12 (December 2002), pp. 244–80; Mark Schultz, 'To the Extreme', *Louisville Paper* (3 February 2012), www.thelouisvillepaper.com; and Sheldon S. Shafer, 'Louisville Extreme Park Rebuild Getting Under Way', *Courier-Journal* (1 April 2014), www.courier-journal.com.

145 Beal, *Skateboarding*, p. 2; 'Black Pearl Skatepark', sitedesigngroup.com; and Hawk, *How Did I Get Here?*, pp. 134–6.

146 www.streetdome.dk.

147 Marni Katz, 'Factoria Joven Skate Park', *Design Milk* (28 October 2011), www.design-milk.com.

148 www.hrhrivieramaya.com; and 'Coming Soon in 2017, Woodward Riviera Maya' (2015), www.youtube.com/watch?v=ZPNrK05FFjU.

149 Bill Bradley, 'Detroit Vying for X Games', *Next City* (28 May 2013), www.nextcity.org; and Phil Wright, 'Is Malmö the Most Skateboarding-Friendly City in the World?', *Huck* (24 August 2016), www.huckmagazine.com.

150 'Guy Hollaway Plans to Put Folkestone on the Map', *Dezeen* (15 May 2015), www.dezeen.com; Liz Stinson, 'Inside a Bonkers Plan to Build a 5-Story Skatepark', *Wired* (20 May 2015), www.wired.com; and Alexandra Gibbs, 'Avoid Brain Drain, Build a Multistory Skate Park' (24 June 2015), www.cnbc.com.

Chapter 9 Super-Architectural Space

1 Merleau-Ponty, *Phenomenology of Perception* (London: Routledge and Kegan Paul, 1962), p. 140

2 Merleau-Ponty, *Phenomenology of Perception*, pp. 138–9.

3 Lefebvre, *Production of Space*, p. 50.

4 Bruce Walker, interview, *SkateBoarder*, v.3 n.1 (October 1976), pp. 40–5.

5 *SkateBoarder*, v.5 n.7 (February 1979), p. 5.

6 Micke Alba, interview, *SkateBoarder*, v.6 n.9 (April 1980), p. 26.

7 Snyder, *Secret History*, pp. 306–19, 641–7, 668, 828–37, *passim*.

8 Kevin Wilkins, in Mullen, interview, *Warp*, p. 48; 'Major Moves', p. 50; Aatish Bhatia, 'The Physics of Doing an Ollie on a Skateboard', *Wired* (5 October 2014), www.wired.com; and Edward Frederick, Jeremy Determan, Saunders Whittlesey and Joseph Hamill, 'Biomechanics of Skateboarding: Kinetics of the Ollie', *Journal of Applied Biomechanics*, v.22 n.1 (2006), pp. 33–40.

9 Jeff Grosso, 'Grosso's Loveletters to Skateboarding – Slide N Roll' (2013), www.youtube.com/watch?v=-B1LTs-xdy0; and 'Jeff Grosso's Loveletters to Skateboarding – Foot Plant' (2012), www.youtube.com/watch?v=GracvV0UK8s.

10 Snyder, *Secret History*, pp. 552–4 and 789; and Allen Losi, interview, *Thrasher*, v.6 n.2 (February 1986), pp. 39–40.

11 Curtis Hesselgrave, '360 – Oasis Easter Classic', *Wired*, v.5 n.12 (July 1979), p. 45.

12 *King of the Mountain* (First On Board, 1980).

13 Hesselgrave, 'Whittier Knights', p. 25.

14 Iain Urquhart, 'Judging: a Special Report', *Skateline*, n.8 (Spring 1982), p. 10.

15 Curtis Hesselgrave, 'The Powell-Peralta Marina Cup', *SkateBoarder's Action Now*, v.7 n.6 (January 1981), p. 65.

16 Mortimer, *Stalefish*, p. 144.

17 '540° McTwist', *Thrasher*, v.4 n.10 (October 1984), pp. 32–3; Craig Ramsay, 'When the Hawk Flies', *Thrasher*, v.4 n.11 (November 1984), p. 22; 'Major Moves', p. 58; and

Marcus and Griggi, *Skateboard*, p. 217.

18 Jocko Weyland, 'Epiphany at Mecca', *Thrasher*, v.17 n.7 (July 1997), p. 63.

19 Hawk, *Hawk*, p. 92; and *Bones Brigade: an Autobiography*.

20 *Bones Brigade: an Autobiography*.

21 *Off Camera with Sam Jones: Episode 10*; Wayne Kerr, 'The Oldest Trick in the Book', *Thrasher*, v.7 n.12 (December 1987), pp. 60–5; and 'Jeff Grosso's Loveletters to Skateboarding – Ben Schroeder' (2011), www.youtube.com/watch?v=P0L3ej7qMts.

22 Danny Way, interview, *TransWorld Skateboarding*, v.9 n.10 (October 1991), p. 109; 'Major Moves', p. 55; 'Tony Hawk – the First 900 Ever at the X Games 1999' (2009), www.youtube.com/watch?v=UnDgQUW1CO0; and Hawk, *Hawk*, pp. 233–41.

23 Weyland, 'Epiphany', p. 62.

24 Hosoi, interview, *Thrasher*, p. 102.

25 Lefebvre, *Production of Space*, pp. 170–6.

26 Curtis Hesselgrave, 'The Dynamics of Skating – Part II', *SkateBoarder*, v.6 n.11 (June 1980), p. 12.

27 Stephen Connor, *A Philosophy of Sport* (London: Reaktion, 2011), p. 18.

28 Georg Simmel, 'The Metropolis and Mental Life', P.K. Hatt and A.J. Reiss, (eds), *Cities and Society* (New York: Free Press, 1951), pp. 642–3.

29 Curtis Hesselgrave, 'Skate Safe: Balance', *SkateBoarder*, v.6 n.6 (January 1980), p. 13.

30 Martin Heidegger, in George Steiner, *Heidegger* (London: Fontana, 1992), p. 89.

31 Peralta, interview, *SkateBoarder*, p. 57; and Snyder, *Secret History*, p. 550.

32 Rodney Mullen, interview, *Thrasher*, v.4 n.3 (March 1984), p. 32; and Rodney Mullen 'Pop an Ollie and Innovate', TED Talk, University of Southern California (May 2012), www.ted.com.

33 'Trickipedia', www.theberrics.com.

34 '2015 Skateboarding World Championships at the Kimberley Diamond Cup Street Finals' (2015), www.youtube.com/watch?v=QFTxr0gN2H8.

35 'Blast From the Past', *Thrasher*, v.17 n.9 (September 1997), p. 54.

36 Britt Parrott, 'Friendship', *TransWorld Skateboarding*, v.6 n.1 (February

1988), p. 6.

37 Mullen, interview, *Thrasher*, p. 61.

38 'Rodney Mullen Debuts New Tricks, Captured in 360 Degrees'.

39 Steiner, *Heidegger*, p. 90.

40 'Are Our Skate Parks Tough Enough?', *Skateboard Scene*, v.1 n.1 (*c.* November-December 1977), pp. 36–9, 52; and Gillogly, 'Skate Parks: Part Eighteen', pp. 68–85.

41 Peralta, interview, *SkateBoarder*, p. 58.

42 Chris Miller, interview, *R.A.D.*, n.77 (July 1989), p. 43.

43 Bill Stinson, e-mail (13 May 1997).

44 www.skatekennesaw.com.

45 www.socalskateparks.com.

46 Davis, 'Del Mar Was', pp. 106–11.

47 Simon Napper, interview, *Skateboard!*, n.19 (June 1979), p. 30.

48 Brian Brannon, 'Viva Las Pools', *Thrasher*, v.8 n.7 (July 1988), p. 72.

49 Lefebvre, *Production of Space*, p. 183.

50 Brian Glenney, 'Skateboarding, Sport and Spontaneity: Toward a Subversive Definition of Sport', Shawn E. Klein, (ed.), *Defining Sport: Conceptions and Borderlines* (Lanham: Lexington, 2017), pp. 147–58; and Brian Glenney and Steve Mull, 'Skateboarding and the Re-Wilding of Urban Space', *Journal of Sport and Social Issues* (forthcoming).

51 Lefebvre, *Production of Space*, pp. 98, 199–200, 286.

52 Paul O'Connor, interview with Aaron McGowen, 'Sk8 O'Clock' podcast (2015).

53 Michel Serres, *The Five Senses* (London: Continuum, 2008); and Thorpe, *Snowboarding Bodies*, pp. 221–2.

54 Peralta, interview, *SkateBoarder*, p. 58.

55 'Who's Hot! Ellen Berryman', p. 90.

56 Napper, interview, p. 54.

57 Merleau-Ponty, *Phenomenology of Perception*, p. 102.

58 August Schmarsow, 'The Essence of Architectural Creation', Robert Vischer, Harry Francis Mallgrave and Eleftherios Ikonomou, *Empathy, Form, and Space* (Santa Monica: Getty Center for the History of Art and the Humanities, 1994), p. 291.

59 Brannon, 'Viva', p. 75.

60 Hesselgrave, 'Dynamics', p. 12.

61 Lefebvre, *Writings on Cities*, p. 220.

62 Lefebvre, *Production of Space*, p. 137.

63 Bernard Tschumi, *Architecture and Disjunction* (Cambridge, Mass.: MIT, 1998), p. 110.

64 Henri Lefebvre, *Rhythmanalysis* (London: Continuum, 2004).

65 Kevin Wilkins, 'NSA Spring Nationals: Kona USA Skatepark', *TransWorld Skateboarding*, v.9 n.10 (October 1991), p. 43.

66 Hosoi and Ahrens, *Hosoi*, p. 7.

67 Jerry Casale, interview, *SkateBoarder*, v.6 n.5 (December 1979), p. 35.

68 Lefebvre, *Production of Space*, p. 206; and 'Major Moves', p. 51.

69 Henri Lefebvre, *Everyday Life in the Modern World* (London: Transaction Publishers, 1984), p. 4.

70 *The Quarterly SkateBoarder*, v.1 n.1 (Winter 1964), p. 7; and John Severson, 'Editorial: Why Speed?', *The Quarterly SkateBoarder*, v.1 n.2 (Spring 1965), p. 7.

71 'Fastest Skateboarder Ever! 89.41 mph/143.89 kph – Kyle Wester' (2016), www.youtube.com/watch?v=QbN_imu_ewA.

72 Charles Stein, 'X Marks the Spot', *Boston Globe* (23 August 1998), magazine section, p. 17.

73 Denis Shufeldt, 'Going for High Speed', *SkateBoarder*, v.2 n.1 (Summer 1975), pp. 26–9; and *Signal Hill Speed Run*.

74 Hamm, *Scarred*, p. 23.

75 Harms and Smith, *Skateboarder's Journal*, p. 236–7.

76 'Crazy Downhill Skateboarders Flying by Cyclists' (2014), www.youtube.com/watch?v=NkXzit3b348.

77 Belinda Wheaton, 'After Sport Culture: Rethinking Sport and Post-Subcultural Theory', *Journal of Sport & Social Issues*, v.31 n.3 (2007), p. 298.

78 Mihaly Csikszentmihalyi, *Flow: the Psychology of Optimal Experience* (New York: Harper and Row, 1990), pp. 3, 6.

79 *Public Domain* (dir. Stacy Peralta and Craig Stecyk, 1988); James Pisano, 'The Tao of Skate', *Concrete Wave* (Winter 2010), pp. 48–53; and *Off Camera with Sam Jones: Episode 10*.

80 T. Seifert and C. Hedderson, 'Intrinsic Motivation and Flow in Skateboarding', *Journal of Happiness Studies*, v.11 n.3 (2010), pp. 277–92.

81 Macdonald, *Dropping In*, p. 123.

82 Harms and Smith, *Skateboarder's Journal*, pp. 32, 247–8.

83 Weyland, *Answer Is Never*, p. 57.

84 Stephen Lyng, 'Edgework: a Social Psychological Analysis of Voluntary Risk Taking', *American Journal of Sociology*, v.95 n.4 (January 1990), pp. 851–86; and Orpana, 'Radical Gestures', p. 115.

85 Tommy Langseth, 'Risk Sports: Social Constraints and Cultural Imperatives', *Sport in Society*, v.14 n.5 (2011), pp. 629–44.

86 Macdonald, *Dropping In*, p. 9.

87 Hawk, *Between Boardslides and Burnout*, pp. 40–1; and Hosoi and Ahrens, *Hosoi*, p. 173, *passim*.

88 *Steep Descent* (dir. Jonatan Lundmark and Sebastian Lundmark, 2010), www.youtube.com/watch?v=Nemgt7phyZw.

89 Teresa Waters, '2013 Skateboarding Fatalities' (2 February 2014), www.skatepark.org; Frank Shyong, 'Los Angeles to Restrict Skateboard Bombing', *Los Angeles Times* (8 August 2012), www.articles.latimes.com; Megan Barnes, 'Rancho Palos Verdes Bans Downhill Skateboard Bombing', *Daily Breeze* (8 July 2015), www.dailybreeze.com; and 'Longboarding Police: Papakura Special' (2013), www.youtube.com/watch?v=ScKmF4NH2AM.

90 Browne, *Amped*, pp. 275–6.

91 Huck, *Paddle Against the Flow*, (San Francisco: Chronicle, 2015), p. 43.

92 Davidson, *Reforming a Counter Culture*, pp. 79–81.

93 Hosoi and Ahrens, *Hosoi*, pp. 40–1; and Browne, *Amped*, p. 219.

94 Hamm, *Scarred for Life*, p. 28.

95 Ian Michna, 'Interview with Almir Jusovic', *Jenkem* (6 November 2012), www.jenkemmag.com.

96 *Signal Hill Speed Run*; Weyland, *Answer Is Never,* photo section, np; 'Jeff Phillips #1', www.vertisdead.blogspot.co.uk (21 December 2008); and Bryan Emery, '10 Exceptional Skateboard Tricks On Drugs', *Jenkem* (19 March 2015), www.jenkemmag.com.

97 Hosoi and Ahrens, *Hosoi*, p. 61.

98 *All This Mayhem*; and Emery, '10 Exceptional Skateboard Tricks'.

99 Lefebvre, *Production of Space*, p. 184.

100 Kent Sherwood, *Jay Boy* (Thornhill:

Concrete Wave, 2006), np; Gillogly, 'Russ Howell', p. 41; and Henderson, interview, *SkateBoarder*, p. 30.

101 'Moments in Time', *Jenkem*, n.12 (December 1996), np.

102 Danny Acton-Bond, interview, *Skateboard!*, n.16 (December 1978), p. 31.

103 Steve Caballero, interview, *Thrasher*, v.9 n.6 (June 1989), p. 49.

104 Balma, *Tracker*, p. 162.

105 *Bones Brigade: an Autobiography*; and Schaffer, 'No One Standing Above You', p. 18.

106 Miller, interview, *Thrasher*, p. 102; Yochim, *Skate Life*, pp. 45–6; and Steve Kane, 'Putting the Style into Freestyle', *Skateboard!*, n.11 (July 1978), p. 83.

107 Dank Magazine, 'Elements of Style', *Ciff Gazette*, (2013), pp. 1–7.

108 'A Matter of Style', *Thrasher*, v.7 n.8 (August 1987), p. 48.

109 Richard Sennett, *The Craftsman* (London: Allen Lane, 2008); and Larsen, 'Parkour Craftsmen?', pp. 295–309.

110 James Fraser, letter, *Skateboard!*, n.16 (December 1978), p. 60.

111 'Sergio Yuppie – King of Downhill Slide' (2014), www.youtube.com/watch?v=qu3I6qJp1Mg.

112 *Thrasher*, n.405 (April 2014), p. 159.

113 *Epicly Later'd*, 'Madness of Andrew Reynolds'.

114 'Nation's Amateur Skateboarders Haven't Landed Trick In 12 Years', *The Onion* (6 May 2013), www.theonion.com.

115 *Off Camera with Sam Jones: Episode 6*.

116 'Any Variations?', *Sidewalk Surfer*, n.14 (March 1997), np.

117 'Freestyle Fanatics', *Thrasher*, v.6 n.3 (March 1986), p. 35; and O'Neal, interview, *SkateBoarder*, p. 68.

118 Dupont, 'From Core to Consumer', pp. 556–81.

119 'Skateboarding FAQ', www.dansworld.com; and 'Trickipedia'.

120 'Moments in Time', np.

121 Lucien Hendricks, interview, *Skateboard!* (second series), n.43 (June 1990), p. 27.

122 Bob Burnquist, *Thrasher*, v.17 n.9 (September 1997), p. 66.

123 John Smythe, 'Opening Day at the Park', *SkateBoarder*, v.4 n.2 (September 1977), pp. 60–8.

124 Harvey, interview, p. 50; and 'Power of London', p. 61.

125 Jonas Ivarsson, 'The Turn-Organization of Pool-Skate Sessions', American Anthropological Association 111th Annual Meeting, San Francisco (14–18 November 2012).

126 *Coping Mechanism*.

127 Ella Shohat and Robert Stam, 'The Politics of Multiculturalism in the Postmodern Age', *Art and Design*, n.43 (1995), p. 12.

128 Petrone, 'Shreddin' It Up', p. 177.

129 Boyle, interview, p. 94.

130 *J. Grant Brittain* (dir. David Fokos and Barbarella Fokos, 2017).

131 Friedman, *Fuck You Heroes*, np; and The Original SkateBoarder.

132 Andrew Norton, 'The Photographer Series: Grant Brittain' (2013), www.vimeo.com/47696545.

133 Ben Kelly, 'TWS 10 Best Cities to Skate in the World', www.skateboarding.transworld.net (7 September 2011).

134 *Bridging the Gap* (2002); and *On The Spot – Warschauer Benches* (dir. Mark Nickels, 2015).

135 Curtis Hesselgrave, 'Hester Finale', p. 23.

136 Garry Davis, Eric Stricker and Mackenzie Eisenhour, 'The TransWorld Timeline', *TransWorld Skateboarding*, 25th anniversary issue (2007), pp. 76–93.

137 Gilbert Angol, interview, *Skateboard Scene*, v.1 n.5 (undated, ca. March 1978), p. 58.

138 Harvey, interview, p. 50.

139 'Upland Pipeline: Closing Comments', pp. 64–72

140 Hawk, *Hawk*, pp. 29, 79.

141 Steve Alba, in 'Upland Pipeline', p. 69.

142 Jeff Grosso, interview, *R.A.D.*, n.64 (June 1988), p. 25.

143 www.noidnoskate.com.

144 'Off the Wall', *SkateBoarder's Action Now*, v.7 n.8 (March 1981), p. 16; Grosso, interview, p. 25; *R.A.D.*, n.83 (January 1990), p. 49; and Way, interview, p. 66.

145 Hawk, *Hawk*, p. 94; and Jeanne Hoffman, in 'Upland Pipeline', p. 66.

146 Jim Gray, in 'Upland Pipeline', p. 70.

147 '1985 Rage at Badlands Part 1 of 5' (2009), www.youtube.com/watch?v=cT4udZed67s; and Craft,

'Interview with Chris Miller'.

148 Alva, interview, *SkateBoarder*, p. 71.

149 Davis, 'Del Mar', pp. 110–11.

150 Lefebvre, *Production of Space*, p. 174.

Chapter 10 Skate and Destroy

1 Miguel Sicart, *Play Matters* (Cambridge, Mass.: MIT, 2014), p. 1.

2 Kevin Thatcher, 'Grab That Board', *Thrasher*, v.1 n.1 (January 1981), p. 6.

3 Izan, 'Aspects of the Downhill Slide', p. 29; and *Future Primitive* (dir. Stacy Peralta, 1985).

4 Stacy Peralta, interview, *Interview*, n.17 (July 1987), pp. 102–3.

5 Craig Ramsay, 'Take, San Jose, For Example', *Thrasher*, v.3 n.5 (May 1983), p. 22.

6 John Smythe, 'Frontier Tales', *SkateBoarder*, v.3 n.2 (December 1976), p. 111.

7 Smythe, 'History', p. 29.

8 Curtis Hesselgrave, 'Curb Grinding and Other Joys', *SkateBoarder*, v.6 n.6 (January 1980), pp. 34–9; Steve Rocco, 'Terror in the Streets: Manifesto for the Masses', *SkateBoarder*, v.6 n.11 (June 1980), pp. 33–9; 'Who's Hot! Tim Scroggs', *SkateBoarder*, v.5 n.9 (April 1979), pp. 78–9; D. David Morin, 'Mutt', *Action Now*, v.7 n.11 (June 1981), pp. 28–31; Stacy Peralta, 'Street Performing', *Thrasher*, v.2 n.3 (March 1982), p. 39; and Lowboy, 'Fear of Freestyle', *Thrasher*, v.2 n.9 (October 1982), pp. 22–33.

9 Mullen, *Mutt*, pp. 115–16; Snyder, *Secret History*, pp. 641–7; and *From the Ground Up: Rodney Mullen* (On Video Magazine, 2002).

10 Mullen, interview, *Warp*, p. 53; Powell-Peralta, advertisement (September 1980), p. 11; Independent, advertisement, *SkateBoarder*, v.6 n.7 (February 1980), p. 3; and Santa Cruz, advertisement, *Action Now*, v.7 n.12 (July 1981), p. 53.

11 John Smythe, 'No Parking', *Action Now*, v.8 n.2 (September 1981), pp. 52–7; and *Thrasher*, v.2 n.4 (April 1982).

12 Lowboy, 'Street Sequentials', *Thrasher*, v.4 n.9 (September 1984), pp. 32–9; Morizen Föche, 'New Blood', *Thrasher*, v.6 n.3 (March 1986), pp.

40–7; *Thrasher*, v.9 n.6 (June 1989), p. 53; Jesse Martinez, 'Venice', *Big Brother*, n.26 (June 1997), pp. 40–5; and Louison, *Impossible*, pp. 116–21.

13 Natas Kaupas, interview, *Thrasher*, v.8 n.5 (May 1988), p. 65.

14 Joel Rice, 'History Lesson – The Gonz Gap', www.xgames.espn.go.com (18 December 2011).

15 'Everything Under the Sun', *Thrasher*, v.7 n.6 (June 1987), pp. 56–9.

16 Harvey, interview, p. 50.

17 Kevin Craft, '16 Things You Didn't Know About Mark Gonzales', *SkateBoarder* (12 October 2005), www.skateboardermag.com.

18 '*Thrasher* Magazine Skater of the Year: a Twenty Year Retrospective, 1975–1995', *Thrasher*, v.17 n.1 (January 1997), p. 60.

19 'Readers' Choice: Rodney Mullen', *TransWorld Skateboarding*, v.20 n.10 (October 2002), pp. 178–83.

20 'Who Killed Vert?', *Thrasher*, v.12 n.7 (July 1992), p. 27; and Morizen Föche, 'San Franciscan Street Style', *Thrasher*, v.3 n.6 (June 1983), pp. 26–31.

21 *Savannah Slamma* (1988).

22 Santa Cruz, advertisement, *Thrasher*, v.2 n.2 (February 1982), inside front cover.

23 'Off the Wall', *SkateBoarder's Action Now*, v.7 n.6 (January 1981), p. 16.

24 Peralta, interview, *Thrasher*, p. 20.

25 Jeanne Hoffman, in 'Upland Pipeline: Closing Comments', p. 66; and Wishon and Oreskovich, 'Bicycles, Roller Skates and Skateboards', pp. 14.

26 *Stuntwood*; John Weyler, 'Action Sports: Why Kids Climb Higher and Jump Farther on Their Own Terms', *OC Family* (February 2003), www.ocfamily.com; Conor Dougherty, 'Skateboarding Capital of the World', *Wall Street Journal* (31 July 2009), www.online.wsj.com; Kurt Badenhausen, 'The Highest-Paid Action Sports Stars', *Forbes* (18 February 2009), www.forbes.com; Clemmit, 'Extreme Sports'; and Whitley, *Public Skatepark Development Guide*, p. 9.

27 Instituto DataFolha, 'Penetração de Praticantes de Skate nos Lares Brasileiros' (2009), www.cbsk.com.brpdf; and Pereira, Siqueira and Stadnik, 'Motivational Factors', pp. 69–78.

28 Domingo Antonio Robledo, 'Globe International Headquarters', *Australian Design Review* (8 June 2011), www.australiandesignreview.com; James Davis and Skin Phillips, *Skateboarding Is Not a Crime* (London: Carlton, 2004); Louison, *Impossible*, p. 225; Giannoulakis, 'Framework for Marketing', p. 2; and O'Connor, 'Skateboard Philanthropy', p. 31.

29 Raoul Vaneigem, 'Introduction', *The Revolution of Everyday Life* (London; Rising Free Press, 1967/1979).

30 Ewan Bowman, 'Comment', *Sidewalk Surfer*, n.13 (January–February 1997), np.

31 Miki Vuckovich, introduction to Mike Vallely, interview, *TransWorld Skateboarding*, v.14 n.1 (January 1996), pp. 92–3; and 'From Surf to Hellbows: the Styling of Street', *R.A.D.*, n.75 (May 1989), p. 60.1

32 *Slap*, v.6 n.1 (January 1997).

33 Sean Young, *Thrasher*, v.16 n.3 (March 1996), p. 55.

34 Edward Said, 'Culture and Imperialism', *Design Book Review*, n.29-30 (Summer/Fall 1993), pp. 6-13.

35 Lefebvre, *Everyday Life in the Modern World*, p. 123.

36 Michel de Certeau, *The Practice of Everyday Life* (Berkeley: University of California Press, 1984), p. 93.

37 Bracali, 'Thanks, Le Corbusier'.

38 Earn Beckinger, 'Baltimore', *TransWorld Skateboarding*, v.15 n.10 (October 1997), pp. 159-64; Wig Worland, 'Milton Keynes', *Skateboard!* (second series), n.48 (November 1990), p. 18; and Jesse Neuhaus, in Leah Garchik, 'The Urban Landscape', *San Francisco Chronicle* (1994).

39 Lefebvre, *Production of Space*, p. 366; and Michel Foucault, 'Of Other Spaces: Utopias and Heterotopias', Joan Ockman, (ed.), *Architecture Culture 1943-1968* (New York: Rizzoli, 1993), pp. 422-3.

40 Lefebvre, *Explosion*, pp. 71-2.

41 Lowboy, 'Skate and Destroy', *Thrasher*, v.2 n.11 (December 1982), p. 25.

42 'Scary Places', *R.A.D.*, n.82 (December 1989), p. 23; and Harry Bastard, *Spots* (Brighton: WJ&T, 2001).

43 'Power of London', p. 65.

44 Lefebvre, *Everyday Life in the Modern World*, p. 184; and Roland Barthes, *Writing Degree Zero* (London: Cape, 1967); Lefebvre, *Writings on Cities*, p. 127; Lefebvre, *Introduction to Modernity*, pp. 116–26.

45 Maggi Russell and Bruce Sawford, *The Complete Skateboard Book* (London: Fontana and Bunch, 1977), p. 7; and Bowman, 'Comment', np.

46 'Scary Places', p. 20.

47 'Searching, Finding, Living, Sharing', *R.A.D.*, n.79 (September 1989), p. 15; and 'Ears', *R.A.D.*, n.98 (July 1991), p. 7.

48 Lowboy, 'Skate and Destroy', p. 25.

49 Thomas S. Henricks, *Play Reconsidered* (Champaign: University of Illinois Press, 2006), p. 1.

50 Hodgkinson, 'Rad, Mad and Dangerous to Know?', p. 10.

51 'In the Streets Today', *Thrasher*, v.1 n.1 (January 1981), p. 16.

52 Steen Eiler Rasmussen, *Experiencing Architecture* (Cambridge, Mass.: MIT, 1959).

53 Beal, *Skateboarding*, p. xi.

54 Empire/Zoo York, advertisement, *Big Brother*, n.19 (undated, ca. late 1995), np.

55 Lefebvre, *Rhythmanalysis*, pp. 97, *passim*; and Lefebvre, *Writings on Cities*, p. 221.

56 Matt Rodriguez, interview, *Heckler*, www.heckler.com (1996).

57 Garchik, 'The Urban Landscape'.

58 Brian Casey, in Paul Mulshine, 'Wild in the Streets', *Philadelphia Magazine*, v.78 n.4 (April 1987), p. 120.

59 Davis, 'Steep Slopes', p. 8; and 'Who's Hot! Steve Rocco', *SkateBoarder*, v.6 n.6 (January 1980), pp. 70-1.

60 Friedman, *My Rules*, np.

61 Foucault, *Discipline and Punish*; Richard Sennett, *Flesh and Stone* (London: Faber and Faber, 1994); and John Urry, *The Tourist Gaze* (London: Sage, 1990).

62 Hamm, *Scarred*, pp. 169-73.

63 Justin Hocking, Jeff Knutson and Jared Maher, (eds), *Life and Limb* (Brooklyn: Soft Skull Press, 2004), p. 94.

64 'Searching, Finding', p. 15.

65 Michael Gumkowski, 'Time Warped', *Thrasher*, v.11 n.9 (September 1991), p. 63.

66 'Let's Go Skate!', *Slap*, v.6 n.1 (January

1997), p. 39.

67 'Power of London', p. 65.

68 Sean Wilsey, *Oh the Glory of It* (London: Viking, 2005), p. 253.

69 'Zered Bassett – Converse CONS Weapon Skate' (Richard Quintero, 2014), www. vimeo.com/99259592; and Matthew Gandy, 'Acoustic Terrains: an Introduction', Matthew Gandy and B.J. Nilsen, (eds), *The Acoustic City* (Berlin: Jovis, 2014), p. 1.

70 Hannah Eed, 'Sanctuary', *R.A.D.*, n.87 (May 1990), p. 70.

71 Henry Hester, in Bill Gutman, *Skateboarding to the Extreme* (New York: Tom Doherty Associates, 1997), p. 13.

72 El Zopilote, 'Garage Tale', *Thrasher*, v.6 n.5 (May 1986), p. 26.

73 T.J. Richter, 'In the City', *R.A.D.*, n.83 (January 1990), p. 62.

74 '15 Tricks You Can't Do on a Snowboard', *Thrasher*, v.16 n.3 (March 1996), p. 20; 'Let's Go Skate!', pp. 39–40; and Mario Solis, 'Deaf Professional Skateboarder Aims to Inspire Others', *NBC Los Angeles* (22 August 2015), www.nbclosangeles. com.

75 Vaj Potenza, 'Smokestack Lightning', *Thrasher*, v.12 n.3 (March 1992), p. 70.

76 *Skate the Night* (Vice, 2016), www. youtube.com/watch?v=EKNs3cojt-A; and Lee Pugalis, Jon Swords, Michael Jeffries and Bob Giddings, 'Toonsformation: Skateboarders' Renegotiation of City Rights', Simin Davoudi and Bell Derek, (eds), *Justice and Fairness in the City* (Bristol: Policy Press, 2016), pp. 125–48.

77 Browne, *Amped*, p. 110.

78 Wilkins, 'New England Hot Spots', p. 43; and 'Skate Junkies', *Thrasher*, v.12 n.1 (January 1992), p. 51.

79 'Where?', *R.A.D.*, n.79 (September 1989), p. 18.

80 John Urry, *Mobilities* (Cambridge: Polity, 2007), p. 48; and Ben Powell, 'Not a Toy', *Sidewalk Surfer*, n.3 (January–February 1996), np.

81 'A Car Full of Monkeys', *Sidewalk Surfer*, n.20 (September 1997), np.

82 Worland, 'Milton Keynes', p. 18.

83 Bowman, 'Comment', np.

84 Jesse Driggs, 'Swamp Trogs from Outer Space', *Thrasher*, v.15 n.9 (September 1995), p. 43.

85 Hamm, *Scarred for Life*, p. 173.

86 Eric Dressen, interview, *TransWorld Skateboarding*, v. 7 n.3 (June 1989), pp. 97–103, 160–72.

87 Jake Phelps, 'Damage Done', *Thrasher*, v.12 n.5 (May 1992), pp. 34–5.

88 Lefebvre, *Production of Space*, pp. 286–8.

89 Lefebvre, *Everyday Life in the Modern World*, pp. 152–4; and Vivoni, 'Contesting Public Space', pp. 72–3.

90 Lowboy, 'Skate and Destroy', pp. 24–9.

91 Mark Gottdiener and Alexandros Lagopoulos, (eds), *The City and the Sign* (New York: Columbia University Press, 1986).

92 Vischer, Mallgrave and Ikonomou, *Empathy, Form, and Space*, pp. 286–7.

93 Chris Smith and Andrew Ballantyne, 'Flow: Architecture, Object and Relation', *ARQ*, v.14 n.1 (2010), p. 22; and Jill Stoner, *Toward a Minor Architecture* (Cambridge, Mass.: MIT, 2012).

94 'Where?', (September 1989), p. 18.

95 Smythe, 'No Parking', p. 57.

96 Smythe, 'History', p. 29.

97 Deleuze and Guattari, *A Thousand Plateaus*, p. 478.

98 'Searching, Finding', p. 15; and Editorial, *Thrasher*, v.3 n.2 (February 1983), p. 4.

99 Lefebvre, *Production of Space*, p. 137; and Henri Lefebvre, *Toward an Architecture of Enjoyment* (Minneapolis: University of Minnesota Press, 2014), pp. xiii–xv, 151–3, *passim*.

100 'Fire and Friends', *Sidewalk Surfer*, n.3 (January–February 1996), np.

101 Wilkins, 'New England Hot Spots', p. 43; and Pete and the Posse, letter, *Thrasher*, v.11 n.9 (September 1991), p. 6.

102 Ron Allen, 'Urban Transcendentalism, Part 2', *Slap*, v.4 n.9 (September 1995), p. 8.

103 Marco Contati, 'New York, New York', *Skateboard!* (second series), n.43 (June 1990), pp. 32–41; and 'Skatetown: New York City', *Thrasher*, v.9 n.10 (October 1989), pp. 58–65, 106.

104 Rud-gr, 'Rotterdam', *Duh*, n.7 (Spring 1995), pp. 21–5; Francisco Martínez, 'Tallinn as a City of Thresholds',

Journal of Baltic Studies, n.10 (2014), p. 24; *This Ain't California*; Russell Waterman, 'Tokyo Listings', *R.A.D.*, n.98 (July 1991), pp. 40-1; '

105 Steven Flusty, 'Thrashing Downtown', *Cities*, v.17 n.2 (2000), pp. 149–58.

106 Santa Cruz, advertisement, *Action Now*, v.7 n.12 (July 1981), p. 53.

107 Ricky Oyola, 'City Skating', *Sidewalk Surfer*, n.2 (November–December 1995), np; and Stacy Peralta, 'Skate of the Art', *Thrasher*, v.5 n.8 (August 1985), p. 40.

108 Adam Abada, 'Adidas' Away Days Premiere', *Monster Children* (14 May 2016), www.monsterchildren.com.

109 'Process: the Technology Behind "We Are Blood"'.

110 'Blast From the Past', p. 56.

111 *Drive: My Life in Skateboarding*.

112 Lefebvre, *Introduction to Modernity*, p. 321.

113 Hocking, Knutson and Maher, *Life and Limb*, p. 94.

114 'Skater's Eye', *Thrasher*, v.17 n.1 (January 1997), p. 71.

115 Edward W. Soja, *Thirdspace* (Oxford: Blackwell, 1996); and Steve Pile, *Real Cities* (London: Sage, 2005).

116 'Where?' (September 1989), p. 18.

117 www.knowhere.co.uk.

118 'Scary Places', p. 20.

119 Gary Davis, 'Radical Manifesto', *Thrasher*, v.2 n.2 (February 1982), p. 18; and Oyola, 'City Skating', np.

120 *Thrasher, Epic Spots*, p. 204.

121 Jon Swords and Michael Jeffries, 'Tracing Post-Representational Visions of the City: Representing the Unrepresentable Skateworlds of Tyneside', *Environment and Planning A*, v.47 n.6 (2015), pp. 1313–31.

122 Guy Debord, 'Introduction to a Critique of Urban Geography', and 'Theory of the Dérive', Ken Knabb, (ed.), *Situationist International Anthology* (Berkeley: Bureau of Public Secrets, 1981), pp. 5–8, 50–4.

123 Hunter Fine, 'The Skateboard Dérive: a Poststructuralist Performance of Everyday Urban Motility', *Liminalities*, v.9 n.3 (2013), pp. 1–20; and Quentin Stevens and Kim Dovey, 'Appropriating the Spectacle: Play and Politics in a Leisure Landscape', *Journal of Urban Design*, v.9 n.3 (2004), p. 361.

124 Rodney Mullen, interview, *R.A.D.*,

n.74 (April 1989), p. 28.

125 Christopher James Pulman, 'An Environmental Issue', *Jenkem*, n.1 (September–October 1995), np.

126 Caine Gayle, 'Multiple Choice Through Words and Pictures', *Slap*, v.4 n.9 (September 1995), p. 33.

127 Driggs, 'Swamp Trogs', p. 43.

128 Lefebvre, *Everyday Life in the Modern World*, pp. 176–7.

129 Smythe, 'No Parking', p. 57.

Chapter 11 Movement Without Words

1 'Insight', *Sidewalk Surfer*, n.23 (January-February, 1998), np.

2 Lefebvre, *Production of Space*, pp. 18–19; and Lefebvre, *Writings on Cities*, pp. 140–1.

3 Lefebvre, *Everyday Life in the Modern World*, pp. 143–93.

4 Peralta, 'Skate of the Art', p. 40.

5 'Easy Riders' (Nine Network '60 Minutes' television story, 1987).

6 Joe Penny, 'Skate and Destroy?: Subculture, Space and Skateboarding as Performance' (MSc dissertation, University College London, 2009), pp. 28–34.

7 'CASTE x Magenta – Part 02' (2014), www.vimeo.com/93339618/201.

8 'Roger "Secondhand Stoke" Pt. 2', *Thrasher* (17 August 2012).

9 *Thrasher*, *Maximum Rad*, np.

10 Smythe, 'No Parking', pp. 52–7.

11 'Shudder Speed', *Thrasher*, v.11 n.11 (November 1991), p. 52.

12 Jane Haas, 'Off the Wall', *SkateBoarder*, v.6 n.6 (January 1980), pp. 74–5.

13 Lefebvre, *Production of Space*, p. 177; and Lefebvre, *Writings on Cities*, p. 171.

14 Gareth Catterick, letter, *Sidewalk Surfer*, n.15 (April 1997), np; and Powell, 'Not a Toy', np.

15 Pat Kane, *The Play Ethic* (London: Macmillan, 2004).

16 Karl Marx, *Capital: a Critique of Political Economy* (Moscow: Progress Publishers, 1867/1887), p. 136.

17 Lefebvre, *Production of Space*, p. 348.

18 Editor's response to letter, *Sidewalk Surfer*, n.14 (March 1997), np.

19 Brad Erlandson, in 'Sacramento', *Slap*, v.6 n.1 (January 1997), p. 53.

20 Lefebvre, *Writings on Cities*, p. 73.

21 Quoted in Garchik, 'The Urban Landscape'.

22 Bleasdale, interview, np.

23 Lefebvre, *Writings on Cities*, p. 131.

24 CSTR, 'Urban Blight', *Slap*, v.4 n.9 (September 1995), p. 60.

25 CSTR, 'Urban Blight', p. 60.

26 Bowman, 'Comment', np.

27 Henri Lefebvre, *Critique of Everyday Life* (London: Verso, 1991), p. 156.

28 'Trash', *Thrasher*, v.11 n.11 (November 1991), p. 90.

29 Mulshine, 'Wild', p. 120.

30 Chris Nieratko, 'Barrier Kult Is the Anonymous Elite Black Warrior Metal Skate Crew Here to Jack Your Shit', *Vice* (9 June 2015), www.vice.com.

31 Iain Borden, 'Thick Edge: Architectural Boundaries in the Postmodern Metropolis', Iain Borden and Jane Rendell, (eds), *InterSections* (London: Routledge, 2000), pp. 221–46; and Erich Fromm, *Man for Himself* (Greenwich: Fawcett, 1967), pp. 75–89.

32 Dan Cates, 'Comment', *Sidewalk Surfer*, n.13 (January–February 1997), np.

33 Bonnie Blouin, 'Skater's Edge', *Thrasher*, v.8 n.7 (July 1988), p. 35.

34 Yochim, *Skate Life*, p. 33; and Leerom Medovoi, *Rebels* (Durham: Duke University Press, 2005).

35 Editorial, *Thrasher*, v.12 n.6 (June 1992), p. 4.

36 James Scott, *Domination and the Arts of Resistance* (New Haven: Yale University Press, 1990), p. 199, in Beal, 'Disqualifying the Official', p. 252–67.

37 Lefebvre, *Introduction to Modernity*, pp. 8–9.

38 Joel Patterson, 'Redeye', *TransWorld Skateboarding*, v.14 n.1 (January 1996), p. 104.

39 Lefebvre, *Production of Space*, pp. 381–2.

40 Benjamin Heim Shepard and Greg Smithsimon, *The Beach Beneath the Streets* (Albany: Excelsior Editions, 2011), pp. 3–23, *passim*.

41 Miki Vuckovich, 'Please Use the Handrail', *Warp*, v.4 n.1 (April 1995), p. 46.

42 Mulshine, 'Wild', p. 126; and Remnick, 'Sisterhood of the Skateboard'.

43 Lefebvre, *Writings on Cities*, pp. 238–9.

44 *The Cinematographer Project* (TransWorld, 2012).

45 Marcus and Griggi, *Skateboard*, p. 35.

46 Davidson, *Skateboard Book*, p. 15; Louison, *Impossible*, p. 13; and Severson, 'Editorial: Skateboarding Comes of Age', p. 9.

47 Beal, *Skateboarding*, p. 11; Marcus and Griggi, *Skateboard*, p. 57; Snyder, *Secret History*, p. 28; Yochim, *Skate Life*, pp. 34–7; and 'Getting Around', *The Quarterly SkateBoarder*, v.1 n.2 (Spring 1965), p. 34.

48 Yochim, *Skate Life*, pp. 37–8; 'Funeral Rites Today', *El Sereno Star*, n.36 (3 September 1964), p. 1; and 'Boy Killed by Shot After Skateboards Anger Man', *Los Angeles Times* (1 September 1964), p. 3.

49 'No More Skateboarding on the Champs Elysées', *SkateBoarder*, v.1 n.4 (1965) p. 19; and Severson, 'Editorial: Skateboarding Comes of Age', p. 9.

50 Inouye, interview, p. 58; Jim W., letter, *SkateBoarder*, v.4 n.4 (November 1977), p. 26; *SkateBoarder*, v.1 n.4 (October 1965), p. 17; and Greg Meisched, *SkateBoarder*, v.4 n.6 (January 1978), p. 105.

51 Peralta, interview, *SkateBoarder*, p. 58; 'An American Bro', letter, *SkateBoarder*, v.5 n.12 (July 1979), p. 18; 'Off the Wall', *SkateBoarder*, v.6 n.10 (May 1980), p. 72; 'World News', *Skateboard!*, n.2 (October 1977), p. 23; *Ultimate Flex Machine*; and *Waverley Gazette*, v.14 n.44 (Wednesday 5 November 1975), pp. 1, 17.

52 *Skateboard!* (1977-8), *passim*.

53 Editorial, *The Times* (7 January 1978), p. 13; and Editorial, *Evening News* (4 January 1978), p. 6.

54 Sally Anne Miller, guest editorial, *SkateBoarder*, v.5 n.6 (January 1979), p. 40; 'Skateboarding and Safety', *Skateboard!*, n.1 (August 1977), p. 53; and Susan King, interview, *US News and World Report* (2 October 1978).

55 Stein Thue, letter, *SkateBoarder*, v.6 n.5 (December 1979), pp. 15–17; Chris Stokel-Walker, 'The Secret Skateboarders Who Defied Norway's 11-Year Ban', *BBC* (19 April 2016), www.bbc.co.uk; Leroy Noll, 'What Am I Doing Here?', *Thrasher*, v.5 n.10 (October 1985), p. 37; Miljøverndepartementet, *Forskrift*

om *Rullebrett* (Oslo, 3 May 1989);
and 'Oslo Punk Ramp', *Skateboard!*
(second series), n.39 (January 1990),
p. 42.

56 'Skateboards', *Which?* (December
1977), p. 643; and Royal Society for
the Prevention of Accidents, 'The
Hidden Dangers' (RoSPA/Fulmer
Research Institute: December 1977).

57 Editorial, *SkateBoarder*, v.3 n.6 (July
1977), p. 20; and National Safety
Council, *Skateboarding* (Chicago:
Bulletin, The Council, 1978), p. 2.

58 Christopher Pick and RoSPA, *Safe
Skateboarding* (London: Evans
Brothers, 1978), p. 56; Pennell,
Skateboarding, pp. 2–3; Wishon and
Oreskovich, 'Bicycles, Roller Skates
and Skateboards', pp. 11–15; and
RoSPA, *Skatcats Quizbook* (London:
RoSPA, 1978).

59 Pennell, *Skateboarding*, p. 3.

60 'The Skateboarding Safety Code',
Skateboard!, n.1 (August 1977), p. 53;
Peralta, interview, *SkateBoarder*, p.
58; 'Off the Wall', *SkateBoarder*, v.3 n.2
(December 1976), p. 123; and Brooke,
Concrete Wave, p. 84.

61 Lara B. McKenzie et al.,
'Epidemiology of Skateboarding-
Related Injuries Sustained by
Children and Adolescents 5–19 Years
of Age and Treated in US Emergency
Departments', *Injury Epidemiology*,
v.3 n.10 (2016).

62 Peacock, *Skateboarding*, p. 141.

63 *The Skateboard Mag*, n.132 (March
2015), p. 77; and Louison, *Impossible*,
pp. 36, 194–8.

64 Curtis Hesselgrave, 'Skate Safe',
SkateBoarder, v.5 n.10 (May 1979), p.
28; Marcus and Griggi, *Skateboard*,
p. 237; and Whitley, *Public Skatepark
Development Guide*, p. 102.

65 Robert Rundquist, 'Street-
Skateboarding and the Government
Stamp of Approval', Arielle
Greenberg, (ed.), *Youth Subcultures*
(New York: Pearson Longman, 2007),
pp. 181–2; and Gail Tominaga et
al., 'Epidemiological and Clinical
Features of an Older High-Risk
Population of Skateboarders', *Injury*,
v.44 n.5 (2013), pp. 645–9.

66 Tony Hawk Foundation, Facebook
post (28 September 2016).

67 Kristin M. Shuman and Michael C.
Meyers, 'Skateboarding Injuries:

an Updated Review', *Physician and
Sports Medicine* (27 May 2015), www.
informahealthcare.com; McKenzie et
al., 'Epidemiology of Skateboarding-
Related Injuries'.

68 Teresa Waters, '2012 Skateboarding
Fatalities' (3 March 2013), www.
skatepark.org; and SPAUSA
'Information Guide to Getting a City
Park Into Your Community', www.
spausa.org.

69 *Thrasher*, 1980s, *passim*.

70 Jesse Neuhaus, 'Chicago', *Big Brother*,
n.28 (September 1997), p. 49–50;
Julian Kates, letter, *Thrasher*, v.4
n.11 (November 1984), p. 4; Kevin
Ogloughlin, letter, *Slap*, v.6 n.1
(January 1997), p. 16; *Deathbowl to
Downtown* (dir. Coan Nichols and
Rick Charnoski, 2009); and Bonnie
and Clyde, 'Savannah Slamma II',
Thrasher, v.8 n.7 (July 1988), p. 46.

71 Diane de Bernardo, 'Monumental
Indifference', *Washington Post* (3
December 1995); and Chris Long
and Travis Jensen, (eds), *No Comply*
(Ventura: FunNotFame, 2006), pp. 97,
165.

72 David Thornton, *Common Criminals*
(Maine: Shoestring Book, 2013), pp.
33-6.

73 Evans, 'Young, Gifted and Board
Stupid', p. 20; Frederick Muir, 'On
a Roll', *Los Angeles Times* (31 May
1989), pp. 1, 8; 'Insight', *Sidewalk
Surfer*, n.13 (January–February 1997),
np; Sarah Nelson, 'Skateboarding Is
Not a Crime', *Asylum*, n.4 (undated,
ca. February 1997), np; David Bell,
'City's War on Skate Menace', *Evening
Mail,* Birmingham (Saturday 26
October 1996), p. 1; Jamie Wilson,
'Skaters Face Ban From City Centres',
The Guardian (6 December 1997),
p. 6; and 'Plymouth Double-Take',
Skateboard!, n.16 (December 1978),
p. 18.

74 Woolley and Johns, 'Skateboarding',
p. 218.

75 'News', Skatin' *Life* (March–April
1989), pp. 26–7; 'Skate não é Crime',
Overall, n.10 (June–July 1989). p. 68;
Jane O'Hara, 'Trouble in Paradise',
Maclean's, v.100 n.14 (6 April 1987),
p. 48; Tom Oho, letter, *TransWorld
Skateboarding*, v.15 n.11 (November
1997), p. 25; Long and Jensen, *No
Comply*, pp. 53–6; John P. Dessing,

letter, *Slap*, v.6 n.9 (September 1997),
np; and Claire Freeman and Tamara
Riordan, 'Locating Skateparks:
the Planner's Dilemma', *Planning
Practice and Research*, v.17 n.3 (2002),
p. 312.

76 Willing and Shearer, 'Skateboarding
Activism', p. 47; Helen Woolley,
Teresa Hazelwood and Ian Simkins,
'Don't Skate Here: Exclusion of
Skateboarders from Urban Civic
Spaces in Three Northern Cities in
England', *Journal of Urban Design*,
v.16 n.4 (2011), pp. 471–87; Tim
Sargeant, '12-Year-Old Boy Stopped
by Police for Skateboarding on
Quiet Street', *Global News* (2 April
2015), www.globalnews.ca; White,
'We Out Here'; and Nic Dobija-
Nootens, 'Madrid Is Banning Street
Skateboarding Next Week', *Jenkem* (21
February 2018), www.jenkemmag.
com

77 Woolley, Hazelwood and Simkins,
'Don't Skate Here', pp. 471–87.

78 Zygmunt Bauman, *Consuming Life*
(Cambridge: Polity, 2007), p. 4.

79 Bauman, *Consuming Life*, p. 56.

80 'News: Ban on City Skating?', p. 4;
'We Are Illegal', *Sidewalk Surfer*, n.15
(April 1997), np; *Rollin' through the
Decades*; and Tim Hoad, 'Wednesday
July 30th 1997', *Sidewalk Surfer*, n.21
(October-November 1997), np.

81 Long and Jensen, *No Comply*, p. viii.

82 Tony Favro, 'Youth Curfews Popular
with American Cities' (21 July
2009), www.citymayors.com; and
Lauren Gambino, 'Outrage Follows
Baltimore's Deeply Flawed Youth
Curfew Decision', *The Guardian* (12
August 2014), www.theguardian.com.

83 'Trash', *Thrasher*, v.6 n.5 (May 1986),
p. 80.

84 'Trash', *Thrasher*, v.12 n.3 (March
1992), p. 74.

85 Fyfe, 'Street Legal?', p. 33.

86 Ducommun, *Skateboarding
Vancouver*, p. 155; Sean Mortimer,
'Meet the Man the World Mistakenly
Believes Invented the Skate
Stopper', *Ride* (3 June 2015), www.
theridechannel.com; Kelvin Ho,
'Skateboarding: an Interpretation
of Space in the Olympic City',
Architectural Theory Review, v.4 n.2
(1999), pp. 98–102; Lombard, 'Skate
and Create/Skate and Destroy',

pp. 482–4; and '15 Things You Didn't Know About Skate Stoppers', *SkateBoarder*, v.15 n.9 (May 2006), p. 120.

87 www.skatestoppers.com.
88 *Stuntwood*; and www. block.com.
89 Beal, *Skateboarding*, p. 100; and Matt Broadley, 'Snail Skate Stoppers: Hungary's New Style of Defensive Architecture', *Kingpin* (4 July 2016), www.kingpinmag.com.
90 www.skatestoppers.com.
91 Ben Quinn, 'Anti-Homeless Spikes are Part of a Wider Phenomenon of Hostile Architecture', *The Guardian* (13 June 2014), www.theguardian.com.
92 David Garland, 'Governmentality and the Problem of Crime', *Theoretical Criminology*, v.1 n.2 (1997), pp. 173–214, cited in Lombard, 'Skate and Create/Skate', pp. 481–2.
93 Smythe, 'History', p. 38.
94 Vivoni, 'Contesting Public Space', pp. 111–14.
95 Carr, 'Legal Geographies', p. 995.
96 Evans, 'Young', p. 19.
97 Alyshah Hasham, 'Cab Driver Convicted of Manslaughter in Longboarder's Death', *Star* (30 October 2015), www.thestar.com; and 'São Paulo Car Driver Mows Down Skateboarders', *Brazil Culture* (26 June 2017), www.plus55.com.
98 Michael C. Scott, 'Disorderly Youth in Public Places' (U.S. Department of Justice: Center for Problem-Oriented Policing, 2011), p. 7.
99 'We Are Illegal', np.
100 Phraeza, 'Fiction?', *Sidewalk Surfer*, n.15 (April 1997), np.
101 Ben Powell, 'The Number One Four Wheeler', *Sidewalk Surfer*, n.9 (August 1996), np.
102 Santa Monica Airlines, advertisement, *Thrasher*, v.8 n.3 (March 1988), p. 7.
103 'We Are Illegal', np.
104 'Trash', (May 1986), p. 80.
105 Tim Cresswell, *In Place/Out of Place* (Minneapolis: University of Minnesota, 1996), p. 58.
106 Long and Jensen, *No Comply*, p. viii; and Lefebvre, *Introduction to Modernity*, p. 23.
107 'Trash', *Thrasher*, v.16 n.11 (November 1996), p. 131; and Munson and Cardwell, *Skateboard Stickers*, pp. 72–3.

108 Manu Berque, 'The Wa: Skate Anti Skate', Chiara Santini Parducci, (ed.), *Do Not Think* (Berlin: Oxylane Art Foundation, 2015), pp. 243–9.
109 Jeff Ferrell, *Tearing Down the Streets* (Basingstoke: Palgrave, 2001), pp. 72–3.
110 Ferrell, *Tearing Down the Streets*, pp. 72–3.
111 '15 Things You Didn't Know About Skate Stoppers', p. 120; *Panhead*, 'Taking Back the Streets', *TransWorld Skateboarding*, v.23 n.4 (2005), 175–84; and Vivoni, 'Spots of Spatial Desire', p. 144.
112 Sean Mortimer, 'Jeremy Klein Talks Selling Skateboards and Stealing Curbs', *Ride* (2 January 2015), www.theridechannel.com.
113 Long and Jensen, *No Comply*, p. 30.
114 Steven Flusty, 'Thrashing Downtown: Play as Resistance to the Spatial and Representational Regulation of Los Angeles', *Cities*, v.17 n.2 (2000), pp. 149–58.
115 Homey, letter, *Thrasher*, v.9 n.6 (June 1989), p. 8.
116 Powell, 'Not a Toy', np.
117 Carr, 'Legal Geographies', p. 991.
118 Mike Davis, *City of Quartz* (London: Verso, 1990); Monica Degen, *Sensing Cities* (Abingdon: Routledge, 2008); Anna Minton, *Ground Control* (London: Penguin, 2009); Neil Smith, *The New Urban Frontier* (London: Routledge, 1996); and Michael Sorkin, (ed.), *Variations on a Theme Park* (New York: Hill and Wang, 1992).
119 Quinn, 'Anti-Homeless Spikes'; 'Remove the Anti-Homeless Spikes', www.change.org (June 2014); and 'Calls to Ban Mosquito Teen Repellent Device Ruled Out', www.bbc.co.uk (28 June 2010).
120 *Neighbourhoods in Action* (Active Living Network, 2003), www.youtube.com/watch?v=Z99FHvVt1G4.
121 Elaine Stratford, 'Mobilizing a Spatial Politics of Street-Skating: Thinking about the Geographies of Generosity', *Annals of the Association of American Geographers*, v.106 n.2 (2015), pp. 350–7; Christopher D. Giamarino, 'Spatial Ethno-Geographies of Sub-Cultures in Urban Space: Skateboarders, Appropriative Performance, and Spatial Exclusion

in Los Angeles' (MSc Urban Planning dissertation, Columbia University, 2017); and Leonie Sandercock, *Cosmopolis II* (London: Continuum, 2003), p. 208.
122 Willing and Shearer, 'Skateboarding Activism', p. 54; and Nolan, 'Ins and Outs', pp. 311–27.
123 Stephen W. Lorimer and Stephen Marshall, 'Beyond Walking and Cycling: Scoping Small-Wheel Modes', *Proceedings of the Institution of Civil Engineers*, v.169 n.2 (2016), pp. 58–66; 'City Passes Motion to Allow Skateboarding on Montreal Bike Paths', *CTV Montreal* (26 May 2015), www.montreal.ctvnews.ca; Michael D'Alimonte, 'Montreal's Peace Park Now Has Signs Officially Allowing Skateboarding' (11 August 2014), www.mtlblog.com; 'Skateboarding Allowed on Downtown Streets', *Wood TV* (17 May 2015), www.woodtv.com; and Bill Cleverley, 'Skateboarding Gets All-Clear in Downtown Victoria', *Times Colonist* (27 March 2015), www.timescolonist.com.
124 Simon Gilbert, 'Online Poll: 88% Say Skateboarding Should NOT Be Banned in Coventry', *Coventry Telegraph* (5 November 2014), www.coventrytelegraph.net; Borden, 'Southbank Skateboarding, London and Urban Culture', pp. 91–107; and 'Green Bay Cop Uses Skateboard to Patrol Beat', *KTVU* (22 June 2014), www.ktvu.com.
125 White, 'We Out Here', pp. 53–9, 74.
126 Vuckovich, 'Handrail', p. 46.
127 Phelps, 'Damage', pp. 34–7.
128 Lefebvre, *Production of Space*, p. 201.
129 'That Thing', *R.A.D.*, n.75 (May 1989), p. 45.

Chapter 12 Artistry

1 Rose, Weaver and Holmes, *Dysfunctional*, p. 22.
2 Cliver, *Disposable Skateboard Bible*, pp. 34–60; and Noll, *Skateboard Retrospective*.
3 Browne, 'Dogtown East'; Beal, *Skateboarding*, pp. xvi, 50–1; and *Deathbowl to Downtown*.
4 Humpston, *Bulldog's Art*.
5 Denike, *Built to Grind*, pp. 40–5.

6   Cliver, *Disposable*, pp. 148–51; Phillips, *Surf, Skate & Rock Art*, p. 71; Phillips, *Skateboard Art*, p. 27–45; and Denike, *Built to Grind*, pp. 22–5.

7   Leslie and Burgoyne, *Bored*, p. 49; 'The Encyclopaedia of Skateboarding', *R.A.D.*, n.93 (February 1991), p. 38; Brooke, *Concrete Wave*, pp. 102–5, 122–3; Cliver, *Disposable Skateboard Bible*, pp. 224–5; Cliver, *Disposable*; and 'Zorlac in Dallas: Skating's Doomiest Brand', *Grave City* (26 July 2016), www.gravecity.wordpress.com.

8   Phillips, *Skateboard Art*, pp. 52–67, 122–3, 188–205; Phillips, *Surf, Skate & Rock Art*, pp. 102–17; and Cliver, *Disposable*, pp. 156–7.

9   Cliver, *Disposable Skateboard Bible*, pp. 114–21.

10   Cliver, *Disposable Skateboard Bible*, pp. 236–47.

11   Lefebvre, *Introduction to Modernity*, p. 298.

12   Cliver, *Disposable*, p. 180–5.

13   Lefebvre, *Introduction to Modernity*, p. 298.

14   Munson and Cardwell, *Skateboard Stickers*, pp. 64–5.

15   Cliver, *Disposable Skateboard Bible*, pp. 310–11.

16   Rudy Vanderlans, 'Design Will Eat Itself', *Emigre*, n.29 (Winter 1994), p. 2.

17   Cynthia Rose, *Design After Dark* (London: Thames and Hudson, 1991), pp. 57–8, 60.

18   Cliver, *Disposable*, p. 39, 48; Carayol, *Agents Provocateurs*, pp. 72–3, 146; and Mullen, *Mutt*, pp. 211–12.

19   Ed Templeton, 'Programming Injection #2', *TransWorld Skateboarding*, v.14 n.1 (January 1996), pp. 104–5; Cliver, *Disposable*, p. 38–71, 158–9; Winston Tseng and Todd Bratrud, *I Hate* (New York: Mark Batty, 2011); and Erik Brunetti, *Fuct* (New York: Rizzoli, 2013).

20   Cliver, *Disposable*, pp. 38, 52, 67; Leslie and Burgoyne, *Bored*, pp. 49–50; Tseng and McKee, *Warning*, pp. 15–18; and Mullen, *Mutt*, p. 214.

21   Homi Bhabha, *The Location of Culture* (London: Routledge, 1994), p. 4.

22   Cliver, *Disposable*, p. 41.

23   Cliver, *Disposable*, p. 78; and *Thrasher*, v.12 n.9 (September 1992),

p. 89.

24   Cliver, *Disposable*, p. 72–3, 79, 214–5; and Tseng and McKee, *Warning*.

25   *Man Who Souled the World*.

26   Carayol, *Agents Provocateurs*; and Tseng and Bratrud, *I Hate*.

27   Carayol, *Agents Provocateurs*, pp. 179–217; and Tseng and Bratrud, *I Hate*, pp. 86–7.

28   Ian Michna, 'Alex Olson Is Starting His Own Company', *Jenkem* (12 August 2103), www.jenkemmag.com; and 'CASTE x Magenta – Part 01' (2014), www.vimeo.com/90116548/2014.

29   David Martinez, 'From Off the Rez to Off the Hook! Douglas Miles and Apache Skateboards', *American Indian Quarterly*, v.37 n.4 (2013), pp. 370–94; and 'I Paint what I Like – Apache Skateboards/Douglas Miles' (2013), www.youtube.com/watch?v=qdvDdzVOHAg&t=12s.

30   J. Namdev Hardisty, *New Skateboard Graphics* (New York: Mark Batty, 2010), p. 9.

31   Cliver, *Disposable*, p. 67.

32   Burgoyne and Leslie, *Bored*, p. 12.

33   Cliver, *Disposable*, p. 84.

34   Bob Colacello, 'How Do You Solve a Problem Like MOCA?', *Vanity Fair* (5 February 2013), www.vanityfair.com.

35   Wilfred Brandt, 'Skateboard Aesthetics: the View from on Board' (PhD thesis, University of New South Wales, 2014), pp. 203–4; Jake Woolf, 'A $15,000 Rick Owens Skateboard You Can't Even Use', *GQ* (16 September 2014), www.gq.com; and Jack Lowe, 'SHUT $15,000 Gold-Plated Skateboard', *Huh* (April 2014), www.huhmagazine.co.uk.

36   Violet Gabor, 'Totally Board', *There Magazine* (April 2014), pp. 30–6; and www.theskateroom.com.

37   Cameron Wolf, 'Goodhood's Skateboarding Exhibit Will Feature Dope Decks from World Famous Artists', *Complex* (6 September 2014), www.complex.com.

38   Brandt, 'Skateboard Aesthetics', p. 9, *passim*.

39   Hosoi and Ahrens, *Hosoi*, p. 44.

40   'Grip Tape Art', *Automatic Magazine* (10 August 2004), www.automaticmag.com.

41   'From Hands that Bite', *Transworld Skateboarding* (December 1987); and

Balma, *Tracker*, p. 234.

42   Aaron Rose, 'Dysfunctional', *Big Brother*, n.19 (*c.* late 1995), np; 'Mandatory Information', *TransWorld Skateboarding*, v.14 n.11 (November 1996), p. 50; Rose, Weaver and Holmes, *Dysfunctional*, p. 18; and Arthur J. Tubb, 'Searching for Animal Chin: Skateboarding as an Artform' (BA Fine Art dissertation, Sheffield Hallam University 1999), pp. 7–8.

43   Aaron Rose and Christian Strike, (eds), *Beautiful Losers* (New York: Iconoclast and D.A.P., 2004), p. 19; and *Beautiful Losers* (dir. Aaron Rose and Joshua Leonard, 2008).

44   Matthew Atencio and Becky Beal, 'Beautiful Losers: the Symbolic Exhibition and Legitimization of Outsider Masculinity', *Sport in Society*, v.14 n.1 (2011), pp. 1–16; and Atencio, Beal and Yochim, 'It Ain't Just Black Kids and White Kids', p. 168.

45   Atencio and Beal, 'Beautiful Losers', p. 11.

46   'Pontus Alv Interview'.

47   Brandt, 'Skateboard Aesthetics', p. 210.

48   Thornton, *Common Criminals*, p. 16.

49   Weyland, *Answer Is Never*, pp. 248–9.

50   *15 Years of Gonz and Adidas*.

51   'Mark Gonzales – Back Worlds for Words' (2013), www.vimeo.com/57637159; and Cameron Hatch, 'Skateboarding in Art Museum', www.thehatchreport.com.

52   'Ratsrepus' (2015), www.vimeo.com/137258888.

53   Jason Moran and Ben Ashworth, 'Finding a Line', www.kennedy-center.org; and David Kettle, 'Scots Skateboarders and Opera Combine in Grind', *Scotsman* (1 June 2014), www.scotsman.com.

54   Laura Bleiberg, 'Skateboard Culture Inspires Diavolo's Dance at the Broad', *Los Angeles Times* (29 September 2012), www.articles.latimes.com.

55   *Stuntwood*; and Silke Wagner, 'Locals Only' exhibition (Kunstraum, Munich, 2004).

56   Raye and Strassburger, *Inside the World of Board Graphics*, pp. 56–7; Zac, 'Haroshi: Pain Exhibition, StolenSpace, London', *Caught in the Crossfire* (15 October 2013), www.

caughtinthecrossfire.com; and 'JAPAN: Haroshi' (2015), www.vimeo.com/134696230.

57 Kelsey Campbell-Dollaghan, 'MoMA PS1's New Playground Is Woven from the Bones of 3000 Skateboards', *Gizmodo Australia* (4 July 2013), www.gizmodo.com.

58 Raphaël Zarka, *Free Ride* (Paris: Editions B42, 2011); and Raphaël Zarka, interview with Sam Griffin, *Grey* (4 April 2011), www.greyskatemag.com.

59 'Raphaël Zarka, 'Espai Pavimentat', www.eacc.es; and Carhartt WIP, 'Paving Space: an Unconventional Encounter between Maths, Art and Skateboarding' (2016), www.youtube.com/watch?v=Pv-xPUVwg98.

60 'Raphaël Zarka', *DesignBoom* (1 January 2010), www.designboom.com; and Zarka, interview.

61 'Art & Motion Shaun Gladwell and Russ Howell', Perth International Arts Festival (2016), www.youtube.com/watch?v=SOax3ksCS-4.

62 Iain Borden, 'Everyday Otherworlds: Rhythm, Detail, Journeys', *Blair French*, (ed.), Shaun Gladwell (Sydney: Artspace Visual Arts Centre, 2007), pp. 32–6; Shaun Gladwell, *Kickflipping Flâneur* (Sydney, 2000); Nicholas Croggon and Charles Green, 'Shaun Gladwell: Critique, Gesture, and Skateboarding', *Australian and New Zealand Journal of Art*, v.11 (2011), pp. 133–54; and Kit Messham-Muir, *Practices of the City and the Kickflipping Flâneur* (Woolloomooloo: Artspace Visual Arts Centre, 2000).

63 Jenny Filippetti, 'D*Face Spraypaint Skateboarding at Ridiculous', *DesignBoom* (11 July 2011), www.designboom.com; 'D*Face Ridiculous Pool Paint Attack' (2011), www.youtube.com/watch?v=ScW5kWzSaSI; and 'Matt Reilly Skateboard Paints Through Mana Contemporary', *DesignBoom* (3 August 2014), www.designboom.com.

64 Kirill Savchenkov, *Museum of Skateboarding* (London: Calvert 22 Foundation, 2016); and Hettie Judah, 'Zen and the (Male) Art of Skateboard Combat', *The Guardian* (22 August 2016), www.theguardian.com.

65 Robin Plaskoff Horton, 'Urban Hacktivism Reinventing Public Spaces', *Urban Gardens* (14 January 2013), www.urbangardensweb.com.

66 Clint van der Hartt, (ed.), *Reclaiming the Street* (Rotterdam: Showroom MAMA, 2011); and Dan Graham, *Two-Way Mirror Power* (Cambridge, Mass: MIT, 2000), pp. 179–80.

67 'EMB Installation', *Thrasher* (August 1992), p. 15; Weyland, *Answer Is Never*, pp. 311–12; *Ohio Online Visual Artist Registry Images*, www.columbuslibrary.org; and Cartner Maness, 'Steve Rodriguez', *Time Out New York* (12 May 2009), www.timeout.com.

68 Anders Smith-Lindall, 'On Exhibit: the Hyde Park Center Picks Up Speed', *Reader*, v.29 n.35 (2 June 2000); and Rita Reif, 'Art/Architecture; A Swimming Pool? A Yacht? No, It's Art', *New York Times* (10 March 2002).

69 Vivoni, 'Contesting Public Space', pp. 109–10.

70 Henrik Edelbo and Rasmus Folehave Hansen, *Dansk Skateboarding* (Copenhagen: Nordstrøms Forlag, 2014), pp. 238–9; and www.jeppehein.net.

71 Kilwag, 'I Don't Know Art but I Know I Like Blowing Out French Skatespots', www.skateandannoy.com (31 July 2007); and www.kogler.net.

72 Edelbo and Hansen, *Dansk Skateboarding*, pp. 137–9.

73 'Stefan Marx Monster Children Show' (2007), www.youtube.com/watch?v=adAbnZ9wRj8; www.jannesaario.com/Striitti; Samantha Melamed, 'At Franklin's Paine Skatepark, Sculptures to Skate On' (6 June 2015), www.articles.philly.com; Zac, 'Zenga Bros – Skate Heads interview', *Caught in the Crossfire* (5 March 2015), www.caughtinthecrossfire.com; and 'Skate Heads' (2015), www.vimeo.com/118643506.

74 Daryl Mersom, 'The Side Effects of Urethane & the New Skateable Architecture', *Kingpin* (26 November 2016), www.kingpinmag.com.

75 Templeton Elliott, 'Skateable Art Comes to Seattle', *The Skateboard Mag* (6 April 2014), www.theskateboardmag.com.

76 Henner Thies, 'Go Behind the Scenes of Philipp Schuster's ICON' (23 June 2016), www.redbull.com; and 'No Skateboarding? More Like GO Skateboarding' (2016), www.youtube.com/watch?v=YgTVzmJdLlY.

77 'PAS House/Skateboard House', *Architizer*, www.architizer.com; 'The PAS House by Francois Perrin and Gil Lebon Delapointe', *Dezeen* (23 May 2012), www.dezeen.com; 'Etnies PAS House for Public Domaine La Gaite Lyrique' (2011), www.vimeo.com/25779239; and Stefan Schwinghammer, 'PAS Haus', *Monster Skateboard*, n.302 (October 2011), pp. 70–5.

78 'Skate Park House/LEVEL Architects', *ArchDaily* (7 September 2012), www.archdaily.com; and 'The Ramp House/Archivirus', *ArchDaily* (26 April 2009), www.archdaily.com.

79 'Skate Villa by Philipp Schuster', *Dezeen* (9 June 2012), www.dezeen.com; and 'Skating in a House – Schuster Skate Villa' (2012), www.youtube.com/watch?v=FUODBXjozdk.

80 *Shepard Fairey* (dir. Brett Novak, 2014); and Friedman, *My Rules*, np.

81 Browne, *Amped*, p. 289.

82 Beal and Weidman, 'Authenticity', p. 343.

83 Mullen, *Mutt*, p. 4; and Louison, *Impossible*, pp. 24–33.

84 Louison, *Impossible*, pp. 24–33, 134–7.

85 *DIY America* (dir. Aaron Rose, 2010).

86 'A Radical Cut in the Texture of Reality', www.radicalcut.blogspot.co.uk.

87 Gregory Shewchuk, 'Finding Balance Through Skateboarding', *Arthur Magazine*, n.30, www.arthurmag.com.

88 Kevin Eason, 'Why I Love Skateboarding', *The Guardian* (17 July 2014), www.theguardian.com.

89 Huck, Paddle *Against the Flow*, p. 69.

90 Claire Cameron, 'Five Ways Being a Writer and Professional Skateboarder Are the Same', *The Millions* (18 March 2015), www.themillions.com.

91 'Skateboarding Tumbles Helped Develop Pace Skills', *DNA India* (15 November 2014), www.dnaindia.com.

92 Corinne Purtill, 'One of the Biggest Toy Companies on Earth Owes Its Turnaround to a Child Skateboarder', *Quartz* (8 March 2016), www.qz.com.

93 'Jeff Grosso's Loveletters to Skateboarding – Skate Art' (2014), www.youtube.com/watch?v=OGJfNffFn98.
94 *DIY America*.
95 Steve Newall, 'Interview: Comedian Tom Green', *The Flicks Interviews* (24 April 2013), www.flicks.co.nz.
96 Huck, *Paddle Against the Flow*, p. 57.

Chapter 13 Do It for Others

1 Howell, 'Creative Class', pp. 32–42; and Nemeth, 'Conflict, Exclusion, Relocation', pp. 297–318.
2 Kerr, 'Death and Life of Great American Skate Plazas'.
3 Long and Jensen, *No Comply*, p. 301.
4 Howell, 'Creative Class', p. 35.
5 Long and Jensen, *No Comply*, p. 108.
6 Adam Jenson, Jon Swords and Michael Jeffries, 'The Accidental Youth Club: Skateboarding in Newcastle-Gateshead', *Journal of Urban Design*, v.17 n.3 (2012), pp. 371–88.
7 Skatepark Advisory Task Force, *City of Seattle Citywide Skatepark Plan* (31 January 2007); and Carr, 'Activist Research', p. 65.
8 Howell, 'Creative Class', p. 32.
9 Howell, 'Creative Class', p. 40.
10 Orpana, 'Steep Transitions' pp. 152–68.
11 Geoffrey Wheatcroft, 'Busk Off', *Spectator* (24 February 1979), p. 28.
12 Long Live Southbank, *Long Live Southbank*.
13 *Long Live Southbank*.
14 *Rollin' through the Decades*.
15 *Long Live Southbank*; and Long Live Southbank, 'Southbank Undercroft'.
16 Southbank Centre, 'Southbank Centre Unveils Plans to Transform Festival Wing', press release (6 March 2013).
17 Iain Borden, 'The Architecture', *Long Live Southbank*, pp. 66–97; *The Bigger Picture* (Long Live Southbank, 2013), www.youtube.com/watch?v=iFaKN98Xg3E; 'Iain Borden on the (Lack of) Festival Wing Consultation' (2013), www.youtube.com/watch?v=EMQwktfjeTA; and *Save Our Southbank* (dir. Winstan Whitter and Toby Shuall 2008).
18 Long Live Southbank, 'Southbank Undercroft'; and Mark Brown, 'Southbank Skate Park Must Stay', *The Guardian* (15 January 2014), www.theguardian.com.
19 Long Live Southbank, 'Southbank Undercroft'; Long Live Southbank, *Long Live Southbank*; and Susannah Butter, 'Wheels of Fortune', *London Evening Standard* (14 April 2014), www.standard.co.uk.
20 Brown, 'Southbank Skate Park Must Stay'.
21 Long Live Southbank, 'Southbank Undercroft'; and Libby Purves, 'Let These Skaters Swoop and Crash and Rattle', *The Times* (13 May 2013), www.thetimes.co.uk.
22 David Harvey, 'The Right to the City', *International Journal of Urban and Regional Research*, v.27 n.4 (2013), pp. 939–41.
23 English Heritage, 'London Sporting Buildings: the Rom Skatepark, London Borough of Havering. Case Number: 1416690' (21 July 2014); English Heritage, 'The Rom Skatepark. List Entry Number: 1419328', *The National Heritage List for England*, www.list.english-heritage.org.uk; Played in Britain, 'The Rom Skatepark, Hornchurch: Britain's First Listed Skatepark' (London: Played in Britain, report, 2014); and Simon Inglis, *Played in London* (London: English Heritage, 2014), pp. 152–3.
24 Borden, 'Pipe Dreams'.
25 Historic England, 'Welcome to Historic England' (2015), www.youtube.com/watch?v=hRIlbL2Lhy8.
26 'London Rom Skatepark Given Listed Status', *BBC News* (29 October 2014), www.bbc.co.uk.
27 Marc Tison and Barry Walsh, *Pipe Fiends* (Montreal: Media MudScout, 2006).
28 'Montreal at 5', *CBC News* (2011), www.youtube.com/watch?v=90Qh2UzXE8w; and 'Big-O Rebirth' (Ethernal, 2013), www.youtube.com/watch?v=feRrG34LWY4.
29 *The Bro Bowl* (dir. Troy Durrett, 2010).
30 Snyder, *Secret History*, pp. 610–13.
31 Fallon Silcox, 'Demolition of Tampa's Historic Bro Bowl Skate Park', *Bay News 9* (20 June 2015), www.baynews9.com.
32 Wixon, *Skateboarding*, p. viii; Dumas and Laforest, 'Skateparks', pp. 19–34; and Taylor and Khan, 'Skate-Park Builds', pp. 489–510.
33 Turner, 'Civilised Skateboarder: a Figurational Analysis', p. 157.
34 Gary Stidder and Sid Hayes, 'Exploring the Social Benefit of Informal and Lifestyle Sports', *Bulletin*, n.68 (2015), pp. 32–44; and Belinda Wheaton and Mark Doidge, 'Exploring the Social Benefit of Informal and Lifestyle Sports', *Bulletin*, n.68 (2015), pp. 45–9.
35 Wixon, *Skateboarding*, pp. 2–6.
36 John Tomlinson, *The Culture of Speed*, (London: Sage, 2009), pp. 146–7.
37 Ducommun, *Skateboarding Vancouver*, pp. 168–9.
38 Wayne Board and Raymond Browning, 'Self-Selected Speeds and Metabolic Cost of Longboard Skateboarding', *European Journal of Applied Physiology*, v.114 n.11 (2014), pp. 2381–6; and Kevin Fang and Susan Handy, 'Skateboarding for Transportation: Exploring the Factors Behind an Unconventional Mode Choice among University Skateboard Commuters', *Transportation* (online July 2017).
39 Welch, 'Gay Skaters'.
40 Harms and Smith, *Skateboarder's Journal*, p. 32.
41 www.longboardgirlscrew.com.
42 Kevin Fang, 'Skateboarding as a Mode of Transportation', *The 92nd Annual Meeting of the Transportation Research Board* (January 2013), www.trb.org; Kevin Fang, 'Skateboarding Down the Street', *The 93rd Annual Meeting of the Transportation Research Board*, Washington DC (January 2014), www.trb.org; and Kevin Fang, 'Skateboarding for Transportation by the Numbers', *The 94th Annual Meeting of the Transportation Research Board*, Washington DC (January 2015), www.trb.org.
43 Dennis Romero, 'Lazy Skaters Rejoice: Electric Skateboards Have Been Legalized', *LA Weekly* (13 October 2015), www.laweekly.com; and Courtney Teague, 'Innovative Skateboard Rack', *Ka Leo O Hawaii* (21 January 2015), www.kaleo.org.
44 Stephen W. Lorimer and Stephen

Marshall, 'Beyond Walking and Cycling: Scoping Small-Wheel Modes', *Proceedings of the Institution of Civil Engineers*, v.169 n.2 (2016), pp. 58-66.

45   Stephanie Mohler and Michael Brooke, 'The New Cooldown', *Concrete Wave*, v.6 n.4 (2008), pp. 50-7; and Francisco Vivoni, 'Waxing Ledges: Built Environments, Alternative Sustainability, and the Chicago Skateboarding Scene', *Local Environment*, v.18 n.3 (2013), pp. 346-7.

46   Vivoni, 'Spots of Spatial Desire' p. 146; and Vivoni, 'Waxing Ledges', p. 351.

47   Giannoulakis, 'Framework for Marketing', pp. 109-11.

48   Carol Tice, 'Growing Up Fast', *Entrepreneur* (1 February 2007), www.entrepreneur.com.

49   www.cometskateboards.com.

50   www.soletechnology.com.

51   www.bureo.co; Hannah Koh, 'There's Something Fishy about This Skateboard', *Eco-Business* (7 December 2016), www.todayeco.com; and D.J. Pangburn, 'Inside the Quest to Make Skateboards 100% Recyclable', *Vice* (12 July 2016), www.creators.vice.com.

52   Jack Lowe, 'A Table Made from Old Skateboard Decks', *Huh* (22 January 2015), www.huhmagazine.co.uk; www.thesplintercell.co.uk; *Day by Day* (dir. Jeremy McNamara, 2017), www.vimeo.com/201019012; www.irisskateboards.com; *Stuntwood*; and Adam Tschorn, 'New Life for Skateboards', *Los Angeles Times* (28 February 2014), www.articles.latimes.com.

53   www.comediansincarsgettingcoffee.com.

54   Turner, 'Transformative Improvisation', p. 183.

55   Brandt, 'Skateboard Aesthetics', p. 73.

56   Lombard, 'Trucks, Tricks, and Technologies', p. 177.

57   Hosoi and Ahrens, *Hosoi*, p. 95-6.

58   Mackenzie Eisenhour, 'The Freestyle Fellowship', *SkateBoarder*, v.11 n.8 (June 2002), p. 70.

59   'Jeff Grosso's Loveletters to Skateboarding – The Freestyle Conspiracy'.

60   www.soletechnology.com.

61   Brooke, *Concrete Wave*, p. 163.

62   Brooke, *Concrete Wave*, pp. 129-30; *Man Who Souled the World*; and Mullen, *Mutt*, pp. 169-87.

63   *Man Who Souled the World*; and Kilwag, 'Postcard from Simon Woodstock', *Skate and Annoy* (16 September 2010), www.skateandannoy.com.

64   Mullen, *Mutt*, p. 194; Marcus and Griggi, *Skateboard*, p. 226; and Hawk, *Hawk*, p. 151.

65   *Man Who Souled the World*.

66   Hawk, *How Did I Get Here?*, pp. xiv, 71-2, 93.

67   www.seismicskate.com; and Harms and Smith, *Skateboarder's Journal*, pp. 191-220.

68   O'Connor, 'Skateboard Philanthropy', pp. 30-46.

69   Harms and Smith, *Skateboarder's Journal*, pp. 56, 74-6; Dave Cornthwaite, *Boardfree* (London: Portico, 2007); Marcus and Griggi, *Skateboard*, p. 153; 'The Return of Board AID', *TransWorld Snowboarding* (9 February 2000), www.snowboarding.transworld.net; Balma, *Tracker*, p. 236; and O'Connor, 'Skateboard Philanthropy', p. 37.

70   www.letitflow.org.

71   Petrone, 'Shreddin' It Up', pp. 167-8, 227-35.

72   O'Connor, 'Skateboard Philanthropy', p. 38.

73   Gillogly, 'Russ Howell', p. 47; and Wixon, *Skateboarding*.

74   www.bryggeriet.org; and *Skate World: Sweden* (Vice, 2010).

75   Meira Harris, 'Skaters Gonna Skate: Skateboarding and Its Influence on Urban Space', *Urban Review* (Fall 2014), pp. 19-23, 28.

76   Tony Hawk, *Hawk*, p. 70.

77   www.skatepass.com; Tracy Loewe, 'Skateboarding Kickflips into PE', *USA Today* (24 June 2008), www.usatoday.com; and Beal, *Skateboarding*, p. 35.

78   www.nsskateboardingleague.org; and Anna Bakalis, 'High School Association Absorbs Liability', *Ventura County Star* (8 June 2007), www.vcstar.com.

79   *Affirmative Action* (Kane Stewart, 2013), www.youtube.com/watch?v=7CJaTJ12wpY; and Willing and Shearer, 'Skateboarding Activism', p. 52.

80   www.createaskate.org; and Beal, *Skateboarding*, p. 35.

81   www.drskateboard.com; William H. Robertson, *Action Science* (Thousand Oaks: Corwin, 2014); www.thefaracademy.co.uk; William H. Robertson, 'The Skatepark Mathematics Extravaganza', *US-China Education Review*, v.5 n.5 (2015), pp. 314-19; and Marco Adriano Dias, Paulo Simeão Carvalho and Deise Miranda Vianna, 'Using Image Modelling to Teach Newton's Laws with the Ollie Trick', *Physics Education*, v.51 n.4 (2016), pp. 1-6.

82   Georgina Badoni, 'Native American Art and Visual Culture Education through Skateboards' (MA dissertation, University of Arizona, 2009); and Dario Baica, 'Saskatchewan Skateboard Company Teaches Riders About Colonial History', *CTV News* (22 August 2015), www.ctvnews.ca.

83   Chris Dart, 'Toronto's Most Unlikely High School is a Skateboard Factory', *Yahoo Canada News* (4 May 2015), www.ca.news.yahoo.com.

84   Doug Brown, *Beyond the Board* (Mustang: Tate Publishing, 2010); and www.dougbrown.org.

85   'Interview – Zachary Sanford, Skateboarding Professor', 'Sk8 O'Clock' podcast (3 February 2015), www.sk8oclock.com; and Curt Sandoval, 'USC Skateboarding Course Merges Business and Fun', *ABC* (3 December 2016), www.abc7.com.

86   Borden, 'Southbank Skateboarding, London and Urban Culture', p. 94.

87   White, 'We Out Here', pp. 80-103.

88   Kilway, 'A Can of Worms: Updated', *Skate and Annoy* (1 August 2012), www.skateandannoy.com; Matthew Lee Johnston, 'Roxhill Meeting #2: Kind of a Disaster', www.seattleskateparks.org (13 October 2011); 'Fraud Charges for Rob Dyrdek's Charity Foundation', *Thronn Sk8 Mag* (9 August 2012), www.thronnsk8mag.com; 'Public Money to Advertise Rob Dyrdek?', www.ripoffwatch.tumblr.com; and Gene Maddaus, 'Joe Ciaglia, Skate Park Builder, to Pay $65,000', *LA Weekly* (4 September 2013), www.laweekly.com.

89   Louison, *Impossible*, p. 206.
90   O'Connor, 'Skateboard Philanthropy', p. 40.
91   Jim Fitzpatrick, (ed.), *Skateistan* (Kabul: Skateistan, 2012); *Skateistan – To Live and Skate Kabul* (dir. Orlando Von Einsiedel, 2011); *Skateistan – Four Wheels and a Board in Kabul* (dir. Kai Sehr, 2010); 'Afghanistan's Girl Skaters – Kabul 2012' (2012), www.vimeo.com/46337060; 'Skateboarding in Afghanistan, Oliver Percovich, TEDxSydney' (2014), www.youtube.com/watch?v=HnYN2yDqZew; and www.skateistan.org.
92   Iain Borden, 'The New Skate City: How Skateboarders Are Joining the Urban Mainstream', *The Guardian*, 'Cities' section (20 April 2015), www.gu.com/p/46yh7/stw.
93   O'Connor, 'Skateboard Philanthropy', p. 38.
94   Fitzpatrick, *Skateistan*, pp. 191, 275.
95   Sophie Friedel, *The Art of Living Sideways* (Berlin: Springer Verlag, 2015), p. 59, *passim*.
96   Fitzpatrick, *Skateistan*.
97   Holly Thorpe, 'Look at What We Can Do with All the Broken Stuff!', *Qualitative Research in Sport, Exercise and Health*, v.8 n.5 (2016), pp. 554–70.
98   Harms and Smith, *Skateboarder's Journal*, p. 316; and www.boardrescue.org.
99   Tracy Smith, 'A Skateboard Company That Builds More Than Boards', *CBS News* (24 August 2014), www.cbsnews.com; 'Cuba Skate' (2014), www.vimeo.com/96121779; www.ethiopiaskate.org; Adrija Bose, 'Why A German Woman Built a Skatepark in Rural Madhya Pradesh', *Huffington Post* (23 August 2016), www.huffingtonpost.in; www.skatepal.co.uk; '7Hills: a Community Skatepark Project in Jordan' (2014), www.vimeo.com/108385034; www.outlangish.com; Bruce Hong, 'UCT Engineering Students', *Cape Talk* (12 March 2015), www.capetalk.co.za; Alex King, 'The Architect

Building His Own Skate Oasis', *Huck* (15 September 2016), www.huckmagazine.com; Jarryd Salem and Alesha Bradford, 'I Gave Up My $120K Job to Build a Skate Park in Cambodia', *Yahoo Travel* (21 September 2015), www.yahoo.com; and Jake Hanrahan, 'The Skateboarders Bringing Peace to Tunisia', *The Guardian* (18 January 2012), www.theguardian.com.
100 'Ride It Sculpture Park: a Success Story' (2013), www.youtube.com/watch?v=ADtErLjggH8; and Matthew Piper, 'Ride It Sculpture Park', *Huffington Post* (14 August 2012), www.huffingtonpost.com.
101 www.askate.org.
102 'Skate Life on an Indian Reservation' (2013), www.youtube.com/watch?v=SYRINJZZqWU; www.strongholdsociety.org; Jeff Ament, 'Jim Murphy', *Juice*, v.22 n.1 (2015), pp. 88–97; Hilary N. Weaver, 'Where Wounded Knee Meets Wounded Knees', *AlterNative*, v.12 n.5 (2016), pp. 513–26; and Chris Nieratko, 'Pearl Jam's Bassist Has Personally Funded More Than a Dozen Skateboard Parks', *Vice* (24 August 2015), www.vice.com.
103 Daniello, 'Plaza at the Forks', pp. 53–63.
104 Hawk, *How Did I Get Here?*, pp. 155–64; and www.tonyhawkfoundation.org.

Chapter 14 Skateboarding – A Magnificent Life?

1   Chantal Mouffe, *The Democratic Paradox* (London: Verso, 2000).
2   Sedo, 'Dead-Stock Boards', p. 282.
3   Gustav Edén, 'Malmö: a City for Skateboarding', Astoria, Helsinki (2016), www.vimeo.com/167716104.
4   'Hull Pledges to Become Skateboard Centre', *BBC News* (24 November 2016), www.bbc.co.uk.
5   City Of Melbourne, 'Skate Melbourne Plan 2017–2027' (Melbourne, draft for consultation, 2016).

6   Sedo, 'Dead-Stock Boards', p. 261.
7   Jan, 'Bigotry in Skateboarding: Embrace the Art, Reject the Hate', *Kingpin* (21 February 2017), www.kingpinmag.com.
8   Zarka, *On a Day with No Waves*, p. 136; and Roland Barthes, 'Toys', *Mythologies* (London: Vintage Books, 2000), pp. 59–61.
9   O'Connor, 'Skateboard Philanthropy', pp. 30–46.
10   Lefebvre, *Introduction to Modernity*, p. 124.

Bibliography

Skateboarding Publications

Dani Abulhawa, 'Female Skateboarding: Re-Writing Gender', *Platform*, v.3 n.1 (2008), pp. 56–72.

Caroline Amell, *Skate Surf & Art* (Barcelona: Monsa, 2017).

Jon Amiano, Fernando Elvira and Javier Mendizabal, *La Kantera 1987–2015* (Gipuzkoa, Euskal Herria: Sugarcane, 2015).

Jake Anderson, *Relapse* (Dublin, Ohio: Coventry House, 2014).

Gerhard Andersson, Tony Hesse and Mikael Nyqvist, *Skateboard I Norköpping* (Linköping: Bax Förlag, 2016).

Jens Andersson, Martin Karlsson and Martin Ander, *Sheraton Years: Stockholm Skateboarding 1990–1999* (Stockholm: Sheraton Years, 2008).

Muriel Andrin, 'Back to the "Slap": Slapstick's Hyperbolic Gesture and the Rhetoric of Violence', Tom Paulis and Rob King, (eds), *Slapstick Comedy* (Abingdon: Routledge, 2010), pp. 226–35.

Julie Angel, *Ciné Parkour: a Cinematic and Theoretical Contribution to the Understanding of the Practice of Parkour* (CreateSpace, 2011).

Matthew Atencio and Becky Beal, 'Beautiful Losers: the Symbolic Exhibition and Legitimization of Outsider Masculinity', *Sport in Society*, v.14 n.1 (2011), pp. 1–16.

Matthew Atencio and Becky Beal, 'The "Legitimate" Skateboarder: Politics of Private-Public Skateboarding Spaces', Kara-Jane Lombard, (ed.), *Skateboarding: Subcultures, Sites and Shifts* (Abingdon: Routledge, 2015), pp. 108–20.

Matthew Atencio, Becky Beal and Charlene Wilson, 'The Distinction of Risk: Urban Skateboarding, Street Habitus and the Construction of Hierarchical Gender Relations', *Qualitative Research in Sport & Exercise*, v.1 n.1 (2009), pp. 3–20.

Matthew Atencio, Becky Beal and Emily Chivers Yochim, '"It Ain't Just Black Kids and White Kids": The Representation and Reproduction of Authentic "Skurban" Masculinities', *Sociology of Sport Journal*, v.30 n.2 (2013), pp. 153–72.

Åsa Bäckström, 'Gender Manoeuvring in Swedish Skateboarding: Negotiations of Femininities and the Hierarchical Gender Structure', *Young: Nordic Journal of Youth Research*, v.21 n.1 (2013), pp. 29–53.

Åsa Bäckström, 'Knowing and Teaching Kinaesthetic Experience in Skateboarding: an Example of Sensory Emplacement', *Sport, Education and Society*, v.19 n.6 (2014), pp. 752–72.

Georgina Badoni, 'Native American Art and Visual Culture Education through Skateboards' (MA dissertation, University of Arizona, 2009).

Stephen Baldwin, *Livin It: Testimonies* (Nashville, Tenn.: B&H, 2006).

Larry Balma, *Tracker: Forty Years of Skateboard History* (Oceanside: Foundry Press, 2015).

Harry Bastard, *Spots: A Guide to Ridable UK Architecture* (Brighton: WJ&T, 2001).

Mikhail Batuev and Leigh Robinson, 'How Skateboarding Made It to the Olympics: an Institutional Perspective', *International Journal of Sport Management and Marketing* (2018).

'Hell On Wheels', *Bay Guardian* (San Francisco) (May 1994).

Becky Beal, 'The Subculture of Skateboarding: Beyond Social Resistance' (EdD thesis, University of Northern Colorado, 1992).

Becky Beal, 'Disqualifying the Official: an Exploration of Social Resistance through the Subculture of Skateboarding', *Sociology of Sport Journal*, v.12 n.3 (1995), pp. 252–67.

Becky Beal, 'Alternative Masculinity and Its Effects on Gender Relations in the Subculture of Skateboarding', *Journal of Sport Behaviour*, v.19 n.3 (1996), pp. 204–20.

Becky Beal, 'Symbolic Inversion in the Subculture of Skateboarding', Margaret Duncan, Garry Chick and Alan Aycock, (eds), *Diversions and Divergences in Fields of Play: Play and Culture Studies Vol. 1* (Greenwich: Ablex, 1998), pp. 209–22.

Becky Beal, 'Skateboarding: an Alternative to Mainstreams Sports', J. Croakley and P. Donnelly, (eds), *Inside Sport* (London: Routledge, 1999), pp. 139–43.

Becky Beal, *Skateboarding: the Ultimate Guide* (Santa Barbara: Greenwood, 2013).

Becky Beal, Matthew Atencio, E. Missy Wright and Zánean McClain, 'Skateboarding, Community and Urban Politics: Shifting Practices and Challenges', *International Journal of Sport Policy and Politics*, v.9 n.1 (2017), pp. 11–23.

Becky Beal and Lisa Weidman, 'Authenticity in the Skateboard World', Robert Rinehart and Synthia Sydnor, (eds), *To the Extreme: Alternative Sports, Inside and Out* (New York: SUNY Press, 2003), pp. 337–52.

Becky Beal and Charlene Wilson, '"Chicks Dig Scars": Commercialisation and the Transformations of Skateboarders' Identities', Belinda Wheaton, (ed.), *Understanding Lifestyle Sports: Consumption, Identity and Difference* (London: Routledge, 2004), pp. 31–54.

Greg Beato, 'The Lords of Dogtown', *Spin*, (March 1999), pp. 114–21, reprinted in Arielle Greenberg, (ed.), *Youth Subcultures: Exploring Underground America* (New York: Pearson Longman, 2007), pp. 21–36.

Matt Berger, *The Handmade Skateboard: Design & Build a Custom Longboard, Cruiser, or Street Deck from Scratch* (Nashville: Spring House Press, 2014).

Aatish Bhatia, 'The Physics of Doing an Ollie on a Skateboard, or, the Science of Why I Can't Skate', *Wired* (5 October 2014), www.wired.com.

Kevin W. Bicknell, 'Examining Perceptions of Authenticity in Museum Exhibits About Skateboarding' (Masters dissertation, University of Washington, 2014).

Michael Blabac, *Blabac Photo: the Art of Skateboard Photography* (Brooklyn: PowerHouse Books, 2009).

Jean-Pierre Blanc, (ed.), *Landskating* (Hyères: Villa Noailles, 2015).

Julian Bleecker, *Hello Skater Girl: Photography by Julian Bleecker* (Pasadena: helloskatergirl.com, 2012).

Eric Blehm, (ed.), *Agents of Change: the Story of DC Shoes and Its Athletes* (New York: ReganBooks, 2003).

Neil Blender and Powell Peralta, *First, I Used to Build Giant Thorns. Correspondence 1983–2017* (Clay Verbs Press, 2017).

Jürgen Blümlein, Daniel Schmid and Dirk Vogel, *Made for Skate: the Illustrated History of Skateboard Footwear* (Berkeley: Gingko Press, 2008).

Jürgen Blümlein and Dirk Vogel, *Skateboarding Is Not a Fashion: the Illustrated History of Skateboard Apparel, 1950s to 1984* (Berkeley: Gingko Press, 2018).

Aaron Bondaroff, *Supreme: Downtown New York Skate Culture* (New York: Rizzoli, 2010).

Douglas Booth, (ed.), *Berkshire Encyclopedia of Extreme Sports* (Great Barrington: Berkshire, 2007).

Iain Borden, 'Beneath the Pavement, the Beach: Skateboarding, Architecture and the Urban Realm', in Iain Borden, Jane Rendell, Joe Kerr and Alicia Pivaro, (eds), *Strangely Familiar: Narratives of Architecture in the City* (London: Routledge, 1996), pp. 82–6.

Iain Borden, *Skateboarding, Space and the City: Architecture and the Body* (Oxford: Berg, 2001). Japanese edition, translation by Miho Nakagawa, Masako Saito and Tsunehiko Yabe, (Tokyo: Shin-yo-sha, 2006).

Iain Borden, 'Everyday Otherworlds: Rhythm, Detail, Journeys', Blair French, (ed.), *Shaun Gladwell: Videowork* (Sydney: Artspace Visual Arts Centre, 2007), pp. 32–6.

Iain Borden, 'A World Apart/Un monde à part', Richard Gilligan, *DIY* (Paris: 19/80 Éditions, 2012), pp. 11–14.

Iain Borden, 'Pipe Dreams: Rom Skatepark', *The Guardian* (1 November 2014), pp. 36–7. Published online as 'Concrete Playgrounds', www.gu.com/p/43vyb/tw.

Iain Borden, 'The Spaces of Skateboarding', *Architect's Journal* (28 November 2014), pp. 56–9.

Iain Borden, 'The Architecture', *Long Live Southbank* (London: Long Live Southbank, 2014), pp. 66–97.

Iain Borden, 'Things That People Cannot Anticipate: Skateboarding at the Festival Wing', Iain Borden, Murray Fraser and Barbara Penner, (eds), *Forty Ways to Think About Architecture: Architectural History and Theory Today* (Chichester: Wiley, 2014), pp. 100–5.

Iain Borden, 'The New Skate City: How Skateboarders Are Joining the Urban Mainstream', *The Guardian*, 'Cities' section (20 April 2015).

Iain Borden, 'An Interview with Professor Iain Borden on the "Long Live Southbank" Campaign and Skatepark Design from the 1970s to the Present', *Fakie Hill Bomb* (22 July 2015), www.fakiehillbomb.wordpress.com.

Iain Borden, 'Southbank Skateboarding, London and Urban Culture: the Undercroft, Hungerford Bridge and House of Vans', Kara-Jane Lombard, (ed.), *Skateboarding: Subcultures, Sites and Shifts* (Abingdon: Routledge, 2015), pp. 91–107.

Iain Borden, 'Ollies at the Olympics: Why Having Skateboarding at Tokyo 2020 Is a Winning Move', *The Conversation* (4 August 2016), www.theconversation.com.

Iain Borden, 'Skateboard City: London in Skateboarding Films', Pam Hirsch and Chris O'Rourke (eds), *London on Film: the City and Social Change* (London: Palgrave Macmillan, 2017).

James Boulter, *Unemployable: 30 Years of Hardcore, Skate and Street* (Sydney: Thames & Hudson, 2015).

John Boykin and Bob Grant, 'Skateboard Acrobatics', *Popular Mechanics* (July 1965), pp. 81–5.

Anthony Bracali, 'Thanks, Le Corbusier (from the Skateboarders)', www.anthonybracali.com.

Graham L. Bradley, 'Skate Parks as a Context for Adolescent Development', *Journal of Adolescent Research*, v.25 n.2 (2010), pp. 288–323.

Scott Bradstreet, *Skateboard Parks: Design & Development* (Atglen: Schiffer, 2009).

Leonardo Brandão and Tony Honorato, (eds), *Skate & Skatistas: Questões Contemporâneas* (Londrina: Universidade Estadual de Londrina, 2012).

Wilfred Brandt, 'Skateboard Aesthetics: the View from on Board' (PhD thesis, University of New South Wales, 2014).

Sean Brayton, 'Resistant to White? "Race", Masculinity, and Representation in Skateboard Culture' (MA, University of Alberta (Canada), 2004).

Sean Brayton, '"Black-Lash": Revisiting the "White Negro" through Skateboarding', *Sociology of Sport Journal*, v.22 n.3 (2005), pp. 356–72.

Sean Brayton, 'MTV's *Jackass*: Transgression, Abjection and the Economy of White Masculinity', *Journal of Gender Studies*, v.16 n.1 (2007), pp. 57–72.

Art Brewer and C.R. Stecyk, *Bunker Spreckels: Surfing's Divine Prince of Decadence* (Los Angeles: Taschen, 2007).

Jamie Brisick, *Have Board Will Travel: the Definitive History of Surf, Skate and Snow* (New York: HarperCollins, 2004).

Eduardo Britto, (ed.), *A Onda Dura: 3 Décadas De Skate No Brasil* (Sao Paulo: Parada Inglesa, 2000).

Michael Brooke, *The Concrete Wave: the History of Skateboarding* (Toronto: Warwick, 1999).

Kevin Brooker, *Way Inside ESPN's X Games* (New York: Hyperion/ESPN Books, 1998).

David Browne, *Amped: How Big Air, Big Dollars, and a New Generation Took Sports to the Extreme* (London: Bloomsbury, 2004).

David Browne, 'Dogtown East', *New York Magazine* (2005), www.nymag.com.

Erik Brunetti, *Fuct* (New York: Rizzoli, 2013).

David Buckingham, 'Skate Perception: Self-Representation, Identity and Visual Style in a Youth Subculture', David Buckingham and Rebekah Willett, (eds), *Video Cultures: Media Technology and Everyday Creativity* (Basingstoke: Palgrave, 2009), pp. 133–51.

Damien Burden, *Cyst* (Middletown: self-published 2015).

Patrick Burgoyne and Jeremy Leslie, *Bored: Surf/Skate/Snow Graphics* (London: Lawrence King and Creative Review, 1997).

Konstantin Butz, *Grinding California: Culture and Corporeality in American Skate Punk* (Bielefeld: Transcript Verlag, 2012).

Claire Calogirou and Marc Touché, 'Les Jeunes et la Rue: les Rapports Physiques et Sonores des Skateurs aux Espaces Urbains', *Espaces et Sociétés*, v.2 n.90–1 (1997), pp. 69–88.

Daniel Campo, *The Accidental Playground: Brooklyn Waterfront Narratives of the Undesigned and Unplanned* (New York: Empire State, 2013).

Antoine Cantin-Brault, 'The Reification of Skateboarding', *International Journal of Science Culture and Sport*, v.3 n.1 (2015), pp. 54–66.

Sebastien Carayol, *Agents Provocateurs: 100 Subversive Skateboard Graphics* (Berkeley: Gingko Press, 2014).

Sebastien Carayol and Todd Francis, *Look Away: the Art of Todd Francis* (New York: Wins Things, 2014).

John Carr, 'The Political Grind: the Role of Youth Identities in the Municipal Politics of Public Space' (PhD thesis, University of Washington, 2007).

John Carr, 'Legal Geographies: Skating around the Edges of the Law: Urban Skateboarding and the Role of Law in

Determining Young Peoples' Place in the City', *Urban Geography*, v.31 n.7 (2010), pp. 988–1003.

John Carr, 'Activist Research and City Politics: Ethical Lessons from Youth-Based Public Scholarship', *Action Research*, v.10 n.1 (2012), pp. 61–78.

John Carr, 'Public Input/Elite Privilege: the Use of Participatory Planning to Reinforce Urban Geographies of Power in Seattle', *Urban Geography*, v.33 n.3 (2012), pp. 420–41.

John Carr, 'Skateboarding in Dude Space: the Roles of Space and Sport in Constructing Gender among Adult Skateboarders', *Sociology of Sport Journal*, v.34 n.1 (2016), pp. 25–34.

Chihsin Chiu, 'Contestation and Conformity: Street and Park Skateboarding in New York City Public Space', *Space and Culture*, v.12 n.1 (2009), pp. 25–42.

Roy Christopher, *Follow for Now: Interviews with Friends and Heroes* (Seattle: Well-Red Bear, 2007), pp. 269–76.

City of Melbourne, 'Skate Melbourne Plan 2017–2027' (Melbourne, draft for consultation, 2016).

Marcia Clemmit, 'Extreme Sports: Are They Too Dangerous?', *CQ Researcher Blog* (3 April 2009), www.cqresearcherblog.blogspot.co.uk.

Sean Cliver, *Disposable: a History of Skateboard Art* (Corte Madera: Gingko Press, 2004).

Sean Cliver, *The Disposable Skateboard Bible* (Berkeley: Gingko Press, 2009).

Sean Cliver, (ed.), *Jackass: 10 Years of Stupid* (New York: MTV Press, 2010).

Sean Cliver and Dave Carnie, (eds), *Shit: the Big Brother Book* (Berkeley: Gingko Press, 2016).

Jay Cocks, 'The Irresistible Air of Grabbing Air: Skateboarding, Once a Fad, is Now a National Turn-on', *Time*, v.131 (6 June 1988), pp. 90–1.

Deborah A. Cohen et al, 'City of Los Angeles Neighborhood Parks: Research Findings and Policy Implications (2003–2015)' (Rand Corporation, Research Report, 2016).

Tait Colberg, *The Skateboarding Art* (Lulu, 2012).

Mark Conahan, *Hopeless Old Men on Skateboards* (Portland: Antigravity Press, 2009).

'Techniques – Skateboard Track', *Constructional Review* (November 1976), pp. 58–9, www.concreteconstruction.net.

Dave Cornthwaite, *Boardfree: the Story of an Incredible Skateboard Journey across Australia* (London: Portico, 2007).

Alex Corporan, Andre Razo and Ivory Serra, (eds), *Full Bleed: New York City Skateboard Photography* (Brooklyn, New York: Vice Books, 2010).

Nicholas Croggon and Charles Green, 'Shaun Gladwell: Critique, Gesture, and Skateboarding', *Australian and New Zealand Journal of Art*, v.11 (2011), pp. 133–54.

Dank Magazine, 'Elements of Style', *Ciff Gazette* (2013), pp. 1–7.

Ben J. Davidson, *The Skateboard Book* (New York: Grosset & Dunlap, 1976, and London: Sphere, smaller format, 1978).

Pete Davidson, *Reforming a Counter Culture: the Flaws and Fallacies of the Skateboarding Industry and How to Fix Them* (Charleston: BookSurge, second edition, 2009).

James Davis and Skin Phillips, *Skateboarding Is Not a Crime: 50 Years of Street Culture* (Buffalo: Firefly Books, 2004).

Matt Dawson, *Sponsored Life: The Ultimate Guide to Skateboarding Sponsorship* (San Juan Capistrano: Luma Publications, 2008).

Josh Dean, 'Skateboarder Bob Burnquist's Far-out Dreams', *Outside* (29 July 2009), www.outsideonline.com.

Bob Denike, (ed.), *Built to Grind: 25 Years of Hardcore Skateboarding. From the Archives of Independent Truck Company* (San Francisco: High Speed Productions, 2004).

Sebastian Denz, *Skateboarding.3D* (Munich: Prestel, 2009).

Marco Adriano Dias, Paulo Simeão Carvalho and Deise Miranda Vianna, 'Using Image Modelling to Teach Newton's Laws with the Ollie Trick', *Physics Education*, v.51 n.4 (2016), pp. 1–6.

Sean Dinces, '"Flexible Opposition": Skateboarding Subcultures under the Rubric of Late Capitalism', *International Journal of the History of Sport*, v.28 n.11 (2011), pp. 1512–35.

Dwayne Dixon, 'Getting the Make: Japanese Skateboarder Videography and the Entranced Ethnographic Lens', *Postmodern Culture*, v.22 n.1 (2011), np.

Dwayne Dixon, 'Posing LA, Performing Tokyo: Photography and Race in Skateboarding's Global Imaginary', Kara-Jane Lombard, (ed.), *Skateboarding: Subcultures, Sites and Shifts* (Abingdon: Routledge, 2015), pp. 73–87.

Pahl Dixon and Peter Dixon, *Your Complete Guide to Hot Skateboarding* (New York: Warner Books, 1977).

Michele Donnelly, 'Extreme Sports Lite? Representations of Women's Skateboarding and Snowboarding on Television' (MA dissertation, Queen's University, Kingston, 2004).

Michele Donnelly, 'Studying Extreme Sports: Beyond the Core Participants', *Journal of Sport & Social Issues*, v.30 n.2 (2006), pp. 219–24.

Michele Donnelly, 'Alternative *and* Mainstream: Revisiting the Sociological Analysis of Skateboarding', Michael

Atkinson and Kevin Young, (eds), *Tribal Play: Subcultural Journeys through Sport* (Bingley: JAI Press, 2008), pp. 197–214.

Michele Donnelly, '"Take the Slam and Get Back Up": *Hardcore Candy* and the Politics of Representation in Girl's and Women's Skateboarding and Snowboarding on Television', Michael D. Giardina and Michele Donnelly, (eds), *Youth Culture and Sport* (Abingdon: Routledge, 2008), pp. 127–43.

David Drissel, 'Skateboarding Spaces of Youth in Belfast: Negotiating Boundaries, Transforming Identities', *Spaces & Flows: an International Journal of Urban & Extra Urban Studies*, v.2 n.4 (2012), pp. 115–38.

Peter Ducommun, *Skateboarding Vancouver: the Skull Skates Collection at the Vancouver Museum* (Toronto: Concrete Wave, 2005).

Paul Duffy and Trawler (Mark Lawler), *Sk8-80's! An Archive of the 80's Skateboarding Scene* (Duffy and Trawler, 2015).

Alex Dumas and Sophie Laforest, 'Skateparks as a Health-Resource: Are They as Dangerous as They Look?', *Leisure Studies*, v.28 n.1 (2009), pp. 19–34.

Stephen Duncombe, *Notes from Underground* (London: Verso, 1997).

Tyler Dupont, 'From Core to Consumer: the Informal Hierarchy of the Skateboard Scene', *Journal of Contemporary Ethnography*, v.43 n.5 (2014), pp. 556–81.

Henrik Edelbo and Rasmus Folehave Hansen, *Dansk Skateboarding* (Copenhagen: Nordstrøms Forlag, 2014).

Gustav Edén, 'Malmö: a City for Skateboarding', Astoria, Helsinki (3 May 2016), www.vimeo.com/167716104.

Aubrey Edwards, 'Swamp Suburbia and Rebellion against a Culture of Crime: the Birth of Black Skateboarding in the Big Easy' (MSc Urban Studies dissertation, University of New Orleans, 2015).

Mackenzie Eisenhour, *Cliché: Résumé – a Decade Plus of Skateboarding in Europe* (Berkeley: Gingko Press, 2010).

El Beardo 'The Never Ending Story: the Ongoing Saga of the Channel Street Skatepark', *Thrasher*, n. 297 (August 2005), pp. 68–73.

Kameliya Encheva, Olivier Driessens and Hans Verstraeten, 'The Mediatization of Deviant Subcultures: an Analysis of the Media-Related Practices of Graffiti Writers and Skaters', *MedieKultur*, n.54 (2013), pp. 8–25.

Yrjö Engeström, 'Wildfire Activities: New Patterns of Mobility and Learning', *International Journal of Mobile and Blended Learning*, v.1 n.2 (2009), pp. 1–18.

English Heritage, 'London Sporting Buildings: the Rom Skatepark, London Borough of Havering. Case Number: 1416690' (21 July 2014).

English Heritage, 'The Rom Skatepark. List Entry Number: 1419328', *The National Heritage List for England*, www.list.english-heritage.org.uk.

Siân Liz Evans, 'Young, Gifted and Board Stupid', *Big Issue*, n.126 (17–23 April 1995), pp. 18–20.

Edwin Faeh and Oliver Drewes, *Dirt Ollies: a Skateboard Trip to Mongolia* (Berlin: Verlag für Bildschöne Bücher, 2007).

Kevin Fang, 'Skateboarding as a Mode of Transportation: Review of Regulations in California Cities and College Campuses', *The 92nd Annual Meeting of the Transportation Research Board* (January 2013), www.trb.org.

Kevin Fang, 'Skateboarding Down the Street: Potential Factors Influencing the Decision to Skateboard as an Active Travel Mode – an Initial Exploration', *The 93rd Annual Meeting of the Transportation Research Board*, Washington DC (January 2014), www.trb.org.

Kevin Fang, 'Skateboarding for Transportation by the Numbers: Quantitative Indications of the Use of Skateboards as an Active Travel Mode', *The 94th Annual Meeting of the Transportation Research Board*, Washington DC (January 2015), www.trb.org.

Kevin Fang and Susan Handy, 'Skateboarding for Transportation: Exploring the Factors Behind an Unconventional Mode Choice among University Skateboard Commuters', *Transportation* (online July 2017).

Jeff Ferrell, *Tearing Down the Streets: Adventures in Crime and Anarchy* (Basingstoke: Palgrave, 2001).

Hunter Fine, 'Underneath the Streets, the Beach: Drifting toward/from a Proto-Poststructuralist Performance of Everyday Spatial Subjectivity' (PhD thesis, Southern Illinois University at Carbondale, 2012).

Hunter Fine, 'The Skateboard Dérive: a Poststructuralist Performance of Everyday Urban Motility', *Liminalities: a Journal of Performance Studies*, v.9 n.3 (2013), pp. 1–20.

Craig Fineman, *Pools* (New York: Dashwood Books, 2014).

Jim Fitzpatrick, (ed.), *Skateistan: the Tale of Skateboarding in Afghanistan* (Kabul: Skateistan, 2012).

Fluff and Nike SB, *1826: Fluff X Nike SB* (Netherlands: United Fluff Press and Nike SB, 2015).

Steven Flusty, 'Thrashing Downtown: Play as Resistance to the Spatial and Representational Regulation of Los Angeles', *Cities*, v.17 n.2 (2000), pp. 149–58.

Nick Ford and David Brown, *Surfing and Social Theory: Experience, Embodiment and Narrative of the Dream Glide* (London: Routledge, 2006).

Jane Forsyth, 'Aboriginal Sport in the City: Implications for Participation, Health, and Policy in Canada', *Aboriginal Policy Studies*, v.3 n.1 & 2 (2014), pp. 214–22.

Edward Frederick, Jeremy Determan, Saunders Whittlesey and Joseph Hamill, 'Biomechanics of Skateboarding: Kinetics of the Ollie', *Journal of Applied Biomechanics*, v.22 n.1 (2006), pp. 33–40.

Claire Freeman and Tamara Riordan, 'Locating Skateparks: the Planner's Dilemma', *Planning Practice and Research*, v.17 n.3 (2002), pp. 297–316.

Sophie Friedel, *The Art of Living Sideways: Skateboarding, Peace and Elicitive Conflict Transformation* (Berlin: Springer Verlag, 2015).

Glen E. Friedman, *Fuck You Heroes: Glen E. Friedman Photographs, 1976–1991* (New York: Burning Flags, 1994).

Glen E. Friedman, *Fuck You Too: the Extras + More Scrapbook* (Los Angeles: 2.13.61 Publications and Burning Flags, 1996).

Glen E. Friedman, *My Rules* (New York: Rizzoli, 2014).

Jessica Fulford-Dobson, *Skate Girls of Kabul* (London: Morland Tate, 2015).

Brian Gaberman, *A Life in Transition. Photography of Brian Gaberman. The Element Years 2006–2013* (USA: Element, 2013).

Trip Gabriel, 'Rolling Thunder', *Rolling Stone* (16–30 July 1987), pp. 73–6.

Leah Garchik, 'The Urban Landscape', *San Francisco Chronicle* (late summer 1994).

Bradley Garrett, *Explore Everything: Place-Hacking the City* (London: Verso, 2013).

Stephanie Geertman, Danielle Labbé, Julie-Anne Boudreau and Olivier Jacques, 'Youth-Driven Tactics of Public Space Appropriation in Hanoi: the Case of Skateboarding and Parkour', *Pacific Affairs*, v.89 n.3 (2016), pp. 591–611.

Daniel Gesmer, (ed.), *The Legacy of Warren Bolster: Master of Skateboard Photography* (Thornhill: Concrete Wave, 2004).

Christopher D. Giamarino, 'Spatial Ethno-Geographies of Sub-Cultures in Urban Space: Skateboarders, Appropriative Performance, and Spatial Exclusion in Los Angeles' (MSc Urban Planning dissertation, Columbia University, 2017).

Chrysostomos Giannoulakis, 'A Framework for Marketing Implementation to Surfing, Skateboarding, and Snowboarding: the Case Study of a Board Sports Company' (PhD thesis, University of Northern Colorado, 2008).

Paul Gilchrist and Belinda Wheaton, 'The Social Benefits of Informal and Lifestyle Sports: a Research Agenda', *International Journal of Sport Policy and Politics*, v.9 n.1 (2017), pp. 1–10.

Richard Gilligan, *DIY* (Paris: 19/80 Éditions, 2012).

Julien Glauser, *Tokyo-Skate: les Paysages Urbains du Skateboard* (Gollion: Infolio, 2016).

Brian Glenney, 'Skateboarding, Sport and Spontaneity: Toward a Subversive Definition of Sport', Shawn E. Klein, (ed.), *Defining Sport: Conceptions and Borderlines* (Lanham: Lexington, 2017), pp. 147–58.

Brian Glenney and Steve Mull, 'Skateboarding and the Re-Wilding of Urban Space', *Journal of Sport and Social Issues* (forthcoming).

Marni Goldenberg and Wynn Shooter, 'Skateboard Park Participation: a Means-End Analysis', *Journal of Youth Development*, v.4 n.4 (2007), pp. 1–12.

Brandon Gomez, 'How Did Nike Get the Swoosh into Skateboarding? A Study of Authenticity and Nike SB' (MA Media Studies dissertation, Syracuse University, 2012).

Jim Goodrich, 'Skateboard History Timeline', www.facebook.com/notes/jim-goodrich/skateboard-hisory-timeline/270818099610316.

Gordon & Smith, *The Gordon & Smith Skateboard Team Book* (San Diego: MLP, 2010).

Gordon & Smith, *One Long Ride* (San Diego: Gordon & Smith, 2014).

Marilyn Gould, *Skateboarding* (Mankato: Capstone, 1991).

Sam Griffin, 'Skateboarding in the Age of Mechanical Image Reproduction: From Powell Peralta to T-Puds', Chiara Santini Parducci, (ed.), *Do Not Think* (Berlin: Oxylane Art Foundation, 2015), pp. 121–40.

David Grogan and Carl Arrington, 'He's Not Lean but His Rap Is Mean, So the Thrashers Relate to Skatemaster Tate', *People Weekly*, v.27 (8 June 1987), pp. 155–6.

Bill Gutman, *Skateboarding to the Extreme* (New York: Tom Doherty Associates, 1997).

Charles Hackenheimer, 'Risk-Taking Behavior of Skateboarders and Traditional Sport Participants in Students Ages 13-16 Years' (MSc Sports Education Leadership dissertation, University of Nevada, 2007).

Miljøverndepartementet, *Forskrift om Rullebrett* (Oslo, 3 May 1989).

Morgan Hall, 'A Cross-Sectional Examination of the Predictors of Commitment in Skateboarders' (MSc dissertation, University of Utah, Exercise and Sport Science department, 2013).

Keith David Hamm, *Scarred for Life: Eleven Stories about Skateboarders* (San Francisco: Chronicle, 2004).

J. Namdev Hardisty, *New Skateboard Graphics* (New York: Mark Batty, 2010).

Catherine Hardwicke, *Lords of Dogtown: Behind the Scenes* (Thornhill: Concrete Wave Editions, 2005).

Jonathan Harms and Jack Smith, (eds), *The Skateboarder's Journal: Lives on Board 1949–2009* (Morro Bay: Morro Skateboard Group, 2009).

Peter Harnik and Coleen Gentles, 'Coming to a City Near You', *Parks & Recreation* (May 2009), pp. 34–8.

Corbin Harris, *Ultimate Guide to Skateboarding* (Sydney: HarperCollins, 2009).

Garth Harris, 'The Belonging Paradox: the Belonging Experience of Committed Uncertain Members' (PhD thesis, Queen's University Kingston, 2011).

Meira Harris, 'Skaters Gonna Skate: Skateboarding and Its Influence on Urban Space', *Urban Review* (Fall 2014), pp. 19–23, 28.

Clint van der Hartt, (ed.), *Reclaiming the Street* (Rotterdam: Showroom MAMA, 2011).

Tony Hawk, *Between Boardslides and Burnout: My Notes from the Road* (New York: HarperCollins, 2002).

Tony Hawk with Pat Hawk, *How Did I Get Here? The Ascent of an Unlikely CEO* (Hoboken: Wiley, 2010).

Tony Hawk with Sean Mortimer, *Hawk: Occupation Skateboarder* (London: ReganBooks, 2000).

Joanna Hearne, '"This Is Our Playground": Skateboarding, DIY Aesthetics, and Apache Sovereignty in Dustinn Craig's *4wheelwarpony*', *Western American Literature*, v.49 n.1 (2014), pp. 47–69.

Neil Heayes, 'All Aboard for the Skateboard Take-Off', *Contract Journal* (19 January 1978), pp. 22–3.

Claudine Heizer, 'Street Smarts', *Parks & Recreation*, v.39 n.11 (November 2004), pp. 74–9.

Annika Amelie Hellman, 'Skateboarding Is Like Dancing: Masculinity as a Performative Visual Culture in Art Education', *International Journal of Education Through Art*, v.12 n.3 (2016), pp. 327–44.

Matt Hensley, *Best of the West: Skatepark Guide* (Thornhill: Concrete Wave, c. 2005).

Stan Hey, 'Wheelers and Dealers', *Time Out*, n.381 (15–21 July 1977), pp. 12–13.

Lynn Hill, *The Guide to Western Skateboard Parks* (La Jolla: Third Eye, 1978).

Peter Hill and Stephen Hill, *Skate Hard* (Fitzroy: Five Mile Press, 1988).

Kelvin Ho, 'Skateboarding: an Interpretation of Space in the Olympic City', *Architectural Theory Review*, v.4 n.2 (1999), pp. 98–102.

Justin Hocking, *Dream Builders: the World's Best Skate Park Creators* (New York: Rosen Publishing, 2005).

Justin Hocking, *The World's Greatest Skate Parks* (New York: Rosen, 2009).

Justin Hocking, Jeff Knutson and Jared Maher, (eds), *Life and Limb: Skateboarders Write from the Deep End* (Brooklyn: Soft Skull Press, 2004).

Tom Hodgkinson, 'Rad, Mad and Dangerous to Know?', *Midweek* (18 January 1990), pp. 10–11.

Hugh Holland, *Locals Only: California Skateboarding 1975–1978* (Los Angeles: Ammo Books, 2010).

Ty Hollett, 'Symbiotic Learning Partnerships in Youth Action Sports: Vibing, Rhythm, and Analytic Cycles', *Convergence* (2017), pp. 1–14.

Sander Hölsgens, 'A Phenomenology of Skateboarding in Seoul, S. Korea: Experiential and Filmic Observations' (PhD thesis, University College London, Bartlett School of Architecture, 2018).

Nick Hornby, *Slam* (London: Penguin, 2008).

Christian Hosoi and Chris Ahrens, *Hosoi: My Life as a Skateboarder, Junkie, Inmate Pastor* (New York: HarperOne, 2012).

Jeff Howe, 'Drawing Lines: a Report from the Extreme World', Robert Rinehart and Synthia Sydnor, (eds), *To the Extreme: Alternative Sports, Inside and Out* (New York: SUNY Press, 2003), pp. 353–69.

Ocean Howell, 'The Poetics of Security: Skateboarding, Urban Design, and the New Public Space', *Urban Action 2011* (2001), San Francisco State University, Urban Studies Department, pp. 64–86.

Ocean Howell, 'Extreme Market Research: Tales from the Underbelly of Skater-Cool', *Topic Magazine* (2004), www.webdelsol.com.

Ocean Howell, 'The "Creative Class" and the Gentrifying City: Skateboarding in Philadelphia's Love Park', *Journal of Architectural Education*, v.59 n.2 (2005), pp. 32–42.

Ocean Howell, 'Skatepark as Neoliberal Playground: Urban Governance, Recreation Space, and the Cultivation of Personal Responsibility', *Space and Culture*, v.11 n.4 (2008), pp. 475–96.

Russ Howell, *Skateboard: Techniques, Safety, Maintenance* (Sydney: Ure Smith, 1975).

Huck, *Paddle against the Flow: Lessons on Life from Doers, Creators and Cultural Rebels* (San Francisco: Chronicle, 2015).

Wes Humpston, *Bulldog's Art by Wes Humpston* (Thornhill: Concrete Wave, 2013).

Simon Inglis, *Played in London: Charting the Heritage of a City at Play* (London: English Heritage, 2014).

'Stacy Peralta', *Interview*, n.17 (July 1987), pp. 102–3.

Jonas Ivarsson, 'The Turn-Organization of Pool-Skate Sessions', *American Anthropological Association 111th Annual Meeting*, San Francisco (14–18 November 2012).

Phil Jackson, Scott Kmiec and Nicholas Orso, *FDR Skatepark: a Visual History* (Atglen: Schiffer, 2012).

Michael Jeffries, Sebastian Messer, and Jon Swords, 'He Catches Things in Flight: Scopic Regimes, Visuality, and Skateboarding in Tyneside, England', Kara-Jane Lombard, (ed.), *Skateboarding: Subcultures, Sites and Shifts* (Abingdon: Routledge, 2015), pp. 57–72.

Adam Jenson, Jon Swords and Michael Jeffries, 'The Accidental Youth Club: Skateboarding in Newcastle-Gateshead', *Journal of Urban Design*, v.17 n.3 (2012), pp. 371–88.

Judith A. Johns, 'The Relationship between Involvement in Unstructured Unsupervised Leisure and Substance Use in a Cohort of Adolescent Male Skateboarders' (PhD thesis, Kent State University, 2011).

Ralph Johns, 'Skateboard City', *Landscape Design*, n.303 (September 2001), pp. 42–4.

Alasdair Jones, *On South Bank: the Production of Public Space* (Farnham: Ashgate, 2014).

Rodney H. Jones, 'Sport and Re/Creation: What Skateboarders Can Teach Us About Learning', *Sport Education and Society*, v.16 n.5 (2011), pp. 593–611.

Stanton Jones and Arthur Graves, 'Power Plays in Public Space: Skateboard Parks as Battlegrounds, Gifts, and Expressions of Self', *Landscape Journal*, v.19 n.1–2 (2000), pp. 136–48.

Lia Karsten and Eva Pel, 'Skateboarders Exploring Urban Public Space: Ollies, Obstacles and Conflicts', *Journal of Housing and the Built Environment*, v.15 n.4 (2000), pp. 327–40.

Deirdre M. Kelly, Shauna Pomerantz and Dawn H. Currie, 'Skater Girlhood and Emphasized Femininity: "You Can't Land an Ollie Properly in Heels"', *Gender and Education*, v.17 n.3 (2005), pp. 229–48.

Deirdre M. Kelly, Shauna Pomerantz and Dawn H. Currie, '"You Can Break So Many More Rules": the Identity Work and Play of Becoming Skater Girls', Michael Giardina and Michele Donnelly, (eds) *Youth Culture and Sport* (Abingdon: Routledge, 2008), pp. 113–25.

Armen Keteyian, 'Chairman of the Board', *Sports Illustrated*, v.65 n.23 (24 November 1986), pp. 46–50.

Steven Kotler, *The Rise of Superman: Decoding the Science of Ultimate Human Performance* (London: Quercus Editions, 2014).

Johan Kugelberg and Ryan Richardson, (eds), *Sounds of Two Eyes Opening. Southern California Life: Skate/Beach/Punk 1969–1982. Photography by Spot* (Los Angeles: Sinecure Books, 2014).

Kyle Kusz, 'The Cultural Politics of Extreme Sports in America', Belinda Wheaton, (ed.), *Understanding Lifestyle Sports: Consumption, Identity and Difference* (London: Routledge, 2004), pp. 197–213.

Kyle Kusz, *Revolt of the White Athlete: Race, Media and the Emergence of Extreme Athletes in America* (New York: Peter Lang, 2007).

Scott Laderman, *Empire in Waves: a Political History of Surfing* (Berkeley: University of California, 2014).

Olivier L'Aoustet and Jean Griffet, 'The Experience of Teenagers at Marseilles' Skate Park: Emergence and Evaluation of an Urban Sports Site', *Cities*, v.18 n.6 (2001), pp. 413–18.

Signe Højbjerre Larsen, 'What Can the Parkour Craftsmen Tell Us About Bodily Expertise and Skilled Movement?', *Sport, Ethics and Philosophy*, v.10 n.3 (2016), pp. 295–309.

Julien Laurent, *Le Skateboard: Analyse Sociologique d'une Pratique Physique Urbaine* (Paris: L'Harmattan, 2012).

Jack Layton, 'Southbank Centre and the Long Live Southbank Campaign: a Study of Public Spaces and Democratic Practices' (MSc Urban Studies dissertation, University College London, 2016).

Florian Lebreton, *Cultures Urbaines et Sportives: Socio-anthropologie de l'Urbanité Ludique* (Paris, L'Harmattan, 2010).

David Leonard, 'To the White Extreme in the Mainstream: Manhood and White Youth Culture in a Virtual Sports World', Michael Giardina and Michele Donnelly, (eds), *Youth Culture and Sport* (Abingdon: Routledge, 2008), pp. 91–112.

Jeremy Leslie and Patrick Burgoyne, *Bored: Surf/Skate/Snow Graphics* (London: Laurence King, 1997).

Jeremy Leslie and Patrick Burgoyne, *Still Bored: Surf/Skate/Snow Graphics* (London: Laurence King, 2003).

Austin Li, 'China's Skateboarding Youth Culture as an Emerging Cultural Industry' (PhD thesis, Loughborough University, 2018).

'Skateboard Mania – and Menace', *Life* (14 May 1965), pp. 126C–126D, 127–30, 132, 134 and front cover.

Kara-Jane Lombard, 'Skate and Create/ Skate and Destroy: the Commercial and Governmental Incorporation of Skateboarding', *Continuum*, v.24 n.4 (2010), pp. 475–88.

Kara-Jane Lombard, 'Trucks, Tricks, and Technologies of Government: Analyzing the Productive Encounter between Governance and Resistance in Skateboarding', Kara-Jane Lombard, (ed.), *Skateboarding: Subcultures, Sites and Shifts* (Abingdon: Routledge, 2015), pp. 169–81.

Chris Long and Travis Jensen, (eds), *No Comply: Skateboarding Speaks on Authority* (Ventura: FunNotFame, 2006).

Long Live Southbank, *Long Live Southbank* (London: Long Live Southbank, 2014).

Long Live Southbank, 'Southbank Undercroft: Cultural & Heritage Assessment Report' (London: Long Live Southbank, September 2014).

Stephen W. Lorimer and Stephen Marshall, 'Beyond Walking and Cycling: Scoping Small-Wheel Modes', *Proceedings of the Institution of Civil Engineers - Engineering Sustainability*, v.169 n.2 (2016), pp. 58–66.

Michael J. Lorr, 'Skateboarding and the X-Gamer Phenomenon: a Case of Subcultural Cooptation', *Humanity & Society*, v.29 n.2 (2005), pp. 140–7.

Michael J. Lorr, 'Skateboarding as a Technology of the Collective: Kona Skatepark, Jacksonville, Florida, USA', Kara-Jane Lombard, (ed.), *Skateboarding: Subcultures, Sites and Shifts* (Abingdon: Routledge, 2015), pp. 139–51.

Cole Louison, *The Impossible: Rodney Mullen, Ryan Sheckler and the Fantastic History of Skateboarding* (Guilford: Lyons Press, 2011).

Lurp Lurpington, 'How Corporations Are Changing Skateboarding and Why It Matters', *Jenkem Magazine* (6 November 2012), www.jenkemmag.com.

Jasmine Y. Ma and Charles Munter, 'The Spatial Production of Learning Opportunities in Skateboard Parks', *Mind, Culture, and Activity*, v.21 n.3 (2014), pp. 238–58.

Andy Macdonald with Theresa Foy Digeronimo, *Dropping In with Andy Mac: the Life of a Pro Skateboarder* (New York: Simon Pulse, 2003).

Ian Macdonald, '"Urban Surfers": Representations of the Skateboarding Body in Youth Leisure', Peter Bramham and Jayne Caudwell, (eds), *Sport, Active Leisure and Youth Cultures* (Eastbourne: Leisure Studies Association, 2005), pp. 97–113.

Steph MacKay, 'Skirtboarder Net-a-Narratives: a Socio-Cultural Analysis of a Women's Skateboarding Blog' (PhD thesis, University of Ottawa, 2012).

Steph MacKay, 'Spreading the Skirtboarder Stoke: Reflexively Blogging Fluid Femininities and Constructing New Female Skateboarding Identities', Kara-Jane Lombard, (ed.), *Skateboarding: Subcultures, Sites and Shifts* (Abingdon: Routledge, 2015), pp. 121–35.

Steph MacKay and Christine Dallaire, 'Skirtboarder Net-a-Narratives: Young Women Creating Their Own Skateboarding (Re)Presentations', *International Review for the Sociology of Sport*, v.48 n.2 (2013), pp. 171–95.

Steph MacKay and Christine Dallaire, 'Skirtboarders.com: Skateboarding Women and Self-Formation as Ethical Subjects', *Sociology of Sport Journal*, v.30 n.2 (2013), pp. 173–96.

Steph Mackay and Christine Dallaire, 'Skateboarding Women: Building Collective Identity in Cyberspace', *Journal of Sport & Social Issues*, v.38 n.548 (2014), pp. 548–66.

Mohd. Shahrudin Abd. Manan and Chris L. Smith, 'Skateboarding with Roland Barthes: Architecture, Myth and Evidence', *Journal for Cultural Research*, v.18 n.3 (2013), pp. 203–15.

Barbara Manning, 'Teenager Tony Hawk Soars Above Everybody in the Scary Sport of Skateboarding', *People Weekly*, v.27 (23 March 1987), pp. 48–9.

Daniel Månsson, *Faces of Skateboarding* (Stockholm: DDMN, 2006).

Ben Marcus and Lucia Daniella Griggi, *The Skateboard: the Good, the Rad, and the Gnarly. An Illustrated History* (Minneapolis: MVP Books, 2011).

Israel Márquez and Ruben Diez García, 'La Cultura Skate en las Sociedades Contemporáneas: una Aproximación Etnográfica a la Ciudad de Madrid', *EMPIRIA*, n.30 (2015), pp. 133–58.

Fiona McCormack and Ben Clayton, 'Engagement and Influence in Local Policy Decisions: an Examination of the Enabling Factors in the Negotiations of a Youth Skateboard Community', *International Journal of Sport Policy and Politics*, v.9 n.1 (2017), pp. 41–54.

Jamie McCullough, *Meanwhile Gardens* (London: Calouste Gulbenkian Foundation, 1978).

Alastair McLellan, *Palace* (London: Idea, 2016).

Donald Meckiffe, 'Mainstreams and Subcultures: the Hidden Histories of Female Bodybuilding, Muhammad Ali, Skateboarding and Black Divas' (PhD thesis, University of Wisconsin, 2003).

Jonathan Mehring, *Skate the World* (Washington: National Geographic, 2015).

Kit Messham-Muir, *Practices of the City and the Kickflipping Flâneur* (Woolloomooloo: Artspace Visual Arts Centre, 2000).

Ian Michna, (ed.), *Jenkem Vol. 1: Skateboarding, Smut, Shenanigans* (Brooklyn: Jenkem Magazine, 2016).

Jody Morris, *20 Plus: the Photography of Jody Morris* (Leucadia: Half Acre, 2014).

Fred Mortagne, *Attraper au vol* (Davenport: Um Yeah Arts, 2016).

Sean Mortimer, *Stalefish: Skateboard Culture from the Rejects Who Made It* (San Francisco: Chronicle Books, 2008).

Oli Mould, *Urban Subversion and the Creative City* (Abingdon: Routledge, 2015).

Robert Muckle and Bruce Emmett, 'Never Say Last Run: Skateboarders Challenging the Terrain and Becoming Involved in Archaeology', Theoretical Archaeology Group Annual Meeting, Southampton University (19 December 2016).

Frederick Muir, 'On a Roll', *Los Angeles Times* (31 May 1989), pp. 1, 8.

Rodney Mullen with Sean Mortimer, *The Mutt: How to Skateboard and Not Kill Yourself* (New York: HarperCollins, 2004).

Paul Mulshine, 'Wild in the Streets', *Philadelphia Magazine*, v.78 n.4 (April 1987), pp. 119–26.

Mark Munson and Steve Cardwell, *Skateboard Stickers* (London: Laurence King, 2004).

National Safety Council, *Skateboarding* (Chicago: Bulletin, The Council, 1978).

Blake Nelson, *Paranoid Park* (London: Penguin, 2006).

Jeremy Nemeth, 'Conflict, Exclusion, Relocation: Skateboarding and Public Space', *Journal of Urban Design*, v.11 n.3 (2006), pp. 297–318.

Nicholas Nolan, 'The Ins and Outs of Skateboarding and Transgression in Public Space in Newcastle, Australia', *Australian Geographer*, v.34 n.3 (2003), pp. 311–27.

Rhyn Noll, *Skateboard Retrospective: a Collector's Guide* (Atglen: Schiffer, 2000).

Rhyn Noll, *Skateboarding: Past-Present-Future* (Atglen: Schiffer, 2003).

Rhyn Noll, *Skateboards That Rock: Graphic Design of a Counterculture* (Atglen: Schiffer, 2003).

Brandon Novak with Joseph Frantz, *Dreamseller: an Addiction Memoir* (New York: Citadel Press, 2008).

Paul O'Connor, 'Skateboard Philanthropy: Inclusion and Prefigurative Politics', Kara-Jane Lombard, (ed.), *Skateboarding: Subcultures, Sites and Shifts* (Abingdon: Routledge, 2015), pp. 30–46.

Paul O'Connor, 'Skateboarders, Helmet Use and Control: Observations from Skateboard Media and a Hong Kong Skatepark', *Journal of Sport and Social Issues*, v.40 n.6 (December 2016), pp. 477–98.

Paul O'Connor, 'Beyond the Youth Culture: Understanding Middle Aged Skateboarders through Temporal Capital' (Lingnan University Staff Publication, 2017).

Paul O'Connor, 'Skateboarding Networks in East Asia: the View from Hong Kong' (draft paper, 2017).

Jane O'Hara, 'Trouble in Paradise', *Maclean's*, v.100 n.14 (6 April 1987), p. 48.

John Oliver, *Anti Gravity Device Company* (Anti Gravity Device Company, 2017).

John O'Malley and Jack Graham, *Skatepark Development* (La Jolla: Skatepark Publications, 1977).

Simon Orpana, 'Radical Gestures: Symbolism, Symptom and Skateboarding' (PhD thesis, McMaster University, 2014).

Simon Orpana, 'Steep Transitions: Spatial-temporal Incorporation, Beasley Skate Park, and Subcultural Politics in the Gentrifying City', Kara-Jane Lombard, (ed.), *Skateboarding: Subcultures, Sites and Shifts* (Abingdon: Routledge, 2015), pp. 152–68.

Patsy Eubanks Owens, 'Recreation and Restrictions: Community Skateboard Parks in the United States', *Urban Geography*, v.22 n.8 (2001), pp. 782–97.

Doug Palladini, *Vans: Off the Wall. Stories of Sole from Van's Originals* (New York: Harry N. Abrams, 2009).

Mike Paproski, *In Your Face: a Collection of Papdog's Favorite Photos* (Papdog, 2017).

Chiara Santini Parducci, (ed.), *Do Not Think* (Berlin: Oxylane Art Foundation, 2015).

Tom Peacock, *Skateboarding: from Dogtown to the X-Games* (Montreal: OverTime Books, 2006).

Olivier Pégard, 'Ethnographie d'une Pratique Ludique Urbaine: le Skateboard sur la Place Vauquelin à Montréal' (PhD thesis, University of Montreal, 1997).

Hazel Pennell, *Skateboarding* (London: GLC Intelligence Unit, London Topics n.24, 1978).

Joe Penny, 'Skate and Destroy?: Subculture, Space and Skateboarding as Performance' (MSc dissertation, University College London, 2009).

Leandro Pereira, João Siqueira and Adriana Stadnik, 'Motivational Factors for Skateboard Adhesion', *International Journal of Science Culture and Sport*, v.2 n.3 (2014), pp. 69–78.

Robert Petrone, 'Shreddin' It Up: Re-Thinking "Youth" through the Logics of Learning and Literacy in a Skateboarding Community' (PhD thesis, Michigan State University, 2008).

Robert Petrone, '"You Have to Get Hit a Couple of Times": the Role of Conflict in Learning How to "Be" a Skateboarder', *Teaching and Teacher Education*, v.26 n.1 (2010), pp. 119–27.

Jake Phelps, (ed.), *Skate and Destroy: the First 25 Years of Thrasher Magazine* (New York: Universe, 2006).

Jim Phillips, *Surf, Skate & Rock Art of Jim Phillips* (Atglen: Schiffer, 2004).

Jim Phillips, *The Skateboard Art of Jim Phillips* (Atglen: Schiffer, 2007).

Christopher Pick and RoSPA, *Safe Skateboarding* (London: Evans Brothers, 1978).

Sarah Pileggi, 'Wheeling and Dealing', *Sports Illustrated* (1 September 1975).

Laura Pipe, 'Moving Concrete: Development, Deployment and Consumption of Skateboarding in the City' (PhD thesis, University of North Carolina at Greensboro, 2017).

Played in Britain, 'The Rom Skatepark, Hornchurch: Britain's First Listed Skatepark' (London: Played in Britain report, 2014).

Kimmy Pletting, 'Have You Zine Me? A Study of Zines as Empowerment for Women within Skateboarding' (BA dissertation, Utrecht University, 2014).

Desmond Poirier, 'Skate Parks: a Guide for Landscape Architects' (Master of Landscape Architecture dissertation, Department of Landscape Architecture/Regional and Community Planning, Kansas State University, 2008).

Shauna Pomerantz, Dawn H. Currie and Deirdre A. Kelly, 'Sk8er Girls: Skateboarders, Girlhood and Feminism in Motion', *Women's Studies International Forum*, v.27 n.5–6 (2004), pp. 547–57.

'Outdoor Plywood Rink Built For Skateboards', *Popular Science* (April 1966), p. 127.

Natalie Porter, 'Female Skateboarders and their Negotiation of Space and Identity' (PhD thesis, Concordia University, 2003).

Natalie Porter, 'She Rips When She Skates: Female Skateboarders as Active Subcultural Participants', Arielle Greenberg, (ed.), *Youth Subcultures: Exploring Underground America* (New York: Pearson Longman, 2007), pp. 121–36.

Natalie Porter, *The History of Women in Skateboarding* (eBook/Kindle, 2014).

Lee Pugalis, Jon Swords, Michael Jeffries and Bob Giddings, 'Toonsformation: Skateboarders' Renegotiation of City Rights', Simin Davoudi and Bell Derek, (eds), *Justice and Fairness in the City: a Multi-disciplinary Approach to 'Ordinary' Cities* (Bristol: Policy Press, 2016), pp. 125–48.

Quartersnacks, *TF at 1: Ten Years of Quartersnacks* (Brooklyn: PowerHouse Books, 2015).

Robynne Raye and Michael Strassburger, *Inside the World of Board Graphics: Skate, Surf, Snow* (Beverly: Rockport, 2011).

Tino Razo, *Party in the Back* (New York: Anthology, 2017).

Lucas Cardoso Dos Reis and Ary José Rocco Jr, 'Abordagem Conceitual Sobre o Comportamento e Envolvimento do Consumidor no Skateboarding Brasileiro', *Revista Intercontinental de Gestão Desportiva*, v.5 n.1 (2015), pp. 35–48.

Robert Rinehart, 'ESPN's X Games: Contests of Opposition, Resistance, Co-option, and Negotiation', Michael Atkinson and Kevin Young, (eds), *Tribal Play: Subcultural Journeys through Sport* (Bingley: JAI Press, 2008), pp. 175–95.

Robert Rinehart, 'Exploiting a New Generation: Corporate Branding and the Co-optation of Action Sport', Michael Giardina and Michele Donnelly, (eds) *Youth Culture and Sport* (Abingdon: Routledge, 2008), pp. 71–89.

Robert Rinehart and Chris Grenfell, 'BMX Spaces: Children's Grass Roots Courses and Corporate-Sponsored Tracks', *Sociology of Sport Journal*, v.19 n.3 (2002), pp. 302–14.

William H. Robertson, *Action Science: Relevant Teaching and Active Learning* (Thousand Oaks: Corwin, 2014).

William H. Robertson, 'The Skatepark Mathematics Extravaganza', *US-China Education Review*, v.5 n.5 (2015), pp. 314–19.

Aaron Rose and Christian Strike, (eds), *Beautiful Losers: Contemporary Art and Street Culture* (New York: Iconoclast and DAP, 2004).

Aaron Rose, Ben Weaver and Andy Holmes, *Dysfunctional* (London: Booth-Clibborn, 1999).

Cynthia Rose, *Design After Dark: the Story of Dancefloor Style* (London: Thames and Hudson, 1991).

Royal Society for the Prevention of Accidents (RoSPA), *The Hidden Dangers* (London: RoSPA, December 1977).

Royal Society for the Prevention of Accidents (RoSPA), *Skatcats Quizbook* (London: RoSPA, 1978).

Jonn Rübcke and Arne Fiehl, *I-Punkt Skateland: Hamburg 1990–2000* (Hamburg: I-Dot, 2012).

Robert Rundquist, 'Street Skateboarding and the Government Stamp of Approval', Arielle Greenberg, (ed.), *Youth Subcultures: Exploring Underground America* (New York: Pearson Longman, 2007), pp. 179–89.

Maggi Russell and Bruce Sawford, *The Complete Skateboard Book* (London: Fontana and Bunch, 1977).

Adam Salo, 'A League of Their Own: How Top Street Skaters Could Turn Their Backs on Contests to Face Street League', *ESPN Action Sports* (21 June 2010), www.espn.go.com.

Kirill Savchenkov, *Museum of Skate-boarding: Practice Manual* (London: Calvert 22 Foundation, 2016).

Bill Schaffer, 'No One Standing Above You: Rodney Mullen and the Ethics of Innovation', Kara-Jane Lombard, (ed.), *Skateboarding: Subcultures, Sites and Shifts* (Abingdon: Routledge, 2015), pp. 17–29.

Michael C. Scott, 'Disorderly Youth in Public Places' (US Department of Justice: Center for Problem-Oriented Policing, 2011).

Tim Sedo, 'Dead-Stock Boards, Blown-out Spots, and the Olympic Games: Global Twists and Local Turns in the Formation of China's Skateboarding Community', Petra Rethmann, Imre Szeman and William D. Coleman, (eds), *Cultural Autonomy: Frictions and Connections* (Vancouver: University of British Columbia Press, 2010), pp. 257–82.

Patty Segovia and Rebecca Heller, *Skater Girl: a Girl's Guide to Skateboarding* (Berkeley: Ulysses, 2007).

T. Seifert and C. Hedderson, 'Intrinsic Motivation and Flow in Skateboarding: an Ethnographic Study', *Journal of Happiness Studies*, v.11 n.3 (2010), pp. 277–92.

Pablo Sendra, 'Rethinking Urban Public Space', *City*, v.19 n.6 (2015), pp. 820–36.

Andrew M. Shanken, 'The Sublime "Jackass": Transgression and Play in the Inner Suburbs', *Places: Forum of Design for the Public Realm*, v.19 n.3 (2007), pp. 50–5.

Charlene S. Shannon and Tara L. Werner, 'The Opening of a Municipal Skate Park: Exploring the Influence on Youth Skateboarders' Experiences', *Journal of Park and Recreation Administration*, n.26 n.3 (Fall 2008), pp. 39–58.

William Sharp and Ozzie Ausband, *Back in the Day* (Berkeley: Gingko Press, 2017).

Kent Sherwood, *Jay Boy: Classic Photographs by Jay Adams' Stepfather, Kent Sherwood* (Thornhill: Concrete Wave, 2006).

Kent Sherwood, *Jay Boy: the Early Years of Jay Adams* (New York: Universe, 2017).

Kristin M. Shuman and Michael C. Meyers, 'Skateboarding Injuries: an Updated Review', *The Physician and Sports Medicine* (27 May 2015), www.informahealthcare.com.

Skatepark Advisory Task Force, *City of Seattle Citywide Skatepark Plan* (31 January 2007).

Dr Skaterock, *Vintage Skaterock: Skateboard Music of the 1960's and 1970's* (Wuerzburg: Skaterock, 2012).

Anders Smith-Lindall, 'On Exhibit: the Hyde Park Center Picks Up Speed', *Reader*, v.29 n.35 (2 June 2000).

Craig B. Snyder, *A Secret History of the Ollie. Vol 1: the 1970s* (Delray Beach: Black Salt Press, 2015).

Gregory J. Snyder, 'The City and the Subculture Career: Professional Street Skateboarding in LA', *Ethnography*, v.13 n.3 (2012), pp. 306–29.

Gregory J. Snyder, *Skateboarding LA: Inside Professional Street Skateboarding* (New York: New York University Press, 2017).

SPAUSA 'Information Guide to Getting a City Park Into Your Community', www.spausa.org, (undated).

C.R. Stecyk III and Glen E. Friedman, *Dogtown: the Legend of the Z-Boys* (New York City: Burning Flags Press, 2000).

Quentin Stevens and Kim Dovey, 'Appropriating the Spectacle: Play and Politics in a Leisure Landscape', *Journal of Urban Design*, v.9 n.3 (2004), pp. 351–65.

Gary Stidder and Sid Hayes, 'Exploring the Social Benefit of Informal and Lifestyle Sports', *Bulletin: Journal of Sport Science and Physical Education*, n.68 (2015), pp. 32–44.

Elaine Stratford, 'On the Edge: a Tale of Skaters and Urban Governance', *Social & Cultural Geography*, v.3 n.2 (2010), pp. 193–206.

Elaine Stratford, 'Mobilizing a Spatial Politics of Street Skating: Thinking About the Geographies of Generosity', *Annals of the Association of American Geographers*, v.106 n.2 (2016), pp. 350–7.

Elaine Stratford and Andrew Harwood, 'Feral Travel and the Transport Field: Some Observations on the Politics of Regulating Skating in Tasmania', *Urban Policy and Research*, v.19 n.1 (2001), pp. 61–76.

J. Strickland, *Shoot to Kill* (New York: Paradise Plus, 2015).

Alex Striler, *X Play Nation: of Actions Sports Game Changers* (San Diego: Striler Publishing, 2011).

Amy Sueyoshi, 'Skate and Create: Skateboarding, Asian Pacific America, and Masculinity', *Amerasia*, v.41 n.2 (2015), pp. 2–24.

Jon Swords and Michael Jeffries, 'Tracing Post-Representational Visions of the City: Representing the Unrepresentable Skateworlds of Tyneside', *Environment and Planning A*, v.47 n.6 (2015), pp. 1313–31.

Myra Taylor and Umneea Khan, 'Skate-Park Builds, Teenaphobia and the Adolescent Need for Hang-out Spaces: the Social Utility and Functionality of Urban Skate Parks', *Journal of Urban Design*, v.16 n.4 (2011), pp. 489–510.

Myra Taylor and Ida Marais, 'Not in My Back Schoolyard: Schools and Skate-Park Builds in Western Australia', *Australian Planner*, v.48 n.2 (2011), pp. 84–95.

Gaurab Thakali and Tom Caron-Delion, *Thik Cha: an Exhibition for Nepal* (London: Our Place, 2016).

Kevin Thatcher and Brian Brannon, *Thrasher: the Radical Skateboard Book* (New York: Random House, 1992).

B.R. Thomas, M. Lafasakis and V. Spector, 'Using Behavioral Skills Training to Teach Skateboarding Skills to a Child with Autism Spectrum Disorder', *Journal of Autism and Developmental Disorders* (2016).

Charlotte Thomas, *Concrete Girls* (Manhattan Beach: Girl is NOT a 4 Letter Word, 2018).

Stuart Thomas and Jason Potts, 'How Industry Competition Ruined Windsurfing', *Sport, Business and Management*, v.6 n.5 (2016), pp. 565–78.

David Thornton, *Common Criminals: the Anthology of Stoke* (Maine: Shoestring Books, 2013).

Holly Thorpe, 'Beyond "Decorative Sociology": Contextualizing Female Surf, Skate, and Snow Boarding', *Sociology of Sport Journal*, v.23 n.3 (2006), pp. 205–28.

Holly Thorpe, *Snowboarding Bodies in Theory and Practice* (Houndmills: Palgrave Macmillan, 2011).

Holly Thorpe, 'Action Sports, Social Media, and New Technologies: Towards a Research Agenda', *Communication & Sport*, v.5 n.5 (2017), pp. 554–78.

Holly Thorpe, 'Look at What We Can Do with All the Broken Stuff!', Youth Agency and Sporting Creativity in Sites of War, Conflict and Disaster', *Qualitative Research in Sport, Exercise and Health*, v.8 n.5 (2016), pp. 554–70.

Holly Thorpe, 'Media Representations of Women in Actions Sports: More Than "Sexy Bad Girls" on Boards', Clarissa Smith, Feona Attwood and Brian McNair, (eds), *The Routledge Companion to Media, Sex and Sexuality* (Abingdon: Routledge, 2017), chapter 26.

Holly Thorpe and Rebecca Olive, (eds), *Women in Action Sport Cultures: Identity, Politics and Experience* (London: Palgrave Macmillan, 2016).

Holly Thorpe and Belinda Wheaton, '"Generation X Games", Action Sports and the Olympic Movement: Understanding the Cultural Politics of Incorporation', *Sociology*, v.45 n.5 (2011), pp. 830–47.

Thrasher, *Ramps: a General Guide to Building a Radical, Wooden Skateboard Ramp* (Berkeley: High Speed Productions, 1985).

Thrasher, *Epic Spots: the Places You Must Skate Before You Die* (New York: Universe, 2008).

Thrasher, *Maximum Rad: the Iconic Covers of Thrasher Magazine* (New York: Universe, 2012).

Gordon A. Timpen, *Longboard: die Kunst des Asphaltsurfens* (Bielefeld: Delius Klasin, 2013).

Marc Tison and Barry Walsh, *Pipe Fiends: a Visual Overdose of Canada's Most Infamous Skate Spot* (Montreal: Media MudScout, 2006).

Gail Tominaga, Kathryn Schaffer, Imad Dandan and Jess Kraus, 'Epidemiological and Clinical Features of an Older High-Risk Population of Skateboarders', *Injury*, v.44 n.5 (2013), pp. 645–9.

Nikki Toole, *Skater* (Heidelberg: Kehrer Verlag, 2015).

Christina Tourino, 'The Leisured Testes: White Ball-Breaking as Surplus Masculinity in *Jackass*', *Journal of Popular Culture*, v.48 n.4 (2015), pp. 691–702.

TransWorld Business, 'The State of Skate' (2015).

Trawler, *Snakes and Moguls: a Scrapbook of Britain's Seventies Concrete Skateparks* (United Kingdom: Mark Lawer, 2016).

Micah Trippe, 'Urban Guerrilla Playfare, or Skating through Empty Cinematic Pools in *Dogtown and Z-Boys* (2001)', Christopher Brown and Pam Hirsch, (eds), *The Cinema of the Swimming Pool* (Oxford: Peter Lang, 2014), pp. 181–90.

Micah Trippe, 'Appropriating Pools: At Play in the Spaces of the City', *Architecture Media Politics Society*, v.10 n.3 (2016), pp. 1–11.

Helge Tscharn, *Possessed* (Münster: Monster Verlag, 2000).

Winston Tseng and Todd Bratrud, *I Hate: the Art of Todd Bratrud* (New York: Mark Batty, 2011).

Winston Tseng and Marc McKee, *Warning: the Art of Marc McKee* (New York: Mark Batty, 2011).

Arthur J. Tubb, 'Searching for Animal Chin: Skateboarding as an Artform' (BA Fine Art dissertation, Sheffield Hallam University 1999).

Daniel Turner, 'The Civilised Skateboarder: a Figurational Analysis of the Provision of Adventure Recreation Facilities' (PhD thesis, Glasgow Caledonian University, 2013).

Daniel Turner, 'The Civilized Skateboarder and the Sports Funding Hegemony: a Case Study of Alternative Sport', *Sport in Society*, v.16 n.10 (2013), pp. 1248–62.

Daniel Turner, 'Performing Citizenship: Skateboarding and the Formalisation of Informal Spaces', Daniel Turner and Sandro Carnicelli, (eds), *Lifestyle Sports and Public Policy* (Abingdon: Routledge, 2017), pp. 13–26.

Thomas Turner, 'Transformative Improvisation: the Creation of the Commercial Skateboard Shoe, 1960–1979', Kara-Jane Lombard, (ed.), *Skateboarding: Subcultures, Sites and Shifts* (Abingdon: Routledge, 2015), pp. 182–94.

Neal A. Unger and Mary Earhart, *Dude Logic* (eBook/Kindle, 2013).

Francisco Vivoni, 'Spots of Spatial Desire: Skateparks, Skateplazas, and Urban Politics', *Journal of Sport and Social Issues*, v.33 n.2 (2009), pp. 130–49.

Francisco Vivoni, 'Contesting Public Space: Skateboarding, Urban Development, and the Politics of Play' (PhD thesis, University of Illinois at Urbana-Champaign, 2010).

Francisco Vivoni, 'Waxing Ledges: Built Environments, Alternative Sustainability, and the Chicago Skateboarding Scene', *Local Environment*, v.18 n.3 (2013), pp. 340–53.

Dirk Vogel, 'The Skateboard as a Medium of Experiencing Urban Space and Appropriating American Public Sites' (Masters dissertation, Johannes Gutenberg University, 2002).

Sergej Vutuc, *Something in Between* (Ghent: Snoeck, 2011).

Jo Waterhouse and David Penhallow, *Concrete to Canvas: Skateboarders' Art* (London: Laurence King, 2005).

LaVada Weir, *Skateboards and Skateboarding: the Complete Beginner's Guide* (New York: Julian Messner, 1977).

LaVada Weir, *Advanced Skateboarding: a Complete Guide to Skatepark Riding and Other Tips for the Better Skateboarder* (New York: Julian Messner, 1979).

Patrick Welch, 'Gay Skaters: the Last Taboo', *Huck* (5 September 2011), www.huckmagazine.com.

Susie Weller, 'Skateboarding Alone? Making Social Capital Discourse Relevant to Teenagers' Lives', *Journal of Youth Studies*, v.9 n.5 (2006), pp. 557–74.

Doug Werner and Steve Badillo, *Skateboarding: New Levels: Tips and Tricks for Serious Riders* (San Diego: Tracks, 2002).

Jocko Weyland, *The Answer Is Never: a Skateboarder's History of the World* (London: Century, 2002).

Belinda Wheaton, '"New Lads"?: Masculinities and the "New Sport" Participant', *Men and Masculinities*, v.2 n.4 (2000), pp. 434–56.

Belinda Wheaton, 'Introduction: Mapping the Lifestyle Sport-Scape', Belinda Wheaton, (ed.), *Understanding Lifestyle Sports: Consumption, Identity and Difference* (London: Routledge, 2004), pp. 1–28.

Belinda Wheaton, 'After Sport Culture: Rethinking Sport and Post-Subcultural Theory', *Journal of Sport & Social Issues*, v.31 n.3 (2007), pp. 283–307.

Belinda Wheaton, 'Introducing the Consumption and Representation of Lifestyle Sports', *Sport in Society*, v.13 n.7–8 (2010), pp. 1057–81.

Belinda Wheaton, *The Cultural Politics of Lifestyle Sports* (London: Routledge, 2013).

Belinda Wheaton, 'Assessing the Sociology of Sport: On Action Sport and the Politics of Identity', *International Review for the Sociology of Sport*, v.50 n.4–5 (2015), pp. 634–9.

Belinda Wheaton and Becky Beal, '"Keeping It Real": Subcultural Media and the Discourses of Authenticity in Alternative Sport', *International Review for the Sociology of Sport*, v.38 n.2 (2003), pp. 155–76.

Belinda Wheaton and Mark Doidge, 'Exploring the Social Benefit of Informal and Lifestyle Sports', *Bulletin: Journal of Sport Science and Physical Education*, n.68 (2015), pp. 45–9.

Katherine White, '"We Out Here": Skateboarding, Segregation and Resistance in the Bronx' (MA dissertation, Fordham University, 2015).

Cindy Whitehead and Ian Logan, *It's Not About Pretty: a Book About Radical Skater Girls* (Los Angeles: Girl is NOT a 4 Letter Word, 2017).

Mark Whiteley, *This Is Not a Photo Opportunity* (Berkeley: Gingko Press, 2009).

Peter Whitley, *Public Skatepark Development Guide: Handbook for Skatepark Advancement* (Portland: Skaters for Public Skateparks, 2009).

Michael Nevin Willard, 'Seance, Tricknowlogy, Skateboarding, and the Space of Youth', J. Austin and M.N. Willard, (eds), *Generations of Youth: Youth Cultures and History in Twentieth-Century America* (New York: New York University Press, 1998), pp. 326–46.

Michael Nevin Willard, 'Skate and Punk at the Far End of the American Century', Beth L. Bailey and David R. Farber, (eds), *America in the Seventies* (Lawrence: University Press of Kansas, 2004), pp. 181–207.

J. Patrick Williams and Heith Copes, 'How Edge Are You? Constructing Authentic Identities and Subcultural Boundaries in Straightedge Internet Forums', *Symbolic Interaction*, v.28 n.1 (2005), pp. 67–89.

Indigo Willing and Scott Shearer, 'Skateboarding Activism: Exploring Diverse Voices and Community Support', Kara-Jane Lombard, (ed.), *Skateboarding: Subcultures, Sites and Shifts* (Abingdon: Routledge, 2015), pp. 44–56.

Sean Wilsey, *Oh the Glory of It* (London: Viking, 2005).

Phillip M. Wishon and Marcia L. Ore-skovich, 'Bicycles, Roller Skates and Skateboards: Safety Promotion and Accident Prevention', *Children Today*, v.15 n.3 (May/June 1986), pp. 11–15.

Ben Wixon, *Skateboarding: Instruction, Programming and Park Design* (Champaign: Human Kinetics, 2009).

Helen Woolley, Teresa Hazelwood and Ian Simkins, 'Don't Skate Here: Exclusion of Skateboarders from Urban Civic Spaces in Three Northern Cities in England', *Journal of Urban Design*, v.16 n.4 (2011), pp. 471–87.

Helen Woolley and Ralph Johns, 'Skate-boarding: the City as a Playground', *Journal of Urban Design*, v.6 n.2 (2001), pp. 211–30.

Emily Chivers Yochim, *Skate Life: Re-Imagining White Masculinity* (Ann Arbor: University of Michigan, 2010).

Alana Young and Christine Dallaire, 'Beware*#! Sk8 at Your Own Risk: the Discourses of Young Female Skateboarders', Michael Atkinson and Kevin Young, (eds), *Tribal Play: Subcultural Journeys through Sport* (Bingley: JAI Press, 2008), pp. 235–54.

Raphaël Zarka, *Free Ride: Skateboard, Méchanique Galiléenne et Formes Simples* (Paris: Editions B42, 2011).

Raphaël Zarka, *On a Day with No Waves: a Chronicle of Skateboarding, 1779–2009* (Paris: Editions B42, 2011).

Raphaël Zarka, (ed.), *Riding Modern Art* (Paris: Éditions B42, 2017).

Skateboarding Films and Videos

Affirmative Action: a Brisbane Skate Documentary (dir. Kane Stewart, 2013).

AKA: Skater Girl (dir. Mike Hill, 2003).

Albion (dir. Kevin Parrott, Morph and Ryan Gray, 2014).

All the Days Roll into One (Volcom, dir. Ryan Thomas, 2008).

All This Mayhem (dir. Eddie Martin, 2014).

American Misfits (dir. Cain Angelle, 2003).

America's Newest Sport (dir. Bruce Brown, 1964).

The Art of Going Sideways (Faltown, 2007).

Avit (dir. Chris Atherton, 2007).

Away Days (Adidas, dir. Matt Irving, 2016).

Back to the Future (dir. Robert Zemeckis, 1985).

Backyard Annihilation (Alva, dir. Kiki, 1988).

Baker 3 (Baker, 2005).

Ban This (Powell-Peralta, dir. Stacy Peralta and C.R. Stecyk, 1989).

Beautiful Losers (dir. Aaron Rose and Joshua Leonard, 2008).

Beers, Bowls & Barneys (Thrasher, dir. Preston Maigetter, 2004).

The Beginning (Birdhouse, dir. Brian Brannon, 2007).

Big-O Rebirth @ the Pipe (Ethernal, 2013).

Blackboard (dir. Marquis Bradshaw, 2016).

Blaze On (dir. Al Benner, 1978).

Blood and Steel: Cedar Crest Country Club (dir. Michael Maniglia, 2017).

Bones Brigade: an Autobiography (Powell-Peralta, dir. Stacy Peralta, 2012).

The Bones Brigade Video Show (Powell-Peralta, dir. Stacy Peralta, 1984).

Bon Voyage (Cliché, dir. Boris Proust, 2013).

Bridge to Bridge (Dreamland, dir. Elias Parias, 2014).

Bridging the Gap: History Goes Down at Carlsbad (On Video, summer 2002).

The Bro Bowl: 30 Years of Tampa Concrete (dir. Troy Durrett, 2010).

'Charlie Brown's All-Stars', television special (CBS, 8 June 1966).

Canvas: the Skateboarding Documentary (dir. Mick Erausquin and Matt Hill, 1987).

Cheese & Crackers (Almost, 2006).

Cherry (Supreme, dir. William Strobeck, 2014).

Children of the Revolution (Osiris, dir. Tony Magnusson, 2008).

Chlorine (dir. Milan Spasic, 2003).

The Cinematographer Project (TransWorld, 2012).

City by the Battlefield: a Film About Fredericksburg Skateboarding (Magic Bullet and Fredericksburg Skateboards, 2007).

City Hunter (dir. Jing Wong, 1993).

Cityscape (Strush, dir. Ryuichi Tanaka, 2012).

Concrete Jungle (dir. Eli Morgan Gesner, 2009).

Coping Mechanism (dir. Philip Evans, 2014).

Cuatro Sueños Pequeños (dir. Thomas Campbell, 2013).

Days Like These (dir. Jenna Selby, 2015).

Deathbowl to Downtown: the Evolution of Skateboarding in New York City (dir. Coan Nichols and Rick Charnoski, 2009).

The DC Video (dir. Greg Hunt, 2003).

Deck Dogz (dir. Steve Pasvolsky, 2005).

Desert Pipes (dir. Steve Pingleton, 2010).

The Devil's Toy (dir. Claude Jutra, 1966).

Dishdogz (dir. Mikey Hilb, 2006).

DIY America: Skate and Create (dir. Aaron Rose, 2010).

Dogtown and Z-Boys (dir. Stacy Peralta, 2001).

DOPE (Death or Prison Eventually) (dir. Chris Ahrens, 2008).

Downhill Motion (dir. Greg Weaver and Spyder Wills, 1975).

Dragonslayer (dir. Tristan Patterson, 2011).

Driftwood (dir. Oliver Payne and Nick Relph, *c.* 1999).

Drive: My Life in Skateboarding (dir. Mark Jeremias, 2002).

Dying to Live (Zero, dir. Lee Dupont and Jamie Thomas, 2002).

'Easy Riders' (Nine Network '60 Minutes' television story, 1987).

The '84 Gordon and Smith Skateboard Team (G&S, dir. Greg Thompson, 1984).

Elementality (Element, dir. Johnny Schillereff, 2005).

The End (Birdhouse, dir. Jamie Mosberg, 1998).

Endless Roads (dir. Juan Rayos, 2014).

Extremely Sorry (Flip, dir. Ewan Bowman, 2009).

'Eye on LA' (Los Angeles television programme, 1981).

1st & Hope (dir. Brian Lotti and The Mallous, 2006).

First Love (TransWorld, dir. Jon Holland and Jason Hernandez, 2005).

Flow (Gravity, 2003).

Footage (G&S, 1990).

Form (dir. Colin Kennedy, 2014).

Format Perspective (dir. Philip Evans, 2012).

Freeling (dir. Andrew Lovgren, 2012).

Freewheelin' (dir. Scott Dittrich, 1976).

From the Ground Up: Rodney Mullen (On Video, 2002).

Fruit of the Vine (dir. Coan Nichols and Rick Charnoski, 2002).

Full Tilt Boogie: the Story of Burnside Skatepark (dir. Chris Bredesen, Brenna Duffy and Julie Gerlach, 2003).

Fully Flared (Lakai and Girl, dir. Ty Evans, Spike Jonze and Cory Weincheque, 2007).

Future Primitive (Powell Peralta, dir. Stacy Peralta, 1985).

A Girl Walks Home Alone at Night (dir. Ana Lily Amirpour, 2014).

Gleaming the Cube (dir. Graeme Clifford, 1989).

Go for It (dir. Paul Rapp, 1976).

Going for It (1980).

Goin' Off (dir. Tony Roberts, 1989).

Goldfish (Girl, dir. Spike Jonze, 1993).

Gnar Gnar (Krooked, 2007).

Grind (dir. Casey La Scala, 2003).

A Guide to Cracks & Curbs: London (dir. Shade Media, 2015).

Guilty (Shorty's, dir. Tony Buyalos, 2002).

Hacking the Streets (dir. Sangam Sharma, 2009).

Hallelujah (TransWorld, dir. Jon Holland and Chris Ray, 2010).

Hall of Meat (dir. Dan Nazzareta, Jake Phelps and Gregory S. Smith, Thrasher, 1999).

Hallowed Ground (Hurley/Poor Specimen, dir. Scott Soens, 2001).

Hard Waves, Soft Wheels (dir. Jim Plimpton, 1977).

Highway Star (dir. Brian Tissot, 1976).

Hill Street: the History of Irish Skateboarding since 1980 (dir. J.J. Rolfe, 2014).

Hokus Pokus (H-Street, dir. Michael Ternasky and Michael McEntire, 1989).

Holy Stokes! A Real Life Happening (Volcom, dir. Russell Houghten, 2016).

Hot Chocolate (dir. Spike Jonze, Ty Evans and Cory Weincheque, Chocolate, 2004).

'Hot Shots' (Itch Production, dir. Toby Keeler, 1981).

Hot Wheels (dir. Richard Gayer, 1978).

How to Go Pro (Shorty's, 2005).

I Am Thalente (dir. Natalie Johns, 2015).

I Had Too Much to Dream Last Night (dir. Dustin Humphrey, 2014).

I Heart MK (dir. Lindsay Knight, 2006).

I Like It Here Inside My Mind, Don't Wake Me This Time (Polar, dir. Pontus Alv, 2016).

In Bloom (dir. Jon Holland and Ewan Bowman, 2002).

Incognito (dir. Mike Atwood, 2013).

In Search of the Miraculous (Polar, dir. Pontus Alv, 2010).

'Jeff Grosso's Loveletters to Skateboarding' (2011–), www.youtube.com.

J. Grant Brittain: 30 Years of Skate Photography (dir. David Fokos and Barbarella Fokos, 2017).

Jump Off a Building (Toy Machine, 1998).

Kenny & Co (dir. Don Coscarelli, 1976).

Ken Park (dir. Larry Clark, 2002).

Kids (dir. Larry Clark, 1995).

Kilian Martin: Freestyle Skateboarding (dir. Brett Novak, 2009).

King of the Mountain (First On Board, 1980).

King of the Road (Thrasher, 2011).

Land of Marble (dir. Simone Verona, 2014).

The Legendary Dead Cat Pool (dir. Steve Pingleton, 2010).

Lenz (dir. Shinpei Ueno, 2012).

Lenz II (dir. Shinpei Ueno, 2013).

Let's Go Skate (Schmitt Stix, dir. Gary Langenheim, 1987).

LHP – Landhausplatz (dir. Stefan Huber, 2012).

Lightbox (dir. Philip Evans, 2015).

Livin Free: the Heart of Longboarding (dir. Marc McCrudden, 2007).

Livin' It (dir. Stephen Baldwin, 2004).

Lords of Dogtown (dir. Catherine Hardwicke, 2005).

The Lovenskate Video (Lovenskate, dir. Samuel Smith, 2012).

Made: Chapter One (dir. Jon Miner, Emerica, 2013).

Made in Venice (dir. Jonathan Penson, 2016).

The Magic Rolling Board (dir. Jim Freeman and Greg MacGillivray, 1976).

The Making of Animal Chin (dir. Don Paul Hoffman, 2005).

The Man Who Souled the World (dir. Mike Hill, 2007).

Meet the Stans (dir. Patrik Wallner, 2012).

Menikmati (éS, dir. Fred Mortagne, 2000).

Mike V's Greatest Hits (dir. Ryan Young, 2003).

Mind Field (Alien Workshop, dir. Greg Hunt, 2009).

Misled Youth (Zero, dir. Jamie Thomas, 1999).

Mongolian Tyres (dir. Henrik Edelbo, 2007).

Mouse (Girl, dir. Spike Jonze, 1996).

MVP: Most Valuable Primate (dir. Robert Vince, 2000).

MVP 2: Most Vertical Primate (dir. Robert Vince, 2001).

A Need for Speed (Thrasher, 1993).

New Ground (Bones Wheels, dir. Jared Lucas, 2013).

Nike SB Chronicles, Vol. 3 (Nike SB, dir. Jason Hernandez, 2015).

911 Emergency (Thrasher, 1995).

Northwest (dir. Coan Nichols and Rick Charnoski, 2003).

Off Camera with Sam Jones: Episode 6 with Tony Hawk (dir. Sam Jones, 2013).

Off Camera with Sam Jones: Episode 10 with Stacy Peralta (dir. Sam Jones, 2013).

Oldog (dir. Tyrell Mills, 2014).

Old School: a Documentary on Cebu's Skateboarders (ZeroThreeTwo, 2013).

On the Spot - Warschauer Benches (Kingpin, dir. Mark Nickels, 2015).

The Original SkateBoarder (Six Stair, dir. Coan Nichols and Rick Charnoski, 2018).

Out of Line: a Short Skate Film (dir. Brett Novak, 2013).

Over Plywood: a Skateboarding History Written in South Wales (dir. Jono Atkinson, 2015).

Paranoid Park (dir. Gus Van Sant, 2007).

Passenger (dir. Angus Leadley Brown, 2004).

Paved for Us (Freebord, dir. Matt Reyes, 2013).

Paving Space (dir. Dan Magee, 2016).

Perpetual Motion (TransWorld, dir. Jon Holland and Chris Thiessen, 2013).

Pidgeon Park (Evergreen, dir. Buddy Pendergast, 2015).

P.J. Ladd's Wonderful, Horrible Life (Coliseum, dir. Arty Vagianos and Matt Roman, 2002).

Police Academy 4: Citizens on Patrol (dir. Jim Drake, 1987).

Pray for Me: the Jason Jessee Movie (dir. Steve Nemsick and David Rogerson, 2007).

Pretty Sweet (Girl and Chocolate, dir. Ty Evans, Spike Jonze and Cory Weincheque, 2012).

Propaganda (Powell-Peralta, dir. Stacy Peralta and Craig Stecyk, 1990).

Public Domain (Powell-Peralta, dir. Stacy Peralta and Craig Stecyk, 1988).

Questionable (Plan B, dir. Mike Ternasky, 1992).

Radical Moves (dir. Larry Dean, 1988).

Raising Helseth: Skateboarding Saved My Life (dir. Josh Becker and Mike Oliphant, 2013).

Ratsrepus (dir. Fabiano Rodrigues and Akira Shiroma, 2015).

The Reality of Bob Burnquist (dir. Jamie Mosberg, 2006).

Really Sorry (Flip, dir. Jeremy Fox, Fred Mortagne and Geoff Rowley, 2003).

The Real Video (Real, 1993).

The Reason (TransWorld, 1999).

The Rebirth of Skateparks (dir. Mike Salinger and Mike Hirsch, 2005).

Reel Life: Saturdays in Film and Sound (SEMLAC, University of Brighton, SEFVA, 2004).

Revers de Tokyo: Images et Imaginaires du Skateboard (dir. Julien Glauser, 2012).

RIDE Channel, www.youtube.com.

Rising Son: the Legend of Skateboarder Christian Hosoi (dir. Cesario 'Block' Montano, 2006).

Road Less Travelled (Fallen, dir. Mike Gilbert, 2013).

Rollin' through the Decades (dir. Winstan Whitter, 2004).

Round Three (Almost, dir. Mike Hill, 2004).

Rubbish Heap (World Industries, dir. Spike Jonze, 1989).

Save Southbank (dir. Winstan Whitter and Toby Shuall, 2007).

Scorchin' Summer (Thrasher, 1999).

The Scrum Tilly Lush (dir. Philip Evans, 2009).

The Search for Animal Chin (Powell-Peralta, dir. Stacy Peralta, 1987).

Searching Sirocco (dir. Brett Novak, 2015).

Second Hand Smoke (Plan B, 1994).

Secondhand Stoke (Roger Skateboards, 2012).*Second Nature* (Sector 9, dir. Colin Blackshear, 2009).

Second Nature: a Documentary Film About Janne Saario (Element, dir. Yves Marchon, 2012).

Service for the Sick (Lifeblood, dir. Bryce Kanights, 2014).

Sex, Hood, Skate, and Videotape (dir. Ian Reid, 2006).

The Seylynn Story (dir. George Faulkner, 2012).

SF Hill Street Blues (Magenta, dir. Yoan Taillandier, 2011).

SF Hill Street Blues 2 (Magenta, dir. Yoan Taillandier, 2012).

Shackle Me Not (H-Street, dir. Tony Magnusson and Michael Ternasky, 1988).

Shepard Fairey: Obey This Film (dir. Brett Novak, 2014).

Sick Boys (dir. Michael McEntire, 1988).

Sierra Highway: a Skateboard Retrospective (dir. Jeff Ryckebosch, 2009).

Sight Unseen (TransWorld, dir. Jon Holland and Greg Hunt, 2001).

Signal Hill Speed Run (dir. Mike Horelick and Jon Carnoy, 2014).

Since Day One (Real, 2011).

Sk8hers (dir. Ethan Fox, 1992).

Skate and Destroy (Thrasher, 1996).

Skate Australia (dir. Anthony Fricker, 2010).

Skateboard Fever (NBC Sports, 1977).

Skateboarding in India (dir. Simon Weyhe and Mathias Nyholm Schmidt, 2013).

Skateboarding in La Paz: Pura Pura Skatepark Build (dir. Simon Weyhe, 2014).

Skateboarding Inside Out (Gullwing, 1988).

Skateboarding in the Eighties (Powell-Peralta, dir. Stacy Peralta, 1982).

Skateboarding vs Architecture: a Study of Public Space and Materiality in Auckland City (dir. Johnny Agnew, 2011).

The Skateboard Kid (dir. Larry Swerdlove, 1993).

The Skateboard Kid 2 (dir. Andrew Stevens, 1995).

'Skateboard Kings' (BBC, 'World in Action' documentary, prod. Horace Ové, 1978).

Skateboard Madness (Hal Jepsen Films, dir. Julian Pena, 1979).

Skateboard Sense (dir. Sid Davis, 1975).

Skateboard – the Movie (dir. George Gage, 1977).

Skateistan: Four Wheels and a Board in Kabul (Skateistan, dir. Kai Sehr, 2011).

Skateistan: To Live and Skate Kabul (Skateistan, dir. Orlando Von Einsiedel, 2011).

Skate More (DVS, dir. Colin Kennedy, 2005).

Skate Near Death (dir. Roma Alimov, 2016).

Skate or Die (dir. Miguel Courtois, 2008).

Skaterdater (dir. Noel Black, 1965).

Skaters from Uranus (Life's a Beach, 1989).

Skatevisions (Vision-Sims, dir. Don Hoffman, 1984).

Skate World: England (Vice, 2010).

Skate World: France (Vice, 2011).

Skate World: Germany (Vice, 2010).

Skate World: Italy (Vice, 2010).

Skate World: Spain (Vice, 2010).

Skate World: Sweden (Vice, 2010).

Skatopia: 88 Acres of Anarchy (dir. Laurie House and Colin Powers, 2009).

Skinned Alive (dir. Bart Saric, 2004).

Skirtboarders: le Film (dir. Mathilde Pigeon, 2007).

Smell the 'Crete (dir. Bart Saric, 2009).

Smell the 'Crete 2: Concrete Dreams (dir. Bart Saric, 2014).

Snake Eyes Die (dir. Joe Gavin, 2013).

The Snake Run (dir. Matt Zafir and Tim Zafir, 2016).

Soleil Levant (Magenta, dir. Yoan Taillandier and Vivien Feil, 2013).

Sorry (Flip, dir. Jeremy Fox, Fred Mortagne and Geoff Rowley, 2002).

So What (With Section, 2016).

Space for Rent (dir. Jeremy Knickerbocker, 2012).

Species of Spaces in Skateboarding (dir. Raphaël Zarka, 2008).

Speed Freaks (Santa Cruz, dir. Tony Roberts, 1989).

Spinn'in Wheels (dir. Chris Carmichael, 1975).

Spirit of the Blitz (Deathbox, dir. Dave Evans, 1991).

Spirit Quest (dir. Colin Read, 2017).

Stand Strong: On the Road with Mike Vallely (dir. Mark Nisbet, 2000).

Static I–V (dir. Josh Stewart, 1999–2014).

Stay Gold (dir. Jon Miner, 2010).

Stoked: the Rise and Fall of Gator (dir. Helen Stickler, 2002).

Strange World (Zero, dir. Jamie Thomas and Mike Gilbert, 2009).

Street Dreams (dir. Chris Zamoscianyk, 2008).

Street Skating with Rob Roskopp & Natas Kaupas (dir. Jack Smith, 1988).

Streets series (dir. Satva Leung, 2003–2008).

Streets on Fire (Santa Cruz, dir. Howard Dittrich, 1989).

Stuntwood: the Birth, Life and Death of a Skateboard (dir. Jeff Roe, 2006).

Sunlight (dir. Jordan Redila, 2012).

Super Charged: the Life and Times of Tim Brauch (dir. Pete Koff, 2010).

Super Session (dir. Hal Jepsen, 1976).

Sydney Pool Services (dir. Dean Tirkot, c. 2011).

Tales from the Street: a California Skateboarding Odyssey (dir. Mike McEntire, 1989).

Teenage Mutant Ninja Turtles (dir. Steve Barron, 1990).

Tent City (dir. Rick Charnoski and Coan Nichols, 2004).

10,000 Kilometers (dir. Patrik Wallner, 2010).

This Ain't California (dir. Marten Persiel, 2013).

This is Qatar: a Skateboarding Tour Documentary (dir. Enrique Mayor & David Moreda, 2010).

This Is Skateboarding (Emerica, dir. Mike Manzoori and Jon Miner, 2003).

Thrasher Vacation: England (Thrasher, 2014).

Thrashin' (dir. David Winters, 1986).

Thrill of It All (Zero, dir. Jamie Thomas, 1997).

Tic Tac 2 Heelflip: Australia's Skateboarding History (dir. Mike Hill, 2001).

Tilva Roš (dir. Nikola Ležaić, Kiselo Dete, 2010).

Timecode (Alien Workshop, 1997).

Tincan Folklore (Stereo, 1996).

Tired Video (2014 and 2015).

Tony Hawk's Secret Skatepark Tour (dir. Morgan Stone and Matt Goodman, 2004).

Tony Hawk's Secret Skatepark Tour 2 (dir. Morgan Stone and Matt Goodman, 2007).

True (Plan B, dir. Erik Bragg, 2014).

The Ultimate Flex Machine (dir. Jason Cameron, 1975).

Underachievers: Eastern Exposure 3 (Dan Wolfe, 1996).

Underexposed: a Women's Skateboarding Documentary (dir. Amelia Brodka and Brian Lynch, 2013).

Under the African Capricorn (dir. Patrik Wallner, 2016).

Under the Bridge: a DIY Skatepark Video (Thrasher, 2009).

Under the Bridge: 25 Years of Fighting for Burnside (dir. Lucas Chemotti, 2015).

Uno (TransWorld, dir. Ted Newsome, 1996).

Urban Isolation (dir. Russell Houghten, 2014).

Useless Wooden Toys (New Deal, 1990).

Vase (Isle, dir. Jacob Harris, 2015).

Video Days (Blind, dir. Spike Jonze, 1991).

Video Nasty (Heroin, 2013).

A Visual Sound (Stereo, dir. Jason Lee and Chris Pastras, 1994).

Waiting for Lightning (dir. Jacob Rosenberg, 2012).

We Are Blood (dir. Ty Evans, 2015).

We Are Skateboarders (dir. Ben Duffy, 2012).

The Weenabago Projekt (dir. Kristian McCue and Tosh Townend, 2005).

Welcome to Hell (Toy Machine, dir. Jamie Thomas, 1996).

What If (Blind, dir. William Weiss, 2005).

Wheels of Fire (Santa Cruz, dir. Scott Dittrich, 1987).

Who Cares: the Duane Peters Story (dir. John Lucero, 2005).

Wide World of Sports (ABC, 1965).

The Work of Director Spike Jonze (dir. Spike Jonze, 2003).

X Games: Evolution of Skate (Monarch, 2005).

X Games: the Movie (dir. Steve Lawrence, 2009).

Yeah Right! (Girl, dir. Ty Evans and Spike Jonze, 2003).

Youth of Yangon (dir. James Holman, 2013).

General

Giorgio Agamben, *Homo Sacer: Sovereign Power and Bare Life* (Stanford: Stanford University Press, 1998).

Aaron Baker, *Contesting Identities: Sports in American Film* (Urbana, University of Illinois Press, 2003).

Roland Barthes, *Writing Degree Zero* (London: Cape, 1967).

Roland Barthes, *Mythologies* (London: Vintage Books, 2000).

Andy Bennett, 'Subcultures or Neo-Tribes? Rethinking the Relationship between Youth, Style and Musical Taste', *Sociology*, v.33 n.3 (1999), pp. 599–617.

Homi Bhabha, *The Location of Culture* (London: Routledge, 1994).

Lee Bofkin, *Concrete Canvas: How Street Art Is Changing the Way Our Cities Look* (London: Cassell, 2014), pp. 6–8.

Iain Borden, 'Beyond Space: the Ideas of Henri Lefebvre in Relation to Architecture and Cities', *Journal of Chinese Urban Science*, v.3 n.1 (2012), pp. 156–93.

Iain Borden, *Drive: Journeys through Films, Cities and Landscapes* (London: Reaktion Books, 2013).

Iain Borden and Jane Rendell, (eds), *Intersections: Architectural Histories and Critical Theories* (London: Routledge, 2000).

Iain Borden, Jane Rendell, Joe Kerr and Alicia Pivaro, (eds), *The Unknown City: Contesting Architecture and Social Space* (Cambridge, Mass.: MIT, 2001).

Pierre Bourdieu, *Distinction: a Social Critique of the Judgement of Taste* (Cambridge, Mass.: Harvard University Press, 1984).

Judith Butler, *Gender Trouble* (London: Routledge, 1990).

Michel de Certeau, *The Practice of Everyday Life* (Berkeley: University of California Press, 1984).

Stephen Connor, *A Philosophy of Sport* (London: Reaktion, 2011).

Tim Cresswell, *In Place/Out of Place: Geography, Ideology and Transgression* (Minneapolis: University of Minnesota, 1996).

Mihaly Csikszentmihalyi, *Flow: the Psychology of Optimal Experience* (New York: Harper and Row, 1990).

Mike Davis, *City of Quartz* (London: Verso: 1990).

Gilles Deleuze and Félix Guattari, *A Thousand Plateaus: Capitalism and Schizophrenia* (London: Athlone, 1988).

Department of Water Resources, 'The 1976–1977 California Drought: a Review' (State of California, The Resources Agency: Department of Water Resources, May 1978).

Umberto Eco, *Travels in Hyper Reality* (San Diego: Harcourt Brace Jovanovich, 1986).

Catherine Elwes, *Video Art: a Guided Tour* (London: IB Tauris, 2005).

Michel Foucault, *Discipline and Punish: the Birth of the Prison* (London: Allen Lane, 1977).

Matthew Gandy and B.J. Nilsen, (eds), *The Acoustic City* (Berlin: Jovis, 2014).

Ken Gelder and Sarah Thornton, (eds), *The Subcultures Reader* (London: Routledge, 1997).

Henry A. Giroux, *Stealing Innocence: Youth, Corporate Power, and the Politics of Culture* (New York: St. Martin's Press, 2000).

Erving Goffman, *The Presentation of the Self in Everyday Life* (Edinburgh: University of Edinburgh Social Sciences Research Centre, 1956).

Mark Gottdiener and Alexandros Ph. Lagopoulos, (eds), *The City and the Sign* (New York: Columbia University Press, 1986).

Dan Graham, *Two-Way Mirror Power: Selected Writings by Dan Graham on His Art* (Cambridge, Mass: MIT, 2000).

David Harvey, *The Condition of Postmodernity* (Oxford: Basil Blackwell, 1990).

David Harvey, 'The Right to the City', *International Journal of Urban and Regional Research*, v.27 n.4 (2013), pp. 939–41.

Dick Hebdige, *Subculture* (London: Methuen, 1979).

Thomas S. Henricks, *Play Reconsidered: Sociological Perspectives on Human Expression* (Champaign: University of Illinois Press, 2006).

Katharine Hepburn, *Me: Stories of My Life* (London: Viking, 1991).

bell hooks, *Black Looks: Race and Representation* (Boston: South End Press, 1992).

Neil Howe and William Strauss, *Millennials Rising: the Next Great Generation* (New York: Vintage Books, 2000).

J.B. Jackson, *Discovering the Vernacular Landscape* (New Haven: Yale University Press, 1984).

Pat Kane, *The Play Ethic: a Manifesto for a Different Way of Living* (London: Macmillan, 2004).

Ken Knabb, (ed.), *Situationist International Anthology* (Berkeley: Bureau of Public Secrets, 1981).

Henri Lefebvre, *The Explosion: Marxism and the French Revolution* (New York: Monthly Review, 1969).

Henri Lefebvre, *The Survival of Capitalism: Reproduction of the Relations of Production* (New York: St. Martin's, 1976).

Henri Lefebvre, *Everyday Life in the Modern World* (London: Transaction Publishers, 1984).

Henri Lefebvre, *Critique of Everyday Life. Volume 1: Introduction* (London: Verso, 1991).

Henri Lefebvre, *The Production of Space* (Oxford: Blackwell, 1991).

Henri Lefebvre, *Introduction to Modernity: Twelve Preludes September 1959–May 1961* (London: Verso, 1995).

Henri Lefebvre, *Writings on Cities* (Oxford: Blackwell, 1996).

Henri Lefebvre, *Rhythmanalysis: Space, Time and Everyday Life* (2004).

Henri Lefebvre, *Toward an Architecture of Enjoyment* (Minneapolis: University of Minnesota Press, 2014).

Stephen Lyng, 'Edgework: a Social Psychological Analysis of Voluntary Risk Taking', *American Journal of Sociology*, v.95 n.4 (January 1990).

Karl Marx, *Capital: a Critique of Political Economy* (Moscow: Progress Publishers, 1867/1887).

Leerom Medovoi, *Rebels: Youth and the Cold War Origins of Identity* (Durham: Duke University Press, 2005).

Maurice Merleau-Ponty, *Phenomenology of Perception* (London: Routledge and Kegan Paul, 1962).

Chantal Mouffe, *The Democratic Paradox* (London: Verso, 2000).

Paula M. L. Moya and Michael Roy Hames-Garcia, *Reclaiming Identity: Realist Theory and the Predicament of Postmodernism* (Berkeley: University of California Press, 2000).

David Muggleton and Rupert Weinzierl, (eds), *The Post-Subcultures Reader* (Oxford: Berg, 2003).

Joan Ockman, (ed.), *Architecture Culture 1943–1968* (New York: Rizzoli, 1993).

Steve Pile, *The Body and the City: Psychoanalysis, Space and Subjectivity* (London: Routledge, 1996).

Steve Pile, *Real Cities: Modernity, Space and the Phantasmagorias of City Life* (London: Sage, 2005).

Steen Eiler Rasmussen, *Experiencing Architecture* (Cambridge, Mass.: MIT, 1959).

Steve Redhead, *The End of the Century Party: Youth and Pop Towards 2000* (Manchester: Manchester University Press, 1990).

Arno Ritter, Marina Treichl and Claudia Wedekind (eds), *Auszeichnung Des Landes Tirol Für Neues Bauen 2012* (Innsbruck: Culture Department, Office of the Provincial Government of Tyrol, 2012).

Paul Rodaway, *Sensuous Geographies* (London: Routledge, 1994).

Edward Said, 'Culture and Imperialism', *Design Book Review*, n.29–30 (Summer/Fall 1993), pp. 6–13.

Leonie Sandercock, *Cosmopolis II: Mongrel Cities in the 21st Century* (London: Continuum, 2003).

Richard Sennett, *Flesh and Stone* (London: Faber and Faber, 1994).

Richard Sennett, *The Craftsman* (London: Allen Lane, 2008).

Michel Serres, *The Five Senses: a Philosophy of Mingled Bodies* (London: Continuum, 2008).

Benjamin Heim Shepard and Greg Smithsimon, *The Beach Beneath the Streets: Contesting New York City's Public Spaces* (Albany: Excelsior Editions/State University of New York Press, 2011).

Rob Shields, *Lefebvre, Love, and Struggle: Spatial Dialectics* (London ; New York: Routledge, 1999).

Ella Shohat and Robert Stam, 'The Politics of Multiculturalism in the Postmodern Age', *Art and Design*, n.43 (1995), pp. 10–16.

Miguel Sicart, *Play Matters* (Cambridge, Mass.: MIT, 2014).

Georg Simmel, 'The Metropolis and Mental Life', in P.K. Hatt and A.J. Reiss, (eds), *Cities and Society: the Revised Reader in Urban Sociology* (New York: Free Press, 1951), pp. 635–46.

Chris L. Smith and Andrew Ballantyne, 'Flow: Architecture, Object and Relation', *ARQ*, v.14 n.1 (2010), pp. 21–7.

Edward W. Soja, *Thirdspace: Journeys to Los Angeles and Other Real-and-Imagined Places* (Oxford: Blackwell, 1996).

Ignasi de Solà-Morales, 'Terrain Vague', Dean Almy, (ed.), *Center 14: On Landscape Urbanism* (Austin: Centre for American Architecture and Design, 2007), pp. 104–13.Michael Sorkin, (ed.), *Variations on a Theme Park* (New York: Noonsday, 1992).

Łukasz Stanek, *Henri Lefebvre on Space: Architecture, Urban Research, and the Production of Theory* (Minneapolis: University of Minnesota Press, 2011).

Łukasz Stanek, Christian Schmid and Ákos MoraváNszky, *Urban Revolution Now: Henri Lefebvre in Social Research and Architecture* (Farnham: Ashgate, 2015).

George Steiner, *Heidegger* (London: Fontana, 1992).

Jill Stoner, *Toward a Minor Architecture* (Cambridge, Mass.: MIT, 2012).

Sarah Thornton, *Club Cultures: Music, Media and Subcultural Capital* (Cambridge: Polity, 1995).

John Tomlinson, *The Culture of Speed: the Coming of Immediacy* (London: Sage, 2009).

Bernard Tschumi, *Architecture and Disjunction* (Cambridge, Mass.: MIT, 1998).

John Urry, *The Tourist Gaze* (London: Sage, 1990).

John Urry, *Mobilities* (Cambridge: Polity, 2007).

Raoul Vaneigem, *The Revolution of Everyday Life* (London; Rising Free Press, 1967/1979).

Robert Vischer, Harry Francis Mallgrave and Eleftherios Ikonomou, *Empathy, Form, and Space: Problems in German Aesthetics, 1873–1813* (Santa Monica: Getty Center for the History of Art and the Humanities, 1994).

Index

California: Laguna Beach 185
California: Laguna Niguel 145
California: Lake Cunningham 145
California: Lake Forest 145
California: Lake Tahoe 138
California: Lakewood 79, *80*, 127, 131, 134
California: Larva Bowl 114
California: Lipton Bowl 100
California: Long Beach 32, *176*
California: Los Altos 106
California: Malibu 106, 185, 259
California: Mammoth Lakes 147
California: Manhole 106
California: Massage Bowl 106
California: Mavericks 98
California: Mike McGill's Skatepark 142
California: Mile High 138
California: Milpitas 127, 145
California: Monrovia 145
California: Montebello 38
California: Monticello Dam 102, 114
California: Morro Bay Skateboard Museum 249
California: Mount Baldy 102, *102*, 104, 114, 127
California: Napa 144
California: National Bahne-Cadillac Skateboard Championships 63, *81*
California: National Skateboard Championships 9, 54, 78
California: Newport Beach 185
California: NHS Skate Museum 249
California: Northridge 114
California: Nude Bowl 145, *146*
California: Orange County 67, 106, 113, 118, 127, 131, 145, 191
California: Oxnard 127
California: Palm Springs 145, *146*
California: Palmdale 138
California: Palo Alto 102, 144
California: Pasadena 228
California: Pearl 106
California: Pink Motel 81, 112
California: Pipeline (1977) 121, *126*, 127, *128-9*, 130-1, 134, 178, 191-2
California: Pipeline (2002) 145
California: Point Loma 32, *87*
California: Point X 140
California: Rabbit Hole 106
California: Raging Waters 139
California: Rancho Mediterrania 127
California: Rancho Palos Verdes 185
California: Rash Bowl 112
California: Reseda *74*, 75, 119
California: Ridiculous 257

California: Runway 121, 134
California: Sacramento 200, 230
California: Sadlands 114
California: San Antonio Dam 102
California: San Bernardino Valley 127, 145, 224
California: San Dieguito 277
California: San Fernando Valley 99, 106, 112, 114, 178
California: San Gabriel Valley 121
California: San Jose 112, 127, 142, 145
California: San Juan Capistrano 106
California: San Leandro 64, 138
California: San Marcos 108
California: San Onofre power station 102
California: San Pedro 162
California: Santa Barbara 112, 116, 150
California: Santa Cruz 11, 100, 108, 133, 157, 168, 230, 249
California: Santa Rosa 231
California: Sepulveda Dam 99
California: Sewers 106
California: Simi Valley 249
California: Skateboard Heaven (San Gabriel) 121
California: Skateboard World (Lakewood) 79, *80*, 127, 131, 134
California: Skateboard World (Torrance) 121, *121*
California: Skate City 127, 130, 134
California: Skatepark Paramount 133
California: Skatepark Soquel 157
California: Skatepark Victoria 127
California: SkaterCross *74*, 75, 119
California: Skatopia *51*, *120*, 121, 134
California: Skipper's 106
California: Soul Bowl 106, 112-13, 127, 133
California: Spring Valley 64, *122-3*, 127, 132-3
California: Stanton 106
California: Sunset 115
California: Surfer's World 118
California: Temecula 140, 144
California: The Ark 138
California: The Galaxy 178
California: The Pit 100
California: Torrance 9, 56, *121*, 249
California: UC Irvine rail 191
California: University Community Park 133
California: Upland 121, *126*, 127, *128-9*, 130, 134, 178, 191-2
California: US Marines Camp Pendleton 102

California: Uvas Spillway 100
California: Vans (Milpitas) 145
California: Vans (Orange) 67, *67*, 130-1, 145
California: Ventura County 119
California: Vermont Drop 99
California: Visalia 118
California: Vista 132, 139, 170
California: Volcom 147
California: West Hollywood 191
California: Whittier 127, 130, 134
California: Winchester 127, 145
California: Yuba City 144
California: Yuvis Dam 100
California Medical Association 228
California Skateboard Parks 131
California Skateparks 144-5, 170, 278
Cal Jam II 49
Calkins, Deanna 38, *40-1*
Cambodia 92, 280-1
camcorders 50, 85-90, 188, 190
Cameron, Jason 78, *100*
Campbell, Dobie 72, 266
Campbell, Thomas 72, *88*, 90, 248, 251
Camp Kill Yourself/CKY 81
Campo Construction 131
Campo, Daniel 162
camps 62, *63*, 139, 169-70, 281
Canada 11, 12, 17, 20, 28, 37-8, 42, 68, 71-2, 92, 94, 106, 133, 144, 147, 152-3, 168, 197, 231, 238, 265, 268, 277-8, 280-1
Canada: AntiSocial 253
Canada: BC Skateboard Championship 63
Canada: Big O 268-70, *271*
Canada: Burnaby 133
Canada: Calgary 147
Canada: Hamilton 265
Canada: Human Rights Museum 281
Canada: Kamloops 153
Canada: Montreal *12*, 42, 168, 228, 238, 268, *271*
Canada: New Spot 232
Canada: Oasis Skateboard Factory 278
Canada: Ontario Skateboard Park 133
Canada: Quebec 231
Canada: Richmond Skate Ranch 142
Canada: Seylynn Bowl 133
Canada: Shaw Millennium Park 147
Canada: Skateboard Palace 133
Canada: The Forks 152, 281
Canada: Toronto 91, 233, 278
Canada: Vancouver 17, 32, 43, 92, 95, 133, 137, 142, 168, 178, *178*, 200, 226, 232, 253

Canada: Victoria 238
Canada: West Vancouver Park 133
Canada: Winnipeg 152, 281
C&K Skateparks *120*
Cannes Film Festival 11
Cannon, Chewy 50
Can't Stop 89
Canvas 144, 149
Canvas 83
Capalby, Tony 116
capitalism 48, 67, 98, 225, 257, 276, 284
Caples, Curren 43
Captain Radical 229, *229*
Cardiel, John 32, 45, 151, 197
Carl Jensen 7
Carlin, Jimmy 104
Carmichael, Chris 78, *100*
Carmona, Arianna 42
Carnel, Chris 210
carnival 67, *67*
Caron-Delion, Tom 75
Caron, Amy 42
Carr, John 159, 165, 168, 233
Carroll, Corky 9
Carroll, Mike 37, 86, 197
cars 14, 57, 71, 89, 90-1, 98, 149, 197, 211, 215, 226, 234, 257
Carson, Johnny 9, 38
Carter, Bill 58, 61
carving 9, 22, 38, 77, *79*, *98-101*, 99-100, *105*, 106-8, 116, *122-3*, 138, *154*, 159, 178, 197, 273
Casale, Jerry 182
Casey, Brian 228
Cash Money Vagrant 89
Cash, Donna 38
Casio 226
Cassimus, James 72
Caster 17, 242
Castle Hill Mob 93, *93*
Castrucci, Joe 264
Cates, Dan 117, 226
Cathey, Steve *103*
Catterick, Gareth 224
Causeway Media 65
Cavaliero, Dan 192
Cayman Islands: Black Pearl 170
CBS 38, 63, 114
CCM 11
CCTV (broadcaster) 81
CCTV (cameras) 121, 232, 266
cease-and-desist 246, 248
CEBRA 170, *171*
Cemetery of Reason, The *253*
Cemporcento Skate 94
Cendali, Richard 277
Certeau, Michel de 36, 200, 257
Česká Asociace Skateboardingu 61
Cespedes, Kim 38
cess slide 174
Chad 276

Tershay, Joey 45
Tesoriero, John 27
Tessensohn, Anita 39
Tête à Tête 254, *255*
Texas 95, 114, 119, 132
Texas: Blue Ramp 138
Texas: Clown Ramp 138
Texas: Corpus Christi 119
Texas: Dallas 138, 142
Texas: EZ-7 100
Texas: Fort Worth 230
Texas: Greenspoint 145, *146*
Texas: Houston 95, 145, *146*
Texas: Jeff Phillips Skatepark 142
Texas: Lipps 100
Texas: Rathole 106
Texas: Skatepark of Houston 142
Texas: Spring/North Houston 145, *146*
Thailand 28, 77, 91, 197
Thailand: Aranyaprathet 153
Thatcher, Kevin 71, 144, 194
That One Day 43
Theeve 22, 280
therapeutic landscapes 280
These 22
Thiebaud, Jim 246
Thiessen, Chris 89
Think 19, 56
ThirtyTwo 274
This Ain't California 196, 197
This Is Skateboarding 89
Thomas, Charlotte 75
Thomas, Jamie 32, 35, 37, 50, 86-7, *87*, 91, 197, 224, 230, *230*, 280
Thomas, Mike *63*
Thomas, Ryan *224*
Thompson, Greg 85
Thompson, Hillary 35, 256, 283
Thompson, Hunter S. 71, 185
Thompson, Pete *216-17*
Thompson, Sheldon 28
Thomson, Rob 92
Thornhill, Laura 38
Thornton, David 230, 253
Thornton, Sarah 46
Thorpe, Holly 35, 37, 95, 280
Thrasher 1, 18, 19, 25, 30-4, *30, 33*, 36, 38-9, 48, 55-60, *59*, 66, 68, *70*, 71-2, 84, 92, 94, 108, 112, 114, 117, 138, *140*, 142, *145*, 158-62, *175*, 178, 182, 188, 194-7, *194*, 200-3, 210, 213-14, 218-19, 222-4, *225*, 226, 238, 242, 254
Thrashin' 80
3M 144-h
Thrill of It All 32, 87, *87*
Thump 39
Thunder 20, 56
Thunderball 9
Tic Tac 2 Heelflip 9, 83

Tilt Mode Army 89
Tilva Roš 80
time 7, 25, 37, 75, 86-7, 90-1, 93, 106-7, 100, 112, 114, 137, 139, 148, 153, 158, 164, 168, 172, 180-4, 188, 192, 210-11, 214-15, 218-20, 232
time collapse 87, *89*, 90
Timecode 86
Time Out 100
Tincan Folklore 86
Tintin 11
Tired 36, 283
Tirkot, Dean *116*
Tissot, Brian 119
TMobile 252
tobacco industry 246
Toft, Lonnie 14, 17, 106
Tongue, Alex 184, *184*
Tonkiss, Fran 30
Tony Hawk Foundation 53, 149, 162, 169, 230, 276, 281, *281*
Tony Hawk Pro Skater 28, *28*, 39, 53, 54, 144
Tony Hawk's Project 8 42
Tony Hawk's Underground 38, 218, 270
Toole, Nikki 75
Torres, Vanessa 39, 42, 197
Torture Chamber 71
Tostenson, Bernie 242
Tourino, Christina 81
tourism 25, 50, 153, 170, 181, 218, 238, 264, 266
Townend, Tosh 92
Toxic 18, 22
Toy Machine 19-20, 37, 39, *39*, 52, 86, 230, *230*, 246
Toyota 50
Tracker 1, 14, *16*, 17-22, 38, 54, 56, 138, *186*
Trafton, George 99, 106
trainers *see* shoes
training 24, 45, 52-3, 62-5, 81, 142, 153, 165, 170, 184, 192, 229, 277, 283
trampolining 153
transformative learning 66
transgender 24, 35
transportation 6, 20-2, 26, 45-6, 98, 238, 270-3
TransWorld Business 61
Transworld Skateboard Championships 178, *178*
TransWorld Skateboarding 21, 22, 48, 55-6, 68, 71, *73, 163*, 178, *178, 186*, 242, *247, 264*
Trant 133
Trauma 248
travel and tours 11, 14, 26, 30, 36-7, 46, 49, 52, 57, 63, 75, 77, 84, 89, 91-2, *91-2*, 144, 149, 153, 187-8, 249, 266

Trefethen, Tina 38
Tress, Arthur 75
trick explosion 174
Trienen, Leaf 39
Triggs, Jesse 220
Trippe, Micah 116
Trocadero Bleu Citron 79
trucks 6-23, *13, 16, 21, 23, 40-1*, 54, 56, 61, 107-8, 127, 180, *186*, 210, 213, 232, 235, 276
True 89, 91, 218
Trujillo, Tony 151
Tscharn, Helge 72, *117, 263*
Tschumi, Bernard 181
TSG 280
Tuffac 138
Tum Yeto 60
Tunisia 281
Tunnel 12, 22, 71
Turkey 61, 197
Turkey: Istanbul 200
Turner SummerSki 20
Turner, Andy *181*
Turner, Daniel 113, 165, 169, 270
Turner, Jovontae 248
Turner, Laura (Laurie) 38
Turner, Peggy 38
Turner, Thomas 58, 273
Turningpoint 104, *137*, 138
Turrell, James 144
Twitter 94
2er 163
Ueda, Lincoln 28
Ueno, Shinpei 32, 218
UFO 17
Uganda 30
Uitto 272
UK 1, 9, 11-17, 36, 38-9, 42-3, 54, 61, 63, 68, 71-2, 75, 79, 83, 92-4, 109, *115*, 116, 118, 132-4, 137-9, 144, 149, 163, 168, 188, 195, 197, 222, 228-9, 231, 257-8, 266, 268, 270, 278, (*see also* London)
UK: Aberdeen 143, 254, *255*
UK: Adrenaline Alley *141*, 143
UK: A Foundation 257
UK: Arrow 133
UK: Barn 133
UK: Barnstaple 133
UK: Barrow-in-Furness 142
UK: Beachcomber 133
UK: Bexhill-on-Sea 256
UK: Big Woody's 54
UK: Birmingham 143, 231
UK: Black Lion 133
UK: Blackpool 54, 143, 229
UK: Bolton 132
UK: Bootle 139
UK: Brighton 43, 109, 133
UK: Bristol 90, 133, 142, *209*
UK: Buszy *151*, 152
UK: Cardiff 200, 229

UK: Chelmsford 92, 139, 231
UK: Chesham 139
UK: Chester 134
UK: Colne 133
UK: Corby *141*, 143
UK: Cornwall 9, 93, *93*, 142
UK: Coventry 238
UK: Creation 143
UK: Croydon Dustbowl 106
UK: Dan Cates pool 117
UK: De La Warr Pavilion 256
UK: Derby 231, 234
UK: Dewsbury 142
UK: Doncaster 133
UK: Dorchester 165
UK: Dread City 109
UK: Dudley 228
UK: Dundee 169, 270
UK: Earth'n'Ocean 133
UK: Edinburgh 92
UK: Empire State Building 138
UK: Essex 142, 268
UK: Everton 150
UK: Evertro 150
UK: Factory 169
UK: Faltown 93, *93*
UK: Farnborough 138
UK: Fast Eddies 142
UK: Fearless Ramp Base 142
UK: F51 170
UK: Folkestone 170
UK: Gateshead 77, 220, 265
UK: Gillingham 133
UK: Glasgow 156, 254
UK: Guildford 133
UK: Harrow 107, *131*, 133, 137, 172, 190, 192
UK: Hastings 138
UK: Hemel Hempstead 133
UK: Hemsby 133
UK: Hereford 133
UK: Hornchurch 133
UK: Hull 142
UK: Ilchester 139
UK: Inner City Truckers 134
UK: Ipswich 214
UK: Kent 54, *278*
UK: Kelvingrove Wheelies 133
UK: Kettering 134
UK: Kidderminster Safari Park 133
UK: Knebworth 133
UK: Langland Bay 9
UK: Leeds 231
UK: Leicester 232
UK: Liverpark 142
UK: Liverpool 142, *208*, 257
UK: Livingston 133, 137, 144
UK: Locomotion 133
UK: Malibu Dog Bowl 132
UK: Malmesbury Abbey 149
UK: Manchester 93, 132, 231
UK: Margate 117